RAND McNALLY

The Atlas of
MANKIND

RAND McNALLY
The Atlas of
MANKIND

RAND McNALLY & COMPANY   CHICAGO · NEW YORK · SAN FRANCISCO

Consultants and Contributors

Editorial Consultants

Professor Ioan Lewis
Department of Social Anthropology
London School of Economics and
Political Science

Professor Christoph von Fürer-Haimendorf
Department of Asian Anthropology
School of Oriental and African Studies
London

Professor Fred Eggan
Department of Anthropology
University of Chicago

Language Consultant

Dr David Dalby
School of Oriental and African Studies
London and CIRELFA
(Conseil international de recherche et
d'étude en linguistique fondamentale
et appliquée)

Historical Consultant

Professor Michael Crowder
Department of History, University
of Botswana and Swaziland and
former Editor of *History Today*

Research Consultants

Dr Michael Sallnow
Department of Social Anthropology
London School of Economics and
Political Science

Robert Dodd
Department of Social Anthropology
London School of Economics and
Political Science

Executive Editor
Lawrence Clarke
Editor
Linda Gamlin
Associate Editor
Joanna Chisholm
Research Editor
Will Gatti
Editorial Researchers
Nigel Morrison
Louise Egerton
Editorial Assistant
Charlotte Kennedy

Executive Art Editor
John Ridgeway
Designer
Niki Overy
Visualizer
Alan Brown
Picture Researcher
Beverley Tunbridge
Cartographers
Terry Allen
Nick Skelton
Martin Brett
Production
Barry Baker

Professor Vladimir Basilov
Academy of Sciences of the USSR
Institute of Ethnography, Moscow
(Turkic-speaking Central Asia)

Dr Catherine H Berndt
Department of Anthropology
University of Western Australia
(Australia and New Zealand—Australian
Aborigines)

Emeritus Professor Ronald M Berndt
Department of Anthropology
University of Western Australia
(Australia and New Zealand—Australian
Aborigines)

Professor John Blacking
Department of Social Anthropology
Queen's University of Belfast
(Southern Africa)

Dr Philip Burnham
Department of Anthropology
University College London
(Cultivators; Mechanized Farming)

Professor Michael Crowder
International African Institute and
London School of Economics and Political Science
(The Colonial Legacy)

Dr David Dalby
School of Oriental and African Studies London and
CIRELFA
(Languages of the World)

Robert Dodd
Department of Anthropology, London School of
Economics and Political Science
(Hunter-gatherers; Taboo; Central Africa)

Dennis J Duncanson OBE
Faculty of Social Sciences
University of Kent
(Southeast Asia)

Professor Fred Eggan
Department of Anthropology
University of Chicago
(North America; Amerindian North America)

Professor Dale F Eickelman
Department of Anthropology
New York University
(Middle East; Arab States, Israel and Iraq)

Professor Nelson H H Graburn
Department of Anthropology
University of California
(Arctic and Subarctic)

Professor Christoph von Fürer-Haimendorf
Department of Asian Anthropology
School of Oriental and African Studies London
(South Asia; India; Mexico and Guatemala)

Dr Joy Hendry
Department of Social Studies
Oxford Polytechnic
(Japan)

Dr Mark Hobart
Department of Anthropology and Sociology
School of Oriental and African Studies London
(Indonesian Archipelago)

Dr Caroline Humphrey
Department of Social Anthropology
Cambridge University
(Central Asia; Eurasian Subarctic; Siberia;
Mongolia and Tibet)

Dr Tim Ingold
Department of Social Anthropology
University of Manchester
(Hunter-gatherers; Pastoralists; Eurasian
Subarctic)

Dr Anthony Jackson
Department of Social Anthropology
University of Edinburgh
(Northern Europe—Faeroese)

Library of Congress Catalog Card Number 82-060973
ISBN 528-83085-6

Typesetting by Tradespools Limited, Frome, England
Reproduction by Adroit Photo Litho Limited,
Birmingham, England
Cartographic reproduction by Grantown Graphics Limited, London
Printed in the United States of America

Professor Grant D Jones
Department of Anthropology
Hamilton College, Clinton
(Central America and the Caribbean)

Professor Jeremy Keenan
Department of Social Anthropology
University of Witwatersrand, Johannesburg
(Saharan Africa)

Professor Jean La Fontaine
Department of Social Anthropology
London School of Economics and Political Science
(East Africa)

Vanessa Lea
Department de Antropologia
Museo Nacional, Rio de Janeiro
(Amazonia and the Eastern Seaboard—
Amerindians)

Professor Ioan Lewis
Department of Social Anthropology
London School of Economics and Political Science
(Africa; Horn of Africa)

Professor Peter C Lloyd
School of Social Sciences
University of Sussex (The Growth of Cities)

Dr Peter Loizos
Department of Social Anthropology
London School of Economics and Political Science
(Europe, Southern Europe)

James Mayall
Department of International Relations
London School of Economics and Political Science
(International Aid and Trade)

Professor John F M Middleton
Department of Anthropology and Sociology
School of Oriental and African Studies, London
(West Africa)

Maryon McDonald
Wolfson College, University of Oxford
(Northern Europe—Bretons)

Dr James P McGough
Department of Sociology-Anthropology
Middlebury College, Vermont
(China and Korea)

Professor Chie Nakane
Institute of Oriental Culture
University of Tokyo
(East Asia)

Dr Stephen Nugent
Department of Anthropology
University College London
(Amazonia and the Eastern Seaboard—favelas)

Dr Roger S Oppenheim
Department of Sociology
University of Auckland
(Australia and New Zealand—Maoris)

Professor E Geoffrey Parrinder
King's College, University of London
(Religious Belief and Ritual; Religions of the
World)

Dr Jonathan P Parry
Department of Anthropology
London School of Economics and Political Science
(Marriage; Death)

Professor John H Paterson
Department of Geography
University of Leicester
(Environment and Survival)

Dr Philip R Payne
Department of Human Nutrition
London School of Hygiene and Tropical Medicine
(Health and Nutrition)

Dr Richard Pennel
School of Peace Studies
Bradford University
(North Africa)

Frances Pine
Department of Social Anthropology
London School of Economics and Political Science
(Eastern Europe)

John Renshaw
Department of Social Anthropology
London School of Economics and Political Science
(Argentina, Paraguay and Uruguay)

Dr David Riches
Department of Geography
University of St Andrews
(Eskimo Zone)

Dr Peter G Riviere
Institute of Social Anthropology
University of Oxford
(South and Central America)

Dr Michael Sallnow
Department of Social Anthropology
London School of Economics and Political Science
(The Andes and the Western Seaboard)

Professor Robert T Smith
Department of History
University of Ibadan, Nigeria
(Northern Europe—general)

Professor Raymond T Smith
Department of Anthropology
University of Chicago
(Canada and the United States)

Professor Andrew Strathern
Department of Anthropology
University College London
(Polynesia, Micronesia and Melanesia)

Dr Marilyn Strathern
Girton College
University of Cambridge
(Oceania)

Professor Eric Sunderland
Department of Anthropology
University of Durham
(Migration and Race)

Nicholas Tapp
Researcher
Chiang Mai, Thailand
(Mainland Southeast Asia)

Dr Richard Tapper
Department of Anthropology and Sociology
School of Oriental and African Studies London
(Turkey, Iran and Afghanistan)

Dr Robert Turner
Department of Social Anthropology
University of Edinburgh
(Pilgrimage and Tourism)

Dr Rubie Watson
Department of Social Anthropology
London School of Economics and Political Science
(The Individual in Society; Kinship and Family)

Philip Windsor
Department of International Relations
London School of Economics and Political Science
(Modern Imperialism)

Dr Sayed Zawwar H Zaidi
Department of History
School of Oriental and African Studies London
(Pakistan)

Contents

Introduction

Never in the history of mankind have men of different nationalities interacted so extensively and intensively. The mass media, package holidays, international labor migration, and the displacement of refugees all contribute to the intercultural exchange that characterizes our age. This global dialogue enriches our own culture and broadens our perspectives on what it means to be human, pointing to an international common denominator of shared humanity. But it also awakens and sharpens our sense of competition for the earth's scarce resources. Rivalry over limited resources, combined with the growing threat of a nuclear holocaust, encourages the pervasive sense of insecurity which drives men to seek their roots in some meaningful cultural heritage. In our shrinking universe, in which people of all nationalities jostle together, blending elements from the heritages of many epochs and civilizations, cultural indentity thus paradoxically clamors for attention.

Community and culture

Today, as in the past, men and women live in groups, and community life presupposes effective communications and some degree of shared culture, particularly a common language. For those who count themselves members of the same community, their language is the most immediate bond, distinguishing their group from others. But all aspects of life, from the most material and tangible to the most immaterial and abstract are invested with unique cultural value. This is particularly pronounced in ideology and political organization, in religious worship and ritual, and in family organization and marriage.

Cultures are thus the distinctive "costumes" of communities, the way those who live together demonstrate their sense of identity. This common identity is not part of our genetic heritage—we have to learn how to speak our native language, how to behave in conformity with our customs and what to think. But while cultural divisions are *not* actually based on biological or genetic differences, people everywhere tend to assume that they are. Thus we speak of "naturalizing," rather than socializing foreigners who are not native to our culture. The attempt to transform racial into cultural distinctions, to transmute culture into nature, reflects the strength of group identity. People value their community and culture so highly that they seek to invest these with unique finality as immutable biological facts.

The human legacy

Human beings everywhere have the same biological needs and vulnerabilities, and thus it is not surprising that there should be common themes underlying the manifest contrasts between different societies. The ease and frequency with which cultural adaptation, borrowing and change all occur attest to these fundamental patterns of human society. Some specific cultural similarities in life style, material technology, religious belief and ideology represent separate and independent inventions, since human beings have often struck on common solutions when faced with the same type of environmental problems. Other similarities are the direct outcome of cultural diffusion, the legacy of trade, migration and conquest in past centuries. Whether borrowed or independently invented, these cultural coincidences reinforce the sense of a panhuman heritage.

We treasure this mixed human legacy from civilizations distant both in space and time. Modern art and music find inspiration in traditional Africa and the Pacific, while western medicine is enriched by alien techniques, such as acupuncture. The West transmits its leading ideologies—Christianity and Marxism, democracy and totalitarianism—importing in

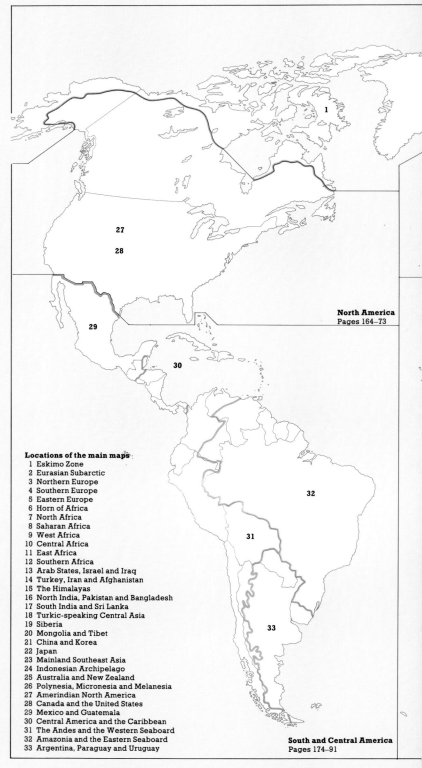

North America
Pages 164–73

Locations of the main maps:
1 Eskimo Zone
2 Eurasian Subarctic
3 Northern Europe
4 Southern Europe
5 Eastern Europe
6 Horn of Africa
7 North Africa
8 Saharan Africa
9 West Africa
10 Central Africa
11 East Africa
12 Southern Africa
13 Arab States, Israel and Iraq
14 Turkey, Iran and Afghanistan
15 The Himalayas
16 North India, Pakistan and Bangladesh
17 South India and Sri Lanka
18 Turkic-speaking Central Asia
19 Siberia
20 Mongolia and Tibet
21 China and Korea
22 Japan
23 Mainland Southeast Asia
24 Indonesian Archipelago
25 Australia and New Zealand
26 Polynesia, Micronesia and Melanesia
27 Amerindian North America
28 Canada and the United States
29 Mexico and Guatemala
30 Central America and the Caribbean
31 The Andes and the Western Seaboard
32 Amazonia and the Eastern Seaboard
33 Argentina, Paraguay and Uruguay

South and Central America
Pages 174–91

return transcendental meditation and other elements of Oriental civilization. These exchanges reaffirm man's common needs and his plasticity as a cultural animal.

At the same time, the sudden acceleration in cultural exchange that has occurred in modern times, has inherent dangers for the more isolated people of the world. The highly complex industrial urban economies of the West have developed from simple hunting and gathering economies by a gradual evolutionary process, taking over 10,000 years to reach their present form. This infinitely slow development is now being repeated, all over the world, in telescoped form and at break-neck speed, as people such as the highlanders of Papua New Guinea or the San of the Kalahari desert are catapulted into the twentieth century.

In our contemporary cosmopolitan era, with its kaleidoscope of cultures, the descendants of great historical empires confront the representatives of small communities lacking recorded history. It is all too easy for us to judge such peoples, with their very simple technology, meager possessions and limited comforts, by our own materialistic standards. If the criteria used by economists to measure the relative well being of different populations were appropriate,

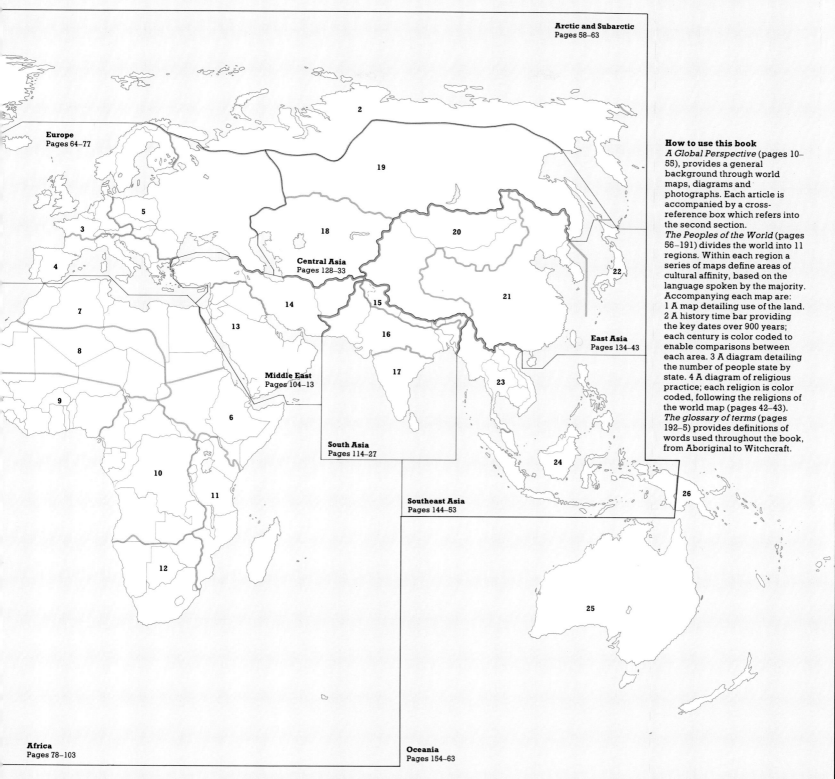

Arctic and Subarctic
Pages 58–63

Europe
Pages 64–77

Central Asia
Pages 128–33

Middle East
Pages 104–13

South Asia
Pages 114–27

East Asia
Pages 134–43

Southeast Asia
Pages 144–53

Africa
Pages 78–103

Oceania
Pages 154–63

How to use this book
A Global Perspective (pages 10–55), provides a general background through world maps, diagrams and photographs. Each article is accompanied by a cross-reference box which refers into the second section.
The Peoples of the World (pages 56–191) divides the world into 11 regions. Within each region a series of maps define areas of cultural affinity, based on the language spoken by the majority. Accompanying each map are:
1 A map detailing use of the land.
2 A history time bar providing the key dates over 900 years; each century is color coded to enable comparisons between each area. 3 A diagram detailing the number of people state by state. 4 A diagram of religious practice; each religion is color coded, following the religions of the world map (pages 42–43).
The glossary of terms (pages 192–5) provides definitions of words used throughout the book, from Aboriginal to Witchcraft.

the level of happiness and contentment of the highly industrialized societies would be much higher than that prevailing among "backward" subsistence cultivations, but the first-hand experiences of anthropologists do not bear out such a conclusion. It is clear that the sense of pleasure and security generated by closely knit communities, and the elation derived from participation in ritual activities, can easily make up for the lack of technological aids and the absence of mass-produced entertainment.

The Atlas of Mankind

We begin this Atlas of Mankind by adopting a comparative, global perspective in which we discuss and analyze general phenomena and processes that have shaped our world. Here we explore common patterns of economic, social and political organization and perennial themes in ritual and religion. This thematic introduction, which emphasizes that culture is a malleable medium for social interaction, rather than an immutable absolute, introduces our geo-historical presentation of the peoples of the world in their respective culture areas. This mixture of the general and particular seems to us essential if we are to begin to understand the dynamic forces which shape and reshape our contemporary world.

General key to the main maps

The main maps in *The Peoples of the World* section are delineated by coastlines or boundary lines marked in pink; these define the areas of cultural affinity. Each map has a key based on language categories from the world language map (pages 18–19). In the general key below entries refer to approximate locations only.

☐ Areas of distribution of languages within a particular language-family (see language key to each map)

⬭ Uninhabited or sparsely populated area

◯ Localized language area (enlarged)

✧ Centre of geographical spread of language(s) spoken by scattered (or nomadic) communities or by important minorities

▨ Area occupied by people(s) featured in the text

▤ Area occupied by people(s) mentioned in captions to each map

■ Capital cities

● Towns and cities with over 250,000 inhabitants

● Towns with 50,000–75,000 inhabitants

○ Towns with less than 50,000 inhabitants

╌ Political boundary

╱ State boundary

╱ River

〜 Lake or reservoir

〜 Seasonal lake

〜 Salt lake

▲ Mountain spot heights in metres

⁘ Historical site

A Global Perspective

A shanty town—Hong Kong harbor

A Global Perspective

Do we live in a miserable world? In one sense, we certainly do. One person in ten does not have enough food. One in four lives in conditions of easily recognizable poverty. The majority of people in the world do not have regular access to safe water, or to medical and hospital facilities.

However, in some respects conditions have not generally deteriorated. Over the last three decades even the low-income countries have experienced a 50 percent rise in income per head, after correcting for price changes, while in the high-income and middle-income countries there has been a rise of about 150 percent. Expectation of life at birth has gone up in the low-income countries from an average of about 37 in 1950 to about 51 in 1980.

Although these averages conceal the abject poverty still suffered by the poorest people of the world, they do point to a general upward trend. But how long that trend can be continued is another matter, for in the coming century the expanding population inevitably threatens to exhaust the earth's natural limitations.

Population and resources

The human population has grown explosively during the twentieth century, largely as a result of the control of disease by modern medicine. In 1900 there were about 1,600 million people on the earth; today there are 4,500 million and, at current rates of growth, there will be almost half as many again by the year 2000—over 6,000 million people. The greatest growth is predicted to occur in developing countries, and the crowded shanty towns that already ring many Third World cities are expected to grow even larger, resulting in massive social problems. Already 25 percent of the world's population lives in cities, but by the end of the century this will have risen to 50 percent

Efforts to curb population growth by family planning programs often fail due to a lack of understanding of the role of the family in developing countries. With high infant mortality and no social security program, parents need to have a great many children to ensure that some survive to look after them in old age. Recent research indicates that people are not likely to utilize birth control facilities effectively unless their general security is assured.

The failure of such family planning schemes highlights a major deficiency in many development projects—an excessive emphasis on technological innovation and insufficient attention to the social implications in their cultural context. Thus, the "Green Revolution" of the 1960s–70s, which was intended to help the poor farmers of developing countries, often had the effect of making them poorer still. The high-yielding strains of wheat and rice that had been developed for their benefit cost so much in fertilizer and pesticide that only fairly prosperous farmers could afford to grow them. These farmers made substantial profits and were able to buy out the smaller farmers, reducing them to landless laborers. In one area of Mexico the Green Revolution resulted in a sixfold increase in food production during a thirteen-year period, during which time the population only doubled. But although more food was available, the poorest third of the community showed no rise in food consumption, and the number of severely malnourished children actually increased. This pattern is repeated throughout the world—there is food enough for everyone but it is distributed according to wealth, not need, so that 570 million people are undernourished.

Almost every aspect of western life is now dependent on the use of fossil fuels—substances that have accumulated gradually over millions of years and that are now being rapidly exhausted. The impressive increases in food production to date rely heavily on the use of fossil fuels, and as these become depleted, yields dependent on them will fall. The development of farming methods that are less reliant on fuel—for example, the biological control of pests rather than chemical insecticides—suggest a possible solution.

The arms race

One of the most controversial ways in which fuel and

Men and machines
On an Indian construction project workers form "human ladders" to lift sand; in the industrialized countries machines are used for such tasks. The replacement of men by machines is widely accepted as a mark of progress. Most Third World countries regard industrialization as a central objective of their economic policy, reflecting a deeply felt need for modernization and economic independence. Yet unemployment and limited fuel resources place a costly price on such uncertain prospects.

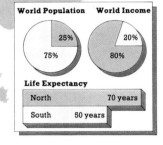

other resources are currently being expended is in the manufacture of arms. Over $450 billion are spent on arms each year—a vast sum which, appropriately used, could solve many major economic and social problems of the Third World. For the price of a single fighter plane 40,000 rural villages could each be equipped with a pharmacy to meet their basic health needs, and this figure excludes the costs of running the plane, which uses several thousand gallons of fuel every hour while in flight.

The stockpiling of weapons by the superpowers has now reached the point where there are sufficient nuclear warheads to devastate all the major cities of the northern hemisphere 400 times over. The total destructive capacity of the world's nuclear weapons is equivalent to 15 billion tons of TNT—over three tons for every man, woman and child on earth. Nevertheless, the arms race continues, providing significant employment in industrial countries and international trade.

While the industrialized western nations are still looking for solutions to their own social ills—unemployment, urban decay and the breakdown of family ties—they are also engaged in contributing to those of the Third World. Western consumerism is being encouraged in the Third World by companies seeking to expand their markets, while the expectations of people in formerly isolated villages are aroused as communications improve. The desire for western consumer goods may produce a disdain for what is local, rural or homemade and accelerate the migration from the countryside to the city slums.

With dwindling global resources, the logic of unfettered consumerism has dangerous implications, and the same has been said of nationalism, seen as another of Europe's legacies to the Third World. However, there are grounds for hope as an increasing number of statesmen in the developed countries recognize the special plight of the underdeveloped. The implications of this North-South dialogue for general prosperity and security are becoming increasingly recognized.

Worlds apart
While the rich industrialized nations (the "North") account for only 25% of the world's population, their share of the world's income is 80%. In these countries life expectancy is around 70 years, while in the developing countries (the "South") it is under 50. Poor diet, inadequate housing, diseases, and lack of sanitation and clean water account for this higher mortality. As many as 20% of children may die before reaching the age of one.

The world map
This world map based upon the Peters Projection is seen as an important step away from the prevailing Eurocentric geographical and cultural concept of the world. The surface distortions that do appear are distributed at the equator and the poles. Unlike other "equal-area" projections, which plot the relative proportion of land surface area, it is claimed that this projection shows densely settled areas in proper proportion to each other.

World Population	World Income
25% / 75%	20% / 80%

Life Expectancy

North	70 years
South	50 years

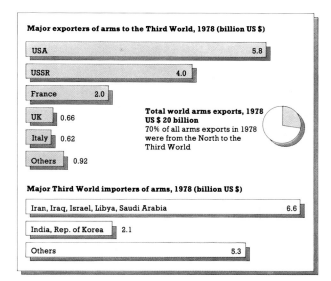

Major exporters of arms to the Third World, 1978 (billion US $)

USA	5.8
USSR	4.0
France	2.0
UK	0.66
Italy	0.62
Others	0.92

Total world arms exports, 1978 US $ 20 billion
70% of all arms exports in 1978 were from the North to the Third World

Major Third World importers of arms, 1978 (billion US $)

Iran, Iraq, Israel, Libya, Saudi Arabia	6.6
India, Rep. of Korea	2.1
Others	5.3

World Population (millions)

6,000
5,000
4,000
3,000
2,000
1,000

The arms trade
Arms are one of the major exports from the North to the South. Servicing weapons and training personnel escalate an already massive financial commitment to the North. The total world spending on arms is almost $450 billion each year. It is estimated that at a cost of one-thousandth of this figure malaria could be eradicated.

The right to work
Rising unemployment in the North is echoed in the South, although there the problem is more one of underemployment, since there is usually some poorly paid work for most people. As world population grows, about 40 million jobs need to be created each year.

The right to food
Enough food is produced to feed everyone in the world, but uneven distribution results in 570 million people going hungry or starving. This victim of the 1974–75 Ethiopian famine is being fed at a refugee camp. Those looking on are not yet weak enough to qualify for food.

North

M   F

Average life expectancy

90 years
80
70
60
50
40
30
20
10

90 years
80
70
60
50
40
30
20
10

South

M   F

Young and old
In some developing countries in the South up to half the population is under 15 years of age. By contrast, in the North the proportion of old people is increasing due to falling birth rates and high standards of medical care; those in the North can expect to live 20 years longer than those in the South.

The population bomb
It is only in the past 200 years that the human population has begun to grow significantly. Before that it was kept at about the same level by disease, but with improvements in food, sanitation and medicine, numbers began to increase dramatically. Although in the North and possibly in China and elsewhere the birthrate is falling, the rate worldwide is still accelerating, and by the year 2000 there may well be 6,000 million people on earth.

3000 BC   2000 BC   1000 BC   Years BC | Years AD   AD 500   AD 1000   AD 1500   AD 2000

Migration and Race

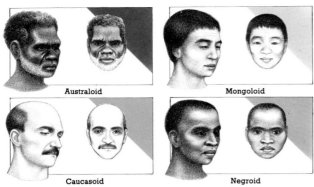

Australoid

Mongoloid

Caucasoid

Negroid

The classification of race
Race is essentially a biological concept and has no cultural implications. Human beings are commonly classified into a number of distinct racial groups, although the basis of such classifications is questioned today, since the so-called races share many physical attributes and are linked by intermediates. A simple racial classification gives four groups: Mongoloid, Negroid, Caucasoid and Australoid. While most of the

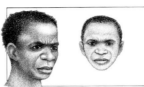

Pygmy

people of the world can be fitted into this scheme, there are certain populations which do not belong to any category, for example the Khoisans, the Ainu and the Veddoids. These are thought to be the relics of ancient racial groups.

Ainu

Veddoid

Human beings vary greatly in size, shape, skin color and facial features, and yet we all belong to a single species—that is, we are all capable of interbreeding to produce fertile, viable offspring. The human species exhibits much more variability than most animal species largely because it inhabits a far wider geographical range. We have, in the course of our evolutionary history, adapted to the intense heat and sunlight of the tropics, to the searing cold of subarctic regions, to the thin air of high mountain ranges, and to every imaginable environment in between. Special characteristics have evolved in response to the demands of different habitats, and these characteristics have spread through migration, or blended through intermarriage, to produce the complex pattern of human features seen today.

It is widely accepted that the human species first emerged in Africa, since most of the fossilized remains of very early man, some over three million years old, are found there. Long after the initial appearance of man there (but over half a million years ago) migrations took some early people, known as *Homo erectus*, to northern parts of Europe and Asia, and into southeast Asia. These people had knowledge of fire, and they inhabited far colder areas of the world than had ever before been possible.

From *Homo erectus* two distinctive human forms evolved—*Homo sapiens neanderthalensis* (Neanderthal Man) and *Homo sapiens sapiens* (modern man), who appeared some 40,000 years ago possibly in the Middle East. Once modern man had emerged, Neanderthal Man disappeared from the fossil record, and it seems that the *sapiens* variety largely absorbed the Neanderthals by interbreeding.

Homo sapiens sapiens migrated into several new areas of the world. A fall in sea level accompanying the Ice Age allowed the ancestors of the Amerindians to migrate from Asia into America via a land bridge where the Bering Straits are now located. The first wave of migration took place at least 12,000 years ago, and perhaps much earlier. Once in America these groups of hunter-gatherers moved rapidly eastward and southward until the whole continent was settled.

The origins of race
Early human populations were small and many were isolated from each other by geographical barriers. Small, reproductively isolated groups such as these can rapidly change their genetic constitution and become markedly different from each other. Toward the end of the last Ice Age small groups in central Asia developed, through natural selection, physical features which equipped them to cope with extremes of cold. They developed short, thickset bodies, round crania, flat faces with little-protruding noses and slit-like eyes—all features which help to reduce heat loss and frostbite. Sparse beard growth in the men was likewise an adaptation to freezing conditions, since beards tend to ice up in extremely cold weather. Once the climate improved after the receding of the ice sheets, these people migrated outward from their homelands into the rest of Asia.

The descendants of these people are known as Mongoloids, one of the four major groups of mankind in many racial classifications. The basis of such classifications is today thought of as questionable, but the four racial groups must nonetheless be dealt with here, since they still have wide usage. Apart from the Mongoloids, the most readily identifiable group is that known as the Negroid. Their characteristics—dark skin color, tightly curled black hair, broad lips and

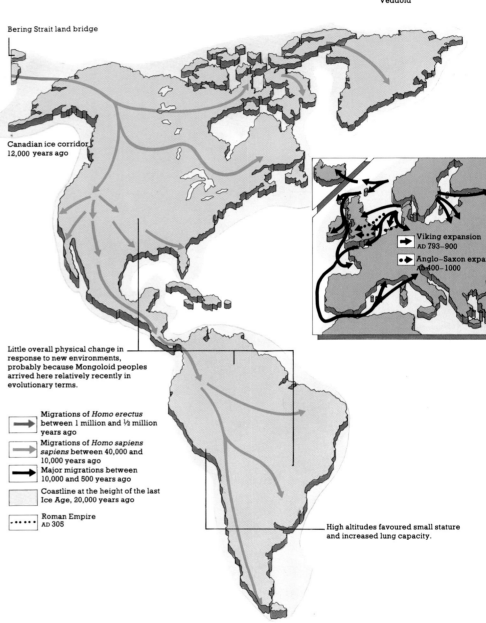

Bering Strait land bridge

Canadian ice corridor 12,000 years ago

Little overall physical change in response to new environments, probably because Mongoloid peoples arrived here relatively recently in evolutionary terms.

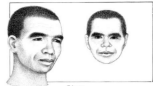

Viking expansion
AD 793–900

Anglo-Saxon expan
AD 400–1000

Migrations of *Homo erectus* between 1 million and ½ million years ago

Migrations of *Homo sapiens sapiens* between 40,000 and 10,000 years ago

Major migrations between 10,000 and 500 years ago

Coastline at the height of the last Ice Age, 20,000 years ago

Roman Empire AD 305

High altitudes favoured small stature and increased lung capacity.

The migrations of man
The human species originated in Africa, our ancestors moving northward into Eurasia half a million years ago. Modern man emerged about 40,000 years ago, perhaps in the Middle East, and moved out from there to colonize the world. Present-day racial differences probably began to evolve after this time. Further migrations since that date have resulted in the complex pattern of racial features seen today. This map shows migrations up to AD 1500—since then there have been migrations on a much larger scale and more widespread intermarriage. As a result of the colonial era, a far greater area of the world is now Caucasoid, and large populations of Negroid ancestry are found in Europe and the Americas, as a legacy of the slave trade.

noses—are an adaptation to high temperatures, high levels of solar radiation and high humidity.

Members of a third group, the Caucasoids, inhabit a broad geographical zone. In the south of their region many are fairly dark skinned, but the northern populations have light pigmentation, an adaptation to the weak sunlight. (Sunlight falling on the skin enables the human body to synthesize vitamin D; very dark pigmentation screens out a great deal of sunlight to protect the skin from the tropical sun, but in weak sunlight it absorbs too much of the light and may cause vitamin D deficiency—rickets.) The fourth major racial group, the Australoids, are characterized by dark pigmentation, wavy hair and broad noses—as with Negroids, adaptations to heat and intense sunlight.

In addition to these four racial divisions there are a number of small groups, such as the Veddoids of southern India, that may be remnants of much older populations. Thus the Bushmen and Hottentots, known collectively as Khoisans, represent a racial group that was once much more widespread in Africa. Their short

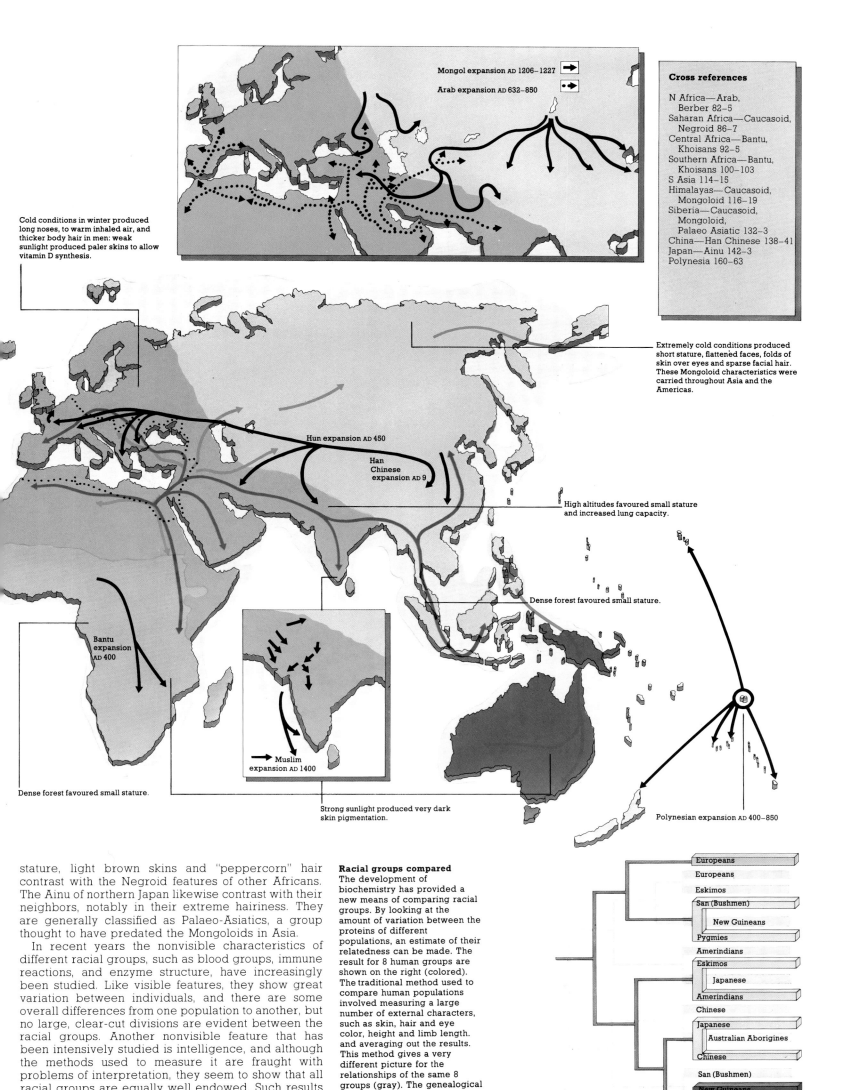

Cold conditions in winter produced long noses, to warm inhaled air, and thicker body hair in men: weak sunlight produced paler skins to allow vitamin D synthesis.

Mongol expansion AD 1206–1227

Arab expansion AD 632–850

Cross references

N Africa—Arab, Berber 82–5
Saharan Africa—Caucasoid, Negroid 86–7
Central Africa—Bantu, Khoisans 92–5
Southern Africa—Bantu, Khoisans 100–103
S Asia 114–15
Himalayas—Caucasoid, Mongoloid 116–19
Siberia—Caucasoid, Mongoloid, Palaeo Asiatic 132–3
China—Han Chinese 138–41
Japan—Ainu 142–3
Polynesia 160–63

Extremely cold conditions produced short stature, flattened faces, folds of skin over eyes and sparse facial hair. These Mongoloid characteristics were carried throughout Asia and the Americas.

Hun expansion AD 450

Han Chinese expansion AD 9

High altitudes favoured small stature and increased lung capacity.

Dense forest favoured small stature.

Bantu expansion AD 400

Muslim expansion AD 1400

Dense forest favoured small stature.

Strong sunlight produced very dark skin pigmentation.

Polynesian expansion AD 400–850

stature, light brown skins and "peppercorn" hair contrast with the Negroid features of other Africans. The Ainu of northern Japan likewise contrast with their neighbors, notably in their extreme hairiness. They are generally classified as Palaeo-Asiatics, a group thought to have predated the Mongoloids in Asia.

In recent years the nonvisible characteristics of different racial groups, such as blood groups, immune reactions, and enzyme structure, have increasingly been studied. Like visible features, they show great variation between individuals, and there are some overall differences from one population to another, but no large, clear-cut divisions are evident between the racial groups. Another nonvisible feature that has been intensively studied is intelligence, and although the methods used to measure it are fraught with problems of interpretation, they seem to show that all racial groups are equally well endowed. Such results are not surprising since members of any of the world's races are capable of freely exchanging genetic material through interbreeding.

Racial groups compared
The development of biochemistry has provided a new means of comparing racial groups. By looking at the amount of variation between the proteins of different populations, an estimate of their relatedness can be made. The result for 8 human groups are shown on the right (colored). The traditional method used to compare human populations involved measuring a large number of external characters, such as skin, hair and eye color, height and limb length, and averaging out the results. This method gives a very different picture for the relationships of the same 8 groups (gray). The genealogical tree based on biochemical features fits in better with what is known about the origins and migrations of the major groups.

Europeans
Europeans
Eskimos
San (Bushmen)
New Guineans
Pygmies
Amerindians
Eskimos
Japanese
Amerindians
Chinese
Japanese
Australian Aborigines
Chinese
San (Bushmen)
New Guineans
Pygmies
Australian Aborigines

Language and Communication

Body language
Unconscious, nonverbal language constantly supplements our speech, especially at emotional moments. Here, a man takes leave of his family at a railroad station. Their smiles, their intense stares, and the way the man inclines his head, all convey meaning about their feelings for each other.

Eloquent gestures
The use of gestures when talking is a universal human trait, and most people find it extremely difficult to talk without moving their hands. This is because our whole body is involved in our relationships with other people; our hands and faces in particular provide key supplements to speech.

Sign language
When communicating across language barriers, gestures are vitally important—here, Amazonian Indians talk with the Villas Boas brothers, founders of the Xingu Park reservation. An elaborate sign language was once used by the Plains Indians of North America, since each tribe spoke a different language.

Animals communicate, but language, strictly speaking, is unique to man, and has played a fundamental role in our development—without language human society as we know it would be impossible. Communication among animals relies on a variety of signals such as sounds, vibrations, bodily postures and movements, facial expressions, and scents. The giving and understanding of these signals is either learned at an early age or inherited genetically—sometimes a combination of the two—but the exchanges that take place are always highly stereotyped. The signal has a specific meaning, such as "this is my territory," and the responses it can evoke are strictly limited. Even the repertoire of signals available is not all that large—for example, the rhesus monkey, a highly social primate, can only communicate about forty distinct messages.

Human speech, in contrast, uses sound signals—words—whose meaning is assigned *culturally*, which makes language highly flexible, since words can readily be adapted to changing needs. The meaning of each word is an entirely arbitrary designation (except in onomatopoeia), whereas a significant number of animal signals bear a direct relationship to their meaning, as when a baboon exposes its massive canine teeth, signifying hostility.

The basic sounds which make up the repertoire of a language are known as phonemes—there are over thirty in most languages, although some have as few as twenty or as many as sixty. The phonemes are put together to make a large number of morphemes, or minimal meaningful units (eg man), and these may be combined or modified to yield other words (eg manly, manhood), so that the total number of words that can be formed is very large. Generally, these basic word signals each carry much less information than a single animal signal, but they can be combined in many different ways. They permit communication at levels of complexity and subtlety which animals never approach, and can convey ideas involving time and space.

The number of items of information which human speech can communicate is potentially infinite. Tone and emphasis modify the meaning of words, and the order in which words are strung together itself conveys information. This structured and meaningful ordering of words is known as syntax, and is a unique property of human speech—although animals sometimes combine two signals there is no known instance of signals being generated in a different order to change their meaning. Although the rules of syntax vary greatly from one language to another, some linguists maintain that there is a fundamental system common to them all, which is an innate, genetically inherited human characteristic. However, such inheritance would be virtually impossible to establish scientifically, and the demonstration of "universal" syntax rules is itself open to doubt.

Talking animals
An interesting perspective on studies of language has come from attempts to teach animals to communicate verbally. It is clear that the more intelligent animals can grasp the principle of *naming*—most dogs can recognize a few words as labels for particular objects,

The human voice
In human speech, the larynx (the "vocal chords") is the basic source of sound, but this sound is modified by changes in the shape of the vocal tract above the larynx. The shape is changed using the muscles of the lips, tongue, pharynx, jaw and velum, as well as muscles which raise and lower the larynx. An enormous variety of sounds can be produced, and each human language uses only a fraction of these. An example of sounds not used in English are the clicking noises, produced by the tongue and palate, of certain African languages. Unlike the vocal tract in humans, the tract in chimpanzees is not specialized for speech; thus it is much shorter and lacks the right-angled bend in the middle. Because of this they cannot make the vowel sounds [ɑ], [i], and [u] (*see below*) which, according to some linguists, are a vital component of human speech. These sounds are produced by moving the tongue so as to constrict the vocal tract near its midpoint above the larynx. However, computer simulations of the chimpanzee's vocal tract show that they could make a number of distinctive sounds—enough on which to base a language of their own, if they had the necessary intelligence and muscular coordination. Human babies have a vocal tract like that of a chimpanzee and it is significant that the sounds made by newborn babies are very similar to those of young chimpanzees.

Neanderthal Man's vocal tract—reconstructed on the basis of fossil skulls—was short and curved, like a chimpanzee's. Computer simulations show that he could not have made precise vowel sounds, although other studies (*below right*) show that he almost certainly had some sort of language. His language, like that of other early hominids, may have had only one vowel, and may have depended on sign language, as well as sound, to convey meaning.

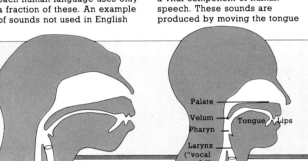

Palate
Velum
Pharyn — Tongue Lips
Larynx ("vocal cords")

The elements of speech
The vowels [ɑ] as in *had*, [i] as in *heed* and [u] as in *who'd* are found in almost all languages. Experiments have shown that someone listening to speech unconsciously uses these vowels to judge the length of the speaker's vocal tract, and that this information is vital in interpreting correctly other vowel sounds that the speaker makes. The three vowels represent the extreme points of a "triangle" containing all other vowel sounds, and depend on the vocal tract being constricted near its midpoint. As a result these three vowels are probably used to "calibrate" speech because they are more stable acoustically than others. The diagrams show where the constrictions occur for each of the three basic vowels. Constrictions like these can be made by modern man because he has a long vocal tract with a right-angled bend in the middle. These vowel sounds cannot be made by chimpanzees, and they could not have been made by Neanderthal Man.

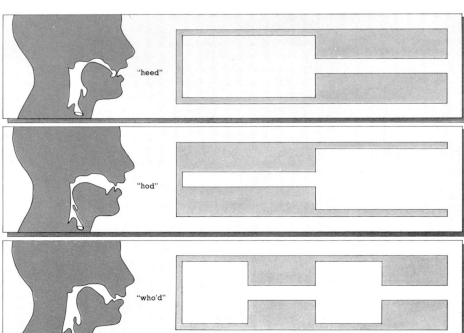

"heed"

"hod"

"who'd"

and experiments with chimpanzees and dolphins show that they too can understand this fundamental principle. Teaching programs with chimpanzees, utilizing deaf-and-dumb sign language, have shown that they can *use* words as well as understand them, but despite years of training, the "talking" chimpanzees still show no sign of grasping the idea of syntax, and only rarely combine the words they know into any novel combinations. The original hope of the experimenters, that the chimps would eventually begin to explain how they felt or what they thought about, now seems extremely remote.

This suggests that there *is* a fundamental difference between animal signals and human language—that our speech represents a radical innovation in forms of communication. Certainly, without speech, and its more durable written form, we could never have achieved the complex organization or technological advances that characterize human society. Language also permits abstract thought and reflection, and the development of language-based art forms. But despite its overriding importance in human life, speech has not displaced nonverbal forms of communication. Although we often underestimate their importance, facial expressions, gestures and bodily posture send out a stream of silent communications that are interpreted unconsciously, sometimes supplementing speech, sometimes taking its place. Close observation of human "body language" and nonverbal sounds (eg grunts and sighs) have led to the surprising discovery that we utilize slightly *more* distinctive signals of this type than even the most communicative social animals—chimpanzees and rhesus monkeys.

Milestones of language

There have been several key developments in human communication since the development of speech itself. The first was the emergence of picture writing and its elaboration into an ideographic script, as still employed for Chinese. With the invention of writing came the possibility of preserving information without the distortion, omission and elaboration that tends to affect oral traditions. The next vital invention, the alphabet, seems to have first occurred in the eastern Mediterranean in the second millennium BC. By representing most relevant sounds using just thirty or so signs, these scripts could capture all the words in a language with ease. Writing was still a painstaking business, however, until the invention of printing—originally in China, but reinvented in the West in AD 1441. It was this which made the mass production of books possible and paved the way for the enormous expansion in communication which has marked the twentieth century. The invention of the telephone in 1876, relying on electrical current for relaying speech, greatly speeded personal communication, but the success of modern forms of *mass* communication is largely due to the use of electromagnetic radiation, which travels at the speed of light. The use of radio and television, combined with satellite transmission, now enables complex messages to be relayed across continents and oceans in a fraction of a second, and to reach something close to entire populations.

Cross references

Horn of Africa—oral culture of Somalis 80–81
Central Africa—oral culture of Pygmies 92–5
East and southern Africa— "click" languages 96–103
Turkic-speaking central Asia—influence of Arabic script 130–31
Siberia—Buryat script 132–3
Mongolia—changes in script 136–7
China—simplification of script 138–41
Japan—learning of script by children 142–3
Amerindian N America— sign languages 166–9
See also
Migration and race 14–5
Languages of the world 18–9

Oral culture
An Australian Aborigine tells an ancient myth in the form of a song, to the accompaniment of his "clapping sticks." This type of oral culture is common among peoples whose language has no written form, and the reciting of stories and legends plays a vital role in binding their communities together.

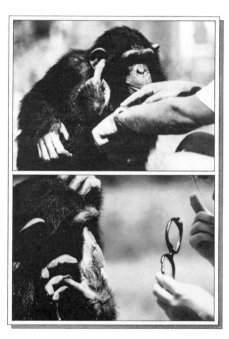

Teaching chimps to talk
An early attempt to teach a chimpanzee human language involved bringing up a young chimp as if it was a human baby. The experimenters hoped that it would begin to talk, but after four years it could only manage rough approximations of four words—"Mama," "Papa," "cup" and "up." More recent experiments have aimed at teaching chimpanzees Amelsan—the sign language used by the deaf in America. Several chimps have been taught this language and have acquired vocabularies of over a hundred words. An experiment in teaching sign language to a gorilla has also been successful. The chimp shown here is making the signs for "hear" and "see." But while the chimpanzees use the signs and understand their meaning, they show no grasp of syntax, which is a fundamental characteristic of human speech—for example, they are as likely to sign "apple give" as "give apple."

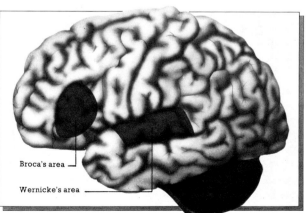

Speech and the brain
The left hemisphere of the brain is primarily concerned with speech and hearing. A raised area, known as Broca's area, is responsible for coordinating the muscle movements that produce speech. Damage to this part of the brain impairs both speech and writing. Wernicke's area is responsible for grammar and vocabulary—damage here may result in nonsensical use of words. The human skull shows the imprint of these two bumps, and fossil skulls have been examined for similar marks. These show up in all hominids, even the very early ones. The marks are large in Neanderthal Man, suggesting that they had a complex language.

Broca's area

Wernicke's area

Russian	Идея использования квантовых систем для ге радиоволн оказалась весьма плодотворной и недостижимые для обычной радиотехники резу.
Burmese	ဤပစ္စည်းကရိယာများ၊ ရှိပြီးဖြစ်လေသည်။ အလယ် ဝိုင်ရ ပဂ္ဂိုလ်များအတွက် အထူးသင်တန်းများ
Greek	Ὁ Ὀδυσσεὺς καὶ οἱ σύντροφοι αὐτοῦ πλοῖα, τὰ ὁποῖα ἦσαν πλήρη λαφύρων, ἀ Τρωάδος, ἐπιθυμοῦντες νὰ φθάσωσιν ὅσο
Hebrew	: יְהוּדִים שָׁמְרוּדִי בָּךְ. כֵּן שֶׁהִגִּיעַ לְאֻנְסְפָּסְרָם זָרְחָה בָּן שֶׁרָאָה אֵת שִׁמְעוֹן הַצַּדִּיק יָרַד מִמֶּרְכַּבְתּוֹ וְהִשְׁתַּחֲוָה
Sanskrit	मंस्कृत नाम देवी वाग् प्रवाक्ष्याम महर्षिभिः। तद्वयम् तन्नमो देशेत्यि मनोक प्रावृतकम्॥ प्राभोरादिगिरि: काव्यस्रवप्रभंश इति स्मृताः॥ शास्त्रे तु संस्कृताद् प्रयद् प्रत्यवगोदितम्॥ इति: प्रमाद: समता माध्यं मुक्कुमारता। अर्थव्यपितर

Chinese
是

帶所及，使英國人的生活習慣也起了變化，
館子吃一頓的，現在大多數改為吃自助餐，
習慣，一星期中，揀了幾天牛油麵包或三文
被迫產生的節約退減情形更嚴重。
至殃及學生們在假期中找臨時工作的出路。
清況都還不錯的華僑們所開發的中國
光是倫敦一地，為去一年來停
倍業。

The written word
These six examples of scripts in use today give some idea of the variety of written forms that can be used for human languages. Apart from Chinese, all these scripts are alphabetic, each symbol representing a sound. All such scripts probably stem from one alphabet, devised in the Syria-Palestine area about 3,500 years ago. The Chinese script is based on ideograms, each of which represents a complete word. A number of ideographic scripts have been devised independently in different parts of the world.

Languages of the World

For most of mankind's history, the distribution of languages has been discontinuous and fragmented, languages diverging and multiplying as human groups dispersed. The foundations of the present language map of the world were laid during the long preliterate period of hunting and gathering, but reshaped and overlaid by the upheavals and migrations of succeeding millennia. As urban societies developed writing systems, and later printing and radio, so human language overcame its former restraints of space and time. Today, with the addition of satellite communications to the complex networks already established, the human race is becoming a single community, for the first time since its early origins. Human communication, in all its forms, can now be considered as a *single* system within which every language, spoken, written or electronic, has its place.

Relationships of languages

Six major language families, or "areas of wider affinity," have been used as a frame of reference in this volume. Each of these covers a wide geographical area, and represents a grouping of languages which share items of vocabulary and which often have similar grammatical rules. The relationship may be readily apparent, as with Spanish and Italian, or it may be more distant, and detectable only by systematic comparisons. Languages excluded from these six areas are described as "unaffiliated," although some of them form less extensive families among themselves (eg Dravidian or Uralic). Certain "unaffiliated" languages may in fact belong within one of the six major areas—Japanese and Korean, for example, are possible members of the Altaic family—but such links are uncertain.

Despite the traditional use of the term "language family," it should be emphasized that languages do not have separate existences, as do individuals within human families. It may seem obvious what "English" is, and yet no two individuals possess (or have ever possessed) an identical knowledge of the English language, and there is no mechanism to prevent another language from adopting any item from English, or *vice versa*. English and French have been linguistic rivals for almost a thousand years, yet they have each changed enormously during that period, and each has absorbed so much from the other that the history of the two cannot be separated. Nor can one say that either language begins, historically, with this or that written text, since unbroken chains of spoken language reach back not only from Modern English to Anglo-Saxon, and from French to Popular Latin, but beyond these to a point of convergence with early forms of other Indo-European languages. It is conceivable that there are further links between major language families, and that cumulative changes by successive generations have now eliminated all trace of their relationship. Indeed, *all* human languages may ultimately share a common origin, but this is a matter for speculation.

The problem of recognizing the boundaries between one language and another is even more pronounced where there has been no attempt to standardize languages, as there has in the nation-states of Europe. In Africa, for example, where few languages have been officially standardized, the dialects of related languages often form a more or less inter-intelligible continuum, so that it becomes a matter of opinion how many African languages there are—estimates vary from less than 1,000 to over 2,000. In the same way, there were once chains of Romance and Germanic dialects in western Europe, but improved communications and formal education through the medium of "standard dialects" have brought greater linguistic unity to each of Europe's nation-states. In the era of radio and television, the dialects which constitute any one of the major languages of Europe are being drawn closer together than ever before.

While some languages are spoken by millions of people, others are restricted to tiny populations, like the languages of the San peoples of the Kalahari, or the Australian Aborigines. However, these languages are as complex in their structure as more widely spoken languages and have intricate grammatical systems. The presence or absence of a complex morphology is in no way related to the type of society or culture involved, whereas much of the vocabulary of a lan-

Major language families
This summary of the distribution of languages in the world today is based on the majority home languages of each area. The languages are classified in terms of the six major "families" now most generally recognized. These families have been used as the unifying framework of reference throughout the atlas. Each family contains varying degrees of complexity, and this is reflected in the maps for each culture area. The Niger-Congo area, for example, includes hundreds of distinct but inter-related languages in Africa, whereas the Indo-European area in the Americas is dominated by only four.

Mother-tongue speakers
Every language in the world has its place within a continuum, its limits determined by the geographical, social and functional roles of adjacent languages. The total of first-language speakers within each of the major language families is given as a percentage of the total world population.

Indo-European 46.5%	
Indo-Iranian	14%
Sino-Tibetan 23%	
Sinitic	
Niger-Congo	6%
Bantu 3%	Others 3%

guage does relate to the culture and value system of its speakers. Thus the languages of pastoralists have many specialized terms relating to the animals herded. However, the size of an average person's active vocabulary shows a remarkable consistency from one language to another, ever though his or her *potential* vocabulary is inevitably larger in a language with a long written tradition than in an unwritten language.

The politics of language

Language serves as a symbol of ethnic or social identity, and the languages of all communities deserve equal respect. Recent centuries have seen the increasing use of language by governments as a means of imposing national unity on a diverse population. English has been used in this way in the United States, for example, and so has Castilian in Spain. Frequently, such policies have involved attitudes of cultural or ethnic superiority by speakers of the dominant language, and have stimulated the use of other languages as rallying points for oppressed or dissatisfied minorities. Armenian has fulfilled this role in Turkey, as have Breton in France, and Basque and Catalan in Spain. Language may also function as a means of reasserting unity among a dispersed population, as with the German speakers of central Europe, or creating a sense of solidarity among people of mixed ethnic background, as in Paraguay, where use of Guarani symbolizes a largely mythical "shared" Amerindian heritage. As the need for worldwide languages increases, so also does the need for minorities to protect their linguistic and cultural heritage.

Major official languages

Indo-European
- English
- French
- Spanish and Portuguese
- Russian

Afro-Asiatic
- Arabic

Sino-Tibetan
- Chinese

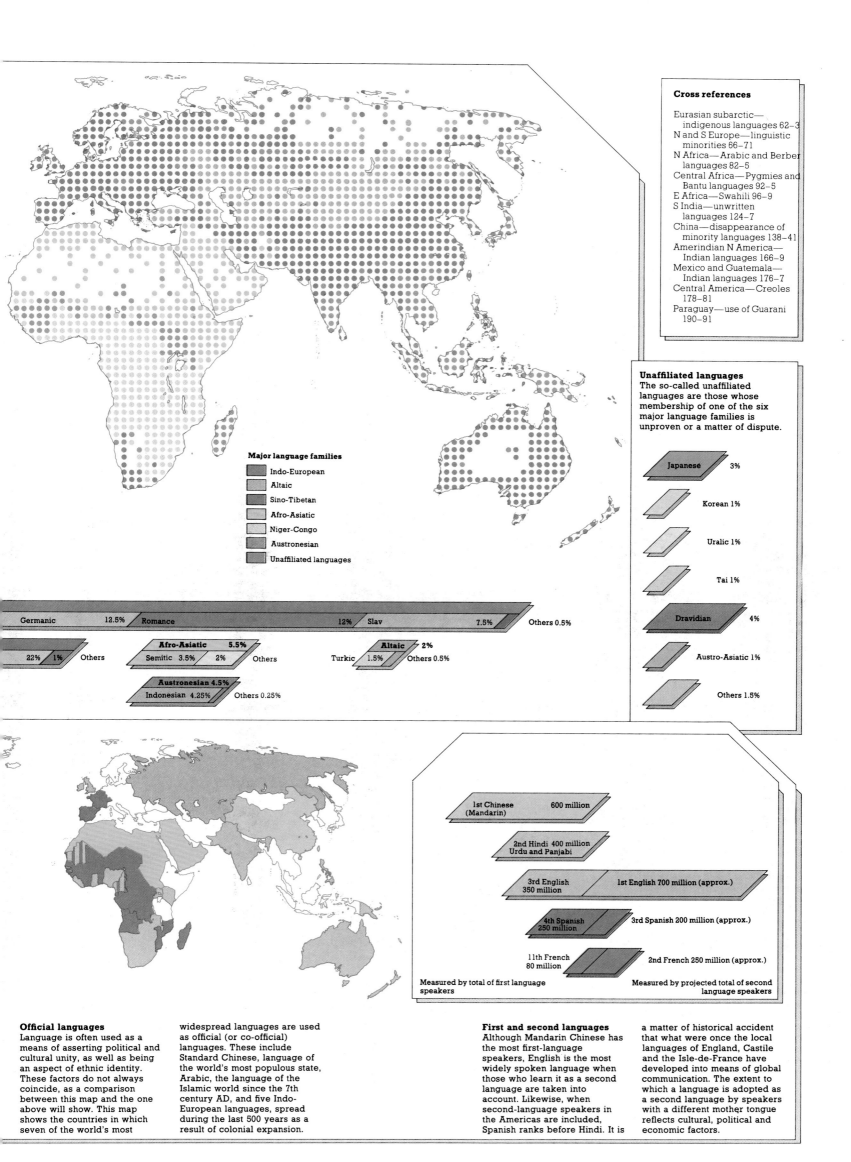

Major language families

- Indo-European
- Altaic
- Sino-Tibetan
- Afro-Asiatic
- Niger-Congo
- Austronesian
- Unaffiliated languages

Cross references

Eurasian subarctic—
  indigenous languages 62–3
N and S Europe—linguistic
  minorities 66–71
N Africa—Arabic and Berber
  languages 82–5
Central Africa—Pygmies and
  Bantu languages 92–5
E Africa—Swahili 96–9
S India—unwritten
  languages 124–7
China—disappearance of
  minority languages 138–41
Amerindian N America—
  Indian languages 166–9
Mexico and Guatemala—
  Indian languages 176–7
Central America—Creoles
  178–81
Paraguay—use of Guarani
  190–91

Unaffiliated languages
The so-called unaffiliated
languages are those whose
membership of one of the six
major language families is
unproven or a matter of dispute.

Japanese	3%
Korean	1%
Uralic	1%
Tai	1%
Dravidian	4%
Austro-Asiatic	1%
Others	1.5%

| Germanic 12.5% | Romance | 12% Slav | 7.5% | Others 0.5% |

| 22% | 1% | Others | **Afro-Asiatic 5.5%** Semitic 3.5% | 2% Others | Turkic 1.5% | **Altaic** 2% Others 0.5% |

Austronesian 4.5%
Indonesian 4.25%   Others 0.25%

1st Chinese (Mandarin)	600 million
2nd Hindi Urdu and Panjabi	400 million
3rd English 350 million	1st English 700 million (approx.)
4th Spanish 250 million	3rd Spanish 200 million (approx.)
11th French 80 million	2nd French 250 million (approx.)

Measured by total of first language
speakers

Measured by projected total of second
language speakers

Official languages
Language is often used as a
means of asserting political and
cultural unity, as well as being
an aspect of ethnic identity.
These factors do not always
coincide, as a comparison
between this map and the one
above will show. This map
shows the countries in which
seven of the world's most
widespread languages are used
as official (or co-official)
languages. These include
Standard Chinese, language of
the world's most populous state,
Arabic, the language of the
Islamic world since the 7th
century AD, and five Indo-
European languages, spread
during the last 500 years as a
result of colonial expansion.

First and second languages
Although Mandarin Chinese has
the most first-language
speakers, English is the most
widely spoken language when
those who learn it as a second
language are taken into
account. Likewise, when
second-language speakers in
the Americas are included,
Spanish ranks before Hindi. It is
a matter of historical accident
that what were once the local
languages of England, Castile
and the Isle-de-France have
developed into means of global
communication. The extent to
which a language is adopted as
a second language by speakers
with a different mother tongue
reflects cultural, political and
economic factors.

Environment and Survival

Climatic patterns

Climate is largely determined by the interaction of the earth's atmosphere and oceans. Geographical features, such as mountain ranges and the distribution of land and sea, modify air pressure systems to a certain extent, and all these factors produce a number of climatic characteristics for each region of the globe. These characteristics determine both the natural vegetation of that area and the crops that man can grow, so that ultimately climate sets limits to the level and intensity of human activity. The cultivation of crops depends on adequate temperatures in spring for germination, adequate rainfall and warmth during the growing season, and a minimum period without frost. Human activities are modifying the climate, however. The burning of fossil fuels, for example, raises temperatures and increases the amount of carbon dioxide in the atmosphere, which may have secondary effects on climate.

London's climate typifies that of the warm, temperate middle latitudes. Maritime influences produce steady rainfall all year and extremes of heat or cold are a rare occurrence.

Cairo experiences the climate of the Egyptian desert. Warm, dry air results from anticyclones, and strong sunshine is interrupted only rarely by thunderstorms.

Calcutta usually receives plentiful rainfall from the summer monsoon of Southeast Asia, but the variability of this rain is a constant threat to this densely populated area.

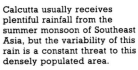

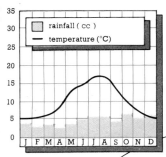

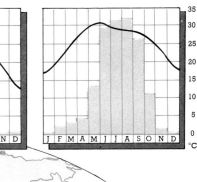

The world of mankind is, by and large, not a particularly suitable world *for* mankind—too much of its surface is unfavorable for settlement. Not only is 70 percent of its surface occupied by oceans, but even on the land areas which account for the remaining 30 percent, there are large parts which are too cold, or too dry, for human comfort. In these parts of the earth sparse settlement is possible only through extreme measures of human adaptation, and dense settlement is not possible at all.

These hostile areas make up over one third of the land surface. In general terms, about 15 percent of the land area is too dry for cultivation or to support sedentary stock raising, and settlement in these areas is limited to oases, mining camps and nomadic tribes. Another 20 percent of the lands are either under polar ice caps or are in the state known as permafrost—frozen throughout the year except for a few inches of soil at the surface. A smaller fraction of the land surface (probably about 3 percent) is either too wet or too liable to flood to be used continuously, and a considerable area consists of highland. Here altitude, exposure, slope, and absence of soil virtually prohibit use, except for seasonal grazing, in some parts, by hardy animals such as goats and yaks.

By the time we have deducted from the total land area all these hostile environments, not much more than a half of the surface is left, whose use and occupation are relatively straightforward. But only relatively so: not only are there natural hazards threatening mankind in most areas—earthquakes, eruptions, tidal waves—but there are long-term influences upon human activity, especially climatic influences, which must be contended with. And then there are problems created, even in the most placid environments, by the mere use of the land in an intensive manner—unforeseen ecological changes, soil erosion, and competition for space or resources.

Climatic regions

Tropical climates

Tropical rainforests experience no seasonal changes, but have steady rainfall and temperature throughout the year; savanna and monsoon areas are also warm throughout the year but have wet and dry seasons.

▦ Rain forest climate

▤ Monsoon climate

▦ Savanna climate

Dry climates

Stable, high-pressure air systems produce cloudless skies and low rainfall in steppes and deserts.

▦ Steppe climate

▦ Desert climate

Warm-temperate rainy climate

Warm, temperate rainy climates occur in the middle latitudes. Winters are usually mild and some rain falls in most months of the year, except in regions of Mediterranean climate, where the summer is hot and dry.

▢ Dry winter climate

▨ Dry summer climate

▨ Climate with no dry season

Cold temperate rainy climates

Humid, cold climates with severe winters are also found in the middle latitudes. Continental interiors have more extreme temperatures, particularly in winter, and less annual rainfall than coastlands.

▢ Dry winter and summer climates

Polar climate

At the poles, icy deserts are found. Adjoining the polar regions are areas of tundra, with limited vegetation, due to the permafrost.

▦ Tundra climate

With all this to overcome, human beings still have succeeded in creating a home for themselves—to be precise, for 4,500 million of them. Dutch engineers building seawalls, Sicilian and Indonesian peasants recolonizing the slopes of a volcano after an eruption, children attending school in the winter darkness north of the Arctic Circle—all these are tributes to the stubbornness of mankind in making the world his home.

The challenge of climate

The impact of climate is not only direct and physiological—not only, that is, a matter of man developing physical characteristics, clothing and housing suited to life in hot climates, cold climates or high altitudes. The indirect impact is much greater: climate imposes rhythms upon life, and sets limits. Whether he is a hunter-gatherer, pastoralist or cultivator, the rhythm of climate establishes his calendar, while the limitations stand as a permanent challenge to his ingenuity in overcoming them.

Among the important climatic variables are two main groups: temperature related and moisture related. Temperature governs the length of the growing season—in cold climates the question is whether enough heat will accumulate for crops to grow between frosts, while in warm climates, it is how many crops can be ripened and harvested in the course of a growing season.

Moisture controls are more complex and almost the least important factor is *how much* rain falls. In areas where moisture is scarce, acceptable ways of life can still be developed, provided that what little moisture there is can be relied upon. More important, at least in dry areas, is the seasonal distribution of rainfall and its variability from year to year. Rainfall during a growing season is useful but rainfall during winter may well be agriculturally useless unless stored in expensive reservoirs and irrigation schemes. Seasonality has its most marked effect in southern Asia, where more than

Cross references

Tropical rainy climates
N India 120–23
SE Asia 144–5
Dry climates
Horn of Africa 80–81
Sahara 86–7
Cold-temperate rainy climates
Arctic and Subarctic 58–9
Siberia 132–3
Natural hazards
Australia and New Zealand 156–7
Caribbean 178–81
Land use
Eskimos 62–3
Argentina, Paraguay and Uruguay 190–91
See also
Migrations and race 14–15
Search for food 22–9
World health 54–5

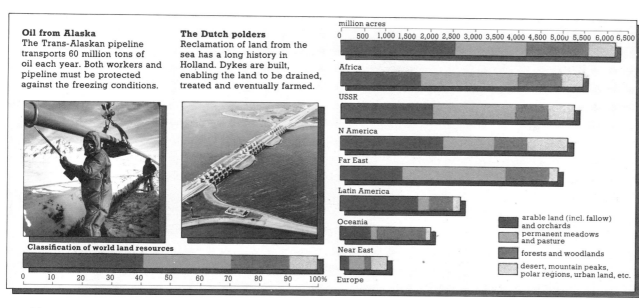

Oil from Alaska
The Trans-Alaskan pipeline transports 60 million tons of oil each year. Both workers and pipeline must be protected against the freezing conditions.

The Dutch polders
Reclamation of land from the sea has a long history in Holland. Dykes are built, enabling the land to be drained, treated and eventually farmed.

million acres

Africa
USSR
N America
Far East
Latin America
Oceania
Near East
Europe

arable land (incl. fallow) and orchards
permanent meadows and pasture
forests and woodlands
desert, mountain peaks, polar regions, urban land, etc.

Classification of world land resources

a fifth of all mankind lives its life by the rhythm of the great monsoon, the three-seasonal division of the year upon which so much depends that men dread the failure of the monsoon rains above all else.

The ecological balance

Apart from hazards and climate, a third kind of problem arises from man's use of the earth, generally from the need to find space and resources for an ever-enlarging population or from a wish to speed up or modify the cycles of nature. Pretechnical man had no means of doing this; he accepted these natural cycles and, with them, a limitation on human numbers. Now we have abundant means, but the means themselves produce chain reactions—chemicals kill pests but pollute streams; new breeds of plant feed more mouths but may require huge inputs of fertilizers to do so; land is cleared of forest and cultivated, but soil erosion results. With a world population of 4,500 million we need more of everything—the problem is how to get it without condemning the next generation or the generation after that to starve.

The world of mankind can be thought of as ringed by frontiers. There is a frontier of cold, which can be

Global land use
Land use reflects both the natural resources and the degree of economic development of the region. Man's activities have reduced forested areas from almost two-thirds to less than one-third of the land surface area. The remaining natural forest consists largely of the northern coniferous forests, where the short growing season does not favor agriculture, and tropical rain forests, where clearance is a barrier to exploitation.

Natural hazards
Destructive forces of nature can have catastrophic results in densely populated regions of the world. However, many people live under continual threat of natural disaster. Hurricanes or typhoons, for example, occur in luxuriant tropical areas that are otherwise highly attractive to human settlement. And the outpourings of volcanoes produce some of the world's most fertile soils, so that man has deliberately chosen to farm volcanic slopes.

pushed back by more efficient heating and by developing hardier crops. There is a frontier of drought, where irrigation, tree planting and moisture conservation are producing real progress. There is a frontier created by the sea, where coastal people have fought a long battle to reclaim land. There is a frontier posed by the forest, where cutting and clearing may well be unwise. There is a health frontier, where disease closes lands to people or livestock, as the tsetse fly does in so much of Africa. There is a technological frontier, where people who once had to conform to natural limitations now work to break free, speed up resource exploitation and raise their standard of living.

The uncomplicated dependence on natural resources with which man began (and after which some Westerners in the twentieth century still hanker) is no longer possible, given the magnitude of the twentieth century's population. Survival for mankind depends on new resource discoveries and on wise resource use. It is fortunate for us that, although there are some glaring examples of misuse, the record of discovery, inventiveness and care in the resource field is, viewed as a whole, an encouraging one.

Natural disasters

tropical storm development regions

volcanoes active since 1900

major destructive earthquakes 1900–79

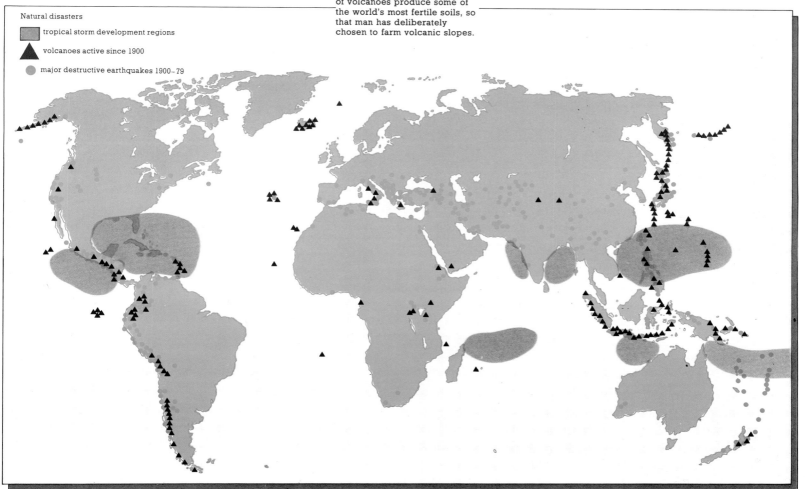

The Search for Food: Hunter-gatherers

For the greater part of human history we have fed ourselves by hunting animals and gathering edible plants from the wild—only in the last 10,000 years or so did man begin to cultivate the land and keep domesticated animals for food. There are two basic differences between these food-production systems. First, all hunter-gatherers *extract* their food from nature whereas cultivators and most pastoralists impose their will on the environment and *manage* natural resources. Second, many hunter-gatherers obtain an immediate return on their labor—the animals they kill or the nuts and berries they gather are consumed on the same day that they are "produced." This is in marked contrast to farming, where there is a delayed return on invested labor. Some hunter-gatherer groups do invest their labor further into the future—hunters and fishers, such as the Eskimo, for example, invest energy and time in the manufacture of their equipment—but not to the same extent as cultivators.

One consequence of this is that, whereas sedentary cultivators tend to have an elaborate structure of social relations to organize and control their labor and assets, hunter-gatherers generally do not. However, social hierarchies can emerge among hunter-gatherers, particularly if there is an abundant supply of food, and this was a notable feature of many groups of North American Indians. The greatest degree of organization was found among the Kwakiutl Indians of the northwest coast, who settled around the salmon streams of Vancouver Island. These provided them with a rich source of food, and because they were able to harvest the streams at particular times of the year, they developed systems of food storage and established permanent villages. Their political structure and ceremonial life became far more complex than that characteristic of "immediate-return" hunter-gatherers.

Hunter-gatherer societies of the immediate-return type include the Hill-Pandaram of southeast India, the Tasaday of the Philippines, the Guayaki of Paraguay, the African Pygmies, the Hadza of Tanzania and the San (Bushmen) of Botswana and Namibia. The immediacy of their economy is reflected in their attitudes—

The hunters' armory
Hunters' weapons are adapted to their particular needs. Here drawn to scale are the bows and arrows of the Baka Pygmies (A) and of the Hadza (B). The bow and arrow is not so important to the Baka, who rely primarily on the very effective 2 meter (7 foot) spear (C).

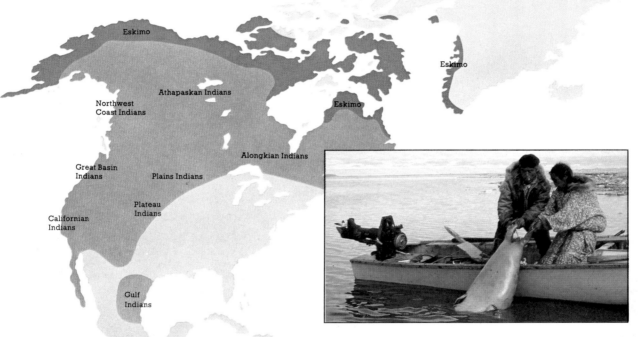

Part-time hunters
An Eskimo couple drag a seal aboard their boat. The Eskimo no longer live solely by hunting, but some still hunt for part of the year and these groups have maintained their hunter identity and traditions of cooperation, although using modern weapons such as rifles.

Meat sharing
!Kung children watch as a young antelope is butchered. The meat will be shared out among the band through a complex chain of gift giving. All hunter-gatherers have a strong ideology about sharing meat which helps to offset the unpredictability of hunting.

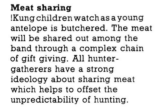

Living in the Kalahari
The main tools for gathering, the digging stick and *kaross* (hide bag), are used here to collect juicy tubers—a valuable source of moisture in the dry season. Surprisingly, many hunter-gatherers work only a few hours a day to collect all the food they need.

they live for the present, make no long-term plans, and do not store food for future consumption. Their shelters, if they have any, are simple affairs that can be erected quickly without much effort.

Most nomadic hunter-gatherers still following their traditional way of life today, live in small, flexible bands. In most groups, rights to land do not exist and there is therefore little need for binding social relationships for the management and transmission of property. The relationship between parents and children tends to be relaxed, while men and women generally have greater equality than in other types of society, although among the Australian Aborigines, with their extremely complex kinship and marriage organization, this is not the case.

Why was hunting-and-gathering abandoned?

As many present-day foragers manage to live surprisingly well even in regions as unproductive as deserts, it may be safe to assume that our hunter-gatherer ancestors, who must have exploited far richer environments, would have been equally successful. Cultivators and pastoralists, on the other hand, work far longer hours and always face the possibility of famine through disease, drought or flooding. Why then, after a successful run of many thousands of years, did most hunter-gatherers abandon this system and turn to cultivation? The possibility that change was forced by some external factor is suggested by the fact that the emergence of sedentary cultivating communities seems to have occurred at about the same time in several different parts of the world—the Middle East, the Far East, Melanesia and Central America.

One theory is that there was a slow but general buildup of population density, but there is not much evidence for any such increase in population at that time. Another argument is that the end of the last Ice Age, about 12,000 years ago, caused ecological changes in which many of the large game animals became extinct so that other food sources had to be sought. Other theories relate the advent of agriculture to the development of more complex societies, requiring food surpluses for exchange and tribute.

Whatever the reasons for the change to agriculture and livestock keeping, its demographic implications were profound. Milk from domesticated animals could be used to feed babies and they did not need to be suckled for so long. This led to an increased rate of ovulation and as the spacing interval between children became shorter the rate of population growth increased sharply.

Hunter-gatherers in the modern world

Today, only a tiny proportion of the world's population continues to practice hunting and gathering and very few depend on it for their entire livelihood. Such groups tend to live in marginal areas—the Arctic zones, the deserts of Australia and southern Africa, and the rain forests of Africa, India, South America and Southeast Asia. The surviving hunter-gatherers face a bleak future as market forces, missionaries and government policies combine to pull them into the wider economy. Programs of sedentarization often result in misery—for people who are used to mobility and to living in small groups, life in large, permanent settlements is a daunting prospect. They are exposed to new diseases and the dangers of alcohol, and some become landless laborers, beggars or prostitutes. Lacking formal institutions for dispute control, they are unable to deal with the tensions that inevitably result from living in larger and more crowded groups.

Cross references

Eskimos 60–61
Baka Pygmies 38, 92–5
San (Bushmen) 100–103
South Indian Hill Marias 125
Australian Aborigines 156–9
New Zealand Maoris 156–9
North American Indians 166–9
South American Chamococo 190
See also
Shifting cultivators 26
Death 36

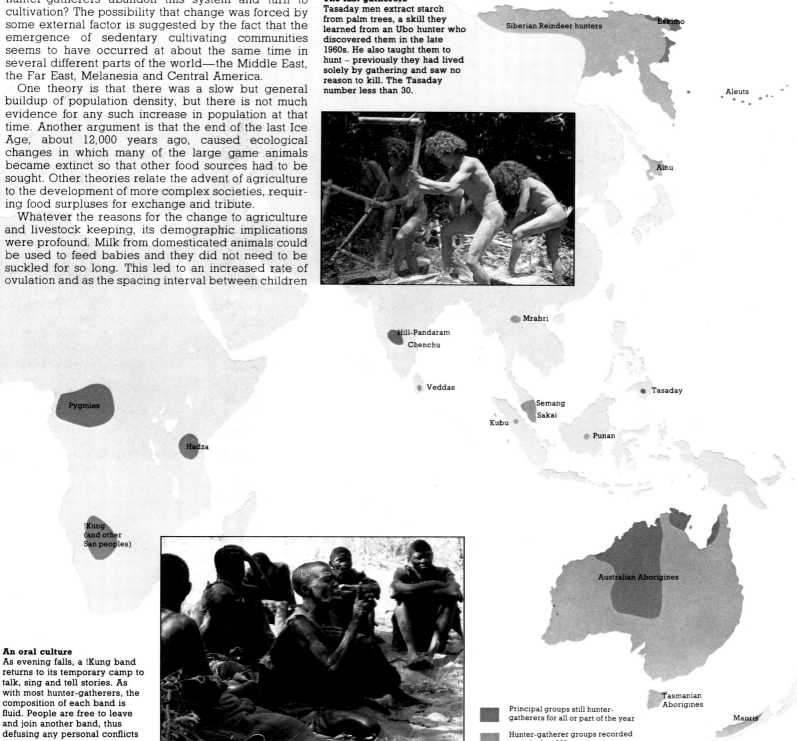

The last gatherers
Tasaday men extract starch from palm trees, a skill they learned from an Ubo hunter who discovered them in the late 1960s. He also taught them to hunt – previously they had lived solely by gathering and saw no reason to kill. The Tasaday number less than 30.

Siberian Reindeer hunters
Eskimo
Aleuts
Ainu
Pygmies
Hadza
!Kung (and other San peoples)
Mrabri
Hill-Pandaram
Chenchu
Veddas
Semang
Sakai
Kubu
Punan
Tasaday
Australian Aborigines
Tasmanian Aborigines
Maoris

An oral culture
As evening falls, a !Kung band returns to its temporary camp to talk, sing and tell stories. As with most hunter-gatherers, the composition of each band is fluid. People are free to leave and join another band, thus defusing any personal conflicts that arise.

■ Principal groups still hunter-gatherers for all or part of the year

■ Hunter-gatherer groups recorded over the last 200 years

The Search for Food: Pastoralists

Pastoralism is a form of livelihood based upon keeping herds of domestic animals—in the Old World cattle, sheep, goats, horses, camels, yak and reindeer, in the New World llamas and alpacas. It is well adapted to semiarid, subarctic or mountainous environments which are unsuited to agriculture. However, few pastoralists are entirely independent of agriculture. Most either cultivate a little themselves, or obtain part of their food from agricultural neighbors in exchange for pastoral produce. It is also common for "pastoralists"—individuals, households or even entire communities—to switch back and forth between pastoral and agricultural sectors of the regional economy.

Even as long ago as the Ice Age, men were involved in very close relationships with the animals they exploited, such as horses and reindeer, and in some cases this involvement could have represented a form of pastoralism. However, true pastoralism in the Old World probably emerged as a result of the intensification of mixed farming. This led to specialization into distinct agricultural and pastoral sectors, and to an overflow of human and animal populations into increasingly arid regions where cultivation was reduced in favor of animal husbandry. Only in the Eurasian subarctic, and possibly in the Peruvian Andes, did pastoralism emerge directly from hunting.

Pastoralists are popularly supposed to be nomadic and it is true that the animals' grazing requirements often force them to make frequent moves. However, the nature and extent of this movement varies considerably from one area to another. In some cases it takes the form of a regular seasonal migration, following a well-worn route, between distinct climatic zones. One very common migratory cycle, which utilizes lowland plains in the winter and upland pastures in the summer, is known as transhumance. In other cases, the pattern of movement is more irregular—a response to the erratic incidence of local rainfall, on which fresh pasture growth depends. Some pastoralists, such as the Maasai of East Africa, move about very little. Nomadism among pastoralists can also be a result of other economic interests—heavy involvement in activities such as long-distance trade or smuggling places a premium on physical mobility, as among many groups of Middle Eastern bedouin. Moreover, nomadic movement may have political significance as a strategy by which tribal groups can escape subjection to government authority.

The local group or "camps" of pastoralists tend to be fluid in social composition, and conflict may be settled by the contestants simply going their separate ways, leaving a trail of unresolved disputes behind them. Whether conflict evokes this response, or leads to protracted feuds, hostility rarely finds expression in the witchcraft accusations so common among cultivators. A fundamental characteristic of pastoralism is the recognition of living animals as a kind of self-reproducing property. Animals can be used to create and cement enduring social relations through their transfer from household to household as gifts, loans or marriage payments. By placing himself at the center of a network of such relations, the successful pastoralist can establish a substantial political following. The possession of animals also influences relations within domestic groups, allowing senior men to exert considerable control over their juniors, who stand to inherit, and who may need animals in order to marry.

The nature and organization of work in pastoral societies depends on the type of animals kept, and on the size and tameness of the herds. Sometimes the animals are so tame that they can almost be regarded as members of the household, as are cattle among the Nuer of southern Sudan, but in other cases they are virtually wild, as among the Sami (Lapps) of northern Scandinavia, who often have to hunt their herds, much as ranchers round up their free-ranging stock. In many pastoral societies there is a pronounced division of tasks and responsibilities by age as well as by sex. The everyday care of tame animals, including milking, often falls to the women, assisted perhaps by young boys. They also have the job of preparing milk and other products for consumption or storage, and carrying out all the chores connected with pitching and breaking camp. Herding is generally entrusted to

young, often unmarried, men. Their task is to protect the herds not only from predators and other natural hazards, but also from the raids of their neighbors. In most pastoral societies, raiding and counter raiding is a recognized means of acquiring property. Senior men in a pastoral society devote their attention to the political and religious affairs of the community.

Pastoral peoples are among the most vulnerable in the modern world, but they have not always been so. In the past they have often held the key to political and economic power in the regions they traversed, by virtue of their military superiority and control over trade. Today their presence is generally considered an embarrassment by the administrations of the territories they inhabit. The pastoral way of life is being progressively eroded by the expropriation of land, restrictions on movement and enforced sedentarization. The growing commercialization of pastoral production has tended to undermine traditional strategies of security—the informal networks of borrowing and lending livestock, and of food sharing, which helped to spread the burden of personal hardship. With increasing pressure on scarce resources, periodic ecological crises, that were previously endured, have turned into disasters of catastrophic proportions. Such was the drought and famine that struck the African Sahel between 1968 and 1973, killing up to 250,000 of the nomadic population, and forcing many of the survivors into shanty towns and refugee camps.

Karimojong—the search for pasture

⬛ Village
● Campsite
— Large family's first herd
— Large family's second herd
— Small family's herd

0   30 km
0   20 miles

The search for pasture
The migratory pattern of the Karimojong depends on family size and wealth. A wealthy man with several adult sons can divide his cattle into two herds. One stays close to home, but the other travels 80 km (50 miles) or more from the homestead, staying at each new campsite for up to 2 years. A less fortunate man keeps his herd near the homestead while the pasture is good, but may make a journey of 15 km (10 miles) during the dry season.

Sami—reindeer migration

Hammerfest

0   100 km
0   60 miles

● Migrations of Mountain Sami
|||||| Settled Sami without reindeer

Reindeer migration
One of life's realities for a reindeer-herding people is that the herd can move 32 km (20 miles) or more a day during the seasonal movements from wintering areas to summer pastures, away from the ravages of heat and mosquitoes. Often, special herdsmen are assigned to the herd by the community.

Blood for strength
A Maasai warrior drinks blood from an ox. To draw blood, an arrow is shot into the jugular vein—this does not harm the animal. Blood is reserved for the warriors or those who have been ill and need strengthening. The preservation of the herd is extremely important to the Maasai and milk, butter and blood are eaten far more often than meat. Animals are only slaughtered occasionally, for example in a ceremony, or during a severe drought.

Division of labor
A Somali woman tends a herd of goats. Goats and sheep are kept near permanent water with the family groups, while camels are herded by unmarried men who range over much more arid country and live on an inadequate diet of camel's milk. The two units only come together during the wet season.

Sorting the reindeer
The Sami (Lapps) sort the reindeer before the spring and autumn migrations, and mark their own animals with a notch in the ear to identify ownership after the journey to the summer pastures. In the autumn the reindeer are herded into corrals where some are chosen for castration or slaughter.

A Dinka settlement
For both Dinka and Karimojong the relationship between cattle and men is close. At initiation the young men are given an "ox name." Cattle are rarely eaten, and for the Dinka "eater of cattle" is an insult. When a Karimojong man dies, he is wrapped in cow hide and buried beneath his cattle corral.

Controlling the animals
Various implements are used to control animals. The wooden neck ring of the Gonds accustoms the beast to a yoke while the hobble prevents straying. The Nuer wean calves by means of a thorn ring, while the Tuareg place a forked stick though the nose—both make suckling painful for the cow.

Modern ranching
These huge US stockyards, geared to producing great quantities of meat, show how ranching in the West differs from traditional pastoralism. Ranching is a business, run for profit, while cattle herding, as practiced by the Dinka, Maasai or Karimojong, is not so much a livelihood as a way of life.

25

The Search for Food: Cultivators

9–10.5 m
(30–35 ft)

4.5–6 m
(15–20 ft)

1.5 m
(5 ft)

up to 23 cm
(up to 9 in)

Oil Palm

Plantain

Maize

Manioc

Squash

Beans

Although the invention of agriculture eventually had a revolutionary impact on the development of human society, recent archaeological research has revealed that the effects of this innovation were not immediate. The domestication of plants was a slow process which occurred independently in several parts of both the Old and the New World. For the peoples involved, the delayed return for their labor represented by the harvest of cultivated crops was not necessarily more advantageous than the immediate returns derived from hunting and gathering. Indeed, even today, this remains true for certain societies that continue to follow a predominantly hunter-gatherer way of life, despite knowledge and limited practice of agriculture.

The Siriono people of the Bolivian Amazon spend most of the year roaming their forested region, hunting and gathering. However, most families also clear and plant small fields of maize, manioc, tobacco and various fruits, although no strict seasonal cycle is followed. Soon after planting is complete, they resume their mobile life, leaving their fields to grow untended. Then, at harvest time, they pass by their fields once again, collecting whatever crops have managed to mature. In effect, the Siriono feel that the advantages of sedentary agriculture do not outweigh those of a nomadic life style.

The form of agriculture practiced by the Siriono is known as shifting cultivation, and is found among many peoples in different parts of the world. In such systems, the natural vegetation is cleared and burned, and the crops are then planted in the ashes, often without preliminary turning of the soil. The fields are cropped for one year, or for a few years in succession, until their fertility begins to decline or weeds become too rampant. Then the fields are allowed to lie fallow, and the natural vegetation reestablishes itself. Typically, the fallow period of a plot is several times longer than the period of cultivation—as much as twenty times longer

The polycrop field
Although the polycrop field may have a haphazard appearance, the diversity of crops fulfils an essential function. The different crop heights give the field a multi-layered character, which helps to prevent weed growth and protects the soil from erosion during torrential rains. Shrub and tree crops provide support for the vines of gourds, squashes and beans, which grow rapidly and are harvested before being shaded. Other annual crops such as maize are also harvested early in the farming cycle. Root crops such as manioc as well as other slower growing crops such as plantain, pawpaw and various palms are harvested from time to time over the next few years as the field gradually reverts to fallow.

Easy weeding
Limited weeding is undertaken as multilayered cropping helps to prevent weed growth; when weeds begin to flourish, the field is allowed to go fallow.

Shifting cultivator's tool kit
Since villages are often moved, possessions are kept to a minimum. Axes and hoes (C), once made with blades of stone or shell, have now been replaced by iron tools, such as the bush knife (D). Tools are also needed for processing food. Manioc root contains a poison which must be removed before eating. The root is crushed (A), grated (G), squeezed (E), dried and pounded (B) before cooking. Other utensils include clay pots and gourds (F).

The moving village
Most shifting cultivators must rebuild their houses every few years, as they move on to cultivate new lands. In many Amazonian tribes, several families live together in a longhouse, each family having a separate hearth, around which their hammocks are slung.

Hard clearing
Undergrowth is cleared first, then the larger trees are felled or girdled. When the cut vegetation has dried sufficiently, it is burned and crops are planted in the ashes. Useful forest trees may be protected from the burning and incorporated into the crop mosaic.

Shifting cultivation in the Amazonian forest
Like other shifting cultivators, those of the Amazonian forest depend on a long fallow period, during which the forest cover regenerates to renew the fertility of the soil. The system therefore requires extensive tracts of land, only a small proportion of which will be under cultivation at any one time—the ratio is 15 fallow fields to 1 cultivated field. The cycle begins with forest clearance and burning, which is followed by planting and gradual harvesting of fields over a period of several years. A new field will be opened every year so that cultivators will be farming several fields at once, each at a different stage in the cycle.

on poorer soils. Such systems therefore require large areas of land, and societies practicing shifting cultivation have low population densities.

Although shifting cultivation is relatively unproductive per unit of land, its productivity per hour of labor expended is relatively high, since shifting cultivation does not require the laborious removal of tree stumps for plowing, nor does it involve extensive ditching and terracing as in irrigated agriculture. Under favorable conditions, especially in tropical root-crop agriculture based on manioc, yams or sweet potatoes, the yield per acre (taking account of the plot under cultivation only) can be high, even rivaling that achieved by mechanized farming in the American Corn Belt. Where human labor is the main source of energy, and where labor is often in short supply, shifting cultivation is therefore highly advantageous, as long as plenty of land is available.

People who practice shifting cultivation often move their settlements every few years, to gain access to new land, but shifting cultivation does not necessarily require regular village relocation, and in some of these societies settlements may remain on the same site for several generations.

Increasing productivity

As population increases and the pressure on land resources becomes greater, agricultural peoples become more concerned to increase productivity per acre, which in nonmechanized systems implies greater labor input and less productivity per hour of labor. Such "intensification" of agriculture offers opportunities for the development of more complex societies. However, the ability to produce more food per acre is not a sufficient explanation for the rise of chiefdoms or empires. In fact, the relationship between the production of agricultural surpluses and the emergence of more complex forms of society is a reciprocal one—the existence of social elites, chiefs, administrators, or craftsmen is ultimately dependent on an adequate production of food, but these incipient political or economic specialists themselves exert pressures for increasing agricultural output.

Agricultural intensification can be brought about in a number of ways—often, fallow time is reduced, the fields are permanently cleared, and the fertility of the soil is maintained by manuring. Mixed farming, in which crop cultivation and livestock keeping are combined, is advantageous for manuring, although the additional work involved in keeping the livestock away from the crops can place a heavy strain on a family's labor resources.

Another means of intensification, particularly in dry regions, is irrigation, the simpler forms of which rely on hand watering with pots or with man- or animal-powered water-lifting devices. More elaborate systems of irrigation require extensive earthworks for dams and canals, and the leveling or terracing of fields. They usually require a relatively centralized society for construction and maintenance of the system. No longer reliant on seasonal rainfall, effective irrigation systems often permit farmers to obtain several harvests from a field in one year and thus contribute substantially to a society's total agricultural production. Systems of irrigated rice production in Asia support staggeringly high densities of population, reaching 2,000 per square kilometer (5,000 per square mile) in parts of Java, but such levels of production are obtained only through tremendous inputs of labor.

[Diagram: Population growth, Taxes, External markets, Ceremonial requirements → Larger surplus]

Why intensify cultivation?
Demands for increased yields may develop for a variety of reasons including population growth, more centralized political control with associated demands for tax or tribute, new opportunities for sales of crops in external markets, and expanding requirements for ceremonial exchange, sacrifices or religious tithes. Often, several of these factors combine to increase pressures on farmers to produce larger and larger surpluses.

Laborious weeding
With more frequent reuse of fields weed growth is more of a problem. Weeding with a short-handled hoe must be carried out several times each season, and the heavy work involved can strain a family's labor resources. Cooperative labor parties of kinsmen and friends help to speed the task.

Domesticated animal power
Animal labor may be substituted for human labor in plowing and hauling, and dung provides valuable fertilizer for the frequently cropped fields. However, animals must be carefully tended to avoid crop damage.

Food storage
Millet and guinea corn are stored in large granaries built above ground level. Sufficient stocks are held to see a family through lean years. Farmers fight a constant battle against mice and insects, which consume substantial quantities of the stored grain.

Essential technology
Irrigation is a widespread method of intensifying agriculture. In West Africa, water is lifted from rivers or wells using a balance beam and bucket, known as a *shaduf*. Such irrigation permits dry-season cultivation of tomatoes, onions, peppers and melons.

Sedentary cultivation in West Africa
In the West African savanna, farms are often arranged in an in-field and out-field pattern. Fields near the village are intensively cultivated, with village wastes and animal dung being used to maintain their fertility. Where adequate water supplies are available, irrigated agriculture is also practiced during the dry season. Further away from the village, fields are farmed on a long fallow, shifting cultivation cycle as labor supplies permit. During the main farming period in the wet season, cattle are pastured in the savanna at the margins of the cultivated area. After the harvest in the early dry season, the herds are allowed to graze crop stubble and manure the fields.

The Search for Food: Mechanized Farming

As the human population of the world has grown so the demand for food has increased, and societies have sought to bring their agricultural land under more permanent and productive cultivation. In less technologically complex societies, this is achieved, primarily by greater input of human labor, but more developed economies rely instead on technological innovation and capital expenditure to raise production.

With the development of agricultural machines such as the tractor and combine harvester, each farmer has been able to cultivate substantially greater acreages than he could by hand. It has therefore become advantageous to combine the smaller scattered plots characteristic of unmechanized farming into a few large, open fields. Whereas in peasant societies the majority of the population is engaged in agriculture, with mechanized farming the highly developed countries manage to produce large agricultural surpluses using less than 5 percent of their work force. Farming in the West today has become "agribusiness," as modern farmers manage heavily capitalized and technologically sophisticated enterprises that produce a very limited number of crops and bear little relation to the traditional family farm.

The price of progress

An integral part of the intensification of agriculture in the developed economies is the use of large quantities of artificial fertilizers to replenish the heavily used soils and to boost yields. Also associated with the development of mechanized agriculture is the practice of monocropping—the cultivation of a single crop species per field. By restricting the planting of a field to one crop in this way, a farmer derives many benefits. These include the possibility of using specialized machinery or chemicals particularly suited to a certain crop as well as the simplification of farm work schedules. A logical development from monocropping is the practice of monoculture—the utilization of uniform varieties of seed so that all the plants grown are very similar genetically. Monoculture has been particularly encouraged by the food processing industry, which demands uniformity of size and quality in a crop grown for canning, freezing or other forms of processing. The most uniform varieties of all are the F_1 hybrids, produced by crossing two heavily inbred lines. These hybrids are very high yielding, and are widely used in certain crops such as maize.

Inevitably, the practices of intensive, mechanized agriculture have a number of disadvantageous side-effects. Large fields planted with a single crop are particularly susceptible to diseases, and must be heavily treated with pesticides to combat these. The chemicals used are expensive and potentially dangerous, both to man and other animals—the harm done to birds of prey by DDT is just one instance of the ecological damage they can cause. With monoculture, susceptibility to disease is an even greater problem, as the genetic uniformity of the crop will allow a disease to which the variety has no resistance to sweep through with devastating effects. This happened in the United States in 1970, when a disease known as southern corn blight spread through 24 million hectares (60 million acres) of maize.

Soil erosion is another problem that accompanies mechanized agriculture, since large, open fields have less protection from wind and rain than small fields surrounded by fencing or hedges. Even fertilizers have their drawbacks—as much as a third of what is applied to the land is washed off again by rain, to finish up in rivers and lakes. Here it stimulates the growth of algae, and causes a process known as eutrophication, as the booming algal population uses up all the oxygen in the water. This kills most fish and the vast numbers of algae create a foul-smelling "soup." Several of the Great Lakes, which lie between Canada and the United States, are seriously affected by eutrophication.

The future of farming

Despite these problems, the productivity of modern agricultural methods does, at first sight, seem impressive. Using such techniques, the farmers of the North American Corn Belt can produce sufficient

The factory farm

Mechanized farming is capital rather than labor intensive. A large landowner in the late 19th century, running a mixed farm, would have provided work for a substantial community, and while producing a surplus, the farmer and his employees would also have been able to exist on their own produce. At its most specialized, a modern farm is geared to the efficient manufacture of one or two products. The farmer will probably buy all his food in the local supermarket, his farm being so specialized that it cannot cater for the needs of his household. On the other hand, with the maximum utilization of modern technology, the factory farmer will be able to produce a surplus undreamed of by his 19th-century counterpart. In the factory farming of poultry, machines are involved at all stages, from incubation, egg laying and sorting, to slaughter, deep freezing, packaging and distribution. The battery hen inhabits a perfect egg-laying environment: controlled lighting simulates days of even length, thus eliminating the fluctuations in laying that normally occur in spring and autumn.

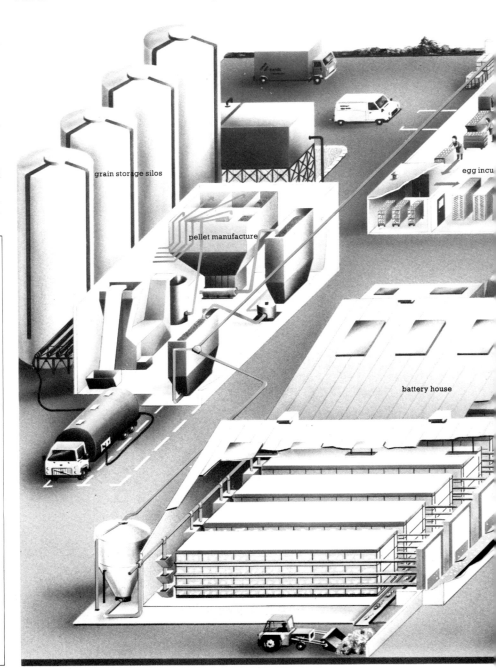

Modern mechanized farming requires heavy capital investment for the purchase and repair of machinery, for the buying of livestock, seed, and the chemical fertilizers and pesticides needed to maintain high yields, and for fuel needed to keep the whole system going. The price paid by the consumer for food items must also cover the costs of packaging and transporting the produce, and the profits taken by the wholesaler and the retailer—in aggregate, these costs may greatly exceed the amount the farmer himself receives. The high capital risks involved in mechanized agriculture are generally alleviated by government intervention in the form of subsidies and price guarantees.

flow of goods
flow of money
Sources of finance: banks, Government subsidies
Suppliers of machinery, fuel, seed, chemicals, etc.
The farm
Processors, packagers and transporters
Wholesaler
Retailer
Consumer

grain storage silos
pellet manufacture
egg incu
battery house

surplus to feed much of the rest of the world, and a dairy farmer in Belgium can achieve more than ten times the milk yield per cow as an East African herdman using traditional methods. These spectacular yields are not as efficient as they seem, however, since they depend on massive inputs of artificially cheap fuels, such as petroleum, which are used directly as fuel as well as in the production of tractors, fertilizers, and the rest of the modern farmer's equipment. It has been calculated that, on the most intensive mechanized farms, every calorie of energy produced in the form of food requires the input of several calories of energy in the form of nonrenewable fossil fuel. With world fuel resources dwindling, it seems clear that western farmers will have to reduce their reliance on petroleum-based fertilizers and pesticides. One approach to this which is currently being investigated is the use of "biological" methods to control diseases—such as introducing natural enemies of insect pests, or planting mixtures of varieties to minimize the impact of disease.

In spite of the rapid technological advance of western farming, agriculturists face their most challenging problems in the next few decades. World food supplies are becoming more and more dependent on the grain production of a few western countries and this production is only maintained by the heavy use of nonrenewable natural resources. Stocks of food have already become political weapons in the international relations between East and West, North and South. It remains to be seen whether modern agriculture can adjust and keep pace with these mounting pressures.

Wind power
This wind pump, being used for irrigation on the Omo River in Ethiopia, is a good example of intermediate technology. The pump comes in kit form and can be assembled locally. As well as being relatively inexpensive to purchase, it also has the advantage of not requiring fuel for its operation. The need to make agriculture less reliant on fossil fuels will become more urgent in the future, not only in the Third World, but for developed countries as well.

Intermediate technology
Intermediate technology, such as this plow supplied to The Gambia under an international aid program, attempts to meet the needs of Third World agriculture in an appropriate way. Ideally, such machinery should be built locally and should increase yields without creating unemployment.

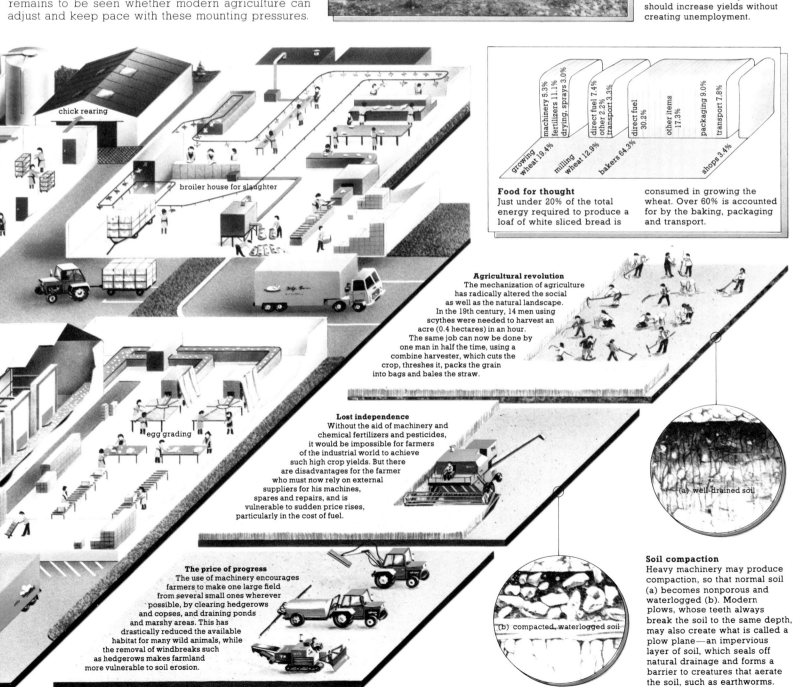

chick rearing

broiler house for slaughter

egg grading

Food for thought
Just under 20% of the total energy required to produce a loaf of white sliced bread is consumed in growing the wheat. Over 60% is accounted for by the baking, packaging and transport.

growing wheat 19.4% — machinery 5.3%, fertilizers 11.1%, drying, sprays 3.0%
milling wheat 12.9% — direct fuel 7.4%, other 2.2%, transport 3.3%
bakers 64.3% — direct fuel 30.2%, other items 17.3%, packaging 9.0%, transport 7.8%
shops 3.4%

Agricultural revolution
The mechanization of agriculture has radically altered the social as well as the natural landscape. In the 19th century, 14 men using scythes were needed to harvest an acre (0.4 hectares) in an hour. The same job can now be done by one man in half the time, using a combine harvester, which cuts the crop, threshes it, packs the grain into bags and bales the straw.

Lost independence
Without the aid of machinery and chemical fertilizers and pesticides, it would be impossible for farmers of the industrial world to achieve such high crop yields. But there are disadvantages for the farmer who must now rely on external suppliers for his machines, spares and repairs, and is vulnerable to sudden price rises, particularly in the cost of fuel.

The price of progress
The use of machinery encourages farmers to make one large field from several small ones wherever possible, by clearing hedgerows and copses, and draining ponds and marshy areas. This has drastically reduced the available habitat for many wild animals, while the removal of windbreaks such as hedgerows makes farmland more vulnerable to soil erosion.

(a) well-drained soil

(b) compacted, waterlogged soil

Soil compaction
Heavy machinery may produce compaction, so that normal soil (a) becomes nonporous and waterlogged (b). Modern plows, whose teeth always break the soil to the same depth, may also create what is called a plow plane—an impervious layer of soil, which seals off natural drainage and forms a barrier to creatures that aerate the soil, such as earthworms.

The Individual in Society

A religious coming of age
The Jewish Bar Mitzwa takes place when a boy is 13. At the ceremony he is required to recite publicly from the Torah benedictions, after which he is acknowledged as an adult in religious life. Observation of the commandments is now the boy's duty—Bar Mitzwa means "Son of the Commandment." A Jew's life is marked by a series of events such as the Bar Mitzwa, where the social group recognizes the passage of an individual from one state to another.

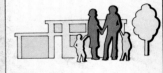

Marriage
In some societies, a man may not marry until he has spent some years in a particular role, such as a warrior. Marriage marks full adult status.

Puberty
Puberty rites do not necessarily coincide with the onset of physical maturity. Initiates may have to prove themselves by enduring an ordeal.

Riding into manhood
An Indian Rajput prince rides through the streets of his local village wearing his father's clothes. The procession is an important part of the initiation ceremony as it marks publicly the transition from puberty into *Brachmachari*, the first stage of manhood. It is also a public affirmation that he may study the Hindu scriptures, and has been invested with the sacred thread, worn only by the higher castes, which signifies spiritual birth.

The long seclusion
This girl of the Mehinacu tribe of Brazil is emerging from 6 months seclusion in a darkened hut—hence her unusually pale skin, and long, unkempt fringe. She has taken part in this rite of passage along with the rest of her age set, and her emergence marks the transition into womanhood and marriageable status. During their long ordeal, the girls learn from the older women the mysteries of life, and what will be expected of them as adults.

Naming
The naming ceremony publicly affirms that society has a new member; in some societies the infant is not a real person until this ceremony takes place.

Baptism
Baptism is the naming ceremony of the Christian churches, a ritual by which the infant is welcomed into the family of Christ. In traditional societies an elder, rather than a priest, usually officiates at the naming ceremony, but the ritual has the same significance in social terms: the society is accepting a new member. Traditionally, a child who died unbaptized could not have a Christian burial, and was placed in unhallowed ground.

Man's ability to obtain a livelihood and to protect himself depends in large part on his membership of a group. Sometimes these groups are based on kinship, sometimes on residence, or economic ties or on other common interests. Whatever their basis, such groups all face similar challenges, namely uniting and integrating their members, and providing a stable group structure that can survive the death of individuals. For the maintenance of the group, it is essential that an individual becomes socialized from an early age. At birth each person becomes part of a set of structural relations, being born into a specific status or class, into a family and into a special position within that family's sibling order. This is particularly true in traditional societies, and although such structural relations have become weaker and more fluid in modern, industrialized countries, they remain important. The individual must be socialized into specific roles appropriate to his or her position, into traditional patterns of behavior and values, all of which make it possible for the group to outlive any of its members.

The process of socialization and enculturation is highly variable. In some societies there are formalized institutions for educating the young, while in others socialization is informal and takes place within the family and community. The acquisition of new roles is

Cross references

Eskimos 60–61
W Africa—Asante 88–91
E Africa—Maasai 96–9
S Africa—Venda 100–103
Australia and New
    Zealand—Aborigines
    156–9
Polynesia—Samoans 160–63
Andes—Quechua 182–5
Amazonia—Xingu Park
    Indians 186–9
Argentina—Mbia 190–91
See also
Marriage 34–5
Death 36–7

Age sets
A Maasai warrior undergoes the initiation ceremony marking his passage into elderhood. Like many of the pastoralists of East Africa, the Maasai organize their society into age sets. A Maasai, with others in his age set, passes through a series of formal stages accepting an increasingly responsible role, and receiving greater prestige up until his retirement from elderhood. After this, his advice will probably be sought only on ceremonial matters.

Elderhood
Elders may achieve their position through election, or seniority may come with age. Elders often have great influence within the group.

The wheel of life,
Buddhist symbol
of reincarnation

Death
In most societies, life and death are seen as part of a continual cycle, and death, like birth and puberty, is marked by specific rites of passage.

Rites of passage
Rites of passage mark symbolically the transition from one important stage in an individual's life to another, and are designed to provide supernatural support for the difficult changeover to a new social role. Rites of passage serve to establish an individual's social position appropriate to his or her age, and like most ritual performances rites of passage have the secondary effect of strengthening the cohesion of the community.

highly ritualized in many parts of the world, but there is a great deal of variation in the specific roles which become the focus of ritual elaboration. Some societies have a set of clearly marked stages through which the individual passes, while in others these stages may be recognized but not ritually elaborated.

At birth or during the first weeks of life there is usually some point at which the infant becomes socially recognized as a person. This may be marked by giving the infant a name, by the ritual of Christian baptism, or by formal presentation to relatives and friends. Among some peoples, such as villagers in traditional China, if an infant died before passing through this stage, there was no mortuary ritual—as far as the society was concerned the person had never existed.

During the first years of life the child is usually socialized within the domestic unit. This unit may include not only parents but also grandparents, aunts, uncles, cousins, and of course siblings. In the rural villages of many countries young children of two or three years quickly become part of a "children's society" made up of their older siblings and neighbors. In such societies child care often becomes the responsibility of older children, thus freeing parents for the heavy household and agricultural tasks.

At some point during the first years of life the child becomes responsible for his or her actions. In most societies there is a marked difference in the way a two-year-old behaves, and is treated, compared with the treatment of, say, five- or six-year-olds. The former has a great deal of freedom ("he doesn't understand") while the latter is expected to know how to behave. The age at which children are expected to "understand" varies from culture to culture and from one historical period to another. In many societies this point coincides with the onset of formal education, in others it begins when the child is given regular chores.

Puberty—gateway to adulthood

In most societies, the major transition of an individual's life is puberty, and very often this is marked by an extremely complex set of rituals. The rituals associated with puberty are a particularly good example of what are known as rites of passage. Such rites celebrate the process of status change, in which the individual becomes socialized into new roles. Like birth, it is not the actual physical change (the onset of sexual maturity) which is celebrated, but the social recognition of that change.

Initiation rites often involve a period of separation from the normal world during which the initiates receive some formal training, often in esoteric knowledge. Particularly among the Plains Indian of North America, and some African peoples, this training may be combined with physical ordeals in which the endurance of the initiates is tested. During this period of seclusion the subjects are in a marginal state—they are no longer children but they are not yet social adults—they are, in effect, outside society. Thus, among the Bugisu of northern Uganda, if one of the initiates should die during his seclusion, the death goes unrecognized—there is no funerary ritual.

After a period of separation the initiates are brought back into the social world with a dramatic flourish, and they assume their new role. It is important to note that these initiation rituals are not really concerned with providing technical knowledge or skills; young people usually come by these in the course of everyday life. Rather, these rites stress the moral obligations which are the responsibility of social adults. Initiation at puberty, or simply the onset of puberty, often marks the beginning of an individual's active sexual life, but in some societies, particularly those influenced by Christian and Muslim teaching, sexual relations, especially for women, are completely prohibited until after marriage. In most Mediterranean countries and Arabic-speaking countries, for instance, a high value is placed on female virginity.

Among many peoples there is a clearly marked and lengthy period between childhood and the attainment of full adult status. This is true not only in the industrialized West, but also in many tribal societies such as those of the Samburu in East Africa or the Lele of Central Africa. Among the Samburu and the Lele it is only males who go through this prolonged adolescence, for in these societies women marry and assume adult status at an early age. Samburu and Lele men spend a number of years as unmarried warriors. It is only after marriage that they become full, social adults.

Kinship and Family

A village of Petersons
As in many isolated communities all the Eskimos of the village of Qeqertag in Greenland bear the same surname—Peterson. The exclusion of any other name might be expected to make the network of relations within the village highly confusing. The Eskimos, however, like people in most traditional societies, employ a system of kin terminology which enables them to classify every relationship. Such a system helps to define responsibilities and the way individuals should act toward each other. Where difficulties do arise in Qeqertag is with the arrival of a stranger with a different family name. The photographers who took this picture had to adopt the name Peterson during their stay in the village.

Some of the most enduring human groups are those based on kinship. Shelter, food and security may only be available within the circle of kinship and those outside this circle are often considered potential enemies. Even in modern industrial societies, where it is generally assumed that kinship is unimportant, people feel they have a right to expect help from kin.

Although the idea of kinship seems simple enough, there is, in fact, tremendous variation in the way people of different societies reckon kinship. Kinship is not simply a matter of biological ties, rather it is the social recognition of those ties. The Chinese may count as near kin someone whom an Englishman had long ceased to regard as a relative. Among many Arabs the father's brother's daughter is an ideal marriage partner, while in other societies the idea of such a union is abhorrent because the kin tie is "too close."

People trace kinship in a variety of ways, but certain ideas and relationships display remarkable uniformity. In nearly all human societies the mother-child relationship is of central importance. A male is usually

attached to this unit, although the intensity and longevity of this attachment is variable. An important feature of kinship is the almost universal censure of mating within the nuclear family. The incest prohibition, as it is known, has been explained biologically, as a mechanism by which the dangers of inbreeding may be avoided, but this is debatable and many anthropologists prefer a cultural explanation. In discussing the incest taboo, most anthropologists emphasize two different, but not necessarily conflicting, points—some stress the confusion which sexual relations within the nuclear family would create, while others emphasize the role which the taboo plays in pushing people out of the family and creating links with other groups.

Within the category of kin, certain ties are given more emphasis than others. In some societies individuals acquire property or a surname from either their father or mother, but not from both. In traditional China, for example, property, surnames and the responsibility to worship ancestors were passed from father to son in the male line—a system of patrilineal descent. In such societies ties to and through women are not denied, but they do not have the economic, political or ideological importance which relations among males hold. Apart from traditional China, patrilineal societies include many of the tribal groups of central Asia, the Middle East and East and North Africa, some Australian Aborigines, and other groups such as the Fox Indians of North America.

While some societies stress the male line, others emphasize relations through women—in these societies matrilineal descent plays the crucial role in determining rights to important resources. However, matrilineal descent is not simply a mirror image of patrilineal descent. Although crucial ties are traced

A Chinese kinship group

♂ Male

♀ Female

⊓ Marriage

■ Ancestors

■ Descent group—
those who trace descent from a common ancestor

▨ Residential group—
those who live together

■ Inheritance line and Ritual group—
those who participate in ritual associated with the lineage

Economic disaster

External threat

Safety in numbers
In isolation an individual is ill-equipped to survive economic disaster or external threat, but as part of a kinship group, with shared economic and political interests, he has a measure of security. In Muslim societies, for example, the death or injury of one individual leads to collective claims of blood compensation. The extended kinship group (here illustrated diagrammatically by a Chinese kinship group) provides an enduring organization transcending the independent family unit. Through the network of consanguineal (blood) relations and marriage or affinal ties, the individual has

access to both economic and political aid. A system of inheritance ensures the continuation of both name and property. The sense of continuing group identity is sometimes furthered by beliefs in reincarnation, or by the belief that the dead become spirits who are concerned with the well-being of their descendants.

1st generation

2nd

3rd

4th

Nuclear family
The isolated nuclear family is the norm among both the rich and poor sections of western society. Nevertheless, kinship remains important in the West, particularly for wealthy, aristocratic families, and it plays a far more significant role in areas such as banking and politics than is often realized.

The ritual group
Chinese men worship at the grave of their ancestors. Only men are present. China is a patrilineal society and women are excluded from any ritual to do with ancestors and the lineage. However, women do participate in rites of passage and in the rites that take place inside the home.

through women, it is usually men who hold positions of authority and power. In many matrilineal systems, positions of importance are passed from a man to his sister's son. The Iroquois of North America, the Bemba of Zambia and the Minangkabau of Indonesia are examples of matrilineal societies.

A few societies have a double-unilineal descent system. Thus, the Yakö of Nigeria trace descent in the female line for some purposes, such as rights to movable property, and in the male line for others, such as rights to immovable property. Many societies do not place any special emphasis on either the male or female line, and they are said to have a system of bilateral kinship. Although many industrialized societies trace kinship bilaterally, such systems are by no means confined to such societies.

In many societies kinship provides much more than just a mechanism for determining one's surname or rights to property. Kinship may serve as the organizational framework for politics and economics. Kinship may play a role in the transmission of political office and it may define where one lives or whom one will marry. One's membership of a kin group may provide access to important resources and it may determine one's most intimate friends or colleagues. In some societies, such as the Tallensi of Ghana or the Nuer of the Sudan, descent dominates the entire social system.

The family

Although the system of tracing descent may influence the composition of domestic units or families, there is no simple correlation between, for example, patrilineal descent and extended families or bilateral systems and nuclear families. It is often pointed out that the nuclear family is particularly suited to the requirements of industrialized societies, where mobility of labor is often necessary and where the government assumes many of the support roles which were once the responsibility of the family—the care of the young, the elderly, the sick, or the unemployed. However, it is important to remember that the nuclear family is found in many different societies, and while it was once assumed that stem and joint families were common in preindustrial Europe, recent research has shown that, for large parts of Europe, this was not the case—in sixteenth- and seventeenth-century England most people were already living either alone or in nuclear families. Work in Africa, India and China has also shown that the stem and the joint family did not necessarily fade away as the process of industrialization increased.

There is a tendency for contemporary Europeans and Americans to underrate the role of kinship in their lives. Nevertheless, kinship continues to provide important emotional and economic supports for most people, and in fields like banking or politics kinship may play a critical, albeit largely unrecognized, role.

Sacrifice and social relations
Rules governing the sharing of food are a clear affirmation of kin status. Among the Dinka of northeast Africa meat is shared in a specific way and each part of the sacrificial bull or ox is reserved for a particular section of the sacrificing group. For example, the youngest sons of the sacrificer's wives will always receive the rump. In this way the beast represents all the people at the sacrifice, and also pinpoints the nature of their individual relationships.

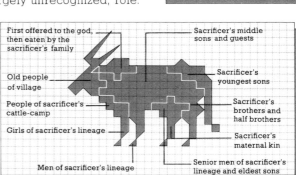

First offered to the god, then eaten by the sacrificer's family
Old people of village
People of sacrificer's cattle-camp
Girls of sacrificer's lineage
Men of sacrificer's lineage
Sacrificer's middle sons and guests
Sacrificer's youngest sons
Sacrificer's brothers and half brothers
Sacrificer's maternal kin
Senior men of sacrificer's lineage and eldest sons

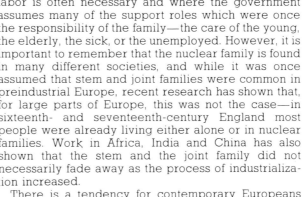

Patrilineal descent

1st generation
2nd
3rd
4th

The extended family
The extended family, a common domestic form here illustrated by the Sakuddai of Indonesia, includes parents, two or more married offspring and their children. The resulting household is well able to support the elderly and cope with sickness or death.

The lineage
A lineage includes the direct descendants from a common ancestor or ancestress. In a patrilineage (*left*), descent is traced through males, while in a matrilineage (*right*), it is traced through females. However, the inheritance of property and position in many matrilineages is from a man to his sister's son.

Matrilineal descent

1st generation
2nd
3rd
4th

Marriage

The label "marriage" has been applied to such widely different arrangements that it is difficult to define. The legitimacy of the offspring of the union between a man and a woman has often been taken as the crucial criterion, but this is by no means always the case.

In certain societies, as among the Kachin of Highland Burma, a man can make a payment so that his children become legitimate members of his own lineage, without in any way "marrying" their mother. The kinds of rights a husband acquires in marriage vary from one society to another. They may include rights to the bride's sexual, domestic and reproductive services, and in a patrilineal society the man usually acquires all three. But in a matrilineal society rights over her reproductive capacity remain with her own lineage, and the husband may not be able to command her labor either. In some cases distinct elements of the bridewealth are payable for each of these rights.

In a few societies forms of marriage exist to provide a childless man with an heir after his death. One of these is the levirate, by which a man has a duty to marry the widow of his childless brother, the offspring of this union being regarded as the children of the dead man. Here, the role of "father" and biological genitor are obviously quite distinct, and this distinction is reiterated by a form of marriage found among the Nuer of southern Sudan in which a woman with cattle of her own may acquire a "wife." She becomes the legal "father" of her "wife's" children, the genitor of whom is a kinsman or friend appointed by her.

In patrilineal societies the wife is generally required to reside with her husband's group, but matrilineal systems display a much greater variation in their residential arrangements. In some of these societies a man is expected to reside with his wife's group or to move at puberty to the village of his mother's brother, where his wife will eventually join him; in others the couple will spend alternate years in the villages of each partner's matriclan. In yet other cases, the couple do not live together at all, and the husband visits his wife only at night.

Multiple marriages

The generic term "polygamy" covers both polygyny, where one husband takes two or more wives, and polyandry where one wife has several husbands. Polyandry is much less common than polygyny, and frequently takes the form of several brothers sharing a common wife. The different forms of polygamy are not always mutually exclusive. In the hill district of Jaunsar-Bawar in northern India, for example, a group of brothers may marry a bride, and the children she bears will recognize all of them as "fathers." The husbands may subsequently acquire additional wives such that the household becomes both polgynous and polyandrous, or one of the men might set up on his own with one of the wives in a monogamous union. Among the matrilineal Lele of the Congo, polyandry is directly related to a shortage of marriageable women, which is created by the polygyny of the elders. Most young men face the prospect of prolonged bachelorhood, and in the past this situation was mitigated by the "village wife," who was the common spouse of the age set. The age set usually abducted her from a neighboring village and initially she was expected to grant her sexual favors to all of its members, who may have numbered up to twenty, later settling down with four or five of them as her recognized husbands. Her position was regarded as an honorable if onerous one.

The politics of marriage

The exchange of marriage partners often plays a vital role in binding potentially hostile descent groups together. Lineages, however, are not invariably exogamous and in much of the Middle East there is a strong preference for marriage within the patrilineage, since this allows property, particularly land, to remain within the group. Such a tendency to marry a member of the same lineage is distinct from compulsory endogamy as practiced by most Indian castes. This is generally found in stratified societies and serves to protect the exclusiveness of those of superior rank. In such societies the integrative function performed by exogamous marriage is lacking, and in the Indian case it is replaced by the division of labor between castes which ensures their interdependence.

Marriage inside one's own group

Marriages arranged by the parents are common in traditional societies. Choice may be restricted to members of the same group, in order to protect group exclusiveness, as in the Indian Hindu caste system, where unions between members of different castes are believed to lead to leprosy. While the ideal Indian marriage is one between equals, where descent is traced patrilineally men may marry rich women of lower status, whose marriageability is enhanced by substantial dowries.

Dinka choice

Dancing is a major feature of a Dinka cattle festival and it provides an opportunity for a girl to make herself known to the man of her choice. The festival can last for 14 days, during which time a relaxed attitude to sexual behavior prevails. A girl may become betrothed as early as 12 years old, but her bridewealth—a number of cattle—will probably not be paid over until she is 16 or 17 years of age, and it is only then that she will leave her village and go to live with her husband's family.

Marriage outside one's own group

A group can assert its own exclusiveness and forge links with opposing groups by ruling that its members *must* marry outside its boundaries. "We marry our enemies" is a common saying in such circumstances. This practice, particularly in Arab cultures, enables rival patrilineal groups to maintain an alliance relationship. In some cases, wife-giving groups are considered to be superior to those who take wives. In other cases, as among Islamic holymen, those who take wives have superior status.

Not all societies expect that the bride and groom should be of equivalent status and some specify that there should be a difference in status—hypergamy refers to a system in which a woman marries "up"; hypogamy to one in which she marries "down." Both are liable to lead to problems at the two ends of the social ladder. In hypergamous regimes the women at the very top have no one to marry while the men at the bottom have difficulty in finding wives. In the past, the highest ranking Rajput aristocrats in northern India solved the first dilemma by practicing female infanticide. The shortage of brides among the lowest ranking Rajputs was alleviated by a form of polyandry, whereby a man had sexual access to his elder brother's wife.

Where a woman is expected to marry a man of higher rank, the payment of a substantial dowry usually accompanies marriage, and this often amounts to a status payment. This is not always the case however, and in many societies dowry represents a premortem inheritance settled on the daughter at the time of her marriage. Dowry payments are often associated with societies where descent is traced bilaterally, whereas bridewealth tends to be pronounced in patrilineal societies.

Climax of the marriage feast

A Chimbu bride and bridegroom from the central highlands of New Guinea take a bite out of a piece of pork—the main food of any ceremonial occasion. This ritual concludes a long series of exchanges of exotic feathers, pigs, money and other goods, signifying that the two parties, previously unconnected, are entering a relationship with each other. The sharing of the pork is a sign of the couple's assent and their willingness to assume the responsibilities and obligations that their relationship will entail. Moments after the pieces of pork have been eaten the bridal party depart for the groom's village: the men in one group, carrying the cooked pork and the goods they have received, and the bride separately, escorted by women from the bridegroom's village.

Theoretically unrestricted individual choice

Where inherited resources are not the key to economic livelihood and there are no significant political considerations, marriage tends to be a matter of individual choice. Romantic love in marriage becomes a significant factor.

Dowry is given by the bride to her husband's family. Where women inherit property, dowry may represent a substantial part of their share of the family estate. Once a common institution in Europe, dowry is still prominent in Mediterranean countries.

Where marriage occurs within the same group, there is likely to be less emphasis on opposition and rivalry between the parties. The change of status of the spouses is marked in rituals which may symbolize the achievement of full adulthood by the wife.

Sometimes dowry is the means by which an independent household is established for the bride and bridegroom. The couple may reside initially at the bride's home, but in most patrilineal societies residence is ultimately with the husband's group.

The nuclear family is usually part of a wider "extended" or "joint-family" in traditional societies. In a polygynous homestead, each wife generally has her own house and resources. Rivalry amongst wives is a classic contributory factor to divorce.

Cross references

N Africa—Rifi 34–5
E Europe—Gorale 74–7
S Africa—Venda 100–3
Turkey—Durrani 110–13
Himalayas—Nishi 116–19
Turkic-speaking central Asia—Uzbek 130–1
Australia and New Zealand—Aborigines 156–9
See also
The individual in society 30–31

Wealth to be worn
Two women of the Hmong, a hill tribe of southeast Asia, display their brideprice in their costumes. Marriage negotiations are complex and involve a great deal of haggling. Considerable sexual freedom is permitted among the Hmong and the wedding is preceded by a period of trial marriage.

Celestial male superiority
The elaborate marriage rituals of the Gimi of Papua New Guinea include a male dance which is a dramatic portrayal of the sun and moon and a deliberate statement of the men's importance. In the same way that the sun and moon dominate day and night, Gimi men see themselves as dominating their society. The men's body decorations display their knowledge of the world beyond the village—a world inaccessible to the women.

Bridewealth secures rights in the person of the bride for the husband and his kin, but rights to the children are never transferred in matrilineal societies. In patrilineal systems the brother of a deceased husband often inherits his widow.

The mutual hostility of the two sides is pronounced in exogamous marriage. The wedding is likely to include symbolic capture of the bride, who has to be forced to join her spouse. The spouse and his kin aggressively boast of their achievement.

Payment of bridewealth in patrilineal societies usually entitles the husband to remove the bride to his home, where she may join his other wives in a polygynous household, or join his extended family, where domestic affairs are often dominated by his mother.

The nuclear family. Divorce is generally easier where descent is traced in the female rather than male line. In patrilineal societies, the husband can claim back his bridewealth, cattle or other goods, but an amount is deducted for each of the children the wife has borne.

A wedding on Bali
Balinese villagers prepare a wedding feast. The decorations on this occasion are particularly elaborate, reflecting the noble status of the betrothed couple, but even in a lower status wedding much care will be lavished on decorations and magnificent cakes: a culinary testament to the importance the Balinese attach to weddings. Preparation is never shouldered by the kin group alone but is shared by the entire village, who spend weeks before the event preparing their cakes and making the decorations. The village also participates in other ceremonies that are regarded as major life events, including cremations. The wedding feast is a lengthy affair, beginning at eight in the morning and lasting the whole day, until about nine in the evening. Eating together is common to most marriages.

Wedding gifts are primarily intended to help the couple establish an independent household. The idea of marriage as an alliance between groups is not present—except to a residual degree in royal and "high-society" unions.

Since marriage primarily concerns the couple themselves the extent to which it is ritualized is largely optional. The civil ceremony is often reduced to a minimum, although any religious affiliation may require more elaborate weddings.

Such marriage generally emphasizes the autonomy of the couple, and even the independence of each partner; wider kin ties are often weak. However, in western societies wider kin ties are maintained among the highest and lowest social classes.

Divorce primarily concerns the two spouses and may be initiated by either, but division of property is often a problem. The frequency of divorce in the West is similar to that found in many traditional matrilineal and bilateral societies.

Death

In almost every culture, the death of an individual represents a breach of the social fabric, a potentially dangerous event that could threaten the well being of the living. The mourning rites and burial procedures that surround death vary greatly from one culture to another, but in general they work to minimize the danger to those left behind and to reintegrate the bereaved into society.

What the majority of cultures seem to abhor above all is the arbitrary and unpredictable nature of death, commonly symbolized by games of chance played by the mourners. Although in the West, a sudden and unanticipated death—at least for the elderly—is often seen as "a good way to go," in most other societies the death for which one is unprepared is viewed with horror. Thus for the pious Hindu the good death is one to which the individual voluntarily submits himself or herself. In the ideal case the terminally sick person is carried to the sacred city of Benares (Varanasi) to die. Having previously predicted the time of his going, he forgoes all food for some days beforehand, and gathers his sons about him. Then, by an effort of concentrated will, he abandons life. Similarly, among the Dinka of southern Sudan, the ideal death for an aging Spearmaster (a religious leader of the tribe) is to preside over his own burial alive—this robs death of its arbitrary power, and enhances the fertility and prosperity of the community. This illustrates the widespread association between ideas of death and fertility. The mortuary rituals of many societies are pervaded by the symbolism of sexuality and birth, and clearly entail a view of death as a source of life.

The way in which the corpse is disposed of is very often imbued with this sort of symbolism. In many areas, including much of pre-revolutionary China, southeast Asia and Madagascar, the corpse is temporarily placed in an isolated grave (or exposed in a tree), and the bones later receive a secondary burial in the collective tomb of the ancestors. In many cases, the cultural logic behind this relates to an opposition between bones, derived from the father, and flesh, from the mother. Such an insistence on separating the flesh from the bones seems to occur in systems with exogamous descent groups, while preoccupation with preserving both characterizes endogamous systems.

The symbolic tomb

The tombs of ancestors often have a symbolic value of their own, and may provide a kind of reference point for the social organization of the living. Among the Merina of Madagascar for example, the fundamental unit of social organization is an endogamous kinship group associated with a specific territory. The central symbol of the continuity of this group, and its enduring relationship with the land, are the collective tombs in which the remains of its members are deposited. Similarly, the social organization of a Spanish Basque village revolves around the farmsteads, which cannot be dismembered by sale or inheritance. Each farmstead is associated with a *sepulturie* on the church floor and this acts as a family stall where the women sit on Sundays, and is the focus of rites to the dead—it is a symbolic family tomb and was their actual burial site in former times. If the farmstead is sold, the new owners assume full control of the *sepulturie*, which thus symbolizes the continuity of the property unit. The significance of tombs as expressions of the prevailing social order is reflected in the fact that since the revolution, the Communist government in China has vigorously (although not altogether successfully) campaigned for the adoption of cremation.

A variation of this symbolism is seen on the Melanesian island of Dobu, where the center of each village is occupied by the burial mound containing deceased members of the matriclan. Residence on Dobu is "alternating" (a married couple spend one year in the village of the husband's matriclan, the next year in the wife's village and so on), and the spouse's village is seen as a dangerous and frightening place, full of treacherous sorcerers. It is only at death that men and women at last attain permanent refuge among their own kin in the village mound, and are freed from the unpleasant necessity of relations with outsiders. The surviving spouse is initially incarcerated in a small enclosure of coconut fronds, and at the end of this period, the house in which the couple had resided is razed to the ground, and the widow or widower is led out of the village and may *never* return. What is represented by the burial mound, then, is not the *actual* social order, but a vision of an ideal world, purged of the necessity for marital alliances.

Death without tears

Whereas in many societies death is a highly visible event, in the industrial West it is an almost furtive affair, except in the case of famous people. Certain hunter-gatherer societies also stand at this pole of minimal elaboration. Among the Hadza of Tanzania, for example, the deceased is either buried in a shallow grave, or a temporary shelter is pulled down over the corpse, and camp is struck. The grave is neither marked nor visited. There are no elaborate beliefs in an afterlife and many Hadza say that when one dies one rots and that's that. Every attempt is made to inhibit any public expression of grief, and the same is true among Mbuti Pygmies. Such a response to death is consistent with the fact that in such societies there are few formalized role positions which require an elaborate process of social replacement. Similarly, in the modern West, where death in old age may now be regarded as the norm, social replacement is not at issue since the deceased will probably have already been superseded in his or her crucial social role.

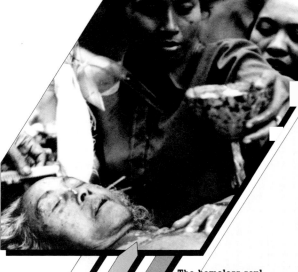

Preparation of the body
The corpse of a Balinese princess is purified by her daughter. In many societies the preburial period is likely to be the most dangerous time of all, and it is striking how often the task of preparing the corpse is assigned to women, who must therefore expose themselves to the pollution of death when it is at its most intense. Men are more likely to preside over those parts of the ritual which emphasize regeneration and the ultimate triumph of life.

The homeless soul
Until the mortuary rituals have been completed and the deceased's soul introduced to the society of ancestors, he is often regarded as a dangerous and malevolent ghost.

Society and the bereaved
The death of Archbishop Makarios, a religious as well as a political leader, was mourned by thousands of Greek Cypriots. The more important a person is, the greater are the social implications of that person's death, and the more widespread the display of grief. For most societies a prime task will be replacement, and this is highlighted in certain societies, like that of the Lugbara of Uganda, where a death is socially recognized before it has actually occurred. The dying man says his last words to his heir, who then emerges, calling the personal chant of the moribund and thus marking the moment of succession.

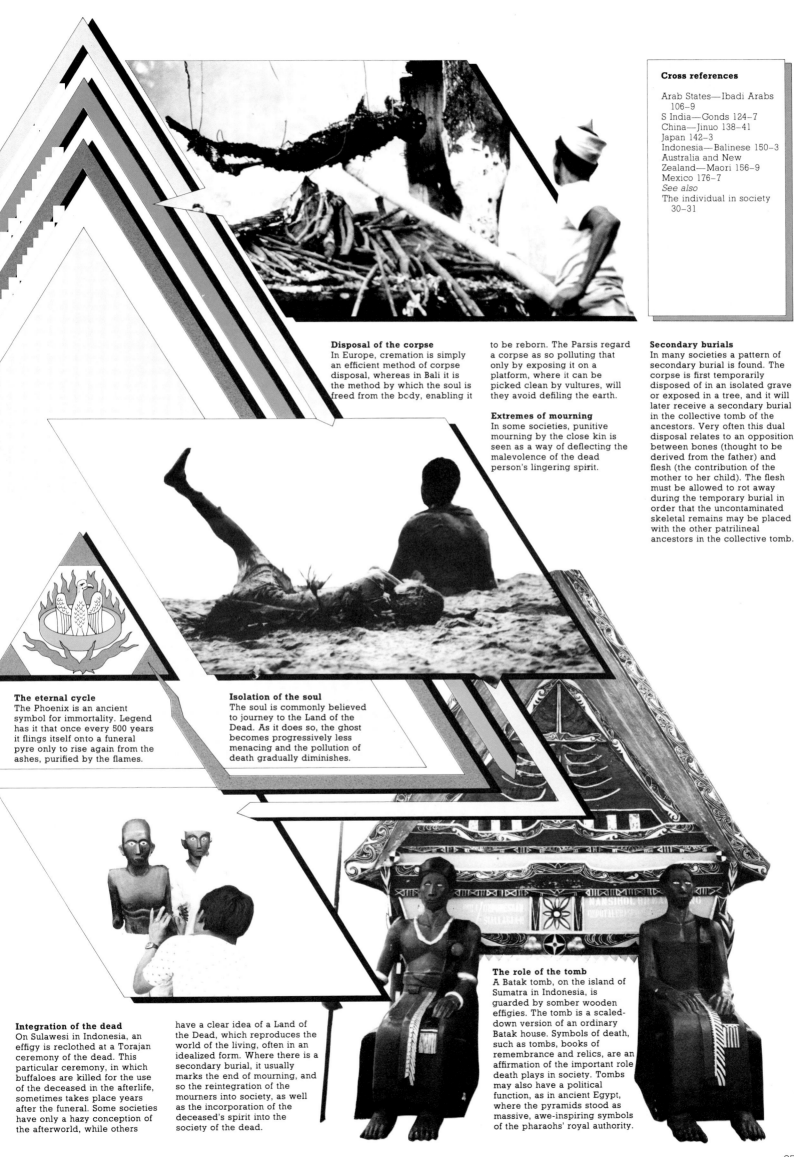

Disposal of the corpse
In Europe, cremation is simply an efficient method of corpse disposal, whereas in Bali it is the method by which the soul is freed from the body, enabling it to be reborn. The Parsis regard a corpse as so polluting that only by exposing it on a platform, where it can be picked clean by vultures, will they avoid defiling the earth.

Extremes of mourning
In some societies, punitive mourning by the close kin is seen as a way of deflecting the malevolence of the dead person's lingering spirit.

Secondary burials
In many societies a pattern of secondary burial is found. The corpse is first temporarily disposed of in an isolated grave or exposed in a tree, and it will later receive a secondary burial in the collective tomb of the ancestors. Very often this dual disposal relates to an opposition between bones (thought to be derived from the father) and flesh (the contribution of the mother to her child). The flesh must be allowed to rot away during the temporary burial in order that the uncontaminated skeletal remains may be placed with the other patrilineal ancestors in the collective tomb.

The eternal cycle
The Phoenix is an ancient symbol for immortality. Legend has it that once every 500 years it flings itself onto a funeral pyre only to rise again from the ashes, purified by the flames.

Isolation of the soul
The soul is commonly believed to journey to the Land of the Dead. As it does so, the ghost becomes progressively less menacing and the pollution of death gradually diminishes.

Integration of the dead
On Sulawesi in Indonesia, an effigy is reclothed at a Torajan ceremony of the dead. This particular ceremony, in which buffaloes are killed for the use of the deceased in the afterlife, sometimes takes place years after the funeral. Some societies have only a hazy conception of the afterworld, while others have a clear idea of a Land of the Dead, which reproduces the world of the living, often in an idealized form. Where there is a secondary burial, it usually marks the end of mourning, and so the reintegration of the mourners into society, as well as the incorporation of the deceased's spirit into the society of the dead.

The role of the tomb
A Batak tomb, on the island of Sumatra in Indonesia, is guarded by somber wooden effigies. The tomb is a scaled-down version of an ordinary Batak house. Symbols of death, such as tombs, books of remembrance and relics, are an affirmation of the important role death plays in society. Tombs may also have a political function, as in ancient Egypt, where the pyramids stood as massive, awe-inspiring symbols of the pharaohs' royal authority.

Taboo

Ever since Captain Cook returned to Europe with the concept of taboo in the eighteenth century, there has been controversy over the exact meaning of the term. In its broadest sense, taboo refers to a prohibition against certain actions; any violation of the taboo is on pain of supernatural punishment or automatic punishment by the rest of the social group.

In the Pacific Islands, Cook observed that certain people were not allowed to eat particular categories of food, that islanders were forbidden bodily contact with their chief, particularly with his head, and that they had to be ritually cleansed after handling a corpse. He also noted that access to specific areas of land was restricted by ritual or magical means. The islanders were afraid of a mystical power which, on the one hand, could be so *sacred* it was dangerous, as in the case of touching the chief's head, and, on the other, so *unclean* as to be defiling, as in the case of contact with a corpse or eating prohibited food. The islanders explained that the objects of these strict prohibitions were "taboo."

The incest taboo – Baka Pygmies

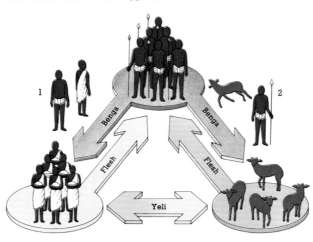

The incest taboo – Asante

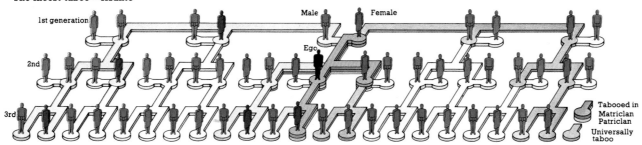

1st generation

Male   Female

Ego

2nd

3rd

Tabooed in
Matriclan
Patriclan
Universally
taboo

The incest taboo
Among the Baka Pygmies of Cameroon, the rule governing incest is analogous to the rule for sharing meat. A hunter must forgo sexual experience with close female kin (1), and he is also tabooed from eating the meat of any animal he has killed himself (2). The two rules are symbolically interrelated, as reflected in the Baka word *benga*, used for both spear and penis. The two rules are crucial to the stability of the social structure. The sharing of meat ensures that nobody goes short of food, and both women and animals become the symbols of exchange and reciprocity between men. Male dominance, however, is balanced by the accepted mystical powers of women over animals: by singing their magical song *yeli* in a forest clearing early in the morning, the women attract the animals that the men will kill. There is an almost universal incest prohibition, which forbids a man from sexual relations with his mother, sister or daughter, but in addition, many societies preclude other liaisons. Among the Asante of Ghana, in addition to the usual incest prohibitions, which are universally taboo, a man may not have sex with women of his matriclan or patriclan on pain of certain death.

It seemed, therefore, that such taboo restrictions were cultural mechanisms which separated men and women from areas of danger. If an individual were to break a taboo he would place himself at the very center of danger and defilement, effecting a negative shift in his ritual status, which would have to be resolved in one of a variety of ways depending on the severity of his offense—death, banishment, illness, bad luck or the performance of a ritual to reverse the setback.

In applying the taboo concept cross-culturally, a number of difficulties arose. First, because no European language had an exact equivalent for this Polynesian word, taboo came to be adopted as a term to cover a whole range of prohibitions. In Polynesia, however, taboo includes the ideas of sacredness and pollution in a single term, whereas in most other languages we find clear-cut oppositions between the sacred and the profane, between purity and pollution, between danger and safety. In such cases, one term would be needed to cover the sacred, the pure and the safe, and another term to cover the profane, the polluting and the dangerous.

Because of the unique meaning of taboo in the Polynesian context, some people have criticized the widespread application of this term to all cultural prohibitions and restrictions. Such purists would point out, for example, that the word taboo is inapplicable to the Indian caste system, where a complex series of prohibitions separates the whole of society into discrete categories. To use the term taboo to explain why a high-caste individual will refuse food from someone of a lower caste would mean applying the same term to both Brahman (priest) and Untouchable, whereas in the culture itself they are polar opposites.

A second objection raised by critics is that taboo is often applied to prohibitions that are not supported by sanctions or ritual requirements. Nevertheless, people throughout the world do divide up the universe into categories of sacredness and pollution.

Universal taboos

The incest taboo is the best known and most universal prohibition. Although the range of incest prohibitions varies from society to society, the same general mechanism is almost always present—this demarcates those categories of close kin between whom sexual intercourse and marriage are strictly prohibited. Violation of this taboo could endanger the whole social fabric, and the punishment of transgressors is therefore severe—they are believed to become ill or die.

Very often offenders feel the weight of their crime so greatly that they actually do become ill as a result; in other instances, an outbreak of illness, particularly leprosy, is attributed to taboo breaking at some time in the past. In some societies the guilty parties or their offspring are expelled or killed by the remaining members of the group.

In many different cultures, certain people are singled out by taboos when they are in specific ritual states. Women are often in a taboo state during menstruation: they may not perform particular actions, enter certain people's houses, eat specific categories of food, and so on. In a number of cultures a man's wife's mother is the object of great respect, even of avoidance. Unless he conforms to culturally prescribed behavior toward her, the woman may influence her daughter and cause her to break off the marriage. Among the Baka Pygmies of Cameroon, a man may not joke with his wife's mother, nor must he enter her shelter, and he is absolutely tabooed from pronouncing her name.

After the birth of a child there is commonly a taboo on sexual intercourse by the parents until the child is weaned; failure to observe this is believed to have an adverse effect on the child's health. As many children in rural societies are not weaned until they are about three years old, this taboo is, of course, frequently broken by the parents, but this does not mean that it is regarded as unimportant. In such cases, the parents generally perform a magical rite in order to restore the infant's benign ritual state.

The magic flutes
In many cultures, the division of the sexes into two quite different spheres is maintained by a series of taboos, prohibiting access by one sex to the secrets of the other. These taboos are often operated by men as a means of dominating women. Here, three Iaualápim dancers of Brazil emerge from the men's house with their sacred flutes. Women are prohibited from viewing the instruments, and contravention is regarded as so serious that the threatened punishment is mass rape by all the men of the village. Apparently the punishment has never been carried out.

Eating people is wrong
Almost as widespread as the incest taboo is a horror of eating human flesh. Apart from specific funerary rituals where some human remains are consumed, or instances where warriors eat the flesh of their enemies in order to humiliate them, cannibalism rarely seems to occur. In 1972, an aircraft carrying a local rugby team crashed in the Andes. With no food supplies on board, some passengers survived by eating the flesh of those who had died on impact. So powerful was the taboo, however, that at least one passenger starved to death rather than indulge in this "unnatural" act.

On the beach
Context is all important to the idea of taboo. Many western cultures have in recent years relaxed the taboo on nudity. These sun worshippers are not self-conscious on a designated "free beach" but would still feel uncomfortable elsewhere.

Sacred cow
The Hindu faith dictates that cows may not be killed, eaten or harmed in any way. The behavior prohibitions that protect this animal afford it a special place in relationships with men. Here a train waits at a station while the guard shares water with a sacred cow.

Religious Belief and Ritual

Religion is the recognition of superhuman or spiritual power or powers, with consequent effects upon human conduct. Although this recognition is expressed in many different kinds of belief and story, its general purpose is to try to make sense of the universe and of life. Most religions have myths of the creation of the world and mankind, either by one act of God or in successive cycles of creation, destruction and re-creation. Underlying them all is a search for truth and intelligibility—religious thinkers believe that a world which contains rational beings must have a rational basis. Myths seek to answer such questions as "What was there in the beginning? Where did people come from? Why is childbirth painful? Why do people die?"

Religion not only tries to answer questions, it also seeks to give strength for life, especially in times of trouble, when it provides support and comfort. God, or the gods, are concerned with human life, showing compassion and providence. Furthermore, religion has always had a strong social side and some of the commonest religious rituals are social occasions, as at birth, marriage and death.

The supernatural world

The Semitic religions—Judaism, Christianity and Islam—are monotheistic, believing in one God who is creator of all things. Zoroastrians and Sikhs also worship one God, and some Hindus revere either Vishnu or Shiva as the sole deity. Other Hindus, like Daoists and Shintoists, recognize the existence of many divinities. Buddhists accept some of the Hindu gods, who they see as attending upon the Buddha, but the Buddha himself is believed to be the "teacher of gods and men," an omniscient and miraculous being, so that functionally he is like a supreme God.

In addition to God or gods, there are common beliefs in supernatural forces that may reside in people, places or things. In most religions, there are holy towns or objects, to which people make pilgrimage or which they use for healing and help. Sacred places and objects are regarded as means by which spiritual power is made accessible, and they are surrounded with taboos to ensure respect.

Perhaps mankind's most universal and oldest religious belief is in life after death, which probably dates back to Neanderthal Man. It is difficult to reconstruct the thoughts of prehistoric peoples, but when the dead were buried in a crouching position as at birth, or painted red like blood, or with tools and utensils beside the body, this strongly suggests belief in another life. All historic religions teach life after death, but the forms of belief vary. Semitic religions believe in heaven for the just, and hell or purgatory for sinners. A basic Indian idea is reincarnation or transmigration, the rebirth of the soul after death in another body—human or animal—with its final goal as deliverance from the chain of rebirth into a timeless Nirvana. Through Buddhism, this belief spread right across Asia. Permeating these different concepts is the belief in the survival of the human spirit, which again helps to strengthen society and provide continuity.

Religious behavior

Religions all have moral teachings which require respect for spiritual forces and correct behavior toward other people. Murder, theft and adultery are commonly proscribed, and the faithful are generally exhorted to care for the sick and needy. Buddhists, Jains and some Hindus are forbidden to take any life and are therefore vegetarians, while Buddhists and Muslims are denied intoxicating drinks.

Belief in superhuman beings results in worship, individual and communal, the latter being conducted by trained and consecrated officials. Islam is notable in having no priesthood, although its worship is led by informed teachers. Priests are nearly always male, but there are orders of nuns in Buddhism and Christianity, and some Protestant churches now ordain women.

All religions allow individual prayers and devotions, which offer praise and petition. There may be meditation or repetition of sacred texts, as well as spontaneous cries for help. The use of prayer beads or rosaries is widespread—this practice seems to have begun in India and was carried by Buddhism as far east as Japan, while to the west it spread with Islam and entered Christianity in the twelfth century.

Buildings used for communal worship have provided some of the greatest monuments of world architecture. The churches and cathedrals of the western world are paralleled by the mosques of Islam, the temples of Hinduism and Buddhism and the shrines of Shinto. Two of the Semitic religions, Judaism and Islam, strongly oppose idolatry, and ban any imagery in statues or pictures in their places of worship. Sikhs also have no idols, reflecting Muslim influence. In Roman Catholicism, however, images are commonly used and in Orthodox Christianity there are icons. Crosses and stained-glass picture windows are common in most, but not all, types of Protestantism. Hindu and Daoist temples have many images of gods, while Jains and Buddhists depict their Jinas and Buddhas as objects of reverence. Shinto shrines have no images but may contain symbols such as mirrors, leaves and water.

Above all, religion is never static, but changes its form according to the needs of society. There are many new religious movements: Ayatollahs in Iran, African prophets and Christian "charismatics." There are notable new religions in Japan, some founded by women, which provide mass congregational worship and centers for personal help in a rapidly changing society. Social movements in many countries are inspired or directed by religious faith, so that the influence of religion is more widespread than its formal organization, buildings or worship.

Aspects of one god
In Christian cultures the forces of good and evil are represented by different beings in constant opposition to each other—Christ on the one hand and Satan or Lucifer on the other. In the Hindu religion they may be aspects of one god. For example, aspects of Devi range from the warlike Durga and bloodthirsty Kali, often depicted with skulls hanging round her neck, to the beautiful and benign Parvati, or Lakshmi, goddess of prosperity.

Virtues personified
Often the attributes of the god or gods are personified in human or animal form. Here the monkey god, Hanuman, stands at the gate of the temple to

Shiva, one of the three major Hindu gods, who represents both reproduction and destruction. Hanuman's devotion to Rama, in mythology the perfect Hindu, is the model for human devotion.

River of a thousand names
For Hindus the Ganges is a holy river—"the destroyer of poverty and sorrow," "the light amid darkness" and "the cow which gives much milk."

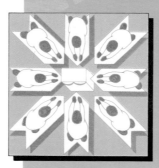

The focus of prayer
The direction of prayer may be important. Many Christians traditionally turn to the east, and Muslims must turn toward the Kaaba shrine in Mecca.

Religion and society
Religion is often closely linked with the structure of society. Thus Muslims speak of "the House of Islam" and identify it with the entire community. The authority of religion serves as a social cement, giving a pattern for the actions of society as well as a coherent structure for the universe and a model for personal living.

Man and God
The Amida Buddha at Kamakura, in Japan, seems to epitomize qualities of serenity and compassion. The Amidists or Pure Land Buddhists are a sect of Mahayana Buddhism. They believe that Amida rules over the Pure Land or Western Paradise. Although Gautama was a historical character, for the Mahayanan Buddhists he is a transcendental being conceived as a supreme deity, above all other gods, embodying absolute truth.

Opposing forces
A recurring theme in both Daoist and Confucian thought is the opposition of two forces, represented by the yin-yang symbol. Heaven is yang, or the active bright, male principle; earth is yin, or the passive, dark, female principle. They are the positive and negative forces of nature reflected in such oppositions as day and night, light and darkness. All things are essentially based on differing combinations of these two principles.

Symbols of faith
Symbols play an important role in concentrating the thoughts of worshipers. The Star of David, symbol of Judaism, has also been used by Christianity and Islam. In Hinduism, the *lingam* (phallus of Shiva) shown with the *yoni* (female organ) is a symbol of fertility and power. In Christian communion, the host symbolizes the body of Christ and, for Roman Catholics, actually *becomes* His body. Here the host is offered up by Pope John Paul II.

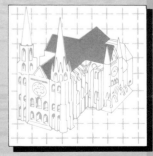

Penance for personal sin
During Easter week in Tasco, Mexico, penitents, bowed down with chains, walk barefoot through the streets. Many religions have sects which believe that physical suffering leads to greater spiritual awareness.

Religious architecture
Many Christian churches, like this Gothic cathedral, incorporate the cross, symbol of Christ's redeeming sacrifice, into their ground plan.

Religions of the World

Those religions which have had the most wide-ranging influence have been scriptural, that is to say not only written down but codified in the form of scriptures. All the major living religions are scriptural and all of them originated in Asia.

Religions from western Asia

In both Judaism and Christianity, man finds the origins for his beliefs in the Bible. Moses, whom the Jews believe to have been the greatest of prophets, received the Law from God on Mount Sinai (c. 1300 BC). After the destruction of their religious center, Jerusalem, by the Romans in AD 70, the Jews were dispersed, mainly into the western world.

Christianity began within Judaism, and Christians accepted the Jewish scriptures, to which they added their "New" Testament. This new part told of Jesus of Nazareth, whom his disciples believed to be the "anointed" of God. He was crucified in Jerusalem, which is therefore also sacred to Christians. After three centuries of persecution, for rejecting the gods of the Roman Empire, Christianity overran Europe and later much of the world. It now has three major divisions: Eastern Orthodox, based in Istanbul; Roman Catholic, based in Rome; and Reformed or Protestant, with centers at Geneva, Canterbury and elsewhere, reflecting the many denominations, such as Presbyterian and Anglican.

The most immediately successful religion was that of Islam—the religion of submission to Allah (God). Its founder, Muhammad, was born in AD 570 in Mecca, Arabia, but he moved to the city of Medina in AD 622. Muhammad's teachings, revealed to him by Allah, are set down in the Qur'an (Recitation). Before he died Muhammad had converted much of Arabia to his teaching and by AD 732, just a century after his death, the Arab Empire stretched from Iran to Spain.

Most Muslims—as all followers of Islam are known—are Sunni, following the Sunna or customs of tradition. They accept as first caliphs (successors or deputies of Muhammad) Abu Bakr, Umar, Uthman and Ali, in that order. The Shia are a second major division of Islam. They believe that Ali, who was the cousin and son-in-law of Muhammad, was the first caliph, and reject the others, but otherwise they differ little from the Sunni.

Religions from India

The major religion of India is known as Hinduism in the western world but is called *sanatana dharma* (eternal truth) by Hindus themselves. Its early history is still little known, but remains of Indian religion are found at Harappa and other sites in the valley of the river Indus. Later, great holy cities were built, of which the most famous is Benares on the river Ganges. The most sacred Hindu texts are the Vedas (Divine knowledge), which are dated from about 1300 BC. They teach yoga (yoking, or discipline), karma (the results of actions) and the reincarnation, or transmigration, of souls.

A north Indian reform movement under Gautama the Buddha (perhaps 563–483 BC) began in a park at Sarnath near Benares, where Gautama taught deliverance from desire and suffering by a Noble Eightfold Path of mental and moral discipline; this would lead to Nirvana (literally the "blowing out" of desire). The place of the Buddha's enlightenment (Buddha means enlightened one) at Gaya near the middle Ganges is also a place of pilgrimage. Gautama renounced his family and formed a community of monks, the Sangha, as the core of Buddhism. Numerous divisions of Buddhism now exist, the major ones being Theravada (doctrine of the elders) and Mahayana (great vehicle).

Contemporary with Buddhism, but now having fewer followers, was Jainism. Jains follow Jinas (conquerors), seeking liberation from karma in Nirvana. Their great center is Mount Abu, Rajasthan.

Another Indian religion is that of the Sikhs, who are disciples of Guru Nanak (AD 1469–1539) but who share some beliefs with Muslims and Hindus. The Sikhs' famous Golden Temple is at their most sacred city of Amritsar in the Punjab.

A small but active Indian religious minority are the Parsis, or Persians, their chief center being at Bombay. They worship Ahura Mazda, the one God, and their beliefs are based on the teachings of Zoroaster, or Zarathustra (c. 628–551 BC), who was perhaps born in Media, near what is now Tehran. His teachings are in the Avesta scriptures and Gatha hymns.

The world map and statistics
Different religions vary in their methods of assessing adherents. Christianity, reflecting western thought, is statistically well documented; Islam, in the mold of eastern philosophy, has no recourse to such analyses—all peoples of Islamic countries are considered Muslim, unless there is a recognized minority. There are no official sources for Buddhism, Confucianism and Daoism. In some cases only adults are numbered; political conflict and persecution also compound the difficulty of compiling accurate statistics. In Communist countries party members, approximately 7% of the total population, are militantly antireligious. The map shows the dominant religion in each country. The cylinders represent the followers of each religion as a percentage of total population.

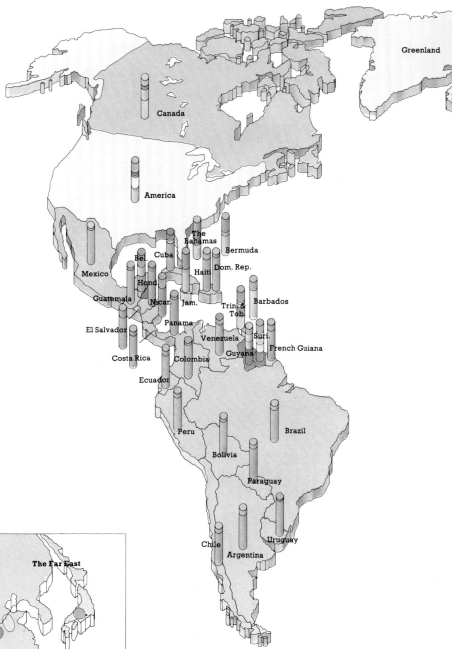

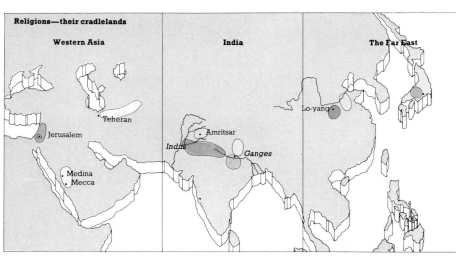

Religions—their cradlelands
There are three related semitic religions (called after the supposed descendants of Shem, son of Noah); Judaism, Christianity and Islam. Indian religions include Hinduism, Jainism, Buddhism and Sikhism and are related to Zoroastrianism, which originated in ancient Iran. The Far East is the home of Chinese Confucianism and Daoism, and of Japanese Shinto. Buddhism, Christianity and Islam are international and missionary faiths. In 1948, the establishment of the state of Israel restored a country and a religious center to Judaism.

Religions from the Far East

Daoism (Taoism) is the most distinctively Chinese religion, the Dao being the "way" or eternal principle of heaven and earth, and life in harmony with it. According to Daoist tradition the founder was Lao-tzu (c. 604–531 BC), but the book associated with him, the *Tao Te Ching*, was probably written later.

From the sixth century BC onward, religious thought in China was deeply influenced by Confucius, or K'ung-fu-tzu (551–479 BC), a moral and social teacher in the state of Lu, Shantung. Confucius was credited with writing Five Classics, but his moral teachings are in the small Analects. His followers subsequently added veneration of ancestors and rituals of state to his teachings. From the fifteenth century, Peking, with its Temple of Heaven, was the center of state rituals that were called Confucian.

Merging sometimes with Daoist nature philosophy was Buddhism, which was brought to China from India in the first century AD and which after some opposition had become rooted in China. This blending of Bud-

dhism and Daoism appeared in meditation sects, Ch'an in Chinese, which is Zen in Japanese (from Indian *dhyana*, meditation). Even more popular were the Pure Land sects, which adored the Buddha of the Pure Land, or Western Paradise, who bestowed salvation.

Shinto (way of the gods) was the native Japanese religion of veneration of spirits of nature and mythology. The chief spirit was Amaterasu the sun goddess and ancestor of the emperor, enshrined at Ise.

Since the beginning of the twentieth century there has been a decline in formal religion in parts of the western world, and a large organized antireligious movement—Communism—has begun to flourish. But whether Communism itself is a form of religion has been debated. It has a belief in a coming Golden Age; it is international and missionary. However Communism has no gods, nor, unlike most religions, has it a belief in life after death, even though two of its major leaders—Lenin and Mao Tse-tung—have great mausoleums, in Moscow and Peking respectively, to which constant pilgrimages are made.

Communism
Members of the Communist party are not differentiated from nonmembers. Although most Communist states recognize some religions, the numbers believing in as well as publicly practicing a religion are not readily available. This particularly applies to minor sects. Albania, which has closed all religious institutions, is the only officially atheist state.

Chinese religions
Confucianism, Daoism and Buddhism formerly coexisted; adherents (approximately 15% of the population) may still practice any one or a combination of all three religions.

Japanese religions
Both Buddhism and Shintoism are practiced by the majority of the population.

The major religions
- Christianity: Roman Catholic
- Christianity: Protestant
- Christianity: Eastern Orthodox
- Islam: Sunni
- Islam: Shia
- Hinduism
- Buddhism: Theravada Mahayana
- Chinese religions
- Japanese religions
- Judaism
- Sikhism
- Communist party members and non-party Communists
- Minority religions, non-scriptural religions and unknowns

The major religions —numbers following each religion in millions

Christianity — Protestant 338.3, Roman Catholic 775, Eastern Orthodox 136.5
Islam — Shia 81.8, Sunni 626.4
Hinduism 449.9
Buddhism: Theravada/Mahayana 200.1
Chinese religions c. 150
Japanese religions 84.7
Judaism 12.9
Sikhism 10.5
Communist party members and nonparty Communists c. 1,050
Minority religions, nonscriptural religions and unknown c. 200

Pilgrimage and Tourism

Both pilgrimage and tourism have expanded considerably in the second half of the twentieth century, owing to improved and cheaper transport. But while tourism as we now know it only began to become popular in the nineteenth century (originally as the "Grand Tour" of Europe, part of a young man's education) pilgrimage thrived in much earlier times. Indeed, there is reason to believe that Stonehenge in southern Britain was a pilgrimage center over 3,000 years ago, as it was a place of worship far larger than the needs of the local population. A more familiar example is pilgrimage to the Holy Land, of special significance to Christians for over 1,500 years, and important also to Jews and Muslims.

It is often difficult to distinguish tourism and pilgrimage and the island of Iona, off Scotland, provides an interesting example of this. As the headquarters of St Columba's mission to convert the Picts to Christianity, it attracts many thousands of visitors each year, but the Church of Scotland, which dominates the island, does not endorse pilgrimage since it contradicts Calvinist ideas of predestination. Are the visitors tourists or pilgrims? What suggests that it is in effect a pilgrimage is that many who visit Iona claim to be transformed by their experience.

In search of healing

The primary motivation for pilgrimage is undoubtedly healing, either direct physical healing—although pilgrims are usually enjoined not to count on miracles—or spiritual healing. A pilgrimage represents a personal and voluntary attempt to recruit supernatural powers for one's own objectives, circumventing religious hierarchies. Personal divisions and rivalries within social groups are subordinated to the overwhelming spiritual power of the shrine.

Although rare among the educated western middle classes, pilgrimage is by no means dying out. One and a half million Muslims a year make the pilgrimage to Mecca, many by chartered aircraft; 750,000 pilgrims arrive at Knock, in Ireland, each year to show their devotion to the Virgin Mary, who is said to have miraculously appeared there in 1879, and 3.5 million came to Lourdes, in France, in 1972. Pilgrimage has an important place in all world religions—Christianity, Islam, Judaism, Hinduism, Sikhism, Buddhism, Jainism, Confucianism, Taoism and Shintoism. Journeys to visit Lenin's grave in Moscow, and Marx's grave in Highgate, London, have also taken on much of the character of pilgrimage, as have the state-subsidized or industrially subsidized "cures" that are widespread in Japan, and in northern and eastern Europe. Here the journey and stay at a spa or seaside resort is justified as restoring the worker to health and thus full productivity. Vast resort hotels have sprung up in German spa towns, such as Baden-Baden, and along the Black Sea coast, at Odessa and elsewhere, to cater for this demand. Frequently the employees of a factory will all take their cure together, a practice often paralleled in Christian pilgrimage.

The tourist phenomenon

What we usually mean by tourism is often better described as sight-seeing. Certain countries, cities, buildings or natural formations (such as sandy beaches, gorges, caves or mountains) are accounted especially worthy of being visited, and become tourist attractions. The process of becoming an attraction is a complex mixture of exchange of travelers' tales, descriptions in guide books, deliberate advertising, and the cumulative attractiveness occasioned by ever-increasing numbers of visitors. Tourist attractions, being socially constructed, can also be socially destroyed. The typical life cycle is discovery by a few articulate and charismatic pioneers, then adoption by an elite capable of coping with inadequate facilities, followed by development (often state sponsored) into a mass tourist site, with large hotels and a concomitant transformation of the local economy. Kenya, for instance, earns more foreign currency from tourism than any other source, including coffee. But many tourist sites pass through this phase, and begin to be abandoned as their charm is destroyed by the presence of tourists in such large numbers. It is instructive to compare Nepal and Bhutan, both tiny Himalayan kingdoms. Bhutan's highly restrictive tourist access policy has provided higher economic returns from tourism, and has enabled the country to remain far more attractive to high-spending tourists than Nepal, which, in the past, has been all too welcoming, resulting in a large influx of "hippies" who deterred wealthier visitors.

Every large city now produces brochures listing its most important tourist attractions. The influential Michelin Guides even rank them using stars—three stars means "worth the journey," two means "merits a detour" and one merely "interesting." This rationalization of attractions provides a means for the tourist to evaluate his own and others' performances as tourists, making sure he has seen all he should. Crucial to this system of gaining social merit by sight-seeing is the ubiquitous camera, since photographs provide acceptable evidence that one has been present at the best attractions. In some American tourist spots, maps and discreet notices even specify where the tourist photographer should stand to get the best camera angles.

The cultural impact

Comparing the social impact of tourism and pilgrimage, it can be argued that on the whole tourism is more culturally disruptive. As a tourist, a person is at leisure, not bent on shaping the world but only on experiencing it. In providing facilities for him, local inhabitants find themselves distanced from their own culture, more aware of the arbitrary nature of its values and prohibitions. A tourist uses a resort as a stage-set for his own freely chosen leisure activities, which may have meaning only in the context of his return to everyday life. By contrast, the pilgrim's often narrowly prescribed actions at a shrine tend to reinforce local values; they are essentially appropriate to the place and have most meaning there.

An uphill pilgrimage
A pilgrim nears the summit of Croagh Patrick, a mountain in County Mayo, in the west of Ireland. Traditionally climbers go barefooted or on their knees. The pilgrimage takes place on the last Sunday of July, when thousands climb the rocky slope to take part in a mass commemorating Saint Patrick, who is said to have fasted for 40 days on the mountain.

Tourism and the economy
These figures for tourist arrivals in 1977, as a percentage of the indigenous population, give an idea of the extent of tourist penetration in any given host country. If the host country has a relatively weak economy, it is likely to suffer rather than benefit from mass tourism. The culture and economy of a rich industrial nation, on the other hand, is secure enough to absorb any number of tourists without their presence becoming disruptive.

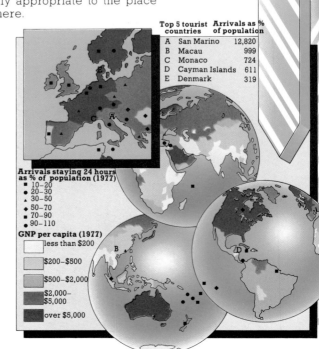

Top 5 tourist countries	Arrivals as % of population
A San Marino	12,820
B Macau	999
C Monaco	724
D Cayman Islands	611
E Denmark	319

Arrivals staying 24 hours as % of population (1977)
- 10–20
- 20–30
- 30–50
- 50–70
- 70–90
- 90–110

GNP per capita (1977)
- less than $200
- $200–$500
- $500–$2,000
- $2,000–$5,000
- over $5,000

Minimal tourism

Remote places attract tourists interested in unspoiled and preferably unexplored territory. The inaccessibility of such regions means that trips are likely to be both costly and arduous; the traveler must live without familiar amenities and be prepared to adapt to different attitudes.

Minimal impact

Where tourists are few in number and are willing to adapt to the local norms, they make little or no impact on the indigenous culture, but will themselves be fully open to the effect of that culture. Consequently the tourist is seen as an individual and judged accordingly.

Observation not participation

Tourists interested in the picturesque aspects of different cultures concentrate on places of local interest, such as the castle-museum circuit. Usually these are popular sites, well equipped to deal with a steady stream of visitors and reflect an officially recognized and controlled local industry.

Keeping the balance

Tourists here tend to make use of local facilities and because their numbers are not great enough to be disruptive, their presence arouses interest rather than resentment. The money they spend will be seen as a welcome addition to local income. Perception on both sides is unhindered by any imposed tourist structure.

Walking the wall

The Great Wall of China, once a defense against the Mongols, is now a major tourist attraction. Most of the people visiting the Wall are Chinese as the government, having seen what damage can be done by uncontrolled mass tourism, is keeping a tight rein on the numbers of foreign tourists.

Recreation

Tourists interested in recreation are attracted by mouthwatering brochures which tend to concentrate on the aquamarine seas and tanned bikini wearers and avoid showing packed beaches or high-rise hotels crowding the waterfront. The emphasis is on relaxation, entertainment and sport.

Tourists expect and receive a certain standard of service and accommodation, and the destination is probably less important than the services that are provided.

Oppressed by numbers

The greater the number of tourists and the more reliant the country is on tourism as an industry the more that country will have to adapt itself to tourist requirements. Indigenous culture becomes molded to tourist expectations and desires, and contact between the tourists and their hosts becomes increasingly stressful. The tourist is seen not as an individual but as a stereotype whose only value to the host is a monetary one.

Waiting for clients

These girls, waiting for clients in a Bangkok "hotel," are trapped in a life of prostitution. Most were sold to traders as children, by their impoverished parents, the average price being about 40 $US. The Vietnam war boosted Bangkok's trade in drugs and prostitutes as American soldiers on leave flooded into Thailand. With the end of the war, business slumped and competition has become intense. Visitors from the West are now offered package holidays in Thailand, with a girl included in the price.

Appealing to all comers

Some of the most popular recreational holidays in the West are skiing trips. This French tourist board poster conveys all the elements in the package – sun, snow, sport and sex – without words. Its simple multilingual statement reflects a confidence in attracting all the tourists required.

The Colonial Legacy

Imperialism has a long history, going back to Hammurabi, King of Babylon, in the eighteenth century BC, and more directly to the massive empire created by Alexander the Great. However, the great empires created between the fifteenth and the twentieth centuries by Europe's expansion overseas were the most extensive in the history of mankind, and it was this colonial era which shaped the face of today's world.

The expansion of Europe overseas began at the end of the fifteenth century as a result of the opening up of sea routes to Africa, Asia and the New World. Generally, the first phase of modern imperial expansion took the form of colonization—settlers from the European powers established colonies in places where there were either no indigenous inhabitants, or where these were so weak that they were easily killed, reduced to servitude, or pushed off their lands. Such was the case in the Americas when they were opened up by the Spaniards and Portuguese, and later by the British and French. This was also the case in Australia, and as in the New World the settlers constructed political units that were modeled on the country from which they came. Only where the settlers were unable to eliminate or decimate the indigenous population and where it contrived, as in Mexico, to be culturally resilient, did the new society diverge from its model.

At an early stage in their expansion overseas, the European imperial powers came up against peoples with whom they wished to trade but whose societies were too well structured for them to dominate. In such cases—notably Japan and most African states before the middle of the nineteenth century—they traded only by consent of the local rulers. In other countries, such as India and Indonesia, the British and the Dutch began to impose forms of political control through their trading representatives. These foreshadowed the colonialism—the political, economic and cultural subjection of non-European peoples—that characterized the European empires of the late nineteenth century.

The Europeans were not alone in their colonialism—America and Australia later became colonial powers, and Japan undertook colonial expansion at the beginning of the twentieth century. In 1905–6 Japan came into conflict with and defeated Russia, which itself had begun to colonize what is now Soviet Asia.

The methods by which the colonial powers administered their colonies differed. Britain, for example, tried wherever possible to rule *indirectly* through the indigenous institutions of the subject peoples, although very often they could not identify or come to terms with suitable indigenous authorities. By contrast, Portugal ruled directly through a hierarchy of civil servants who took little account of the indigenous political structures, while the colonies as a whole were considered as overseas provinces. But whatever the method employed, the goal was the same: the exploitation of the resources of the colonies for the benefit of the motherland. What benefits accrued to the colonies themselves were largely incidental—roads, railroads and ports for the export of their produce, or medical and educational services designed to produce healthy and literate workers for commerce and government.

Development designed mainly to benefit the inhabitants of the colony was not undertaken on a significant scale until World War II, when nationalist opposition to the colonial rulers in Asia and Africa was beginning to pose a threat. The nationalists sought an end to their political, economic and cultural subservience. They thus sought control of the political units which had been instituted by the colonial powers, rather than independence for the original states or peoples from which the colonies had been created. In a few cases the colonial state and the precolonial state were essentially the same, for instance in Cambodia or Morocco. But in the vast majority of cases the independent states that emerged from the colonial era were radically different from those that had existed on the eve of colonial rule. In a very real sense the European powers had redrawn the map of the world.

Nationalism in the European colonies was essentially a reaction to political domination, but political independence only brought about a nominal change in the relationship between the former imperial powers and their ex-colonies. There now existed a *neocolonial*

The causes of colonialism

Marxists argue that the scramble to colonize the undeveloped world stemmed from the capitalists' need to expand their markets. Colonies offered a perfect opportunity to utilize cheap labor and acquire cheap raw materials, thus cutting the costs of production and increasing profits. In order to protect their overseas investments it was often necessary to impose formal political and military control. A more pluralistic interpretation of imperialism suggests that it sprang from a variety of motives: securing frontiers, protecting overseas markets, establishing naval bases, controlling vital natural resources, fulfilling military ambitions, satisfying national honor or evangelizing and "civilizing" foreign peoples.

Empires of the colonial powers 1914

Belgian	Dutch
British	Ottoman
French	Portuguese
German	Russian
Italian	Spanish
Japanese	United States

Major raw materials from colonies

Meat	Rubber
Tea	Wool
Cane sugar	Copra
Dairy produce	Diamonds
Veg. oil	Gold
Grain	Copper
Silk	Tin
Cotton	
Jute	

Slave trade 1790

British
French
Portuguese
Dutch

"Since trade ignores national boundaries and the manufacturers insist on having the world as a market, the flag of his nation must follow him, and the doors of the nations which are closed against him must be battered down. Concessions obtained by financiers must be safeguarded by ministers of state, even if the sovereignty of unwilling nations be outraged in the process. Colonies must be obtained or planted, in order that no useful corner of the world may be overlooked or left unused."

Woodrow Wilson 1907

The Panama Canal

Having supported a Panamanian independence movement, the US signed a treaty with the new government which gave them the right to build a canal on a strip of land granted to them in perpetuity. The canal was completed in 1914. In return the US guaranteed to defend Panama's independence.

Pacific Islands

Midway
Hawaii
Wake
Solomon
Guam
Gilbert
Ellice
Samoa
Fiji

British Empire 1909

Area	Population
20%	23%

Partition of the world 1914

Area: 11%, 21%, 68%
Population: 22%, 18%, 60%

Independent states
Semi-colonial states
Colonial territories

Foreign investment 1914 (in millions US$)

UK
France
Germany
Holland
USA
Belgium
Russia

500 3,510 4,100 5,650 9,280 19,935

Foreign investment

Before 1914 Britain led the field in foreign investment, a reflection of her vast empire. Such investment often gives control over supposedly independent countries—in the 19th century, 20% of Britain's overseas investment was in Latin America, which was thus largely controlled by Britain.

Slavery

The lucrative sugar plantations of the Caribbean relied on slave labor, and between 1670 and 1786 more than 2 million slaves were transported to the British colonies alone. Some African peoples, such as the Asante, came to depend on the slave trade, preying on weaker neighbors to supply the traders.

Colonialism before 1870
Before 1870 the European colonies were of limited extent, but millions of slaves had already been shipped from Africa to the Caribbean. European explorers, such as Stanley and Speke, paved the way for the hectic scramble for colonies which took place between 1870 and 1914.

A warning to Japanese girls
This 19th-century Japanese poster, warning against mixed marriages, reflects the intense antiforeign feeling that the forcible ending of 200 years of isolation caused. In 1853 a US naval squadron "requested" that Japan open her ports and permit trade, making it clear that the alternative was war.

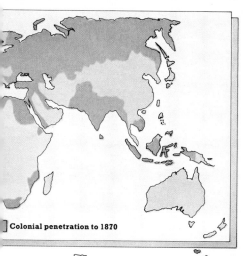

Colonial penetration to 1870

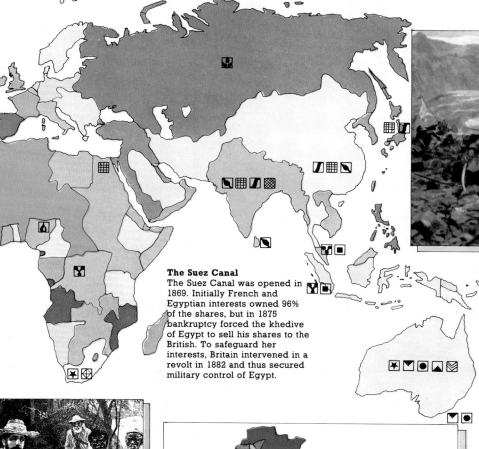

The Suez Canal
The Suez Canal was opened in 1869. Initially French and Egyptian interests owned 96% of the shares, but in 1875 bankruptcy forced the khedive of Egypt to sell his shares to the British. To safeguard her interests, Britain intervened in a revolt in 1882 and thus secured military control of Egypt.

On the northwest frontier
A painting entitled "Last stand of the 44th foot at Gandamuk," depicts the grim reality of life for the British soldier on India's northwest frontier. The need for a colonial power to secure its frontiers produced a cyclical effect: once a zone had been subdued it needed to be made secure, often leading to conflict with neighboring peoples. Once they had been subdued, the frontier expanded and new neighbors were encountered, so that the problem arose again. The Afghan wars of the 19th century were also the result of Britain's need to create a buffer zone between her Indian territories and the expanding Russian Empire.

British crown colony of India, c. 1914

△ possessions
▲ Portuguese possessions

0   800 Kms

British possessions 1805
British possessions by 1858
British possessions by 1914
Dependent Indian principalities 1914
-- Area of Mutiny 1857

The white man's burden
Bishop Mackenzie, as depicted by a Victorian artist, preaching to African children. Britain saw its role as civilizing the world—an impulse which conveniently paralleled its economic and political interests. The "white man's burden" was to take over the running of supposedly uncivilized countries.

India—creeping imperialism
Established in 1600, the British East India Company became the unofficial organ of British colonial policy. To safeguard its trading interests, the company extended its influence, interfering in the power struggles of the Indian princes in order to secure administrative control and the right to levy taxes. A power struggle between the French and British ended with Robert Clive's victory at Plassey in 1757, which secured complete British domination. The East India Company was dissolved in 1858 and India became a viceroyalty. Where possible the British exercised control through traditional local rulers.

relationship in which the economic resources of the "independent" state were still controlled by the former metropolis or other western industrialized powers. The colonies had simply now moved from the formal to the informal control of the colonial powers. Just as in the nineteenth and twentieth centuries the European imperialists had succeeded in controlling the economies of most Latin American countries without imposing formal political control over them, so they continued to exercise a major influence over the economies of their former colonies in Africa and Asia.

The way in which the economies of the colonies had been shaped by the colonial powers often made it difficult for them to break away from continued economic dependence on their former metropolis despite formal independence. Large areas of land, once used for subsistence farming, had been devoted to export crops during the colonial period, and many colonies became dependent on a single export crop, such as cocoa, sugar, tea or bananas, for foreign exchange. Their inability to control the price they obtained for these crops on the world market, coupled with their dependence on imported machinery and, in a growing number of cases, on imported foodstuffs, has condemned many former colonies to a cycle of poverty from which it is difficult to escape.

The present-day struggle in the ex-colonies is for real economic independence. In many, there is also a struggle against the strong cultural bonds with which they are tied to their former rulers, through language, education and religion. Gaining control of their economies is matched in importance by the difficult task of establishing an independent cultural identity.

Modern Imperialism

In its broad sense, imperialism has remained as much a fact of international life after World War II as it was before. Great powers still seek to dominate vast areas of the world, and small powers seek to dominate their weaker neighbors. At the same time, imperialism has changed its meaning. The old colonial empires—which were a curious mixture of economic profit and loss, of arrogance and idealism—have vanished. Their last remnants, such as the British outposts in Hong Kong or Gibraltar, persist by the will of the inhabitants and not that of the colonial power. Instead, a different kind of imperialism has emerged—one based upon ideological rivalry. Ironically, the two opposing ideologies are headed by powers which have traditionally thought of themselves as anti-imperialist: the United States, which came into existence through revolt against an imperial power, and the Soviet Union, which was born in revolution against the Tsarist Empire. Today, the United States stands for capitalist democracy, the Soviet Union for universal socialism, and it is their ideological rivalry that makes the struggle so intense.

Ideologies do not merely compete for power; whereas older imperialist conflicts were very often settled by territorial compromise, ideological competition cannot be resolved in this way. It is concerned with people's beliefs, with an appeal to the soul of the world and the direction of its future. In this sense the struggle is about everything, although at the same time it is modified and limited by the realities of power and the overriding need to avoid nuclear war.

On the one hand, these two great powers seek to spread their messages, to recruit new allies in the socialist cause or to win new adherents to democracy. But at the same time each is trying to contain the power of the other and, in so doing, will support regimes or countries whose ideologies they detest. For many years, the Soviet Union exercised enormous influence

in Egypt through the support it gave to President Nasser, even while he imprisoned his own Egyptian communists. The United States continues to support an Islamic royal system in Saudi Arabia which makes no secret of its contempt for the idea of democracy.

Both powers, however, are determined to maintain control, and to safeguard either capitalism or socialism in their own immediate neighborhood. This is most clearly the case in eastern Europe, over which the Soviet Union acquired complete control between 1945 and 1947. It did not merely impose its own military power there but also its ideological system. Only one sizeable east European state, Yugoslavia, was able to break out of the system effectively, and since 1948 it has become a leading member of the neutralist nations, opposed to the imperialism of both sides. Other eastern European countries have not been allowed to deviate very far from the Soviet path.

A similar pattern can be seen in the relations of the United States to Latin America. Like the Soviet Union, it has suffered one major setback, when Cuba successfully launched a socialist and anti-American revolution in 1960. But in other countries the United States has intervened either directly, as in the Dominican Republic in 1968, or, as in El Salvador in the 1980s, by sending arms supplies and military advisors to back up repressive and unpopular governments.

Beyond their immediate neighbors, the two superpowers seek influence and allies throughout the world. In many cases, they have been accused of indirect imperialism by supplying arms and maintaining regimes in other countries. Iranians, for example, blame the United States for the repressions of the Shah. More generally, the two systems they represent have come to confront each other, and even engage in prolonged fighting, as in Korea (1950–53) and Vietnam (1960–73).

In the years after the Vietnam war, the United States was a relatively quiescent power, but it was in the

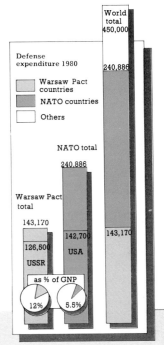

Defense expenditure 1980

- Warsaw Pact countries
- NATO countries
- Others

World total 450,000

World total

NATO total 240,886

Warsaw Pact total 143,170

240,886

USSR 126,500

USA 142,700

143,170

as % of GNP

12%   5.5%

Arms and ideology
Ideological rivalry has polarized the modern world, and resulted in the massive stockpiling of arms by the two major military alliances, NATO and the Warsaw Pact. Both the US and USSR tend to exaggerate estimates of each other's expenditure on military equipment and use these claims to justify further increases. The superpowers now have enough weapons to annihilate each other, and all of Europe, several times over.

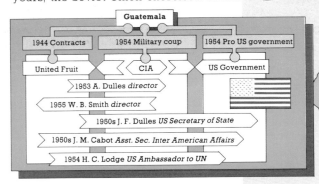

Guatemala

| 1944 Contracts | 1954 Military coup | 1954 Pro US government |

| United Fruit | CIA | US Government |

1953 A. Dulles *director*
1955 W. B. Smith *director*
1950s J. F. Dulles *US Secretary of State*
1950s J. M. Cabot *Asst. Sec. Inter American Affairs*
1954 H. C. Lodge *US Ambassador to UN*

Guatemala and United Fruit
In 1944, Guatemala's economy was dominated by foreign business interests, operating under the most favorable conditions—the United Fruit company, for example, had a 99-year tax-free concession. The wealth generated by this foreign investment did not benefit the majority of the people. In the 1950s, the reformist government of Jacobo Arbenz attempted to radically alter this, primarily through land reform, and declared its

intention of expropriating 152,000 hectares (380,000 acres) of unused United Fruit land. The company was to keep any land under cultivation plus 35,200 hectares (88,000 acres) for future clearance. The close links that existed between United Fruit, the US Government and the CIA helped to bring about a military coup in which Arbenz was overthrown. Following the coup in 1954, US aid to Guatemala suddenly increased and concessions to foreign business were restored.

The Cuban missile crisis
East confronts West, as the USS *Barry* steams alongside the Russian freighter *Anosov*, carrying military equipment for Cuba. The hostility of the US toward Fidel Castro's left-wing regime forced Cuba, an ex-colony with massive financial problems, into increasing economic dependence on the USSR. In 1962, American planes observed Soviet missile bases on Cuba, but after pressure from the US, the missiles were withdrawn.

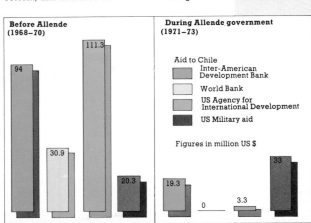

| Before Allende (1968–70) | During Allende government (1971–73) |

94
111.3
30.9
20.3

Aid to Chile
- Inter-American Development Bank
- World Bank
- US Agency for International Development
- US Military aid

Figures in million US $

19.3
0
3.3
33

After coup (Sept 1973–March 1974)

201
18.3
4
11

The US and Chile
In 1970, when Salvador Allende came to power, Chile's economy was dominated by US business interests and crippled by a massive foreign debt. Private investment from the US stood at $1.1 billion out of a total of $1.72 billion, and the copper industry—Chile's only significant export earner—was 80% US owned. Faced with Allende's plans to nationalize the copper mines, the US applied a credit squeeze. As a result, Chile's imports were cut by 75%, crippling the economy. At the same time, support was given to those in Chile who opposed Allende, which was reflected in increased military aid.

Salvador Allende
Salvador Allende was the first democratically elected Marxist president in the western hemisphere. He died during the military coup in 1973.

End of the "Prague Spring"
In 1968 the tanks of her Warsaw Pact allies rolled into Czechoslovakia, bringing to an end the brief "Prague Spring" of Alexander Dubcek's regime. His democratization program was seen as a threat by the USSR despite widespread national support. Dubcek and his fellow leaders were arrested and finally replaced in 1969.

same period that the Soviet Union embarked on a more vigorous policy. Its ally, Cuba, with the aid of Soviet transport and equipment, intervened successfully in conflicts in Angola in 1976 and Ethiopia in 1977. In the following year there were coups in South Yemen and Afghanistan which pulled these countries more closely into the Soviet orbit, while Vietnam invaded Cambodia and set up a puppet government there. In December 1979 Soviet forces invaded Afghanistan, producing the strongest vote of condemnation that the United Nations has ever seen. Many countries from the neutralist bloc now accuse the Soviet Union of outright imperialism, and Cuba and Vietnam of being imperialists masquerading as neutralists.

Apart from the rivalry of the two superpowers and their allies, other countries, many of them ex-colonies themselves, have engaged in activity which is widely regarded as imperialist. In 1980–81, Libya aroused anxiety in West Africa through its support of revolutionary forces in Chad and attempts to extend its influence elsewhere. Israel is accused by most Third World countries of imperialism because it continues to occupy the West Bank of the Jordan, which it seized in 1967. In 1977, Somalia and Ethiopia went to war because Ethiopia continues to rule over large territories which are inhabited by Somalis. There are a number of similar instances, reflecting a new driving force—nationalism—which is impelling many ex-colonies to activities which other governments regard as imperialist. As in Somalia, these problems often stem from the arbitrary boundaries which the new states inherited from the colonial powers. The difficulty for most countries which regard themselves as anti-imperialist is that they are involved in contemporary struggles for power, while at the same time still trying to free themselves from the economic and psychological legacy of the colonial era. Imperialism has changed its form, but it is still a fact of life.

Cross references

Horn of Africa 80–81
Saharan Africa 86–7
Southern Africa 100–103
Middle East 104–113
N India, Pakistan and
  Bangladesh 120–23
Mongolia and Tibet 136–7
China and Korea 138–41
Mainland southeast Asia
  146–9
Pacific Islands and New
  Guinea 160–63
Mexico and Guatemala
  176–7
Central America and the
  Caribbean 178–81
See also
A global perspective 12–13
The colonial legacy 46–7
International trade and aid
  52–3

The promised land
From the 1890s, Jewish immigrants settled in Palestine, swelling the original Jewish minority. After World War I, Palestine became a British mandate, and Britain's qualified support for a Jewish National home in Palestine increased tension between Jews and Arabs. In 1948 Britain withdrew; the Zionists proclaimed their new state of Israel and seized ⅔ of Palestine. Since then Israel has confronted Arab opposition; the 1967 war brought massive territorial gains which, with the exception of the Sinai, relinquished in 1982, have not yet been surrendered.

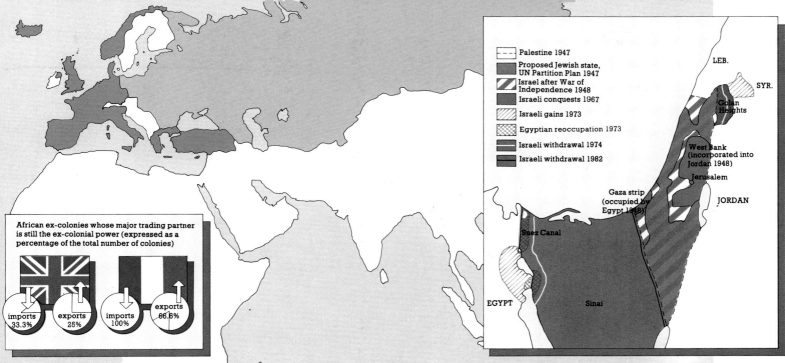

Palestine 1947
Proposed Jewish state, UN Partition Plan 1947
Israel after War of Independence 1948
Israeli conquests 1967
Israeli gains 1973
Egyptian reoccupation 1973
Israeli withdrawal 1974
Israeli withdrawal 1982

LEB.
SYR.
Golan Heights
West Bank (incorporated into Jordan 1948)
Jerusalem
JORDAN
Gaza strip (occupied by Egypt 1948)
Suez Canal
EGYPT
Sinai

African ex-colonies whose major trading partner is still the ex-colonial power (expressed as a percentage of the total number of colonies)

imports 33.3% exports 25% imports 100% exports 66.6%

Neocolonialism
Political independence rarely coincided with economic independence for the former colonies. These new countries found themselves still tied economically to their former colonial masters, and thus still vulnerable to political pressure. The degree to which they are still dependent is reflected in their trade figures. The disparity that exists between the British and French trade figures for their former African colonies reflects their differing aspirations. France wished to assimilate her colonies, while Britain aimed, in theory at least, to create a commonwealth of equal nations.

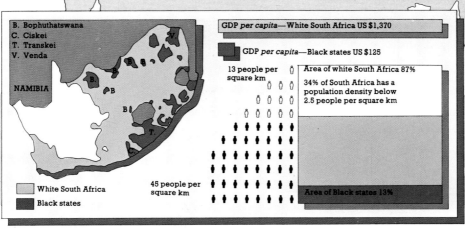

B. Bophuthatswana
C. Ciskei
T. Transkei
V. Venda

NAMIBIA

White South Africa
Black states

GDP *per capita*—White South Africa US $1,370

GDP *per capita*—Black states US $125

13 people per square km

Area of white South Africa 87%
34% of South Africa has a population density below 2.5 people per square km

45 people per square km

Area of Black states 13%

The price of independence
Between 1951 and 1971 ten Bantustans were created—the "black homelands" intended for independence within South Africa. The result is further control of the movement of the black population and, in the event of the extension of the vote, a considerable reduction in the number of potential black voters. The poor resources of most of the homelands mean that they have no hope of economic viability. Many men officially classified as part of the "temporarily absent economically active population" work outside their Bantustan, and are separated from their families for 49 weeks each year.

International Aid and Trade

"Development" only emerged as an issue in world politics with the dismantling of the European empires at the end of World War II. Before 1945, governments had been reluctant to accept any responsibility for the management of the international economy, but after the experience of mass unemployment in the industrial world during the 1930s, and the practical involvement of governments in industrial management during World War II, there could be no return to unrestrained *laissez-faire*. Under the leadership of the United States the governments of the western powers were determined to establish an open world economy, in which trade and investment would flow as freely as possible. It was to achieve this goal that the International Monetary Fund (IMF), the International Bank for Reconstruction and Development (IBRD) and the General Agreement on Tariffs and Trade (GATT), were established in 1944 and 1948.

Although this institutional structure was primarily designed to further the interests of the West, the question arose as to how the poor states of the world, mostly former colonies, were to be accommodated within the new system. Indeed, the question could not be avoided because the United Nations now provided these countries with a public platform. During the debates leading to the establishment of the UN it had become clear that economic development was not viewed by these countries merely as a technical problem but as a continuation of the anticolonial struggle. The developing countries, as they came to be called, claimed that the industrial world had an obligation to assist in their development, both from humanitarian concern and as a restitution for past exploitation.

These claims did not meet with an immediate response in the West, although in Britain and France the pressure of liberal public opinion (which led to the establishment of such voluntary agencies as Oxfam in 1948), combined with a desire to maintain influence in former colonies, ensured that requests for aid were received sympathetically. In the mid-1950s, however, the logic of cold-war rivalry between the two superpowers projected foreign aid to the forefront of the international agenda. Nonaligned India provided the test case. In 1955, halfway through the second five-year development plan, the Indians exhausted their currency reserves and sought international assistance to enable them to complete the plan. In the same year, the new Soviet leaders, Kruschev and Bulganin, toured Asia promising development assistance for non-Communist countries, and India subsequently became one of the major recipients of Soviet aid. The western response was the Aid India Consortium, organized by the IMF to coordinate western aid. This was the model for numerous later consortia.

By the early 1960s, however, enthusiasm for foreign aid was declining in both western countries and the Soviet Union. In the United States, the Administration found it increasingly difficult to persuade Congress that development aid to nonaligned countries was in the general security interest. In the Soviet Union, the political benefits from aid were questioned when the leaders whom they had supported were overthrown.

Partly in response to this change of mood, the governments of the developing countries attempted to change the emphasis of the development debate from aid to trade. They argued that it was pointless for the West to support their industrial development plans if they then discriminated against their exports. In an attempt to negotiate new trading rules the United Nations Conference on Trade And Development (UNCTAD) was set up in 1964, and by the end of the 1960s a series of preferential trade schemes were implemented. However, it soon became clear that these would benefit only a tiny minority of developing countries—those which had already developed an industrial sector with an export potential, such as Taiwan, Hong Kong, Mexico and Brazil. The majority would continue to be dependent on exports of raw materials and tropical foodstuffs—often crops that had been forced on them during the colonial period—the prices of which were determined on world markets beyond their control.

The quadrupling of the oil price by the Organization of Petroleum Exporting Countries (OPEC) in 1973 had

Rich world, poor world
The major influences on a country's wealth are its fuel resources, its history of industrialization and colonization, and its sense of national unity. Former colonial powers still benefit from the economic relations established during the colonial era, and from being in the forefront of industrialization, while for Third World countries industrialization is hampered by trade barriers. Oil has brought wealth to many Middle Eastern countries, but in Nigeria, for example, the legacies of colonialism—underdevelopment and friction between ethnic groups—preclude real prosperity despite oil revenues. For the least developed countries, the remittances of citizens working abroad are often a major factor in the economy.

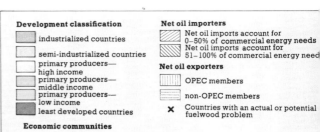

Development classification
- industrialized countries
- semi-industrialized countries
- primary producers—high income
- primary producers—middle income
- primary producers—low income
- least developed countries

Economic communities

A Andean Common Market (Founded 1969)

B Caribbean Community and Common Market—CARICOM (Founded 1973)

C Central American Common Market—CACM (Founded 1960)

D Council For Mutual Economic Assistance—CMEA or COMECON (Founded 1949)

E Economic Community of West African States—ECOWAS (Founded 1975)

F European Economic Community—EEC (Founded 1957)

G European Free Trade Association—EFTA (Founded 1960)

H l'Union Douanière et Economique de l'Afrique Centrale–UDEAC (founded 1964)

Net oil importers
- Net oil imports account for 0–50% of commercial energy needs
- Net oil imports account for 51–100% of commercial energy needs

Net oil exporters
- OPEC members
- non-OPEC members
- X Countries with an actual or potential fuelwood problem

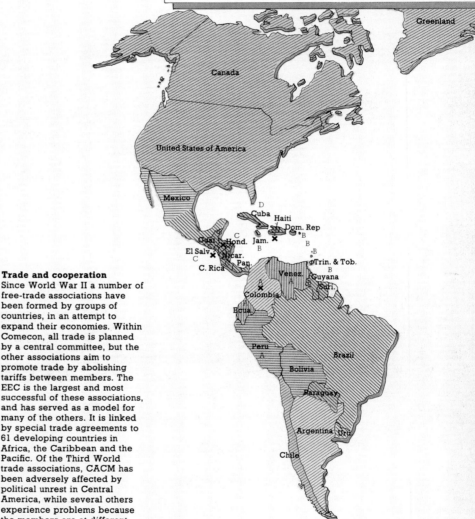

Trade and cooperation
Since World War II a number of free-trade associations have been formed by groups of countries, in an attempt to expand their economies. Within Comecon, all trade is planned by a central committee, but the other associations aim to promote trade by abolishing tariffs between members. The EEC is the largest and most successful of these associations, and has served as a model for many of the others. It is linked by special trade agreements to 61 developing countries in Africa, the Caribbean and the Pacific. Of the Third World trade associations, CACM has been adversely affected by political unrest in Central America, while several others experience problems because the members are at different levels of development.

The wood fuel shortage
Over 2,000 million people depend on wood, or on crop and animal wastes, for fuel. As the forests are gradually diminished, people have to spend more and more time collecting wood, at the cost of working the land. In poor countries, with limited areas of forest, cropping patterns have changed in favor of growing foods that require less cooking. As wood becomes scarcer, people use wastes which should be employed as fertilizer, and yields fall. This creates a need to cultivate more land, which may speed up the process of deforestation. Removal of trees may also result in soil erosion, and the silting up of canals and rivers.

far-reaching consequences for the developing countries. Encouraged by the success of the oil producers in joining forces to demand higher prices, other commodity producers called for a New International Economic Order (NIEO) mediated by a new institution, The Common Fund. The purpose of the Fund would be to manage international commodity trade and reverse the deterioration in the terms of trade between rich and poor countries. At first the western powers, who had been forced to acknowledge their vulnerability to Third World pressure by the oil crisis, were sympathetic. But the depth of the world recession (itself triggered by oil-price rises) transformed the boom market of 1973–74 into a buyer's market, thus reducing the pressure on the industrial world to reach an accommodation. Paradoxically, therefore, the major consequence of OPEC—the first successful blow by

The transnationals
Shell is one of the three largest transnational companies in the world. Transnationals control between 25% and 35% of all world production, while trade within such companies accounts for about 30% of all world trade. The extent of their operations allows them to avoid effective control by nation-states.

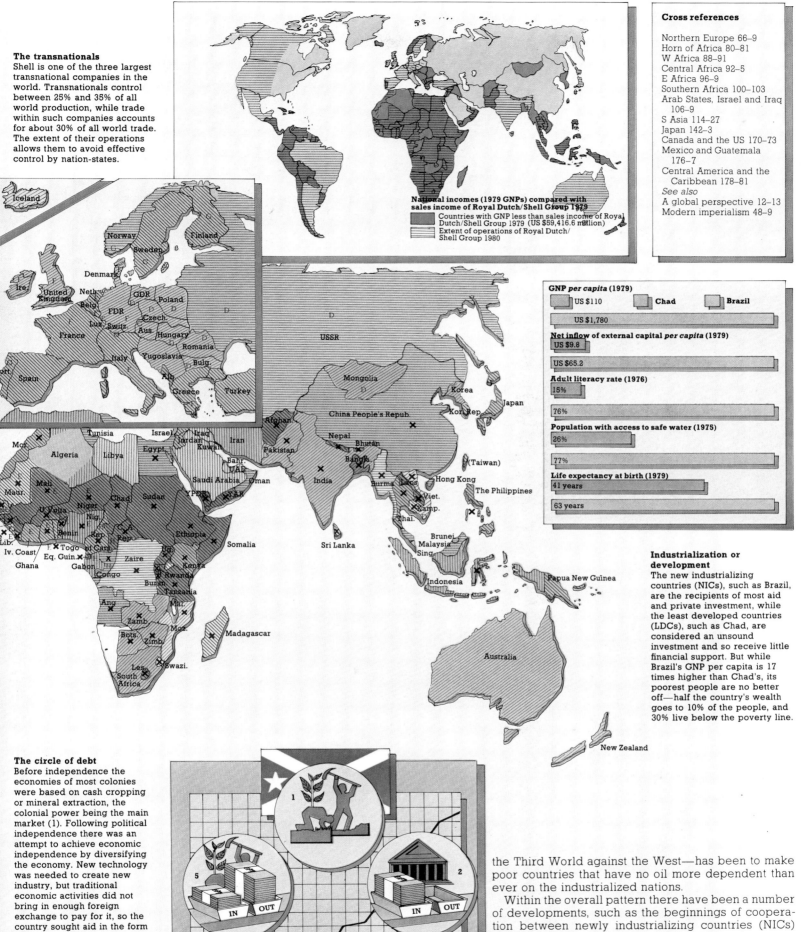

National incomes (1979 GNPs) compared with sales income of Royal Dutch/Shell Group 1979
Countries with GNP less than sales income of Royal Dutch/Shell Group 1979 (US $59,416.6 million)
Extent of operations of Royal Dutch/Shell Group 1980

GNP per capita (1979)
US $110 — Chad — Brazil
US $1,780

Net inflow of external capital per capita (1979)
US $9.8
US $65.2

Adult literacy rate (1976)
15%
76%

Population with access to safe water (1975)
26%
77%

Life expectancy at birth (1979)
41 years
63 years

Industrialization or development
The new industrializing countries (NICs), such as Brazil, are the recipients of most aid and private investment, while the least developed countries (LDCs), such as Chad, are considered an unsound investment and so receive little financial support. But while Brazil's GNP per capita is 17 times higher than Chad's, its poorest people are no better off—half the country's wealth goes to 10% of the people, and 30% live below the poverty line.

The circle of debt
Before independence the economies of most colonies were based on cash cropping or mineral extraction, the colonial power being the main market (1). Following political independence there was an attempt to achieve economic independence by diversifying the economy. New technology was needed to create new industry, but traditional economic activities did not bring in enough foreign exchange to pay for it, so the country sought aid in the form of loans (2). New technology was acquired (3), but since it required servicing, spare parts and fuel, the import bill increased (4). Interest payments accumulate on loans and, as a result of dependence on foreign technology and imported fuel, the country becomes vulnerable to price changes. More debts accumulate, and the ex-colony is forced to concentrate on traditional exports in order to service the debts (5).

the Third World against the West—has been to make poor countries that have no oil more dependent than ever on the industrialized nations.

Within the overall pattern there have been a number of developments, such as the beginnings of cooperation between newly industrializing countries (NICs) such as Taiwan, Mexico and India, and in a few cases the consolidation of economic relations with the Soviet Union and its allies. But the overall pattern remains one of dependence by poor countries on the West. The Brandt Commission Report, published in 1980, was an attempt to rekindle western enthusiasm for transfers of wealth from rich to poor nations on the basis of interdependence. However, the outcome of the Mexico summit conference in 1981, which met to consider this report, showed that official support had sunk to a lower level than at any time since the debate began.

The Growth of Cities

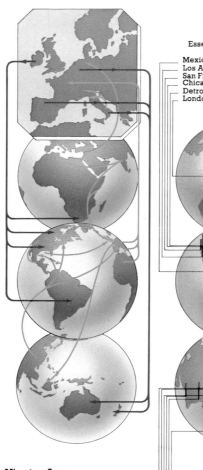

Philadelphia 2.9m/4.4m
New York 12.3m/16.1m
Cairo 2.5m/5.6m
Paris 6m/8.7m
Essen-Dortmund 4.6m/6.8m
Moscow 5.5m/6.7m
Mexico City 4m/14m
Los Angeles 4m/9.5m
San Francisco/Oakland 2m/4.5m
Chicago 4.9m/7m
Detroit 2.7m/4.4m
London 10.4m/11.5m

Djakarta 1.5m/4.5m
Calcutta 5.1m/7.3m
Bombay 3.3m/5.1m
Wu Han 1.2m/4.2m
Tientsin 2.2m/4.5m
Peking 2.1m/8m
Hong Kong 1.6m/4.1m
Shangai 5.3m/8.5m
Seoul 2m/6.9m
Tokyo 6.3m/12.2m
Buenos Aires 5.2m/9.4m
Sao Paulo 2.4m/8.4m
Rio de Janeiro 3m/7.2m

Migratory flows
→ 19th century
E Europe, S Europe, Ireland
to US, Canada, Australia,
New Zealand, S Africa, S America
→ mid-20th century
Spain, Portugal, Algeria to France
S Italy to N Italy, Switzerland
Turkey to Germany
W Indies, India, E Africa to UK
Indonesia to Holland
China to US, W Europe
India, Pakistan to Gulf
Mexico, Puerto Rico to US

The search for work
The pattern of migration to
cities has changed over the last
two centuries. However, the
underlying motive for migration
is the same—the continuing
search for work.

The world's largest cities
In the last few decades the
rate of growth of Third World
cities has far outstripped that of
the industrial nations; here
numbers in millions are
compared for years 1950/1970.

For millennia men and women have lived in cities. The
urban revolution originated in the valley civilizations of
the Middle East and in the Indian subcontinent in the
third or fourth millennium BC, while in Mexico and the
Andes cities first began to develop in about 1000 BC.
These cities were the imperial capitals of a dominant
aristocracy or priesthood, and they housed their administrative cadres as well as the artisans who furnished their elaborate life styles. The inhabitants were
maintained by tribute exacted from rural areas, where
the vast majority of the population were still to be
found, their way of life relatively unchanged.

The cities brought together many skilled and intelligent people who had the leisure and the resources to
develop new art forms and to enquire into the world
about them. Thus the early cities fostered the study of
architecture, astronomy, mathematics, philosophy,
medicine and a great many other subjects. The invention of writing, which first occurred in Sumer in about
3000 BC, allowed their conclusions to be recorded and
a store of knowledge built up within urban centers.

With the industrial revolution of the eighteenth and
nineteenth centuries, vast new urban agglomerations
were created as manufacturing was located near to
sources of power, usually coalfields. These new centers were populated from the surrounding rural
areas within the nation and the migrant peasants
quickly lost their ties to the villages and became a
culturally homogenous urban workforce. Within a few
decades the urban population of northwest Europe
came to exceed that of the countryside.

1940　**1970**

Towns and cities

	Over three million
	250,000 – one million
	50,000 – 250,000
	20,000 – 50,000
	2,000 – 20,000

Rural population

Flight from the country
Peru is the extreme example of
the redistribution of a
developing nation's population.
In the 1950s, two thirds of the
people lived in the country, by
1972 a quarter of the population
of 14 million lived in the capital,
Lima. Like many other Third
World cities, it has acted like a
magnet to people in the outlying
impoverished villages and so
has more than quadrupled in
size, swallowing up the
neighboring town of Callao in
the process.

Life in these new cities was very different from that of
the earlier medieval towns and from that which the
migrants had experienced in the rural areas. Work-
place and home were separated and people lived
in single-class neighborhoods—slums for the poor,
pleasant suburbs for the rich. All had access to
improved services—water, lighting, schools and hospitals—but the differential provision of these tended to
perpetuate the stratification of society.

The new cities were places of opportunity, offering
new forms of employment and freedom from many
social constraints, but the cities also brought problems.
One major problem was congestion and high costs of
transporting people from home to work. By 1950 a
quarter of Europe's population lived in cities of over
100,000 inhabitants, but with the technological advances of the mid-twentieth century many of these
urban centers are now in a state of decline, as industry
moves to newer cities offering better living conditions
and services.

The development of the new industrial nations—the
United States, Canada and Australia—in the late nineteenth century drew people from the more backward
parts of Europe into their rapidly expanding urban
centers. By a similar process, in the mid-twentieth
century, the highly advanced industrial nations of
Europe have attracted the peasantry of the Mediterranean fringe and people from former colonies in Africa,
Asia and the Caribbean to swell the workforce of their
towns and cities. The great cultural differences, both
between immigrant and host populations and within
the immigrant community, have led to various political
and social problems in these countries.

In the poorer countries of the southern hemisphere,
the pattern of urbanization in the nineteenth and
twentieth centuries has differed markedly from that in
the older, wealthier, industrial nations. To a great
extent the industrial development of these poor countries has been consequent upon economic processes
within the industrialized nations, and this in turn has
affected urban development. In the early stages of
colonization administrative capitals were established,
and in the second half of the twentieth century transnational companies have found in these capitals a
source of cheap labor for light industrial manufacturing. Mining towns also grew up in the colonial
era and have continued to expand, producing raw
materials for export to the industrialized nations.

Meanwhile agriculture has remained stagnant with
little investment, while better health care has led to a
lower death rate and overpopulation in many areas.
More widespread education and the penetration of the
mass media even into remote villages have brought a
vision of urban prosperity to the rural poor, resulting in
an unprecedented migratory flow to the cities.

Since 1945, many of the capital cities of developing
nations have grown at a rate of 5 to 10 percent per
annum, a staggering increase when one considers that
a 7 percent growth rate doubles the size of a city in
each decade. About half of this growth can be attributed to fresh immigration, and half to natural increase. This growth has generally been confined to
one or two cities in each country—the administrative
centers, which are often also ports and centers of
skilled labor.

A direct consequence of this rapid growth is urban
poverty, since the immigrants have few skills and
resources, and cannot find employment in the capital-
intensive industrial complex. They therefore turn to
informal economic activities for their livelihood, and
live in vast peripheral slums or shanty towns. In the
informal sector of the economy one finds a vast range
of small-scale activities—petty trading, artisanry and
personal services for both rich and poor. These are
created by the poor themselves who continually find
new opportunities within the urban economy.

Individual or family enterprises predominate and
personal relationships are seen as important for success. Most of the adult residents of these settlements
are migrants and they retain strong ties of affection
with their villages of origin. With social security
systems limited or nonexistent for the poor, their
relationships with their kin and compatriots are vital,
and ethnic associations—village clubs—proliferate.

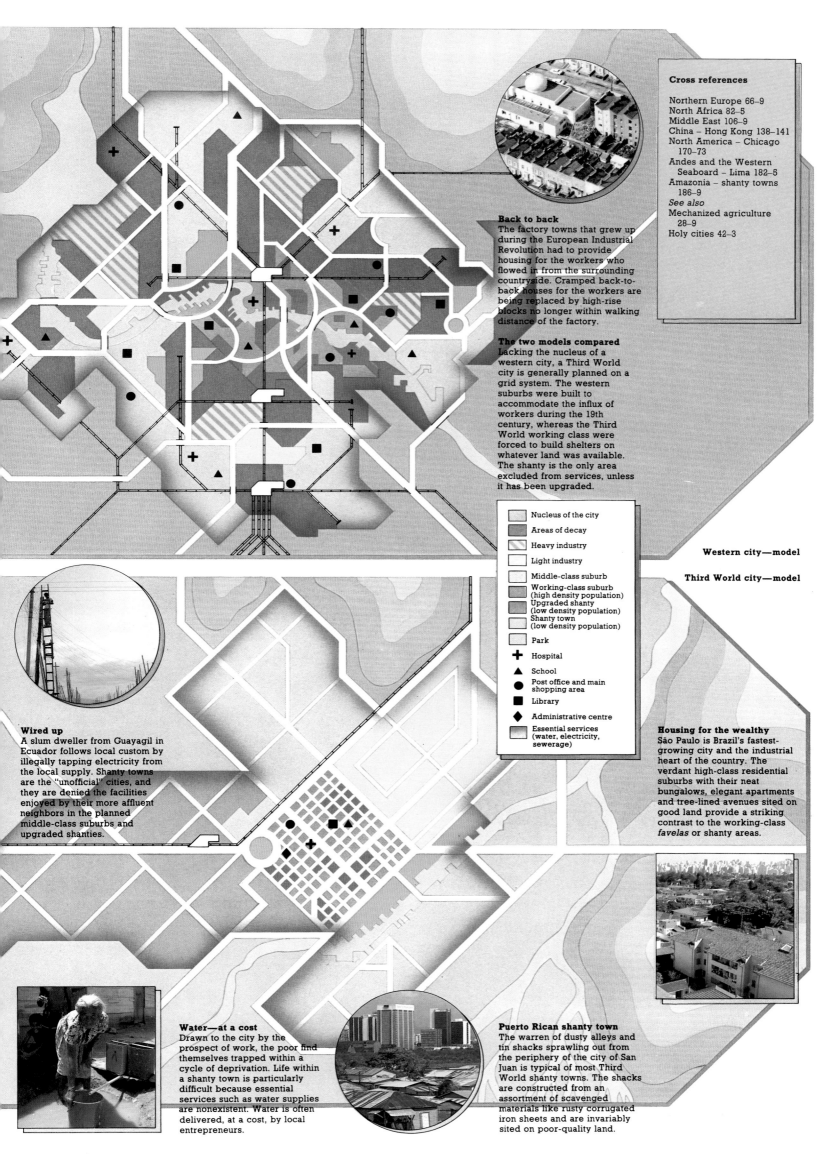

Back to back
The factory towns that grew up during the European Industrial Revolution had to provide housing for the workers who flowed in from the surrounding countryside. Cramped back-to-back houses for the workers are being replaced by high-rise blocks no longer within walking distance of the factory.

The two models compared
Lacking the nucleus of a western city, a Third World city is generally planned on a grid system. The western suburbs were built to accommodate the influx of workers during the 19th century, whereas the Third World working class were forced to build shelters on whatever land was available. The shanty is the only area excluded from services, unless it has been upgraded.

Western city—model

Third World city—model

Nucleus of the city

Areas of decay

Heavy industry

Light industry

Middle-class suburb

Working-class suburb
(high density population)

Upgraded shanty
(low density population)

Shanty town
(low density population)

Park

+ Hospital

▲ School

● Post office and main
  shopping area

■ Library

◆ Administrative centre

Essential services
(water, electricity,
sewerage)

Wired up
A slum dweller from Guayaqil in Ecuador follows local custom by illegally tapping electricity from the local supply. Shanty towns are the "unofficial" cities, and they are denied the facilities enjoyed by their more affluent neighbors in the planned middle-class suburbs and upgraded shanties.

Housing for the wealthy
São Paulo is Brazil's fastest-growing city and the industrial heart of the country. The verdant high-class residential suburbs with their neat bungalows, elegant apartments and tree-lined avenues sited on good land provide a striking contrast to the working-class *favelas* or shanty areas.

Water—at a cost
Drawn to the city by the prospect of work, the poor find themselves trapped within a cycle of deprivation. Life within a shanty town is particularly difficult because essential services such as water supplies are nonexistent. Water is often delivered, at a cost, by local entrepreneurs.

Puerto Rican shanty town
The warren of dusty alleys and tin shacks sprawling out from the periphery of the city of San Juan is typical of most Third World shanty towns. The shacks are constructed from an assortment of scavenged materials like rusty corrugated iron sheets and are invariably sited on poor-quality land.

Health and Nutrition

People in developed countries today live longer, on average, than did their forefathers and suffer far less pain and inconvenience from diseases. This improvement has mainly occurred over the last century, partly through advances in medical science and partly from a more general improvement in economic and social conditions. Life expectancy in England in 1700 was about thirty-seven years. This low figure was caused primarily by high infant mortality, as smallpox, dysentery, croup, malaria and other acute disorders killed about 40 percent of children before the age of five.

The building of isolation hospitals represented an early attempt to control epidemic diseases, and smallpox was further controlled from the 1720s by direct inoculation and later by vaccination. Ideas of cleanliness and sanitation became more important from the mid-eighteenth century onward, and as the Industrial Revolution accelerated population movement toward the towns, various pressure groups campaigned for improvements in waste disposal, water provision, factory conditions and housing standards. Most infectious diseases were already in decline by the 1870s, when Louis Pasteur, Robert Koch and others elaborated the germ theory of diseases, but once the role of bacteria was understood, more effective sanitary measures were possible. From the 1890s, the development of immunology permitted vaccination against certain diseases, including rabies, tetanus, diphtheria and, more recently, polio. Malaria disappeared from Europe largely through the drainage of fenlands and control of mosquitoes, while increased personal hygiene helped eradicate louse- and flea-borne diseases such as typhus. The development of antibiotics such as penicillin, which was first used in the 1940s, has further enhanced our control over infectious diseases.

Eating in Britain
Often the criterion used for defining an adequate diet has been based on what is eaten in affluent nations, and this is likely to be well above any sort of minimal need. Affluent nations have their own nutritional problems, such as obesity, heart disease, gout, bowel cancer and chronic tooth decay.

United Kingdom

100%
13%
46%
41%

Average daily calorie intake 2,650

At the same time, the expectations of the early bacteriologists have not been entirely realized. Although most people now survive into old age, life expectancy for those over forty has improved only slightly during the past century. Cancer and cardiovascular diseases have increased markedly and are often impossible to treat. Civilization has its own diseases, related to stress, sedentary jobs and environmental pollution, while the concomitants of affluence—unbalanced diet, obesity, alcohol and cigarettes—also take their toll. These problems are not amenable to the relatively simple measures used to combat infectious diseases and have confounded earlier dreams of disease eradication.

Health in the developing countries
The magnitude of the difference in health between the people of developed and developing countries is at first difficult to grasp. A child born in an affluent nation is ten times as likely to reach the age of one year as a child born in a developing country, and twelve to fifteen times as likely to reach the age of five. In the very poorest regions of the developing countries, 50 percent of children die during the first year of life. These high mortality rates are caused by the greater prevalence and severity of diseases combined, very often, with poor diet. Different factors are interrelated in a complex fashion—children under five, for example, often become malnourished after a bout of gastroenteritis, which both reduces the absorption of nutrients from the food eaten and depresses appetite. The resulting malnutrition then weakens the body's defenses against fatal diseases such as diarrhea, measles and pneumonia.

Water and excreta are key factors in the transmission of many serious diseases in developing coun-

Eating in Papua New Guinea
The people of the highlands of Papua New Guinea are subsistence farmers. The major part of their carbohydrate intake comes from the sweet potato and at least 35 varieties are distinguished on the basis of color, texture and leaf shape. The sweet potatoes are baked on an open fire or in a pit-oven lined with banana leaves and heated stones. Hunting and fishing are the main sources of animal protein apart from domesticated pigs.

100%
7%
13%
80%

Upper Volta

Average daily calorie intake 1,850

Average daily calorie intake per head

- less than 1,750
- 1,750–2,000
- 2,000–2,500
- 2,500–3,000
- over 3,000
- No data available

- Protein
- Fat
- Carbohydrate

100%
7%
10%
83%

Papua New Guinea

Average daily calorie intake 2,300

Birth–1 year
1–2 years
2–3 years

GOOD   DANGEROUS   VERY DANGEROUS

Eating in Upper Volta
The subsistence farmers of the Upper Volta experience their highest energy needs during the rainy season, when their fields have to be cultivated. This period of hard work often coincides with food shortages, since most of the previous year's harvest will have been eaten. This period is often known as "the hungry season" and is the time when the incidence of malnutrition is highest. The meal which provides much of the daily energy intake consists of a bowl of sorghum or millet porridge with a spicy sauce made from sorrel and okra. Occasionally fish or meat may be added.

Monitoring nutrition
Growth charts are now widely used by health clinics in poor areas—by recording weight at regular intervals, malnutrition can be diagnosed before symptoms appear. In the example shown, growth at A is satisfactory, weight change at B is unsatisfactory and further weight loss at C would be dangerous. Recovery in response to supplementary feeding is shown at D.

The essentials for health
Although the importance of adequate nutrition is well recognized, there is still much controversy over what constitutes an adequate diet. There is a wide range over which adaptation to different diets can take place and basic nutrient requirements appear to vary widely from one individual to another. Estimates of nutrient requirements are constantly being modified, the present trend being toward reductions in the requirements for energy, protein, calcium and iron. Until the mid-1960s for example, nutritionists thought that inadequate protein intakes were the major nutritional problem in the world and efforts were made to bridge the "protein gap." During the 1970s, however, estimates were reduced to about 70% of previous levels, so that there no longer seemed to be a protein gap. A calorie deficit or a general shortage of food is now believed to be the major nutritional problem. The calorie is the unit used for measuring energy values of food. The daily calorie intake per person is plotted on the world map. The figures are averages at the national level and do not show the extent to which food is unequally distributed within each country—the calorie intake of the poorest will be much lower.

tries, particularly those contributing to the development of malnutrition, and the prevalence of infectious disease is related more to water availability than to any other factor. There is evidence that rates of diarrheal diseases tend to be highest in those households which are farthest from a water supply. The dimensions of this problem are reflected in figures from a study in Kenya, in which it was reported that over 20 percent of rural households spent six hours or more each day collecting water.

Inadequate diet is another major cause of the heavy disease burden found in developing countries, but malnutrition, as seen in the world today, is not the simple result of food shortage—rather it is a manifestation of abject poverty. A *world* food shortage does not actually exist—there is enough food produced each year to satisfy the needs of the present world population and, up to now at least, food production has increased so as to keep pace with the continuing growth of that population. Poor people experience hunger as a result of maldistribution of food supplies

both between and within countries, reflecting differences in income, at the national and individual levels.

The poorest people in developing countries are often trapped in a cycle of poverty from which it is very difficult to escape. Lack of income causes families to live in crowded, insanitary conditions on poor diets, and greatly increases the number and severity of many diseases. The debilitating effect of these diseases in turn affects human productivity and reduces the possibility of improving the family income. Rapid growth in population adds to the problems of the developing countries, but the decision to have a large family is often a rational attempt to cope with the poverty trap. For the poor, human labor is the only resource and large families provide more labor.

Clearly, on a global scale, the problem of hunger and health require solutions which are primarily of a political and social nature. These should ensure that everyone can afford to buy (or have the resources to grow) sufficient food, and that a healthy environment is provided as a basic human right.

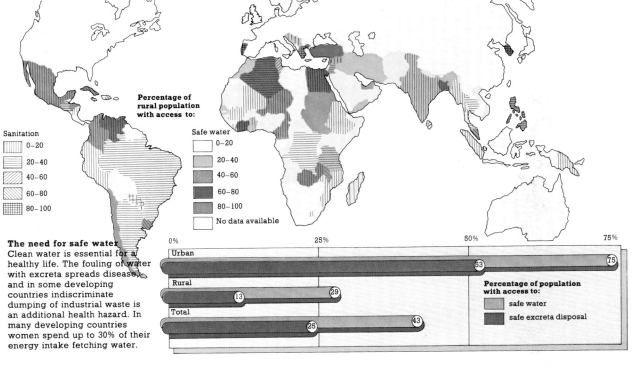

Sanitation
- 0–20
- 20–40
- 40–60
- 60–80
- 80–100

Percentage of rural population with access to:

Safe water
- 0–20
- 20–40
- 40–60
- 60–80
- 80–100
- No data available

The need for safe water
Clean water is essential for a healthy life. The fouling of water with excreta spreads disease, and in some developing countries indiscriminate dumping of industrial waste is an additional health hazard. In many developing countries women spend up to 30% of their energy intake fetching water.

	0%	25%	50%	75%
Urban			53	75
Rural	13	29		
Total	25	43		

Percentage of population with access to:
- safe water
- safe excreta disposal

Safe water and sanitation
Data on the availability of adequate sewerage and safe water are far from complete. A survey carried out in 1975 indicated that only a quarter of the 2,000 million people living in developing countries (excluding China, for which no data are available) had access to safe water and adequate waste disposal facilities. The 1,500 million without these basic services consisted of more than 80% of the total rural population and between 50% and 65% of the urban population. The map shows the percentage of the rural population in each country with access to safe water and adequate sanitation.

The need for sanitation
In developing countries 75% of the population have no kind of sanitary facility—not even a pit or bucket latrine. Feces are commonly disposed of in lakes and rivers which are also used as sources of drinking water. The resultant diseases may claim as many as 25 million lives a year.

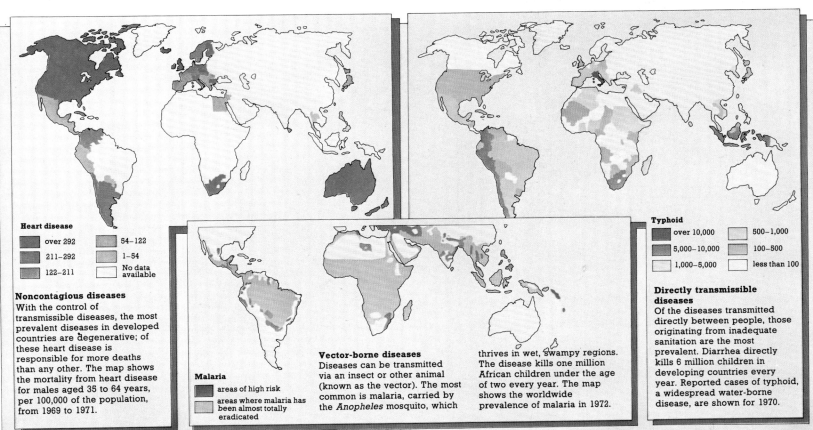

Heart disease
- over 292
- 211–292
- 122–211
- 54–122
- 1–54
- No data available

Noncontagious diseases
With the control of transmissible diseases, the most prevalent diseases in developed countries are degenerative; of these heart disease is responsible for more deaths than any other. The map shows the mortality from heart disease for males aged 35 to 64 years, per 100,000 of the population, from 1969 to 1971.

Malaria
- areas of high risk
- areas where malaria has been almost totally eradicated

Vector-borne diseases
Diseases can be transmitted via an insect or other animal (known as the vector). The most common is malaria, carried by the *Anopheles* mosquito, which thrives in wet, swampy regions. The disease kills one million African children under the age of two every year. The map shows the worldwide prevalence of malaria in 1972.

Typhoid
- over 10,000
- 5,000–10,000
- 1,000–5,000
- 500–1,000
- 100–500
- less than 100

Directly transmissible diseases
Of the diseases transmitted directly between people, those originating from inadequate sanitation are the most prevalent. Diarrhea directly kills 6 million children in developing countries every year. Reported cases of typhoid, a widespread water-borne disease, are shown for 1970.

The Peoples of the World

The 1972 Munich Olympic games

Arctic and Subarctic

In the Arctic and subarctic zones lies one of the last frontiers between man and nature—the boundary where human ingenuity meets with the unconquerable cold of earth's northernmost lands. Mongoloid peoples carved out a niche for themselves in these frozen wastes many thousands of years ago, and survived, often precariously, by hunting, fishing or reindeer herding. Equipped with modern technology, Europeans have now penetrated the area and established a very different way of life, as they extract oil and other precious resources from beneath the frozen soil. For the indigenous people, such as the Eskimos, their arrival has brought the traditional way of life to an end.

The subarctic region is commonly divided into tundra and taiga zones, Russian words which describe the areas north and south of the tree line. The tree line itself is determined by the extent of the permafrost (permanently frozen ground),

since in the tundra it lies so close to the surface that only shallow-rooted plants, mainly mosses and lichens, grow while in the taiga zone the permafrost lies deeper down and is discontinuous, allowing the slow growth of coniferous trees, dwarf willow and birch. The frozen layer also prevents the drainage of melting snow and summer rains, and in flat areas the tundra is covered with ponds and lakes during the summer, providing nesting sites for the millions of birds which come here to breed.

The continental interiors have extremes of cold, but the western shores are bathed by warm currents (the Gulf Stream in the Atlantic and the Japan Current in the Pacific), giving them a milder, wetter climate. The lack of vegetation limits the number of land animals, but the seas and lakes contain a wealth of fish and mammals. In addition, migratory species, such as caribou/reindeer, whales, geese, ducks, swans, salmon and char, permit the existence of native populations, who harvest food in times of plenty and store some of their catch for the barren seasons.

Strategies for survival

Except for the center and north of Greenland and some of the Canadian High Arctic Islands, the circumpolar regions were all inhabited by Mongoloid peoples before the penetration of Europeans. However, the low biological productivity only allowed very sparse human populations—in the interior Arctic lands less than one person per 100 square kilometers (2.5 per 100 square miles) and even in the most favored areas on the warmer western coasts, rarely as many as one per square kilometer.

The total population of the whole area was less than 600,000 people, of whom nearly half were Yakut. The North American Arctic was inhabited by less than 70,000 Eskimo and Aleut peoples, while other hunting, gathering, and fishing groups inhabited northeast Siberia—the Chuckchi, Koryak, Kamchadal and Yukaghir, known collectively as Palaeo-Siberian peoples. The rest of Arctic Eurasia was inhabited by nomadic reindeer herders—the 40,000 Sami (Lapps) of Finland and Scandinavia, the Samoyed (Nentsi) peoples of northern Russia, and many Turkic-speaking peoples, such as the 70,000 Tungus (Evenki) of central Siberia.

The technological adaptations of these peoples enabled them to lead a nomadic life and thus harvest temporary concentrations of food. Nearly all groups had some form of sled, sometimes pulled by hand, usually drawn by domesticated animals—dogs or reindeer. Boats with skin covers (kayaks, umiaks) or birchbark canoes were also present in most parts of the region, and hunting devices included bows and arrows, spears, traps, snares, corrals and, in Eurasia, nets. All groups used tailored clothing made of skins, usually those of caribou/reindeer. Portable dwellings with wooden poles and skin covers were common in all areas, but other types, such as wood or sod houses and, in North America snow-block igloos, were used during sedentary periods.

With the need for frequent movements, social organization and leadership were flexible, allowing the groups to split up and reform during the annual cycle. The most widely dispersed groups had bilateral kinship, but in central Asia the Yakuts, Tungus and others had patrilineal clans and fixed territories. Division of labor was marked, with women responsible for domestic tasks and gathering, while men did the hunting and trapping. All groups enjoyed a rich religious and ritual life, with a common belief in the presence of souls or spirits in humans, animals and the natural world. The real world was seen as but one layer connected to others often by a tree or river of life. Religious specialists or *shamans* (a Tungus word) could visit the spirits, the heavens and the depths through soul flight. This occurred during a trance or similar performance that was often carried out publicly for the benefit of the whole community.

Oil beneath the ice

European expansion into the circumpolar regions began over one thousand years ago in Scandinavia, where the Norwegians, Swedes and Russians pushed the Sami (Lapps) into ever smaller areas, forcing them to trade and pay taxes in skins. The Russians expanded eastward in the seventeenth century, subduing the peoples of Siberia for trade and missionization, and colonizing Alaska, which they later sold to the United States. In the twentieth century the colonizing powers have tightened their administrative hold in these strategically important northern areas, attempting to assimilate the aboriginal peoples through formal education and government controls. The enormous resources of many of these areas—hydroelectric power, oil, gas, asbestos and metallic ores—have increased their economic importance in recent decades. At the same time the education of the northern peoples has allowed them to see their own predicament, and to demand greater autonomy and control over their lands.

A winter afternoon at Frobisher Bay in northern Canada

Eskimo Zone

For one people the Ice Age never ended. Pitting themselves against a daunting and heartless landscape, the Eskimos exploited to the full the meager resources of their *homeland, and evolved a tough, uncompromising attitude to life that enabled them to survive. With the introduction of guns, snowmobiles and central heating this attitude is changing dramatically.*

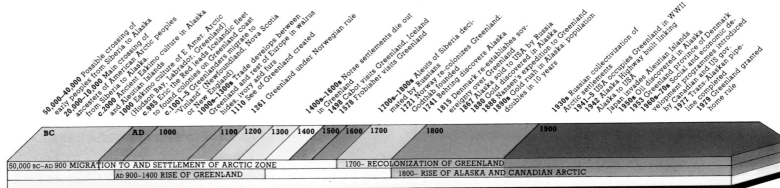

Timeline events:
- 50,000-40,000 Possible crossing of early peoples from Siberia to Alaska
- 20,000-10,000 Main crossing of ancestors of American Arctic peoples from Siberia to Alaska
- c.2000 Ancient Eskimo culture in Alaska and Aleutian Islands
- 1000 Eskimo culture of E. Amer. Arctic (Hudson Bay, Labrador, Greenland)
- c.985 Eric the Red leads Icelandic fleet to found colonies on Greenland coast
- c.1001-5 Greenlanders migrate to "Vinland" (Newfoundland, Nova Scotia or New England)
- 1000s-1300s Trade develops between Greenland and rest of Europe in walrus hides, ivory and furs
- 1110 See of Greenland created
- 1261 Greenland under Norwegian rule
- 1400s-1600s Norse settlements die out in Greenland
- 1498 Cabot visits Greenland, Iceland
- 1578 Frobisher visits Greenland
- 1700s-1800s Aleuts of Siberia decimated by Russians
- 1721 Norway re-colonizes Greenland; Godthåb founded
- 1741 Bering discovers Alaska
- 1815 Denmark re-establishes sovereignty over Greenland
- 1867 Alaska sold to USA by Russia
- 1880 Gold discovered in Alaska
- 1888 Nansen's expedition to Greenland
- 1890s Gold rush in Alaska: population doubles in 10 years
- 1930s Russian collectivization of Arctic settlements
- 1941-5 USA occupies Greenland in WWII
- 1942 Alaska Highway built linking Alaska to USA
- 1950s Oil discovered in Alaska
- 1953 Greenland province of Denmark
- 1960s-70s Social and economic development programmes introduced by Canadian and US gov.
- 1977 Trans-Alaskan pipeline completed
- 1979 Greenland granted home rule

Timeline bands:
- BC | AD | 1000 | 1100 | 1200 | 1300 | 1400 | 1500 | 1600 | 1700 | 1800 | 1900
- 50,000 BC–AD 900 MIGRATION TO AND SETTLEMENT OF ARCTIC ZONE
- 1700– RECOLONIZATION OF GREENLAND
- AD 900–1400 RISE OF GREENLAND
- 1800– RISE OF ALASKA AND CANADIAN ARCTIC

Population by Country
Total: 1 million

N Canada 57%   N USA 38%
Greenland 5%

Population by Religion

Protestantism 70%   R Catholicism 30%

Modern technology
In spite of the high cost of fuel, the Eskimos now travel by snowmobile, a faster and more easily handled vehicle than the dog-drawn sled.

Eskimos are the descendants of hunters who moved from Siberia into Alaska at the close of the last Ice Age, about 12,000 years ago, when the two continents were linked by a bridge of dry land. As these hunters colonized different areas, they developed distinctive cultural traits, although the various groups still had much in common. Today, the Eskimo people straddle the political boundaries of Greenland, Canada, the United States and the Soviet Union. They have long been influenced by traders, explorers and missionaries, and in the twentieth century have been affected by the policies of the states into which they have been absorbed. Yet they have maintained a sense of common cultural identity, most still having similar hunting techniques, social customs and folklore.

This broad tundra region is characterized by freezing arctic conditions for up to eight or nine months of the year, and relatively infertile soils, which preclude the development of agriculture. The traditional Eskimo economy was therefore based on hunting and fishing. Whales, seals and fish were a major source of food, while birds and land animals such as caribou (a close relative of the European reindeer) were also hunted. The economy of the Aleuts, the other indigenous group in the Eskimo zone, depended almost entirely on molluscs and sea mammals, such as the sea otter, the fur seal and the now extinct northern sea cow.

Except in Greenland, national governments had shown little concern for improving the traditional economy until the 1960s and 1970s, when substantial economic and social development programs were introduced in many Eskimo regions. The money invested in these programs has generally far exceeded any economic returns, while burgeoning oil,

mineral and hydroelectric interests in several areas have not always provided a great deal of employment for local inhabitants. They have, however, stimulated interest in the question of whether the Eskimos hold legal title to the land they have customarily occupied and, if so, whether royalties from oil and mineral extraction are owed to them. Eskimo political pressure has secured certain land rights in Alaska, Quebec and especially Greenland, which in 1979 was granted Home Rule status by Denmark. The Eskimos living in Siberia are sea-mammal hunters, numbering about 1,500. Since the Revolution, they have been concentrated into three or four villages and their economy collectivized. They are organized into teams of ten to twelve kinsmen who together operate a single boat.

Eskimos of eastern Canada

In each of the twenty-three small coastal communities in northern Quebec and Baffin Island, the European inhabitants seldom number more than fifty, whereas the Eskimo population varies from 100 to 700 people. However, in the administrative centers, Frobisher Bay and Fort Chimo, the populations of both whites and Eskimos are much higher. Before 1960 the life style of the Eskimos in this area was strikingly different from that of today. They were grouped in small nomadic communities, seldom comprising more than fifty people, and mostly organized along kinship lines. They lived mainly in snowhouses and tents, and their economic existence was precarious. Since the early 1900s they had exchanged fox furs with local trading companies to secure such equipment as firearms, strong wooden sleds and motorboats, all of which were subject to substantial price variation. At the same time, the traditional subsistence resources, especially caribou and walrus, were becoming increasingly scarce, for a variety of reasons, including overhunting by Eskimos who were now equipped with guns. Since subsistence hunting was particularly difficult and the Eskimos' material aspirations were rising, they became increasingly dependent on government welfare.

In the 1960s the Canadian government provided oil-heated prefabricated houses, schools and health facilities in all settlements. In order to diversify and capitalize the Eskimo economy, money was loaned for fish-freezing plants, sewing equipment and sizeable fishing boats. Eskimo-owned cooperatives and community councils were established. European teachers, engineers, administrators, nurses and resource development officers were installed in each settlement.

Except in the few settlements where Eskimos fully subscribe to the rules laid down by their cooperatives and councils, their social organization is flexible. There are no descent groups, and no rules enjoining people to align with specific kin or neighbors, or with particular leaders. A leader owes his position solely to people's recognition of his exceptional abilities in some field—hunting, for example. In Eskimo society, the most important social relations are those among kinsmen, who assist one another in times of difficulty and share the food they have hunted. As far as social

obligations are concerned, Eskimos make no distinction between kin on the mother's or the father's side and do not normally recognize kin beyond first or second cousins; as in the traditional period, marriage between close kinsmen is not favored. Traditionally, marriage was not accompanied by any formal ritual, but it is now marked by a Christian service and community celebration.

In the smaller settlements the men are engaged year-round in a variety of hunting and fishing activities, visiting different localities within 150 kilometers (100 miles) of the settlement. It is only when the men remain for several days in one locality that traditional snow-houses are constructed. During the summer, if the men plan to be away from the settlement for a long time, women and children usually accompany them. Since the children normally attend school for most of the year, the summer is an important period when they can be taught the skills of hunting and traveling.

In these smaller settlements traditional food is highly valued. The Eskimos cannot afford most European foods and locally secured meat and fish provide a major part of their diet. In the larger administrative towns, where relatively little time is devoted to hunting, European foods are far more important. Here, lack of education means that many people make unwise purchases, resulting in an unbalanced diet. There is no doubt, however, that government economic intervention has benefited the Eskimos materially. Although their incomes do not nearly match those of the local Europeans, they are now substantially higher than in the days of the fur trade. Since wage labor and social welfare are also fairly readily available, many Eskimos enjoy a fair degree of material comfort.

Yet modernization has also encouraged serious social problems, particularly alcohol abuse. In traditional Eskimo society kinship ties linking members of a community ensured a high degree of mutual protection and support, and nonkinsmen could also establish a supportive relationship with one another, often exchanging wives as a sign of their friendship. The large modern settlements, however, house people

of very diverse origins, and wife exchange and some of the other means of linking nonkinsmen have largely fallen into disuse, in part through pressure from missionaries. There are, consequently, fewer restraints on disruptive behavior.

Eskimos still frequently participate in community events. One tradition that has survived is the practice of ritual sponsorship—an adult who, if possible, assists at the birth of a child, subsequently acts on the child's behalf. When the child reaches maturity and successfully accomplishes an adult task, such as killing an animal, everyone in the community takes part in a ritual in which the sponsor's contribution to the child's development is acknowledged. Apart from Christian festivals and card gambling parties, other important recreational activities are square dances, film shows and television watching, all reflecting the Eskimo absorption of European cultural traits. Up until fifty years ago Eskimos practiced a shamanistic religion akin to that of Siberian peoples, but this has now ceased, partly as a result of intense missionary activity. Themes from the traditional religion are, however, still evident in Eskimo ideas and certain taboos remain.

Eskimo artists
An Eskimo artist pulls a print in a cooperative printshop. The traditional crafts of carving and engraving in bone and ivory have now been largely replaced by more commercial creative activities. A number of notable Eskimo artists have emerged, and their work commands high prices in the US and Canada.

The hunter's role
Two Eskimos, having killed a walrus, drag it onto the ice. In the past, many walruses were killed to feed the dog teams on the long journeys necessitated by the fox-fur trade. With the decline in the fur trade and the introduction of snowmobiles, walrus numbers have increased dramatically. In spring the men hunt birds, especially ptarmigan and geese, as they migrate northward into the Arctic to their breeding grounds. They also fish for trout through holes cut in the frozen lakes and hunt seals as they come up for air at breathing holes or bask on the ice. Eskimos stalk seals by creeping very slowly across the ice toward them, imitating the movements of a seal.

The Ammassalimiut of eastern Greenland have largely retained their traditional way of life, unlike the Eskimos of western Greenland who now live in prefabricated houses and work in factories or offices, although the men still hunt occasionally.

Indo-European
[ ] Germanic languages (English, Danish)

Unaffiliated languages
[ ] Inuit, Aleut

Featured peoples
Eskimos of eastern Canada

Peoples and languages
There are two major linguistic groups among the 100,000 Eskimo. The Yupik live south and west of the Yukon river and include 1,500 Eskimo living on

collectives in Siberia; only 60% of the latter now speak their traditional language. The Inupik are scattered across the whole of the rest of the Arctic from Alaska to Greenland, but show

little variation in dialect or culture since they are all descendants of one group, the Thule Eskimo, who migrated across America into Greenland between AD 1000 and 1400.

S I B E R I A
ST LAWRENCE IS.   Bering Strait
Bering Sea
Nome   BROOKS   Beaufort
RANGE   Sea
Barrow
ALEUTIAN IS.
A L A S K A
Mt McKinley 6194 ▲
Anchorage   Valdez
KODIAK IS.
Whitehorse
Yukon
Dawson
Great Bear Lake
Tuktoyaktuk
VICTORIA IS.
Coppermine
Pt Radium
Cambridge Bay
Mackenzie
Ft Simpson
Yellowknife
CANADA
Ft Nelson
ROCKY MTS
Nelson
Churchill
Baker Lake
Hudson Bay
ELLESMERE IS.
Thule
QUEEN ELIZABETH IS.
GREENLAND
ARCTIC CIRCLE
Scoresbysund
Baffin Bay
Upernavik   Angmagssalik
Umanaq
Arctic Bay
BAFFIN IS.
Davis Strait
Godthåb
Foxe Basin
Frobisher Bay
Ungava Bay
LABRADOR
Ft Chimo
Ft George   NEWFOUNDLAND
Q U E B E C
Moosonee

The 2,000 Aleuts on the Aleutian Islands (USA) and the few hundred on the Commander Islands (USSR) are culturally very similar to the Eskimo. Before the Russian incursions of the 18th and 19th centuries they numbered about 20,000.

Woods and forests
[ ] Coniferous trees used for timber, pulp and paper.

Rough grazing land
[ ] Wild reindeer on the tundra

Nonagricultural land
[ ] Ice cap and coastal tundra.

0   600 km
0   600 miles

Land use
Hunting sea mammals, birds and land animals is the traditional means of exploiting the tundra, which is too cold, boggy and infertile for agriculture.
Recently there have been some successful experiments in musk ox and reindeer ranching, and in attracting tourists, particularly for the fishing.

The administrative centers, Frobisher Bay and Fort Chimo, have communities of up to 1,000 European traders, teachers, missionaries and administrators; they tend to lead separate lives from the Inuit living in these centers.

Most of the Inuit of eastern Canada live in small coastal communities and the men engage in seasonal hunting and fishing tasks. These activities have been largely modernized by the use of improved technology, and wage labor is also available.

Eurasian Subarctic

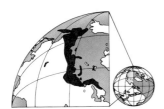

The myriad tribes of the Eurasian subarctic have lived for millennia by fishing and hunting or herding reindeer across the cold, boggy, mosquito-ridden tundra. Here the sun never sets during the brief summer months, but vanishes entirely in the desolate midwinter. Once the shaman's sorcery was the only defense against disaster, now Soviet collective farms provide security.

c.10,000 Ancestors of European Arctic peoples move north and west into Europe
c.2000 Ancestors of Eurasian Arctic peoples move north into Siberia
c.1000– Trade develops with Central Asian and Far Eastern civilizations
Reindeer domesticated; development of pastoralism
c.900 Norwegian settlements as far north as Tromsø; Swedes gradually moving north
c.1300 Norwegians settle Vardø
1400s European traders in W Siberia
1500s Russian traders in W Siberia
1500–1700 Trade develops with Europe
in Lapland; missions established
1553–4 Sir Hugh Willoughby explores Novaya Zemlya via Lapland
Richard Chancellor reaches Russia via Arkhangelsk
1600s–1700s Wild reindeer diminished; tame reindeer bred
1696–1706 Russia conquers Kamchatka
1744 Russians settle Alaska
1750 Norway/Sweden border defined
1800s Kola Peninsula settled
1826 Russia/Norway border defined
c.1850 Spitsbergen claimed by Russia, Sweden and Norway
Lapps displaced by Finns as far north as top of Gulf of Bothnia
1860 Emancipation of peasants (Russia): large-scale settlement of Siberia
1891–1904 Trans-Siberian Railway built; incorporated into Soviet system
1917 Russian Revolution: Siberia
1919 Russia/Finland border defined
1930s Collectivization in USSR settlements in Arctic

BC	AD	1000	1100	1200	1300	1400	1500	1600	1700	1800	1900

900–1900 EUROPEANS DISPLACE INDIGENOUS PEOPLES NORTHWARDS
1930s– RUSSIAN ARCTIC UNDER SOVIET SYSTEM
10,000–2,000 BC MIGRATION TO AND SETTLEMENT OF ARCTIC ZONE
1860– SIBERIA SETTLED BY EUROPEANS

Population by Country
Total: 4 million

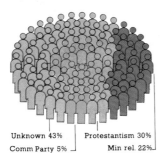

N Sweden 7%
N Norway 16%
N USSR 72%
N Finland 5%

Population by Religion

Unknown 43%
Comm Party 5%
Protestantism 30%
Min rel. 22%

Nentsi hunter
The Nentsi hunt deer, arctic foxes, hares and ermine, the last of these being particularly important because of its valuable fur. To keep themselves warm, they wear elaborate, tentlike fur clothes. Along the coast they hunt seals and whales and they fish the rivers for salmon and sturgeon.

The vast expanse of forest and open tundra that makes up the Eurasian far north has from prehistoric times been the home of small, scattered bands of hunting, trapping and fishing peoples. It also constitutes the zone of natural distribution of the reindeer, on which most of these peoples have been vitally dependent. As a result of the domestication of the reindeer, which probably occurred along the southern margins of this zone during the first millennium BC, a unique form of pastoralism emerged along the northern limits of the forest, all the way from Lapland to Kamchatka. Reindeer herding is one of the major differences between the societies of subarctic Eurasia and those of subarctic North America. Another is the long period of involvement with European agents of trade and colonization (since the fifteenth century) and, less directly, with the great civilizations of Central Asia and the Far East (for the last 2,000 years). Apart from the Sami (Lappish) population of the Nordic countries, all the peoples of this zone now fall within the domain of the Soviet Union.

Most of the Eurasian north is covered by a broad belt of taiga (virgin coniferous forest). Along its southern margin the taiga adjoins the steppes of Asia and the temperate forests of Europe. To the north it gives way to a strip of arctic tundra, about 350 kilometers (400 miles across at its widest, between the tree line and the Arctic Ocean. Both taiga and tundra zones are remarkable for their homogeneity, and the tundra in particular for its unique ecological conditions. In climate there is a pronounced gradation from the maritime northwest, with relatively high precipitation and only moderately cold winters, to the continental heart of northeastern Siberia, where mean midwinter temperatures are the lowest in the world, and where the precipitation is only a little higher than in the world's desert regions. Topographically, much of the arctic and subarctic consists of a vast plain, dissected by three huge rivers—the Ob', Yenisei and Lena. However, there are some notable mountain ranges, including the Scandinavian chain, the Urals and the Kolyma mountains of northeastern Siberia.

Despite the cold, the taiga and tundra are not unproductive. During the summer of almost continuous daylight, the tundra supports a striking abundance of animal and plant life. The innumerable lakes and rivers of the taiga are plentiful in waterfowl and fish, and along the warmer arctic coasts around Scandinavia and the Bering Straits there are rich maritime resources. However, edible plants are few, and plant foods are mainly limited to berries; with the exception of parts of the European subarctic, no cultivation is possible. As throughout the circumpolar north, commercial interests currently focus on the enormous mineral and energy reserves of the region, and these interests often conflict with the continuation of traditional modes of subsistence.

The cultural configuration of arctic and subarctic Eurasia has always been in continuous flux. Successive migrations, dispersals and assimilations have generated an ethnic map of considerable complexity, and the extensive crosscutting of economic, cultural and linguistic divisions make it difficult to identify separate "peoples." Despite this cultural and linguistic diversity, there is a striking degree of similarity in basic modes of subsistence, which may be linked to the homogeneity of environmental conditions throughout the taiga and tundra. Thus, as can be seen in the lives of the Nentsi, any one ethnic group may practice some combination of land- and sea-mammal hunting, coastal and riverine fishing, reindeer herding and fowling.

Nentsi of northwestern Siberia

The Nentsi, who numbered 30,000 in 1979, speak a Samoyedic language. They are divided into two groups: the tundra Nentsi, who are hunters of sea mammals and herders of reindeer, and the forest Nentsi, a much smaller group, who live mainly by river fishing and, in recent times, farming.

The Nentsi were already trading with the Russians by the fifteenth century, and by the sixteenth century they, along with other Siberian peoples of the area, were paying a tribute in furs to the Cossacks who had conquered the Siberian kingdom of Kuchum. Under the Tsarist system of indirect rule the Nentsi were scarcely affected by outside influence until the second half of the nineteenth century. Then, Russian Orthodox missionaries converted many people, merchant fur traders established shops and markets, replacing barter with the use of money, fishing enterprises grew up and the hunting of wild reindeer was disrupted. By the twentieth century the Nentsi were mainly breeders of domestic reindeer, which they used for meat and skins, and also for pulling sleds.

Before the Russian Revolution in the early twentieth century, their social organization was based on patrilineal clans, each having its own summer and winter reindeer pastures, its own cemetery and sacrificial sites. The Nentsi practiced polygyny, and paid a brideprice of reindeer for their wives until these practices were declared illegal after the Revolution. Their religion of shamanism has survived in covert form, and it now incorporates Russian saints such as St Nicholas into the native pantheon.

Since the 1930s the Nentsi have been moved onto collective farms and state farms, but they have still kept up their traditional pursuits of hunting and reindeer herding. Previously, the Nentsi lived in small camps dispersed over a large area, and there was some resistance to the idea of large, settled villages containing 1,000 to 3,000 people. Settlement onto these collective farms has changed the social structure, although it is difficult to say exactly what kinds of social groups have emerged. In the past, some Nentsi tried to return to their traditional nomadic life, but today all live within the Soviet system.

Each family has a permanent house on the collective farm, even if much of the year has to be spent moving across the tundra with the herds. The farm has to fulfill an obligatory quota of meat and furs for the state, but each family is also allowed to own a few animals

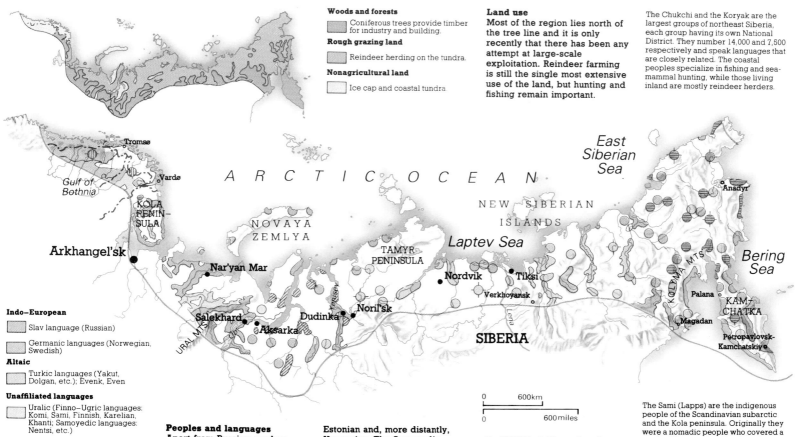

Woods and forests

Coniferous trees provide timber for industry and building.

Rough grazing land

Reindeer herding on the tundra.

Nonagricultural land

Ice cap and coastal tundra.

Land use

Most of the region lies north of the tree line and it is only recently that there has been any attempt at large-scale exploitation. Reindeer farming is still the single most extensive use of the land, but hunting and fishing remain important.

The Chukchi and the Koryak are the largest groups of northeast Siberia, each group having its own National District. They number 14,000 and 7,500 respectively and speak languages that are closely related. The coastal peoples specialize in fishing and sea-mammal hunting, while those living inland are mostly reindeer herders.

Indo–European

Slav language (Russian)

Germanic languages (Norwegian, Swedish)

Altaic

Turkic languages (Yakut, Dolgan, etc.); Evenk, Even

Unaffiliated languages

Uralic (Finno–Ugric languages: Komi, Sami, Finnish, Karelian, Khanti; Samoyedic languages: Nentsi, etc.)

Chukchi, Koryak, etc.

Featured people

Nentsi

Additional peoples

Peoples and languages

Apart from Russian, spoken throughout the region, the indigenous languages include members of the Uralic group and other unaffiliated languages. Of the Uralic group, the Finno-Ugric language of the Sami is related to Finnish, Estonian and, more distantly, Hungarian. The Samoyedic languages spoken by the Nentsi are also distantly related to the Finno-Ugric languages. Other peoples, like the Ket, and the few Eskimo and Aleut near the Bering Strait, speak languages unrelated to the Uralic group.

The 30,000 Nentsi live scattered across a vast area. Although their lives have changed greatly in this century and they now live on collective farms as sea-mammal hunters, reindeer herders, farmers and fishermen, they are far from being the most Russified of the Soviet peoples and only 9% count Russian as their mother tongue.

The Sami (Lapps) are the indigenous people of the Scandinavian subarctic and the Kola peninsula. Originally they were a nomadic people who covered a much wider area, but they have been pushed farther north by the spread of farmers from the south. Furthermore, their migratory routes have been blocked by the closure of international frontiers. Today there are about 40,000 Sami. Most are sedentary and work as farmers or fishermen; only a few are still nomadic reindeer herders.

---

privately. Wages are paid in roubles, and Nentsi people now have access to a wide range of Russian goods. They use snowmobiles, motorboats and modern nets as well as the old equipment, such as reindeer sleds. All farms have schools, hospitals and clubs attached to them.

Within the farm the production brigades are the most important socioeconomic units beyond the family. Each brigade comprises a number of *artels* (production teams) containing two or three herdsmen/hunters. It has its own production plan, to which all *artels* are subordinate. The brigades, which can vary greatly in size, are each led by a brigadier, who is appointed by the farm committee. When out in the tundra, the brigadier keeps in touch with his herdsmen and hunters by radio. Each brigade takes part in "socialist competition" for the number of furs, number of surviving deer fawns, weight increase of deer, and other production targets.

When on the move, the Nentsi live either in traditional conical, bark-covered tents (now often covered with tarpaulin) or in modern Soviet-designed tents and wooden huts built by the *kolkhoz* (collective farms) along the migration routes. Much of their food is hunted *en route*; the rest is either brought with them or stored in the huts. Wives who accompany the expeditions to look after the men are paid for their work. Children rarely go—they are left at boarding schools, and many parents are worried that traditional Nentsi skills will be lost due to lack of experience by the children in the forests and tundra.

Nentsi folklore and mythology are still passed on to the younger generation, although shamanism has lost its former authority. The traditional Nentsi view of the world is that there is an upper, middle (earthly) and lower world. *Ngu eru* (master of heaven) created the world, and then *ja minju* (a female spirit) made the mountains. She and her sons are the main sources of good in earthly life, and she lives with one son, *juba perca* (master of the south), the producer of warmth. Other good spirits are the master of reindeer and the master of birds. Evil spirits are responsible for various diseases and natural phenomena. Another of *ja minju's*

sons is *ja eru* (master of the underground) who is dark and unclean. *Uma budi* (master of the north) tried to marry his son to the daughter of the master of the south. The sun and moon also have their masters, who are offered sacrifices of reindeer. Stones, meteorites, single trees and hills are sacred and have their own spirit masters. Three categories of shaman deal with these spirits of the upper, middle and lower world.

Alongside old festivals, such as the cult of the reindeer, the Nentsi now celebrate all-Soviet festivals such as May Day, and there are numerous lesser celebrations that combine Nentsi and Soviet elements.

The Nentsi population has risen significantly since the Revolution and many Nentsi take advantage of educational opportunities—to the extent that it is now difficult for all the trained doctors, pilots and engineers to find jobs in their own national areas.

Deer for the sleds

Before the herds migrate, a number of the reindeer are lassoed, castrated and used for pulling the sleds. Despite the introduction of snowmobiles, the Nentsi still use reindeer sleds, although now these tend to be pulled by two rather than one reindeer. The reindeer are made to exchange places at frequent intervals, because they pull with only one shoulder. Renowned for their efficient methods of herding, the Nentsi have also introduced certain new techniques, such as separating the calves and barren does from the pregnant does, and enriching the herd's diet with fish meal.

Europe

Europe was once largely forested and inhabited by hunter-gatherers, but about ten thousand years ago agriculture, which had originated in the Middle East, slowly diffused northward. The hunters retreated into the dwindling forests as intensive farming and livestock herding flourished on the plains. Today little remains of Europe's native forests, for they have been cleared to build houses and ships, to warm the inhabitants through the cold, damp winters, and to make room for ever-increasing agricultural production.

The Indo-European-speaking peoples, who started to enter Europe from Anatolia and the Caucasus over 4,000 years ago, have given rise to most of the peoples of contemporary Europe and to their racial label, "Caucasoids." Successive waves of migration, and extensive population movements within the continent, have contributed to the diversity of physical characteristics, such as height, build and eye color.

The Roman legacy

The Roman Empire has been a powerful force in the continent's history, giving Europe the Latin language, which allowed a flow of ideas between scholars of different countries. Even today a Spaniard and an Italian can communicate basic ideas to each other thanks to the common origins of their languages. The Romans also gave much of Europe a basic legal system, and helped to spread Christianity from its birthplace to the distant lands of northern Europe.

Europe has been deeply marked by Christianity, which it has elaborated and exported to many different parts of the world. Local pre-Christian practices have sometimes been violently suppressed, as during the Albigensian Crusade of the early thirteenth century, but in other times and places have been tolerated and even incorporated. Christmas trees, Easter eggs and Lenten carnivals, all common throughout Europe, are probably older than Christianity, and represent "little traditions" with which the great churches have come to terms and even smiled upon.

European Christianity has three distinct movements: the Eastern Orthodox Church, dominant in Russia, Greece and the Balkans, which sees itself as the original form of Christianity; the Catholic Church, dominant in southern Europe, which looks to the Pope in Rome for spiritual authority; and finally the Protestant Churches, which rebelled against Rome in the sixteenth century Reformation and predominate in northern and parts of western Europe. Despite the overrunning of most of Spain and the Balkans by Muslims, Christianity eventually fought off the challenge of Islam to Europe. While the Crusaders struggled against Islam, Christianity, down the ages, has vacillated in its treatment of Jewish minorities, ignoring, persecuting or tolerating them by turns.

European nation-states

In the wake of the Roman Empire, a feudal order emerged in Europe, and when this in turn decayed, the nation-states of Europe were slowly born. From the late fifteenth century onward the development of such states, particularly England, France and the Netherlands, accelerated. The long coastline of Europe, with its many natural harbors, encouraged seafaring and the vigorous "modern" states of western and northern Europe began to found colonies in other continents, as they pursued gold, silver, slaves, foods and spices. The Industrial Revolution, powered by the rich seams of coal found in northern Europe, stimulated colonial enterprise, since the colonies provided new sources of raw material as well as new markets. Hardly any part of the earth was left untouched by the European powers during the colonial era, and in those continents populated mainly by hunter-gatherers or shifting cultivators—Australia and the Americas—Europeans very largely replaced the indigenous peoples. Elsewhere, European influence transformed existing economic and social relations.

The process of nation-state formation has projected the ideal of a uniform national state, in which all citizens share a single language and body of customs. In reality, however, only a few states, such as Iceland, conform to this image, and most contain some groups for whom the national language is a second tongue, while nation-state frontiers often cut through cultural groups. If today all French citizens are proficient in French, it is because the tongues of Provence, Languedoc, Aquitain, Brittany and other regions have withered—or been pruned by an imposed, uniform educational system.

The nation-states also sharpened the contest for territory within Europe that had been a recurrent feature of medieval Europe. The two world wars of this century were, in a sense, epic versions of the imperial wars the major European powers had been fighting for several hundred years. Since World War II, European world supremacy has waned, and most of the European colonies were granted independence between 1945 and 1965. However, the economic relations established in the colonial era still contribute to Europe's prosperity. Immigrants from the former colonies have established themselves in most European countries with mixed results—some have experienced discrimination while others have been well received.

The peace which has prevailed in Europe since 1945 has been an armed, tense peace. The Europeans are deeply divided by two political philosophies—Marxism and representative democracy. Marxism dominates eastern Europe, whose governments belong to the Warsaw Pact and Comecon. Most western European states have a long democratic tradition and are members of the North Atlantic Treaty Organization and of the European Economic Community. The United States of America, a state largely created by emigrants from Europe, is NATO's most powerful member, and the threat of nuclear war between the United States and the Soviet Union now overshadows the politics of Europe.

The city center, Warsaw

Northern Europe 1

Out of the grime of the Industrial Revolution emerged a new world power creating vast empires and spreading her Christian beliefs and materialist philosophy to the ends of the earth.

For centuries a pioneer in science and political thought – the birthplace of both parliamentary democracy and Marxism – northern Europe's dominance is only now beginning to be eclipsed.

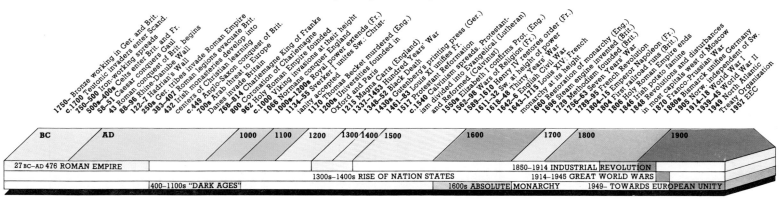

Timeline events:
1750: Bronze working in Ger. and Brit.
c.1700: Teutonic invaders enter Scand.
750–500: Iron-working spreads
500–400s: Celts enter Brit. and Fr.
58–51: Caesar conquests Gaul
43: Roman conquest of Brit. begins
88–98: Rhine–Danube Wall
122–7: Hadrian's Wall
250s: Ger. tribes invade Roman Empire
383–407: Roman legions evacuate Brit.
432: Irish monasteries develop into centers of Christian learning
c.449: Anglo-Saxon conquest of Brit.
700s: Arab threat to Europe
768–814: Charlemagne King of Franks
800: Coronation of Charlemagne
962: Holy Roman Empire founded
c.1000: Viking invasions at their height
1066: Normans conquer England
1000s–1200s: Royal power extends (Fr.)
1134–55: Sverker unites Sw.; Christianity accepted into Sw.
1170: Thomas Becket murdered (Eng.)
1200s: Universities founded at Oxford and Paris
1215: Magna Carta (England)
1337–1453: Hundred Years' War
1348–52: Black Death
1430s: Gutenberg's printing press (Ger.)
1461–83: Louis XI unifies Fr.
1517: Protestant Reformation
c.1540: Calvinism spreads; Protestantism divided into Evangelical (Lutheran) and reformed (Calvinist)
1550s: Elizabeth I confirms Prot.
1562–98: Wars of Religion (Fr.)
1589–1610: Henry IV restores order (Fr.)
1611–32: Sw. at height of power
1618–48: Thirty Years' War
1642–3: English Civil War
1643–1715: Louis XIV – French monarchy at its height
1660: Restoration of monarchy (Eng.)
1696: Steam engine invented (Brit.)
1729: Methodism founded (Brit.)
1756–63: Seven Years' War
1789–95: French Revolution
1804–15: Emperor Napoleon (Fr.)
1806: Holy Roman Empire ends
1846: Irish potato famine
1848: Revolutions west of Moscow – in most capitals famine and disturbances
1870: Franco-Prussian War
1800s: Bismarck unifies Germany
1905: Norw. independent of Sw.
1914–18: World War I
1939–45: World War II
1949: North Atlantic Treaty Organization
1957: EEC

Timeline bands:
- 27 BC–AD 476 ROMAN EMPIRE
- 400–1100s "DARK AGES"
- 1300s–1400s RISE OF NATION STATES
- 1600s ABSOLUTE MONARCHY
- 1850–1914 INDUSTRIAL REVOLUTION
- 1914–1945 GREAT WORLD WARS
- 1949– TOWARDS EUROPEAN UNITY

(BC / AD / 1000 / 1100 / 1200 / 1300 / 1400 / 1500 / 1600 / 1700 / 1800 / 1900)

Population by Country
Total: 218 million

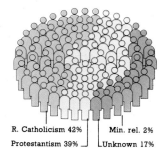

FDR 29%
Aus./Switz./Liech. 6.5%
UK/Ire. 27%
Neth./Belg./Lux. 11%
N Fr. 16.5%
S Sw./S Den./S Fin./S Norw./Ice. 10%

Population by Religion

R. Catholicism 42%
Min. rel. 2%
Protestantism 39%
Unknown 17%

North of the Alps, Europe is a region of varied, but rarely extreme, physical character. Its long, indented coasts offer good harbors which have encouraged seafaring among its inhabitants, while navigable rivers give easy inland access. The climate is generally mild, due to the warm waters of the Gulf Stream, while frequent rainfall and adequate sunlight, combined with good soils, make successful agriculture possible nearly everywhere. Useful minerals abound, some of which have been exploited since the Bronze Age while others, such as North Sea oil, are of recent discovery.

Although man's ancestors have inhabited northern Europe for over 200,000 years and farming villages were in existence some 8,000 years ago, it was not until the first millennium BC that the sparse population began to increase. This was largely due to the expansion of the Celts, whose knowledge of iron working enabled them to open up heavy soils for agriculture.

Toward the end of the first millennium BC a considerable part of the region was absorbed into the Roman Empire, whose limits were marked by the Rhine–Danube fortification and in Britain by Hadrian's Wall, built across the island. The fourth and fifth centuries AD saw the breakdown of Rome's empire under the assaults of Germanic invaders, and the Romanized inhabitants were either overrun or, like the Bretons, retreated into the remoter areas of the west. Amid the ruins of the empire there arose new political units under Germanic rulers, of which the Frankish kingdom was the most prominent. These in turn had to meet the onslaught of further invaders. In AD 736 a Frankish army turned back the Arabs, but the Viking raids in the ninth and tenth centuries were more successful, giving rise to numerous settlements.

The states which emerged in northern Europe exhibited Roman influence in varying degrees. In the western half of the Frankish kingdom, France, Popular Latin formed the basis of the local language, but elsewhere Germanic languages prevailed. The most widespread legacy from the Roman past was the Christian Church, whose organization mirrored that of the imperial administration. The imperial idea survived too in Charlemagne's Holy Roman Empire, which was revived in the tenth century by the Saxon emperor Otto, and lasted, in various forms, from the tenth to the early nineteenth century. But neither in the "Dark Ages" nor the Middle Ages of northern Europe was it possible to create a strong and lasting central authority, and the characteristic political and economic system was feudalism, whereby land was held in return for service. Only in the late fifteenth and sixteenth centuries were the increasingly ineffective medieval governments transformed into national monarchies—a development to which Germany was the important exception. This change was accompanied by, and associated with, other momentous developments—the spread of ideas from Renaissance Italy, the invention of printing, the split in the Church initiated by the German monk Luther, and the growth of nationalism.

The nation states of early modern Europe embarked on voyages of discovery overseas, and then on programs of settlement in the newly discovered lands. In the seventeenth century leadership in overseas exploration passed from Spain and Portugal to the French, British and Dutch. Prosperity steadily increased in northern Europe, aided by the trade in slaves and tropical products. Population was increasing too, but until the late eighteenth century the basis of society remained agricultural. However, this changed with the Industrial Revolution which, beginning in Britain during the reign of George III (1760–1820), led to a dramatic rise in the production of coal, pig iron, engineering goods and textiles. Continental Europe, plagued by wars and customs barriers, followed only slowly until the second half of the nineteenth century, when a second Industrial Revolution occurred. Steel, chemicals and electrical goods now came to the fore and Germany, having achieved unity in 1871, took the lead. Throughout northern Europe capitalism provided the framework for an industrialized and urbanized society, and new technology vastly increased manufacturing production. Efficient government and the possession of overseas empires gave northern Europe leadership of the world.

Meanwhile, an ever-growing population, reflecting healthier living conditions, inhabited the swollen towns. These people were fed partly by the increased food production resulting from the Agrarian Revolution, which had accompanied the Industrial Revolution, and partly by cheap imports. They contributed to a flow of emigrants who carried European technology, culture and values to all parts of the world.

The twentieth century has seen this world leadership diminished, due both to problems within northern

North Sea oil
Six tugboats maneuver one of the giant North Sea oil rigs into position. The extraordinary industrial boom which took place in Europe in the 19th century was only possible because of the accessibility of substantial quantities of coal—then the prime source of industrial energy. By the 1950s, however, coal had been replaced by oil as the main source of energy. Oil had two main advantages: it could be handled more easily than coal, and it could be refined into many products. North Sea oil should have a major impact on the economy of the North Sea countries, and might also provide a measure of security from political rationing by other oil producers. The finds, although not comparable with those of the Middle East, are nonetheless substantial. The giant Ekofisk petroleum field off southern Norway—discovered in 1970—has a capacity of about 300,000 barrels a day.

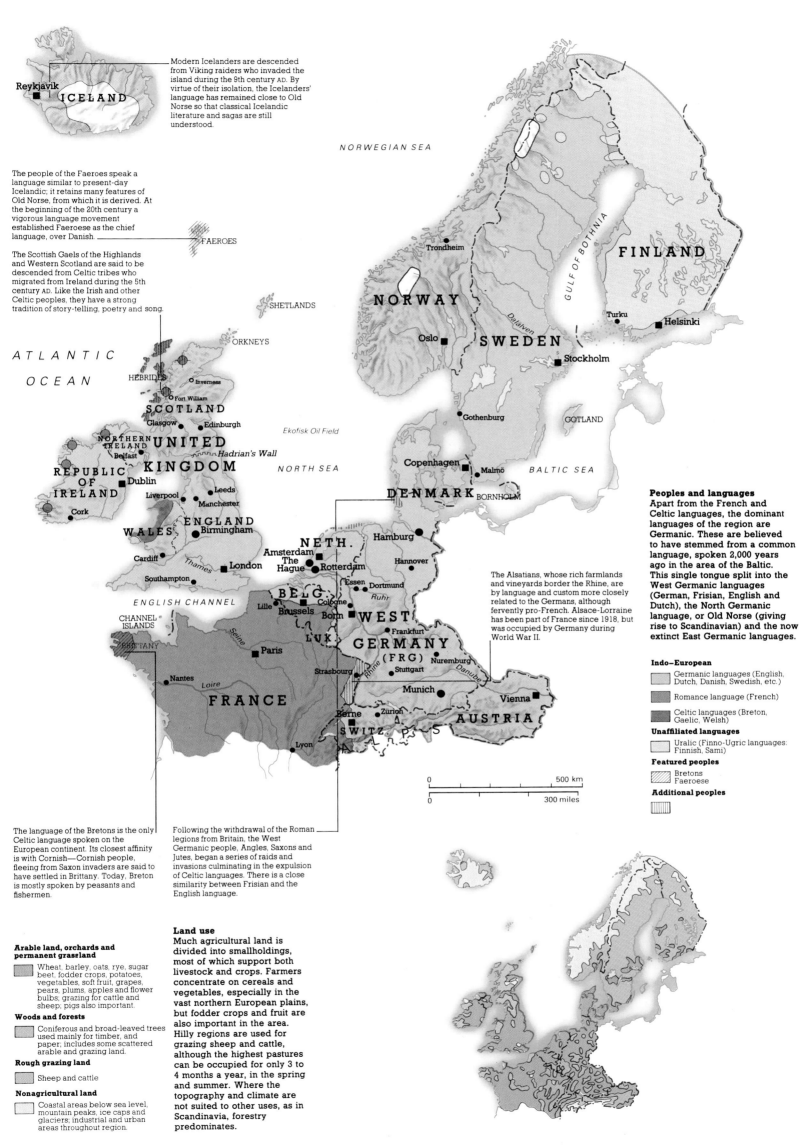

Modern Icelanders are descended from Viking raiders who invaded the island during the 9th century AD. By virtue of their isolation, the Icelanders' language has remained close to Old Norse so that classical Icelandic literature and sagas are still understood.

The people of the Faeroes speak a language similar to present-day Icelandic; it retains many features of Old Norse, from which it is derived. At the beginning of the 20th century a vigorous language movement established Faeroese as the chief language, over Danish.

The Scottish Gaels of the Highlands and Western Scotland are said to be descended from Celtic tribes who migrated from Ireland during the 5th century AD. Like the Irish and other Celtic peoples, they have a strong tradition of story-telling, poetry and song.

Peoples and languages
Apart from the French and Celtic languages, the dominant languages of the region are Germanic. These are believed to have stemmed from a common language, spoken 2,000 years ago in the area of the Baltic. This single tongue split into the West Germanic languages (German, Frisian, English and Dutch), the North Germanic language, or Old Norse (giving rise to Scandinavian) and the now extinct East Germanic languages.

Indo-European
- Germanic languages (English, Dutch, Danish, Swedish, etc.)
- Romance language (French)
- Celtic languages (Breton, Gaelic, Welsh)

Unaffiliated languages
- Uralic (Finno-Ugric languages: Finnish, Sami)

Featured peoples
- Bretons
- Faeroese

Additional peoples

The Alsatians, whose rich farmlands and vineyards border the Rhine, are by language and custom more closely related to the Germans, although fervently pro-French. Alsace-Lorraine has been part of France since 1918, but was occupied by Germany during World War II.

The language of the Bretons is the only Celtic language spoken on the European continent. Its closest affinity is with Cornish—Cornish people, fleeing from Saxon invaders are said to have settled in Brittany. Today, Breton is mostly spoken by peasants and fishermen.

Following the withdrawal of the Roman legions from Britain, the West Germanic people, Angles, Saxons and Jutes, began a series of raids and invasions culminating in the expulsion of Celtic languages. There is a close similarity between Frisian and the English language.

Arable land, orchards and permanent grassland
- Wheat, barley, oats, rye, sugar beet, fodder crops, potatoes, vegetables, soft fruit, grapes, pears, plums, apples and flower bulbs; grazing for cattle and sheep; pigs also important.

Woods and forests
- Coniferous and broad-leaved trees used mainly for timber, and paper; includes some scattered arable and grazing land.

Rough grazing land
- Sheep and cattle

Nonagricultural land
- Coastal areas below sea level, mountain peaks, ice caps and glaciers; industrial and urban areas throughout region.

Land use
Much agricultural land is divided into smallholdings, most of which support both livestock and crops. Farmers concentrate on cereals and vegetables, especially in the vast northern European plains, but fodder crops and fruit are also important in the area. Hilly regions are used for grazing sheep and cattle, although the highest pastures can be occupied for only 3 to 4 months a year, in the spring and summer. Where the topography and climate are not suited to other uses, as in Scandinavia, forestry predominates.

Europe and to the rise of powers outside the region. Nationalism, and hence international rivalries, brought two world wars in which ever more efficient armaments increased the devastation. Europe's overseas empires have crumbled and economic expansion has been checked by the growth of world competition. Other developments have been more positive—under the protection of the North Atlantic Treaty, European unity has prospered, resulting in the formation of the European Economic Community. Within the EEC, democratic forms of government continue to prevail, and the material welfare of the people has become a primary concern of all governments.

In the twentieth century, the disruptions of war have resulted in major population movements, while the dissolution of Europe's overseas empires has brought new immigrants from the former colonies, adding to the existing ethnic diversity. Meanwhile, some aspects of the ancient indigenous cultures of northern Europe have been preserved in isolated regions, as on the Faeroe Islands, where the descendants of Viking adventurers still live, and among the Celtic inhabitants of Brittany in northwest France.

The Faeroese

The Faeroe Islands, stark crags of basalt rising precipitously out of the sea, were discovered and colonized by the Vikings in about AD 850. Because the only means of communication was by boat, the eighty villages that comprise the total settlement were all built close to the shore. Up to 1800 the population remained stable, but during the nineteenth century their numbers rose as a result of better health care and an increasing export market for fish. Today there are 43,000 Faeroese living on seventeen islands.

For nearly a millennium the Faeroes were governed by Norway, but after the Napoleonic wars they were ceded to Denmark. The official language was Danish and all trade with the outside world was conducted through the Royal Danish monopoly, so that produce such as knitted stockings, butter, fish oil and dried fish was bartered for flour, salt, iron and liquor.

Like other Scandinavians the Faeroese became Christian in AD 1000, while in AD 1540 they accepted the Reformation that had found favor in Norway. One important consequence was that the extensive lands of the Catholic Church were confiscated by the Crown and then leased out. These Crown farms were passed on as a single unit from father to son and remain the largest farms in the Faeroes. Other farmland was subject to a law whereby children inherited equal shares, and was quickly fragmented.

Until this century, farming was the keystone of the social structure since there were few alternative forms of livelihood. The sparse resources of each village—grazing, peat, birds, birds' eggs and seaweed—were shared out in proportion to the amount of land each farmer owned. The Crown farmers naturally had a clear advantage and more or less ruled the villages.

Angling for leisure
Anglers on the River Avon in Warwickshire, England, attempt to hook a prize-winning fish during the 1981 world championship. Angling is one of the most popular participation sports in northern Europe and there are great claims for its therapeutic value, particularly for those living in the stressful environment of modern cities. Like the other field sports, such as hunting, shooting and hare coursing, it evolved from the necessary search for food. What is striking about leisure activities in industrialized countries is the amount of time, energy and money people spend on them. This is in marked contrast to the developing countries, where the working day is often almost twice as long as the average in the West, and incomes are much smaller. With increasing automation, the increase in leisure time in the wealthy industrialized nations is expected to create serious social problems.

Ruhr valley
The Ruhr valley is the most densely populated region in Germany and is particularly important for the production of coal and steel. The coal field, which first began to be worked during the Middle Ages, is one of the largest in the world. The industrialization of the area really began in the 19th century, when large-scale coal-mining and steel production were started by the Krupp and Thyssen firms. Since then it has, in a sense, become Germany's industrial backbone; it provided the basis for the massive military effort of World War II and suffered the consequences of heavy Allied bombing, which destroyed 75% of the mining area. The whole region is served by an extensive rail and canal system which transports its goods and raw materials.

Breton coif
A Breton woman, wearing a traditional lace coif to catch the eye of tourists, sells oysters in one of the many small harbor towns of this region. In the past, different coifs and costumes clearly signified local identity within Brittany, but they are no longer everyday wear, except among some of the older women. Many of the traditional aspects of Breton life have been glamorized and romanticized by virtue of their near disappearance in modern times.

The break-up of this paternalistic rule began with the abolition of the Royal Monopoly in 1856. With free trade many entrepreneurs looked for new ways of expanding the economy and an obvious answer lay in fishing. The first sloop was acquired in 1870 and sailed to Iceland to catch cod for export as dried fish. So successful was this enterprise that by 1939 there were a hundred sloops engaged in seasonal fishing.

During World War II the Faeroes were occupied by the British, and the islanders supplied Britain with Icelandic fish, thus building up a massive credit. At the end of the war the Faeroese voted, in a referendum, for independence, but this was overruled by Denmark, who instead granted them partial autonomy in 1948.

After the war the Faeroese reequipped their fishing fleet and embarked on an ambitious modernization program, which included electrification and the building of roads and harbors. This has totally changed the infrastructure of the economy and the Faeroes are now thriving. A third of the workforce is engaged in fishing, while the rest work mainly in the service industries. Agriculture is now of negligible importance—a complete reversal of the situation a century ago.

In the 1880s another movement was gathering strength—nationalism. Although Faeroese had always been spoken it had never been written down, but in the 1880s a script was invented, based upon the Icelandic one. As a result the Faeroese started a newspaper and began writing poems and novels. Today there are six newspapers and many volumes of poetry and novels are published annually. All the arts blossomed and painters, sculptors and novelists won renown in Scandinavia. This efflorescence of activity is remarkable for such a small population.

There is no traditional musical instrument in the Faeroes, but they have preserved songs and melodies from the Middle Ages about the deeds of Charlemagne, Roland and the Viking heroes. These songs have been passed down orally and are the accompaniment to a form of medieval ring dance where everyone links arms and stamps out the beat in unison. Such performances were a typical expression of collective feelings at the high points of life—weddings, harvesttime, Christmas, New Year, the catching of pilot whales and the Faeroese national day. The consumption of large quantities of spirits was the inevitable accompaniment to these celebrations and abuse of alcohol led to a referendum in 1907 which prohibited the sale of liquor in the Faeroes.

The Bretons

Brittany, which became a French province in the early sixteenth century, is the foremost agricultural region of France, and an important fishing area. Until the late 1960s, the population was predominantly rural, although the movement away from agriculture first began in the 1950s. In 1954 over 50 percent of the total active population of Brittany was still engaged in agriculture, but by 1975 this had fallen to 21 percent. Many of those who have stayed on the land are elderly people working small, barely viable units. Special government indemnities are paid to those who retire and sell or rent out their land to form larger units. Likewise, an improved system of credit facilities has enabled some heirs to buy out their departing coheirs and to enlarge and modernize. Even so, most farms in Brittany are still 20 hectares (50 acres) or less and although larger, more efficient farms are becoming more common, agriculture is still heavily subsidized. Farming remains a family concern and there is a division of labor within the family—women do the milking while the men generally tend the machines and work in the fields. However, women help out in the fields when neighboring farms cooperate for major agricultural tasks.

The traditionally rural character of Brittany has contributed to the survival of the Breton language, which is still spoken by an estimated 500,000 people. However there has been an overall drop of about 62 percent in the number of Breton speakers during the last hundred years. Compulsory schooling, officially in French, was launched in the 1880s, and education is commonly seen as the principal reason for the demise of Breton. The rural, peasant world was, for a time, less schooled than the rest of the population, and Breton is still considered to be predominantly the language of the countryside. Peasants commonly speak Breton to each other locally, while French is spoken to anyone who is not a close acquaintance. Since the late 1960s, it has been rare to speak Breton to children.

There is a movement in Brittany which has, for almost 150 years, fought to conserve a Breton identity in terms of traditional costume, song, dance, music and language. The Celtic roots of the Breton language have gained significance, and Breton historians have keenly researched Breton origins in fifth-century emigrations of ancient Britons to the old Armorican peninsula, now Brittany. These origins have given Brittany the character of a distinct, minority world in France, and are important for those in the modern Breton movement who now seek Breton autonomy.

Breton costumes, including white lace coifs of the women, are now donned mainly for tourists, although coifs are still worn locally by some older women, and they are not uncommon at annual *pardons* (religious processions). Breton music and dance have attracted far greater numbers of young enthusiasts—revived *festoù-noz* ("night festivities," once linked to the agricultural cycle) are frequent, with simple country dances performed to the accompaniment of progressive folk music. For most in the modern Breton movement, however, it is their language that is most important. More and more young people are learning Breton at school, university, or in militant groups, and a few have set up independent Breton-medium schools for their children.

Preying on puffins
Sea birds are valuable to the Faeroe islanders. Puffins and their eggs are an important source of food, and the eider duck is hunted for its feathers.

The village of Mykines
This cluster of austere cottages, some of which still have traditional turf roofing, is typical of a Faeroese village. Although today the people of the Faeroes rely almost exclusively on the sea for their livelihood, there are few natural harbors on the islands. However, most villages have a point from which a boat can be launched and this is usually close to the local church. The juxtaposition of these two points is significant: one is the economic and the other the spiritual heart of the village. The Faeroes have no protection from the strong westerly winds and the frequent gales which build up over the Atlantic. As a result all the islands are naturally treeless. Frequent storms can isolate the islands for several weeks at a time.

Whale kill
In the agricultural era, whale meat was an essential part of the Faeroese diet, and pilot whales are still captured today, although more as a sport than out of necessity. The whales, which swim in large groups, are driven into shore by men banging loudly against the sides of their small boats. The underwater vibrations they set up panic the whales, who swim headlong into shallow water, where they are harpooned and slaughtered. This method of catching pilot whales was originally devised by the Vikings and was once practiced in Iceland, and in the Orkney and Shetland Islands, as well as in the Faeroes.

In the warm lands of southern Europe, olive grove and vineyard are set against the azure of the Mediterranean Sea. Here the Christian Church holds sway, and in colorful festivals images of the saints are carried through the streets. The spirit of machismo, epitomized by Spanish bullfights, lives on, and there are sharp contrasts between the roles of men and women.

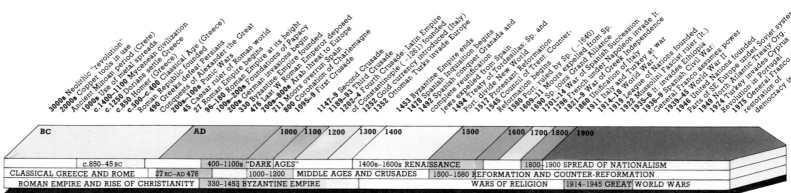

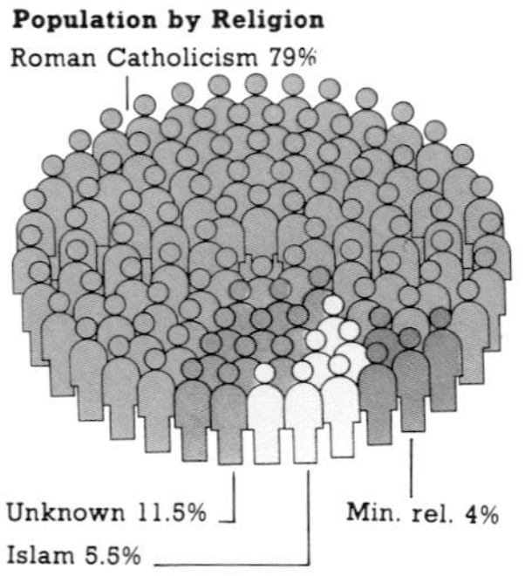

Timeline entries:
3000s Neolithic "revolution"
2000s Copper tools in use
1000s Use of metal spreads
Ancient Minoan period (Crete)
c.1400–1100 Mycenaean civilization
c.1250 Dorians settle Greece
c.850 Homer (Classical Age)
c.500–c.400 Classical Age (Greece)
Roman Republic founded
490 Greeks defeat Persians
Conquests of Alexander the Great
45 Cassar ruler of Roman world
27 Roman Empire begins
96–180 Roman Empire at its height
100s–200s Punic Wars
200s German invasions begin
330 Byzantine Empire founded
476 Last W Roman Emperor deposed
700s–800s Arab threat to Europe
711 Moors overrun Spain
800 Coronation of Charlemagne
1095–9 First Crusade
1147–9 Second Crusade
1189–93 Third Crusade
1202–4 Fourth Crusade: Latin Empire of Constantinople (–1261) founded
1252 Gold currency introduced (Italy)
1352 Ottoman Turks invade Europe
1453 Byzantine Empire ends
1478 Spanish Inquisition begins
1492 Spanish conquer Granada and complete reunification Granada and Jews expelled from Spain
1494 Treaty of Tordesillas: Sp. and Port. divide New World
1517 Protestant Reformation
1545 Council of Trent: Counter-Reformation begins (–1640)
1580 Port. ruled by Sp. (–1640)
1609–11 Moors expelled from Sp.
1690 Sp. joins Grand Alliance
1701–14 War of Spanish Succession
1796 French under Napoleon invade It.
1821–9 War of Greek Independence
1860 Unification of Italy
1911 Italy and Turkey at war
1914–18 World War I
1919 League of Nations founded
1922 Mussolini Fascist ruler (It.)
1935–6 It. invades Ethiopia
1936–9 Spanish Civil War: General Franco assumes power
1939–45 World War II
1946 United Nations founded
Parts of SE Europe under Soviet system
1949 North Atlantic Treaty Org.
1974 Turkey invades Cyprus
Revolution in Portugal
1975 General Franco dies: restoration of democracy in Sp.

BC		AD		1000	1100	1200	1300	1400		1500		1600	1700	1800	1900	

c.850–45 BC
CLASSICAL GREECE AND ROME
ROMAN EMPIRE AND RISE OF CHRISTIANITY
27 BC–AD 476
330–1453 BYZANTINE EMPIRE
400–1100s "DARK AGES"
1000–1200 MIDDLE AGES AND CRUSADES
1400s–1600s RENAISSANCE
1500–1580 REFORMATION AND COUNTER-REFORMATION
WARS OF RELIGION
1800–1900 SPREAD OF NATIONALISM
1914–1945 GREAT WORLD WARS

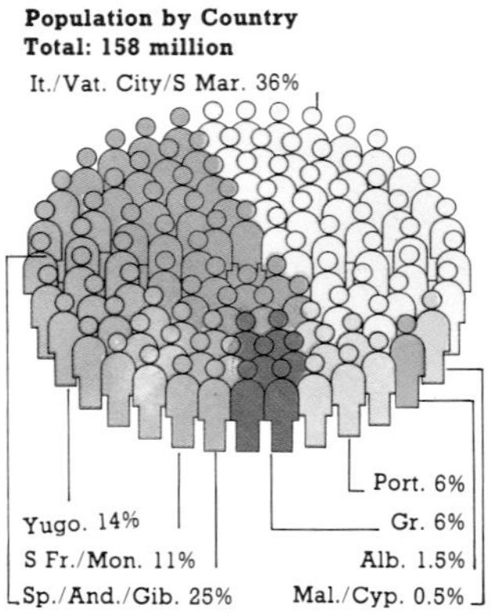

Population by Country
Total: 158 million

It./Vat. City/S Mar. 36%

Port. 6%
Gr. 6%
Alb. 1.5%
Mal./Cyp. 0.5%
Yugo. 14%
S Fr./Mon. 11%
Sp./And./Gib. 25%

Population by Religion
Roman Catholicism 79%

Unknown 11.5%
Islam 5.5%
Min. rel. 4%

It is well over a thousand years since southern Europe was inhabited by "peoples" who resembled, in the homogeneity of their cultures, the tribal societies of South America or Africa. The Roman Empire emerged out of the political unification of diverse tribes and, as it expanded throughout Europe, it conquered other tribal peoples. But for the last eight centuries southern Europe has seen the pioneering emergence of the modern nation-state out of the wreckage of decaying empires. Since the French Revolution the inhabitants of southern Europe have gradually become citizens of modern states, rather than "peoples" or "folk." This has two crucial implications: first, they are economically highly differentiated (so that even a simple village may produce lawyers and physicists, as well as shepherds and peasants) and second, although their citizens may share a common national language, they do not share a common culture. They are often deeply divided by political allegiances, as well as by attitudes for and against religion.

The region has given its name to the "Mediterranean climate" characterized by mild winters and hot, dry summers. A large area was once forested, but the trees have long since been felled to provide timber for shipbuilding. The drier parts of the region are now covered with a type of scrub vegetation known as maquis. The lack of summer rainfall is the main factor limiting agricultural production, but cereals, grapes,

Moving with the seasons
Pastoralists throughout this area tend to practice transhumance—regular seasonal movements between fixed points. In summer they drive their herds up from the bare, dry plains to the cooler, greener, hill pasture. As winter approaches they return to the warmer conditions of the plains, where, once again, the land will provide adequate grazing for the herds as it has done for centuries.

Galician is more closely related to Portuguese than Spanish; there are an estimated 2,500,000 speakers. Its lyrical, poetic literature developed during the Middle Ages but then degenerated into folk song and peasant patois until interest was revived in this century.

Basque, with over 500,000 speakers, is an isolated language, unrelated to any other. It is the only surviving remnant of the languages used in the area before the arrival of Indo-European speakers. Basque separatists continue to seek independence from Spain by emphasizing their unique heritage.

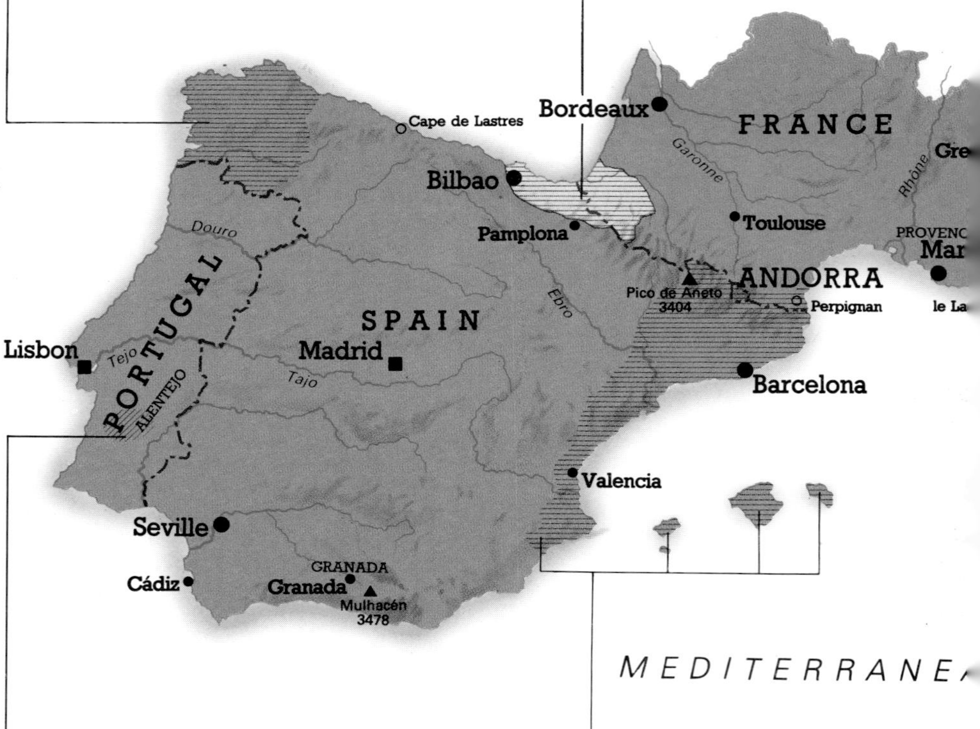

The Alentejo is a poor region of Portugal dominated by large estates or *latifundia*; most men are seasonal laborers and many must migrate to find work. This area was the scene of major land occupations after the revolution of 1974; a political tug-of-war over land ownership continues.

Catalan has nearly 5 million speakers in Spain and 300,000 in France and Sardinia. In the tiny Pyrennean state of Andorra it is the official language. Recently there has been a revival of interest in the language, which of all the Latin-based tongues, retains most of its original characteristics.

Sard is the most conservative of the Romance languages, having closely preserved words and forms from the original Latin. Although spoken by most of the 147,000 Sardinians, only older people use it in daily life and most of its speakers can only read and write Italian.

Map labels: FRANCE, SPAIN, PORTUGAL, ANDORRA, Bordeaux, Bilbao, Pamplona, Toulouse, Perpignan, Barcelona, Valencia, Madrid, Lisbon, Seville, Cádiz, Granada, GRANADA, Cape de Lastres, Pico de Aneto 3404, Mulhacén 3478, Douro, Tejo, Tajo, Ebro, Garonne, Rhône, ALENTEJO, PROVENCE, Mar, Gre, le La, MEDITERRANEA

Peoples and languages

Apart from the Basques, Slavs, Albanians, Greeks and Maltese, who make up roughly 10% of the region's population, the majority of people speak Romance languages. These are all derived from Latin, and have many similar words, so that a certain amount of understanding is possible between speakers of different Romance languages. Most states have a single national language, but this does not mean that each state is linguistically homogenous—the whole of southern Europe is a patchwork of regional languages and dialects. These linguistic regions rarely correspond to national boundaries. Many groups have retained their cultural and linguistic traditions, particularly in mountainous areas.

Indo–European

- Romance languages (Spanish, Portuguese, French, Italian, Occitan, Catalan, Sard, etc.)
- Slav languages (Serbo–Croat, etc.)
- Other languages (Albanian, Greek)

Altaic

- Turkic language (Turkish)

Afro–Asiatic

- Semitic language (Maltese)

Unaffiliated language

- Basque

Featured peoples

- Peasants of the Alentejo Greek Cypriots

Additional peoples

The Ladin language flourishes among the mountain peasants of northern Italy. It is spoken by up to 20,000 people and has its own newspapers. Friulian, with around 500,000 speakers, is closer to Italian and has a vigorous literature. Other minority languages in Italy include French and German.

citrus fruit and vegetables of many kinds are grown on the fertile soils of the plains. The mountainous regions have poorer soil and are used for pasturage, and for fruit and nut trees.

The extensive maritime coasts have always been exploited for fish, but have also encouraged long-distance trade, piracy and colonization. These activities have contributed to the growth of cities such as Lisbon, Cadiz, Bilbao and Genoa. The expansion from southern Europe also transformed the cultural patterning of the New World and produced the Hispanic saturation of South America that we see today. In more recent times, the migration of Italian and, to a lesser extent, Greek workers to the United States of America has left its mark on the cultural pattern of that country.

At first glance, the nation-states appear to have won the battle for a uniform national culture: for example, each country has a single official national language, which virtually all of its citizens must learn in school. But underneath this uniformity is the reality of dialect. Italians, for example, may read Italian and understand it when it is spoken over the radio, but in their homes and their piazzas they mostly speak distinctive regional dialects that deviate very markedly from the official language. In this sense they are best regarded as bicultural, almost bilingual. In some parts of southern Europe true bilingualism exists, for example, some Basques speak both Basque and Spanish.

There are now, moreover, a number of movements for cultural autonomy that show how far the uniform culture of the nation-state has failed to bind the local minorities. The movements of Basques, Catalans, Corsicans and Tyrolese all bear witness to this. In all of them, language is a decisive factor, determining allegiances and acting as the symbol of nationality.

Southern Europe today has two distinctive political zones. From Portugal to Italy there has been relative stability of frontiers since the Napoleonic Wars ended

Slovene is a Slav language written in the Roman alphabet. It is closely related to Serbo-Croat although the two are not mutually intelligible. There are 1½ million speakers in Yugoslavia, around 40,000 speakers in the Trieste province of Italy, and 22,000 in Austria's southernmost province.

in 1815, and the process of building a uniform national culture is mostly well advanced. In the Balkans, however, the frontiers have twice been redrawn in the twentieth century. The ethnic composition of Yugoslavia is a patchwork medley of minorities, while in Albania and Greece the minorities' problems are reproduced in a lesser form and there are still tensions over national boundaries.

Over the whole region the strongest cultural feature is the dominance of Roman Catholicism and Orthodox Christianity. The Catholics insist on a celibate clergy, and the supreme authority of the Pope as head of a centralized, unified Church, while in the Orthodox Church there is no equivalent figure to the Pope and the parish priest is normally married.

Godparenthood, with its roots in the early Christian Church, has profound spiritual and secular implications for both Roman Catholics and Orthodox Christians. It is known as *compadrazgo* in Spain, *comparaggio* in Italy, *kumstvo* in the Balkans and *koumparia* in Greece. Between parents and godparents who are social equals it works as a kind of superfriendship, and between unequals it is a disguise for the "lopsided friendship" known as patronage, or patron-client relations.

Even in the twentieth century, women are markedly subordinate to men in southern Europe: they are virtually excluded from public places and public life. Strong emphasis is placed on female premarital chastity and marital fidelity, although the husbands often expect to enjoy sexual escapades which they forbid their wives. This is known variously as the honor-and-shame complex, *machismo* (from the Spanish word for masculinity), or the double standard.

The Roman Catholic Portuguese of the Alentejo and the Orthodox Greeks in Cyprus illustrate the contrasting ways of life within this region as well as its many common cultural themes.

Serbo-Croat is an official language of Yugoslavia, alongside Slovene and Macedonian. Serbian and Croatian are dialects of the same language; their written forms reflect religious influences: the Orthodox Serbs use a modified Cyrillic script, the Catholic Croatians use the Roman alphabet.

Arable land

- Cereals, especially wheat and maize; potatoes, sugar beet, fodder crops; vegetables such as peppers and tomatoes.

Orchards and vineyards

- Olives, grapes, citrus fruits, apples, pears, peaches, almonds, hazelnuts and figs.

Rough grazing land

- Mainly beef and dairy cattle; sheep and goats often graze on rocky pasture.

Woods and forests

- Coniferous and broad-leaved trees used for timber; also provide limited grazing areas for livestock.

Nonagricultural land

- Mountain peaks; industrial and urban areas throughout region.

Land use

A variety of soils combined with local variations in rain and temperature produce a range of micro-climates suited to specific crops. The poorer mountain land is used mainly as pasture, but the wetter hill and mountain regions specialize in cereals and fruit, nut and olive trees. The plains, watered by winter rainfall, produce cereals and citrus fruits. Wherever there is enough water in summer, a wide selection of vegetables are grown including peppers and tomatoes.

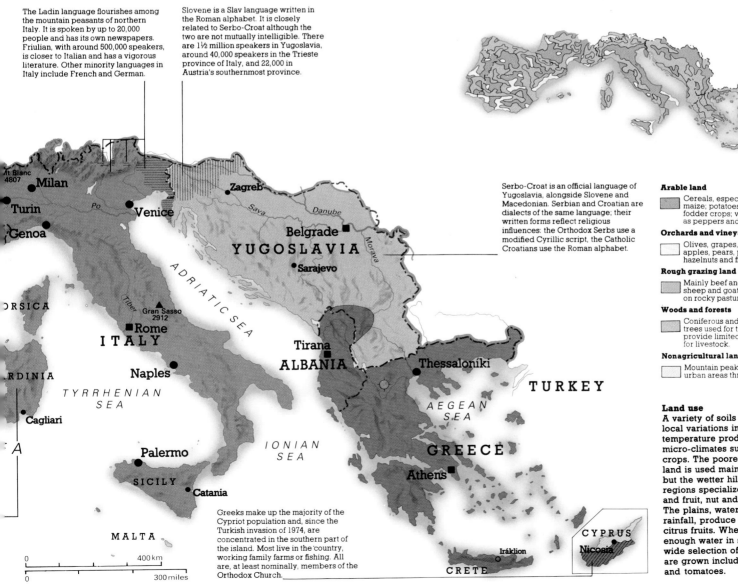

Greeks make up the majority of the Cypriot population and, since the Turkish invasion of 1974, are concentrated in the southern part of the island. Most live in the country, working family farms or fishing. All are, at least nominally, members of the Orthodox Church.

Southern Europe 2

Greek Cypriots

In the island of Cyprus, 78 percent of the population are Greek Cypriots, 18 percent are Turkish Cypriots and the remainder are Armenians or Maronites. The two major ethnic groups lived in close association throughout the island until 1974, but following an invasion by Turkey, the *de facto* separation of Greeks and Turks took place and a form of partition occurred.

Most Greek Cypriots live in the countryside, where their predominant occupations are cultivating the land and fishing. The remainder live in the major cities and are mainly employed in light industry, trade, crafts, services and government. Greek Cypriot farmers grow cereals, citrus fruits, grapes, potatoes, carrots, carobs and such early vegetables as tomatoes, cucumbers, artichokes, eggplant, onions and okra. Most of the agricultural land is in small holdings and a typical family may own between eight and twelve small plots dispersed around a village. The Greek Orthodox Church is the largest single landowner, with some of the choicest urban and sea-coast property, as well as agricultural land, which is rented to farmers.

Land is owned and worked by both men and women. In general, men undertake irrigation and plowing, which is now frequently done with a tractor, although draft animals are still employed in some hilly areas. Women are responsible for the weeding, and the harvesting of fruit and vegetables on the land of their own families. If they are forced to accept wage labor on the land of other people, this is taken as a sign of family poverty. As elsewhere in the region, men prefer to keep their womenfolk secluded from contact with nonrelatives, since their own social status as providers and protectors largely depends on this.

Although roughly half the Greek Cypriots support left-wing political parties, virtually all follow the marriage, baptism and funeral rituals of the Orthodox Church. The religious year is punctuated by two major fasts; the first, of fifty days, precedes Easter, the most important event of the year, and the other, of forty days, precedes Christmas. In rural communities everyone attends the dramatic candle-lit midnight mass at Easter, and relatives or neighbors of late arrivals will search the village for them and bring them to the church. After this ceremony, the traditional greeting on all sides is "*Christos onesti*," "Christ is risen."

The two most striking features of Greek Cypriot marriage are that children usually receive their share of parental property on marriage, rather than at the death of a parent, and that the girl's family provides a dowry house—a new household set up for her and her husband. As the provision of dowry houses for daughters places an immense burden on the poorer families, some girls are left in the humiliating position of spinsters, and others marry relatively late in life, after years of thrift and hard work.

The provision of a dowry is a major spur to economic enterprise as it is the lifelong ambition of most Greek Cypriot parents to marry off their children. Once this is

The man in the square
The traditional Portuguese saying "*A mulher em casa, o homen na praça*" ("the women at home, the man in the square") could apply to the whole southern European area. This scene, of a game of petanque being played in le Lavandou, Provence, illustrates the point. Whereas men, when not working, gather in the cafés around the village square, the women sit outside their houses chatting to their neighbors.

Baptism—a spiritual rebirth
With the adoption of Christianity by the Roman Empire in AD 313, Rome became the center of the Church in the west, while Constantinople was its center in the east. In the 11th century, the Church split into Roman Catholic and Orthodox, but there are still many similarities between them. Baptism is very important to both faiths and Greek Cypriots are seen here in an Orthodox ceremony. The Orthodox archbishop of Cyprus, Archbishop Makarios, was at the forefront of the independence movement and became the first president of Cyprus in 1960.

done, and all their property has been divided among the children, the parents retire to very small houses on the properties of one or more of their children. It is then quite common for them to visit their children in turn, helping to look after the grandchildren. In line with Greek Orthodox teaching, a Greek Cypriot must not marry a second cousin or closer relative and there are no dispensations from this. Traditionally marriages have been arranged by the families involved, and only recently have young people started to acquire some rights to veto the partner proposed.

Cyprus is a class-stratified society with extremes of wealth and poverty, but, since most land is not held in large estates, the proportion of landless families is relatively small. The partition of Cyprus in 1974, however, turned about one third of the entire population into refugees. These people have made an extremely painful transition in life style, which will leave its scars on public life for generations to come. While only relatively small numbers of Greek Cypriots have remained in refugee camps, as many as one in five may have emigrated in search of security and income elsewhere. The others have been absorbed into the resilient Greek Cypriot economy, although not necessarily in the same occupations as before. The island's Greek and Turkish communities have understandably become obsessed with the refugee problem and with their political divisions, and the prosperity of the island has become a victim of intercommunal conflict.

Portuguese of the Alentejo

The Alentejo is a distinctive region of southeastern Portugal. The population is Roman Catholic and the large majority are either employed locally in agriculture or migrate in search of a better income. Unlike the north of Portugal, a region of small family farms, the Alentejo is dominated by *latifundia* (large estates). In one rural district with 8,700 hectares (21,700 acres) of arable land, some fifteen families own two thirds of the land in estates of 100 hectares (250 acres) or more. The remaining two thirds of the inhabitants are either landless or have holdings which are not usually large enough to support a family. Most of these people have to sell their labor—for which the demand fluctuates seasonally—to the large landowners.

The main crop of the Alentejo is wheat, although the yields have been steadily declining due to poor farming methods and low prices. Oats, barley and rye are also grown, watered by winter rainfall, as are olives and wine grapes. Where there are sources of perennial water the Portuguese grow cucumbers, melons, tomatoes, onions and other vegetables on small plots for domestic consumption.

Men do most of the agricultural tasks, whether on their own land or on the *latifundia*. The women are

responsible for cooking, laundering clothes and cleaning the home. They must also whitewash their homes (and those of their employers) several times a year, although they are not permitted to do this when they are menstruating. There has been a recent attempt to introduce craft activities to the Alentejo, and some women have started weaving bedcovers, which are dyed with local vegetable dyes.

Most households consist of husband, wife and children; sometimes a grandparent may also live in the house. Among the poorer people, who are the majority, houses are generally rented. Marriages are not arranged, the young choosing each other freely from among members of their own class. *Namoro* (courtship) often starts at a dance and usually lasts for at least three years, sometimes seven or eight. It is a formal relationship and during this time the young couple save carefully for the costs of setting up an independent home. There is no dowry, only a trousseau. Girls begin their *namoro* at fifteen or sixteen, but boys wait until they are three or four years older. A girl known to have slept with her fiancé would, if he jilted her, have difficulty in finding another.

Traditional customs and ceremonies have been much eroded in recent years, but *Carnaval* is still celebrated in February. This once involved antagonistic masquerades of sexual role reversal in which women would dress in men's clothes and then chase and abuse the menfolk, but this is now almost extinct. However, the suggestive *baile da pinha* (pinecone dance) is still performed when the King and Queen of Carnaval are chosen.

In summer, during the *festa* (celebration) for the patron saint of the local community, young men will, at some risk to themselves, bait an angry bull, which is finally slaughtered by a local butcher and eaten. The event continues with dancing and firework displays until early morning. The next day the secular atmosphere gives way to church services and a procession for the patron saint.

Although the population are nominally Catholic and turn to the Church for marriage, baptism and funeral ceremonies, there is also a pronounced anticlerical spirit. Priests are mistrusted by their poorer male parishioners since their commitment to celibacy is questioned—or their masculinity, if they appear truly celibate. The poor also believe that the priests side with the rich, and the men are understandably reluctant to attend Confession.

Men seem to pride themselves on an anticlerical, and at times irreligious, stance and leave the task of seeking divine protection for their families to their wives. Women, while having reservations about official religion, are generally ready to make *promessas* (vows) to the saints, offering them masses (which must be paid for) in return for intercession with God, who is seen as too distant and powerful to be approached directly. The requests are typically for help when a member of the family is unwell.

Eastern Europe 1

Now separated from the rest of Europe by an "iron curtain," the people of eastern Europe are no strangers to war and unrest. Lacking natural frontiers, their lands have fallen victim to a succession of different armies, from the Magyar horsemen who swept in from Asia over one thousand years ago, to the invading tanks of Germany and Russia in the twentieth century.

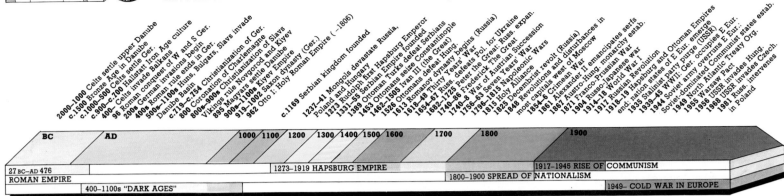

Timeline events:
2000–1000 Celts settle upper Danube
c.1500 Bronze Age in Danube
c.1000–500 Celts settle Iron Age culture
c.900–c.700 Hallstatt Iron Age in Ger.
400 Celts invade Balkans
96 Roman conquest of W and S Ger.
200 German invasions begin
400s Roman rule ends in Ger.
500s–1100s Huns, Bulgars, Slavs invade
Danube Basin
c.719–c.754 Christianization of Ger.
800 Coronation of Charlemagne
800s–900s Christianization of Slavs
Vikings rule Novgorod and Kiev
895 Magyars settle Danube
900s–1100s Kiev Empire
919–1002 Saxon dynasty (Ger.)
962 Otto I: Holy Roman Empire (–1806)
c.1169 Serbian kingdom founded
1237–41 Mongols devastate Russia,
Poland and Hungary
1273 Rudolph first Hapsburg Emperor
1331–55 Serbian Empire founded
1389 Ottoman Turks defeat Serbians
1453 Ottomans seize Constantinople
1462–1505 Ivan III (the Great)
1526 Ottomans defeat Hung.
1613 Romanov dynasty begins (Russia)
1618–48 Thirty Years' War
1654–67 Russ. defeats Pol. for Ukraine
1682–1725 Peter the Great: Russ. expan.
1740–86 Frederick The Great
1740–8 War of Austrian Succession
1756–63 Seven Years' War
1796–1815 Napoleonic Wars
1815 Holy Alliance
1825 Decembrist revolt (Russia)
1848 Revolutions and disturbances in most capitals west of Moscow
1854–6 Crimean War
1861 Alexander II emancipates serfs
1867 Austro-Hung. monarchy estab.
1871 Franco-Prussian War
1904 Russo-Japanese war
1914–18 World War I
1917 Russian Revolution
1918–19 Hapsburg and Ottoman Empires end: nation states of E. Eur. emerge
1935 Stalinist party purge (USSR)
1939–45 WWII: Ger. occupies E. Eur.
1944 Soviet army overruns E. Eur.: Soviet-dominated Communist states estab.
1949 North Atlantic Treaty Org.
1955 Warsaw Pact
1956 USSR invades Hung.
1968 USSR invades Czech.
1981 Russ. interenes in Poland

Timeline bar:
BC | AD | 1000 1100 1200 1300 1400 1500 1600 | 1700 | 1800 | 1900

27 BC–AD 476 ROMAN EMPIRE
400–1100s "DARK AGES"
1273–1919 HAPSBURG EMPIRE
1800–1900 SPREAD OF NATIONALISM
1917–1945 RISE OF COMMUNISM
1949– COLD WAR IN EUROPE

Population by Country
Total: 317 million
W USSR 65%
Bulgaria 3%
Romania 7%
Czech. 5%
GDR 5.5%
Hungary 3.5%
Poland 11%

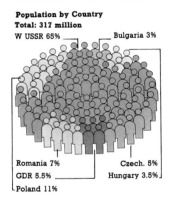

Population by Religion
Eastern Orthodox 20%
Prot. 5%
Islam 11%
Non-party Comm. 39%
R.C. 17%
Comm. Party 8%

Traditional Gorale housing
Two-roomed timber huts such as these, with a central wood-burning stove for both heating and cooking, are now giving way to modern brick houses.

The lands of eastern Europe form a vulnerable buffer zone between Europe and Asia, and they have had a long and troubled history, marked by migrations, invasions, and the rise and fall of great empires. Wars and political bargains have redrawn national boundaries repeatedly throughout the area, often separating ethnically similar peoples, and uniting others who are both diverse and antagonistic. Traditionally, the gap between the urban and rural populations has been wide. The old cities have been centers of learning and culture, while the rural mountains and plains have been the home of pastoralists and peasants, who were far removed culturally from the ruling urban elite. Since the end of World War II, however, eastern Europe has fallen within the sphere of influence of the Soviet Union, and this has led to great social and economic changes.

The region contains ecological features as diverse as its population. On the vast Russian and Polish plains, peasants have long cultivated wheat, rye and other grains and vegetables, while along the Danube the climate and soils are suited to a great variety of vegetables and fruits, notably grapes. The mountainous Carpathian and Balkan regions, on the other hand, are characterized by poor soils and harsher climate. Traditionally these areas were occupied by transhumant pastoralists, raising livestock and growing only a few crops for subsistence.

The majority of eastern European peoples are Slav speaking, reflecting the slow, steady migration of Slavs westward from Russia to the Vistula River, and then south across the Carpathians. A Romance language is spoken in Romania, however, a legacy of the expansion of the Roman Empire into the Balkans. The Romans were succeeded as rulers of this region by the Byzantine Empire and later the Ottoman Empire, but farther north stable states did not develop until much later—during the Middle Ages, German, Scandinavian, Lithuanian and Slav principalities competed for power, and a coherent pattern only emerged with the growth of the Grand Duchy of Moscow, and the kingdoms of Poland and Hungary.

Incursions from Asia occurred throughout this period—marauding Magyar horsemen swept through the Danube valley in the ninth century and eventually settled there, while Mongol horsemen invaded Russia, Poland and then Hungary in the thirteenth century, causing great destruction. The Polish king subsequently opened his country to outsiders, if they would come and repopulate its devastated lands, and millions flocked in from western Europe, including many Jews fleeing persecution. The Mongol advance into Europe halted abruptly following the death of the Great Khan Ogedei in 1241, but Mongol Khanates continued to rule Russia for over 200 years.

The eighteenth century saw the steady growth of two great empires—the Prussian and the Austro-Hungarian—and eastern Europe became divided up between these two powers, and the empires of Russia and Turkey. At the same time the gulf between the peasantry and the landed gentry increased, and the general climate of inequality and repression culminated in several mid-nineteenth century national rebellions. In 1917, severe hardships created by World War I exacerbated the situation and led to the Russian Revolution. Following World War I, the massive blocks of territory of the four great powers were fragmented. Poland was once more independent, and several new nations—including Latviya, Lithuania and Czechoslovakia—came into being, only to fall under total or partial Soviet domination again after World War II.

Eastern Europe is predominantly Christian, the main denominations being Roman Catholic and Orthodox, with strong Protestant minorities in Czechoslovakia and Hungary. Prior to World War II, there were large Jewish populations in eastern Europe, but during the war millions of Jews fled or were massacred by the Nazis. However, Jewish minorities still exist, especially in Russia, Poland, Bulgaria and Romania. Bulgaria, which was part of the Ottoman Empire from the fourteenth century until the nineteenth century, still has a substantial Muslim minority, as does Russia.

Despite strong government opposition to organized religion, the Church continues to play an important role in the lives of many eastern Europeans. In Poland, where the greatest level of compromise and co-existence between Church and State has been achieved, the Roman Catholic religion is a major unifying force. In other eastern European countries, organized religion is less prominent, but at Easter and Christmas, village churches are full, and local religious festivals are carried out with the same colorful pageantry as in the past. Throughout rural eastern Europe, traces of ancient pre-Christian ritual are apparent in most religious festivals.

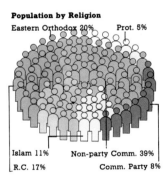

Land use

The rolling plains of Poland and Russia produce mainly cereals and vegetables, but in the Danube valley a greater variety of crops can be grown. Here the landscape is dotted with vineyards, and the villagers' orchards and fields produce apricots, peppers, lentils and tobacco, as well as more standard vegetables, fruits and grains. In the mountainous regions, nomadic pastoralists raise livestock and grow some crops for subsistence, while along the shores of the many rivers, and along the coast, fishing has always been an important occupation.

Arable land and orchards
Cereal and root crops, primarily wheat, rye, barley and sugar beet; potatoes, other vegetables; grapes, apples, plums, pears and apricots.

Permanent grassland and rough grazing land
Beef and dairy cattle; sheep raised in the Balkans and Carpathians; pigs are also important.

Woods and forests
Coniferous and broad-leaved trees mainly provide timber; some areas in northwest are mixed with arable and grazing land.

Nonagricultural land
Mountain peaks; industrial and urban areas throughout region

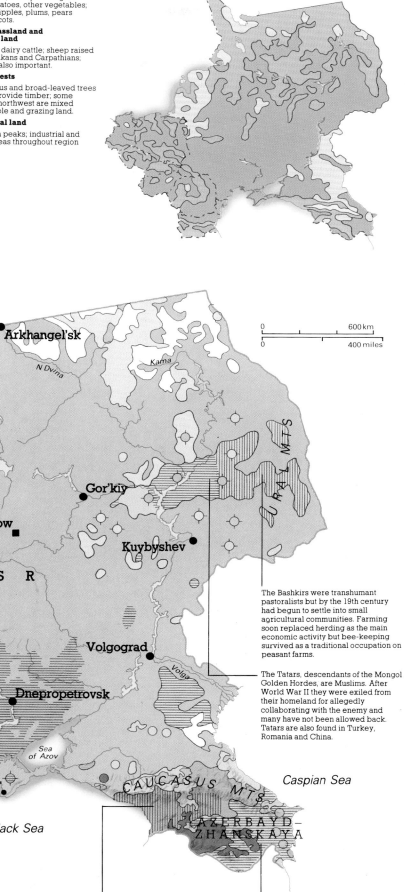

The largest Roma (Gypsy) populations are found in the Balkans—70,000 live in Romania, and even more in Yugoslavia. The roots of their language, Romany, have been traced to an archaic Sanskrit dialect; their ancestors migrated from the Indus valley probably in the 10th century.

The Estoniyans enjoy the highest standard of living in the USSR, largely due to their successful manufacturing industry. They have close linguistic and cultural links with Finland and westernized attitudes. Estoniya was an independent republic between the two world wars.

About 25% of Hungarians are farmers, despite the country's official policy of industrialization. The collectivization of most Hungarian peasant farms has eliminated uneconomic holdings. It has also disrupted the traditional organization of the family workforce, except on private plots.

The Gorales' farms have never been collectivized, but many farmers now belong to the United Peasants' Party, and distribute their produce through local cooperatives. Less than a quarter of Polish farmland has been successfully collectivized, due to strong opposition.

The Bashkirs were transhumant pastoralists but by the 19th century had begun to settle into small agricultural communities. Farming soon replaced herding as the main economic activity but bee-keeping survived as a traditional occupation on peasant farms.

The Tatars, descendants of the Mongol Golden Hordes, are Muslims. After World War II they were exiled from their homeland for allegedly collaborating with the enemy and many have not been allowed back. Tatars are also found in Turkey, Romania and China.

Indo–European
Indo-Iranian languages (Tat)

Slav languages (Polish, Czech, Russian, Bulgarian, etc.)

Romance languages (Romanian, Moldavian)

Germanic language (German)

Baltic languages (Lithuanian, Latvian); Armenian

Altaic
Turkic languages (Chuvash, Tatar, Bashkir, etc.); Mongolian language (Kalmyk)

Unaffiliated languages
Uralic (Finno-Ugric languages: Hungarian, Karelian, etc.)

Caucasian languages (Georgian)

Featured peoples
Gorale

Hungarian peasants

Additional peoples

Peoples and languages

The majority of peoples are Slav-speaking, but Romanian is a Romance language, a relic of the Roman Empire's penetration into the Balkans. The Baltic languages, Latviyan and Lithuanian, form a separate group within the Indo-European family. Hungarian, a Finno-Ugric language related to Finnish and Estoniyan, has its roots in the 9th-century invasions of Magyar horsemen from the east.

The Ukrainians form the second largest ethnic group in the USSR after the Russians. They have retained their own language and distinctive folk traditions. The Ukraina is a major grain-producing area, with vast collective farms, and an important industrial region.

The Georgians are a culturally diverse group of people drawn from more than a dozen tribes, although their differences are slowly fading with increased urbanization. They are renowned for their generosity and hospitality, as well as their world-famous longevity.

The Turkic-speaking Azarbayjanis are Muslims whose culture retains its Turkish and Persian elements, despite the influence of Soviet education. The drought-prone Azarbaijani Republic has vast oil and gas fields where many work; cotton-farming is the other major activity.

Map labels
Arkhangel'sk
N Dvina
Kama
Onega
L. Ladoga
Leningrad
Tallinn
ESTONIYA
Novgorod
Gor'kiy
Riga
LATVIYA
LITVA
Moscow
Kuybyshev
URAL MTS
Baltic Sea
Gdańsk
USSR
EAST GERMANY
Berlin (GDR)
POLAND
Warsaw
Vistula
Prague
Pilsen
Kraków
L'vov
Bohemia
CZECH
Bratislava
CARPATHIAN MTS
Budapest
HUNGARY
Dnepr
UKRAINA
Kiev
Volgograd
Volga
Dnepropetrovsk
Odessa
Sevastopol'
Sea of Azov
CAUCASUS MTS
Caspian Sea
ROMANIA
Danube
Black Sea
BULGARIA
Sofiya
AZERBAYD-ZHANSKAYA

Eastern Europe 2

Although this area contains several major ethnic groups, as well as many minorities, there are basic similarities in the social organization and culture of rural areas. The household, often comprising three generations, traditionally provides most of the labor for the family farms or herds. Authority over domestic affairs generally lies with the senior woman, while labor in the fields or with livestock is under the direction of the senior man. This cultural pattern persists wherever production has not been collectivized, and even where this has occurred, the old ways are followed in working the private family plot. Collectivization has been implemented with varying degrees of success in the postwar years. The peasantry on the whole opposed the change, and in Poland, resistance was so strong that the movement was abandoned in the mid-1950s, and today less than a quarter of Polish farmland is socialized.

All the countries of eastern Europe entered the twentieth century with a low level of industrialization. Intensive campaigns to industrialize were instigated by the socialist governments, and nonagricultural wage labor became available in the rural areas, often for the first time. Today a new group of "peasant workers"—part-time farmers and part-time wage laborers—has emerged. One result of this is that women tend to take over traditional male activities, and assume responsibility for farm management. Young people in all areas are tempted to leave their rural homes and seek work in the towns and cities. As such movement is strictly controlled, the exodus to urban areas is not as pronounced as in parts of western Europe, but it is a growing trend.

The different states of the Soviet bloc have responded with varying degrees of passivity and opposition to Russian supremacy. Bulgaria has closely followed the Soviet model, while Romania has managed to maintain a degree of political independence. In Hungary and in Czechoslovakia, attempts to develop more autonomous forms of socialism were repressed, and in Poland periods of instability and at times violent unrest have marked the past twenty-five years. The Gorale of Poland provide an example of a traditional eastern European rural society whose agricultural methods have been little changed by socialism, while the economy of the peasants of the Hungarian plains has been more radically affected by the Soviet system.

Gorale—Polish highlanders

The Gorale, whose name means "highlanders," live in the southwest region of Polish Galicia known as the Podhale. This area, reaching from the foothills to the high peaks of the Carpathians, is characterized by very poor soil, and an alpine climate of long, snowy winters and short, clear summers. The Gorale were traditionally pastoralists, raising sheep and cultivating only a few crops, such as oats, barley and potatoes, for their own consumption. Today more modern agricultural methods have fostered some agricultural development and dairy farming predominates.

Roma—the traveling people
Found throughout Europe, the Roma people have a strong patrilineal organization and their own legal code. They have always kept apart from the established social and economic order and as a result have been frequent victims of repression. In Romania, despite restrictions on movement, many Roma still live in horse-drawn caravans, and eke out a living in their traditional trades, as coppersmiths, sieve makers and showmen.

The Gorales at work
A husband and wife team work together cleaning and spinning wool—the various stages in the manufacture of woollen clothes are often carried out by different families. Gorale women play an active role in the social and economic life of the village.

People of the fields
Poland's name comes from the word *Polani*, meaning "people of the fields." Industrialization has not led to agricultural mechanization, and scythes and horse-drawn plows are still common. In spite of this, agricultural production is fairly high—Poland is the world's fifth largest exporter of dairy produce, and an important exporter of meat. Food is exported to generate foreign currency, and this results in domestic shortages.

Most Gorale live in small villages, where clusters of houses are surrounded by long strip fields, pastures and forest. The old two-roomed wooden huts stand side by side with modern multistory brick houses, but even in the latter, the entire family still tends to live, eat and sleep in one or two rooms, renting the rest out to tourists. The Podhale also has several market towns, and a few tourist resorts. Since World War II the area has been opened to light industry, and many villagers work part-time in local factories.

The Gorale have managed to maintain many of their traditions despite years under Austrian rule during the partition of Poland, occupation by Nazi forces during World War II, and integration into the Polish socialist state since 1947. Distinguished from other groups of Polish peasants by dialect and various aspects of culture and social organization, the Gorale are an autonomous people, with a reputation of interfamily and intervillage blood feuds, and for generally rebellious behavior. Their history, however, is a bleak one—emancipated from serfdom in 1848, they followed a system of land tenure with equal inheritance by all offspring, which soon led to the fragmentation of small holdings. Population pressure on the land was exacerbated by periods of plague and famine, and by the early twentieth century many Gorale had emigrated to America. The area continued to be one of the poorest in Poland until the 1950s, when improvements in agriculture, industry, and an expanding tourist industry began to promote economic growth.

Although there is a growing tendency for young couples to establish their own households shortly after marriage, the three-generation extended family is still common. On the farm, the division of labor is based on age and gender. Men perform the labor that involves horses, machinery and tools such as scythes, while women and young children rake and turn hay, plant and gather potatoes and weed vegetable patches. These categories are flexible, however, and there is no shame attached to men doing most kinds of women's work, or women doing men's work.

The Gorale are uniformly Catholic, and religious events and ceremonies are the most important occasions of the year. During Easter, Christmas and May (the month of the Virgin Mary's ascent into heaven) the village churches and wayside shrines are beautifully decorated, and people don traditional costumes to attend Mass and join in processions around the church.

Weddings are especially important to the Gorale. Traditional rituals, including a long blessing by the parents before the church ceremony, the greenery on the bride's headdress (representing her virginity), the gates of greenery through which the couple must pass on their way home from church, and the greeting of the bride by her mother-in-law, with bread, salt and greenery, are still maintained. A good wedding feast lasts for two or three days, with over a hundred guests, and is remembered by the entire village for years.

The most important relationship, other than those of kinship and affinity, is that of *kumoter* (co-godparenthood). In the past, poorer peasants established patron-client type relationships with richer neighbors by means of *kumoter*, while richer peasants chose godparents from among their peers. Today it is equally common for close kin to be godparents.

Peasants of the Great Hungarian Plain
The Great Hungarian Plain has long been the home of sedentary agriculturists, raising cattle and cultivating grains, fruits and vines. Following the Turkish wars and invasions of the sixteenth and seventeenth centuries, very large villages replaced the small, scattered settlements of medieval times. Typically, these later villages held over 2,000 inhabitants, living either in central clusters of thatched mud-brick houses, or in small *tanya*—isolated dwellings outside the main cluster. The household consisted of the extended family, usually comprising the parental couple, two or more married sons and their families, and other unmarried children. Each married couple had their own room and kitchen, or a separate house within the compound.

Villages were stratified between *gazda*, wealthier peasants owning enough land to be self-sufficient, and *zseller*, peasants with very small holdings or no land at all. The division of labor was strict, with men working in the fields and women in the household. Only in poor families, or in families lacking sons, did women do men's work. The division between the sexes was reflected even in sleeping arrangements—at maturity, boys left the house and joined their father and brothers sleeping with the animals in the stable. Today the farmlands are collectivized, and the traditional family structure has been undermined by the loss of the cohesive focus of the family farm. However, individuals still farm small plots of their own, and here the old patterns remain.

The plains are populated primarily by Roman Catholics and Calvinists. Although less ardent in their practice than the Gorale, Hungarian villagers continue to attend church on major feast days and holidays, and to place importance upon ceremonies such as church weddings. In recent years, religious faith has become an area of contention between the old and the young, with older villagers still attending church, while the younger ones spurn it on most occasions.

The two most important relationships outside the family kin group are those of *nasz* (co-parents-in-law) and of *keresztkoma* (co-godparents). *Nasz* are expected to attend each other's major life events, and to treat each other with respect and mutual support, and a similar degree of involvement exists between *keresztkoma*. A man chooses one of his closest friends, generally a man who has worked with him or served with him in the army, to become godfather. Often this is arranged before either of the two men have children, and the role of godparent is reciprocal and lifelong. Two couples become godparents to all of each other's children and, should one of the godparents die, his or her obligations are taken over by a son or daughter. Godparents are expected to be the chief guests at their godchild's wedding, and to provide aid and support if necessary.

Herdsmen of the Great Hungarian Plain
In the past, herding was a specialized profession whose skills were handed down from generation to generation within certain families. As well as caring for animals, they would also be the leatherworkers, making whips, sandals and satchels. These herdsmen did no agricultural work, and tended to form an independent group within the peasant community, with their own distinctive style of dress as shown here. Their herds were made up of animals owned by a number of different villagers, and they were paid in kind, visiting all the owners after the harvest to collect their share. As a result of collectivization and the migration of young people to the towns, herding is rarely a family profession today.

Heavy industry in Pilsen
Since World War II most of the countries of eastern Europe, whose economies in the past were based primarily on agriculture, have concentrated on developing heavy industry. Czechoslovakia, however, already had a legacy of industrialization, based on the mid-19th century industrial revolution in the Austro-Hungarian Empire and on reserves of coal and iron ore found in Bohemia, now eastern Czechoslovakia.

The Church in Poland
Polish villagers gather outside the church for an elaborate Palm Sunday parade. Links between Poland and western Europe were forged in the 10th century when Poles accepted Roman Catholicism rather than the Orthodox Christianity adopted by the Russians. Although young people have increasingly adopted denim jeans and other modern fashions, Sundays and important social ceremonies are still celebrated in traditional dress.

PEOPLES OF THE WORLD
Africa

Africa is a continent of striking geographical contrasts, incorporating large areas of desert and scrub, as well as rolling savanna and dense tropical rain forest. Linguistically and culturally, it is just as diverse, although centuries of trade, migration and conquest have given certain features—such as architectural styles, techniques of herding and crop cultivation, and forms of kinship and political organization—a very wide distribution.

The largest areas of cultural homogeneity, however, are the result of foreign conquest and colonization, first by Arabs and then by Europeans. The impact of such conquests is reflected in the fact that most of Africa's contemporary states are products of foreign colonization, and traditional ethnic solidarities and divisions often cut across their boundaries. With such exceptions as Morocco, Egypt and Ethiopia, these states do not generally correspond to precolonial political units.

Earlier generations of Europeans were fascinated by the achievements of Pharaonic Egypt, with its intricate Nile Valley irrigation and its remarkable monuments, the Pyramids, whose construction is still a baffling feat of engineering. This brilliant Egyptian legacy encouraged the widespread European tendency to regard sub-Saharan Africa as a "dark continent," where any signs of progress or cultural advancement should be traced to Egyptian or other foreign influence. The Arab invasion and settlement of North Africa in the seventh and eighth centuries AD installed the literate Arabic language and complex culture of Islam, so renewing this ancient distinction between North Africa—essentially part of the Middle East and Mediterranean Europe—and the supposedly "barbaric" tropical zone to the south.

Although black Africa seems often in the past to have been the recipient rather than the exporter of ideas and techniques, the north-south dialogue has not in fact been quite so one sided as appears at first sight. It is true that the desert caravan trade of nomadic pastoralists spread Islam to the south and helped stimulate the rise and expansion of sub-Saharan states, particularly those on the southern fringes of the desert. But, as Islam spread south, so elements from the indigenous African religions it displaced were carried back to the north as, for instance, in the case of the Hausa *bori* cult and the Ethiopian *zar* cult. It was black slaves, transported across the Sahara, who were largely responsible for the introduction of these religious cults.

While North African influences played a part in the growth of states in sub-Saharan Africa, it is simplistic to assume that divine kingship is a unique legacy of Pharaonic Egypt, diffused throughout Africa from this source. The impressive early African civilization at Nok, in northern Nigeria, with its famous terracotta sculptures, goes back to the first millennium BC and may well have developed independently of North African influences. Similarly, the state which flourished in what is now Zimbabwe from the eleventh to the fifteenth century, and whose capital, Great Zimbabwe, boasted a magnificent stone temple and palace, was a largely autonomous development, despite trade contacts with the east coast.

The colonial era

The partition of Africa by Christian European powers, which reached its peak in the late nineteenth century, gave additional impetus to the spread of Islam as the religion of resistance to European colonization. The powers which then established their respective territories—Belgium, Britain, France, Italy, Portugal and Spain—were partly inspired by national rivalries in Europe itself and partly by their desire to gain access to resources (including labor) and markets in Africa. Of the various European settler communities, the most entrenched of all proved to be those of predominantly Dutch origin, settled at Table Bay since the seventeenth century, who became the Afrikaner ethnic group which still controls South Africa and Namibia. Only Ethiopia, whose rulers had been Christian since the fourth century AD, escaped this high point of European colonial partition, and actually extended rather than diminished its territories under its forceful Emperor, Menelik.

By the mid-1960s, most of the European colonies in Africa had become self-governing, the most recent member of the Organization of African Unity being Zimbabwe, formerly Southern Rhodesia, which achieved independence under Black majority rule in 1980. These new African states are the direct legacy of colonization, their frontiers being those established by the European colonizers when they carved out their possessions, and, with the exceptions already noted, they bore little relation to Africa's traditional ethnic frontiers. Despite the colonial emphasis on assimilation to the dominant metropolitan culture, strongest in French, Belgian, Spanish and Portuguese colonies, these new states are usually characterized by ethnic and linguistic pluralism and are far from achieving viable nationhood in the sense of possessing a single homogenous national culture. Yet traditional ethnic loyalties, often heightened rather than diminished by the postindependence struggle for power and resources, remain a strong feature, threatening to destroy fragile state cohesion if disregarded.

These circumstances seem to encourage a marked attachment to frontiers in the quest for distinctive identity, and to foster authoritarian regimes which rely heavily on a personality cult of the leader. Such factors are not conducive to steady, equitable development or rational use of available resources. Hence development, which is frequently associated with neocolonial patterns of trade (as, for instance, within the Francophone or Anglophone network), is often distorted and shows little promise of being able to provide adequately for the population of the continent which, with modern medical resources, is now rapidly increasing.

Turkana nomads watering their herd near Lake Turkana in Kenya

Horn of Africa

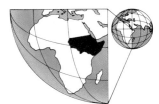

Source of myrrh and frankincense for the Egyptian Pharaohs, the Horn of Africa straddles the worlds of Africa, Europe and the Middle East, embracing ancient legacies of both Islam and Christianity. Today, desert nomads face an uncertain future, plagued by drought and war, as centuries-old tensions between Muslim herder and Christian farmer erupt in bitter conflict.

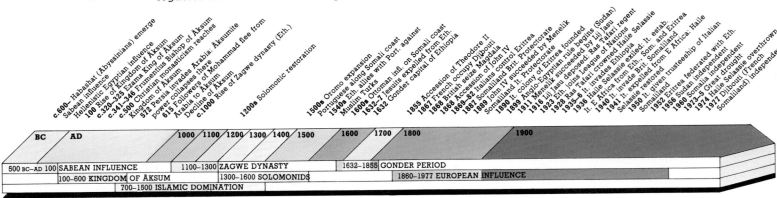

Timeline events:
c.600s Habashat (Abyssinians) emerge
Sabean influence
Hellenistic Egyptian influence
100 Rise of Kingdom of Aksum
c.320–325 Ezana King of Aksum
c.341–346 Frumentius Bishop of Aksum
c.500 Christian monasticism reaches Kingdom of Aksum
372 Persia invades Aksum
Kingdom of Aksum power collapses there
615 Followers of Mohammad flee from Arabia to Aksum
Decline of Aksum
c.1000 Rise of Zagwe dynasty (Eth.)
1200s Solomonic restoration
1500s Oromo expansion
Portuguese along Somali coast
1540s Eth. allies with Port. against Muslim Turks
1600s Ottoman infl. on Somali coast
1632–7 Jesuits expelled from Eth.
1632 Gonder capital of Ethiopia
1855 Accession of Theodore II
1867 French occupy Djibouti
1868 British seize Magdala
1869–82 Accession of John IV
1881 Italians control Eritrea
1887 Somaliland Brit. Protectorate
1889 Accession of John IV
1889 Menelik II succeeded by Menelik
1890 It. colony of Eritrea founded
1899 Anglo-Egyptian rule begins (Sudan)
1911 Menelik succeeded by Lij Jasu
1916 Lij Jasu deposed by Ras Tafari regent
1923 Ras Tafari crowned Ras Tafari regent
1928 Ras Tafari crowned Haile Selassie
1935 It. invades Ethiopia
1936 Haile Selassie exiled. It. estab. It. E Africa from Eth., Som. and Eritrea
1940 It. invade Brit. Somaliland
1941 It. expelled from E Africa. Haile Selassie restored
1950 It. given trusteeship of Italian Somaliland
1952 Eritrea federated with Eth.
1956 Sudan independent
1960 Somalia independent
1973–5 Great drought
1974 Haile Selassie overthrown
1977 Djibouti (French Somaliland) independent

	BC	AD	1000	1100	1200	1300	1400	1500	1600	1700	1800	1900

500 BC–AD 100 SABEAN INFLUENCE
1100–1300 ZAGWE DYNASTY
1632–1855 GONDER PERIOD
100–600 KINGDOM OF ĀKSUM
1300–1600 SOLOMONIDS
1860–1977 EUROPEAN INFLUENCE
700–1500 ISLAMIC DOMINATION

Population by Country
Total: 50 million

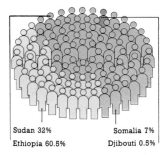

Sudan 32%   Somalia 7%
Ethiopia 60.5%   Djibouti 0.5%

Population by Religion

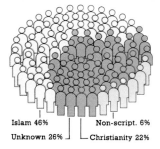

Islam 46%   Non-script. 6%
Unknown 26%   Christianity 22%

Water for the Danakil desert
Both Somalia and Ethiopia suffered severe drought in 1973–5. The Somali government responded by setting up fishing and agricultural settlements, and introducing literacy schemes for the nomads. In Ethiopia the government, with UN help, attempted to set up an irrigation scheme on the fringe of the Danakil desert, one of the most inhospitable parts of the world. The long-term intention was to provide the Afar nomads of Ethiopia and Djibouti with a more reliable source of water as well as giving immediate relief by encouraging them to work on the scheme with payments of food and supplies. It was also hoped that the Afars would give up their traditional way of life as pastoral nomads and settle under the control of central government. However, the Afars, a fiercely independent people, were not easily persuaded and many returned to the drought-stricken area as soon as it began to recover. In the Somali Republic, as a result of war and drought, about a million nomads are living on international relief rations in refugee camps.

South of the Sahara, the Horn of Africa juts out into the Red Sea and the Indian Ocean, occupying a unique position in the African continent. Known to the ancient Egyptians as the fabled "land of Punt," source of exotic myrrh and frankincense; its Judao-Christian and Islamic legacies make it the natural bridge between Africa, the Middle East and Europe. The contemporary states of the region—Christian Ethiopia and the Islamic Republics of Somalia and Djibouti—have their roots in the distant past, and the centuries-old rivalry between Christian agriculturists and nomadic Muslim pastoralists is reflected in the tensions between them.

The central landmass of Ethiopia is extremely mountainous, with the Simien Massif reaching an altitude of over 4,500 meters (15,000 feet). The well-watered northern and central highlands are mainly inhabited by Semitic-speaking and largely Christian Tigreans and Amharas, who combine stock raising with cereal cultivation. On the more arid coastal plains the Cushitic-speaking Oromo, Somali, Afar, Saho and Beja live, mainly as pastoral nomads. Sheep, goats and camels are herded, as well as cattle in the better-watered regions.

With an extremely diverse population of about thirty million, Ethiopia has had a history of almost continuous independence. The "holy city" of Āksum in Tigre was the ancient center of Ethiopian kingship, probably founded by immigrants from southern Arabia in the first millennium BC. In the fourth century AD, Ezana, king of Āksum, became a Christian, introducing the religion which has been politically dominant ever since, despite the arrival of Islam 500 years later.

Ethnic competition in the region always has tended to follow religious lines. In the Middle Ages the Christian kingdom was surrounded by hostile Islamic states and almost foundered in the protracted holy wars of those countries. With Portuguese aid, however, the Muslims were defeated, and the Christians gradually expanded, conquering surrounding peoples.

This process of expansion and consolidation was interrupted in the sixteenth century by the Cushitic-speaking Oromo advancing irresistibly northward from their earlier base in southeast Ethiopia. This huge ethnic group, today numbering ten million, was pastoralist in origin, but as they moved northward they adjusted to the environment of the local Amhara peasantry and many groups became cultivators. A number of these people were gradually converted to Christianity and adopted the Amharic language, thus becoming part of the expanding Amhara empire. As the state grew, the capital moved farther and farther south, reaching its present site of Addis Ababa in the nineteenth century, when Emperor Menelik (1889–1911) made further conquests, establishing Ethiopia's present frontiers.

At this time, France and Britain were competing for control of the Nile, with Russia and Italy acting as satellite partners. Menelik exploited the rivalry between these European powers and retained control over his expanded empire, while the coastlands that now constitute Somalia, Djibouti and Eritrea were divided up between France, Britain and Italy. The Italians briefly seized control of Ethiopia from 1935 to 1940, but this only served to reinforce Ethiopia's image as a symbol of African independence. Thus Haile Selassie, who succeeded as emperor in 1928, became the "Black Messiah" of Rastafarians in the West Indies, the United States and Britain. Their name derives from his precoronation title, "Ras Tafari." Haile Selassie continues to be venerated despite his death in captivity following the 1974 revolution.

After World War II, Italy's former colony, Eritrea, was ceded to Ethiopia, creating the basis for the Eritrean nationalist struggle, and the Somali Republic was established by uniting the former British and Italian Somali territories. Two expansive states, Ethiopia and Somalia, were thus set to confront each other in the Horn of Africa. The adoption of socialism by both states did little to solve the ensuing conflict.

Somali nomads of Somalia, Djibouti and Ethiopia

The Cushitic-speaking Somali, numbering about four million, are Muslims. Unlike the Christian cultivators of Ethiopia, living in their well-constructed, circular, mud-and-wattle homes, the Somali nomads form temporary settlements around wells, using tents with wooden frames covered by mats and skins. The settlements are most concentrated in the dry season while in the wet season they disperse as widely as possible to their pastures. Here the young men, who are the traditional fighting and defence force, tend the

Somali nomadic life
The Somali pastoral nomads move over vast distances with their herds, which provide milk and meat and, through their export, imported tea, sugar, clothes and other commodities. The bulk of the camels, which in the dry season can go for two weeks or more without water, are herded by the young men. Low and unreliable rainfall, aggravated by tribal feuds and conflict between Ethiopia and Somalia, make the nomad's lot extremely precarious.

camels. They are often separated by several days' journey from the married men, their wives, daughters and younger children, who remain near permanent wells with the sheep, goats and milch camels.

This separation is reflected both in their social organization and in the role of women. The Somali are organized politically by a combination of patrilineal loyalties and explicit defense agreements. Some groups have developed petty sultanates, but the prevailing pattern is for all the adult males of a group to meet together, when necessary, to determine common policy. Their democratic traditions contrast sharply with the hierarchical system of the Christian Amhara.

Although women are traditionally excluded from these assemblies they nevertheless still exercise a great deal of informal influence. Because they are responsible for the herding of sheep and goats, women enjoy considerable freedom of movement and independence. In urban settings, however, they tend to lead more restrictive lives, unless they have salaried employment. It is in towns particularly that some women succumb to afflictions which are diagnosed as possession by spirits. A standard precipitating situation occurs when a married man is about to negotiate an additional marriage. If his first wife is suddenly possessed by spirits this may entail such expensive therapy that he cannot afford the payments required to secure his new bride.

Although Islam has made Arabic available for centuries as a script, only a minority of Somalis—mainly religious teachers—have used it. Since 1972, the Somali language has been written in a Roman script. The greatest riches of Somali culture are found in the poetry of the nomads, who are, without exaggeration, a nation of bards. Poetic competitions regularly take place and poetry is the most effective medium for political polemic. All the great leaders in Somali history have been poets and orators.

Although war and drought can quickly reduce the Somali nomads to destitute refugees, in good times their valuable livestock not only provides most of their subsistence needs but also, through the export of livestock and produce, contributes to the national economy. However, with the vast difference in salaries between the Horn of Africa and the oil-rich Gulf states, many nomads now join the "muscle drain" to Saudi Arabia and neighboring countries. Other nomads who lost their herds in the 1974 drought have been settled in government-organized cooperatives for both fishing and agriculture.

Amhara highlanders number about 5 million. Their political domination has been tempered by their tendency to absorb other groups, such as the Oromo, through intermarriage. Until the revolution, the Amhara peasants had hereditary rights to till the soil.

The Black Jews, or Falasha, of Ethiopia, number about 50,000. They specialize in ironwork and pottery, and speak a Cushitic language. Ethiopia's strong Judaic legacy led to political links with Israel during Haile Selassie's reign.

The Beja are Muslim pastoralists who, like the Tigre, straddle the border between Eritrea and the Sudan. In alliance with the Tigreans, the warlike Beja have played a vital role in the Eritrean movement seeking independence from Ethiopia.

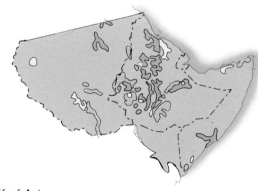

Afro–Asiatic
- Semitic languages (Amarinya, Tigre, Gurage, Arabic, etc.)
- Cushitic languages; Omotic languages; Chadic languages

Niger–Congo
- Fulfulde; Kordofanian languages

Unaffiliated languages
- Nubian languages (Hazara, Midob, etc.)
- Nilotic languages (Jieng, Naath,))
- Other "Nilo-Saharan" languages (Fur, Bongo, Moru, etc.)

Featured people
Somali nomads

Additional peoples

Peoples and languages
Most peoples speak Semitic or Cushitic languages. Apart from some Tigre-speakers in Tigre and Eritrea, most Semitic-speaking Ethiopians are Christians. Muslim speakers of Cushitic languages such as the Oromo, Afar, Saho and Beja are concentrated in the coastal regions. To the south, peoples and languages are very varied; here Nilotic languages and northernmost pockets of Bantu languages are found.

The Oromo number about 10 million and are traditionally pastoral nomads although many have been assimilated by the Amhara of Ethiopia. Their unique system of social organization dictates a rotation of power every eight years between groups of elders and juniors.

Somali nomads, who number about 4 million, herd sheep, goats and camels. Camels are the medium for making marriage payments and compensations for injuries or deaths— 100 camels in the case of a man, 50 for a woman. A herder with 100 camels is considered well-to-do.

Arable land and gardens
- Wheat, barley, maize, millet, teff, sorghum, vegetables, pulses, groundnuts and cotton.

Plantations
- Sugarcane, bananas, coffee and citrus fruits such as grapefruit.

Woods and forests
- Coniferous and broad-leaved trees mainly provide timber, charcoal, paper, gums and resins.

Rough grazing land
- Sheep, goats and camels in arid areas; cattle in better watered areas; some shifting cultivation is practised in this area.

Nonagricultural land
- Desert, areas below sea level, swamps and mountain peaks.

Land use
The well-watered north and the central highlands of Ethiopia are the best agricultural lands in the region, and here wheat, barley, maize, millet, *ensete* (the false banana) and the indigenous cereal *teff* are grown. At lower altitudes coffee is produced for export. To the east and west the land is more arid, and pastoral nomadism is the dominant land use. However, there is some mixed farming in Somalia, particularly along river valleys in the south; sorghum is the staple crop. There are a few commercial plantations, growing sugarcane, bananas and grapefruit.

Map labels: RED SEA, Khartoum, Kassala, Mits'iwa, Aksum, ERITREA, DANAKIL DEPRESSION, SUDAN, Gonder, TIGRE, Gulf of Aden, El Obeid, L. Tana, Magdala, DJIBOUTI, Marra Mts 3071, Blue Nile, ETHIOPIA, Djibouti, Berbera, Harer, ETHIOPIAN HIGHLANDS, Addis Ababa, White Nile, SOMALIA, Juba, Mogadishu, INDIAN OCEAN, Chisimaio

0 — 600 km
0 — 400 miles

North Africa 1

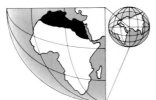

To the Romans this was a fertile colony from which came figs, dates and grain. Armies of conquest have marched across North Africa many times since then, and the sweeping Arab conquests converted the entire region to Islam. Yet, despite centuries of Arabization, proud Berbers in their mountain retreats have kept alive their own language and colorful traditions.

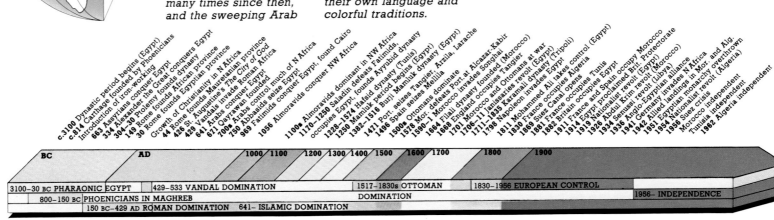

c.3100 Dynastic period begins (Egypt)
c.814 Carthage founded by Phoenicians
Introduction of iron-working
663 Assyrians conquer Egypt
334 Alexander the Great conquers Egypt
304–30 Ptolemy founds dynasty
149 Rome founds African province
30 Rome founds Egyptian province
Growth of Christianity in N Africa
44 Rome founds Mauretanian province
426 St. Augustine's *The City of God*
429 Vandals invade Roman Egypt
641 Arabs conquer Egypt
670s Qayrawan founded
700s Arabs control much of N Africa
750 Abbasids seize Egypt
969 Fatimids found Cairo
1056 Almoravids conquer NW Africa
1100s Almoravids dominant in NW Africa
1170–1250 Saladin defeats Fatimids, occupies Egypt, founds Ayyubid dynasty
1228–1574 Hafsid dynasty (Tunis)
1382–1516 Mamluk period begins (Egypt)
1471 Port. seizes Tangier, Arzila, Larache
1496 Spain seizes Melilla
1500s Ottomans dominate
1517 Burji Mamluk dynasty (Egypt)
1578 Mor. defeats Port. at Alcazar-Kabir
1590–1 Morocco invades western Songhai
1664 England occupies Tangier
1668 France occupies Port at Alcazar-Kabir
1701 Morocco and Ottomans at war
1706–11 Janissaries revolt (Tripoli)
1711–1835 Karamanli dynasty (Tripoli)
1798 Napoleon invades Egypt
1811 Mohammed Ali takes control (Egypt)
1830 France occupies Algeria
1869 Suez Canal opens
1882 Britain occupies Tunis
1881 France and Spain occupy Morocco
1911 France and Spain occupy Morocco
1912 Egypt occupies Egypt
1914 Egypt proclaimed Brit. Protectorate
1919 Nationalist revolt (Egypt)
1926 Abdul Krim revolt (Morocco)
1936 Anglo-Egyptian Alliance
1942 Senussi revolt (Libya)
1942 German invades in Africa
1942 Allied landings in Mor. and Alg.
1951 Egyptian monarchy overthrown
1954 Nationalist revolt (Algeria)
1956 Suez crisis
Morocco independent
Tunisia independent
1962 Algeria independent

BC	AD	1000	1100	1200	1300	1400	1500	1600	1700	1800	1900

3100–30 BC PHARAONIC EGYPT
429–533 VANDAL DOMINATION
1517–1830s OTTOMAN DOMINATION
1830–1956 EUROPEAN CONTROL
800–150 BC PHOENICIANS IN MAGHREB
150 BC–429 AD ROMAN DOMINATION
641– ISLAMIC DOMINATION
1956– INDEPENDENCE

Population by Country
Total: 89 million

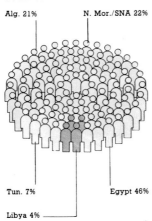

Alg. 21%
N. Mor./SNA 22%
Tun. 7%
Egypt 46%
Libya 4%

Population by Religion

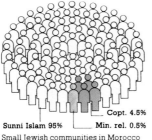

Sunni Islam 95%
Copt. 4.5%
Min. rel. 0.5%

Small Jewish communities in Morocco are all that remain of the large numbers of Jews who once lived in cities throughout the region. Their numbers have been greatly reduced since mass emigration to Palestine began in 1948. Like other minorities the Jews occupied their own quarter in each city.

Isolated evidence of the passage of peoples across the desert survives in the oasis of Tabelbala where descendants of Negro slaves speak Belbali, a dialect of Songhai which is spoken in the Niger river region of Mali, on the other side of the Sahara. Belbali is the only language of black Africa spoken north of the Sahara.

From the time of the first Pharaohs in Egypt (*c.* 3100 BC to 332 BC), North Africa has seen some of the ancient world's most advanced civilizations. The Romans conquered the whole area from 30 BC and it became one of the great grain-producing regions of their empire, but it was the Arab invasion of the seventh and eighth centuries AD that had a longer-lasting effect on North Africa, giving it a common language, Arabic, and a common religion, Islam. Islamic North Africa now bridges two distinct areas: Africa and the Middle East. Although geographically in Africa, in many ways this area identifies itself more with the Islamic world. The people have a traditional self-confidence, based on their Islamic beliefs and the continuity of the Islamic past. European colonialism in the nineteenth and twentieth centuries divided the area between Spain, France, Italy and Britain; this did not result in any mixing through intermarriage but did introduce French and English as second languages in the area.

North Africa contains three very different geographical regions. In the northwest lie the fertile regions of the Maghreb countries—Morocco, Algeria and Tunisia—where the combination of mountains and sea bring an adequate rainfall and a largely Mediterranean climate. To the south, the Sahara takes up most of Algeria, and in central Libya it extends northward almost to the shore of the Mediterranean. In the east, the desert reaches to Egypt and Sudan, which are bisected by the Nile valley, with its fertile banks and alluvial delta.

Through major economic change, the whole of North Africa is now characterized by a sharp contrast between the "modern" minority, involved mainly in mineral production and industrial development, and

The 500,000 Berbers of the Rif are a fiercely independent group of about 20 tribes whose dialect is not always intelligible to other Berber speakers. The irrigated valleys of their rugged, mountainous terrain are fertile and produce grain, citrus fruits, nuts and olives. To increase the land available for agriculture the hillsides are terraced and irrigated. Sheep and goats are herded on the dry hillsides, mainly by the children. The area is densely populated and many men now leave to find work in Europe, mainly in France and Holland, but return for 3 months each winter. On the coast the men fish, usually with nets from boats or the shore.

The underground water supply at Awjilah supports a population of 2,000 people, mainly Arabized Berbers. Most grow grains and vegetables in irrigated gardens, and date palms provide a cash crop. The discovery of oil and the building of a metalled road have brought new prosperity to this isolated oasis.

0 ————— 600km
0 ————— 400miles

Arable land, gardens and orchards
Wheat, maize, rice and cotton along Nile; wheat, barley, olives, grapes, figs and citrus fruits in the Maghreb; dates, wheat and vegetables in oases (not marked).

Woods and forests
Used for timber, firewood, charcoal, paper and cork.

Rough grazing
Sheep, goats and camels.

Nonagricultural land
Desert; occasional grazing.

Land use
North Africa contains three very different regions—the Maghreb, the Sahara and the Nile valley. The coastal plain of the Maghreb has a largely Mediterranean climate and is well-suited to agriculture; cattle are also kept here. In the mountains, sheep are herded on the slopes and vegetables, fruit and grain grown in the valleys. The Sahara, traditionally peopled by groups of nomadic pastoralists, is now a rich source of oil and natural gas. To the east, the desert is bisected by the Nile, and here grains and cotton are cultivated on the fertile soil.

the traditional majority, comprising peasants involved in agriculture. For the minority, oil has made a great economic impact on the area, especially in Libya and Algeria. New industries have developed, but they have not absorbed all the people who have moved into shanty towns around the major cities.

North African cities reflect the new economic environment. Previously they were renowned for their highly developed crafts: leatherwork and metalwork in Fez, carpets in Tunis and goldsmithing in Tripoli. Several cities, notably Fez and Cairo, were great centers of learning, while at the same time they were social centers and markets for the surrounding countryside. Today some traditional cities have been overtaken in size and importance by new towns, such as Casablanca, growing up around modern industry. The lack of employment in such towns has forced many to emigrate to find work: to France and to northern Europe from the Maghreb (meaning "west" or "sunset" in Arabic), and to the oil-rich states of Libya and Saudi Arabia from Egypt and Sudan.

The principal indigenous people of North Africa before the Arab invasion were the Berbers, who show considerable variation in both language and appearance; some have dark hair and eyes, but others have pale skin, green or hazel eyes, and light brown hair. As a result of intermarriage, however, Arab and Berber physical characteristics can no longer be clearly distinguished, and it is primarily the Berber language which separates Berbers from Arabs. In the fertile lowlands, where Arab settlement was concentrated, extensive Arabization occurred, but in the less accessible mountainous regions the Berbers preserved much of their own culture.

Among the cultural differences which can still be discerned are the geometric patterns used by Berbers to decorate their pottery, rugs and blankets—these contrast with the floral designs introduced by the Arabs. Additionally there are vestiges of Berber pre-Islamic religion, syncretized into the practice of Sunni Islam. This syncretized religion is well illustrated by

Unlike most other peoples of the region, the Christian Copts never converted to Islam. Today they form a large minority among the urban people of Egypt. For religious purposes this community uses the Coptic language, a derivative of ancient Egyptian, although they speak Arabic in their daily lives.

Awqaf, land held as religious endowments, existed in Egypt until the 19th century when European notions of landed property and the introduction of cash crops forced many people off the land, disrupting rural communities and swelling the cities of Cairo and Alexandria with a new poverty-stricken urban proletariat.

A Moroccan souk
The larger *souks* (markets) attract traders from outside the area selling utensils and luxuries, as well as specialists such as dentists, fortune tellers and smiths. The smaller *souks* provide an outlet for surplus crops grown by the Berbers. Each *souk* has an appointed official to check weights and measures being used. The different vendors are divided according to their produce. Butchers tend to be sited away from other stallholders because they are traditionally associated with the presence of evil spirits. Markets that have been established exclusively for women still exist in many areas.

Peoples and languages
Arab language, culture and religion are the dominant features of North Africa. The two major groups of peoples are the Arabs and the Berbers, the indigenous people of the Maghreb before the Arab invasions of the 7th and 8th centuries. Language is the main distinction between Arab and Berber today, although there are some cultural differences. Unlike the Maghreb, Egypt is completely Arabized. Tribal structures have been largely broken down, because the population has been under firm central control since the Middle Ages, and most tribes were forcibly settled early in the 19th century. In northern Sudan people of mixed Arab and Negro ancestry are found.

Indo-European

▨ Romance language (Spanish)

Hamito-Semitic

▨ Semitic language (Arabic)

☐ Berber

Unaffiliated languages

☐ Nubian

▨ Songhai (Belbali)

Featured peoples

▨ Berbers of Awjilah Rifi

Additional peoples

▤

The fertile land on the banks of the Nile has supported glittering ancient civilizations. Today over 50 million people depend on the grains and vegetables grown on the rich silt along its banks. Most speak Arabic, although in the south live Nubian speakers, descendants of the original inhabitants of the Middle Nile.

the Berbers of the Rif, a rebellious and independent people who were fierce opponents of Spanish colonialism in northern Morocco. Their traditions appear to have a good chance of survival, but for the Berbers of the Awjilah oasis in Libya, oil, a new road and the transistor radio seem set to complete the centuries-long process of Arabization.

Berbers of the Rif
The Rifi, who number about half a million people, live in rugged mountainous terrain, isolated from the rest of Morocco by sharp escarpments and deep valleys, which form natural defenses and a place of refuge. Among the dense population in this confined region, a definite social and political identity has developed. The Rifi dialect of Berber, for example, is not always intelligible to people speaking other dialects of the language and they sometimes get round the difficulty by using Arabic to converse with other Berber groups.

Rifi society is based primarily on kinship—territorial considerations having a secondary but important position. The hierarchical structure of their society is divided into three main levels. Overall, there are about twenty *qabilas* (tribes), and these vary from the very small (about 7,000 people) up to the very large (30,000 people). Each *qabila* lives within a defined area and is divided patrilineally into *rba'a* (clans); the *rba'a* are in turn made up of extended families within a number of *dshar* (local communities). In precolonial times, the basic political assumption in each area was that the nearest community of comparable size was probably hostile, and there existed a more or less formal arrangement of alliances, *liffs*, between each community and its next neighbor but one, so that help could be provided if feuding broke out.

In fact fighting was generally avoided through councils of notables at each of the three levels. Less important men formed the councils of *dshar* and took care of everyday problems—irrigation, minor crimes and grazing rights. Notables in the *rba'a* dealt with matters such as major thefts, fighting and running the markets. The most important and powerful notables met in the council of the *qabila* to deal with only the most serious crimes—murder and adultery. The council maintained order by levying fines on criminals and, in cases of murder, by confiscating their property and forcing them into exile. If the fines were not collected or not paid, however, then feuding might start, with the possibility of many deaths. Today, although northern Morocco is administered by the central government in Rabat and policed by a rural *gendarmerie*, local affairs are still informally under the control of the traditional councils of notables.

This degree of local autonomy is reflected in the Rifi laws of land ownership. Land owned by the mosques, *awqaf*, is made up of donations from pious individuals and the income from the sale of its produce is then used for religious purposes, such as education. Land is also owned collectively by the *dshar*, when it is usually used for pasture, or by individuals, when it is often farmed on a share-cropping basis. Land is rarely

Alexandria
Port Said
Suez Canal
Damanhûr
Giza
Suez
Cairo
Beni Suef
Gulf of Suez
ilah
OASIS
El Minya
Mallawi
Red Sea
EGYPT
Qena
Aswân
Lake Nasser
SUDAN

North Africa 2

transferred to people outside the group and this means that women are often deprived of their rights of inheritance under Islamic law (one half the share of male inheritors); for the same reason marriage is often confined within the clan.

Such deviations from the letter of Islamic law are paralleled by differences in religious practices. Like other North African Muslims, the Rifi depend heavily upon *marabuts* (local saints), whose powers are based on *baraka*, their own personal holiness or that inherited from their ancestors. These holy men function as mediators in disputes, as healers and as casters out of the *jinn* (malevolent spirits) in whom all Rifi believe. When they die, their tombs may become the object of local pilgrimages. These practices are integrated with Islam, the Rifi being devout Muslims; although not everyone prays the required five times a day, all fast during the month of Ramadan.

Despite their inferior social position and the denial of their land-ownership rights in Islamic law, women preserve a considerable amount of power for themselves. This is done through involvement in magic, medicine and fortune telling, and also in some parts through the existence of a secondary system of women's markets, which men are not permitted to enter. These not only provide a place for exchange of goods, but also for arranging marriages. Much of traditional medical practice is based on protecting people from the *jinn* and the "evil eye," particularly pregnant women and recently born infants, for whom great precautions are taken. The placenta and umbilical cord of a child are securely and secretly buried, to prevent the dogs from eating them, which it is believed would cause barrenness.

One particular series of rites, peculiar to the Rifi, reflects the importance of agriculture and the dependence, in a dry area, on irrigation. The timely arrival of the rain is a matter of considerable importance, and should it be late there are two rituals that are followed—one is carried out by the men and the other by the women, and both are highly formal. For the men's ceremony, all the men of a *dshar* go to the mosque and sacrifice a goat. They then make a collective offering of such foods as olive oil and sugar, while the goat is being cooked. After the men have eaten the goat, they take off their shoes and turbans, turn their *jillabas* (ankle-length robes) inside out and put them on back to front. They then walk around the mosque seven times in a counterclockwise direction, chanting a formula asking for rain. The ritual begins at noon and lasts for five hours; it is held every day until the rain arrives. Turning the *jillaba* inside out symbolizes the idea of turning the sky inside out, bringing rain.

In the second ritual, unmarried girls take a long-handled shovel of the type used for putting bread into ovens, and dress it up in fine clothes and necklaces. It is then called the Bride of the Rain, and is taken from house to house while a verse asking for rain is recited. In some places the Bride is then taken to the mosque, and the verse is chanted while walking round it counterclockwise. In both rituals the verses are chanted in Arabic, not Berber, Arabic being the language of religion, even in a Berber-speaking area.

Berbers of Awjilah oasis

Awjilah, although isolated and surrounded by desert, has always been important as an oasis at the crossroads of two historic trade routes across the Sahara—between the Mediterranean and tropical Africa, and between Egypt and the Maghreb. The trans-Saharan trade declined in the nineteenth century and was almost destroyed by the Italian invasion of Libya in 1911, but the discovery of oil in the 1960s and the building of a metaled road in the 1970s brought new prosperity to Awjilah which is now a staging post for the desert oil fields to the south. Thus its inhabitants have been exposed to a series of outside cultural influences, especially Arab ones.

Awjilah is surrounded largely by level stony plains, and its climate is harsh. Temperatures reach 60°C (140°F) on summer days and fall to 16°C (60°F) at night. The oasis lies in a depression, between 0.75 and 1.5 kilometers (½ mile–1 mile) wide, and running 16 kilometers (10 miles) northwest to southwest. It is sited over an underground water supply, which supports a population of around 2,000 people living in a main village and four dispersed hamlets.

The population is divided among four *qabilas*. The *qabilas* are not localized and depend on patrilineal descent. Each *qabila*, which is divided into lineages, is led by a *shaykh*, theoretically chosen by consensus among the lineages and rotating between them—in fact, strong men have emerged in the past to dominate the oasis. Power now lies mainly in the hands of the official appointees.

Although there is almost no rainfall, many Berbers grow crops in and around Awjilah by utilizing the water table, between 6 and 12 meters (20–40 feet) below the surface, to irrigate their sandy gardens. Most gardens are very small, around 200 square meters (240 square yards), but two crops a year are possible, especially now that mechanized pumping systems have stabilized the water supply.

Light agricultural work, such as picking vegetables and weeding, is done by women, who also prepare the meals and milk the goats and sheep. The women of Awjilah are, however, very secluded and spend much of their time indoors, as a result of male attitudes which seek to protect not only the women's virtues but also the honor of their menfolk. Women do not, for example, go to the mosque or shop in the market area. This is done by men, who perform all the heavy agricultural work, store keeping and teaching as well as

A place of worship and study
Muslims are called to prayer five times a day—a constant reminder of the presence of God and of the equality of all in the sight of God. The main prayers of the week take place on a Friday, when the faithful go to the mosque. Traditionally, the mosque is not only a place of worship but also an educational center. Famous mosque universities exist in Cairo (al-Azhar, founded 972), Tunis (Zaytuna, 9th century) and Fez (Qarawiyyin, 859).

Camels—beasts of value
Camel markets are held throughout the region; at the large weekly camel market in Nabeul, Tunisia, horses, mules and donkeys as well as camels are bought and sold. Although motorized transport is now widespread in North Africa, the camel remains a valuable animal, used primarily for short hauls, especially in regions too arid for mules. Despite tough competition from Algerian lorries, Tuareg nomads are still able to supply the Sahel region with North African dates and salt mined in the Sahara, exchanging these goods for grain—as recently as 1976 a camel train of 200 animals was seen crossing the desert. Camels are also used for plowing and their hair is made into blankets.

working in the oil fields. As a result of their seclusion, some older women, unexposed to outside cultural influences, still speak Berber, although the majority of Awjilah's population speak Arabic.

In the choice of marriage partners for their children, women are very influential, as it is they who decide who is acceptable. Suitability as a potential bride encompasses virginity, good reputation, good health and ability to carry out domestic duties. A potential groom must be able to provide for a family and to maintain his economic position. Marriage is usually within the *qabila*, and often within the lineage. Marriage between cousins is common, in order to keep property intact, and, as with the Rifi, women hardly ever inherit land.

Girls first marry at about fourteen years old and men at about twenty-five years old. Fairly modest bride-wealth is paid to the bride's family, who repay most of it in the event of the wife leaving her husband and returning to her parents' home. About one in four marriages do end in divorce, a common reason being that the marriage is childless—barrenness always being assumed to be the woman's fault.

Although devout Sunni Muslims, wedding festivities reflect traditional Berber practices. The festivities last for seven days and during this period the bride and groom never appear together in public. On *laylat al-hanna* (night of the henna), the bride and her female relatives have their hands and feet dyed red, using henna. The bride literally lets her hair down, and the other women sing and dance to her. On the wedding night itself, an egg is cracked as the bride crosses the threshold of her new home, where her virginity is then tested. Virginity is proved by bloodstains on a white cloth, which is exhibited to show the bride's purity.

The wedding ends with at least three days of dancing. At first the men dance alone, with a highly sexual dance form. The women meanwhile are in another room with the bride. The women then send in one of their number—often the groom's younger, virgin sister, his younger cousin or the daughter of a neighbor. She is dressed in a white blouse, black skirt, red stockings and a veil and carries a white baton. The baton is held in both hands over her head while she dances by twisting her hips from side to side, shuffling up the line of male dancers on her heels. When the dance is finished, one of the males begins a highly sexual song about her, in which he feigns overwhelming emotion. Should this song become too impertinent or offensive, the girl may strike him over the head with the baton. Once the song is over she returns to the women's party. She or another dancer may return two or three times during the evening. The whole dance is highly symbolic of the importance of female honor, the white stick representing a physical check to the suggestiveness of the men.

Although, as with the Berbers of the Rif, religion is as strong as ever, the Awjilah oasis is now changing. Better communications with the coast, state-run education, employment on the oil fields and the use of Arabic as the predominant language are encouraging the demise of Berber, a process which is being completed through the influence of the radio.

Popular culture
Every day, from early morning until sundown, people congregate in the main square of Marrakesh to watch jugglers, snake charmers, acrobats and dancers, and to listen to story tellers acting out their tales.

Protection from the sun
By building their dwellings around a sunken courtyard, the troglodyte Arabs of the Tunisian Martmata mountains are able to protect themselves from the extreme heat of the desert sun.

Marriage—Rifi style
On the third day of the marriage festivities the bride, heavily veiled, rides to the groom's house. If the girl proves not to be a virgin, she will probably be sent home and her bridewealth returned. Marriages are arranged by the fathers of the bride and the groom, and the bridewealth is paid by the father or family of the groom to the father of the bride. For remarried women the amounts are considerably less than for first-time brides. An unmarried woman can be distinguished by her embroidered headband tied at the back, with its widest part above the middle of the forehead. A married woman wears cords of black wool attached to her hair at the nape of the neck and hanging down her back in two braids.

Saharan Africa

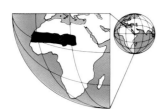

The arid expanses of the Sahara cut across North Africa to create a daunting barrier between the fertile Mediterranean coastlands and the dense equatorial forests. In this barren terrain,

drought, heat and violent sandstorms make human life all but impossible. Carving out a way of life despite such hardships, resilient and ruthless nomads have dominated this region for centuries.

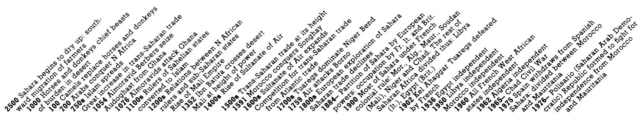

| BC | AD | 1000 | 1100 | 1200 | 1300 | 1400 | 1500 | 1600 | 1700 | 1800 | 1900 |

700–1500 RISE OF AFRICAN EMPIRES AND TRANS-SAHARAN TRADE

1600–1800 EUROPEAN COMMERCIAL COMPETITION

1800–1956 EUROPEAN OCCUPATION

1960– INDEPENDENCE DECLINE OF TRANS-SAHARAN TRADE

Population by Country
Total: 4 million

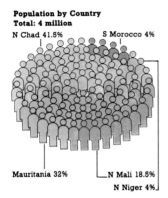

N Chad 41.5%   S Morocco 4%
Mauritania 32%   N Mali 18.5%
N Niger 4%

Population by Religion

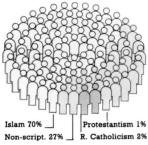

Islam 70%   Protestantism 1%
Non-script. 27%   R. Catholicism 2%

Precious moisture
The valleys of seasonal streams in the Aïr region support plants such as the acacia tree, a vital source of fodder for the herds of the Southern Tuareg.

The Sahara desert is one of the least hospitable regions on earth. Only along its southern fringes, known as the Sahel, and in highland regions such as Ahaggar, is there enough rainfall to support human life. Since few areas are suitable for agriculture, the herding of goats and camels is the primary economic activity, traditionally combined with trading in such goods as salt, grain and dates. In the past another major source of income was raiding and exacting tribute from passing caravans, but stronger central governments have put an end to these activities, while the introduction of motorized transport has undermined the caravan trade. A further blow has been dealt to desert peoples such as the Tuareg by the severe droughts in the Sahel, and their hierarchical society and unique cultural traditions, developed in the isolation of this hostile and forbidding environment, are now rapidly disappearing.

The areas of highest rainfall in the Sahara are the mountains of Ahaggar in southern Algeria, and those of Tibesti in northern Chad, which both reach heights of 3,000 meters (10,000 feet), and are relatively well populated. In these mountains natural rock water holes and small areas of cultivable land in the valley bottoms are relatively common. The mountains of the Adrar des Iforas (Mali) and Aïr ou Azbine (Niger), although not as high, are also fairly well populated. As one moves south from these mountainous areas into the country around the Niger Bend, and the plains of central and southern Niger, the rainfall, vegetation and population all increase. This same population pattern is found throughout the Sahel. In Mauritania, for example, 80 percent of the country's population lives in the south of the country near the Sénégal River.

In the Middle Ages most of the western and southern Sahara fell within the domains of the great Sudanic empires—Ghana, Mali and Songhay. These, however, were gradually wiped out by the successive invasions of Berber and Arab peoples from the north. The Berber-speaking Almoravids invaded the western Sahara in the eleventh century and other peoples, probably Berber speaking, came into the region during the following two centuries. Beginning in the fifteenth century, there was a further influx, this time of Arabic-speaking peoples, into what is now Mauritania.

By the beginning of the twentieth century, nearly all the land around the Niger Bend, much of Mali and Niger, as well as southern Algeria, was completely dominated by Berber-speaking Tuareg. Even in areas such as Aïr the Tuareg influence overshadows the original Hausa population. The same general demise of the Negroid population took place in the Libyan Sahara at the end of the eighteenth century, and now only the Teda of the Tibesti testify to the earlier dominance of Negroid peoples in the Sahara.

In the nineteenth century a large part of this region was colonized by France, resulting in many economic, social and political changes, especially in regard to the relationship between noble and subordinate tribes and peoples. At the purely economic level, raiding was banned, nomads were confronted by administrative boundaries, and the influx of agriculturists, as for example in Ahaggar, was encouraged.

Since independence, Mauritania, Mali, Chad, and to a lesser extent Niger, have all been characterized by conflict between the northern, predominantly Caucasoid, Islamic populations and the predominantly Negroid Christian south. In Chad this conflict has erupted in a festering war which has dragged on since 1960. Meanwhile, the imposition of effective government and modern legislation has further eroded the power of the once dominant Tuareg. Their reduced status, both economically and politically, is well illustrated by the Kel Ahaggar, once reputed to be the fiercest of all the Tuareg tribes.

The Tuareg of Ahaggar

The Tuareg of the Ahaggar massif, known as the Kel Ahaggar, number about 6,000. When they were finally defeated by the French in 1902 the total population of Ahaggar numbered about 5,000, comprising about 3,000 to 3,500 Tuareg (nobles and vassals) with about 1,000 to 1,500 of their slaves, and about 500 Harratin cultivators, who, like the slaves, were predominantly Negroid. At that time the Harratin had only been in the area for about forty years. By the 1970s the Ahaggar population was over 20,000, with the Kel Ahaggar being outnumbered by Harratin, ex-slaves, and other recent immigrants, by at least two to one.

At the turn of the century, the Kel Ahaggar were heavily dependent on pastoralism. Goat herds, sometimes with a few sheep, were the domain of the vassals, who were generally referred to as *Kel Ulli* (people of the goats); through various forms of tribute, they provided the nobility with meat, milk and skins. This subsistence was augmented by trade with nearby oases which supplied dates and grain. The economy was also supplemented by hunting and the raiding activities of the nobility.

At that time the contribution of the Harratin gardens was small, and the salt trade was not a vital part of the economy as it was for other Tuareg groups—indeed, the Ahaggar salt trade only began in 1896. Under French rule, however, raiding and warfare were prohibited and the Kel Ahaggar increasingly relied on trade, transporting locally mined salt to southern Niger, where they exchanged it for millet. By the 1920s the caravan trade was organized on a regular basis and was a crucial part of the Kel Ahaggar's economy.

By the 1950s both nobles and vassals faced economic difficulties, largely due to a decline in the rate of exchange between salt and millet. Thus they turned increasingly to the exploitation of the Harratin, who had been encouraged to settle in Ahaggar in greater numbers by the French, and who cultivated the land for the Kel Ahaggar on a contract basis. Most Harratin were reduced to abject poverty, and up to one hundred of them died each year from malnutrition.

Since 1962 the general policy of the Algerian government has been to break the power of the Ahaggar nomads. Slavery was abolished and the gardens were reorganized on a cooperative basis, with land being declared "free" to those who worked it. As a result the Kel Ahaggar became a political minority more or less overnight. At the same time, border disputes with Niger resulted in a virtual termination of the salt caravans. These factors, in conjunction with the onset of fairly prolonged drought conditions, forced most Kel Ahaggar to abandon their nomadic existence. Today all nobles are completely sedentarized and most vassals are now only seminomadic. Many cultivate gardens alongside former slaves and Harratin, something that was unthinkable a generation ago.

The traditional form of political organization among all Tuareg groups was founded on the "drum group," which consisted of a noble descent group and a number of vassal descent groups. Under French colonial rule the political structure of the drum group was retained and vassals continued to make their tributary payments to the supreme chief, Amenukal, through whom the French governed. Today, the Amenukal has no effective political power, but the descent groups

still provide the basic framework of social organization. Vassal groups have clearly defined territories in which they traditionally held pastoral rights.

Descent group membership is reckoned matrilineally, as is succession to political office, but inheritance is patrilineal in accordance with Koranic law. Because of their traditional class interests the organization of the nobility emphasized matrilineality, while the organization of the vassals was basically patrilineal. Among the nobility the importance of matrilineality itself is diminishing, as the traditional structure of society gives way to more individualistic life styles.

Many of the basic Tuareg attitudes and traditions have survived however. Prestige and position remain of paramount importance, and, as in the past, they are expressed through nuances of physical pose and gesture, as well as through speech. Tuareg men still wear the veil, covering their mouths in the presence of strangers, or their parents-in-law. The women go unveiled, but wear a headcloth which is used to cover the mouth in similar circumstances.

People of the veil
Nothing is wasted in the desert. After this Ahaggar Tuareg has drunk his tea, the leaves will be given to the camel to eat. "Tuareg" is an Arabic word which may derive from the root *terek*, meaning "those abandoned by God," since these nomads have a reputation for not being particularly devout Muslims. A more likely explanation is that it derives from *Targa*, a region of the Sahara now called Fezzan. In fact the Tuareg call themselves *Kel Tagelmoust*, "people of the veil." The veil, worn only by the men, symbolically distances the wearer from others or indicates deference. It is also believed that covering the mouth keeps out *Kel Asouf*, evil spirits that haunt dark, lonely places. Harratins and ex-slaves of the Tuareg also wear veils.

The Moors are divided into the *Bidani*, whose name means "Whites", and the subservient *Sudani*, who are of Negroid origin. The Bidani themselves are split into the *Hassani* warriors who hold earthly power, and the *Zawiya* who are the spiritual guardians.

The Tekna are a large tribe of Arabized Berber nomads who inhabit northern Mauritania and southern Morocco. Some of the Tekna now labor in the iron ore mines in northern Mauritania, but most are still nomadic or seminomadic.

The lives of the Northern Tuareg have changed dramatically, particularly for the nobles, but many vassals still breed goats. Their camps follow traditional patterns, with 2–6 tents housing 15–20 people. The camp herd is tended by the women.

Arable land, gardens and rough grazing

◻ Barley in Western Sahara, millet and vegetables around the Senegal and Niger rivers; there are also some gardens in highland areas and around oases (not marked).

Rough grazing

◻ Camels, goats and sheep; some cattle in south Mauritania.

Nonagricultural land

◻ Desert; occasional grazing.

Land use
Most of the region is arid and remains uninhabited except when rare rain provides nomads with temporary grazing. In mountainous areas. notably the Ahaggar, there is greater rainfall and even snow. These mountains are populated by pastoralists and some cultivators, who grow wheat, barley, sorghum, tomatoes, and other vegetables. On the southern fringes of the Sahara, known as the Sahel, rainfall and vegetation increase. Pastoralism is still predominant here, but subsistence farming is also possible around the rivers Senegal and Niger. In scattered oases throughout the region dates, wheat and vegetables are grown.

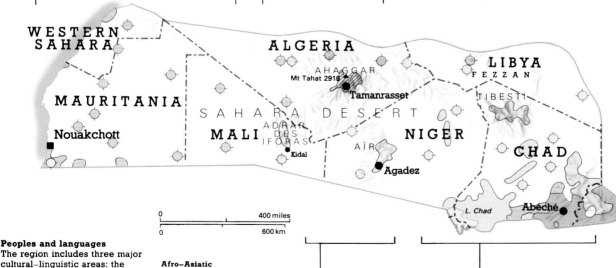

WESTERN SAHARA

ALGERIA

LIBYA

FEZZAN

MAURITANIA

AHAGGAR
Mt Tahat 2918
Tamanrasset

TIBESTI

Nouakchott

S A H A R A   D E S E R T

ADRAR DES IFORAS

MALI

NIGER

AÏR

CHAD

Kidal

Agadez

Abéché

L. Chad

0 ——————— 400 miles
0 ——————— 600 km

Peoples and languages
The region includes three major cultural–linguistic areas: the predominantly Arabic-speaking and Arabized tribes, known as the Moors, to the west; the Berber-speaking Tuareg who inhabit Niger, Mali and southern Algeria; and the Teda (Tebu) in the Tibesti and Borku regions to the east, who are of Negroid origin and whose language is related to the Kanuri and Kanembu languages spoken around Lake Chad.

Afro–Asiatic

◻ Semitic language (Arabic)

◻ Berber language (Tamasheq). Chadic language (Hausa)

Unaffiliated languages

◻ East Saharan languages (Teda, Kanembu, etc.)
◻ Other "Nilo–Saharan" languages (Maba, Tamo, etc.)

Featured people

▨ Tuareg of Ahaggar

There are 6 Southern Tuareg groups who, like the 2 Northern Tuareg groups, speak *Tamasheq*, a Berber dialect with its own traditional alphabet, known as *Tifinagh*, possibly of Phoenician origin. The Tuareg have never formed a united kingdom.

The Teda, descendants of the ancient Negroid inhabitants of the Sahara, number about 22,000. Half live in the Tibesti, and half live south of the desert in Chad and Sudan. Like the Tuareg, the Tibesti Teda are divided into noble and vassal groups.

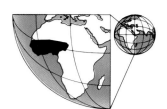

North of the Equator, the African continent bulges out westward into the Atlantic, producing a southern belt of humid tropical forest and a zone of arid savanna to the north.

Here live one third of all Africa's people. In the north, once rich from trade in ivory and gold, many now expect drought and famine, while in the south the forest people work their fertile lands.

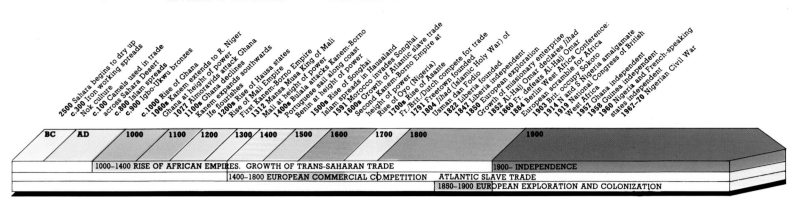

BC | AD | 1000 | 1100 | 1200 | 1300 | 1400 | 1500 | 1600 | 1700 | 1800 | 1900

1000–1400 RISE OF AFRICAN EMPIRES. GROWTH OF TRANS-SAHARAN TRADE

1400–1800 EUROPEAN COMMERCIAL COMPETITION   ATLANTIC SLAVE TRADE

1900– INDEPENDENCE

1850–1900 EUROPEAN EXPLORATION AND COLONIZATION

West Africa has the longest history of contact with Europe of any part of Africa, except the Mediterranean littoral, and it contains more than 30 percent of the total population of Africa. It is composed of two main geographical and ecological zones, which run east to west. The savanna zone extends from the southern Saharan borderlands, often known as the Sahel, down to the tropical rain forest zone of the Atlantic coastlands. Between the two zones there are considerable differences in crops and means of communication. The northern savanna or Sahel is dry for much of the year, so that droughts and famine are frequent. The forest zone has heavy annual rainfall, so it is rich and fertile, but livestock, especially cattle, are not as important as they are in the north, owing to tsetse fly. These flies transmit a serious disease, tripanosomiasis, in both humans and cattle; the common name for the human disease is sleeping sickness. In the north both

Population by Country
Total: 134 million

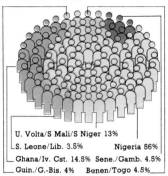

U. Volta/S Mali/S Niger 13%
S. Leone/Lib. 3.5%   Nigeria 56%
Ghana/Iv. Cst. 14.5% Sene./Gamb. 4.5%
Guin./G.-Bis. 4%   Benen/Togo 4.5%

Population by Religion

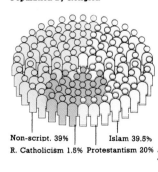

Non-script. 39%   Islam 39.5%
R. Catholicism 1.5% Protestantism 20%

Numbering about 2 million, the Wolof are an important Muslim people of Senegal and the Gambia. Traditionally agriculturists of the savanna region, they have become a highly educated, wealthy and largely urbanized people who control much of modern Senegalese economic and political life.

The Fulbe, who number over 7 million, have migrated across the whole of the savanna. They are known by a variety of names. Fulani is the Hausa and common English name for them. They often act as herdsmen for other peoples of the area, including the Hausa and the neighboring Wolof.

The Dogon, numbering about 250,000, live in the remote mountainous areas of southeast Mali and are skilled farmers and weavers. Their densely clustered villages are built in the shelter of formidable rock faces, where they took refuge from the powerful societies situated in the Niger valley.

Arable land, gardens and rough grazing
Millet, sorghum, yams, rice, maize, cowpeas, vegetables; cotton and peanuts grown for cash in north; cattle, goats and sheep are kept.

Plantations and orchards
Coffee, cocoa, oil palms, citrus fruits, kola-nuts, rubber.

Woods and forests
Mahogany and other hardwoods; rice fields and scattered plantations of cocoa and oil palms; also gardens growing root crops.

Rough grazing
Goats, sheep and cattle; some subsistence farming.

SENEGAL
Dakar
THE GAMBIA
Banjul
GUINEA-BISSAU
Bissau
MALI
Bamako
GUINEA
Conakry
UPPER VOLTA
Ouagadougou
SIERRA LEONE
Freetown
IVORY COAST
GHANA
BENI[N]
TOGO
LIBERIA
Monrovia
L. Volta
Kumasi
Porto Novo
Abidjan
VOLTA DAM
Lomé
Sekondi
Accra
Takoradi
Nia[...]

ATLANTIC OCEAN

Grain Coast
Ivory Coast
Gold Coast
Slave C[oast]

0   400 km
0   300 miles

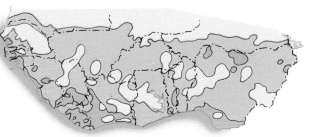

Land use
Cassava and yams are the staples in the forest zone except in the far west and the Niger valley where rice is more important. In the southern part of the savanna zone, yams are the staple crop; in the north millet and sorghum take over.

The one million Mende are farmers in the rain forest regions of Sierra Leone. Although divided into many chiefdoms, the real power is held by the so-called "secret societies," which control their members' social behavior. Today, Mende leaders are among the most powerful politicians in the country.

The Asante are the most numerous of the Akan peoples. Most are farmers who grow yams, oil palms and other forest foods as staples. They export cocoa, gold and timber. They have a rich history and culture; their matrilineal clans are presided over by the Asantehene from the central town of Kumasi.

Life-supporting technology
The peoples of the Sahel rely heavily on the rainy season. To guard against the threat of drought the relief agencies have built wells and lakes. The Volta Dam has been built to create one of the biggest man-made lakes in the world, irrigating 178,000 hectares (440,000 acres) of land.

The Hausa are grain farmers and traders who were converted to Islam in the 14th century. Although most Hausa live in villages, their society has always centered on important towns, notably Kano. Learning is greatly valued and there are many highly skilled craftsmen found in urban areas.

Niger–Congo

Niger–Congo languages (Fulbe, Yoruba, Ewe, Asante, etc.)

Afro–Asiatic

Chadic languages (Hausa, etc.); Berber

Unaffiliated languages

East Saharan languages

Songhai

Mande languages

Featured peoples

Igbo, Asante, Hausa

Additional peoples

Peoples and languages
West Africa is one of the most linguistically complex areas in the world, containing hundreds of separate individual languages. All the states in the area retain a major European language for official and educational purposes since today's postcolonial political boundaries bear little relation to the distribution of either the peoples or their languages. Nigeria alone has several hundred languages within its borders. However, most languages in the area belong to two great "families," or areas of wider affinity. The languages of the southern area (known as Niger-Congo) include Fula, spoken by the Fulbe people throughout the region, Wolof in Senegal, Temne in Sierra Leone, Dogon in Mali, Mossi in Upper Volta, Senufo in the Ivory Coast and Mali, and the so-called "Kwa" languages of the forest belt. The latter include the Akan languages of Ghana and the Ivory Coast, Ewe and Fon to their east, and Yoruba and Igbo in Nigeria. Languages of the northern area of wider affinity (known as Afro-Asiatic or Hamito-Semitic) include Hausa, one of the two most widely spoken languages of black Africa. Languages that fall outside the two areas include the Mande languages in the west and Songhai from the middle Niger.

The Fulbe are seminomadic pastoralists who are widely distributed in West Africa. They live interspersed with the sedentary Hausa with whom they are closely linked, both historically and economically. Since the Fulbe conquered the Hausa in the last century, most Hausa emirs are of Fulbe descent.

The Ewe, of Ghana, Togo and Benin, number about one million. Most are fishermen. They are divided into many small chiefdoms, but they are essentially egalitarian in outlook. Almost half are Christians, the remainder observing the traditional religion.

The Igbo are successful intensive farmers who grow a wide range of crops. They are renowned for their trading and entrepreneurial talents and have migrated all over Nigeria and beyond in search of opportunity. They retain strong links with their home villages through migrants' associations.

The 12 million Yoruba live in the forest belt and grow yams and root crops as staples; cocoa is the main cash crop. They are divided into many kingdoms, each with a sacred king. Today these kings are nationally important political figures. Women, as traders, are wealthy and have high status.

the open savanna and rivers provide easy and quick means of communication, and there has always been much movement of peoples from the south, through the Sahel, and from there across the Sahara to northern Africa. Communications along the forest zone have proved more difficult: there are few natural harbors and until quite recently, with the arrival of Europeans, the sea was hardly used as a means of travel.

The patterns of settlement in both zones have always

included urban centers as well as scattered villages, and large towns such as Kumasi and Kano have been a marked feature of West African society. They have been centers for long-distance trade and the seats of kingdoms that have drawn on the surrounding areas for their goods, whether gold, kola, ivory or slaves.

The cultural history of the West African peoples is a complex one; it has been determined both by ecological variations and by the economic and political institutions associated with trade. The earliest West African states were in the savanna zone; their inhabitants were essentially middlemen, trading gold and slaves from the forest zone for salt, weapons, horses and metal goods from the Mediterranean countries. From the seventh century onward, wealthy and powerful empires were established by Muslim rulers. Arabic was used as a trade language, standing armies protected the caravan routes, and weaker peoples provided taxes, soldiers and slaves. From the fifteenth century, however, the appearance of European traders saw the rise of new trading states in the forest zone. Four centuries later the Europeans, by a series of colonial wars, took control of the inland trade; the growth of cities, industrial centers, plantations and modern transport became concentrated in the forest zone. This development gave the southern peoples the opportunity to grow into new independent nations in the mid-twentieth century.

Today the ethnic picture remains a complex one, in that linguistic divisions do not correspond to political or national ones. There has also always been much movement and intermingling of peoples from their original homelands. Of the many hundreds of languages in West Africa, more people speak Hausa than any other, and it is a language with a long written tradition, using either Arabic or Roman script. Hausa is widely spoken by traders and serves in many areas as a *lingua franca*.

Most of the savanna peoples, such as the Hausa, are Muslims or have been under strong Muslim influence for a long time. They are thereby distinct from the non-Muslim peoples of the forest zone, such as the Igbo and Asante. Except for Arabs in some parts of the savanna zone, and Lebanese and Syrians along the coast, non-West African peoples are very few.

Hausa of the savanna zone

The Hausa, who number some fifteen million, live mainly in villages in the dry savanna country of northern Nigeria and southern Niger. Most of the Hausa are sedentary farmers, who produce surpluses large enough to support a densely settled population; many others are craft specialists, such as weavers, ironworkers, leatherworkers and silversmiths.

In addition to grains, the Hausa grow other subsistence crops and cash crops such as cotton and peanuts; all agricultural work is done by the men, who also raise cattle, horses, donkeys and chickens. Sheep and goats are tended by the younger children. Women pound, thresh and winnow the grain and exchange foods in the market, while men trade the livestock.

The Hausa are divided into a series of autonomous emirates, each of which has a complex bureaucratic organization. A markedly hierarchical system of social stratification exists, especially in towns: there are chiefs of many degrees, officials of noble lineages, commoners and former slaves. The nobles wield great authority and have charge of various bureaucratic functions. The chiefs, officials and commoners are Hausa, but those of slave descent are non-Hausa.

As most Hausa are Muslims, marriage follows Islamic rules; cross-cousin marriages are the preferred form. The groom's father provides the bridewealth for the first wife, the groom having to provide it himself for any subsequent wives. Men remain in the villages of their birth, and the wives have to move in and live communally, although the men and women eat separately. In some noble families women may be kept in purdah, and even in some modern families and in towns, a husband and wife are not permitted to be seen together in public. Divorce, which can be sought by either party, is frequent, divorced women becoming courtesans until remarriage.

The Hausa have been closely linked with the Fulbe, or Fulani, who are pastoralists and who conquered them in the eighteenth and nineteenth centuries. The two peoples have developed a symbiotic relationship; for example the Fulbe cattle provide manure for the Hausa grain farmers. However, some Hausa known as the Maguzawa were not converted by the Fulbe and have thus retained their pre-Islamic religion.

Igbo of the forest zone

The traditional homeland of the Igbo (or Ibo) is on the thickly forested tableland that lies east of the Niger river in southern Nigeria. Most of the ten million Igbo live there, the others having migrated throughout the rest of Nigeria and beyond to take up jobs as traders, clerks and teachers.

The Igbo, who have a very high population density, are highly skilled intensive farmers whose main crops are yams, cocoyams, cassava and palm oil (an export crop). Foodstuffs such as maize, beans, okra, red pepper and gourds are also produced, and the Igbo are self-sufficient as regards basic foods. Yams are cultivated mostly by the men, the women tending the other crops. Any surplus is traded, mainly by the women, for cash, although barter often enters into transactions between kin.

The basic social unit is the village, occupied by a cluster of patrilineal kin in individual compounds. Each compound might consist of a man, his wives and children, his widowed mother, and his younger brothers and sisters. Land is owned by the households, within the area of tenure of the village. The compound head commands the labor of the compound members to work on his land in return for representation and protection. Traditional authority of the compound head has, however, been undermined by Christianity, modern education and the migration of young Igbo men and women to the towns.

Some dozen or more villages form a "village group," the traditional basis of government, averaging some 5,000 people. The village group may be dispersed over a wide area, but it shares a common market, a single guardian deity and, in theory, common ancestry. It is controlled by a council of elders, who acquire "titles" by lineage, seniority, public respect and wealth. In some areas with important long-distance trade, as at Onitsha on the Niger, forms of kingship have developed.

Formal political and domestic authority is held by men; women, who do most of the trading, largely control the domestic economy and are able to acquire wealth independently of the men. In some areas there is a caste of descendants of former cult slaves, who were attached to various religious cults as a result of offenses or of being sold by their kin. They are known as *osu*, and they are largely avoided by ordinary Igbo; marriage with them is strongly disapproved. Nor must Igbo marry their own kin. The men may have more than one wife, and they must pay bridewealth to each wife's family; to marry without bridewealth, means that any children belong to the mother's kin.

Throughout Nigeria the Igbo maintain associations based on the village groups, which provide welfare benefits, help migrants find work and housing, and link urban and rural areas. Through them money earned in the cities is channeled back for the advancement of the overcrowded rural villages: self-help and self-advancement are strongly held Igbo values.

Igbo traditional religion includes beliefs in a creator God, a goddess of the Earth, ancestors and many kinds of spirits. As a result of extensive missionary work since the mid-nineteenth century, most Igbo are now Christians. Igbo art, mainly in wood, is associated with religious masquerades and festivals, the latter being important as a sign of unity within village groups. In recent years, despite the traditionally fragmentary nature of their political organization, a strong sense of ethnic identity has emerged, culminating in the civil war of 1967–70, in which the Igbo tried, unsuccessfully, to establish an independent state of Biafra. Since then they have again become part of the economic and political life of the Nigerian nation.

Asante of the forest zone

The Asante (or Ashanti) of Ghana's fertile rain forest zone number about 850,000 and are the most numerous of the Akan peoples—the only matrilineal groups in West Africa. The Asante have considerable political leverage because most of them are wealthy cocoa farmers, and thus wield great economic power.

Asante work on their own plantations and farms, which are owned on a family and community basis. A woman has her own land and may sell her crop surplus in the market. Like other Akan peoples, in addition to cocoa the Asante grow yams, cassava, plantain and oil palms as subsistence crops, as well as a great array of forest food and cash crops. Livestock are relatively unimportant. Both men and women work in the fields, on subsistence and cash crops, the small children often being cared for by their older sisters.

Cash crops are sold to traders, both individual entrepreneurs and trading companies, who use trucks to transport the goods along the excellent road system. Cocoa is the most important export, an economic depression resulting if world prices fall, but gold and timber are also exported.

The Asante are divided into eight basic social groups. These *abusua*, or clans, are dispersed throughout both the Asante and other Akan peoples. Land, house and village rights are vested in the *abusua*, although all but the latter can be individually held. The mother's *abusua* gives a person his "blood"

Asante tradition personified
Many taboos surround the Asantehene to demonstrate his sacred quality: he must never touch the ground so must always wear sandals, and when outdoors he must always be covered by an umbrella and carried in a palanquin. He is adorned in specially woven cloth, usually of gold, and wears massive golden ornaments. He speaks only through spokesmen, and is said never to sleep or die. Since colonial rule most of the jural and military authority of the Asantehene has been given by the central government to elected officials, but the role of the Asantehene as the focus of traditional state religion persists and is very much a living institution. His ceremonial Golden Stool is believed to embody the soul of the Asante nation.

A wealth of Asante craft
The Asante are world renowned for their art, with its liberal use of gold. Besides their famous woodcarvings, Asante craftsmen weave and dye kente cloth and make umbrellas and pots. They also cast in brass and gold. Weights were made from brass and used for weighing gold-dust. Their shapes and styles represent characters in folk tales and proverbs; the various animals and traditional motifs are used in weaving as well as in metalwork.

Sun-baked Hausa village
The high walls of the houses enclose each Hausa compound, affording seclusion to the women, who have less independence than in societies of the forest zone, due to the teachings of Islam. Hausa architecture displays influences from the Middle East that spread across North Africa. Within the compound the buildings are arranged to accommodate a changing family structure. Distinctive features of Hausa architecture, both rural and urban, are the pear-shaped mud and straw bricks laid along the top of the walls with the points uppermost. The Hausa like to decorate their walls and elaborately painted or sculptured facades are often found around doorways. Corrugated sheeting has become a popular new building material for roofs and doors.

The emir's household cavalry
The pomp and ceremony that surround the emirs of Hausaland reflect their powerful political and religious position. During the 18th and 19th centuries the Fulbe, under the leadership of Uthman dan Fodio, carried out a series of Holy Wars to purify the lax Muslims of West Africa and conquered most of the Hausa states. They established emirates over them which were consolidated by a military made especially effective through the use of the cavalry. The current Fulbe rulers now speak Hausa and have adopted Hausa customs and forms of political organization. The emirs are at the top of each state government apparatus. Accountable to each are titled officers, who hold sets of villages as fiefs from which they extract taxes.

A burden of gold
This Fulbe woman's weighty earrings signify her family wealth. Support may be needed if more gold is added later.

Cash bargaining and barter
The Igbo are well known for their trading and entrepreneurial skills and for their mobility. At local markets selling is most commonly done by the women. Besides being centers of trade, markets are meeting places for social and jural discussions. For married women they are especially important as it is here that they can keep in touch with friends and relatives from their respective home villages.

and his formal social position, including rights in land (of use, sale and inheritance), in other property and in lineage and state offices. Inheritance is through the sister's children, except for certain craft tools. Patrilineal descent is also important, the father's *ntoro*, or line, giving a person his moral and spiritual qualities and his personal name.

The head of a segment, or "house," of the *abusua* is a man, elected for his ability by the head of the local *abusua*, who is the genealogically senior woman. Asante most often marry someone within their own town or village, although marriage cannot take place within either the *abusua* or the *ntoro*. Several wives are permitted to an Asante man, and divorce is frequent, the children being affiliated to the *abusua*. On marriage, the groom's family makes only a token payment of bridewealth, one or two bottles of drink and a small sum of money being typical. For childbirth the wives return to live with their own *abusua*. When a baby is eight days old, the father comes to bestow a name on it—before this it is not considered truly human, but is thought of as a "ghost child." Many Asante rituals have now weakened on contact with the West.

The *Asantehene* is the nominal ruler of all Asante. The Asantehene's authority is largely based on his being believed to be the living representative of a line of royal ancestors; in clan matters he is, however, under the authority of his queen mother, usually not his own mother but a senior woman of the *abusua*.

Chiefs no longer arbitrate over anything much except chieftaincy disputes; civil and criminal cases go to magistrates. Traditional chiefs did arbitrate, except in intra-clan disputes, which were settled by the senior man and family council. This still applies in most areas if disputes are between close kin. At all times a chief or king has to listen to his queen mother, to the head of the ruling family and so to his ancestors.

All chiefs and family heads have stools, carved of wood, in which their ancestors "reside"; the ancestors receive sacrificial offerings placed on the stool. In many houses there is also a special room set aside for the worship of ancestors, where the stool is kept. The Asantehene has a Golden Stool, in which it is thought his royal power and spiritual qualities reside; it is never used as an actual stool, even by the Asantehene.

Asante believe traditionally in Onyame, a High God, and in Asase Yaa, the goddess of the Earth. Ancestors are important in traditional ritual, and at times of any family decisions their spirits are offered libations of palm wine and gin. There are also beliefs and rites to do with nonancestral powers and spirits of many kinds. Christianity is now widespread, both in its more orthodox forms and in that of many prophetic sects.

Central Africa 1

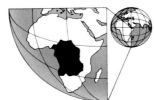

Creeping stealthily in pursuit of forest antelope as diminutive as themselves, the Pygmies live in harmony with the African rain forest, respecting its spirit, the terrifying Njengi. Once the Pygmies alone lived here, but then came the Bantu, who cleared land for their crops. Today power saws make even greater inroads on the trees and the Pygmy way of life may soon end.

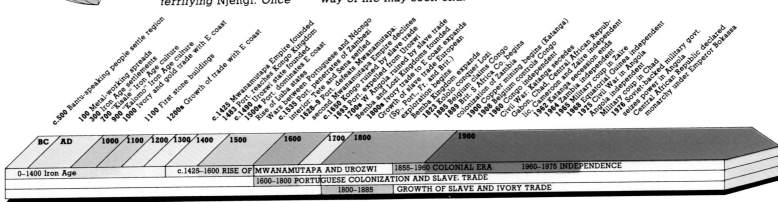

Population by Country
Total: 55 million

Zaïre/Zambia 61%
Eq. 0.5%
CA Rep. 4%
S Chad 5%
Angola 12%
Congo/Gabon 3.5%
Rep of Cam. 14%

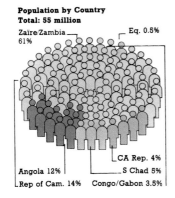

Population by Religion

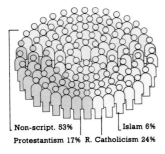

Non-script. 53%
Islam 6%
Protestantism 17% R. Catholicism 24%

The arid plains of Zambia
The Zambian savanna is prone to drought and is infested with tsetse fly. Subsistence farming and copper mining are the main economic activities.

The Central African region is characterized by a wide belt of dense and humid tropical rain forest that almost bisects the African continent, while to the north and south of this lie areas of open woodland and savanna. The heartland of the region is dominated by the River Congo (or Zaïre), which flows from the east in a massive arc, crossing the equator in the north before descending to the central swamplands and the Atlantic.

The original inhabitants of Central Africa were Pygmies who lived in the forest by hunting and gathering and knew nothing of agriculture. About 2,500 years ago, much taller Bantu-speaking people began to spread into the region. No one is certain what triggered off this migration, but one theory is that it followed the development of trade with other parts of the world which brought the Bantu knowledge of iron working, allowing them to make tools that could clear forest lands. This trade also brought crops from Southeast Asia that could withstand the wet, hot climate of the tropics—particularly successful in the forest were plantain bananas and macabo (cocoyams).

Armed with these new materials, the Bantu speakers are believed to have moved down into the rain forest, gradually displacing the hunter-gatherers and spreading southward, by riverine routes, through what is now Gabon, the Congo and Zaïre, into southern Africa. Although today the population of the Central African region is ethnically very diverse, it is predominantly Bantu speaking. The original languages of the Pygmies have long since disappeared, and most Pygmy groups now speak the language of their Bantu neighbors.

The Portuguese began trading along the western coast of Africa in the late fifteenth century, and established settlements on the Angola coast in the sixteenth century. During the scramble for Africa in the late nineteenth century, Portugal extended its control over the interior to cover what is modern Angola, while the rest of Central Africa was divided between Belgium, France, Germany, Britain and Spain. Some cash crops were introduced, notably coffee, cotton and cocoa.

Central Africa is for the most part thinly populated, and agriculture, fishing, hunting and forestry account for most of the economic activity. There are few towns and cities considering the size of the area, and the bulk of the population live in small villages and settlements. In the forest regions, women grow the basic foodstuffs, while the men produce coffee and cocoa, which are purchased from them by the state. In the savanna regions to the north and south of the forest the cash crops include cotton, sugarcane, rubber and tobacco. These are often grown on large industrial plantations, the local population providing wage labor. Mineral wealth is of increasing importance, particularly aluminum, diamonds and copper, uranium and various rare elements are also mined. Hydroelectric power is now being developed in Zaïre, and oil has been found in Angola.

Cameroon, Gabon and Zambia have enjoyed a relatively long period of political stability, but the other states of this region have, in recent years, suffered from civil wars, *coups d'etat* and other internal problems. All nine states have been hard hit by the international oil crisis and great efforts are now being made toward national unity and economic growth. Angola in particular is engaged in a long-term program of reconstruction after the war of independence in the 1970s. Chad has been devastated by a civil war which has lasted for over a decade, and the Central African Republic impoverished by years of dictatorial misrule.

For the great majority of people, the standard of living has improved very little in modern times, as shown by the Bemba of northern Zambia. Meanwhile, the gradual erosion of the ancient hunter-gatherer life style by Bantu agriculturists continues, and is perhaps in its final stages. The slow decline of the Pygmies is well illustrated by the Baka people of the Congo and Cameroon forests.

The Baka Pygmies of the Congo and Cameroon
In the forest belt of Central Africa are found the remnants of the ancient Pygmy population. They live in small groups and are found in Cameroon, Gabon, the Congo, the Central African Republic and Zaïre; their numbers are estimated at 150,000 to 200,000.

The Baka Pygmies live in southeast Cameroon and in the northern forests of the Congo. Unlike most other African Pygmies, the Baka do *not* speak the language of their immediate neighbors and thus they have maintained a degree of isolation from the Bantu cultivators. Most other African Pygmies have adopted villager hunting technology, using nets, and their ritual and religious life have become dominated by Bantu cultural traditions. However the Baka have never taken up net hunting and although in the last generation they have adopted the villager practice of setting traps, they still hunt largely with spears and dogs. Their ritual

Land use

The region is generally thinly populated and agriculture, fishing, hunting and forestry are the main occupations. As tsetse fly infests the entire region, few cattle are kept; game and fish are important sources of protein. Most people are subsistence farmers who also grow a few cash crops. In the humid tropical rain forest, women are mainly responsible for growing food for domestic consumption—plantains, macabo, manioc and peanuts—while men grow coffee and cocoa for cash. In the hot dry savanna to the north and south, maize, sorghum and millet are the staples; cash crops include cotton, sugar cane, rubber and tobacco, often grown on large plantations.

Arable land and gardens

Maize, sorghum, millet, cotton and tobacco in savanna areas; manioc, yams, taro, groundnuts and plantains elsewhere.

Plantations

Sugarcane and rubber in savanna areas; coffee, cocoa and oil palms in the forest.

Woods and forests

Mainly broad-leaved trees used for timber; manioc, plantains and groundnuts grown in gardens cleared in the forests; coffee, cocoa and oil-palm plantations are also found in this area.

Rough grazing land

Goats and sheep; crops also grown in this area.

Nonagricultural land

Desert and semidesert.

The Fali number around 10,000 and live in small enclosed villages of less than 1,000 people. Each nuclear family has its own compound where husband and wife have separate sleeping huts. Millet is their staple food and they also grow peanuts, tobacco and vegetables on the rocky hillsides. The men hunt and the women make pottery—large, elegant storage jars—but otherwise there is little division of labor.

Unlike most other Pygmies, the Baka do not speak their neighbour's language, but a language related to one that is spoken today in the Central African Republic. This indicates that the Baka moved into their present area from the Central African Republic at some time in the past, bringing their adopted language with them.

Peoples and languages

Although the people of Central Africa are ethnically diverse, they are predominantly speakers of Bantu languages. Central and southern Cameroon is dominated by Bantu-speaking peoples including the Duala, the Basa, and the great Fang nation in the western coastal region, and the Ewondo, Eton and Bulu in central and eastern areas. In the Central African Republic the Banda are the predominant group while the Fang make up the bulk of the population in Equatorial Guinea and Gabon. Elsewhere tribal populations spread across political boundaries.

Niger–Congo

Bantu languages (Fang, Kongo, Bemba, etc.)
Other Niger–Congo languages (Zande, Banda, etc.)

Afro–Asiatic

Semitic language (Arabic)
Chadic languages (Kuang, etc.)

Unaffiliated languages

East Saharan language (Kanuri)
Other "Nilo–Saharan" languages
Languages of the San or "Bushmen" ('Kung, Kedi, Kwadi)

Featured peoples

Bemba
Baka

Additional peoples

The Kongo are descendants of a once-powerful kingdom. They retain a strong sense of identity and play a major part in the affairs of both Zaïre and Angola. Women do most of the agricultural work and are often economically independent through their participation in the wide network of weekly markets.

The Ovimbundu, once one of Africa's greatest trading peoples, were very seriously affected when rubber prices fell in 1911. As cash-crop farmers and urban workers they are once again a powerful force and form 40% of Angola's population. The nuclear family has replaced the kinship group as the basic social unit.

The Zande originally consisted of many different tribes. Today they number over 2 million people in over 100 scattered clans. The ruling clan, the Avongara, form a privileged élite who, unlike commoners, can never be accused of witchcraft—a dominant element in the social life of the rest of the community.

The Bemba are a warrior people, derived from an ancient Congo empire, who established a powerful state in what today is Zambia. From early colonial times they were involved in migrant labour in the mines and subsequently were in the forefront of the struggle for independence. They remain a powerful political force.

93

Central Africa 2

life, too, is intact and many of their ceremonies are secret and take place deep in the forest. The dramatic initiation ceremony, in which young boys are introduced to the terrifying spirit of the forest, *Njengi*, has rarely been witnessed by an outsider.

In the forest the Baka live in small groups of twenty-five to forty. The blue duiker is the most common animal killed but other small animals are hunted. The men also climb high into the forest canopy to search for honey, which is often eaten when hunting is poor. Women dam the streams to catch fish, crabs, shrimps and small crocodiles, and they gather vegetable foods, termites and grubs. Failure in the food supply is only occasionally experienced with respect to meat and honey and never in the case of other types of food.

Marriage among the Baka is a simple affair and there is no ceremony. A young man must prove his hunting ability by presenting the bride's family with meat from a large animal he has killed. He is expected to work for and hunt with his wife's father and brothers until their first child is born and weaned—then he is free, if he wishes, to return to his own group with his family. The early years of first marriages are often stormy, with frequent conjugal disputes and accusations of adultery. Divorce is easy and marriages only begin to stabilize once a family has been started.

The Baka say that the forest is bountiful and they contrast the peace and cleanliness they find there with the constant disputes and poor health that they experience in the Bantu villages. They believe that the forest was made for them by *Komba* (God) and they like to talk about how good and powerful their deity is. As darkness descends on a Baka forest camp people sit around their fires and talk about the day's events. Sometimes an old man or old woman will gather the youngsters around a fire and recount Baka myths, handed down for generations, and the children and others in the camp will sing the set-piece chorus. Or, when the moon is full and rises high above the trees, out will come the drums and the men will decorate themselves with gleaming, newly cut raffia ribbons and dance until the early hours, while the women sing their hauntingly beautiful polyphonic melodies. No day will end without an old person, man or woman, giving a

Exporting the forest
The tall, straight trees of the rain forest supply prime timber for European furniture makers, and wood is a major export of several central African countries, including the Central African Republic, where this timber factory is sited. Deforestation has now begun to be a problem and the steady destruction of their natural habitat may soon affect the livelihood of those Pygmies, who remain hunter-gatherers. France takes over half of the CAR's exports, and this small country is totally dependent on her former colonial master in economic terms. Agricultural production is disorganized and there is a steady migration of young people to the main town; as a result, rural labor is in short supply and the production of cash crops has slumped.

The artery of Central Africa
Dugout canoes assemble for a market on the Congo (Zaïre) river, which provides over 9,000 miles of navigable waterways for Central Africa and has long been the main means of transport and communication. However, with the development of mining, roads and railways are becoming more important.

Instant housing
When they have chosen a suitable site for their temporary camp, the Baka men clear away the undergrowth and small trees and then leave the women to build huts while they go off hunting with their dogs. The huts have sapling frames and are covered with leaves. There are no domestic secrets in a Baka camp, the huts being far from soundproof. After individual families have retired for the night, interhut conversation carries on until all are asleep. If two families fall out they will change the entrances to their huts so that they no longer face each other. Today the Pygmies are spending more and more time living near the Bantu villages where they work as laborers. The Bantu are anxious to get the Pygmies in their power, for example by selling them kerosine lamps—the Pygmies then have to work for the Bantu to obtain kerosine. The Bantu have also introduced the Pygmies to marijuana for the same purpose. The Bantu regard the Pygmies as primitive, because they do not worship their ancestors.

formal speech of advice to the rest of the camp. He or she advises the people who are in dispute to settle their differences and to live in peace, praises the beneficence of *Komba*, or comments on traditional Baka values. In a society where no one has the right to issue orders to others, nor has the power of coercion, the advice speech helps to maintain orderly life.

In the past the Baka were elusive and avoided all contact with the newly arrived Bantu, but over the years they have gravitated more and more toward the Bantu villages. Today about 80 percent of Baka could be described as semisedentary—they spend about five months a year living a nomadic life of hunting and gathering in the forest but the rest of the year is spent in semipermanent camps, close to a village. They live in these camps for periods of six or seven weeks at a time, working as laborers for the Bantu. For their wages they receive plantain bananas and other village foods, secondhand clothing, cooking pots and other goods. During their stay in village camps they continue to exploit the forest for meat and vegetable foods.

Because of economic, cultural, political and linguistic differences, the relationship between Pygmy and villager is colored with suspicion and mistrust. Whereas the villagers regard the Pygmies as lazy, dirty, feckless primitives, the Baka ragard the Bantu as overbearing and stupid. They recognize the good things that village life can bring but they also see that the Bantu suffer from occasional meat shortages, crop failure, disease and polluted water supplies. In the villages, their cherished value of peace evaporates and they are harassed by missionaries, but the pull of the transistor radio and other material goods of the modern world has begun to equal the pull of the forest—they want good clothes, bicycles and health care. In abandoning the forest they risk losing both their self-sufficiency and their traditional culture—in a few decades, they may become the new landless proletariat in an area of Africa where once *only* they could survive.

Bemba of northern Zambia

The Bemba of northern Zambia number about 250,000 and are one of the two most prominent ethnic groups in the country. Inhabiting regions where the presence of tsetse fly militates against cattle raising, they practice shifting cultivation of finger millet on relatively poor soils. Plots of land are traditionally cultivated for four or five years before being left to regenerate.

A typical Bemba village once consisted of a cluster of thirty to fifty thatched mud-and-wattle houses, but today sun-dried bricks are used in some areas, and roofing of corrugated iron is not unusual. The Bemba remain a predominantly rural people, although most of the male population are migrant workers who live in

Bemba village life
The Bemba practice shifting cultivation of millet on plots which have to be abandoned every 4 to 5 years as the soil becomes exhausted. Men do the bulk of the work of clearing the ground for the new garden, and the women plant and harvest the crops. The core of a village consists of a village headman, his married daughter and her children, his divorced or widowed sisters and other matrilineal dependants. At marriage the groom initially goes to live with his wife in her maternal village and works for her kin in the first few years of marriage. Only after some years can the husband return with his wife to his own village. Today this form of marriage payment is often replaced by remittances from migrant labor in the copper mines.

Manhood through hunting
Two boys emerge from the forest with an antelope which they have killed. A strong taboo, linked with the taboo against incest, forbids any Baka from eating the meat of an animal he has killed himself. The meat is given away and the taboo has the effect of sharing meat out among the members of the band. When a large animal, such as an elephant, is pursued all the hunters cooperate, but only one man goes forward to make the kill, so that as many as possible can benefit from the meat. The transition from boyhood to manhood is marked by the successful hunting of animals. With the first kill, none of the boy's family can eat the meat, but with the next kill it is just the boy and his father, and finally just the boy himself (now considered a man) who is subject to this taboo. Elephants are regarded differently, however, and a father will never eat the meat of an elephant killed by his son. Many Pygmies now practice circumcision as an additional mark of the transition to manhood, because it makes them seem manly in the eyes of their Bantu neighbors.

large towns for part of the year. As with other related Central African peoples, kinship is traced matrilineally, a man passing his inheritance to his sister's son rather than his own.

Despite their mobility and low population density, the warlike Bemba have an elaborate, centralized political system which traces its origins to the ancient Luba Kingdom in the neighboring Congo. This state is presided over by the *Citimukulu*, a member of the royal crocodile clan whose name expresses the aggressive power of this ruling group. The king is "owner" and "father" of the land and is looked to as a source and guarantor of fertility and prosperity. Assisted by a group of traditional advisors, his position is that of a divine king, on whose personal well being and health depend those of his people.

With the aid of powerful sacred relics, the *Citimukulu* traditionally performed ritual sexual intercourse, releasing energy for the benefit of his land and people. His death was believed to threaten their well being and tradition records that infirm, aged monarchs were ritually strangled to prevent their taking the vitality of the country away with them to the grave. Speedy and smooth appointment of a successor has always been of the utmost importance to avoid a general crisis. As with Papal succession in the Catholic Church, each new ruler assumes the position of founder of the dynasty—hence the latest incumbent could speak of meeting the nineteenth-century English missionary Livingstone as though it was a direct personal encounter and not that of one of his ancestors.

The introduction of firearms in the midnineteenth century encouraged the expansion of the Bemba warrior state and made the rulers less dependent on mystical power. After British colonization, the growth of the copper mining industry on the edge of Bemba territory attracted large-scale migration of Bemba men, depriving their agricultural system of much of its manpower and creating new class tensions.

The involvement of the Bemba in mining and industry also led to their early prominence in trade union activity and thus in nationalist politics, and it was from the Bemba that many nationalist leaders came. These developments have cast the *Citimukulu* and his supporters in a conservative role *vis à vis* the new political leaders of modern Zambia. As in the past, many Bemba work in mining and industry, and they have seized modern educational opportunities wherever possible, but Zambia's unhealthy economy combined with the infertile soil of their homelands mean that most Bemba are still very poor.

East Africa 1

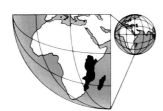

On the plains of Africa man's ancestors were born, as much creatures of the savanna as the antelope, zebra, cheetah or lion. Today, haughty, elegant Maasai warriors herd their cattle there

and descendants of powerful ancient kingdoms tend their crops. The societies of the coastlands, cosmopolitan, literate and urbane, are a legacy of the centuries-old Arab trade in ivory and slaves.

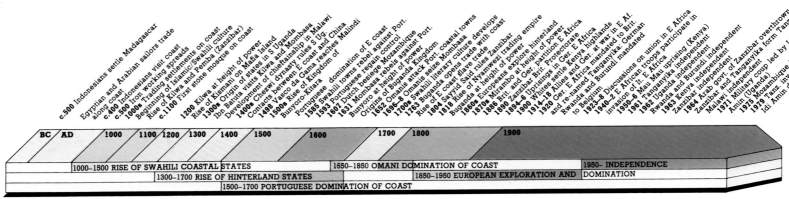

c.500 Indonesians settle Madagascar
Egyptian and Arabian sailors trade along coast
c.400 Indonesians visit coast
c.500 Iron working spreads
1000s Trading settlements on coast
Beginning of Islamic/Swahili culture
Rise of Kilwa and Pemba (Zanzibar)
c.1100 First stone mosque on coast
1200 Kilwa at height of power
Rise of Kismani on Mafia Island
1300s Origin of states in S Uganda
Ibn Batuta visits Kilwa and Mombasa
Development of chieftainship in Malawi
1400s Chezwi dynasty rules S Ug.
Contacts between E coast and China
1498 Vasco da Gama reaches Malindi
1500s Rise of Kingdom of Bunyoro-Kitara
Portuguese domination of E coast
1585 Swahili towns rebel against Port.
1593 Portuguese regain control
1607 Dutch besiege Mozambique
1631 Mombasa rebels against Port.
Origins of Buganda Kingdom
1652 Omanis seize Mombasa
1696-8 Omanis attack Port. coastal towns
1700s Swahili literary culture develops
1763 Buganda opens trade with coast
Rise of E. coast slave trade
1804 Sayyid Said rules Zanzibar
1818 Rise of Nyamwezi trading empire
Buganda at height of power
1860s Europeans explore hinterland
1870s Mirambo at height of power
1886 Brit. and Ger. partition E Africa
1890 Zanzibar Brit. Protectorate
1894-6 Uprisings in Ger. E Africa
1900 Whites settle Kenya highlands
1914-18 Allies and Ger. at war in E Af.
1920 Ger. E Africa mandated to Brit. and re-named Tanganyika; German Rwanda and Burundi mandated to Belgium
1923-8 Discussions on union in E Africa
1940-2 E African troops participate in invasion of It. E Africa
1950-6 Mau Mau uprising (Kenya)
1961 Tanganyika independent
1962 Uganda and Burundi independent
Rwanda independent
1963 Kenya independent
Zanzibar and Tanganyika form Tanz.
1964 Arab govt. of Zanzibar overthrown
Malawi independent
1971 Military coup led by Idi Amin (Uganda)
1975 Mozambique independent
1978 Tanz. invaded by Idi Amin depo

BC/AD	1000	1100	1200	1300	1400	1500	1600	1700	1800	1900

1000–1500 RISE OF SWAHILI COASTAL STATES
1300–1700 RISE OF HINTERLAND STATES
1500–1700 PORTUGUESE DOMINATION OF COAST
1650–1850 OMANI DOMINATION OF COAST
1850–1950 EUROPEAN EXPLORATION AND DOMINATION
1950– INDEPENDENCE

Population by Country
Total: 71 million

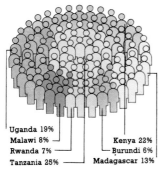

Uganda 19%
Malawi 8%
Rwanda 7%
Tanzania 25%
Kenya 22%
Burundi 6%
Madagascar 13%

Population by Religion

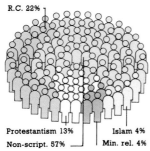

R.C. 22%
Protestantism 13%
Non-script. 57%
Islam 4%
Min. rel. 4%

Samburu boys herding cattle
The Samburu resemble their southern neighbors, the Maasai, but lead a more nomadic life, since grazing is scarce in their arid lands.

Variety is the main characteristic of East Africa, whether considered geographically, linguistically, or in terms of its traditional cultures and recent history. Although clearly defined to the east by the Indian Ocean and to the west by the western arm of the great Rift Valley with its chains of lakes and mountains, the northern and southern boundaries of East Africa are not so easily delineated; there are no dramatic changes in terrain, and languages and ethnic groups cross national frontiers.

Most of East Africa lies at 900–1,500 meters (3,000–5,000 feet) above sea level, and high altitude, together with the pattern of rainfall, modifies the climate and vegetation from that typical of equatorial regions—tropical rain forest—to scrub and grassland. Where rain forest did once prevail, such as on the well-watered central plateau to the east of Lake Victoria, this has now disappeared as a result of the activities of agricultural peoples. To the north of the region, a much lower rainfall produces semidesert conditions, except in the west where the Nile flows through the swamps north of Lakes Albert and Kyoga.

Where the annual rainfall permits, agriculture is practiced, often combined with animal husbandry. In recent times, population pressure in these regions has caused cultivators to move into less favorable areas where they do not obtain reliable harvests. On the central plateau millet, sorghum and maize have been the staples for generations, but at lower altitudes, and particularly to the north and west of Lake Victoria, the banana is the staple. Bananas crop for a long period and require little labor once they are established, so that where they are the staple, people are freed from the demands made by annual crops.

In areas of lower rainfall, and where the tsetse fly is not endemic, pastoralism is practiced. A few pastoral peoples, such as the Karimojong, supplement the products of their livestock with agriculture, but others, such as the Turkana, Maasai, Samburu and the pastoral peoples of Kenya's northern border, trade with agricultural peoples for their produce, particularly grain. By contrast, the coastal economy has for centuries been based on long-distance sea trade, and the coastlands have had a mixed, international population for centuries. Arab trade in ivory and slaves is documented from about AD 80 and by the eleventh century there was a chain of Arab coastal colonies stretching all along the coast, from Mogadiscio to Beira.

These colonies were subject to no single overlordship until the arrival of the Portuguese in the sixteenth century, which coincided with a period of decline in the fortunes of many towns. Except in Mozambique, Portuguese domination lasted little more than a century, after which dynasties from Oman became the overlords. But it was only in the middle of the nineteenth century that there was any form of unification when, under Seyyid Said, control became centered on Zanzibar. At the same time, attempts to suppress the slave trade, largely by the British, and the increasing interest in East Africa as a market for manufactured goods, led to European powers taking over the whole area by the end of the nineteenth century.

The influence of the Arabs during their long period of settlement and rule over the coastal region resulted in a distinct coastal culture, whose language, Swahili, is Bantu in structure but contains many Arab and some Portuguese words; it was traditionally written in Arabic script. Writings that survive from earlier periods show that coastal society was sophisticated, literate and open in its outlook.

Most of East Africa came under British control for the sixty- to seventy-year period of colonial rule. During this period the cultivation of crops for export was encouraged and coffee, cotton, tea, sugar and sisal rapidly became major exports. Migrants from the Indian subcontinent soon formed a distinct community in Kenya, Uganda and Tanzania, while white settlement was largely confined to Kenya and Mozambique. A simplified form of Swahili provided the *lingua franca* for much of East Africa in the colonial period.

Before the colonial period both the western and eastern boundaries of East Africa were characterized by more complex sociopolitical systems than the center. In the west there were the traditional kingdoms of the interlacustrine Bantu, such as the Ganda, Nyoro, Toro, Rwanda and Rundi. Between these kingdoms and the complex maritime society of the east coast lay a large area occupied by peoples whose only common characteristic was a lack of centralized authority. Elders in councils decided policy and settled disputes. This, and the absence of a hereditary aristocracy, makes these people assert that they are more democratic and progressive by tradition than the former subjects of kings, an assertion vehemently denied by those who have always considered a lack of kingship to be evidence of backwardness. These attitudes

The Ganda, who are the largest single people in Uganda, suffered heavy losses in the period of turmoil during and after the rule of Idi Amin. Many fled the country and are still refugees, and many were killed. Most Ganda are peasant farmers who grow cotton and coffee as cash crops. Potatoes, maize, beans and manioc are subsistence crops, with bananas the staple food. Goats and chickens are kept for their meat and wealthy people also keep cattle. The prosperity of the Ganda and their pre-eminence in Ugandan society accounts in part for the persecution they have suffered in recent years.

The Hadza, who number less than 1,000, are hunter-gatherers who live in small, highly flexible and mobile bands, moving camp every 2 to 3 weeks. They speak a language with many click sounds, like those of the Nama and San peoples in southern Africa. Attempts by the Tanzanian government to settle the Hadza as farmers have met with little success

The Maasai, who number about 190,000 are a cattle-herding people, whose remote, arid territories straddle the Kenya–Tanzania border. Cattle are rarely killed for food; they have very high symbolic value as the source of prestige and wealth. Milk and blood are the staple foods for men; the women eat milk, vegetables, grain and sometimes blood.

Peoples and languages
Speakers of Bantu languages, including the Swahili speakers of the coast, form the majority. In northern Tanzania there are pockets of languages found nowhere else in the area such as the click languages of the Sandawe and Hadza. Speakers of Nilotic languages include the Acoli, Lango and Luo, while speakers of Paranilotic languages include the Karimojong, Kalenjin, and Maasai. Swahili is the official language of Tanzania and with English remains a joint official language in Kenya, where it is also used by Europeans and Indians. Luganda, the language of the Ganda people, was the language of administration and education in Uganda until independence. Uganda uses English as its official language today, while Rwanda and Burundi use French, alongside Kinyarwanda and Kirundi. The use of French tends to divide these states from the rest of East Africa and orientate them more toward Zaïre, their western neighbor. Portuguese is the official language of Mozambique and is spoken as a second language by many people. In Malawi, Cewa, a Bantu language, is widely spoken but English is the official language.

Niger–Congo
Bantu languages (Swahili, Ganda, Rwanda, Kikuyu, etc.)

Afro–Asiatic
Cushitic language (Iraqw)

Austronesian
Malagasy

Indo–European
Romance languages (Indian Ocean French Creoles)

Unaffiliated languages
Nilotic and Paranilotic languages (Acoli, Turkana, Maasai, Karimojong, etc.)
Sandawe
Hadza

Featured peoples
Ganda
Maasai

Additional peoples

Arable land
Maize, millet, sorghum, rice, plantains, cotton and tobacco.

Plantations
Coffee, sisal, tea, sugarcane, citrus fruits and mangoes.

Woods and forests
Coniferous and broad-leaved trees, used for timber and charcoal.

Rough grazing land
Goats and cattle (where tsetse fly is not endemic).

Land use
Where there is sufficient rainfall, agriculture or mixed farming is practiced, cereals or bananas being the staple crops. Cash crops, such as tea, are also grown. The keeping of animals is restricted by tsetse flys, which transmit a disease known as tripanosomiasis from wild animals to cattle.

ETHIOPIA

L. Turkana

KENYA

UGANDA
Kampala
Entebbe
L. Albert
L. Kyoga
L. Edward
L. Victoria

Mt Kenya 5200

Nairobi

Kigali
RWANDA
Bujumbura
BURUNDI

Malindi
Kilimanjaro 5895
Mombasa

Tabora
Ujiji
L. Tanganyika

TANZANIA

MAASAI STEPPE

ZANZIBAR

Dar es Salaam

Kilwa Masoko

Lindi

INDIAN OCEAN

Mirambo

L. Nyasa

MALAWI
Lilongwe
Zambesi

Blantyre
Tete

MOZAMBIQUE

Moçambique

Quelimane

Limpopo

Maputo

Diégo-Suarez

Tananarive

MADAGASCAR
(MALAGASY REPUBLIC)

Tuléar

Malagasy, the language spoken by most of Madagascar's 8 million people, does not belong to any African language group but is related to Austronesian languages. The islanders are believed to be the descendants of traders from Indonesia who journeyed to Indian, Arab and East African ports and settled on the uninhabited island about 2,500 years ago.

MAURITIUS
RÉUNION (Fr)

0   400 km
0   300 miles

East Africa 2

underlie much of the strife in Uganda, although Kenya, which had no traditional kingdoms, and Tanzania, where the kingdoms were weak and remote from the modern centers of power, have suffered less from this form of rivalry. The contrast between a centralized state and a loose federation of tribes is well illustrated by the Ganda cultivators of Uganda and the Maasai pastoralists of Kenya and Tanzania.

Ganda of Uganda

The Bantu-speaking Ganda are the largest single group in Uganda. They numbered nearly two million at the last census, but the population suffered heavy losses during the rule of Idi Amin in the 1970s and in the fighting that followed his downfall. Many Ganda are still refugees elsewhere in Africa or overseas; there are no reliable figures for those killed.

Buganda, the country of the Ganda, lies on the well-watered, fertile north shore of Lake Victoria. The staple crop, the banana, is a reliable and easily cultivated source of food; traditionally it supported a dense population in the south. Today most Ganda are still farmers or part-time farmers. Cotton, introduced in 1905, and coffee, introduced later, rapidly became important sources of cash income, bringing prosperity to the area. This early development resulted in the establishment of schools and in the siting of both Kampala, the commercial capital, and Entebbe, the administrative center, in the heart of Buganda; this perpetuated the preeminence of the Ganda in the political and commercial worlds of modern Uganda.

The Ganda are proud of their long history; the Kabaka (King) traces his succession through thirty-six predecessors to the founder of the kingdom. Even before modernization accompanying British rule, the Ganda state was both centralized and firmly controlled. In this it differed from similar kingdoms to the west and southwest, where the rulers were weaker and the political structure much looser. The Ganda also lacked the castelike division into agricultural peasants, cattle-owning nobility and royalty, which characterized most of the interlacustrine kingdoms, Rwanda being the most extreme example. The Ganda political and social hierarchy was more fluid and it depended on the king's power to promote or dismiss. Such a system encouraged an emphasis on individual achievement and political skills, which enabled the Ganda to adapt easily to their changing world.

The treaty with the British in 1901 gave the Ganda further political influence and for two or more decades at the beginning of the century they formed an administrative class under British direction, which in part accounts for the antipathy felt to them in areas where they formerly ruled. Their traditional system was remolded into a three-tier bureaucratic structure with all but the village headmen being paid officials who were subject to transfer and promoted on merit rather than through the personal favor of the Kabaka. Tribute was abolished, but many of the early chiefs benefited from the registration of title to land, for the British authorities mistook the system of administration for one of landholding, and some administrative areas became private estates. There was thus established a class of wealthy landowners where once the system allowed an individual to rise by his own efforts.

In spite of many changes since the British Protectorate of 1901 a system of patrilineal clanship still

The ordeal of circumcision
A 17-year-old Gisu boy is watched by a crowd of male relatives and neighbors as he undergoes circumcision. Among the Gisu of eastern Uganda, this initiation remains important as it marks the assumption of full adult status. The circumcisor is usually a stranger to the neighborhood. As with the Maasai and other tribes, circumcision is an ordeal which must be endured without flinching. Among the Gisu, even those young men who have been to university feel that unless they have been circumcised their maturity will not be recognized.

***E unoto*—Masai promotion**
A Maasai woman shaving the head of her son—the penultimate act in the *E unoto* ceremony at which 49 selected junior *moran* are promoted into the senior age set. The ceremony takes place once every 15 years and begins with a feast, followed by a sexually symbolic ritual where the initiates enter the ceremonial hut and urinate into a hole. At the sound of the Kudu horn, the dancing begins and as the dance climaxes the *laibon* blesses each warrior with milk and spittle. *E unoto* lasts for 4 days and ends with the burning of the ceremonial hut.

Warriors without a war
The *moran* were once the Maasai's standing army. A Maasai boy becomes a *moran* after circumcision—armed with spear and sword he is then the defender of the tribe. He lives outside the village's thorn stockade and is not allowed to marry. Traditionally the life of a *moran* was devoted to herding cattle and to cattle raiding, but raiding has now been outlawed. Lions were hunted as a test of courage, but these animals are becoming scarce. A few Maasai in the more favored parts of Maasailand have broken with their pastoralist traditions and taken to commercial farming, largely of wheat.

persists. Clans are few in number and members live dispersed throughout Buganda. The dead are buried in clan land and all clan members observe certain food taboos and a restriction on marriage within it. Women have strong ties with their own clan through their brothers, and remain attached to it even after marriage.

Religious belief and practice, however, have changed significantly. Traditional religious cults centered on the spirits of dead kings or persons who were supposed to manifest supernatural powers when alive. These spirits possessed mediums who might become powerful figures in their own right but the Kabaka himself was a secular ruler. He sent gifts to the shrines where the spirits of his predecessors were located at set times but royal spirits, unlike those of dead commoners, did not possess their heirs.

Today virtually all Ganda are Christian, with a minority of Muslims. Conversions began at the end of the nineteenth century and subsequently Buganda suffered religious wars between political factions espousing one or other of the new faiths, during which many Ganda Christians were martyred. However, it was the kingship as a symbol of tradition and history, rather than religion that was the unifying institution in traditional Buganda and this has remained the focus of Ganda national loyalties.

Maasai of Kenya and Tanzania

The Maasai are the largest of a number of distinct groups who speak dialects of the same language. Their territory, much reduced since the nineteenth century, straddles the Kenya-Tanzania border. Although usually described as cattle herders they also keep smaller animals, usually for slaughter, and trade with neighboring peoples for grain, beads, cloth and iron weapons. The cattle are herded and protected by the men while the women milk them and prepare the curdled milk which, together with blood, is the staple food of the men. The cattle are only occasionally killed for food and have high symbolic value as the means to create social bonds as well as being a manifestation of wealth and a means of subsistence.

The grazing and watering needs of the stock influence the movements of the Maasai settlements, but they move within known and clearly demarcated territories. Thus this loose federation of tribes is divided into sections, areas whose residents respect one *laibon* (prophet) and have joint rights in available resources. Sections are subdivided into smaller subsection territories, in which there is greater solidarity and a common leader; subsections are formed of clusters of settlements which use the same grazing and watering places. The Maasai age-set system, characteristic of most pastoralists in East Africa, involves formal rituals of initiation. Every adult belongs to an age set, several of which form the larger unit or class. Each class is progressively promoted to the two senior social grades, known as *moran* (warriors) and elders.

The basis of the system is the settlement with its associated *moran* encampment, where the *moran* live and eat apart. The settlement is surrounded by a circular thorn fence, inside which the low rectangular huts are built by the women, leaving a central space for the stock. The enclosure is pierced by gates, each of which belongs to an elder, a household head; the huts of his wives flank the gate in order of seniority, the first to the right. Co-wives are thus grouped into two divisions, known as right and left hand, of which the right is senior. Similar divisions mark the age classes.

Boys are circumcised at puberty and those of one locality circumcised in one season are formed by a ritual into an age set. Four consecutive sets are the right-hand section of an age class and establish a *moran*'s encampment. The three subsequent sets make up the left-hand section. After the class is complete a closed period marks an end to its recruitment. The class is now in the position of junior *moran*, undertaking herding and fighting duties as subordinates of senior *moran* and elders. After eight to twelve years as juniors, the class is ritually promoted to senior moranhood and the next junior class begins to recruit.

The system may entail a long bachelor period for men, who during moranhood are marginal to domestic life. Girls may live with their lovers in the *moran* encampments but leave the area permanently when they marry outside the clan. They marry men of the class senior to their lovers and although they are not expected to be virgins, premarital pregnancy is regarded with horror. Senior warriors are finally promoted to elderhood when their junior class is complete, and they may then marry and begin establishing themselves as householders. It is not until the next class is promoted to elderhood that they become senior elders, with some of their number becoming recognized leaders in a wider sphere.

Within each class and age set, *moran* leaders are chosen for their fulfillment of the ideals of moranhood: courage, physical strength and beauty. Among the elders other qualities are demanded, and those who are wealthy and make effective use of wealth and oratorical skills emerge as leaders. The *laibon* are drawn from one clan; they hold both ritual and political authority and some of them have been very powerful. While the *moran* are admired by all Maasai as the epitome of Maasai manhood, it is the elders who exercise power in Maasai society.

Like other pastoral peoples in East Africa the Maasai have a reputation for conservatism; they live in remote, dry and thinly populated areas with few incentives to economic and social change. Today some are growing wheat in the areas of more reliable rainfall and more of their young people are being drawn away by modern education into other occupations. Attempts to improve their productivity as cattle breeders are frustrated by the unreliability of water and grazing. Recent famines have caused much suffering, but in general the Maasai traditional way of life is still their best chance of surviving without massive outside investment.

Independence of Ganda women
On the shores of Lake Victoria a Ganda woman is clearly distinguished by a long wrap known as a *busuti*, introduced by European missionaries. Ganda women have a reputation for independence and many support themselves by farming or commerce. Even in traditional Buganda divorce was fairly common and childless women are not a new phenomenon. Women retain strong ties with their own clan after marriage.

Accepting change
Like other Bantu-speaking peoples, the Kikuyu are quick to accept change and have adopted new crops and agricultural techniques from European settlers; here, farmers harvest a cash crop of rice. Their ambition is reflected in their concern for education—many Kikuyu have become lawyers, doctors and academics. A Kikuyu leader, Jomo Kenyatta, led Kenya to independence in 1963.

The search for energy
Mombasa has a long history as an important center of trade. Kilindini, Mombasa's deep-water harbor is now the base for the huge American oil rig, Apollo One, but so far no oil has been found. The cost of Kenya's energy needs are crippling the economy—over 75% of fuel is imported. Wood and charcoal are still widely used for fuel and are even exported so that deforestation is now a serious problem.

Southern Africa 1

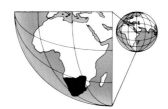

In its southernmost latitudes Africa is a land of sunshine, of good grazing and rich crops, with gold, diamonds and other treasures beneath the soil. Small wonder then that so many have battled for its possession, or that its history is one of conflict and bloodshed. Even in the Kalahari Desert, once a haven of peace for the nomadic Bushmen, the demands of the modern world intrude.

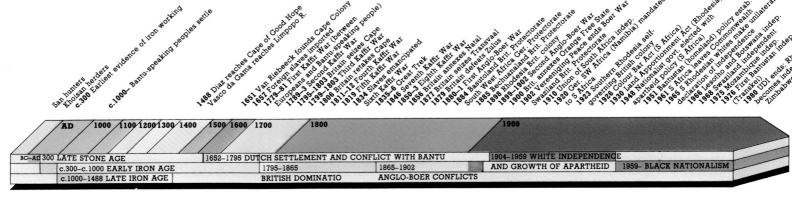

San hunters
Khoisan herders
c.300 Earliest evidence of iron working
c.1000– Bantu-speaking peoples settle
1488 Diaz reaches Cape of Good Hope
Vasco da Gama reaches Limpopo R.
1652 Van Riebeeck founds Cape Colony
1657 Foreign slaves imported
1779–81 First Kaffir War (between Europeans and Bantu-speaking people)
1789–3 Second Kaffir War
1795–1803 Britain seizes Cape
1806 Britain retakes Cape
1811–12 Third Kaffir War
1819 Fourth Kaffir War
Sixth Kaffir War
1834 Slaves emancipated
1835–6 Great Trek
1846 Seventh Kaffir War
1850–3 Eighth Kaffir War
1856 Britain seizes Natal
1877 Britain annexes Transvaal
1879 Britain defeats Zulus
1880–1 First Anglo-Boer War
1884 Basutoland Brit. Protectorate
South West Africa Ger. colony
1885 Bechuanaland Brit. Protectorate
1889 Rhodesia Brit. colony
1899–1902 Second Anglo-Boer War
1902 Vereeniging Peace ends Boer War
Swaziland Brit. Protectorate
1910 Union of South Africa indep.
1920 Ger. SW Africa (Namibia) mandated to S. Africa
1923 Southern Rhodesia self-governing British colony
1926 Colour Bar Act (S Africa)
1930 Land Apportionment Act (Rhodesia)
1948 Nationalist govt. elected with apartheid policy (S Africa)
1951 Bantustan (homeland) policy estab.
1961 S Africa leaves Commonwealth
1965 S Rhodesian whites make unilateral declaration of independence
1966 Lesotho and Botswana indep.
1975 Mozambique indep.
1976 First Bantustan independent (Transkei)
1980 UDI ends; Rhodesia becomes indep. Zimbabwe

AD	1000	1100	1200	1300	1400	1500	1600	1700	1800	1900

BC–AD 300 LATE STONE AGE	1652–1795 DUTCH SETTLEMENT AND CONFLICT WITH BANTU	1904–1959 WHITE INDEPENDENCE
c.300–c.1000 EARLY IRON AGE	1795–1865	1865–1902	AND GROWTH OF APARTHEID	1959– BLACK NATIONALISM
c.1000–1488 LATE IRON AGE	BRITISH DOMINATIO	ANGLO-BOER CONFLICTS	

Population by Country
Total: 46 million

S Africa 51%
Namibia 2%
Zimbabwe 16%
Botswana 2%
Mozambique 25%
Swaziland 1%
Lesotho 3%

Population by Religion

Non-script. 48%

R. Catholicism 12%
Min rel. 5%
Protestantism 35%

Tradition on the Bantustan
A Venda chief's house surrounded by those of his wives—each wife has her own living house and kitchen within the chief's compound.

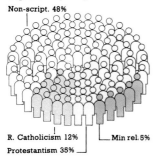

Where the tip of Africa extends southward, beyond the Tropic of Capricorn, latitude and topography combine to produce deserts in the northwestern part but elsewhere an almost ideal climate with long hours of sunshine and temperatures that rarely fall too low or rise too high for human comfort. This pleasant land is stocked with riches beneath its soil—diamonds, gold and other valuable minerals—and its recent history is one of conquest and warfare as different peoples have fought for its possession. Today, the economic development of the whole area is dominated by South Africa, the wealthiest and most highly industrialized nation in Africa. Much of this country's prosperity is based on the cheap labor of its black inhabitants and South Africa's failure to grant even the most basic rights to these people has been the cause of severe international criticism.

Geographically, most of southern Africa is a high, saucer-shaped plateau, drained by the Orange river, the Limpopo and the Zambezi. The rim of this vast plateau is known as the Great Escarpment and it encircles southern Africa, reaching heights of over 3,000 meters (10,000 feet) in the Kingdom of Lesotho. Beyond this high escarpment lie the narrow coastlands whose climates range from subtropical in the east to Mediterranean around Cape Town in the southwest. North of Cape Town lies an arid region, a southerly extension of the uninhabitable Namib desert. The Namib and the Kalahari make Namibia one of the most arid countries on earth, and the Kalahari also covers most of Botswana.

A fairly low level of rainfall throughout the region means that only a small area of southern Africa is suitable for arable farming but over 80 percent can be used for grazing, and cattle raising is an important economic activity, particularly in Botswana. The staple crops are corn or millet, while citrus fruits, cotton and tobacco are grown for cash, often with the help of irrigation. On the moist and fertile east coast bananas, mangoes and sugarcane are produced.

The original inhabitants of Africa were of the Khoisan race, people of small stature and light brown skins speaking languages that contain click sounds. They are represented today by the Nama herders of Namibia, and the San (Bushmen), some of whom still live as hunter-gatherers in the semiarid, but surprisingly productive, fringes of the Kalahari. Hunter-gatherers and pastoralists such as these once roamed the entire region, but about 2,000 years ago Bantu-speaking agriculturists began to enter what is now Zimbabwe and by the twelfth century large numbers had settled in the Transvaal. This was the last phase of the Bantu expansion in Africa and as a result the original inhabitants survived in greater numbers here than elsewhere on the continent.

Communities of Bantu had been established in the Cape area for several centuries before the Dutch East India Company set up their staging post at Table Bay in 1652, but most of the local inhabitants were the so-called Cape Hottentots, a Khoisan people who practiced pastoralism. The Dutch settlers either drove these people away or absorbed them by intermarriage. By the late eighteenth century the settlers numbered 15,000 and had evolved a distinctive way of life; they became known as the Boers (farmers) or Afrikaners.

In the early years of the nineteenth century, the British seized control of Cape Province and thousands of British settlers arrived. The new administration attempted to control the way in which the Boers treated their black laborers, and this caused great resentment among the Dutch settlers. In 1835–36, they began the Great Trek, moving north and east to settle the interior.

At first the whites were often accepted by the indigenous peoples of the interior as a new ruling clan whose administration might increase prosperity, and they were allocated land for grazing and cultivation. Rule by a minority clan, often an alien one, had been a common feature of many southern African political systems, but exploitation had always been checked. Trouble began when the new rulers ignored the traditions of land tenure and assumed they had been given land that was in fact communally owned.

In 1852 and 1854 the Boers annexed the areas that later became the republics of the Transvaal and the Orange Free State. Thus they were outside the range of British influence, but when diamonds and then gold were discovered in these regions in the late nineteenth century the British sought to gain control of them, leading to the Anglo-Boer Wars of 1880 and 1899. During this period the British also established a protectorate in Bechuanaland (now Botswana) while the German government ruled Namibia from 1884 onward. The four regions of South Africa were united in 1910 and following World War I South Africa administered Namibia under a League of Nations

mandate. This mandate was withdrawn in 1946, but South Africa continues to occupy Namibia. Rhodesia (now Zimbabwe) was a British colony from 1898 until 1965 when the white minority seized power and declared independence. Their policies, modeled on those of South Africa, brought widespread criticism and they were toppled by black nationalists in 1980.

All the indigenous people of southern Africa have been affected by the European colonists, and their economy and social life have been disrupted and often destroyed by the effects of organized migrant labor. Because the whites took most of the good land in Zimbabwe and South Africa, the traditional subsistence activities—horticulture and pastoralism—had to be supplemented by wage labor, often carried out hundreds of miles from home. This process increased ethnic intermarriage and brought about the rapid modernization of African cultures. There is now widespread employment of men and women in industry, public services, stores, hotels, restaurants and domestic work. Public-service workers are generally recruited for specific periods and compelled to live in compounds, like mine workers.

Land use
Grazing of cattle, sheep and goats is the predominant land use, but the Transvaal can also produce citrus fruits, cotton and tobacco. Tropical fruits are grown along the east coast and in the Cape Town region grapes are the main crop. Fishing is important, 90% of the catch being exported.

Arable land and gardens
Maize, wheat, sorghum, forage crops, groundnuts, vegetables, cotton and tobacco.

Orchards and plantations
Sugarcane, grapes, citrus and deciduous fruits, pineapples.

Woods and forests
Coniferous and broadleaved trees, especially eucalyptus for timber, paper and tannin.

Rough grazing land
Sheep, goats and cattle; some subsistence farming.

Nonagricultural land
Desert, sand-dunes, swamps, industrial and urban areas.

The 450,000 Ovambo make up nearly half the Namibian population, and the South West Africa People's Organization (SWAPO) was originally a movement of Ovambo workers. The Ovambo (and indeed the economy of Namibia as a whole) depend heavily on wage labor in the mines towns of South Africa for survival. Another 150,000 Ovambo live in Angola.

Shona-speaking people have lived for centuries in Zimbabwe, Mozambique, and parts of Botswana and Zambia. The Ndebele are the descendants partly of Shona speakers and partly of the Ndebele, who moved north across the Limpopo after coming into conflict with the Zulu kingdom and the Boers. "Shona" was the name given by the Ndebele to the 19th-century rulers of

the Changamire state in southwest Zimbabwe. This large state was one of several which arose, as a result of increased trading activities, from the small states of various Shona-speaking groups. However, in the 1890s, Shona lands were taken over by Europeans. In 1980, the new state of Zimbabwe was formed under the Shona prime minister Robert Mugabe.

The 450,000 Venda possess a rich and sophisticated culture. Before colonial times they consisted of a loose federation of tribes, living in a small area of mountainous land and basing their economy on shifting cultivation. Today many work in urban areas and on white farms. Their "homeland" is one of a number established as part of the policy of apartheid.

The Zulu are the descendants of an empire created in the early 19th century from several tribes of northern Natal, by Shaka, a brilliant military leader. Many of the 5½ million Zulu today live in towns and cities outside their homeland, which they have refused to accept as a Bantustan. The urban Zulu play an important role in African political movements.

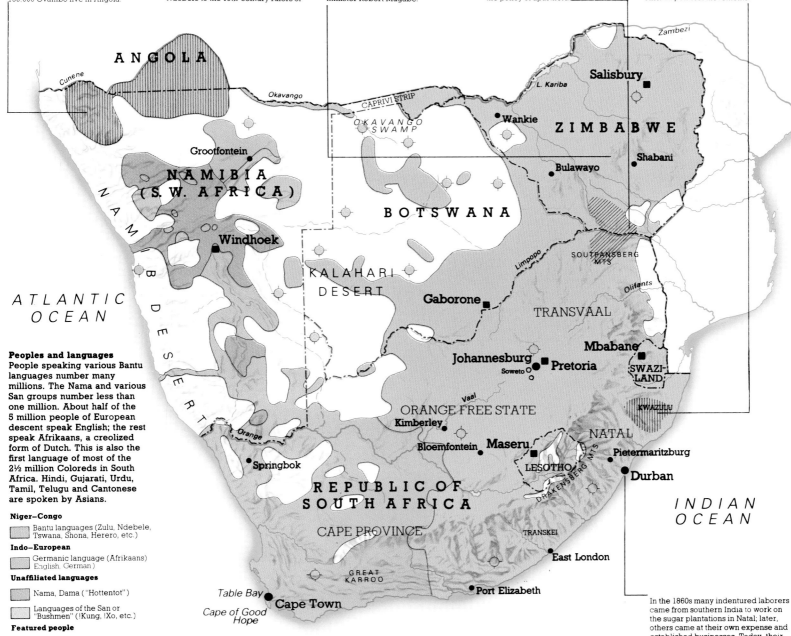

Peoples and languages
People speaking various Bantu languages number many millions. The Nama and various San groups number less than one million. About half of the 5 million people of European descent speak English; the rest speak Afrikaans, a creolized form of Dutch. This is also the first language of most of the 2½ million Coloreds in South Africa. Hindi, Gujarati, Urdu, Tamil, Telugu and Cantonese are spoken by Asians.

Niger–Congo
Bantu languages (Zulu, Ndebele, Tswana, Shona, Herero, etc.)

Indo–European
Germanic language (Afrikaans) English, German.

Unaffiliated languages
Nama, Dama ("Hottentot")

Languages of the San or "Bushmen" (!Kung, !Xo, etc.)

Featured people
Venda

Additional peoples

In the 1860s many indentured laborers came from southern India to work on the sugar plantations in Natal; later, others came at their own expense and established businesses. Today, their descendants number almost 800,000 and are prominent in commerce and the professions throughout the region, especially in Durban.

Southern Africa 2

Since 1948, South Africa has pursued a rigorous segregationist policy of *apartheid* ("separate development") toward the nonwhites, that is, the blacks, coloreds and Asians. Laws restrict their freedom of movement, freedom of residence, freedom of employment, and all manner of other personal freedoms. Beginning in the 1950s the government set up Bantustans, or black homelands, which are nominally independent. In 1977 there were ten such Bantustans, covering less than 13 percent of the total area of South Africa. These regions are too small to be economically viable and many of the people who are now officially designated as their citizens have never ever visited them. One Bantustan, Transkei, was declared independent in 1976, whereupon its people, over one million of whom actually live outside its boundaries, lost their South African citizenship. Since then, three other Bantustans have been declared independent.

Ethnic groups in many parts of southern Africa have become united by modern urban life, ethnic intermarriage, European-style education and Christian beliefs and practices. But there are also parts of southern Africa where members of particular ethnic groups predominate and some traditional institutions are practiced in modified forms. The Venda living on the northern border of South Africa are a clear example, having a language and sophisticated culture distinct from all others in South Africa.

Venda of South Africa

The traditional home of the Venda is in and around the Soutpansberg mountains and it forms the most compact of the South African Bantustans. Vendaland has a tropical to subtropical climate, with January and February the hottest and wettest months. The cattle-grazing country to the north of the Soutpansberg is flat and dry, but the southwestern plateau of the Soutpansberg has high rainfall and fertile soil suitable for forestry, and for citrus fruit and vegetable production.

Before the period of colonization, self-sufficiency in food and threats from hostile neighbors encouraged the Venda to remain concentrated within the mountain areas, although a few moved farther afield in order to

Cheap labor in the mines
Gold is the most valuable mineral in South Africa, although diamonds, asbestos, copper, iron, platinum, tin and zinc are also mined. Uranium is a by-product of gold mining and large coal reserves are also exploited. Of the 400,000 workers in the gold mines, 90% are nonwhite, including many migrant workers from neighboring states. Black workers must live on the mining compound. Enforced separation from their families and a low wage—one twentieth of that received by white workers—result in severe hardship. Until recently, blacks could not achieve "skilled" status.

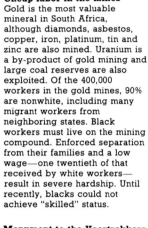

Monument to the Voortrekkers
In 1835–36 many Afrikaner families—the *Voortrekkers*—traveled north across the Orange river in search of land free from British control. The harsh 2-year trek is proudly commemorated each year, reinforcing the Afrikaners' fierce sense of independence.

Botswana women
Since large numbers of men migrate annually from Botswana to South Africa in search of work, a growing proportion of the households have to be managed entirely by women. To supplement their income many women take up heavy work, such as bricklaying.

trade. After the whites began to administer their homeland in 1902, however, the Venda tended to move away from the villages of their rulers and live in homesteads scattered over the hills and mountains. In the 1960s, many Venda were again regrouped in villages, as part of a scheme for developing the country. Other Venda remained on the white farms and in the urban areas to which they had migrated.

The white colonists brought poverty to the Venda, who had previously been self-sufficient. The traditional Venda economy had been based on shifting cultivation in cycles of five years or so, for which plenty of land was needed. Maize and millet were the main crops and cattle and goats were raised. The Venda also hunted several different kinds of antelope and, occasionally, elephants. The white settlers took much of the Venda's land and removed male labor, thus shattering the traditional economy and disrupting the pattern of family life. However, since the mid-twentieth century, there have been moves to help the Venda restore their agricultural output and also to develop cash crops such as bananas, peanuts, avocados, tea and coffee.

In 1979 the Venda were granted a measure of independence in their homeland, but land to the west and south, which had been taken over by white colonists for farming and mining, was not returned to them. One third of the Venda population, estimated at 450,000, now live in "white" areas, in the Soweto suburbs of Chiawelo and Meadowlands, and in towns in the Transvaal or occasionally farther afield. However, most Venda return to their homeland at least once a year.

Although working in gold is part of their culture, the Venda have never cared to labor in the gold mines; they prefer teaching, clerical jobs, labor for the municipalities, or work in stores and factories. They are not always easily identified in the towns and cities, because many have changed their names as a result of the rather arrogant attitudes of the numerically dominant Sotho-Tswana and Nguni peoples. The modern Venda have managed to blend the values of the past with the technological developments and bureaucratic organization that are necessary for the future of their homelands. Venda Christians, and especially members of the independent black churches, have taken up the social and spiritual message of the gospels with fervor. Modern education has been pursued with enthusiasm. School life is enriched by sports activities and the performances of choral music, often composed by Venda teachers.

There was a time when educated Venda were expected to reject the artistic achievements of their people, because of their associations with "pagan" beliefs. By the 1960s, however, some Venda were beginning to regard traditional music, dance, religion and folklore as the embodiment of their cultural heritage, and to appreciate that the expression of their own values and ideas must form the basis of their national development. In the 1960s their clan rituals were still important and they continued to practice public initiations, for example at puberty, but these traditions are now dying out.

The apparent homogeneity of Venda society masks a variety of clan rituals, many of which go back several centuries to the time when autonomous clans were grouped around hills or mountains that were regarded as clan centers. Acknowledgment of the past is contained in stories and songs, and especially the ritual song of the premarital initiation school. An important Venda custom is *murula*, in which *vho-makhulu* (wife-givers) regularly visit *vhakwasha* (wife-takers) and beer, food and, more recently, money are exchanged. This ritual can begin in childhood when a marriage is arranged between the families and go on until the death of one of the partners. Marriage is formalized by the removal of the bride by night to her husband's home. Cross-cousins can marry, and the marriage of a man with his mother's brother's daughter is especially favored. Divorce is permitted, as is marriage between two women, despite missionary disapproval. Patrilineal descent is strong, but the mother's patrilineage is also influential.

The Venda have always been politically alive and often more successful than other South African blacks in maintaining their independence. Their future prospects, however, are dependent on the extent to which they are really able to make their own free decisions and plan a future that benefits the whole population, without widening the gap between the traditionalists and those with modern education.

Surviving with style
Herero women from Namibia wear 19th-century dress, introduced by the wives of missionaries. In 1904 the Herero rebelled against their German rulers and over 70% were massacred. Once pastoralists, the Herero are today crowded onto reservations and some work as servants or laborers.

Public initiations
This picture of Venda girls during a premarital initiation ceremony was taken in 1958. The ceremony retained its importance at least until the late 1960s, but is now dying out. The Venda are very musical—traditional songs and dances thrive and choral singing is of great importance in the schools.

Middle East

The wars, revolutions and political upheavals that afflict the Middle East today are in part an echo of its turbulent past, a past dominated by the power of religion, which here is often inextricably bound up with politics. The Middle East was the birthplace of three great universal faiths, Judaism, Christianity and Islam, and all these religions have in turn deeply affected the region's history, culture and traditions. This same region has fostered some of the world's most ancient civilizations—the earliest evidence of agriculture is found here, and the oldest forms of writing. The Middle East has been the setting for major developments that have shaped the course of human history, and in the twentieth century the discovery of oil has guaranteed its renaissance and its continuing importance in international affairs.

Much of this region is desert or almost featureless, semi-arid plains, but in the north and northeast the land rises

steeply, and Turkey, northern Iraq, Iran and Afghanistan are dominated by massive mountain ranges. These extend from the Mediterranean Sea round to the Gulf, and from there up into the Himalayas. Here rainfall is more plentiful, and for centuries sheep, cattle and goats have been kept on the fertile, grassy slopes and crops such as millet, barley and wheat grown.

In most of the rest of the region, however, irrigation is essential for farming, and the major civilizations of the past sprang up around great rivers—the Tigris, the Euphrates and, in North Africa, the Nile. Here settled cultivators lived in simple, mud-brick houses and grew wheat, barley, dates and vegetables. They also kept a few goats and sheep, and traded some of their produce with the nomadic bedouin who herded camels across the more arid regions of steppe and desert. Since many communities of nomads and peasants were almost self-sufficient, rulers of empires and city-states under whose jurisdiction they fell often had to extract their tribute by force.

Invasions and empires

The linguistic and ethnic complexities of the Middle East are due in part to its lack of natural boundaries. Land and sea trade routes have crossed the region since ancient times and these have also served as invasion routes on many occasions. At the same time the Middle East's mountainous zones and deserts have provided places of refuge and aided the survival of minority groups, which continue to play an important political role.

The most momentous conquests in this region were the swift Arab invasions of the seventh century AD that brought Islam from the Arabian peninsula to the rest of the Middle East, North Africa and parts of Europe. The first Muslim empires were Arab dominated, but the civilizations and traditions of the vast Byzantine and Persian conquered territories were partially absorbed and contributed to the newly emerging Islamic civilization. After the initial Arab conquests, non-Arab Islamic empires such as the Ottoman Empire emerged. Turkish tribes from the north, who began gradually to move southward in AD 1000, adopted Islam and formed the basis of the Ottoman Empire, which subsequently dominated much of the Middle East and adjacent regions, including Arab lands.

The first Islamic empires often relied upon nomadic cavalries, and by the fifteenth century these began to adapt to gunpowder weapons. However, the European powers were quicker than Middle Eastern ones to exploit new military technology and changing economic opportunities, and by the late eighteenth century the Middle East began to fall prey to European demands and incursions. Only in the midtwentieth century did the last vestiges of direct colonial rule disappear.

The role of religion

Islam has played a major role in shaping the politics of this region and in giving its people a sense of common destiny. Most Muslims share the "five pillars" of belief and practice: the declaration of faith, the five daily prayers, almsgiving, the month-long Ramadan fast and the pilgrimage to Mecca. The Feast of Abraham occurs at the time of the annual pilgrimage to Mecca, and on this day every household with the means to do so, throughout the Muslim world, sacrifices an animal and shares its meat, distributing some to the poor. The Middle Eastern Muslim population is about equally divided between the Sunni and Shia sects—Shia Muslims are prevalent in Iran and southern Iraq, and significant numbers live in other countries of the region, although these are predominantly Sunni. Although keenly felt, the differences between them, in both belief and practice, are not in fact all that great. However, as the Iranian revolution showed, Shia religious leaders can exercise far-reaching political influence more readily than their Sunni counterparts.

There are also numerous regional and local variations in Islamic belief and practice. Especially in rural areas, many people believe in spirits and powers not regarded as elements of Islamic faith by educated Muslims. In the Northern Tier countries many adhere to one of the Sufi—mystical, religious brotherhoods—although these have been declared illegal in Turkey. Except on the Arabian peninsula, many countries have significant Christian and Jewish communities. Since the creation of the state of Israel in 1948, however, the size of Jewish communities elsewhere in the Middle East has been greatly reduced.

Today much of the Middle East is ruled by monarchs and military dictators. The endemic political crises in the region, including the Arab-Israeli conflict, the Iran-Iraq dispute, the Iranian revolution and the Soviet intervention in Afghanistan, ensure that the Middle East will continue to face profound internal and external challenges. At the same time, the rapid social transformations engendered by massive oil revenues offer this region tremendous opportunities for the future.

Nodūshan - a small town in central Iran

Arab States, Israel, Iraq 1

Since prehistoric times, these lands have been a crucible of invention and innovation, the birthplace of agriculture, irrigation and writing. They have also long been a crossroads of mankind; *here three of the world's most influential religions— Judaism, Christianity and Islam—had their origins. Dominated today by Islam, the oil-rich Arab states now have immense wealth and power.*

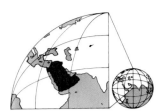

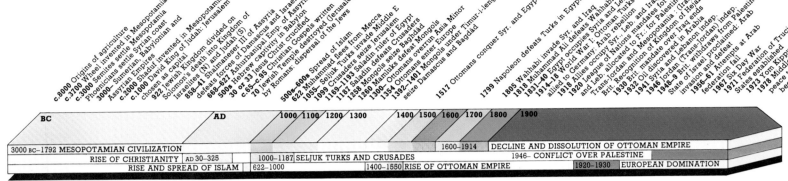

The timeline reads:

c.8000 Origins of agriculture in Mesopotamia · c.3700 Wheel invented in Mesopotamia · c.3000 Semites settle Syrian coast · Phoenicians settle Syrian coast · 3000– Sumerian Empires · Assyrian Babylonian and Sumerian Empires · c.2000 Shadul invented in Mesopotamia · c.1000 David King of Judah; Jerusalem chosen as capital · Solomon's Kingdom divided on Solomon's death into Kingdom of Israelites (N) and Judah (S) · 922 Jewish Kingdom divided of Israel and Judah · 858–11 Shalmaneser III of Assyria defeats forces of Damascus and Israel · 668–627 Ashurbanipal Emp. of Assyria · 500s Hebrew captivity in Babylon · 30 or 33 Jesus Christ crucified · c.65–c.95 Christian Gospels written · 70 Jewish Temple destroyed (Jerusalem) by Romans; dispersal of the Jews · 500s–600s Spread of Islam · 622 Muhammad flees from Mecca · 1055– Seljuk Turks invade Middle E. · 1099 Crusaders seize Jerusalem · 1169–1193 Saladin ruler of Egypt · 1187 Saladin defeats Crusaders · 1258 Mongols seize Baghdad · 1260 Mamluks defeat Mongols · 1300– Ottomans overrun Europe Asia Minor · 1354–1401 Mongols under Timur-i-leng · 1392–1401 Ottomans seize Damascus and Bagdad · 1517 Ottomans conquer Syr. and Egypt · 1799 Napoleon defeats Turks in Egypt · 1805 Wahhabi invade Syr. and Iraq · 1818 Muhammad Ali defeats Wahhabi · 1831–40 Egypt occupies Syria and Leb. · 1914–18 World War I; Ottoman Turks allied to Germany; Arab rebellion · 1918 Allies occupy Syr., Leb. and Iraq · 1920 League of Nations mandates for Syr. Trans-Jordan and Mesopotamia (Iraq) to Brit. Recognition of Kingdom of Hejaz · 1930 Brit. mandate over Iraq ends · 1932 Oil discovered in Arabia · 1941 Syria and Lebanon indep. · 1946–9 Brit. withdraws from Palestine; State of Israel proclaimed; Arab invasion and defeat · 1948– Jordan (Trans-Jordan) indep. · 1956–61 Attempts at Arab federation fail · 1967 Six Day War · 1971 Federation of Trucial States established · 1973 Yom Kippur War · 1918 Middle East peace talks begin

BC	AD	1000	1100	1200	1300	1400	1500	1600	1700	1800	1900

3000 BC–1792 MESOPOTAMIAN CIVILIZATION · 1600–1914 DECLINE AND DISSOLUTION OF OTTOMAN EMPIRE
RISE OF CHRISTIANITY AD 30–325 · 1000–1187 SELJUK TURKS AND CRUSADES · 1946– CONFLICT OVER PALESTINE
RISE AND SPREAD OF ISLAM 622–1000 · 1400–1550 RISE OF OTTOMAN EMPIRE · 1920–1930 EUROPEAN DOMINATION

Population by Country
Total: 50 million

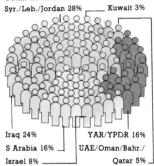

Syr./Leb./Jordan 28% — Kuwait 3%
Iraq 24%
S Arabia 16%
Israel 8%
YAR/YPDR 16%
UAE/Oman/Bahr./
Qatar 5%

Population by Religion

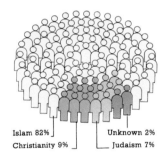

Islam 82%
Christianity 9%
Unknown 2%
Judaism 7%

Cross, crescent and star
Lying on the watershed separating the Mediterranean from the desert, Jerusalem, as an ideal natural fortress, was chosen by David for the capital of the kingdom of Judea after 1000 BC and thus became the spiritual heart of the Jewish nation. Following the period of Christ's ministry, it also became the symbolic home of the Christian faith. With the destruction of the city by the Romans in AD 70 and the dispersal of the Jews, Jerusalem became a Christian city, first under the domination of Rome and later the Byzantine Empire. Ironically it was the heavy yoke of Byzantine rule that encouraged the Christian patriarch Sophronius to open the city gates to the less oppressive overlordship of Islam in AD 638. Just over 60 years later the mosque known as the Dome of the Rock (which dominates this view of Jerusalem) was completed. The rock on which the mosque is built, is both the legendary site of Abraham's offered sacrifice of Isaac and the site from which the prophet Muhammad is believed to have ascended.

The Arabian peninsula and its neighboring lands to the north form a complex region which has long been a crossroads of trade and religion. Agriculture originated here, about 10,000 years ago, in the so-called Fertile Crescent, an arc of land that stretches from the Dead Sea in the west, through the foothills of the Taurus and Zagros mountains, to the confluence of the Tigris and the Euphrates in the east. Irrigation, a separate and later development, probably also originated in the Tigris-Euphrates valley and did much to encourage permanent human settlement.

In ancient times, Mesopotamia was the setting for a number of civilizations, including the Sumerian, Akkadian, Babylonian and Assyrian. The eastern Mediterranean was dominated by a succession of other Semitic-speaking peoples, notably the Phoenicians, Arameans and Hebrews. The latter was a group of seminomadic tribes that ruled ancient Palestine intermittently between the thirteenth century BC and the conquest of Jerusalem by the Romans in AD 70. A distinct Jewish ethnic identity and religion first emerged among the Hebrews in the Palestine area about 3,000 years ago.

Christianity sprang from Judaism about 2,000 years ago and in the early centuries of the Byzantine Empire (AD 330–1453), this new religion won many adherents in Palestine, Syria and Mesopotamia. A few of these people retained their faith and distinct community identity to present times, but about 1,400 years ago Islam arose in southwest Arabia, and less than a century after the death of the Prophet Muhammad in AD 632, it encompassed the entire region, as well as North Africa, Persia and parts of India and Spain. Arabic, the language of the Arabian peninsula, spread dramatically with the rapid expansion of Islamic domains after the seventh century AD so that it soon became the language of the majority of the region's inhabitants. Classical Arabic is still understood by educated Arabs, from Morocco in the west to Iraq and Oman in the east, and acts as a valuable unifying force.

For relatively brief periods after the Islamic conquests most of the region was under one rule, but it was too large and diverse for any central government to be effective everywhere. Inaccessible regions such as Oman, central Arabia and the Yemen remained largely autonomous. In the eighteenth and early nineteenth centuries the Wahhabi movement—puritanical Islamic reformists—united much of the Arabian peninsula politically and expanded rapidly into neighboring regions until checked by Egyptian forces in 1818.

With the break-up of the Ottoman Empire after World War I, Britain and France assumed control of much of the region, but by the late 1940s all countries except the Gulf states were free from colonial domination. Earlier boundaries remained largely unchanged, but for the founding of the state of Israel in 1948, which resulted in an influx of Jewish settlers and the flight or removal of up to 700,000 Arab Christians and Muslims.

Oil was discovered on the Arabian peninsula in 1932 and by the 1950s, when the revenues from production began to be applied in earnest to development projects, it had a major impact upon both the oil-producing countries themselves, and upon neighboring countries which supplied much of their labor force. Major inequalities of wealth characterize most of the oil-producing states, but in the last two decades extensive educational, health, housing and welfare programs have made significant inroads upon poverty.

Over 95 percent of the rural population are settled cultivators, most of whom live in small villages, while the remaining 5 percent are nomadic pastoralists. However, there has been a reduction of the rural work force in all countries as a result of wage labor becoming available in cities and abroad. Urbanization has proceeded rapidly throughout the region, the most spectacular growth of cities and towns occurring in Saudi Arabia and the Gulf states. All the states of the region seek to foster a sense of national identity among their citizens, but religious, class, tribal and linguistic differentiations remain important. Tribal distinctions are especially strong in northern Yemen and Saudi Arabia and here, as in other countries of the region, persistent efforts are being made to reduce the authority of tribal leaders.

There are cultural variations throughout the region, but several common elements prevail. Because marriages often imply political alliances and transfers of control over land and property, they involve long deliberations between the extended families of both parties. In rural and tribal contexts, these deliberations

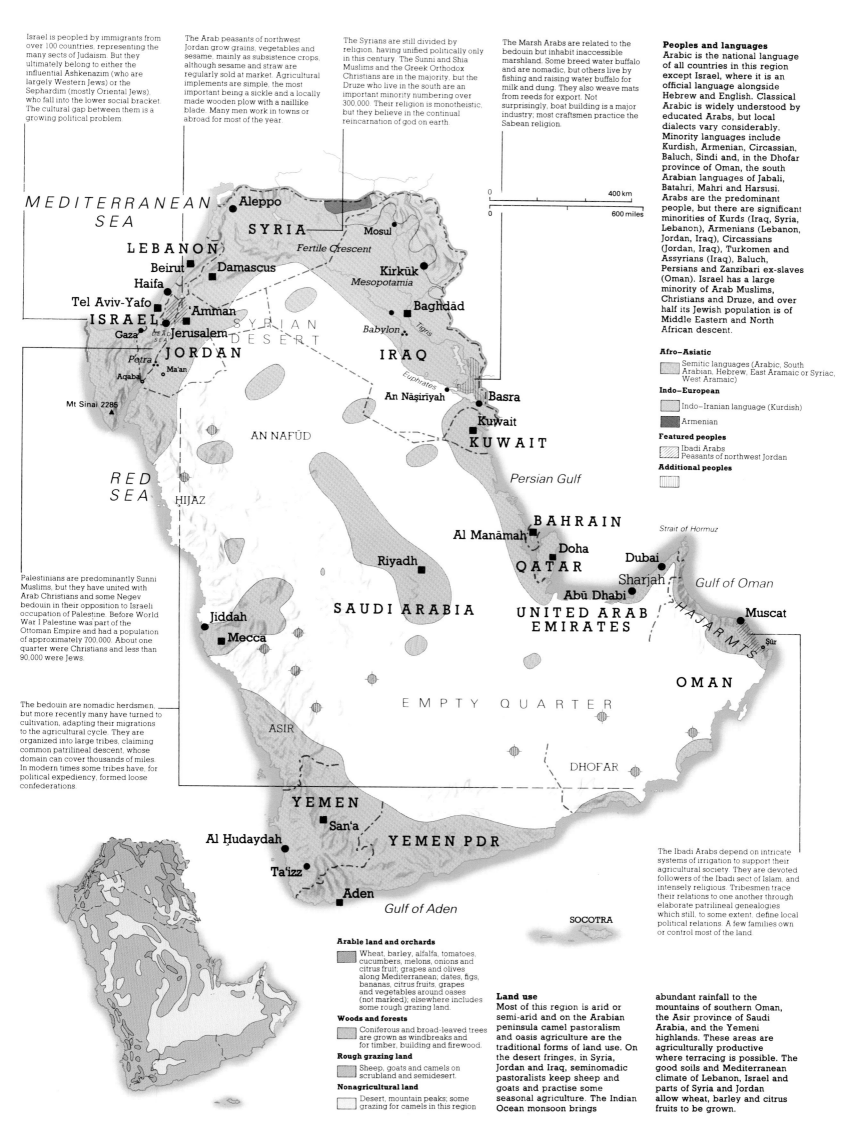

Israel is peopled by immigrants from over 100 countries, representing the many sects of Judaism. But they ultimately belong to either the influential Ashkenazim (who are largely Western Jews) or the Sephardim (mostly Oriental Jews), who fall into the lower social bracket. The cultural gap between them is a growing political problem.

The Arab peasants of northwest Jordan grow grains, vegetables and sesame, mainly as subsistence crops, although sesame and straw are regularly sold at market. Agricultural implements are simple, the most important being a sickle and a locally made wooden plow with a naillike blade. Many men work in towns or abroad for most of the year.

The Syrians are still divided by religion, having unified politically only in this century. The Sunni and Shia Muslims and the Greek Orthodox Christians are in the majority, but the Druze who live in the south are an important minority numbering over 300,000. Their religion is monotheistic, but they believe in the continual reincarnation of god on earth.

The Marsh Arabs are related to the bedouin but inhabit inaccessible marshland. Some breed water buffalo and are nomadic, but others live by fishing and raising water buffalo for milk and dung. They also weave mats from reeds for export. Not surprisingly, boat building is a major industry; most craftsmen practice the Sabean religion.

Peoples and languages
Arabic is the national language of all countries in this region except Israel, where it is an official language alongside Hebrew and English. Classical Arabic is widely understood by educated Arabs, but local dialects vary considerably. Minority languages include Kurdish, Armenian, Circassian, Baluch, Sindi and, in the Dhofar province of Oman, the south Arabian languages of Jabali, Batahri, Mahri and Harsusi. Arabs are the predominant people, but there are significant minorities of Kurds (Iraq, Syria, Lebanon), Armenians (Lebanon, Jordan, Iraq), Circassians (Jordan, Iraq), Turkomen and Assyrians (Iraq), Baluch, Persians and Zanzibari ex-slaves (Oman). Israel has a large minority of Arab Muslims, Christians and Druze, and over half its Jewish population is of Middle Eastern and North African descent.

Afro–Asiatic

Semitic languages (Arabic, South Arabian, Hebrew, East Aramaic or Syriac, West Aramaic)

Indo–European

Indo–Iranian language (Kurdish)

Armenian

Featured peoples

Ibadi Arabs
Peasants of northwest Jordan

Additional peoples

Palestinians are predominantly Sunni Muslims, but they have united with Arab Christians and some Negev bedouin in their opposition to Israeli occupation of Palestine. Before World War I Palestine was part of the Ottoman Empire and had a population of approximately 700,000. About one quarter were Christians and less than 90,000 were Jews.

The bedouin are nomadic herdsmen, but more recently many have turned to cultivation, adapting their migrations to the agricultural cycle. They are organized into large tribes, claiming common patrilineal descent, whose domain can cover thousands of miles. In modern times some tribes have, for political expediency, formed loose confederations.

The Ibadi Arabs depend on intricate systems of irrigation to support their agricultural society. They are devoted followers of the Ibadi sect of Islam, and intensely religious. Tribesmen trace their relations to one another through elaborate patrilineal genealogies which still, to some extent, define local political relations. A few families own or control most of the land.

Arable land and orchards

Wheat, barley, alfalfa, tomatoes, cucumbers, melons, onions and citrus fruit; grapes and olives along Mediterranean; dates, figs, bananas, citrus fruits, grapes and vegetables around oases (not marked); elsewhere includes some rough grazing land.

Woods and forests

Coniferous and broad-leaved trees are grown as windbreaks and for timber, building and firewood.

Rough grazing land

Sheep, goats and camels on scrubland and semidesert.

Nonagricultural land

Desert, mountain peaks; some grazing for camels in this region

Land use
Most of this region is arid or semi-arid and on the Arabian peninsula camel pastoralism and oasis agriculture are the traditional forms of land use. On the desert fringes, in Syria, Jordan and Iraq, seminomadic pastoralists keep sheep and goats and practise some seasonal agriculture. The Indian Ocean monsoon brings abundant rainfall to the mountains of southern Oman, the Asir province of Saudi Arabia, and the Yemeni highlands. These areas are agriculturally productive where terracing is possible. The good soils and Mediterranean climate of Lebanon, Israel and parts of Syria and Jordan allow wheat, barley and citrus fruits to be grown.

Arab States, Israel, Iraq 2

may involve the entire community. In most countries of the region, notions of Islamic law pervade both formal legal systems and popular expectations, and political action, whether radical or conservative, tends to be justified by appeal to religious principles. There is significant variation in the status of women. Saudi Arabia is in some ways the most restrictive, although there, and in most other countries, education and modernization have resulted in a dramatic rate of improvement in women's status.

The Ibadi Arabs of Oman and the peasants of northwest Jordan emphasize the contrasting economic and political contexts of this region. Oman was one of the poorest countries of the world until 1970, but in the past decade oil revenues have brought dramatic changes in the material conditions of life. Jordan has no oil, but in recent years, many Jordanians have found urban life and work abroad more attractive, leading to rural stagnation typical of the region. In both cases, traditional cultural and religious values continue to shape the course of development.

Ibadi Arabs of Inner Oman

Most of the Ibadi tribes of Oman are settled cultivators living in oasis towns and villages on the eastern side of the Hajar mountain range. Inner Oman has been a stronghold of Ibadi Islam since the sect was first established there in AD 730. Since then the community has, with few exceptions, been ruled by an *imam* (religious and political leader), formally qualified by religious learning and personal piety, and informally selected by other learned men from among the *shaykhs* (leaders) of dominant tribes. Imamate rule over the interior ended when the Sultan of Muscat and Oman forced the last *imam*'s abdication in 1955, but Ibadi doctrine continues to have a significant influence on political structure and organization in Oman.

Inner Oman has approximately 235,000 inhabitants, most of whom live in small villages of a few hundred persons each. A minority of *shaykh* families own or control most of the land and water rights, leaving the majority of tribesmen dependent upon them. Although the Sultan has sought to limit the political role of *shaykhs* in recent times, they are still indispensable as intermediaries between government and tribesmen

and constitute the pool of talent from which local government officials are drawn. Some of the inhabitants of larger towns and villages are ex-slaves of African origin (also Ibadi Muslims) who act as servants, armed retainers and agricultural laborers for the wealthier tribal *shaykhs*, or work as blacksmiths, butchers and barbers. With recent economic and social changes, ex-slaves are seeking more prestigious employment, particularly in the army and the police.

Each village is built around at least one underground irrigation channel, which conducts water by gravity flow from the hillsides to the orchards and fields. Some additional lands are irrigated by wells, today often equipped with motor pumps. Dates and limes are the principal crops but melons are also grown, together with a few vegetables. Many households keep small herds of sheep and goats, and some tribesmen specialize in herding them in the more remote mountain valleys. Bedouin from adjacent desert areas, sometimes Ibadi but often Sunni Muslims, live during the summer on the outskirts of the larger towns and villages, where they maintain gardens.

Rural stagnation
In northwest Jordan a woman collects fodder for goats. Cash sent back by men working elsewhere is vital to the economy of this region.

Palestinian refugees
This farmer from Palestine lost his lands in the Arab-Israeli war of 1967, and his home is now a camp just outside Ma'an on the road to Petra. Many similar camps have been in existence since 1948 and their amenities are poor. Underemployment is severe, making these camps natural recruiting sites for the Palestine Liberation Organization.

The cradle of civilization
Bounded by the Tigris and the Euphrates, the region of Sumer in Iraq is a landscape of lagoons and giant reeds extending over 15,500 square km (6,000 square miles). The Ma'dan Arabs live in the central marshes, in reed houses built on man-made islands of reeds and mud. Their high-prowed canoes have not changed in design for centuries.

In general the region is not self-sufficient agriculturally, so that many adult males are compelled to emigrate in search of work. Following the oil boom in Saudi Arabia and the neighboring Gulf states, such work was readily available on the Arabian peninsula, and it is only recently that villagers have been able to find work in their own country. Oil was not discovered in Oman until 1964 and its revenues were not significantly used for development until 1970. Local clinics and schools have only been built in the last few years.

The Ibadi Arabs' strict code of etiquette and public conduct indicates a profound respect for personal honor and integrity. In villages and tribal centers *shaykhs* and their deputies meet regularly with tribesmen in *Jama'a* (informal council), an institution which pervades all levels of Omani society. Here local conflicts are resolved or regulated. The final decisions of *shaykhs* are rarely openly opposed, since they allow thorough discussion of all issues to ensure consensus.

Great emphasis is placed on cooperation within the extended family, and marriages, many of which take place when children are in their early teens, are arranged by parents within the extended family itself. Because the households of close relatives are clustered together, women fetch water, herd animals near their houses, and perform their domestic chores without breaching the strict rules of sexual separation that prevail outside the extended family. Men, for their part, perform most of the agricultural labor, visit the market, and attend the daily coffee sessions at the *sabla* (guest room) of the tribal *shaykh* or, in the case of smaller settlements, the village headman.

The Ibadi are intensely religious, and men and women wake before dawn to perform their ablutions and the first of the five daily prayers. Each village has at least one mosque, and most also have Qur'anic schools for children. On major feast days tribesmen assemble for communal prayers, while women congregate nearby but do not pray publicly. Except for persons of slave origin, there is no public dancing, even at weddings. Community life is invariably intense—every village man and woman, regardless of status, visits any household in which there has been a death. The unmarked stones of Ibadi cemeteries symbolize the formal equality of all persons before God.

Arab peasants of northwest Jordan

There are over 200 villages in the cereal-growing region of the eastern foothills of the Jordan valley. The area is heavily populated, with about 300 people per square kilometer (780 per square mile). Irrigation is not practiced, and the 20–30 centimeters (8–12 inches) of rain which falls annually between November and March is considered the bare minimum for cultivation. Peasants follow a two-crop system, growing wheat,

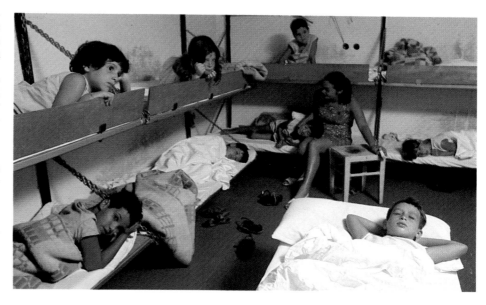

Children of the kibbutz
The first kibbutz, or collective settlement, was founded in 1909 by Jewish settlers in Palestine who sought the ideal society based on equality. This was to be achieved by group living, communal ownership and co-operative enterprise. In essence the family unit was to be replaced by the kibbutz. With subsequent generations, however, family ties and awareness have become the norm, while the original framework remains. Mothers keep their newborn babies for up to six weeks after birth. They then hand them over to the communal nursery, and join the rest of the kibbutz at agricultural or, more commonly, industrial work. The mothers have a short visiting period in the morning and at night, when they put their children to bed.

Oil and affluence
Sharjah was one of seven poor emirates in the 1950s. Now part of the United Arab Emirates it benefits from the oil wealth of the richest emirates, Abu Dhabi and Dubai, although it has no oil of its own. Oil has radically transformed the area, as reflected in the modernistic style of this newly built souk.

The price of oil and water
Omani tribesmen bring fleeces and vegetables into the market at the coastal town of Sur, Oman. Paved roads have recently been built, as the revenue from oil has begun to be applied to development, and camels and mountain donkeys are now used for transport only in the most isolated areas. Although oil production now dominates the economy, Oman is not oil rich by OPEC standards—Saudi Arabia's production is 30 times greater. On the other hand, it is fairly fertile, but even here agriculture is limited by water shortages. During periods of drought, some farmers are compelled to buy water for their crops at auctions. Dates and limes are the principal crops, but vegetables such as onions, radishes, garlic and cucumbers are also grown. Rice, a staple of the Omani diet, has to be imported from Pakistan. The infusion of oil wealth into the local economy has created a greater interdependence between communities. They now share such amenities as schools, clinics, electricity and other government services.

barley and fodder crops in the winter and vegetables, maize and sesame during the summer.

Until the 1930s a system of land tenure called *musha'* was common, in which the village collectively owned the land and each household was allocated a certain area each year. This system was replaced by individually registered, inherited plots in the 1930s. Because of land shortages and insufficient incomes derived from agriculture, much of the adult male population works elsewhere, in the army, the police or in other occupations, in Jordan or abroad. Remittances from these workers are a mainstay of the rural Jordanian economy, but because so many men have left, there is a shortage of agricultural labor, and Palestinian refugees are hired as sharecroppers and day laborers.

Most villages are made up of between three and six patrilineal descent clusters, each of which tends to have a separate residential quarter in the village. Men spend much of their free time in the guest house of their descent cluster. Men and women are normally expected to marry within their own descent cluster, although marriages are sometimes arranged with other descent clusters in the village for political reasons. Marriages involve complicated transfers of land and property, and thus entail extensive discussions among the relatives involved. Since nearly 80 percent of marriages are between villagers, they can trace intricate relationships to one another through both men and women.

Most villages are Sunni Muslim (although there are a few Christian ones) and they hire a preacher to deliver Friday sermons and to instruct children in the Qur'an. Ramadan, the month of fasting, is an intensely social time when villagers offer hospitality to their friends, neighbors and the village poor. Men and women separately visit their relatives and friends. It is also a time for reconciliation of quarrels, and young men who may not regularly attend Friday prayers during the rest of the year will participate alongside their elders.

Turkey, Iran, Afghanistan 1

As the craggy mountains of the Northern Tier rise up from the dry Arabian plains a cloak of green pasture begins to soften the landscape. Here, too, the austere face of Islam is softened and changed by the mysticism of the Sufis, and by the colorful clothes and music of the nomadic tribesmen. The area's rich ethnic mix is a legacy of its position as a crossroads of migration since the dawn of man.

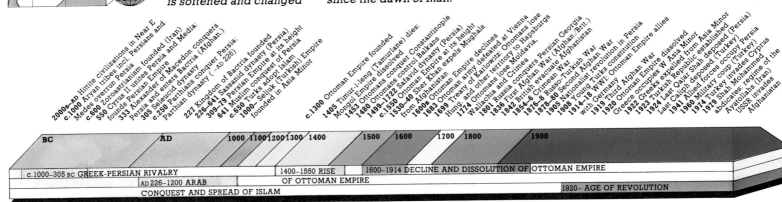

Population by Country
Total: 98 million

Turkey 46%
Iran 38%
Afghanistan 16%

Population by Religion

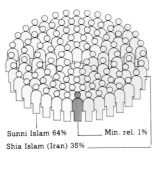

Sunni Islam 64%
Shia Islam (Iran) 35%
Min. rel. 1%

Turkey, Iran and Afghanistan, the three non-Arab countries of the Islamic Middle East, all have long frontiers with the Soviet Union and have become known as the Northern Tier. Since the earliest migrations of mankind, this region has been a crossroads for the movement of peoples, and the result is a highly complex mixture of cultures.

Two mountain systems cross the region, connecting the Alps of Europe with the Hindu Kush and the Himalayas of Asia. One range passes through northern Turkey, becomes the Elburz chain in Iran and joins the Hindu Kush in Afghanistan; the second crosses southern Turkey as the Taurus range, western and southern Iran as the Zagros, and becomes the Suleyman mountains in Afghanistan. These two mountain systems provide extensive high-altitude pasturelands. Between the two stretch the steppes and semideserts of the Anatolian and Iranian plateaus, marked by continental climates, while to the north in Central Asia, and to the south in Arabia and Baluchistan, lie further deserts and steppes. Much of the region is thus suitable only for seasonal grazing, with scattered patches of cultivation where water can be provided. In great contrast are the warm, wet, Mediterranean, Aegean and Black Sea coastlands of Turkey, and the Caspian coastland of northern Iran, where rich farmlands, forests and fisheries are all found. The southern coasts of Iran, however, are among the hottest and driest places on earth.

In a long history of invasions and empires, the most momentous were those of the Arabs from the south, who introduced Islam in the seventh century AD, and those of the Turkish tribes from the north from around AD 1000, who adopted Islam and dominated the whole

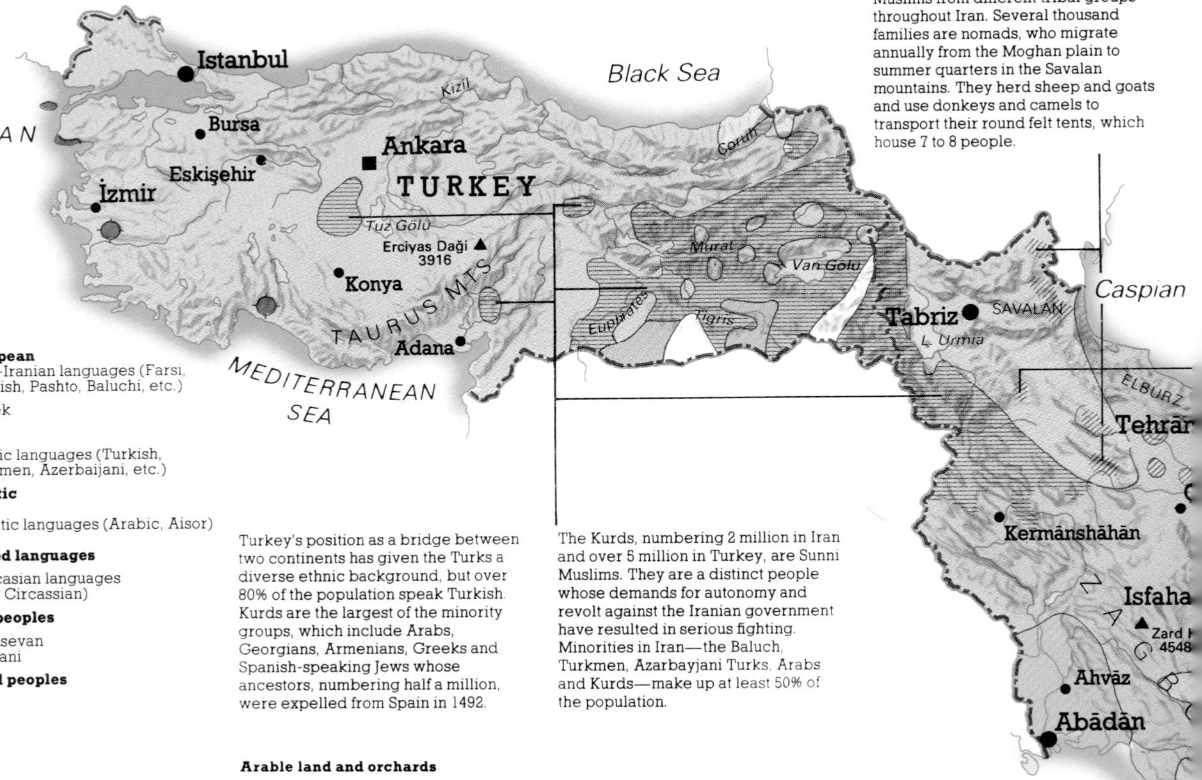

Shahsevan are Turkish-speaking Shiite Muslims from different tribal groups throughout Iran. Several thousand families are nomads, who migrate annually from the Moghan plain to summer quarters in the Savalan mountains. They herd sheep and goats and use donkeys and camels to transport their round felt tents, which house 7 to 8 people.

Peoples and languages
Of the region's nearly 100 million inhabitants, 45 to 50 million speak Turkic languages. Anatolian Turks account for 35 million of these and Azarbayjanis 8 million. Speakers of Persian and related languages number over 45 million, including 20 million Persians, 12 million Kurds and Lurs, 6 million Pukhtuns and 6 million Tajik, Aymak and Hazara. Among Pukhtuns, Kurds, Lurs, Baluch, Aymak, Hazara, and many Turkic groups in Iran and Afghanistan, forms of tribal organization are still important.

Indo-European
Indo-Iranian languages (Farsi, Kurdish, Pashto, Baluchi, etc.)
Greek
Altaic
Turkic languages (Turkish, Turkmen, Azerbaijani, etc.)
Afro-Asiatic
Semitic languages (Arabic, Aisor)
Unaffiliated languages
Caucasian languages (Laz, Circassian)
Featured peoples
Shahsevan
Durrani
Additional peoples

Turkey's position as a bridge between two continents has given the Turks a diverse ethnic background, but over 80% of the population speak Turkish. Kurds are the largest of the minority groups, which include Arabs, Georgians, Armenians, Greeks and Spanish-speaking Jews whose ancestors, numbering half a million, were expelled from Spain in 1492.

The Kurds, numbering 2 million in Iran and over 5 million in Turkey, are Sunni Muslims. They are a distinct people whose demands for autonomy and revolt against the Iranian government have resulted in serious fighting. Minorities in Iran—the Baluch, Turkmen, Azarbayjani Turks, Arabs and Kurds—make up at least 50% of the population.

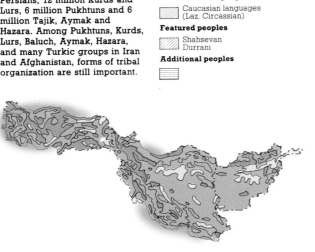

Arable land and orchards
Wheat, barley, sugar beet, potatoes, vegetables, cotton, tobacco, tea, poppy seed (for opium), grapes, citrus fruits and mulberry trees (for silk).
Woods and forests
Coniferous and broad-leaved trees for firewood and timber.
Rough grazing
Seasonal grazing primarily of sheep and goats.
Nonagricultural land
Mountain peaks, desert.

Land use
Seasonal nomadism and pastoralism are the traditional forms of land use over much of this region of high mountains, steppe and semidesert. There are dry-farmed areas in the north and west but most cultivation is on scattered pockets of irrigated land; rich farmlands and forests cluster along most of the sea coasts.

Map labels:
Istanbul, Black Sea, AEGEAN SEA, Bursa, Eskişehir, Ankara, İzmir, TURKEY, Tuz Gölü, Erciyas Daği 3916, Konya, Van Gölü, Murat, TAURUS MTS, Adana, MEDITERRANEAN SEA, Tabriz, SAVALAN, L. Urmia, Caspian, ELBURZ, Tehran, Kermānshāhān, Isfaha, Zard 4548, Ahvāz, Abādān, Persian Gu, Sh, Kizil, Çorum, Euphrates, Tigris

Timeline labels (top):
2000s–AD Hittite civilizations in Near E.
c.1000 Aryan tribes incl. Persians and Medes overrun Persia: Persians and Media.
c.650 Zoroastrianism founded (Iran).
550 Cyrus II unites Persia and Media: founds Persian Empire.
333 Alexander of Macedon conquers Persia and enters Bactria (Afghan.)
305 Seleucid dynasty (Afghan.)
c.250 Parthian dynasty (–AD 226)
227 Kingdom of Bactria founded
226–641 Sassand dynasty (Persia)
309–79 Persian Empire at its height
641 Muslim conquest of Persia
c.650 Turks adopt Islam
1000– Seljuk (Turkish) Empire founded in Asia Minor
c.1300 Ottoman Empire founded
1405 Timur-i-leng (Tamurlane) dies:
Mongol Empire dissolved
1453 Ottomans conquer Constantinople
1480 Ottomans control Balkans
1499–1722 Safavid dynasty (Persia)
c.1530–40 Ottoman Empire at its height
1600s Ottoman Empire declines
Sher Khan expels Mughals from Afghanistan
1683 Ottoman army defeated at Vienna
1699 Treaty of Karlowitz: Ottomans lose Hung. and other territory to Hapsburgs
1774 Ottomans lose Moldavia, Wallachia and Crimea
1801 Russia conquers Persian Georgia
1836 First Afghan War (Afghan./Brit.)
1842 British evacuate Afghanistan
1854–6 Crimean War
1876–8 Russo-Turkish War
1878–80 Second Afghan War
1905 Nationalist revolution in Persia
1908 Young Turks constitution
1914–18 WWI: Ottoman Empire allies with Germany
1919 Third Afghan War
1920 Ottoman Empire dissolved
Greece occupies W Asia Minor
1922 Greeks expelled from Asia Minor
1923 Turkish Republic established
1924 Last Qajar Shah deposed (Persia)
1941 Allied forces occupy Persia
1960 Military coup (Turkey)
1974 Turkey invades Cyprus
1979 Shah Mohammed
abdicates: regime of the Ayatollahs (Iran)
USSR invades Afghanistan

Timeline era bands:
BC | AD | 1000 | 1100 1200 1300 | 1400 | 1500 | 1600 | 1700 | 1800 | 1900
c.1000–305 BC GREEK-PERSIAN RIVALRY
AD 226–1200 ARAB CONQUEST AND SPREAD OF ISLAM
1400–1550 RISE OF OTTOMAN EMPIRE
1600–1914 DECLINE AND DISSOLUTION OF OTTOMAN EMPIRE
1920– AGE OF REVOLUTION

0 400 km
0 200 miles

region politically by the sixteenth century. Rapidly replacing earlier Christian, Zoroastrian and Buddhist faiths, Islam imposed a degree of uniformity in culture and religion, although local traditions have persisted and developed in all areas.

The advent of the Turks brought together two major nomadic cultures, the Central Asian with its round, white, felt-covered tents and Bactrian camels, and the Middle Eastern with its rectangular, black, goat-hair tents and dromedaries. After the rise of the Ottoman Empire and the fall of Constantinople in 1453, Turkish became the main language of Anatolia. In Safavid Iran and Afghanistan (*c.* 1500–1722), however, Turkic dialects were confined to certain districts and tribal elites, while Persian remained the main language of literature, administration, and urban and peasant society. The larger indigenous tribal groups accepted

Kala—an Afghan village
This fortified *Kala* is situated on the foothills of the Hindu Kush. Afghanistan is a mountainous land with an inhospitable terrain and a harsh climate and yet, because of its strategic position as the main gateway through the Hindu Kush mountain barrier, it has suffered a series of invasions. It is not surprising, given its violent history, its tradition of inter-village feuding and the prevalence of bandits, that many *Kala* resemble medieval forts. With their high outer walls flanked by square corner towers, these *Kala* provide shelter and protection for the entire community especially in time of danger.

Islam, but not Turkish culture, and continued to speak languages related to Persian, such as Pushto, Kurdish and Baluchi, as their descendants do today. Arabic, the language of scholarship, has never been the vernacular of more than a small minority in each country. However, Arabic script is used for the major languages of the region, except in Turkey where a Roman alphabet was introduced in 1928.

All three countries entered the nineteenth century as empires with a history of conquest, only to confront expanding European and Russian powers who defined their present frontiers, although without subjecting them to full colonial domination. Each country achieved formal political independence in the twentieth century under a reformist ruler: Ataturk in Turkey, Amanullah Durrani in Afghanistan, and Reza Pahlavi in Iran. The Durrani were ousted by an unpopular Soviet-supported regime in 1978, and the Pahlavis were replaced by an Islamic Republic in 1979, but Ataturk's western-oriented Republic of Turkey survives. The economy of Iran has been transformed by the oil boom, while Turkey, with a broad base of development, and Afghanistan, with very few resources, remain dependent economies. In recent decades there have been large-scale movements of labor, from Turkey to Europe and the Arab oil states, and from Afghanistan to Iran and the Gulf. The events of 1979 in Iran have led to a revival of pastoral nomadism and a middle-class exodus to Europe and the United States. In the wake of the Russian occupation of 1979, over two million Afghans of all ethnic groups and classes have fled to Pakistan and Iran, and many more have been displaced inside the country.

Ethnic categories are still used in all three countries as a major basis for social differentiation, despite efforts by recent governments, in the interest of national integration, to deny the existence of tribal or ethnic minorities. Ethnic differences, however, are increasingly cross-cut by class differences, particularly in major groups such as the Anatolian Turks, the Persian-speakers of Iran and the Pukhtuns. Each of these includes a wide spectrum of people, from the wealthy and educated urbanites to the poor and illiterate peasants.

The rural populations—now numbering around 40 percent in Turkey, 50 percent in Iran and over 80 percent in Afghanistan—tend to live in villages of a few hundred people. Most of them are cultivators and they rely on irrigation, either from surface water courses or by means of *qanat* or *karez* (underground channels) in the barren foothills. In spite of recent land reform measures, land is frequently owned by absentee landlords, who take the bulk of the crop. Major crops are grain, fruit and vegetables of all kinds, and more recently cash crops such as cotton, tobacco, tea and opium. Cultivators often produce silk and items such as carpets, and they usually keep some livestock. Extensive pastoralism, however, is the concern of nomads, who raise sheep and goats, producing meat, skins, wool and various milk products, both for home consumption and for the market. Villagers and nomads conduct direct exchanges, but also meet in the market towns, which are scattered throughout the region and function as craft and distribution centers. These market towns are linked to the cities and hence to a network of intercontinental trade routes.

No single way of life is typical of any of the major ethnic groups, whose main distinguishing features are language and religion—Anatolian Turks, Kurds, Tajiks and Pukhtuns being Sunni, while Persians and Azarbayjani Turks are Shiite. However, broad common themes emerge in major institutions such as marriage and religious festivals, and these can be seen in the contrasting ways of life of the Durrani cultivators of Afghanistan and the Shahsevan nomads of Iran.

Durrani of Afghanistan

The Durrani, a major branch of the Pushto-speaking peoples, number around two million and live in southern, western and northern Afghanistan intermingled with many other ethnic groups. In all areas Durrani, however poor, claim social if not political superiority through genealogical connection with the rulers, high officials and military leaders of Afghanistan, who from 1747 to 1978 came mainly from the Durrani tribes. Most

The 2 million Durrani are a major branch of the Pushto-speaking peoples; most live by farming and nomadic pastoralism. Durrani landowners commonly employ Uzbek Turks, Hazara and Tajiks as share-croppers, for up to half the crop. Sheep, goats and camels kept by villagers are often sent with nomads to pasture.

The Afghani Kirgiz inhabit the mountainous Wakhan corridor of northeast Afghanistan, but their original homeland is the Soviet Republic of Kirgizia, several hundred kilometers to the north. They are pastoral nomads, sheltering on the lower mountain slopes in winter but moving up to higher plateau grasslands in the summer.

The Hazara, who number over one million, speak a Persian dialect with many Turkish and Mongolian words; according to legend they are descendants of Chingghis Khan's army. They remained independent in their harsh, isolated mountains until 1892. With the help of irrigation they grow grains, pulses and fodder for their cattle, sheep and goats.

Turkey, Iran, Afghanistan 2

Durrani are rural people, living by settled farming or nomadic pastoralism, or by a combination of the two.

The village cultivators use simple farming techniques involving the iron-tipped plow, the smoothing-board drawn by oxen, and the spade and sickle. Durrani men may work in the fields (although many take on laborers from other ethnic groups) while women and small children carry out domestic tasks within the high-walled compounds. Each village is based on a patrilineage and only members of that patrilineage can own village land, though not all do so. Resident nonmembers are known as *hamsaya* (neighbors), but are treated as clients. Each household jealously guards its independence in controlling its resources. Land is inherited by sons, but cousins and even brothers may be bitter rivals over patrimony or marriage decisions.

Sons and daughters are married off early. Wealthy family heads usually choose spouses for their children, particularly for elder sons, thus hoping to further family interest through alliances. Brideprices are very high except among close kin, and may delay a poor man's marriage unless an exchange of girls can be arranged. Much of the brideprice is spent on the bride's trousseau. Every married woman should have a room of her own, though married men rarely become independent of their father before his death. Only the very wealthy, or those whose first wives have failed to produce sons, marry further wives. Weddings are spectacular affairs, at which anyone who can hear the drums and pipes is welcome. The very poor can often survive the winter on wedding fare.

Durrani are devout Sunni Muslims. Every village has a mosque (for men only) and a resident mullah to lead prayers, contract marriages and conduct burial and mourning ceremonies. He also teaches all children how to perform their religious duties, and sometimes imparts basic literacy skills. Major ceremonies are held at the feast concluding Ramadan and the Feast of Sacrifice, with mass gatherings at the mosque, followed by games, competitions and dances. Many villagers belong to a Sufi brotherhood and when their *pir* (spiritual leader) visits to collect tithes and hold ceremonies, his younger followers achieve ecstasy through controlled breathing and movement, an experience held to be a proper complement to the sober, impersonal, formal religion of the mosque.

Ordinary daily life is intense—Durrani men and women hate to be alone, and delight in heated conversation. Men regularly invite each other to meals, and so do women. Leading men in any community keep separate houses or rooms for guests, and here their male friends will gather on winter evenings.

A man with wealth and personality may be recognized as a *malik* (village leader), officially responsible for dealings with government, but formal authority belongs to the *jirga* (assembly of adult males), which may be called by the *masharan* (elders) to determine common action in a crisis or to consider a dispute

Buzkashi—a national sport
Buzkashi is the dramatic national sport of the Afghans. It is played as a team game in the cities, but in the country it is often a sport for individuals. A headless calf or goat carcass is placed in the middle of a circle of horsemen who then fight to pick it up. The successful rider, gripping the carcass under one leg, has to ride around a post, sometimes as much as a mile away, and back to the winning circle while staving off the other competitors.

Wedding dance of the Durrani
Dancing, games and feasting precede the actual wedding ceremony. At the climax of a Durrani village wedding, after the bride's trousseau has been displayed to the assembled guests from both sides, the groom is dressed by an elder in new white clothes, before the bride herself is brought out to be taken to the groom's home. Durrani weddings are elaborate and expensive affairs; brideprices are high and divorce is almost unknown.

To the harvest
These Turkish women from the Black Sea area are on their way to the harvest. Women are usually confined to domestic tasks in and around the home— the harvest is the only time of year when couples work side by side. These women are carrying their babies in carved cradles on their backs. While they are busy in the fields, they leave the cradles hanging from the branches of an olive or a carib tree. Each village in the area has a cradle maker.

Isfahan's labyrinthian bazaar
Isfahan's bazaar is a bewildering maze of enclosed alleys and is renowned as a center for metal crafts—an essentially male activity. Carpet making, for which the whole region is famous, remains an industry carried out by women and children at home.

Tents of the nomads
The Kirgiz of northern Afghanistan use a tent similar to the *alachigh* of the Shahsevan, although among the Kirgiz it is called *oey*. With their wooden frames and outer covering of thick felt they provide better protection from extreme conditions than the rectangular tents made of woven goat-hair cloth that are used by the majority of nomads in this region. The tent has a hole in the roof to allow smoke to escape.

Milk, wool and surplus animals, especially young rams, are sold to visiting merchants or in the towns, to obtain wheat flour and other supplies. Care of the animals, marketing, and the erection of the tents are tasks for men and boys. Women and girls may fetch water but normally stay in camp; their tasks include baking bread, making cheese, yogurt and butter, and weaving colorful rugs and bags.

Brothers, sometimes cousins and occasionally other relatives and hired shepherds, cooperate in small herding groups, but the most important group in nomadic society is the community of about thirty households, mostly descended patrilineally from a common ancestor a few generations back. Each community has its own winter and summer pastures, migrates between them as a unit, and forms a congregation, with a specially erected mosque tent, at religious ceremonies such as the Ramadan fast and the mourning in Muharram.

Unlike the Durrani, neither egalitarian assemblies nor the mediation of respected holy men are part of Shahsevan culture. Community affairs are directed by an elder, who also organizes religious ceremonies and deals with outside authorities. He is usually the wealthiest member, and maintains a life style that embodies the honor of the community, for example by receiving important guests and financing lavish entertainment at weddings and funerals attended by outsiders. He also controls marriages, up to half of which are between community members. Women too have elders, whose opinions and decisions may be respected by the whole community. Communities are grouped into about thirty tribes, averaging a few hundred families and headed by a chief. The tribes are not linked genealogically, and many comprise patrilineages of disparate origins.

The Shahsevan were prominent over the last 250 years in the history of Azarbayjan, often a battleground between Iran and her neighbors. In the nineteenth century, after Russia deprived the nomads of the better part of their winter quarters, their raids disrupted trade and settlement far into both Iran and Russia, causing friction between the powers. Following disarmament in 1923, the Shahsevan, like other nomad tribes in Iran, underwent government reforms, the most dramatic of which was a ban on migration and the use of tents. This forced settlement was disastrous for the nomads and their flocks, and by 1941 they had resumed their former way of life. Between 1950 and 1978 the construction of massive irrigation schemes in Moghan brought a more gradual settlement, but this was reversed once again by the revolution of 1979.

The nomads are far outnumbered by the local peasants and townsmen, whom they call *Tat*. Although culturally distinct, Shahsevan and *Tat* share the same language and religion and are closely linked economically and administratively. Shahsevan nomads often abandon their tribal identity soon after they settle, and indeed many *Tat* are Shahsevan by origin.

arising from theft, trespass, sexual offense or murder. Penalties and compensation for such offenses are specified in a strict code of personal honor. Women may not normally attend assemblies, but their opinions can be made known and their causes pleaded there by respected old ladies. At such assemblies—which have become institutionalized at all levels of Afghan politics—no man can enforce his will, since decisions should be reached by consensus and persuasion. These egalitarian ideals are sometimes confounded, however, when a man accumulates land and followers and becomes recognized as a *khan* (chief), able to impose his authority on a tribal community. But the authority of chiefs, and disputes between them, are checked by the influence of respected holy men.

Shahsevan of northwestern Iran

The name Shahsevan means "lovers of the Shah," and dates from the seventeenth century, when Shah Abbas the Great of Iran made personal appeals to the loyalty of unruly tribesmen. Today, 200,000 to 300,000 people, all Turkish-speaking Shiite Muslims, but from a number of distinct tribal groups in various parts of Iran, still call themselves Shahsevan. Most are settled, but in Azarbaijan several thousand families of nomadic pastoralists continue to migrate from winter quarters in the Moghan plain near the Soviet frontier to summer pastures 160 kilometers (100 miles) south at heights of 3,000 meters (10,000 feet) in the Savalan mountains.

These nomads have distinctive round felt-covered tents of the Central Asian type, resembling upturned saucers. Large households are preferred, and the average tent contains seven or eight people, married brothers often staying together after their parents have died. The only partition in the tent is the curtain behind which a new bride and groom sleep in the first year of marriage.

The Shahsevan herd sheep and a few goats, with camels and donkeys to transport their possessions.

The thriving small business
Like most of the manufacturers in Afghanistan, this cutler in Kandahar produces and sells his wares in a small, open-fronted shop. It is by craftsmen such as this that people's everyday needs are met, since imported foreign goods are luxuries which most people can rarely afford. The country possesses rich mineral resources, but political problems and the difficulties of access and transport have, up to now, made exploitation uneconomical.

South Asia

South Asia represents an intriguing paradox, for it is a region of great racial diversity with innumerable cultures, languages and religions, yet it is a region that has a distinctive and unmistakable identity. Two of mankind's major religions, Hinduism and Buddhism, developed within its borders, and these, particularly Hinduism with its rigid caste system, have left their mark on its unique cultural pattern.

South Asia is clearly delimited by a massive arc of mountain ranges separating it from Afghanistan and Iran to the west, from Central Asia and Tibet to the north, and from Burma and China to the east. Its human diversity is partly due to the periodic immigrations of peoples from the northwest and, to a lesser extent, from the east. Once immigrant populations had entered the Indian subcontinent they were caught in a trap, for the vast oceans extending to the south, east and west barred any further southward movement

except to the island of Sri Lanka, which, geographically and culturally, forms an extension of southern India.

Thousands of dialects of the main language families are spoken in South Asia, and several of the world's principal racial types are represented. There are traces of Negroid elements, and an archaic type known as Veddoid occurs in many tribal groups. Populations of Mongoloid race are found in the Himalayas and the eastern highlands, and a branch of the Caucasoid race accounts for many of the populations of both north and south India. Their skin color is usually darker than among Caucasoids in other parts of the world, but in some northern regions, such as Kashmir, people as light-skinned as Europeans are found.

Religion and society

The most important element in Indian culture, Hinduism, resulted from the merging of the beliefs of the ancient

Aryans, who reached India between 1500 BC and 1200 BC, with the cults and practices of earlier populations. Knowledge of the Aryans is derived from the Vedic hymns, composed by their Brahman priests and handed down from generation to generation by oral tradition.

The structure of present-day Indian society can be directly traced to the division of Vedic Aryan society into four *varna*—Brahman (priests), Kshatriya (warriors), Vaishya (merchants and peasants), and Shudra (serfs). A fifth group, the Untouchables or outcastes, came at the bottom of the social order. This simple caste system of the Aryans has proliferated into an exceedingly complex structure in which there are several hundred castes. These castes can be broadly divided into three major groups—high, middle and low caste, the high caste group corresponding to the Brahman, Kshatriya and Vaishya *varna* of the Aryans. Membership of a caste is hereditary and marriage outside the caste is prohibited. This rigid system of social compartments remains the foundation of Hindu society, and it is an important factor in political life. Although active discrimination against Untouchables is now officially forbidden, it is still widely practiced, especially in rural areas.

In the first millennium BC a new religion, Buddhism, sprang from Hinduism and soon won over many of its adherents. The doctrine preached by the Buddha retained many Hindu concepts, such as that of reincarnation, with deeds done in one life affecting future existences. Other ideas, however, such as monasticism and the renunciation of secular life, were innovations. Although Buddhism has now virtually died out in India, it is the major religion of Sri Lanka and is strongly represented in Nepal alongside Hinduism.

The empire builders

From AD 997 onward, Muslim invaders harassed northern India with periodic raids, which destroyed the Hindu political system, and between the thirteenth and the early seventeenth centuries the greater part of South Asia was under the rule of Muslim dynasties, all of foreign origin: first the Turks, then Pathans and Afghans, and finally the Mughals. Muslim architectural styles, exemplified by the magnificent Taj Mahal, dominated northern India, and large sections of the population converted to Islam. In the Deccan and the extreme south, however, Hindu civilization continued to flourish. Where Hinduism and Islam came into confrontation attempts were made to reconcile the two belief systems, and one such attempt produced the Sikh religion.

In its final phase, the Mughal Empire was subjected to Persian and Afghan invasions from the north, and was threatened by a resurgence of Hindu power under the leadership of the Marathas, a martial people of western India. However, the final replacement of Mughal rule came from the British, who founded an empire that united the entire subcontinent. At first British rule was exercised through the machinery of the East India Company, a mercantile organization based in London, but in 1858 the responsibility for government was assumed by the British Crown.

British rule lasted until 1947 and the unity of India might have been preserved if a deep-seated hostility between Hindus and Muslims had not flared up as the end of British dominance seemed imminent. The Muslims demanded a state of their own, and Pakistan, consisting of two halves separated by more than 1,600 kilometers (1,000 miles) of Indian territory, was constituted. Hostility between India and Pakistan continues, particularly over the status of Kashmir.

Pakistan in its original shape lasted for only twenty-four years, and in 1971 the eastern wing became independent, as the People's Republic of Bangladesh, after a short but bitter civil war, in which many thousands of people died. Both Pakistan and Bangladesh have experienced long periods of military rule, but India and Sri Lanka are democratic republics under presidents, their parliamentary systems a legacy of British colonialism.

Hindus bathing in the Ganges at dawn

Himalayas 1

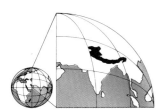

From the north, the Himalayas are scoured by the cold, dry winds of Tibet, while from the south come the warm, moisture-laden winds of the monsoon. Thus these majestic mountains are a dividing line for climate, as well as for language, religion and race. Here Mongoloid and Caucasoid meet, while Hinduism, Islam and Buddhism mingle with the mysterious spirits of ancient faiths.

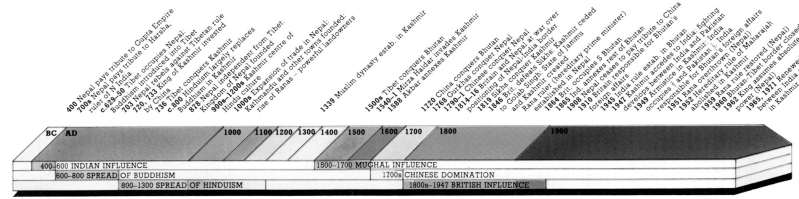

Timeline events:
400 Nepal pays tribute to Gupta Empire
700s Nepal pays tribute to Harsha, ruler of N India
c.625–50 Tibet occupies Nepal; Buddhism introduced into Tibet
703 Nepal rebels against Tibetan rule
720, 733 King of Kashmir invested by China
736 Tibet conquers Kashmir
c.800 Hinduism largely replaces Buddhism in Kashmir
878 Nepal independent from Tibet: Kingdom of Nepal founded
900s–1200s Kashmir centre of Hindu culture
1000s Expansion of trade in Nepal; Kathmandu and other towns founded; rise of Ranas – powerful landowners
1339 Muslim dynasty estab. in Kashmir
1500s Tibet conquers Bhutan
1540–1 Mirza Haidar invades Kashmir
1588 Akbar annexes Kashmir
1720 China conquers Bhutan
1768 Gurkhas conquer Nepal
1790–1 Chinese conquer Nepal
1814–16 Britain and Nepal at war over positioning of Nepal-India border
1819 Sikhs conquer Kashmir
1846 Brit. defeats Sikhs; Kashmir ceded to Golab Singh: State of Jammu and Kashmir created
1864 Rana ruler (hereditary prime minister) established in Nepal
1865 Brit. occupies S Bhutan
1908 Ind. annexes rest of Bhutan
1910 Nepal ceases to pay tribute to China
1945 Britain responsible for Bhutan's foreign affairs
1947 India rule estab. in Bhutan
1949 Kashmir accedes to India; fighting develops between India and Pakistan over Armistice in Kashmir; India occupies and Pakistan responsible for Bhutan's foreign affairs
1951 Rana overthrown (Nepal); India responsible in Kashmir
1952 Hereditary rule of Maharajah abolished in Kashmir
1959 Rana rule restored (Nepal)
1960 Bhutan; foreign affairs power (Nepal)
1962 King assumes absolute power (Nepal)
1965, 1971 Indo-Tibet border closed
1965, 1971 Renewed fighting between India and Pakistan in Kashmir and...

	BC / AD	1000	1100	1200	1300	1400	1500	1600	1700	1800	1900	

400–600 INDIAN INFLUENCE
600–800 SPREAD OF BUDDHISM
800–1300 SPREAD OF HINDUISM
1500–1700 MUGHAL INFLUENCE
1700s CHINESE DOMINATION
1800s–1947 BRITISH INFLUENCE

Population by Country
Total: 25 million

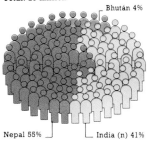

Bhutan 4%
Nepal 55%
India (n) 41%

Population by Religion

Hind. 73%
Islam 13%
Budd. 10%
Christ. 2%
Sikh. 0.5%
Min. rel. 1.5%

Peoples and languages
To the south are Caucasoid peoples, speaking Indo-Aryan languages and practicing Hinduism or Islam. Elsewhere Mongoloid speakers of Tibeto-Burman languages are found and in the mountainous regions these people have always been influenced by Tibetan culture and Buddhism. To the east, however, dense forests have enabled small tribal groups, who closely resemble the highland peoples of Burma and other parts of Southeast Asia, to preserve their own way of life, free from either Buddhist or Hindu influence.

Indo-European
Indo-Aryan languages (Hindi, Nepali, Kashmiri, etc.)

Sino-Tibetan
Tibeto-Burman languages (Rai, Bhotia, Tamang, Lepcha, etc.)

Unaffiliated languages
Burushaski

Featured peoples
Nishi
Bhotia

Additional peoples

The Himalayas, the world's highest and most majestic mountain range, have always played an important role as a natural boundary between two of the principal cultural and racial divisions of Asia: the Mongoloid speakers of Tibeto-Burman languages, practicing Buddhism, and the Caucasoid speakers of Indo-European languages, adhering to Hinduism and, to a lesser extent, Islam. The interaction of these ethnic complexes and of their great civilization has produced the racial, linguistic and cultural kaleidoscope that can be seen in the region today.

Areas of different altitude lie so close together in the Himalayas that a people's habitat may comprise several entirely distinct environments, a situation which favors seasonal migrations to make best use of the different zones. Apart from contrasts in altitude, there are also completely different climates prevailing on the northern and the southern sides of the Himalayan range, which separates the humid monsoon conditions of South Asia from the cold, dry climate of the Central Asian highlands. This arid zone extends into the western Himalayas and the northern valleys of Nepal, but the eastern Himalayas have much higher rainfall and are covered in a totally different type of vegetation—thorny thickets and dense subtropical forest.

Whereas the central Himalayas have for centuries been traversed by trade routes between Nepal and Tibet, the tangle of pathless wooded hills stretching from eastern Bhutan to the extreme northeast corner of India have served as a refuge for simple tribal communities, practicing shifting cultivation. In this region there are no caravan routes because of precipitous river gorges, and these people, who resemble some of the highland populations of Burma in race, language and culture, have developed their own economic and social institutions.

To the west of this zone lies the Kingdom of Bhutan, today an independent state linked by treaty with India. There Buddhist culture of the Tibetan type was superimposed on tribal populations, perhaps as early as the twelfth century AD. Until recently Sikkim was also dominated by a population of Tibetan stock and

Kashmir is in marked contrast to other highland regions. Here, a predominantly Muslim population has developed intensive irrigated agriculture. The beauty of the landscape attracts many tourists and these people provide a ready market for the products of urban craftsmen, who are highly skilled in weaving, embroidery, carpet making, wood carving and lacquerwork.

The arid highland region of Ladakh is one of the few remaining places where traditional Tibetan Buddhism (Lamaism) still thrives. Up to 20% of the male population are Buddhist monks, and other traditional features of Tibetan culture, such as polyandry, flourish with undiminished vitality, even though links with Tibet were severed following the conflict between China and India in the 1960s.

The 30,000 Lepcha are the indigenous people of Sikkim. Waves of Bhotia immigrants during the early 16th century converted these shifting cultivators to Buddhism, and Nepali immigrants during the past 100 years have brought elements of Hindu culture. The result today is a distinctive Sikkimese culture. Sikkim—called *Denjong*, The Valley of Rice, by its people—was an independent state until the monarch was deposed in 1974 and it was incorporated into India.

The Bhotia inhabit a vast region from Himachal Pradesh to Sikkim. They practice agriculture and pastoralism, but also depend heavily on trade between the Himalayan region and Tibet. They have been hard hit by the closure of the Indo-Tibetan border and by improved communications between Nepal and India. No longer the sole traders in the region, their traditional way of life is now under threat.

The Newar farmers, traders and craftsmen of Kathmandu valley are descended from the original inhabitants of the area who were conquered by Nepali hill tribes in the 18th century. They speak their own Tibeto-Burman tongue, and their religion is a combination of Buddhist, Hindu and indigenous elements.

Map labels: KARAKORAM MTS, Indus, Nanga Parbat 8126, Srinagar, INDIA, Simla, Ganges, Dehra Dun, Dhaulagiri 8172, Annapurna 8078, NEPAL, Kathmandu, Mt Everest 8848, Kanchenjunga 8598, Darjeeling

Buddhist religion, but immigrant Hindus from Nepal have multiplied so rapidly that they now form the majority of the population and political control has passed into their hands. Although they have the same farming technology as the indigenous Lepchas and Bhotias, the Nepalis are capable of accumulating more capital because they are frugal and hardworking, and devote far less time to religious activities.

In Nepal itself, the largest of the Himalayan states, the population is growing at an alarming pace, causing a shortage of land, erosion owing to deforestation, and unemployment. Unlike the territories to the east, Nepal has a long history of Indian penetration, and it is believed that as early as 270 BC Buddhist missionaries came there from the Gangetic plain. When, in the thirteenth century, northern India was invaded by Muslim armies many Hindu princes and chieftains sought refuge in the hills of Nepal, and subsequently established principalities there. The interaction of disparate ethnic groups has played an essential part in the formation of the civilization of Nepal, and through-

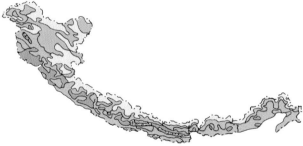

Land use
Fertile irrigated valleys across the western two thirds of the region are skilfully farmed to provide rice, wheat, maize and millet. Above 3,600 m (12,000 ft) only hardy crops such as buckwheat, barley and root vegetables can be grown. Here, the keeping of animals,

particularly yaks, is of great importance. Plows are generally used, but at very high altitudes some peasants continue to till the soil with iron hoes. In the dense forests of the eastern hills people hunt and practice shifting cultivation, growing rice, millet, maize, taro and sweet potatoes.

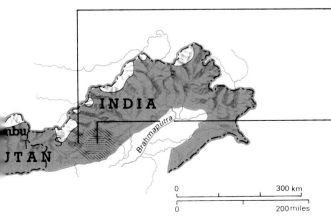

0 ____ 300 km
0 ____ 200 miles

Village in the clouds
The Bhotia village of Kermi in Humla, northwestern Nepal, lies at an altitude of 3,300 m (11,000 ft). Seen from a distance it resembles a large fortress, but it is made up of many houses, a maze of narrow lanes within the village giving access to each one. The houses are built of stone and timber and the ground floor of each serves as a cattle shed. On the first floor, reached by a notched ladder, is the main living room. Such compact villages have advantages, for in winter the inhabitants can move from one house to the next across the roofs without having to trudge through deep snow. In summer the roofs, often enclosed on two sides by covered galleries, are used for threshing crops and for carrying out the various household chores.

Arable land
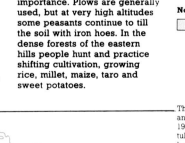
Mainly millet, maize, wheat, buckwheat, barley, sweet potatoes and taro are grown.

Rice fields
Irrigated and dry rice.

Woods and forests
Broad-leaved and coniferous trees, mainly for timber; shifting cultivation in eastern forests; some forests are being destroyed by uncontrolled felling.

Rough grazing land
Seasonal grazing for yaks, sheep and goats in high summer pastures; year-round grazing on lower slopes for cattle, pigs, mithan sheep, goats and yaks.

Nonagricultural land
Mountain peaks.

The 50,000 Nishi remained free from any outside political control until the 1940s. Shifting cultivation of grains and tubers, and animal husbandry form the basis of their economy. The men are skilled hunters and aggressive warriors. Although theirs is a patrilineal society, Nishi women have considerable independence.

The 15,000 Apa Tani are strikingly different from their neighbors, the Nishi. Although racially and linguistically related, they are skilled and industrious sedentary farmers who lovingly tend every available patch of earth in their valley. The valley floor is covered with rice fields irrigated by a network of canals. Maize, millet and tobacco are also grown and bamboo and pine groves planted.

out the country speakers of Indo-Aryan languages live side by side with populations speaking the many Tibeto-Burman tongues.

To the west of Nepal lie two areas of contrasting religion and culture which add further to the complexity of the Himalayan region. One is Kashmir, where a prosperous Muslim population practices intensive irrigated agriculture, and the other is Ladakh, whose population is of almost entirely Tibetan stock and whose culture has resisted both Hindu and Muslim influences. Since the suppression of Tibetan Buddhism by Communist China, Ladakh is one of the few areas where lamaistic Buddhism has flourished.

During the past thirty years development projects and the improvement of road and air communications have brought about dramatic changes in the Himalayan region, but the many different areas and peoples still have their own distinctive characters. The Nishi, shifting cultivators of the eastern Himalayas, and the Bhotia, Buddhist traders of the central region, demonstrate some of the contrasts to be found in what is perhaps the most culturally diverse region of the world.

Nishi of the eastern Himalayas
The Nishi, or Dafla, are one of the Mongoloid hill peoples of Arunachal Pradesh in the extreme northeast of India; they speak a Tibeto-Burman language. The total number in the Subansiri district is about 50,000 although a very similar group known as Bangni and numbering 22,000 live in the neighboring Kameng district.

Arunachal Pradesh, with its luxurious forest growth, subtropical climate and heavy rainfall, provides ideal conditions for shifting cultivation, the traditional basis of the Nishi economy. The Nishi sowing cycle starts in late April, both men and women cooperating in this task. They first sow maize and sorghum in holes dug with crude digging sticks, and then broadcast millet. Women also sow rice and plant taro and sweet potatoes. Most Nishi are self-sufficient in grain, although in bad years they also eat wild tubers.

The Nishi breed mithan (a domesticated form of the gaur) as well as common cattle, goats and pigs. They trade cattle and pigs for rice grown by neighboring peoples such as the Apa Tani. Mithan are kept principally for their meat and for sacrifice, and they are neither milked nor used for traction. The Nishi are expert hunters, a man seldom leaving his village without carrying a bow and poisoned arrows to kill wild bears and leopards. They are also skilled in setting traps and snares. They catch fish in bamboo traps inserted into dams by stunning them with poison.

Whereas several peoples of Arunachal Pradesh, such as the Apa Tani, live in large compact villages, the Nishi live in small settlements of up to fifty widely dispersed houses. Each longhouse stands on a separate site, preferably on the highest point of a hillock or spur, surrounded by granaries and pigpens. Most of the houses are joint family dwellings in which forty or fifty men, women and children live.

Nishi women enjoy a position of considerable independence within this patrilineal society. Before marriage they can engage in farming and petty trade on their own. Once married they have their own cultivation plot and granary and take charge of their husbands' valuables, which they secretly bury. Marriage ties with other wealthy families greatly strengthen a man's position. Previously a network of alliances gave security from attack, but even though this is no longer needed because of effective government control, it is still not unusual for a Nishi to have six or seven wives.

No one has individual rights to land and the inhabitants of a settlement are free to cultivate wherever they choose. Thus wealth cannot be invested in land and until recently a Nishi's possessions, consisting of cattle and valuables, could easily be stolen. None were born into a situation of lasting security, and status depended almost entirely on skill, energy and ruthlessness. There was no permanent social stratification and a man born a slave might be given his freedom and rise to the position of a respected householder, while a rich man could be totally ruined by an adversary or captured in a raid and sold as a slave. Slavery was abolished in the 1960s and raiding has now stopped under the effective control of government.

Himalayas 2

There is no leader among the Nishi, but conventions prescribe the conduct of kinsmen, limit the extent of feuds and provide for the safety of gobetweens engaged in negotiating peace settlements. Sexual offenses are unimportant to the Nishi unless they interfere with what is considered a man's property. Thus a girl's elopement will concern her father only if it deprives him of his brideprice, which may amount to ten or more mithan. A man whose wife leaves him for another man will only be outraged because he may have difficulties in recovering the price he paid to her parents. A husband who learns of the infidelity of his wife will scold and beat her, but will neither kill nor divorce her, as he would lose an economic asset. It is therefore not unusual for the young wife of a rich elderly man to have sexual relations with one of his sons or younger brothers.

When hostile parties meet to settle a feud, both keep to details of custom, each trying to prove that their own actions were justified and those of their opponents were a breach of custom. Oaths and ordeals are sometimes used to establish the guilt or innocence of an offender. An appeal to supernatural powers may also be made to strengthen the credibility of an oath, but there is otherwise no suggestion that gods and spirits are concerned with the moral conduct of human beings. Animal sacrifices are tendered in propitiation of deities believed to have afflicted people with illness, but never in atonement of wrongful conduct.

Consistent with this absence of any sense of guilt or sin are Nishi beliefs about the afterlife: that the final destination of the departed depends solely on the manner of their death and not on their record in this life. Those who die a violent death are believed to go to a different place from the ordinary Land of Death.

The traditional life style of the Nishi is gradually giving way to modernization. Since the 1960s Nishi country has been opened up by the construction of roads, and cash transactions have replaced much of the barter trade. Many Nishi have attended school and some of them have received higher education in universities outside Arunachal Pradesh. In no other part of India has social change been so rapid as in Arunachal Pradesh, where a small elite of the tribal population has achieved the transition from an archaic way of life to an entirely modern one within the brief span of thirty-five years.

Wives for prestige
Most affluent Nishi men have several wives, for this raises their prestige and gains them allies—in the lawless times before government rule, such allies were of assistance in feuds. When a man dies his wives are often inherited by his younger kinsmen.

Nishi longhouse
Longhouses are characteristic of the Nishi and several other peoples found in the eastern Himalayas. Each house stands by itself with the granaries of individual families built in groups, some distance away. The interior of a longhouse is not subdivided, even when several related families share it. Fields on which millet and rice are grown occupy nearby slopes, while carefully tended groves provide bamboo.

Bhotia ceremonial headdress
The frame of this elaborate headdress is silver and the top is covered with flat pieces of turquoise. A screen of silver chains hides the face of the wearer, while a silver casket worn on the chest contains amulets and slips of paper bearing sacred Buddhist texts.

Two husbands
Bhotia women of Yakba, a village in a remote part of Humla, wear valuable necklaces of turquoise, amber and coral. Some women have two or even three husbands, often brothers. Most women prefer polyandry because it gives them greater wealth and security.

Bhotia of the central Himalayas

Like the Nishi, the Bhotia are a Mongoloid people; their population outside Tibet numbers about 400,000 and they speak various dialects of Tibetan which are not always mutually intelligible. Most Bhotia live in areas of high altitude, and although they share many ecological and cultural features, they are not a homogenous ethnic group but comprise many different populations. Some groups are hardly distinguishable from Tibetans; others, such as the Sherpas of Nepal, have intermarried with neighboring non-Mongoloid populations. The name Bhotia is derived from "Bhot," the Indian name for Tibet, from whence these people are known to originate.

The great majority of Bhotia have long been involved in the caravan trade, since they inhabit the gap between two complementary economic zones—the arid Tibetan plateau and the more fertile Himalayan middle-range and foothills. Until the 1960s, they were the main agents of trans-Himalayan commerce in many regions, supplying the Tibetans with grain and many other Nepalese products in exchange for salt, wool and livestock. The pack animals used to carry this trade depended on the nature of the environment—yak were best at high altitudes while mules were more suitable for lower lying routes. On difficult paths only sheep or goats with small bags strapped to their backs could be used.

In addition to trading, many Bhotia communities practiced agriculture and animal husbandry, and this they continue to do—the herding of yak, involving frequent movement in search of new pastures, is especially important. Bhotia agriculture may also necessitate a seasonal shifting of labor from one place to another. Barley, buckwheat and potatoes can be grown as high as 4,000 meters (3,000 feet) and these are the main crops. Most agricultural tasks, including reaping, are performed by the women, the men being responsible for plowing and the care and herding of livestock. Plows are usually drawn by yak or cross-breeds of yak and cattle, although in a few areas teams of three or four men may do this work.

The Bhotia system of transhumance also determines their settlement pattern. The people of Khumbu as well as the Bhotia of western Nepal own several houses, all solidly built, in widely separated localities at different altitudes. There are three types of permanent settlements: main villages, winter settlements and summer settlements. The main villages are inhabited throughout the year by at least some families, and there the people have their principal houses, which contain their valuable possessions and most household goods.

Involvement in long-distance trade compels most Bhotia men to be away for much of the year, and in their absence the women are responsible for running the household and farm. As a result there is a high degree of equality between the sexes. Bhotia may marry anyone not closely related to them and the women may take two or three husbands, often brothers. There are no restrictions on the sexual adventures of unmarried boys and girls.

Bhotia society, which is patrilineal, is basically egalitarian. Civic tasks are taken up in rotation and the government of a village community is based on the concensus of its inhabitants. Authority is delegated to elected village dignitaries, whose term of office is strictly limited and whose duties are clearly defined. They have power to impose fines on those whose actions run counter to the interests of the community.

To the outside world a person is identified by the valley he inhabits, and the valleys were the main sociopolitical units of traditional Bhotia society. One of the few large political entities which survived into recent times was the domain of the Raja of Mustang which was, until 1951, virtually an independent state within the Kingdom of Nepal. The Raja still wields great influence, and the ancient walled city of Mustang remains the center of Bhotia civilization and a focal point of Buddhist culture.

Buddhism is the traditional religion of virtually all Bhotia and the gaining of merit is considered man's most important aim in life. Behavior believed to result in such gain includes religious and ritual practices, good deeds to other people and kindness to animals. A skilful mediator is more admired than a "strong" man, for the Bhotia ideal is not the heroic personality but the wise, restrained and peaceful man.

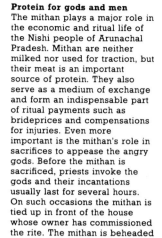

Protein for gods and men
The mithan plays a major role in the economic and ritual life of the Nishi people of Arunachal Pradesh. Mithan are neither milked nor used for traction, but their meat is an important source of protein. They also serve as a medium of exchange and form an indispensable part of ritual payments such as brideprices and compensations for injuries. Even more important is the mithan's role in sacrifices to appease the angry gods. Before the mithan is sacrificed, priests invoke the gods and their incantations usually last for several hours. On such occasions the mithan is tied up in front of the house whose owner has commissioned the rite. The mithan is beheaded and the meat is then divided between the priest and the participants.

The multipurpose yak
Yaks are extremely hardy animals that can be kept in the open throughout the winter, surviving even in heavy snow. Milk products constitute a major part of the Bhotias' diet; butter is the principal cooking fat and is also required for the preparation of salted Tibetan tea. Lamps using butter as fuel are an essential element of Buddhist ritual, and images decorated with butter are used as offerings. Cattle-owning Bhotias are expected to donate butter for use in temple services. The hair of the yak is made into coarse blankets and into bags that are used for the transport and the long-term storage of grain.

In memory and for merit
Religious monuments, known as *chorten*, are numerous in Mustang, a district of northern Nepal. They are a characteristic feature of Tibet and regions influenced by Tibetan Buddhism. Derived from the *stupa* of India, which were connected with early Buddhist civilization, chorten are primarily shrines in which relics and sacred scriptures are enclosed. By their construction, merit is gained, and chorten are often built in memory of lamas of special saintliness. Many chorten are built of stone and left unplastered, but some are plastered and painted in white and red.

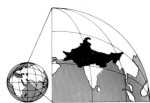

South of the Himalayas lies the vast plain of North India, broken only by great meandering rivers and their many tributaries. Swelled by the monsoon rains, these rivers often break their banks, with devastating effect. Here the simplicity of Islam confronts the richness and complexity of Hinduism, and the equality of all men before Allah opposes the rigid hierarchy of the Hindu castes.

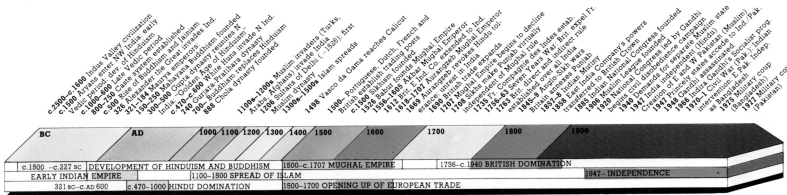

c.2500–c.1600 Indus Valley civilization
c.1500 Aryans enter NW India: early Vedic period; dev. of Hinduism
c.1000–600 Late Vedic period
800–750 Caste system established
c.500 Rise of Buddhism and Jainism
326 Alexander the Great invades Ind.
321–184 Maurya empire
150–250 Maurya dynasty reunites N. India; 'Golden Age of Hinduism'
300–500 Gupta dynasty emperors:
c.470–c.600 White Huns invade N Ind.
740 Gujara-Pratihara dynasty founded
700 Buddhism replaces Hinduism
888 Chola dynasty founded
1100s–1200s Muslim invaders (Turks, Arabs, Afghans) invade N India
1206 Sultans of Delhi (–1526); first Muslim dynasty
1300s–1500s Islam spreads
1498 Vasco da Gama reaches Calicut
1500– Portuguese, Dutch, French and British establish trading posts
c.1500 Sikhism spreads
1526 Babur founds Mughal Empire
1556–1605 Akbar Mughal Emperor
1612 Brit. E Ind. Co. extended to Ind.
1618–1707 Aurangzeb Mughal Emperor
1669 Aurangzeb revokes Hindu tol- erance; unrest in India
1690 British trade expands
1707 Mughal Empire begins to decline
1708 Sikhs make Punjab virtually independent of Mughal rule
1735 Fr. Compagnie des Indes estab.
1756–63 Seven Years War: Brit. expel Fr. established over all India
1763 Brit. direct and indirect rule
1845–9 Anglo-Sikh wars
1849 Britain annexes Punjab
1857–8 Indian Mutiny
1858 East India Company's powers transferred to British Crown
1885 Indian National Congress founded
1906 Muslim League founded
1920 National Congress led by Gandhi begins civil disobedience campaign
1940 Demands for separate Muslim state
1947 India independent (Hindu); Creation of E and W Pakistan (Muslim)
1947 Princely states accede to Ind./Pak.
1948 Gandhi assassinated
1966 Indira Gandhi's Socialist prog.
1970–1 Civil War (Pak.); Indian intervention; E Pak. indep. as Bangladesh
1975 Military coup (Bangladesh)
1977 Military coup (Pakistan)

	BC	AD		1000	1100	1200	1300	1400	1500	1600	1700	1800	1900

c.1500 –c.227 BC DEVELOPMENT OF HINDUISM AND BUDDHISM | 1500–c.1707 MUGHAL EMPIRE | 1756–c.1940 BRITISH DOMINATION
EARLY INDIAN EMPIRE | 1100–1500 SPREAD OF ISLAM | 1947– INDEPENDENCE
321 BC–c.AD 600 | c.470–1000 HINDU DOMINATION | 1500–1700 OPENING UP OF EUROPEAN TRADE

Population by Country
Total: 562 million

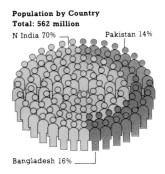

N India 70%   Pakistan 14%

Bangladesh 16%

Population by Religion

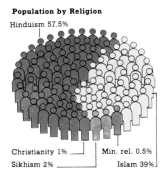

Hinduism 57.5%

Christianity 1%   Min. rel. 0.5%
Sikhism 2%   Islam 39%

Indo–European

◻ Indo–Iranian languages (Hindi, Gujarati, Bengali, Pukhtun, etc.)

Sino–Tibetan

◼ Tibeto–Burman languages (Naga, Boro, Kuki-Chin, Garo, etc.)

Unaffiliated languages

◻ Dravidian languages (Brahui, Kurukh, Malto)
◻ Austro–Asiatic: Munda languages (Santali, etc.); Mon–Khmer language (Khasi)

◻ Kisan

Featured peoples

▨ Sikh
▨ Pukhtun

Additional peoples

▨ ▥

Peoples and languages

Indo-Aryan languages (a subdivision of the Indo-Iranian group) gives unity to this huge region. Hindi has by far the widest currency, being the main language of Uttar Pradesh, Haryana and Rajasthan, and the dominant language in Bihar and Madhaya Pradesh. In the highlands of Bihar, tribal peoples speak Munda languages (including over 3 million Santal and over one million Munda) and Dravidian languages (including over one million Oraon). The Chittagong hills are also the home of tribal peoples who speak Tibeto-Burman languages. The people of Pakistan fall into four main ethno-linguistic groups—the Punjabis and the Sindhis, who have loose ethnic boundaries, and the Pukhtuns and Baluchis, who both have a strong sense of cultural identity.

To the south of the Himalayan mountain range lies a region of vast plains traversed by some of Asia's major rivers. For the traveler flying from Karachi to Calcutta the entire region presents the same monotonous view of undifferentiated plains dissected only by meandering rivers. During the monsoon many of these rivers tend to spill over their banks and flood huge tracts of land, with the result that millions lose their homes and suffer devastation of their farmland.

Although geographically homogenous, politically the region is less uniform. It was unified by the Mughal empire and under British rule, but because the Muslims of the north feared Hindu dominance, the country was divided in 1947 and Pakistan was founded as a separate state from India. Further fragmentation occurred in 1971 when East Bengal broke away from Pakistan and formed the state of Bangladesh. This newly emerged political configuration does not always coincide with the ethnic and linguistic pattern—thus the Indian state of West Bengal has much in common with Bangladesh, while the cultural pattern of the Indian Punjab resembles that of the western Punjab, now forming part of Pakistan.

A clear divide does exist, however, between Islam (largely Sunni Islam) shaping the way of life in Pakistan and Bangladesh, and Hinduism which is dominant in

After partition, millions of Urdu-speaking refugèes, *Muhajirs*, poured into Sind and settled in the towns, particularly in the port of Karachi. As most Sindhi are rural subsistence farmers and artisans, the Sindhi language has given way to Urdu as the main language of education and communication in the province.

The Pukhtun economy is based on the cultivation of wheat and maize, as well as cash crops such as tobacco, sugar cane and fruits. The Pukhtuns also raise sheep and goats. Much of their land is irrigated by canals and although traditional farming methods predominate, in certain areas modern machinery and methods have now been successfully introduced.

Punjabis make up 62% of Pakistan's population. A representation of over 70% in the army and more than 50% in the bureaucracy gives them virtual domination of Pakistan's political system. With the spread of education in Urdu, Punjabis have become bilingual, and although most are urban, still country dwellers, growth has been rapid.

CHITRAL
DIR
BAJAUR
Khyber Pass
● Peshawar
■ Islamabad
WAZIRISTAN
Lahore ● ● Amritsar
● Multan
PUNJAB
Sutlej
HARYANA
Delhi ■
PAKISTAN
Churu ○
UTTA
PRADE
Kalat ○
THAR DESERT
Bikaner ○
Yamuna
BALUCHISTAN
Jaipur ●
Kanp
Indus
RAJASTHAN
INDI
SIND
Hyderabad ●
Karachi ●
Mouths of the Indus
VINDHYA MTS
Jaba
Ahmadabad ●
● Indore
GUJARAT
Narmada
MADH
PRADE

0   600km
0   400 miles

northern India. Despite centuries of Muslim rule, life in the villages of northern India retains the Hindu pattern, characterized by the caste system. Indians believe that in the plain drained by the sacred rivers Ganges and Yamuna there lies the cradle of Hindu civilization, and this belief reinforces the claim of Hindi speakers that their way of life should be emulated by all Indians.

Each village community in northern India is typically composed of several castes, each with its traditional rights and duties, its privileges and its special functions within the community. The position of a man's caste determines the range of his career prospects and his social relations. Marrying a member of another

The British legacy
Bombay's railroad station is a splendid example of Victorian colonial architecture closely modeled on London's St Pancras station. India's vast network of railways holds the subcontinent together and is the most obvious legacy of British rule. Because of the railroads it has been possible to relieve those areas afflicted by flood, drought or famine—the perennial ailments of one of the most densely populated areas of the world.

caste remains virtually unthinkable except in sophisticated urban circles. Equally, a man's close social contacts are almost exclusively with his caste fellows, for even sharing a meal with a person of lower caste status pollutes a Hindu and may necessitate elaborate and expensive purification rites. Yet business transactions frequently involve members of different castes, as do exchanges between cultivators and artisans in the villages.

The villages in northern India are compact, with many homesteads of mud, brick or stone crowded around a central courtyard. In Bangladesh, however, they are more widely dispersed with single homesteads of bamboo or reeds surrounded by palm groves and paddies. This visible change highlights a fundamental difference in the rural society of Bangladesh, which is far less rigidly structured than in the west of the region. In general Bangladeshis have a spirit of independence that, together with their faith, Islam, has prevented the growth of the extreme class distinctions found in the caste system. The vast majority of Bangladeshis belong to the larger ethnic community of Bengali speakers, and this ethnolinguistic unity played a great role in Bangladeshi nationalism.

In marked contrast, Pakistan, which lies at the crossroads of central and southern Asia, has a diverse racial composition, caused by successive currents of migration. Of the four main ethnolinguistic groups, two are mainly agrarian societies living in the Indus valley, the dominant group, the Punjabis, having almost total domination of the country's political destiny. The remaining two, the Pukhtun and Baluch, live in the western borderlands and have retained their distinctive tribal structures. In both Pakistan and Bangladesh, Islamic beliefs impose rigid restrictions on women, who are generally dominated by their male relatives.

Two major cultural themes dominate northern India—the mixing of many different peoples through migration, and the conflict between Islam and Hinduism. The Pukhtuns of Pakistan illustrate the first of these themes, with their tribal society and warrior traditions whose roots are clearly in the mountainous lands to the northwest, while the Sikhs, with their conglomerate faith, are living symbols of the religious rivalry that for centuries has torn this region in two.

Sikhs of northwest India
Sikhs are members of a religious sect, about eleven million strong, that over the centuries has grown into an ethnic group with a pronounced sense of corporate identity. Founded by Guru Nanak in the fifteenth century, the sect believes in one supreme creator and, contrary to Hinduism, opposes the worship of images; it does, however, retain the Hindu belief in rebirth, and the doctrine that a man's fortune is shaped by his deeds in a previous existence.

The Punjab's 6 million Sikhs are members of a religious sect which over the centuries has grown into a distinct group with a strong cultural identity. They are successful, progressive farmers and enterprising businessmen who are found in all major Indian cities and in many foreign countries, as well as here in their original homeland.

The art, architecture, climate, and people of Bangladesh reflect the country's position as a bridge between South and Southeast Asia. It is a small country, most of whose 80 million people are subsistence farmers growing rice and jute on the delta, although there is some industry around the larger towns. Bengalis make up 97% of the population, the density of

which is very high—as many as 600 people per square km (1,500 per square mile).

Although the delta land is fertile, rainfall of up to 1,520 mm (60 in) a year, devastating floods and the occasional cyclone all bear heavily on the people—factors which keep Bangladesh among the world's poorest countries.

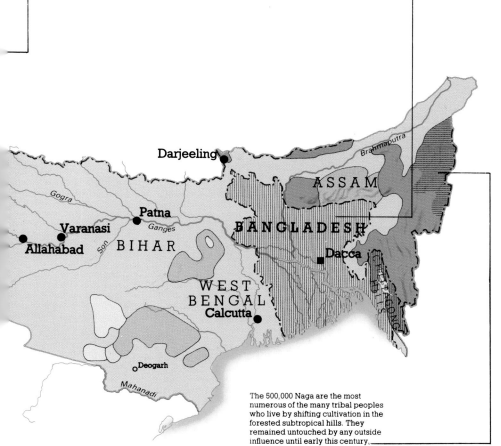

The 500,000 Naga are the most numerous of the many tribal peoples who live by shifting cultivation in the forested subtropical hills. They remained untouched by any outside influence until early this century.

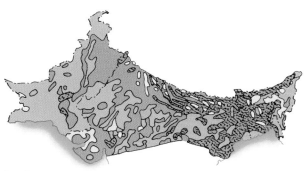

Land use
Agriculture consists mainly of rice cultivation in irrigated fields, and on low-lying, flooded alluvial land. Overpopulation has led to great pressure on the land, and there is a density of 400 to 600 people per square km (1,000 to 1,500 per square mile) in many areas. Most of Pakistan's population is today concentrated in the Indus valley, an area which was too arid for cultivation until the completion of the world's most extensive canal irrigation system in the early twentieth century.

Arable land
⬛ Wheat, millet, maize, pulses, vegetables, cotton and jute.

Rice fields
⬛ Rice grown with irrigation or on flooded alluvial land.

Plantations
⬜ Sugar-cane, bananas, tea and spices.

Woods and forests
⬛ Used mainly for timber; some shifting cultivation practised.

Rough grazing land
⬛ Cattle, buffalo, sheep and goats on desert and semi-desert areas.

Nonagricultural land
⬜ Salt- and mud-flats, mountain peaks.

North India 2

The Sikhs' original homeland is the Punjab, where the greatest concentrations of them are still found. However, when the Punjab was divided between India and Pakistan in 1947, most Sikhs fled to India, where Sikh communities already existed, widely dispersed over many of the northern states. In 1966 the Sikhs' craving for a separate political unit was largely satisfied when the government of India split the East Punjab into a Punjabi-speaking state and the Hindi-speaking state of Haryana.

Sikhism compels its male adherents to distinguish themselves by a number of visible marks. Thus Sikh men wear long hair like the old sages, on the grounds that a man with long hair is like a lion—since a lion never allows anyone to pluck his hair, it is a great sin for a Sikh to have his hair or beard cut. Long beards are sometimes tied up in a net and held in place with the turban. Sikhs are also required to wear a *kangsha* (wooden comb) for keeping the hair clean, a *kara* (steel bangle) as a symbol of the honest and correct use of the hands, a *kirpan* (dagger) for protection and *kachha* (tight shorts) as a symbol of continence. Such shorts are sometimes worn as an outer garment by men, but more usually as underwear, by men as well as women. Unlike men, Sikh women have no specific dress distinguishing them from Hindu women. However, the traditional dress for women in the Punjab is the *shalwar-kameez* (loose tunic) and wide trousers; the sari, too, is becoming popular.

Although Sikhism arose as a movement opposed to the Hindu caste system, castelike divisions developed as a result of the conversion and incorporation of members of Hindu communities. Hence there are now among Sikhs such endogamous divisions as farmers, merchants, artisans, laundrymen and sweepers; the latter having been recruited from Hindu untouchable castes are still subject to social discrimination. Caste distinctions are suspended in the practice of religion however, and even the lowest can enter the *gurdwara* (temple) and sit with members of higher divisions. Women can worship side by side with men, and they enjoy a much higher status and greater freedom of movement than the women of orthodox Hindu and Muslim communities.

Among Sikhs there are three important domestic rituals: the name giving, the wedding and the funeral. The name-giving ceremony takes place in the *gurdwara*. A reading is taken from the Guru Granth Sahib, the Sikh holy book, which is then reopened at random. The first word on the left-hand page is read to the parents of the child to be named. The parents must then decide on a name beginning with the first letter of that word, adding *Singh* (lion) for a boy or *Kaur* (princess) for a girl. As many names are common to boys and girls, the appended names Singh and Kaur are essential.

Social interaction between the sexes is restricted in traditional Sikh society, although not as rigidly as among Muslims. Marriage is usually arranged once a child reaches fourteen or fifteen years of age, Sikhs preferring to marry within their own castelike divisions. Any kinship ties within the past four generations are a bar to marriage. Sikhs are monogamous, and a marriage is a religious ceremony and not the conclusion of a social contract. Divorce, though possible, is strongly discouraged. The remarriage of widows is permitted, but when they remain unmarried widows are respected and, in contrast to Hindu practice, are allowed an active role in the life of the family and the community. A widow may even hold the position of family head and controller of property, the eldest son executing his mother's decisions.

When a Sikh dies there is continual chanting of hymns until the body is prepared, and the funeral is normally held on the following day. Cremation is the favored method of disposing of the corpse but burial is also possible. At a cremation a final prayer is said before the pyre is lit and the ashes of the dead are then usually cast into the waters of the Beas, or into one of the sacred Hindu rivers, preferably the Ganges. Monuments to the dead are never built.

Sikhs have always shown a considerable mobility, and many have abandoned farming for town life and the occupations that go with it. Tens of thousands of

Sikhs are taxi drivers and motor mechanics. In the Indian army and the central civil service Sikhs have established a secure position, and many have risen to high office. Their industriousness and their entrepreneurial skills have encouraged them to seek favorable economic openings overseas, and as early as the beginning of the twentieth century some Sikhs had emigrated to Britain, Canada, California or East Africa.

Pukhtuns of Pakistan

The Pukhtuns, or Pathans, are a vast tribal society, numbering about thirteen million, spread mainly over Afghanistan and Pakistan. The seven million Pukhtuns of Pakistan live in a complex tangle of mountains and valleys lying between Pakistan's western borderlands and Afghanistan. Their settlements on the traditional invasion route to India have brought them into contact with, and under the ephemeral sway of, numerous conquering powers including the Turks, the Mughals, the Sikhs and the British. War has therefore become part of the way of life of the Pukhtun, who are expert guerrilla fighters.

The Mughal legacy
Delhi, the present-day capital of India, was at the center of the Mughal Empire, established by Babur in 1526. Its Red Fort was built by Shah Jahan in the 17th century, and includes a palace, mosque, administrative buildings and barracks. Within the massive sandstone walls is found the magnificent white marble *Diwan-i-Khas*, or Hall of Private Audience, in which the famous Peacock throne once stood. Shah Jahan personified the high point in the distinctive art and architecture of the Mughals, reflected in the magnificent Taj Mahal. However, his successors' religious bigotry heralded the collapse of the Mughal Empire. Today the Red Fort is primarily a tourist attraction, although a small part is still used as an army barracks.

The warrior people
Blood feuds still exist in the tribal area and it is rare for Pukhtuns to travel unarmed. Most of their guns are made at Darra, where, using primitive machinery, craftsmen make precise copies of western small arms. The .303 Lee Enfield is preferred—the rifle used against the Pukhtuns by the British at the turn of the century.

Survival in the Khyber Pass
As the traditional invasion route to India, the Khyber Pass has been the scene of much violence, and the Pukhtuns have been briefly ruled by various conquering powers. Their walled villages overlooking the Pass serve as easily defensible places of refuge. No outside force has ever succeeded in imposing effective continued control over the area.

The Pukhtuns are divided into a number of different tribes, such as the Afridis and Wazirs, and each tribe is split into a constellation of communities known as *khels*. There is no central, unifying leader for an entire tribe, political leadership being both fluid and competitive. A *khan* presides over a number of *khels* and his status denotes a position of power sustained by political and economic control over his followers. Below him are the headmen of the *khels* known as *maliks*, who are responsible for controlling their group members and for assisting the *khan* in the management of tribal affairs. The main source of the *khan's* wealth and power is land.

According to Pukhtun custom, equality is very important, and *shamilat* (pasture) is collectively owned. The rest of the tribal land is divided equally among each community in the tribe, and it is then redistributed among the major families, who allocate *bukhra* (individual plots) to adult males. Property is normally inherited in the male line, and women are excluded from inheriting shares in land. Rivalry over property is common between cousins contending for the inheritance of their paternal grandfather.

Most Pukhtuns are very devout Sunni Muslims of the Hanafi school, although the Turis of the Kurram valley are Shia. The practice of orthodox Islam is usually tempered with tribal and local customs, and the shrines of *pirs* (saints) are often visited to ask for help and assistance. The Pukhtuns have a strong sense of cultural unity, reinforced by their literature, which goes back to the sixteenth century. One famous Pukhtun warrior-poet of the seventeenth century was Khushhal Khan Khattak, who, as well as being a philosopher, wrote on medicine and religion. In addition to literature, the Pukhtuns are notable for their songs and dances, which mirror their martial traditions.

The dominant elements of Pukhtun culture are the warrior tradition of *izzat* (male honor) and the exacting code of social behavior, known as *Pukhtunwali*. The main elements of this code are *badal* (vengeance), *melmastia* (hospitality) and *nanawati* (generosity to anyone, even an adversary begging for peace or sanctuary). *Pukhtunwali* is enforced through the *jirga*, an assembly of tribal leaders who decide disputed matters. Disputes are typically over *zar* (gold), *zan* (woman) and *zamin* (land). In tribal culture women, as sisters and wives, embody the honor of men.

The Pukhtun economy is primarily based on crop growing, although sheep and goats are also raised, especially in the less productive mountainous areas of Chitral, Dir, Bajaur and Waziristan. With few manufactures and no significant agricultural surplus, the region owes its limited commercial importance to trade routes that connect it with the markets of Afghanistan and with other parts of Pakistan.

Since the late nineteenth century the Pukhtuns have had to seek work away from their homeland—seasonal work and military service being the most popular. They have also seized the opportunities offered by the spread of education and the opening of Peshawar University in 1952, and many have become doctors, engineers, lawyers or teachers, while others earn their living as businessmen or merchants. Large numbers of Pukhtuns are now engaged in various occupations in the Arab states. This new source of income has had an important impact not only on the economic life of the Pukhtuns areas but also on their traditional culture, which is now in the process of transformation.

Hallmark of the true Sikh
The turban is both functional—containing the uncut hair and beard—and symbolic—as in the exchange of turban lengths of cloth at weddings and funerals.

The Golden Temple
Any building housing a copy of the Sikhs' holy book is regarded as a *gurdwara* or temple. The temple at Amritsar contains the original holy book and is the Sikhs' most sacred shrine. The temple stands in the *amrit-sar* (pool of nectar), an artificial lake, and is linked to the perimeter by a marble causeway. It has entrances on all sides, signifying that it is open to all castes and creeds.

Temples of modern culture
Bombay is the center of India's huge film-making industry, with an output greater than Hollywood's. Cinemas are found in all cities and most large villages. Nearly all films are produced for the home market and are in Hindi. However, by keeping to a formula story of love and valor interspersed with song and dance, language is never a barrier to appreciation. One result of such popularity is the creation of a new aristocracy of film stars.

South India and Sri Lanka 1

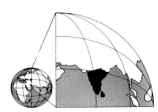

Far from the steely grip of Muslim emperors, Hindu traditions once flourished in South India, where magnificent temples were erected. Integral to the Hindu way of life was the caste system, which grew here as nowhere else. Official policy now curbs the power of the once omnipotent Brahmans and protects the despised Untouchables—Gandhi's "Children of God."

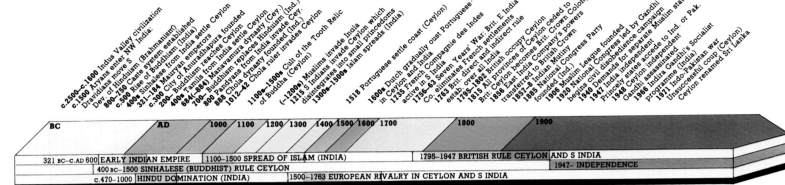

Timeline events:
c.2500–c.1600 Indus Valley civilization
c.1500 Aryans enter NW India.
Dravidians move S
Dev. of Hinduism (Brahmanism)
800–750 Caste system established
c.500 Rise of Buddhism (India)
400s Sinhalese from India settle Ceylon
321–184 Mauryan emperors
c.300 City of Anuradhapura founded
200– Buddhism reaches Ceylon
684(-884) Tamils from India settle Ceylon
700– Buddhism replaces Hinduism (Cey.)
800 Pandyans from India invade Cey.
868 Chola dynasty founded (Ind.)
1012–42 Chola ruler invades Ceylon
1100s Cult of the Tooth Relic of Buddha (Ceylon)
(~1200s) Muslims invade India which disintegrates into small princedoms
1215 S Indians invade Ceylon
1300s–1500s Islam spreads (India)
1518 Portuguese settle coast (Ceylon)
1600s Dutch gradually oust Portuguese in Ceylon and S India
1735 French Compagnie des Indes active in S India
1756–63 Seven Years' War: Brit. E India
Co. eliminates French settlements
1763 Brit. direct and indirect rule estab. over all India
1795–1802 British occupy Ceylon
Brit: Ceylon becomes Brit. Crown Colony
1815 All provinces of Ceylon ceded to Brit. East India Company's powers transferred to British Crown
1856 Indian Mutiny
1857–8 British Crown
1885 National Congress Party founded (Ind.)
1906 Muslim League founded by Gandhi
1920 National Congress led by Gandhi begins civil disobedience campaign
1940 Demands for separate Muslim state
1947 India independent
Princely states accede to Ind. or Pak.
1948 Ceylon independent
1966 Indira Gandhi's Socialist programme (India)
1971 Indo-Pakistan war
Unsuccessful coup (Ceylon)
Ceylon renamed Sri Lanka

Timeline bar:
BC | AD | 1000 | 1100 | 1200 | 1300 | 1400 | 1500 | 1600 | 1700 | 1800 | 1900

321 BC–C.AD 600 EARLY INDIAN EMPIRE | 1100–1500 SPREAD OF ISLAM (INDIA) | 1795–1947 BRITISH RULE CEYLON AND S INDIA
400 BC–1500 SINHALESE (BUDDHIST) RULE CEYLON | 1947– INDEPENDENCE
c.470–1000 HINDU DOMINATION (INDIA) | 1500–1763 EUROPEAN RIVALRY IN CEYLON AND S INDIA

Population by Country
Total: 258 million

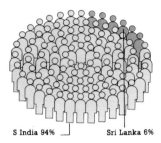

S India 94% | Sri Lanka 6%

Population by Religion
Hinduism 80%

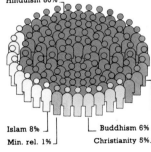

Islam 8% | Buddhism 6%
Min. rel. 1% | Christianity 5%

Gond cultivation
The Gonds raise livestock and grow cotton. Subsistence crops include grains and oil seeds. Irrigation is alien to their traditions and is rarely practiced.

The peoples of southern India are distinguished from those of the north more by physical features, language and culture than by the nature of their environment. Both regions are characterized by large plains, drained by networks of rivers, where fertile lands support dense populations. South of the Vindhya mountains much of the land is a large plateau, known as the Deccan, which simply means "the South." This plateau, dissected by such major rivers as the Godavari and Krishna, was the cradle of ancient civilizations. Today, within such states as Andhra Pradesh, contrasts in levels of material and social development are sharper than they are in most parts of northern India. There are enormous differences, both culturally and economically, between the inhabitants of the modern cities and the people of the hills.

While northern India derives its basic character from a variety of immigrant groups who, since the second millennium BC, moved from their central Asian homelands into the Gangetic plains, southern India has been largely unaffected by these population movements. As a result its dark-skinned inhabitants contrast sharply with the lighter-skinned people of the north. Indigenous languages and cultural forms, too, have survived here in relatively undiluted form. Thus the Deccan plateau remains the preserve of speakers of such Dravidian languages as Telugu, Kannada and Tamil—languages that have no apparent connection with any other language family either inside India or in any other part of Asia. In Sri Lanka, a relic of the most ancient ethnic stratum is found in the Veddas, who still lived as hunter-gatherers at the beginning of the twentieth century, but have now been largely absorbed by the rural Sinhalese population.

Although part of the Deccan was at times subject to Muslim rule, the influence of Islam always remained superficial, and this accounts for the preservation of Hindu centers of worship, such as the great and still thriving temple complexes of Tamil Nadu. Here Brahman priests steeped in the traditions of Vedic Hinduism cater to the needs of pilgrims. Freedom from the impact of puritanical Muslim ideology explains also the favorable position of southern Indian women, who have never been subjected to the male domination and the seclusion accepted by women in northern India. Parts of southwest India, such as Kerala, are centers of matrilineal societies, in which women own and inherit land. In these societies polyandry prevailed until recently but is now declining.

The difference between northern and southern social practices extends above all to the kinship system. Whereas in northern India cousins and even inhabitants of the same village are debarred from marriage, so that men must seek their brides in distant places, in the south marriage partners are chosen from a narrow circle of relatives. The preferred type of union is that of a man with the daughter of either his mother's brother or his father's sister (cross-cousin marriage). Hence people live in small, self-perpetuating clusters of families, a system that gives great stability to the entire social structure.

In contrast to the equality of the sexes characteristic of Dravidian society, caste distinctions have remained more rigid than in other parts of India. Discrimination against the lower strata of society, particularly against Untouchables (Harijans), used to be extremely severe. With urbanization and industrialization, such discrimination is gradually disappearing, but the rural areas of southern India remain bulwarks of traditional Hindu society. A caste system is even found among the Buddhists of Sri Lanka, although here castes, such as that of the Karavas, have no ritual function. By contrast, the Gonds of the Deccan, and most other tribal people of South India, are casteless, and their egalitarian traditions have survived in the midst of the highly stratified and hierarchical society of Hindus.

Karavas of western Sri Lanka

The Karavas are one of the principal Sinhalese castes of Sri Lanka, and their contribution to the island's economy is substantial. Originally a group of seafarers and warriors, they developed both deep-sea and coastal fishing. There is no census of individual castes, but it is estimated that the Karavas now number approximately two million. This figure includes those of the coastal regions, where most of the Karavas live, as well as those dispersed over the highlands, who do not follow the traditional occupation of fishing.

For deep-sea fishing the Karavas use *oru*, outrigger canoes fashioned from large trunks of breadfruit and jackfruit trees. The art of boat building is confined to certain families, and so great is the skill of these artisans that their fragile-looking, elegant boats stand up to the rough seas of the monsoon. For coastal fishing the Karavas use a much simpler craft known as a catamaran, which is a kind of raft made of five logs;

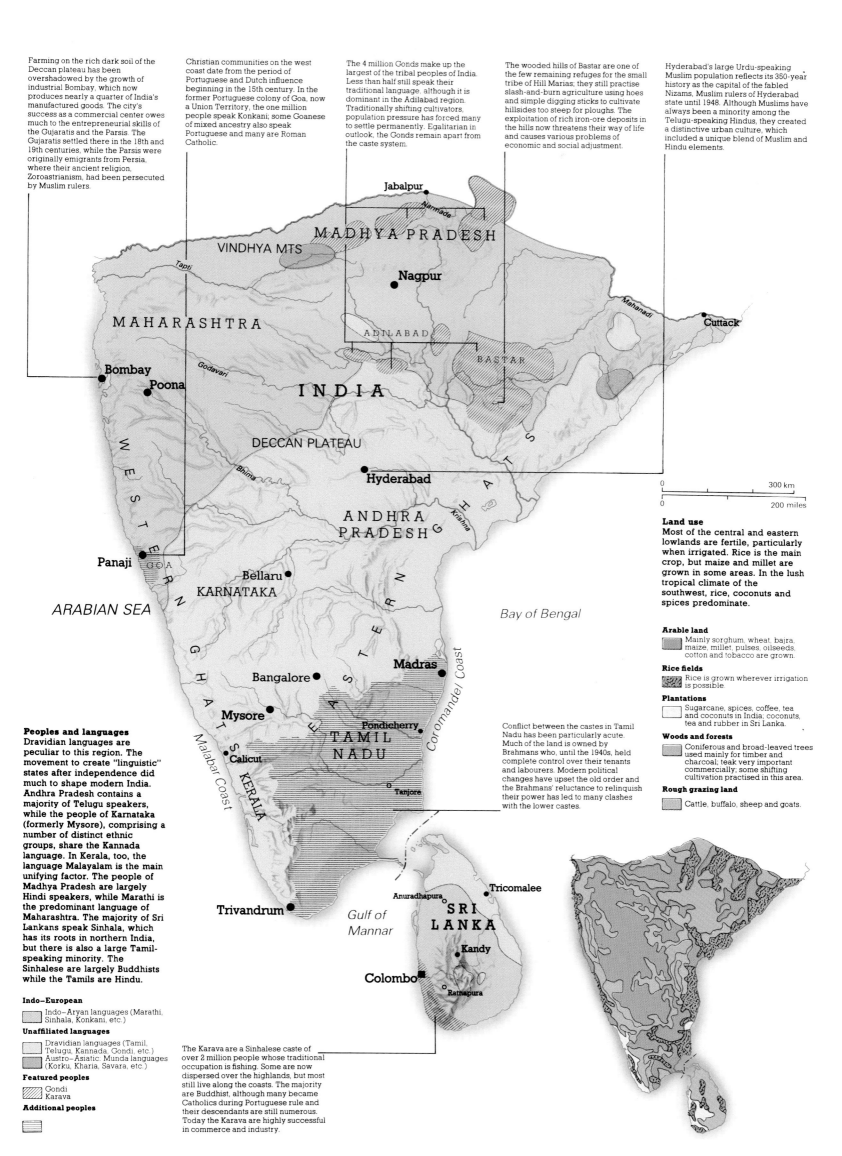

Farming on the rich dark soil of the Deccan plateau has been overshadowed by the growth of industrial Bombay, which now produces nearly a quarter of India's manufactured goods. The city's success as a commercial center owes much to the entrepreneurial skills of the Gujaratis and the Parsis. The Gujaratis settled there in the 18th and 19th centuries, while the Parsis were originally emigrants from Persia, where their ancient religion, Zoroastrianism, had been persecuted by Muslim rulers.

Christian communities on the west coast date from the period of Portuguese and Dutch influence beginning in the 15th century. In the former Portuguese colony of Goa, now a Union Territory, the one million people speak Konkani; some Goanese of mixed ancestry also speak Portuguese and many are Roman Catholic.

The 4 million Gonds make up the largest of the tribal peoples of India. Less than half still speak their traditional language, although it is dominant in the Adilabad region. Traditionally shifting cultivators, population pressure has forced many to settle permanently. Egalitarian in outlook, the Gonds remain apart from the caste system.

The wooded hills of Bastar are one of the few remaining refuges for the small tribe of Hill Marias; they still practise slash-and-burn agriculture using hoes and simple digging sticks to cultivate hillsides too steep for ploughs. The exploitation of rich iron-ore deposits in the hills now threatens their way of life and causes various problems of economic and social adjustment.

Hyderabad's large Urdu-speaking Muslim population reflects its 350-year history as the capital of the fabled Nizams, Muslim rulers of Hyderabad state until 1948. Although Muslims have always been a minority among the Telugu-speaking Hindus, they created a distinctive urban culture, which included a unique blend of Muslim and Hindu elements.

Land use
Most of the central and eastern lowlands are fertile, particularly when irrigated. Rice is the main crop, but maize and millet are grown in some areas. In the lush tropical climate of the southwest, rice, coconuts and spices predominate.

Arable land
Mainly sorghum, wheat, bajra, maize, millet, pulses, oilseeds, cotton and tobacco are grown.

Rice fields
Rice is grown wherever irrigation is possible.

Plantations
Sugarcane, spices, coffee, tea and coconuts in India; coconuts, tea and rubber in Sri Lanka.

Woods and forests
Coniferous and broad-leaved trees used mainly for timber and charcoal; teak very important commercially; some shifting cultivation practised in this area.

Rough grazing land
Cattle, buffalo, sheep and goats.

Peoples and languages
Dravidian languages are peculiar to this region. The movement to create "linguistic" states after independence did much to shape modern India. Andhra Pradesh contains a majority of Telugu speakers, while the people of Karnataka (formerly Mysore), comprising a number of distinct ethnic groups, share the Kannada language. In Kerala, too, the language Malayalam is the main unifying factor. The people of Madhya Pradesh are largely Hindi speakers, while Marathi is the predominant language of Maharashtra. The majority of Sri Lankans speak Sinhala, which has its roots in northern India, but there is also a large Tamil-speaking minority. The Sinhalese are largely Buddhists while the Tamils are Hindu.

Indo–European
Indo–Aryan languages (Marathi, Sinhala, Konkani, etc.)

Unaffiliated languages
Dravidian languages (Tamil, Telugu, Kannada, Gondi, etc.)
Austro–Asiatic: Munda languages (Korku, Kharia, Savara, etc.)

Featured peoples
Gondi
Karava

Additional peoples

Conflict between the castes in Tamil Nadu has been particularly acute. Much of the land is owned by Brahmans who, until the 1940s, held complete control over their tenants and labourers. Modern political changes have upset the old order and the Brahmans' reluctance to relinquish their power has led to many clashes with the lower castes.

The Karava are a Sinhalese caste of over 2 million people whose traditional occupation is fishing. Some are now dispersed over the highlands, but most still live along the coasts. The majority are Buddhist, although many became Catholics during Portuguese rule and their descendants are still numerous. Today the Karava are highly successful in commerce and industry.

South India and Sri Lanka 2

they may also use a seine net attached to the shore. Traditional Karava fishing craft, however, are now rapidly being superseded by motorboats.

Karava women do not participate in deep-sea fishing, but busy themselves with the making and repairing of nets, and the cleaning and marketing of fish. It is also the women who do most of the work in the kitchen gardens. The system of land tenure is based on small holdings, which are inherited in the male line. Most children now go to school at least for three or four years but older ones help with their parents' work.

While many Karavas are still fishermen or farmers, more recently they have turned to trade and become a mercantile community of great wealth and enterprise. Some have adapted to urban living, and there are Karavas who hold important positions in commerce and national politics. Yet the Karavas feel a strong sense of identity and display no tendency to split into subcastes; in this respect they differ basically from most Indian castes. They have also assimilated western styles of living very successfully.

Unlike most peoples of southern India, the majority of Sinhalese, including the Karavas, still adhere to the Buddhist faith. Monks drawn from the Karava community have enriched Buddhist scholarship and are held in high esteem by their caste fellows. Karavas also participate in the cult of local *deva* (deities) and *yakku* (demons). Their belief in gods and demons is reflected in their Kolam dances. Carved wooden masks, depicting the traditional features of gods, demons and legendary personages, are worn by dancers who enact mythological stories to the drumming of musicians and chanting of singers.

In spite of Buddhist beliefs, Karava social customs are strongly reminiscent of those of Hindu societies, especially at marriage. Monogamy is the usual form of marriage and divorce is rare. In the event of separation the wife does not accept any maintenance from the husband, but is supported by her natal family.

Karavas are very pollution conscious and at the time of menstruation a woman is regarded as impure for seven days, during which time she takes no part in household duties, and stays in an outhouse. A course of purificatory baths is required to remove the pollution.

Gonds of the Adilabad district of Andhra Pradesh
Among the tribal populations of southern India, the group known as the Gonds is by far the largest numerically, there being more than four million members spread over several different regions. Gonds vary in levels of economic development and do not form a culturally homogenous group; less than half speak their traditional unwritten Dravidian language.

Architecture of a living faith
The prevailing architectural style in northern India is Indo-Islamic, but southern India escaped Muslim influence and it is here that magnificent Hindu temples are found, such as the Brihadiswara temple, built at Tanjore during the period of the Chola Kings (907–1053).

People of the sea
As well as deep-sea and coastal fishing, the Karavas practice beach seine-net fishing, in which one end of the net is attached to the shore, while a flat-bottomed boat feeds out the net in an arc, returning to shore with the other end. To haul in a big catch 40 to 50 men are needed on the shore.

Working the tea plantations
During the 19th century, British entrepreneurs established plantations of tea, coffee and rubber in the central highlands of Sri Lanka. Local labor was inadequate and so large numbers of Tamil laborers were recruited from southern India. A longstanding animosity exists between the indigenous population and the Indian Tamil minority, who are generally very poor and lack political power since they cannot vote. An attempt to resolve the problem through repatriation— the Indian government is willing to accept 600,000—and the offer of Sri Lankan citizenship to the rest may go some way toward alleviating their discontent.

Most Gonds were once shifting cultivators—as long as the population was sparse and they had a free run of large stretches of forest, they could periodically abandon their cultivated land, and even their settlement, and carve new fields and a new village site from the forest a few miles away. Pressure of population, however, and the invasion of the Gonds' habitat by more advanced populations, have forced many to alter their settlement pattern and to attach themselves more firmly to the land.

One group of Gonds who have retained their tribal language and culture inhabit the Adilabad district of Andhra Pradesh. Although their farming economy is very similar to that of the surrounding Hindu peasants of the Deccan, the basis of their society is completely different. The society is divided into a large number of exogamous clans, within which descent is in the male line. The mainspring of clan solidarity lies in rituals performed for deities that are linked with each clan's mythological origins. Each clan has a common cult center, usually a thatched hut containing ritual objects. It is there that the clan deity is worshiped, and members gather here for worship and feasting twice a year. The symbol of ritual unity is the priest, who is responsible for the performance of rites and is supported by a bard, preserving by oral tradition the myths and legends that reflect clan history.

A man's membership of his natal clan is clear and immutable, but a woman's clan status is subject to change. As a girl she is attached to her father's clan, but at her wedding she is transferred to her husband's. After her death she is ritually joined to her husband's clan god and to his ancestors. In the mind of the Gonds, the deceased members of a clan dwell in the company of the clan deities and thereby remain part of their community. The living, through ritual acts such as animal sacrifices, can influence the fate of the departed, and the dead are thought capable of aiding their kinsmen in the world of the living. The funerary rites that accompany cremation or burial are the visible expression of this belief.

The Gonds believe in the existence of a multitude of supernatural beings who are not normally visible,

A question of caste
It is hard for an outsider to tell the caste of an Indian, but caste determines both his economic and social prospects. What distinguishes members of one caste from another is the work they do. Marriages must take place within the caste, and what binds these endogamous units together is their economic interdependence. Through distribution of his crops at harvest time, the land-owning Indian can call on the community to provide him with services.

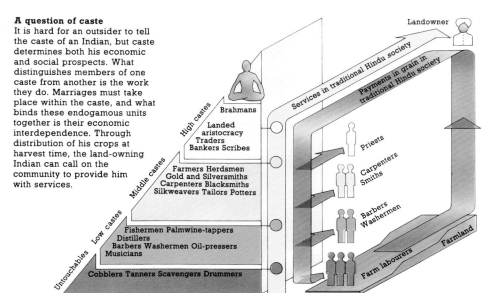

Gond music, ritual and poetry
A Pardhan musician plays one of their massive traditional horns. The Pardhan, while being a separate people, live among the Gonds and provide the musicians and bards who perform at all Gond marriages and other festivities. The major occasion for such festivity is the twice-yearly meeting of the clan members at their shrine. The clan spends several days in worship and feasting, during which time the souls of the recently deceased are formally introduced to the company of other ancestors and the clan deities. In the 15th and 16th centuries the Gonds' kingdoms were magnificent and powerful, equalling those of Hindu princes in wealth and status, but their power was slowly eroded by the Mughal Emperors and later the Maratha Kings.

though on occasion they appear to seers in dreams or visions, and at certain rites speak through the mouths of oracle priests. Their impact on human life is felt in a number of ways. On a level different from that of clan gods and local deities is Bhagavan, the lord of the gods and supreme deity, who presides over the court of immortals and is the giver of life and death. Although the Gonds consider him superior to all other gods, they do not accord him as much worship as they do to many lesser deities, and there is a strong likelihood that the concept of this supreme deity is derived from Hindu ideas. The Gonds also expect gods and spirits to bless their crops, and they relate agricultural work to many activities directed toward these deities. Tillage of the soil with the help of plow and bullock, for example, is inextricably caught up with ritual observances.

Unlike neighboring Hindu peoples, the Gonds believe in equality of sexes, particularly when it comes to taking part in religious rites and choosing a marriage partner. Relations between boys and girls are not hemmed in by many restrictions, and no great premium is placed on virginity, but youthful affairs are considered stepping stones to permanent unions. Marriage, not adventure, is the aim of courtship, and all Gonds expect to be married by the time they reach their midtwenties. A first marriage can take place by negotiation, by service or by capture. The first type is the most prestigious, but involves heavy expenditure on an elaborate wedding by the groom's family. Men may have two or three wives, but this practice is declining in popularity. Divorce is easy, and both men and women can remarry. It is still not unusual for a woman to have a succession of husbands.

Growing contact with politically advanced communities and the opening up of their habitat by newly constructed roads have not proved beneficial to the Gonds of Andhra Pradesh. Much of their ancestral land has been acquired by newcomers, and their economic and social life has been largely disrupted, causing a great deal of unrest in some regions.

Cotton—a Gond cash crop
The high price cotton fetches has induced the Gonds to devote a large part of their land to cotton rather than the traditional subsistence crops—grains and oil seeds. Before cotton is sent to the ginning mills it has to be gleaned and graded by hand. This task is done exclusively by women.

Gem sieving
Sri Lanka is famous for gems such as sapphires, rubies and garnets. Using bamboo sieves, the gravel is sifted from muddy pits, rivers and even holes scraped at the edge of paddies. While the gem center is Ratnapura, gems are sought all over the island, often as a part-time activity.

Central Asia

Central Asia and Siberia have few natural frontiers cutting them off from surrounding regions, and historically these have been areas which lay between great civilizations, rarely at the center of them. The empires of the Middle East and Russia to the west were counterbalanced by those of Mongolia and China to the southeast and numerous cultural influences passed through these lands.

Turkic-speaking central Asia—the Uzbek, Tadzhik, Kazakh, Turkmen and Kirgiz Republics of the Soviet Union—is a dry region with a sharply continental climate. It is an area of desert and mountain, interspersed with fertile valleys. The northernmost of the republics, Kazakhstan, is a region of open grassland, now covered by vast wheatfields. North of this again is the taiga (virgin coniferous forest) of Siberia, a cold inhospitable land where settlement is mostly along the great rivers draining northward to the Arctic Ocean.

The forests of Siberia, the vast open steppes, and the fertile oases and valleys of the south, constitute three very different ecological zones, each with its own economic opportunities. The people of the oases adopted agriculture about 6,000 years ago, and by 3,000 years ago fairly large towns had grown up in these regions. The steppes, on the other hand, were ideally suited for grazing animals and were inhabited by tribes of nomadic pastoralists. In the taiga lived other nomadic tribes, who largely relied on hunting, trapping and fishing for their livelihood.

This region has a long history of invasion, conquest and instability, beginning in about the fifth century BC, with attacks on the oasis dwellers by the nomadic tribes of the steppes. Between the second century BC and the seventh century AD a succession of nomadic peoples—Huns, and later Turks—dominated the steppes. These events affected south-

ern Siberia, which was conquered successively by the Huns, by the Chinese, and by several Turkic Khanates, but the hunting and fishing tribes further north remained outside the influence of such empires. In the eighth century AD, Arab armies poured northeastward across the Kopet-Dag mountains and conquered a broad strip of territory extending as far as the Syr-Dar'ya river. Their legacy was the Muslim faith, to which the various tribes of the steppes and oases were all converted, and the Arabic script, which allowed the culture of the urbanized south to flourish and grow.

The rise and fall of the steppe empires between the ninth and the thirteenth centuries drove some Turkic-speaking groups southward, where they merged with the local Iranian-speaking population and formed the ancestors of the present-day Uzbek and Turkmen. Other Turkic-speaking groups spread into the Altai mountains, and yet others, the Yakut, abandoned the comparatively mild Lake Baikal region to venture north into Siberia. The Yakut horsemen took with them the southern steppe economy of cattle herding, and it is possible that the development of reindeer herding by several Siberian tribes was stimulated by their example.

The Mongol armies of Chinggis Khan conquered two of the more important steppe empires at the beginning of the thirteenth century, and by the middle of the century they had divided Turkic-speaking central Asia into three parts, the area of the Golden Horde in the northern steppes, the Chagatai Ulus in the region of Tashkent and Samarkand, and the fiefdom of the Il-khans in the south and west. Meanwhile, certain Mongol tribesmen who sought to escape the hold of the Mongol Empire, moved northward out of Mongolia into southern Siberia, taking with them their pastoral economy and their religion, Tibetan Buddhism. The Mongol state fell apart in the fourteenth century, but a new ruler—Timur, or Tamburlane—established a vast empire which stretched as far south as India. This empire was finally defeated in the late sixteenth century by the Uzbek tribes, who ruled Turkic-speaking central Asia for the next 300 years.

The Russian influx

The Russians began their conquest of Siberia in the sixteenth century and a definite border was established with Mongolia, then under the rule of the Manchu Empire, in the early eighteenth century. The individual Khanates of Turkic-speaking central Asia came under the control of the Tsar in the second half of the nineteenth century and large numbers of Russian immigrants moved into the area. A similar influx took place in western and southern Siberia, where the new settlers established farming communities despite the opposition of the native peoples. Today, Russians greatly outnumber the indigenous people in Siberia, and constitute a third of the population of Turkic-speaking central Asia.

Since the 1917 Revolution, many of the social customs of the indigenous people of these regions have been swept away, and the practice of their religions—Islam among the steppe and oasis peoples, Buddhism among the Buryat of Siberia, and shamanism among other Siberian tribes—has been actively discouraged. However, their traditional economic pursuits have been retained, particularly among the native Siberians, although they are now carried on in collectives and state farms. Among the Uzbek, Tadzhik and Turkmen there has been a great expansion in the production of cotton, silk, vegetables and fruit, making these regions very prosperous. The development of new economic ventures, such as heavy industry in Siberia or wheat growing in Kazakhstan, has largely been the responsibility of Russians and Ukrainians.

Politically, this area is part of the Soviet Union which is dominated numerically by Slavic peoples, but many nationalities, such as the Tatars, the Altains and the Yakut, have their own administrative units, and the peoples of Turkic-speaking central Asia have their own republics. Throughout the region cultural traditions remain strong and show every sign of continuing alongside Soviet culture.

A Kirgiz band cross the Soviet Union-Afghanistan border

Turkic-speaking Central Asia

Around the fertile oases of central Asia, literate urban societies grew up, while merchants prospered from the fabled Chinese silk route. To the north, warlike nomads roamed the *steppes, united with the oasis dwellers only by their common Muslim heritage. Today, fields of wheat cloak the wild steppelands, and Soviet education has weakened the power of Islam.*

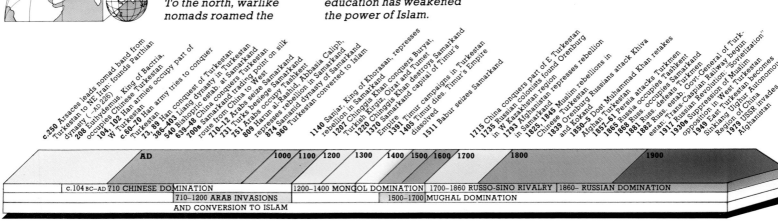

c.250 Arsaces leads nomad band from Turkestan (–AD 226): founds Parthian dynasty
208 Euthydemus, King of Bactria, occupies Chinese Turkestan
104, 102 Han armies occupy part of W Turkestan
c.60–70 Han armies try to conquer Turkestan
73, 89 Han conquest of Turkestan
386–403 Liang dynasty in Turkestan
540 Bishopric estab. at Samarkand
639–48 China conquers Turkestan
c.700s Samarkand trading point on silk route from China to West
710–12 Arabs seize Samarkand
731 Turks besiege Samarkand
751 Arabs occupy Tashkent
809 Harun al-Rashid, Abbasid Caliph, represses rebellion in Samarkand
874 Samanid dynasty of Samarkand
960 Turkestan converted to Islam
1140 Sanjar, King of Khorasan, represses rebellion in Samarkand
1207 Chingis Khan conquers Buryat, Turkish Kirgiz, Oirat and Tumet
1220 Chingis Khan conquers Samarkand
1370 Samarkand capital of Timur's Empire
1391 Timur campaigns in Turkestan
1405 Timur dies, Timur's Empire dissolved
1511 Babur seizes Samarkand
1715 China conquers part of E Turkestan
1735 Russian colonists found Orenburg in W Kazakhstan region
1793 Afghanistan represses rebellion in Samarkand region
1825, 1845 Muslim rebellions in Chinese Turkestan
1839 Orenburg Russians attack Khiva and Kokand
1850–5 Dost Muhammad Khan retakes Afghan Turkestan
1857–61 Persia attacks Turkmen
1865 Russia occupies Tashkent
1868 Russ. occupies Tashkent
1881 Russ. defeats Turkmen estan: Trans-Caspian Railway begun
1882 Russ. estab. Govt-General of Turkestan
1917 Russian Revolution: "Sovietization"
1930s Suppression of Muslim opposition in West Turkestan
1949 East Turkestan becomes Sinkiang Uighur Autonomous Region of China
1979 USSR invades Afghanistan

	AD	1000	1100	1200	1300	1400	1500	1600	1700	1800	1900

c.104 BC–AD 710 CHINESE DOMINATION
710–1200 ARAB INVASIONS AND CONVERSION TO ISLAM
1200–1400 MONGOL DOMINATION
1500–1700 MUGHAL DOMINATION
1700–1860 RUSSO-SINO RIVALRY
1860– RUSSIAN DOMINATION

Population of Union Republic
Total: 40 million

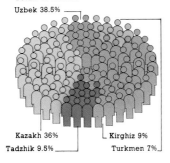

Uzbek 38.5%
Kazakh 36%
Kirghiz 9%
Tadzhik 9.5%
Turkmen 7%

Population by Religion

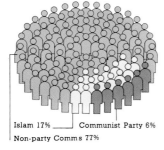

Islam 17%
Communist Party 6%
Non-party Comms 77%

Turkmen folk singers
The Turkmen, like other central Asian peoples, have a strong oral tradition, of epic poetry, myths and folk songs. In the past, these reflected Muslim influence. Today, in addition to their traditional arts, they also enjoy cinema, theater and ballet. Formerly, the Turkmen were seminomadic pastoralists, a life style that was particularly well suited to their arid environment. Now, with the help of intensive irrigation, crops such as cotton, maize and millet are grown. A massive shipping and irrigation canal—the largest in the world—is being built across the Kara Kum (Black Sands) desert.

Central Asia, at least until the twentieth century, was a land of contrasts: arid deserts and mountains were interspersed with green fruitful valleys; nomadic tribes kept links with the busy urban bazaars, where produce from all over Asia could be found; relics of shamanism and belief in ancestor spirits continued to exist together with the ideas of Islam. The economic differences between the sedentary and nomadic worlds, as well as the geographical position of the region, gave trade an important role—the northern ways of the famous "silk route" passed from Sinkiang through central Asia to the Middle East.

Central Asia is rimmed by mountains to the south and east, and these give rise to the great rivers which are the source of the oases in the central valleys. The sharply continental climate of much of the region and its general dryness make agriculture possible only on irrigated land. However, the northern expanses of Kazakhstan have a higher, though sporadic, rainfall. Formerly steppe grassland, much of Kazakhstan is now given over to nonirrigated grain production.

The central Asian oases saw the appearance of one of the world's earliest cultures. Irrigated agriculture was practiced from about 4000 BC, and by 1000 BC there were complex urban societies in the area. North of the oases, in the steppelands, lived tribes of pastoralists, and in the sixth century the entire region was conquered by the mighty Turkic Khaganate, a confederation of tribes of the southern Siberian steppes. These Turkic-speaking peoples mixed with the Iranian-speaking inhabitants to form the amalgamation found today. Always vulnerable to attack, central Asia was again conquered by the Arabs in the eighth century, and they left a lasting cultural heritage—the religion of Islam and the Arabic script. From this time until the appearance of the Mongols in the thirteenth century, the region was subject to upheavals, as the tribes of the northern steppes struggled for supremacy.

When the Mongol Empire in turn disintegrated there arose a new world conqueror in central Asia, Timur, or Tamburlane, who gained power over an area stretching from China to the Volga, and from Syria into India. His capital was Samarkand, and he brought artists, craftsmen and architects from the conquered lands to create the beautiful mosques and mausoleums of the city. At the end of the sixteenth century this brief empire was destroyed by a union of steppe tribes called "Uzbek." It was the Uzbek Khans who ruled most of central Asia for the next three centuries.

From the early nineteenth century onward, Tsarist Russia had an economic interest in central Asia as a market for its manufactured goods and a source of raw materials, particularly cotton. Between 1860 and 1880 the Khanates of Kokand, Bukhara and Khiva came under Russian rule and there were large migrations of Russians into the towns. Following the 1917 Revolution, the Bolshevik Government assumed control of the region, despite the resistance of various guerrilla groups, known as "Basmatchis." Soviet republics were set up in the early 1920s.

The main Turkic-speaking peoples of central Asia today are the Uzbek, the Kirgiz, the Turkmen, the Kara-Kalpak and the Kazakh. The Uzbek were once the most urbanized, having descended in part from the original Iranian-speaking oasis dwellers. The Kazakh and Kirgiz traditionally lived a nomadic pastoral life, raising herds of sheep, goats and horses, while the Turkmen, some groups of Uzbek and the Kara-Kalpak lived a semisedentary life with some subsidiary farming. The only large Iranian-speaking group surviving in central Asia is the Tadzhik (Tajik).

In prerevolutionary times all the people of this region followed the Sunni branch of Islam, although earlier religious practices continued, often in an Islamicized form. Some of the pre-Islamic gods assumed the likeness of Muslim saints, for example, the patron of agriculture, Boboi-Dehkan, revered everywhere. *Shamans* conducted rituals concerned with fertility, health, good luck and wealth. Despite the opposition of the Muslim clergy, shamanic sacrifices to spirits continued, especially in rural areas. Since the Revolution, Islamic observances have suffered a widespread decline, although a significant number of people still regard themselves as Muslims.

The towns of central Asia have retained their traditional crafts, such as metalwork, jewelry, carpet making, pottery and woodwork, although these are now carried out in factories rather than small workshops. There has been a great development of industry, particularly iron and steel production, mining and cotton processing. In the countryside, farming is now carried out by collectives, many of which have over 5,000 members; most operations are mechanized. Livestock herding remains the major occupation of the steppes and mountains, the grazing area having been expanded by the introduction of artesian wells.

The indigenous people of these regions have preserved a great deal of their traditional way of life, but education and modern communications, particularly radio and television, are bringing them closer both to one another and to Soviet culture as a whole, as shown by the changing lives of the Uzbek.

Land use
In the deserts and semideserts pastoralists raise sheep, cattle, goats, horses and camels. Agriculture occurs mainly in irrigated areas such as oases. Non-irrigated farming, largely of wheat, is practised in northern Kazakhstan. In other parts of the region the main crop is cotton since the Revolution. As in the past, oases support orchards, vineyards and mulberry trees.

Arable land, orchards and permanent grassland
Wheat, maize, sorghum, cabbages, tomatoes, sugar beet, fruits, grapes, cotton and mulberry trees (for silk); some grazing for beef and beef-dairy cattle.

Wood and forests
Coniferous and broad-leaved trees, important economically for timber.

Rough grazing land
Mainly sheep, cattle and camels on desert and steppe.

Nonagricultural land
Coastal areas below sea level, mountain peaks.

The Kazakh, numbering about 5 million, still practise pastoralism but are no longer nomadic. Their republic is now a major industrial and grain-producing area; the influx of Russians has made the Kazakh a minority.

The Kirgiz inhabit one of the highest plateaus in the world; their remotest grazing lands are at 3,000 m (10,000 ft) and are accessible only on foot or by helicopter. Some Kirgiz are found in China and Afghanistan.

```
0        600 km
0        400 miles
```

Altaic
Turkic languages (Kazakh, Turkmen, Uzbec, Kirgiz, etc.)

Indo-European
Slavic languages (Russian, Ukrainian, Bulgarian, etc.)
Indo-Iranian languages (Tajik, Persian)

Featured people
Uzbeks

Additional people

Peoples and languages
For nearly 2,000 years, until the 1st century AD, the area was inhabited by tribes speaking Iranian languages, but these people were later absorbed by Turkic-speaking nomads of whom the Kirgiz are perhaps the oldest group. Uzbek is the most widely spoken non-Slavic language in the USSR; like other Turkic languages, it was written in Arabic script, but the Roman alphabet was introduced in 1927, and then replaced by the Cyrillic script in 1940.

The Turkmen never experienced political unity until 1924. They were divided into numerous tribes who were constantly at war. This allowed them to be rapidly conquered by the Russians in the 1860s–70s.

The Uzbek ruled Central Asia for 300 years and the constant wars of their khans exhausted the local economy. The Uzbeks are still numerically dominant, although some moved to Afghanistan after the Revolution.

The Uzbek of Uzbekistan
The Uzbek number over thirteen million in total, and of these over ten million live in the Uzbekistan Soviet Socialist Republic, where they account for 70 percent of the population. Another two million live in neighboring republics of central Asia, and over one million are found in northern Afghanistan.

Like many other ethnic groups in the Soviet Union, the people who now call themselves Uzbek did not recognize themselves as a single people until classified as such by the central government. They represent a mixture of Turkic and Iranian stock and speak a Turkic language.

Islam has profoundly affected the lives of the Uzbek, particularly the sedentary people, whose women once occupied a very low position in society. They were assigned to the internal rooms of the house, which male outsiders could not enter. During holidays or the performance of rites, women sat in a separate building, hidden from the eyes of men. A woman could go out only with the permission of her husband, and she was obliged to wear a cloak and a horsehair veil. Among the nomadic pastoralists the women did not wear the veil and generally had more freedom, since their way of life made seclusion impossible.

In the past all marriages were arranged, the girls marrying when thirteen or fourteen years old and the boys at the age of fifteen or sixteen years. Marriages between cousins were favored to avoid the fragmentation of land. Extensive negotiations took place beforehand between the parents of the couple and a brideprice was paid—this was particularly high among the nomads. The wedding usually took place in the house of the bride and was followed by a feast. Then the bride was taken to the home of the groom, all the while being guarded against witchcraft and evil spirits. The wedding feast was repeated in the groom's house, this time with the relatives and neighbors of his family present.

The married couple sometimes continued to live with the groom's parents even when their own children were born, and the male head of the house had unlimited authority over all members of his family. Among the nomads the families were grouped into patrilineal tribes, whose members gave mutual assistance and joined in communal rites such as weddings, burials and circumcision. For the sedentary Uzbek, too, a strong sense of community existed in all the villages and towns, based on the need to maintain and operate the common irrigation network. In the towns, the bazaar was the center of public life, the place for entertainments and meetings, but its importance has now been eroded by the state shops.

The social changes of the Soviet period have contributed to a rapid dissolution of tribal and community ties, and the fragmentation of extended families. Women now have equal rights and young people marry out of choice, although the vestiges of match-making linger in that the families meet to discuss the wedding and future life of the young couple. The number who still adhere strictly to Islamic practices is falling, even though most still consider themselves Muslim. Education, once the domain of religion, has been made freely available to all, and the literacy rate has increased dramatically. However, the old traditions are still seen in everyday life—the social nature of family occasions such as weddings, the reverence paid to old men, the desire for a great many children, and the mutual assistance among neighbors are all typical of the Uzbek's former social patterns.

The Uzbek people
The Uzbek national costume of a flowing, striped robe, baggy drawstring trousers, colorful waistcoat or waistband and a length of cloth wound around the head in a turban is still worn. However, European-style clothes are now common, especially in the cities, as a result of Russian influence.

Mountain pastoralists
Like the other pastoralists of the region, the Kirgiz were nomadic. But whereas the Kazakh and Turkmen migrated from north to south, the Kirgiz practiced transhumance, using high-altitude pastures in the summer months and the more sheltered valleys during the winter. The Kirgiz now belong to herding collectives, and lead a largely sedentary way of life. Since the Revolution many roads have been built, so that livestock can now be transported by truck; helicopters are also used to carry animals to the highest pastures. Agriculture has been introduced in many parts.

Siberia

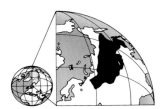

When the Cossacks first penetrated the dark forests of Siberia, they found innumerable tribes of hunters, fishermen and reindeer herders, who worshiped the spirits of the sun and moon, of rivers and mountains. Today, the mountains are mined for precious ores and the rivers harnessed for hydroelectricity, but vast tracts of wilderness remain, where the ancient ways of life are preserved.

c.1500 Bronze Age in E Siberia
c.500–300 Altaic culture
100–AD Nomadic population overrun by Huns

1300–1400 Novgorod merchants venture beyond Urals into W Siberia
1400–1500 Russ. Cossacks, mainly military adventurers, explore Siberia
1558 Tsar grants land along river Kama to Stroganov family
1584 Don Cossacks defeat Khanate of Sibir: Russia annexes Siberia
late 1500s, 1600s Russian fur trappers, traders and Cossack explorers reach Bering Sea
1689 Russo-Chinese Treaty of Nerchinsk limits Russ. expan.
1696–1700 Russians led by Peter the Great conquer Kamchatka
1699 Siberia organized as one of Russia's govemates
1700s Siberia used as place of exile for criminal and political prisoners
1860 Far Eastern territory (beyond Amur River) ceded by China
1861 Emancipation of peasants: settlement of Siberia accelerates
1867 Alaska sold to USA by Russia
1891–1904 Trans-Siberian Railway built from European Russia to Pacific: large-scale settlement begins
1917 Russian Revolution: Siberia passes under Soviet system as Russian Soviet Federated Socialist Republic
1928–32 First Five Year Plan accelerates industrial development
1960s Petroleum deposits opened of Siberia (western Siberia)

BC AD 1000 1100 1200 1300 1400 1500 1600 1700 1800 1900

1300–1558 RUSSIAN EXPLORATION AND TRADE
1584–1700 RUSSIAN OCCUPATION
1700–1917 RUSSIAN SETTLEMENT OF SIBERIA
1917– ECONOMIC DEVELOPMENT

Population by Union Republic
Total: 13 million

E RSFSR 100%

Population by Religion
Non-party Comm. 87.5%

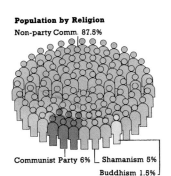

Communist Party 6%   Shamanism 5%
Buddhism 1.5%

The word Siberia conjures up a vision of dark, silent forest and desolate tundra, always cold, windswept and inhospitable, with a thinly scattered population. This, today, is a completely misleading picture, and in some ways Siberia is one of the most developed regions of the Soviet Union. It is in Siberia that we find the largest hydroelectric installations, the mining complexes for rare "strategic" ores, university and academic towns, and the most developed systems of communication. The great majority of the Siberian population is Russian, but they coexist with the native Siberians, many of whom still follow traditional occupations—hunting, reindeer herding and fishing—within the new conditions created by the Soviet state.

The climate of Siberia is characterized by extremes of temperature. In summer, many places in the south reach 20–25°C (68–77°F), but winter temperatures are around −30°C (−22°F) on average. In the coldest part of Siberia, Verkhoyansk, temperatures may reach −80°C (−112°F). Permafrost—permanently frozen soil —reaches as far as the northern end of Lake Baikal.

Despite its immense area, Siberia is geographically fairly homogenous. Taiga (virgin coniferous forest) covers virtually all of it, although in the far north the trees give way to tundra. Immense rivers flow northward into the Arctic Ocean and until the advent of air traffic, these were the main channels of transport and communication. Along the river valleys, agriculture is possible, although farming has never been productive enough to be a sole occupation, and has always been combined with fishing, hunting or reindeer herding. Almost none of the forest was cleared in prerevolutionary times but some areas have now been cleared and more land is under cultivation than ever before.

Very little is known about the early history of Siberia, but its present-day ethnic complexity indicates that there were many waves of migration from several different directions. The native Siberians show a varying mixture of Caucasoid, Mongoloid and Palaeo-Asiatic features, with Caucasoid elements more strongly represented in the west and Palaeo-Asiatic predominant in the northeast.

The earliest inhabitants of Siberia were nomads, who were conquered, in the first century BC, by the Huns spreading northward from Mongolia. The Huns were themselves pursued by the Chinese and the region later fell under the temporary and tempestuous sway of various Turkic empires. By the twelfth century it was involved in the fringes of the Mongolian Empire. Throughout this period the great empires of the south affected only those people living adjacent to them, and the vast northern forests were inhabited by hunters and fishers who were largely untouched by war.

Russian Cossacks first began to venture into western Siberia in the fifteenth century and by the beginning of the sixteenth century they were regularly collecting a fur tax from the peoples of the Urals. Gradually they spread farther and farther east. They traveled down the great rivers, used dogsleds to cross the forest, and rapidly subdued the native people by means of guns. Once Siberia had been opened up by these traders and adventurers, the Russian Tsars were eager to include it in their empire. They sent their own armies on expeditions with the aim of military conquest, and by 1648 they had already reached the Pacific Ocean.

The Russians collected the fur tax and put down native risings when necessary, but otherwise did little to affect the lives of the Siberian natives. During the nineteenth century, however, Russian peasants began to settle in western and southern Siberia in large numbers. These peasants took much of the best farmland, and by the beginning of the twentieth century serious confrontations occurred between Russian settlers and native peoples, especially the Buryats.

The Revolution of 1917 had little immediate effect on the native peoples of Siberia, but it was fought with tenacity and desperation by the Siberian Russians. Since the Revolution the economies of the native Siberians have been collectivized and modernized. The government has poured financial aid and expert advisers into the area, and as a result the conditions of life for these people have improved greatly, especially in the field of health and education. Whereas their population levels were declining, they are now on the increase, although in some areas there is a loss of ethnic identity, and social problems such as alcohol abuse are encountered. The native Siberians have on the whole benefited under the Communist system, and they tend to be more fervently pro-Communist than many Russians.

In the 1950s thirty-one different native peoples were described in Siberia. Some of these live in the extreme north, such as the Nentsi, Entsi, Nganasan and Chukchi (see pages 62–3) and the Asiatic Inuit or Eskimo (see pages 60–61). The cultural and linguistic patterns of Siberia are extremely complex and do not correspond to economic divisions.

The religion of all of the native peoples of Siberia centered on *shamans*, who could communicate with and manipulate spirits. However, the southernmost peoples of Siberia, the Buryats, Tuva and Altaians,

Facing the Siberian winter
On Siberian collectives, logs for winter fuel are provided free to every family. Although the nomadic Buryat once lived in round, wood-frame, felt-covered tents, they now build 2- or 3-roomed winter houses of logs, plastering earth and moss into the chinks to keep the wind out and provide insulation. Simple one-roomed summer houses, owned by the collective, are scattered across the pastures; a herding family will use as many as four or five of them in the course of one season. Married couples qualify for a house and their own livestock, the produce of which they can keep, so people tend to marry early.

were heavily influenced by Tibetan Buddhism (Lamaism), which reached them from Mongolia, and here shamanism was overlaid by a fairly powerful organization of Lamaist monasteries. The Russians attempted to convert the Siberian peoples to Orthodox Christianity, but on the whole this was unsuccessful. This religious conflict epitomizes the meeting of East and West that has occurred in southern Siberia, and which has been a powerful cultural influence, as demonstrated by the Buryats of Lake Baikal.

The Buryats of the Lake Baikal Region

The Siberian Buryats, who number about 350,000, consists of an amalgamation of groups of Mongolian origin, who migrated north to escape the rule of the Mongolian Empire. They were really formed as a people during the seventeenth and eighteenth centuries, when the establishment of a guarded border between Tsarist Siberia and the Manchurian Empire cut them off from their kin to the south.

The Buryats, traditionally herders of cattle, sheep and horses, lived a seminomadic existence. During the long Siberian winter, they lived in scattered communities, each dwelling surrounded by its hayfields. In summer they moved to different pastures, allowing the grass to grow for hay near the winter quarters. To the west of Lake Baikal the Buryats were concentrated in narrow valleys in the taiga forest; they had comparatively little land for pasture and during the nineteenth century increasingly took up agriculture. To the east of Lake Baikal, however, there was ample pastureland and the Buryats practiced very little agriculture. These groups were highly mobile, especially those living near the Mongolian and Manchurian frontiers, and they lived in round felt tents, whereas those near Lake Baikal built wooden houses.

The underlying religion of the Buryats was shamanism, but in the eighteenth century Tibetan and Mongolian Buddhist monks penetrated Buryatskaya, and by the middle of the nineteenth century the Tsarist government was so alarmed at their success that it tried to limit the number of monasteries. Despite prohibitions, the number of monks grew, until by the time of the Revolution they numbered up to one in six of all males among the Eastern Buryats.

Some Buryats at the beginning of this century had a university education in Russian cities, and some traveled to Tibet for education in the monasteries. By the time of the Revolution the Buryats were unique among Siberian peoples in the number of learned men they had produced, even though a large proportion of the population was illiterate. The Western Buryats, were not exposed to Buddhism and their dialects were never written down, but the eastern dialects were sufficiently close to Mongolian for the Mongol alphabet to be widely used. The written form of their language proved to be a strong unifying force for these people.

Today the Buryats are still to a large extent rural, and they still specialize primarily in livestock farming. Rural Buryats are members of *kolkhoz* (collective farms) or *sovkhoz* (state farms). The farming tasks have been divided into specializations and, where possible, mechanized. This has been difficult for livestock tasks, so that the traditional Buryat occupations remain largely manual, and therefore low paid. The more skilled jobs are done by the younger people, and competition is intense for educational opportunities, the main avenue, apart from political activism, to economic advancement. Side by side with this Soviet reality there remains a Buryat cultural identity, based on language, history and kinship traditions.

The heritage of the Buryat
The Buryat originated in Mongolia, as the features of this *kolkhoz* chairman clearly show. Buddhism was a powerful and beneficial influence for the Eastern Buryat. Their language was recorded in Mongol script, their mythology written down, and a tradition of scholarship established.

Northern outpost of Buddhism
Outside a modern monastery in Siberia stands a Buryat monk or lama. The practice of Buddhism was forbidden by the Soviet government and all the monasteries closed down, but since World War II this policy has been reversed. Two monasteries have been reopened with a limited number of monks. Ironically, it was Buddhist monks who founded the very first communes among the Buryats in the wake of the 1917 revolution—in the face of fierce opposition from older monks, they decided to divest the church of its property and return to the original doctrines of the Buddhist faith.

Peoples and languages
It is doubtful whether many of the smaller groups of Siberian peoples ever thought of themselves as one people before the Soviet government began to classify them for administrative reasons. Since that first period of classification in the 1920s many small groups have disappeared, coalesced, or been assimilated by the Russians. However, in the 1950s, Soviet ethnographers distinguished 31 different native peoples of Siberia. The Buryat and the Yakut, with populations around 300,000, are the most numerous, while most other groups are numbered in thousands, or even hundreds. Russians, who number 12 million and live scattered all over Siberia, are the majority people.

Indo–European

	Slav languages (Russian, etc.)
	Baltic language (Latvian)
	Germanic languages (German, Yiddish)

Altaic

| | Turkic languages (Tatar, Shor, Yakut, Altai, Tuva, Khakas, etc.); Mongolian language (Buryat); Tungus languages (Evenki, Eveni, Ul'chi, Nania, Udege, etc.) |

Unaffiliated languages

| | Uralic (Finno–Ugric languages: Khanti, etc.; Selkup) |
| | "Paleosiberian" (Ket, Nivkhi) |

Featured people

| | Buryat |

Additional peoples

| | |

Arable and permanent grassland

| | Sheep, cattle, horses and camels on steppe; wheat, maize, vegetables and fodder crops. |

Woods and forests

| | Mainly coniferous trees providing timber and building; includes some rough grazing land. |

Rough grazing land

| | Mainly reindeer on tundra; some cattle. |

Nonagricultural land

| | Mountain peaks, swamps and steep slopes. |

Land use
Taiga covers virtually all Siberia. Most people in the west live by fishing, reindeer herding or a combination of fishing, farming and herding. The northern peoples live by reindeer herding, hunting and fur trapping. In the southeast, farming, fishing and pastoralism on the steppe grassland predominate.

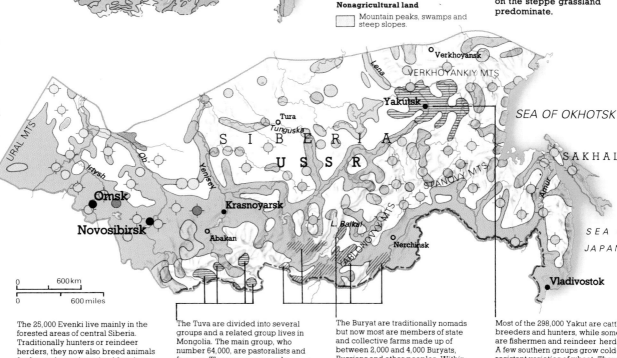

0   600km

0   600 miles

The 25,000 Evenki live mainly in the forested areas of central Siberia. Traditionally hunters or reindeer herders, they now also breed animals for fur, and practice mixed farming. The related Eveni are reindeer herders, hunters and fishers, numbering about 12,000.

The Tuva are divided into several groups and a related group lives in Mongolia. The main group, who number 64,000, are pastoralists and farmers. They were very early converts to Buddhism and for a long time their land was a province of the Manchurian Empire.

The Buryat are traditionally nomads but now most are members of state and collective farms made up of between 2,000 and 4,000 Buryats, Russians and other peoples. Within the farms, the household, which owns a small private plot of land, remains the basic social unit.

Most of the 298,000 Yakut are cattle breeders and hunters, while some are fishermen and reindeer herders. A few southern groups grow cold-resistant varieties of wheat. There is a university at Yakutsk and many Yakut hold administrative and educational posts.

East Asia

In the vast lands of east Asia almost one quarter of the world's population is found. Although encompassing wide varieties in the basic pattern of life as dictated by climate and terrain, the region shows a remarkable continuity of cultural themes. Both now and in the past, this cultural pattern has flowed largely from China which, with its long tradition of strong, bureaucratic government, has dominated its immediate neighbors. However, Japan has remained largely free from Chinese political control, and today its highly industrialized, capitalist society stands in stark contrast to the Communist regimes which predominate in mainland east Asia.

East Asia can be divided into three major areas: Mongolia and Tibet, predominantly occupied by pastoral nomadic peoples, the wheat-growing area of northern China, together with the oases of Sinkiang and cultivated valleys in central and southern Tibet, and finally the area of irrigated rice

cultivation stretching throughout southern China, Korea and Japan. East Asia also contains many different ethnic groups, although most of them belong to the Mongoloid race, except in Sinkiang, where a Caucasoid element is found. The dominant people are the Han Chinese, who characterize Chinese society and culture. The Han are thought to have originated in northern China around the Huang Ho (Yellow River) and to have spread southward over the last 2,000 years, gradually absorbing southern populations.

The influence of China and Confucianism
East Asia is, broadly speaking, the region covered by Chinese civilization. The subregions situated around China —Korea, Japan, Mongolia and Tibet—formed their ancient states as a result of the influence of Chinese civilization, and their international status was confirmed by their official relationship with China. Thereafter Chinese influence con-

tinued in these countries, at least until the eve of their modernization. Consequently, these states developed bureaucratic institutions along Chinese lines, with the centralization of administrative power, based on Confucian ethics. This was particularly manifested in the Yi Dynasty of Korea (1392–1910) and, to a lesser degree, in the Tokugawa regime of Japan (1603–1867).

So strong was the influence of Confucian ethics in China and Korea that orthodox religion failed to gain significant power, as it did in south Asia or Europe for example. Religious power, in the form of an institution or of a priestly community, never succeeded in overcoming political power. Religions remained mostly under the patronage of the state authority or at the level of folk belief. Thus in these countries the most prestigious occupation has always been a post in the bureaucracy, and professionals, in whatever field, have traditionally been subjected to political control.

In contrast to these regions, the people of Tibet, Mongolia and Sinkiang did not accept Confucianism, and there religion played a significant role in social and political affairs. In Tibet, Buddhism, which was originally an Indian religion, developed into Lamaism, with an elaborate pantheon of spirits and gods added to the basic Buddhist beliefs. Lamaism was the focus of Tibetan life, and maintained a hierarchical structure based on a network of monasteries. The hierarchy was headed by the Dalai Lama, under whom the Tibetan government was institutionalized. Tibetan Buddhism also influenced most of Mongolia and the bordering areas between China proper and Tibet, such as Chinghai and Sikang. It even spread northward into Siberia, where a Buddhist people, the Buryat, are still found today. The "corridor" of Sinkiang lay on the major route of Buddhism from India to China, and the ancient states established around the oases also practiced Buddhism, but at a later date the people of this region were converted to Islam.

Despite these religious influences, Tibet, Mongolia and Sinkiang were all within the Chinese sphere of influence throughout their history, and occasionally under direct military and political control. Chinese rule of Tibet, Sinkiang and Inner Mongolia was firmly established in the years after Mao Tse-tung's Communist party came to power in 1949. As a result religion, particularly Tibetan Buddhism, was largely eradicated, and the commune organization of China introduced.

According to the Chinese Institute of the National Minorities, there are fifty-five non-Han ethnic groups in China at present. Some of the ethnic groups now listed as minorities were once the rulers of China, such as Mongolians of the Yuan Dynasty and Manchus of the Quing (Ch'ing) Dynasty, but most minority groups occupy the outskirts of China proper, being particularly numerous in the mountainous areas of southwest China, such as Yunnan and Sichuan. The minorities vary considerably in size, from larger groups with millions to smaller groups with only a few thousand. Many non-Han groups have slowly become Sinicized, and as the Chinese administration penetrates the more remote areas, contacts with the Han Chinese are increasing. Nevertheless, in the heart of each minority group community the traditional culture, including language and social customs, has generally been preserved. Some groups even possess their own script, which helps to preserve their cultural identity.

While almost the entire area of mainland east Asia is under Communist rule, Japan stands apart, both politically and economically. These islands have been inhabited, since prehistoric times, by people with a language, culture and social system quite different from those of the Chinese. Although Japan was heavily influenced by Chinese civilization, the native social system and beliefs have been largely maintained. Japan's social and geographical distance from China, and the homogeneity of the Japanese people (excluding the Ainu), have made possible its unique development, and contributed to its success in industrialization.

Paddies in the Kwangsi region, southern China

Mongolia and Tibet

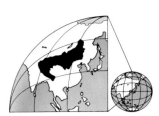

On the high bleak plains of Mongolia and Tibet the nomadic way of life reached its zenith; here the proud and warlike tribesmen despised farmers and tradesmen alike. Lamaism, with its rich pantheon of ghosts and spirits, was their religion, and wealthy monasteries dominated society. Today the monasteries have been abandoned and the nomadic life collectivized.

Population by Region
Total: 18 million

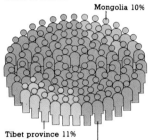

Mongolia 10%
Tibet province 11%
Sinkiang province 79%

Population by Religion

Buddhism 30% | Communist Party 4%
Non-party Communists 66%

Palace of the Dalai Lama
The Potala, towering over 200 m (700 ft) above Lhasa, was once the palace of the Dalai Lama. He had practically no contact with the ordinary people and rarely left the seclusion of his massive, thousand-roomed palace. When he did, he was carried in a curtained sedan chair and was guarded by horsemen, foot-soldiers and monk policemen armed with staves. Prior to the revolution, approximately one sixth of the male population were monks. The monasteries, together with the aristocrats, owned most of the land and were the country's ruling class; the peasants were little better off than serfs.

For at least 4,000 years Mongolia and Tibet have been inhabited by tribes of pastoral nomads. These people roamed the dry, barren uplands of Tibet and the wide rolling grasslands of Mongolia. Although they speak different languages, the Tibetans and Mongolians were brought together by a common religion and culture. The chief unifying force was Tibetan Buddhism (Lamaism) and there was once a great traffic of pilgrims, missionaries, scribes and artists between them. Tibetan was understood, at least in its written form, by all Mongolian monks, who at one time accounted for one sixth of the male population. Although Tibet is now part of China and has experienced great political changes, its people have retained much of their ethnic identity, as have the Mongolians in their Soviet-oriented People's Republic.

Separating these two regions is a series of oases, running from east to west, and these were settled by intensive agriculturists and traders—people with a fundamentally different way of life. Chinese people spread westward into this corridor during the first century BC, and it became one of the great trading routes of the world, connecting Imperial China with India, Afghanistan and Europe. The people of the oasis belt were Muslim, Confucian or Daoist, and culturally quite distinct from the nomads. They are now part of the People's Republic of China.

Most of Mongolia is steppe, watered by occasional rainfall in summer, but extremely cold and dry in winter, and scoured by sand storms in the spring Tibet consists largely of a high plateau, divided into two regions. To the north is the vast Tibetan tableland, much of it over 4,800 meters (15,800 feet), and dotted with snowy peaks, salt lakes, and stretches of desert. To the south is the Tsangpo valley, where the climate is relatively damp from the monsoon rains. Tibetan civilization developed in this valley, where agriculture is possible, and most of the population, both agriculturist and pastoralist, live there.

The pastoral nomads of Mongolia and Tibet evolved a system of production based on the flexible use of several different kinds of livestock: sheep, cattle, yaks,
goats, camels and horses. This variety of livestock protected them against epidemics, which could kill off one type of animal. They ate milk and meat, supplemented by wild berries, bulbs and the proceeds of hunting. The agriculturists of Tibet, known as *shing-sa-wa* (people of the fields), engaged in regular trade with the high-altitude pastoralists. They grew barley, potatoes and vegetables, and their houses, of wood or stone, were grouped in villages. Although their sedentary life style was fundamentally different from that of the nomads, they were very similar to them culturally, and the two groups were bound together by their religion. In general, however, nomadism was thought of as a superior way of life, both by the nomads and the villagers. Kinship, based on the patrilineal principle, was of great importance throughout this area. The patrilineage was known in many places as *yasan* (bone), and it was considered that the father's semen made the bone of the child, while the mother contributed the flesh. The nomadic pastoralists have long genealogical memories, tracing their ancestors back as far as Chingghis Khan and the Tibetan kings.

The earliest steppe empires were founded by the Huns between the third and first centuries BC and they were followed by a series of others, culminating in the Mongolian Empire of the twelfth century. The Mongols, under Chingghis Khan, conquered Tibet, and spread rapidly into China, where the Yuan Dynasty was established. The Mongolian Empire broke up in the fourteenth century, and internal wars divided the Mongols until the seventeenth century, when a new empire, that of the Manchus, united the tribes.

Throughout this period Buddhism flourished in Tibet, and it spread north to Mongolia, first during the Yuan Dynasty in the twelfth century, and again during the Manchurian Dynasty in the seventeenth and eighteenth centuries. Tibetan Buddhism was of the Mahayana school, but had a complex, hierarchical organization. The Buddhist doctrine that the world is illusory developed into a belief in unseen forces—spirits, gods and ghosts—whose worship became part of the religion. The Manchus encouraged the growth of monasteries and established feudal relations in the steppes, but during the eighteenth and nineteenth centuries they were gradually undermined in power and influence by the Chinese. Traders from China spread into the steppes and involved the people, both administrators and individuals, in mounting debts. By 1911, when the Manchurian Dynasty was overthrown, Mongolia owed a colossal debt to these traders.

After 1911, both Tibet and Mongolia were nominally independent and ruled by "Living Buddhas": the Dalai Lama in Tibet, and the Jebtsundamba Khutukhtu in Outer Mongolia. Outer Mongolia underwent a revolution in 1921 and established a socialist government having close ties with the Soviet Union. Inner Mongolia remained within the Chinese sphere of influence, and in 1959 the Chinese reestablished control over Tibet.

Great social and economic changes have taken place since the respective revolutions of Mongolia and

Tibet's population of 2,700,000 are mostly engaged in raising livestock, mainly sheep and yaks. Tea growing, mining and hydroelectric schemes have now been introduced. Many thousands fled to India and Nepal after the Chinese invasion of 1959.

Khalkha is the most widely spoken Mongol dialect. Its modern script was devised from the Russian Cyrillic script, but traditionally Khalkha was recorded in a Mongolian alphabet written in vertical columns, the result of centuries of Chinese influence.

Traders, pilgrims, artists, doctors and missionaries crossed Sinkiang's oasis corridor between Mongolia and Tibet for centuries, yet the oasis peoples, dominated by Muslim Uighurs since the 7th century, remained culturally distinct from their Buddhist neighbors.

Arable land

Wheat, barley, millet, potatoes and vegetables in the north; barley, wheat, peas, oats and tea in the south; wheat, cotton, maize, rice and melons in the oasis corridor.

Woods and forests

Mainly coniferous trees, used for timber.

Rough grazing land

Mainly sheep, cattle, goats, camels, horses and yaks; includes some permanent grassland and arable land.

Nonagricultural land

Deserts, mountain peaks, salt lakes and marshland.

Land use

The predominant form of land use in this region is pastoralism, although agriculture has always been practiced in some areas, notably the Tsangpo valley and the oasis corridor of Sinkiang. The Mongolian People's Republic has now introduced cereal growing in many areas.

Peoples and languages

Mongols speaking Khalkha make up 76% of Mongolia's population; another 15% speak other Mongol dialects. The remainder speak mostly Turkic languages and tend to live in the northwest provinces; Kazakhs form the largest minority group. Uighurs are the majority people in Sinkiang. Tibet's population is mainly Tibetan apart from a few Mongols, Nepalese and Chinese.

Altaic

Mongolian languages (Khalkha, Buryat, Barga, etc.); Turkic languages (Uighur, Kazakh, Kirghiz, etc.)

Sino-Tibetan

Tibeto-Burman language (Tibetan)

Chinese languages

Indo-European

Indo-Iranian language (Tadzhik)

Featured peoples

Khalkha Mongols

China. Apart from a few token monasteries, Buddhism has been swept away in both countries. The Mongolian People's Republic has developed mining and heavy industry as well as a certain amount of agriculture. Inner Mongolia was settled by Chinese farmers during the 1920s and 1930s, and has long since lost its distinctive nomadic character. Tibet has perhaps changed least in what it produces—wool, meat and barley—but all agriculture and herding now takes place within cooperatives producing toward planned delivery targets.

The social structure and political organization of Tibetan and Mongolian life have been radically transformed, but those more indefinable aspects of culture, or "ways of looking at the world," that have been distinctive through the centuries, have survived. This mixture of cultural continuity and political transformation is well illustrated by the Khalkha Mongols.

The Khalkha Mongols of Mongolia

The main Mongol ethnic group is the Khalkha, and together with other Mongol groups in the Mongolian People's Republic, these people number just over one million. In the past, Mongols generally lived in groups of two to four households, known as *ail*, and these families would cooperate in pasturing their animals, moving camp at least four times a year. During the winter there was a danger that snow might cover the pasture, so the camp was situated on a south-facing slope, where snow would quickly melt in the sun. As soon as the young grass started to sprout, the herdsmen would hasten to move camp to the best pastures, moving on when the grazing was exhausted. In September, they moved to autumn camps, where they prepared hay for the winter, and killed the animals they would need to keep them in meat until the spring. The meat was dried or frozen, and the people returned to winter camp to face the rigors of wind and ice.

The Mongols were largely self-sufficient in this way of life. Each *ail*, or group of *ails*, contained people who knew leather, wood and metal working, and the techniques of castration, veterinary medicine, hunting and trapping. However, they needed some items from outside (such as cotton, silk, tea, tobacco, opium, sugar, flour, guns and religious objects) and these they obtained from Chinese traders on credit, at terms which greatly favored the traders. The traditional Mongol way of life began to disintegrate in the nineteenth century, partly as a result of this trade with the Chinese. The Mongols seldom engaged in trade themselves, and showed no inclination toward farming, for they prized the life of the herdsman.

The Revolution of 1921 brought socialization and industrialization of the Mongol economy. The nomads, particularly in the west of Mongolia, showed some resistance, but by the 1950s the government was able to persuade most people to join a *negdel* (collective). A state university was set up in the capital of Ulan Bator, staffed in part by ex-monks, and aid for building factories, roads, bridges, electricity plants and modern housing began to pour into the country from both China and the Soviet bloc.

A typical herding family in a *negdel* still lives in the traditional round white felt tent and moves seasonally with the herds. Now, however, each family is part of a *suur* (production team) and does specialized work looking after one type of animal only. Although not all jobs in the *negdel* are paid at the same rate, the great gulf between "rich" and "poor" that existed before the Revolution has been lessened considerably. Many Mongols go for training in the Soviet Union and other socialist countries, but very few ever emigrate or marry outside their own Khalkha community.

Sports of the nomads

In the summer, when the new grass began to grow, the Mongol nomads would celebrate with festivities that included wrestling, horse racing and archery. Still popular today, wrestling bouts conclude with the victor performing an "eagle dance," flapping his arms like a bird.

A mobile home

The *ger* can be assembled or taken down by 2 to 3 people within 30 minutes; its wooden framework, round shape and felt covering provide warmth and shelter during the severe winter storms. For these reasons it is still widely used by the Mongols; even the suburbs of Ulan Bator entirely comprise permanently sited *gers*. Inside the *ger*, men and objects considered masculine, like hunting and riding equipment, still occupy the western half, in accordance with tradition; women and objects associated with female tasks, such as cooking pots, occupy the eastern half

China and Korea 1

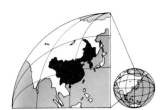

Shielded from marauding nomads by the Great Wall, and inspired by the teaching of Confucius, who extolled obedience to family and state, the Chinese Dynasties grew steadily in power, wealth and learning for over two thousand years. With the victory of Mao Tse-tung came a new era for China, in which paddies and factories replaced imperial aspirations as the focuses of society.

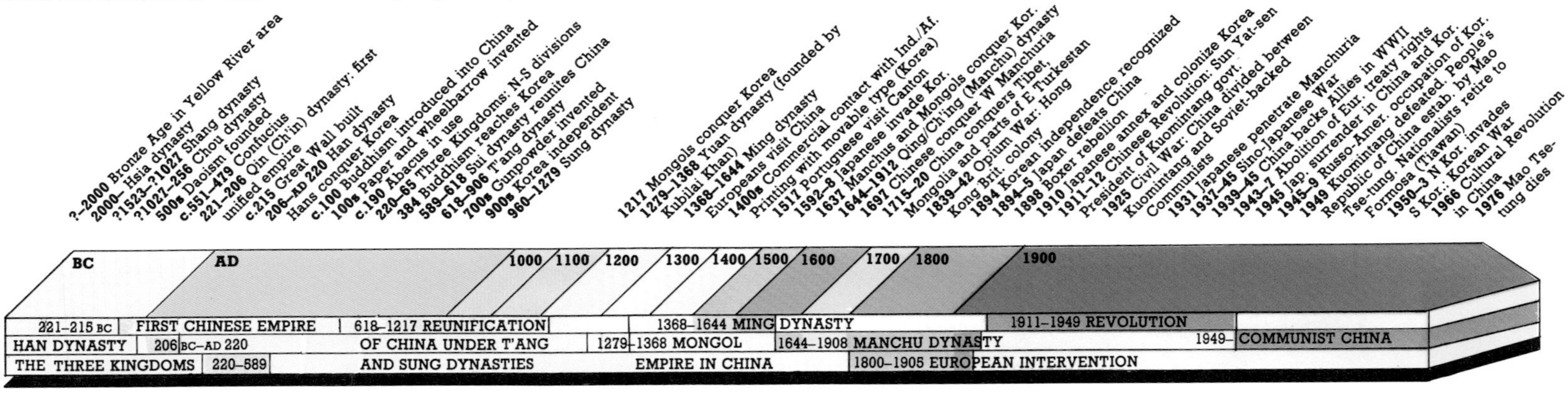

Timeline entries:
2–2000 Bronze Age in Yellow River area
2000 Hsia dynasty
?1523–?1027 Shang dynasty
?1027–256 Chou dynasty
500s Daoism founded
c.551–479 Confucius
221–206 Qin (Ch'in) dynasty: first unified empire
c.215 Great Wall built
206–AD 220 Han dynasty
Hans conquer Korea
c.100 Buddhism introduced into China
c.100 Paper and wheelbarrow invented
c.190 Abacus in use
220–65 Three Kingdoms: N-S divisions
384 Buddhism reaches Korea
589–618 Sui dynasty reunites China
618–906 T'ang dynasty
700s Gunpowder invented
900s Korea independent
960–1279 Sung dynasty
1217 Mongols conquer Korea
1279–1368 Yüan dynasty (founded by Kubilai Khan)
1368–1644 Ming dynasty
1400s Commercial contact with Ind./Af.
Europeans visit China
1517 Portuguese visit Canton
1592–8 Japanese invade Kor.
1637 Manchuria invade Kor.
Printing with movable type (Korea)
1644–1912 Qing (Manchu) dynasty
1697 Chinese conquer W Manchuria
1715–20 China conquers Tibet,
Mongolia and parts of E Turkestan
1839–42 Opium War: Hong Kong Brit. colony
1894 Korean independence recognized
1894–5 Japan defeats China
1898 Boxer rebellion
1910 Japanese annex and colonize Korea
1911–12 Chinese Revolution: Sun Yat-sen President of Kuomintang govt.
1925 Civil War: China divided between Kuomintang and Soviet-backed Communists
1931 Japanese penetrate Manchuria
1937–45 Sino-Japanese War
1941 China backs Allies in WWII
1943–5 Jap. surrender in China and Kor.
1945–9 Russo-Amer. occupation of Kor.
1949 Kuomintang defeated: People's Republic of China estab. by Mao Tse-tung; Nationalists retire to Formosa (Taiwan)
1950–3 N Kor. invades S Kor.: Korean War
1966 Cultural Revolution in China
1976 Mao Tse-tung dies

Timeline bar:
| BC | AD | 1000 | 1100 | 1200 | 1300 | 1400 | 1500 | 1600 | 1700 | 1800 | 1900 |

221–215 BC	FIRST CHINESE EMPIRE	618–1217 REUNIFICATION		1368–1644 MING DYNASTY		1911–1949 REVOLUTION	
HAN DYNASTY 206 BC–AD 220	OF CHINA UNDER T'ANG	1279–1368 MONGOL	1644–1908 MANCHU DYNASTY		1949– COMMUNIST CHINA
THE THREE KINGDOMS 220–589	AND SUNG DYNASTIES	EMPIRE IN CHINA	1800–1905 EUROPEAN INTERVENTION	

Population by Country
Total: 1,035 million

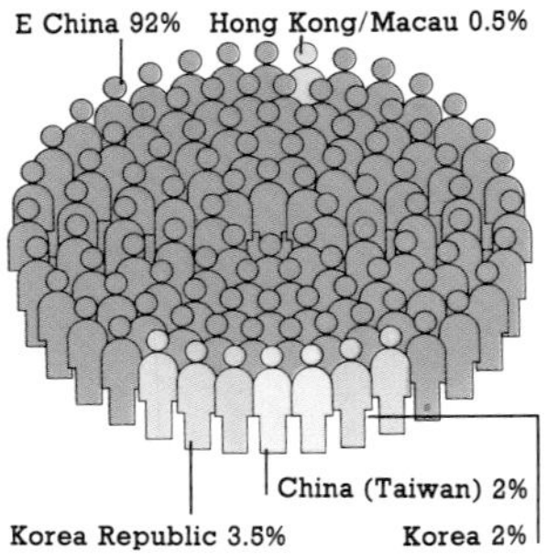

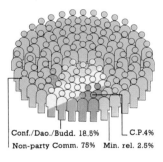

E China 92% Hong Kong/Macau 0.5%
China (Taiwan) 2%
Korea Republic 3.5% Korea 2%

Population by Religion

Conf./Dao./Budd. 18.5% C.P. 4%
Non-party Comm. 75% Min. rel. 2.5%

Taming China's rivers
The most notable achievements of modern China include flood prevention and the provision of navigable waterways and hydroelectric power.

The geography of eastern Asia has had a profound effect on the societies found in the area. The huge Eurasian landmass generates powerful meteorological cycles, known as the monsoon system, in which warmed air rising from the land in summer sucks in moisture-laden air from the seas to the south and east. The southeast thus receives the most rainfall, and the northwest the least. The terrain slopes gradually down to the sea, and rivers therefore tend to drain to the east. Over the millennia they have formed extensive fertile alluvial plains in many parts of eastern China, where elaborate civilizations have developed, based on intensive irrigated agriculture.

In the hilly mountainous areas of the south and southwest, however, the terrain does not permit the construction of large-scale irrigation systems, and shifting cultivation is widely practiced. By contrast, some parts of the north and west receive too little rainfall for any type of agriculture, so that here pastoralism forms the basis of the traditional economy. The pastoral nomads of the north have played a major role in China's history, but in the uplands of the southwest live many small ethnic groups, who until recently remained outside the mainstream of Chinese culture.

The prehistoric origins of Chinese civilization, dating back as far as the second millennium BC, are found in the northern part of the lowland area, along the Huang Ho (Yellow River). Centuries of intermittent warfare among many small kingdoms culminated in the victory of the Qin (Ch'in) Kingdom in 221 BC, and the establishment of China's first unified bureaucratic empire, controlling an area that stretched from the Pacific coastlands as far as Tibet. Although the Qin Dynasty was short lived it established the pattern for centralized government which was consolidated and developed by its successor, the Han Dynasty. It was under the Qin Dynasty that much of China's Great Wall was constructed, although parts of it had been built by earlier states as a defense against raids from the north.

The Han Dynasty ruled China from 206 BC to AD 220 and was responsible for conquering much of what is now Korea, as well as increasing China's wealth through overseas trade and encouraging philosophy, art and scholarship. These traditions were furthered by later dynasties such as the T'ang (AD 618–906) and the Ming (AD 1368–1644). In 1644 the Ming Dynasty was conquered by the Manchus, pastoral nomads from the north who established the Qing (Ch'ing) Dynasty. In the nineteenth century the Manchu dynasty suffered a steady decline and became oppressive and corrupt, leading to its overthrow by revolutionary forces.

The power of successive Chinese dynasties depended, at least in part, on the influence of Confucianism, a peculiarly Chinese religion with its major focus on the relationship of the individual to the family, society and the state. Two other religions, Daoism and Buddhism, have also been influential in China. Daoism refers to a rather heterogeneous set of ideas and practices, of considerable historical depth, ranging from shamanism to complex philosophical concepts. Buddhism, a foreign import, was quickly Sinicized, and in its Chinese form incorporates both a complex pantheon of supernatural beings and a sophisticated philosophy. In the everyday religious life of the Chinese, these three teachings were inextricably mixed.

From the sixteenth century onward, foreign expansion threatened China's isolation. Macau was colonized by the Portuguese in 1557, but China's independence was not significantly affected until the midnineteenth century, when the western powers effectively gained control of much of the mainland. Following China's defeat by Japan in 1894–5 foreign domination increased, leading to the Boxer rebellion of 1898. The Manchu Dynasty finally fell in 1911 and China was plunged into civil war from which the Communist Party emerged triumphant in 1949.

China has long been an agrarian state and the great majority of the people (75–80 percent) are still directly involved in farming. In Imperial times agricultural production was carried out in millions of small-scale domestic units by peasant families. A portion of this production was siphoned off through taxes, rents and the profits of the grain merchants, to end up in the state coffers and the pockets of a small elite. These people derived their position from a monopoly on education, political power and landownership.

Since 1949 leaders of the People's Republic of China have aimed at erasing such deep-seated class divisions, at shifting production from domestic to communal units, and at increasing industrial production. Their reforms have transformed the economic conditions of the Han Chinese, the dominant people, without seriously disrupting their traditional culture, but for ethnic minorities such as the Jinuo, economic advancement has been accompanied by rapid Sinicization.

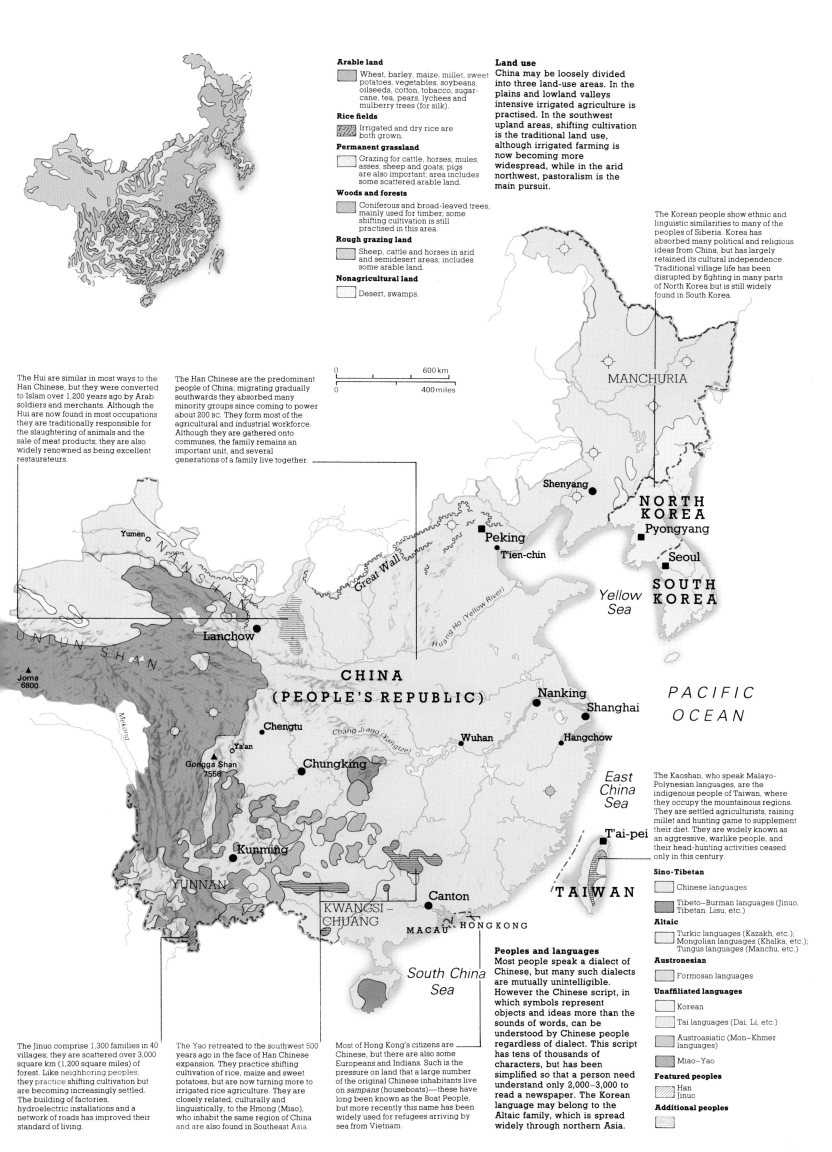

Arable land
Wheat, barley, maize, millet, sweet potatoes, vegetables, soybeans, oilseeds, cotton, tobacco, sugar-cane, tea, pears, lychees and mulberry trees (for silk).

Rice fields
Irrigated and dry rice are both grown.

Permanent grassland
Grazing for cattle, horses, mules, asses, sheep and goats; pigs are also important; area includes some scattered arable land.

Woods and forests
Coniferous and broad-leaved trees, mainly used for timber; some shifting cultivation is still practised in this area.

Rough grazing land
Sheep, cattle and horses in arid and semidesert areas; includes some arable land.

Nonagricultural land
Desert, swamps.

Land use
China may be loosely divided into three land-use areas. In the plains and lowland valleys intensive irrigated agriculture is practised. In the southwest upland areas, shifting cultivation is the traditional land use, although irrigated farming is now becoming more widespread, while in the arid northwest, pastoralism is the main pursuit.

The Korean people show ethnic and linguistic similarities to many of the peoples of Siberia. Korea has absorbed many political and religious ideas from China, but has largely retained its cultural independence. Traditional village life has been disrupted by fighting in many parts of North Korea but is still widely found in South Korea.

The Hui are similar in most ways to the Han Chinese, but they were converted to Islam over 1,200 years ago by Arab soldiers and merchants. Although the Hui are now found in most occupations they are traditionally responsible for the slaughtering of animals and the sale of meat products; they are also widely renowned as being excellent restaurateurs.

The Han Chinese are the predominant people of China; migrating gradually southwards they absorbed many minority groups since coming to power about 200 BC. They form most of the agricultural and industrial workforce. Although they are gathered onto communes, the family remains an important unit, and several generations of a family live together.

The Kaoshan, who speak Malayo-Polynesian languages, are the indigenous people of Taiwan, where they occupy the mountainous regions. They are settled agriculturists, raising millet and hunting game to supplement their diet. They are widely known as an aggressive, warlike people, and their head-hunting activities ceased only in this century.

Sino-Tibetan
Chinese languages
Tibeto–Burman languages (Jinuo, Tibetan, Lisu, etc.)

Altaic
Turkic languages (Kazakh, etc.); Mongolian languages (Khalka, etc.); Tungus languages (Manchu, etc.)

Austronesian
Formosan languages

Unaffiliated languages
Korean
Tai languages (Dai, Li, etc.)
Austroasiatic (Mon-Khmer languages)
Miao–Yao

Featured peoples
Han
Jinuo

Additional peoples

Peoples and languages
Most people speak a dialect of Chinese, but many such dialects are mutually unintelligible. However the Chinese script, in which symbols represent objects and ideas more than the sounds of words, can be understood by Chinese people regardless of dialect. This script has tens of thousands of characters, but has been simplified so that a person need understand only 2,000–3,000 to read a newspaper. The Korean language may belong to the Altaic family, which is spread widely through northern Asia.

The Jinuo comprise 1,300 families in 40 villages; they are scattered over 3,000 square km (1,200 square miles) of forest. Like neighboring peoples, they practice shifting cultivation but are becoming increasingly settled. The building of factories, hydroelectric installations and a network of roads has improved their standard of living.

The Yao retreated to the southwest 500 years ago in the face of Han Chinese expansion. They practice shifting cultivation of rice, maize and sweet potatoes, but are now turning more to irrigated rice agriculture. They are closely related, culturally and linguistically, to the Hmong (Miao), who inhabit the same region of China and are also found in Southeast Asia.

Most of Hong Kong's citizens are Chinese, but there are also some Europeans and Indians. Such is the pressure on land that a large number of the original Chinese inhabitants live on *sampans* (houseboats)—these have long been known as the Boat People, but more recently this name has been widely used for refugees arriving by sea from Vietnam.

MANCHURIA

Shenyang

NORTH KOREA
Pyongyang

Seoul

SOUTH KOREA

Yellow Sea

Yumen

NAN SHAN

K'UNLUN SHAN

▲ Joma 6800

Mekong

Lanchow

CHINA (PEOPLE'S REPUBLIC)

Peking
T'ien-chin

Great Wall

Huang Ho (Yellow River)

Chengtu

Ya'an

▲ Gongga Shan 7556

Chungking

Nanking

Shanghai

Chang Jiang (Yangtze)

Wuhan

Hangchow

East China Sea

Kunming

PACIFIC OCEAN

T'ai-pei

TAIWAN

YUNNAN

Canton

KWANGSI-CHUANG

MACAU HONG KONG

South China Sea

0   600 km
0   400 miles

China and Korea 2

Han Chinese

The dominant people of China today are the Han Chinese, whose cultural complex has expanded widely over the millennia, and in the process assimilated a large number of other ethnic groups. It has long been, and still is, largely dependent on intensive irrigated agriculture, and so its expansion has been limited to regions with sufficient and controllable water resources. Dry and upland regions have typically been exploited by other ethnic groups. Limited in the north and west by sparse and unpredictable rainfall, the Han Chinese cultural complex has moved south over the last 2,000 years into areas with greater rainfall, permitting the higher productivity responsible for China's growth and cultural achievements.

In imperial society, the family was a very important part of the social structure and so was the Confucian code of behavior which reinforced the authority of the male family head. In some areas of China, families were typically confederate, forming large-scale units of kin related through males. Such lineages, or clans, sometimes comprised entire villages.

Much of this has now changed, and with the establishment of communes many of the production functions of the family were lodged in other institutions, notably the production team. This transition is not complete, however—between 10 and 30 percent of agricultural production in China is private, carried out by families on small plots they own. Since the family still plays an important, though reduced, role in production and distribution, many traditional forms connected with it persist. Care of the aged, for example, is largely the responsibility of the children, so there is good reason for rural couples to have large families.

Religious life shows a similar pattern of modification of traditional forms rather than wholesale elimination. The general trend seems to be one of simplification, accompanied by a shift of focus to domestic observances and away from clan and community rituals. Family-oriented rituals associated with birth, marriage, death and ancestor worship, and such annual festivals as the lunar new year, are still practiced.

The Jinuo of Yunnan Province

In June 1979 the people known as the Jinuo became China's fifty-fifth officially recognized ethnic minority. The Jinuo, numbering around 10,000, speak a Tibeto-Burman language and inhabit the subtropical forests of Yunnan province in the extreme southwest of China. Yunnan is China's most ethnically diverse province—a full third of its population belongs to one or another of twenty-two ethnic minorities.

The Jinuo village was traditionally the most important economic and political unit, land being owned by the village and farmed communally by its members. The Jinuo originally practiced shifting cultivations, in which the land was divided into thirteen sections, each of which was cleared, burned, planted and harvested in rotation while the remaining twelve lay fallow. Crops grown included millet, maize and cotton, but

High-density living
The commercial bustle of Hong Kong is in marked contrast to the austerity of towns and cities in mainland China. Hong Kong, a British Crown Colony, consists of 3 parts: the island of Hong Kong, which was ceded to Britain in 1842, the tip of the Kowloon peninsula, acquired in 1860, and the New Territories, 946 square km (365 square miles) of the mainland which were leased to Britain in 1898 for 99 years. Hong Kong has one of the most perfect natural harbors in the world and is now very densely populated. Land has been reclaimed from the sea and even steep hill slopes have high-rise housing.

Chinese opera
The elaborate makeup, headdress and costume of this star of the Peking opera, require at least 4 hours preparation before each performance. Opera is still highly stylized but the themes may have a socialist content and the plot may be based on recent historical events.

The greatest resource
One of the most ambitious reforms of the People's Republic of China was the creation of a network of communes, averaging 5,000 households in each. These are subdivided into production brigades, and the brigades into production teams of 20 to 40 families each. This social reorganization served to harness China's greatest resource—its people. Here a team of men and women carry stones to shore up the banks of a river. Previously, annual flooding had prevented this commune from fully exploiting the potential of its fertile lands.

hunting and gathering of wild foods represented a crucial supplement to the people's livelihood, as indeed they still do. Since the seventeenth century an important source of income has been the production of Pu'er tea, a variety widely appreciated in China.

Jinuo villages were traditionally made up of groups of patrilineally related kinspeople residing together in large bamboo houses. These longhouses once measured as much as 60 meters (200 feet) long by 10 meters (33 feet) wide. As many as twenty or thirty families lived in rooms along either side of a central corridor, each room having its own cooking hearth. Such large longhouses are no longer in use, but ones 30 meters (100 feet) long are still found. At one time there were also large communal houses where young people of both sexes lived together in temporary liaisons. Although such adolescent sexual freedom seems to be in decline, the communal houses often remain as community and entertainment centers.

Shamanism and the worship of indigenous spirits, both elements of the traditional religion, seem to be less common now than in the past, but ancestor worship is prevalent. When someone dies, a small bamboo house is built over the grave, where descendants put the personal effects of the dead person, and leave daily food offerings for as long as three years.

Jinuo is the everyday language and few adults speak Chinese. The Jinuo language has no written form, however, and while the great majority of teachers in the primary and middle schools are of Jinuo origin, the language of instruction is Chinese, so it is likely that the use of Chinese will spread, to some degree at the expense of Jinuo. Other symbols of Jinuo ethnic identity, such as staining the teeth and the use of ear ornaments, are falling more rapidly into disuse.

These changes have taken place in recent decades and will no doubt accelerate in the future as the Jinuo become less isolated. The journey to the Jinuo area from the provincial capital, Kunming, once took twenty-five days, but it can now be accomplished in only a few days thanks to the network of roads totalling more than 2,000 kilometers (1,240 miles) built by the People's Liberation Army. More than 180 factories have been established in the Jinuo area, producing such things as machines, fertilizer, sugar, paper, herbal medicines, rubber and shoes.

In 1958 the Jinuo Luoke People's Commune was established, and the government helped to construct an irrigation system so that the Jinuo could switch some of their efforts from shifting cultivation to the more productive irrigated rice agriculture. Two local hydroelectric power plants have brought electricity to the commune center, and outlying villages will soon be supplied with electricity as well. The results of these and other changes have been improvements in health, education and standard of living. If previous experience is any guide, however, another result will be the increasing Sinicization of the Jinuo.

Traditions of the Jinuo
Jinuo sports include walking on stilts and catapulting bamboo spears. These Jinuo peasants will present the cocks as prizes. They wear traditional clothing for the occasion—for the women, a colorful jacket and white peaked bonnet, resembling the thatched roofs of the longhouses. For everyday wear, however, most have adopted contemporary Chinese clothing. Two Jinuo customs which are gradually dying out are staining the teeth black with the sap of the lacquer tree (said to prevent tooth decay as well as enhance beauty), and the enlargement of pierced earlobes to hold ornaments.

The education revolution
Since 1949 mass education has been a key goal for the People's Republic of China. Today, schooling is free and available to everyone. Babies and toddlers are cared for in a crèche attached to the office or factory where the mother works. Children between 2 and 7 years old attend kindergarten,

and those between 7 and 12 years old attend primary school. This is followed by middle school, where students stay until they are 17 years of age. Middle school students spend 2 months of the year working in a factory as part of their education—here children are helping to sort out raw material for use in the manufacture of silicone.

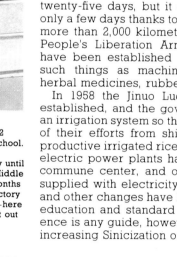

Entertainment—old and new
These citizens of Hangchow are listening to traditional tales told by a blind storyteller accompanying himself on a two-string violin. During the Cultural Revolution of the late 1960s this would have been considered reactionary, but there has been considerable relaxation of such austere attitudes. In the parks of Peking and other cities, people gather early in the morning, before they go to work, to listen to storytellers, to play musical instruments, or to participate informally in such traditional activities as sword dancing and shadow boxing. In addition, official classes are now held to teach the ancient Chinese art of puppetry. The stories enacted are taken from folk tales and opera, or reflect contemporary socialist ideals with titles such as "Celebrating a Bumper Harvest." Elsewhere, on China's more prosperous communes, the weekly entertainment is a free film, usually with a highly political content.

Japan

The huge, symmetrical cone of Mount Fuji aptly symbolizes Japan, a land where orderliness and power are the basis of society. Isolated from the rest of the world for centuries, the Japanese *have made an astounding leap into the twentieth century. Grafting capitalism onto their hierarchical society they have created an economic machine of awesome efficiency.*

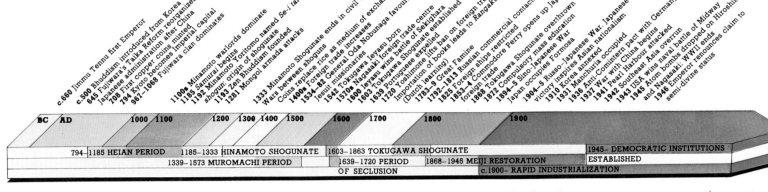

BC/AD	1000 1100	1200 1300 1400 1500	1600 1700	1800	1900				

794–1185 HEIAN PERIOD 1185–1333 HINAMOTO SHOGUNATE 1603–1863 TOKUGAWA SHOGUNATE 1945– DEMOCRATIC INSTITUTIONS
1339–1573 MUROMACHI PERIOD 1639–1720 PERIOD OF SECLUSION 1868–1945 MEIJI RESTORATION ESTABLISHED c.1900– RAPID INDUSTRIALIZATION

**Population by Residence
Total: 116 million**

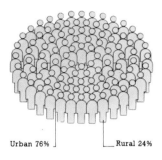

Urban 76%   Rural 24%

Population by Religion

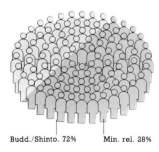

Budd./Shinto. 72%   Min. rel. 28%

Reclaiming land from the sea
Japan's economy is based on industry and technology. Here an industrial complex is being built on reclaimed land at Muzushima, near Kurashiki.

In just over a hundred years, the Japanese have grown from a feudal people, closed to the outside world, to a modern industrial nation respected as a major power in international economic affairs. The inhabitants of the islands of Japan are a remarkably homogenous people, unified as subjects, although at times in the past only nominal subjects, of a long and unbroken Imperial Line. They have had a complex independent civilization since they began to record their history in the early eighth century AD, and they share a unique language, religion and general attitude to life. Japan has absorbed and adapted foreign artifacts and ideas while retaining a core of Japanese character, now actually reinforced through the mass media and through a standardized education system, originally imported from the West.

Japan suffers not only from a scarcity of natural resources but also from the occasional ravages of typhoons, earthquakes and volcanic disturbances. Only one sixth of the land is suitable for cultivation, the terrain being largely mountainous and often of spectacular beauty. This restricts the majority of the one hundred million population to the narrow coastal plains and to land reclaimed from the surrounding ocean. Close living quarters result, and this encourages an extremely economical use of space and a strong emphasis on order and harmony in relations between people who live and work together. Japanese society functions to maintain a complex hierarchy without the need for orders to be given.

Rural Japanese

In rural communities, members of each household have traditionally worked small plots of land using little more than family labor. As successful cultivation depends on the skillful use of irrigation techniques, neighboring farmers cooperate over the matter of water distribution and this pattern of cooperation persists, although modern machinery and chemicals have been adopted wherever possible.

The chief principle of social organization is the importance of the continuity of the household, and this explains some of the characteristics of Japanese communities. Despite changes in the inheritance laws since World War II, rural property is usually still passed on to one child, preferably the eldest son. He is then responsible for the care of his parents in their old age, for the commemoration of his ancestors, and for the provision of an heir to maintain the household. His marriage may well be arranged by his parents and by those of his wife-to-be through the offices of a go-between, although the principals nowadays play a considerable part in the decision.

A household successor will usually bring his bride into the family home after the wedding. A noninheriting son will take the opportunity of marriage to set up his own home. Families who have no male heir try to adopt a successor—even introducing a total stranger is thought better than letting the household die out. Traditionally this household (known as the *ie*, a Japanese concept that includes the idea of continuity) has been the most important element of Japanese society, and individuals have been expected to put the household's needs before their own personal desires.

Relationships between households are maintained, where possible, through successive generations, since this helps to maintain the stable nature of community life. Such relationships are based on kinship, affinity, age, residence in the same neighborhood and comparable occupation. They form the basis of cooperation for endeavors beyond the resources of the household alone, such as the performance of religious rites, housebuilding and the celebration of life crises and ancestral memorials. Groups of households in a village take it in turns to look after the local shrine and to arrange the local Shinto festival.

Each village elects a head and a committee to make decisions about day-to-day affairs including the maintenance of village property and the running of the local volunteer fire brigade; this system ensures a certain amount of security and the resolution of internal disputes. The village head also respresents the community to the higher powers of local government.

Most villages would claim to be Buddhist, calling on priests to celebrate funerals and the rituals associated with ancestral memorials, but community festivals usually take place at the Shinto shrine. Shinto and Buddhism are complementary faiths, the former concerned with activities of the living, the latter with those of the dead.

Offerings are made daily in many Japanese homes to departed members of the family whose names are inscribed on tablets kept in a *Butsudan* (a Buddhist household altar). A recently dead member of the household is remembered individually for a while, but eventually merges into the category of "ancestors."

A Shinto fire festival
The Shinto religion has many gods and spirits, and reveres natural phenomena such as mountains and waterfalls.

Japanese schoolchildren used to be taught that the emperor was descended from the Shinto sun goddess, but in 1945 the present emperor publicly rejected this.

Shamanism is not uncommon in rural areas, and decisions about marriage partners or house design, or personal problems such as sickness may be taken to a diviner of either Shinto or Buddhist persuasion.

Urban Japanese

Many Japanese towns that grew up around castles during the feudal period (from the twelfth to nineteenth century) still retain some of their old charm. However, most of urban Japan is now so sprawling that in the southern part of the mainland, and certain other densely populated regions, it is almost impossible to distinguish the end of one city from the beginnings of another. Modern roads and railroads carry a seemingly endless stream of traffic through the jungle of reinforced concrete.

Urban employees frequently see their allegiance to a firm as a lifetime commitment, involving loyalty comparable to that of family members to the household. The company provides general fringe benefits and also takes care of such matters as accommodation, recreation, holidays for its employees and sometimes even the finding of a suitable spouse. Many workers rent accommodation in the "bed towns" (accommodation areas specially built by the Japanese Housing Corporation) where they live with their immediate families. The wife normally stays at home to look after the children.

Each employee fits into a hierarchy based on position and length of service, and each maintains relations of superiority and inferiority with his immediate colleagues. In this way, an individual establishes a long-term relationship with a superior, owing him unerring loyalty in exchange for his superior's special concern for all aspects of his life. Similar principles of loyalty operate in schools, universities, political parties and many other social groups. An important Japanese tradition is that of working in harmony toward a common goal, whether it be the company's productivity or the harvesting of the rice. The resulting conflict between an individual's duties and his personal desires is a theme often depicted in novels, plays and films.

Many Japanese in cities now choose their own marriage partners, but others are still introduced by a third party such as a relative or a company superior, who acts as a go-between. Nuclear families are common in cities since noninheriting males often move to urban areas to seek employment, and company employees may also be transferred away from their home town or village. Elderly parents are sometimes moved to a son's or a daughter's home when they can no longer take care of themselves, and ancestral tablets may be moved if a family home is abandoned.

Neighborly cooperation continues in cities, particularly in traditional communities, but often on a much smaller scale than in the country. While a man's first allegiance is more likely to be to his company or other place of employment, women tend to center their activities on the schools of their children, typically in the parent-teacher association, education

Peoples and languages
The origins of the Japanese language are uncertain, but the pictographic script was adopted from China over 1,300 years ago. Over the centuries many words have been adopted from Chinese and Korean, from Portuguese in the 16th century and more recently from English. Variations of regional dialect are relatively slight, and standard Japanese is used everywhere. Much of the first six years at school are spent mastering the script's 881 characters, a task that is estimated to add two years to the acquisition of literacy, by comparison with European languages. The 20,000 Ainu speak a language entirely unrelated to Japanese.

Unaffiliated languages

☐ Japanese; Ryukyu

▨ Ainu

Featured peoples
Urban and rural Japanese

Additional peoples

Hokkaido, almost exclusively inhabited by Ainu hunter-gatherers until the 19th century, remains the home of a dwindling number of their descendants. Despite some discrimination, they are gradually becoming integrated into wider Japanese society.

Land use
Rice is the major crop and it is still grown on hillsides that were terraced hundreds of years ago. Generally, however, agriculture is less labor intensive than it once was. New crops have been introduced, while meat and dairy products, rarely eaten by the Japanese 40 years ago, now account for 20% of the total output. Fish is still the major source of protein in the diet. Forests covering most of Japan provide timber and wood pulp.

Arable land and orchards
☐ Vegetables, pulses, oilseeds; wheat and barley on uplands; tea, mandarin oranges and mulberry trees (for silk).

Rice fields
☐ Largely on terraced hillsides.

Permanent grassland
☐ Cattle and pigs.

Woods and forests
☐ Used for firewood, charcoal and wood pulp.

Nonagricultural land
☐ Mountain peaks; industrial and urban areas throughout region.

being the wife's responsibility. Many mothers spend their time investigating and pursuing various possibilities for their children's education. Competition for top jobs is high, and children are often under pressure to achieve demanding standards. Although in rural areas and in urban family businesses it is common for women to work, among white-collar workers men are expected to be the breadwinners, and girls generally give up their jobs when they marry. Women, however, retain complete control of the family finances and the running of the home.

City dwellers generally claim not to practice a religion, although most of them celebrate New Year and the midsummer festival Obon as holidays, and may well participate in local Shinto festivals. During the Obon holiday, when ancestral spirits are said to visit their old homes, people who have moved away from their birthplace often travel back to be with their relatives, living and dead. The Japanese express an intense, almost spiritual love of nature and parties to view the full moon or the cherry blossom are still a feature of Japanese life. City dwellers also often turn to Buddhism for funerals and they generally show respect for their ancestral tablets.

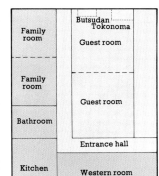

Tradition in a modern society
Japanese country houses retain their traditional character with a corridor dividing the house in two. Sliding doors and *tatami* matting remain, as does the *tokonoma*, an alcove displaying a single *object d'art*. Modern additions of a bathroom, a room furnished in western style, and a second floor are common.

Southeast Asia

Divided between the southeast corner of the Asian continent and the long chain of volcanic islands that make up Indonesia and the Philippines, southeast Asia's 250 million people are predominantly of one ethnic stock. They owe their present linguistic and cultural diversity to small groups of immigrants and to the preaching of religious teachers of diverse faiths. These religious teachers were often hired by ambitious local state builders in need of legitimating symbols with which to overawe their new subjects. Hindu ritual and law spread through southeast Asia—to Dvaravati, Angkor and Champa on the mainland, to Srivijaya and Majapahit on Sumatra and Java. Thereafter, successive waves of immigration brought Buddhism to the emerging plains states of Burma, Thailand and Cambodia, while oceanic commerce infused Atjeh and Malacca, Minangkabau and Jogjakarta with the teachings of Islam.

It would be a mistake, however, to view southeast Asia as simply a recipient of imported cultures. There is an underlying common heritage of material culture—tools, clothes and agricultural methods—and of connected magical practices and beliefs. These are most easily detected in the remoter tribal societies, but also show through the imported technologies, religions and art of the more sophisticated states. The field in which this dualism has been studied most fully is that of law: Hindu, Buddhist and Islamic legal systems have had to come to terms all over the region with persistent customary laws. These laws often have a directly opposite effect to the officially adopted norms, in such matters as family relationships and inheritance. Although harder to analyze, a similar dualism shapes religious practice: Hindu, Buddhist and Muslim teachers have had to tolerate shamanism, agricultural rites, taboos and lucky and unlucky days,

and to give their blessing to amulets and talismans that protect against evil. These ancient beliefs and practices vary little from one southeast Asian people to another.

Discoveries to shape the world

Two vastly significant discoveries were made originally in southeast Asia. The first, made on the mainland, was how to cultivate irrigated rice. The great rivers of southeast Asia rise in eastern Tibet, and when the snows there melt, the torrents flood down to the plains, creating conditions ideal for the growing of rice. The specialization of the rice plants and the development of methods for growing them—control of the annual floods, arduous transplantation of seedlings, ingenious hill terraces and waterwheels—constitute a gift to mankind which, in due course, enabled India and China, as well as southeast Asia itself, to support vast populations.

The other discovery, made in the archipelago in the first century BC, was the twice-yearly reversal of the prevailing monsoon winds in the tropical belt, from northeast during the months when the sun's zenith is in the southern hemisphere, to southwest when the sun is in the northern hemisphere. By this alternation, early Malay mariners learned to sail from southeast Asia to southern India in "winter" and to sail back home in "summer"; the discovery was passed on to the South Arabians, and thence to the Romans, with incalculable benefit to early intercontinental trade. Malay merchants exploited this discovery for the export of southeast Asia's spices, timber and aromatic oils, and their journeys to distant countries resulted in the communication of political and religious ideas. Some Malays settled the island of Madagascar in about AD 500, and their descendants still occupy its interior plateaus.

Colonialism and beyond

The most recent general cultural influence in southeast Asia was the technical revolution wrought during colonial rule, which was established in all countries except Thailand. The coming of the Europeans in search of pepper and camphor was itself a by-product of the centuries-old monsoon trade: the early Portuguese, Dutch, English and French merchants differed little from the Arab and Indian traders. After two hundred years, however, they moved from the traditional trade relationship of equality, to the imposition of their own administration on those with whom they traded. European dominion lasted less than a century, but it forced southeast. Asia into the progressive westernization of its social, political and economic institutions. It also brought World War II in its train, as well as the Japanese occupation (1942–45) and the international Communist movement.

The chief agents of modernization during the colonial period were the Chinese. There are nearly twenty million of them scattered throughout the region today, and in the great city-state of Singapore, with its banks, factories, shipyards and oil refinery, they account for 80 percent of the population. China is in fact the most enduring of all the external influences in southeast Asia; the Chinese emperor received tribute missions from petty rulers in southeast Asia, and arbitrated in their quarrels until they were subjected to the authority of the European colonial powers. Although Chinese spiritual and artistic culture is confined to Vietnam, which alone has learned from China in the manner the other countries have learned from India, the supernatural world of southeast Asia is more like that of China than India.

The Chinese populations are generally assimilated with their hosts on the mainland, but the Malaysian and Indonesian governments still regard them as a potential Trojan horse in the event of some future conflict with Peking—for example over exploitation of the mineral resources under the South China Sea. The quest for unity against this perceived threat was the stimulus for the non-Communist states (with the exception of Burma) to found the Association of Southeast Asian Nations (ASEAN) in 1967. This organization represents the first attempt at political cooperation in the entire history of the region.

Rice terraces in the Philippines

Mainland Southeast Asia 1

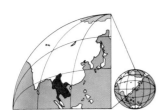

Delicate, multicolored temples adorned with gold leaf dot the landscape of Southeast Asia, raising spires of hope to the sky. Saffron-robed monks walk the streets and country roads, for here Buddhism in its purest form reigns supreme. Sadly war and destruction also prevails, marking those caught in the bloody confrontation between Communism and its enemies.

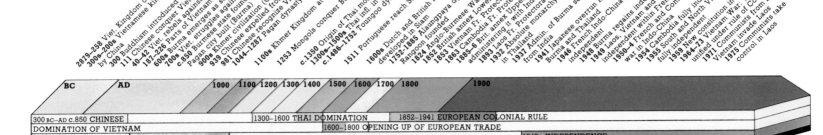

Timeline events:
2879–258 Viet: Kingdom of Van Lang
300s–200s Vietnamese kingdoms ravaged by China
300 Buddhism introduced into Burma
111 Chinese conquer Vietnam
40–42 Viet: rebels against Chinese
187–226 Parts of Vietnam regain indep.
600s Burma emerges as separate entity
700s Viet: struggles against China
c.850 Burmese state founded
900s Khmer civilization (Cambodia)
939 Chinese expelled from Vietnam
981 Chinese recognize Viet. indep.
1044–1287 Pagan dynasty (Burma)
Pagan city built (Burma)
1100s Khmer Kingdom at its height
1253 Mongols conquer Burma
c.1350 Origin of Thai monarchy
1309s–1500s Thai infl. in Indo-China
1486–1752 Toungoo dynasty (Burma)
1511 Portuguese reach Siam (Thailand)
1600s Dutch and British interests developed in Siam
1752–1885 Alaungpaya dynasty (Burma)
1824 Anglo-Burmese Wars begin
1852 British annex Lower (S) Burma
Rangoon founded
1853 Vietnam Fr. Protectorate
1863 Cambodia Fr. Protectorate
1885 Brit. annex Upper (N) Burma, administering it with Ind.
1893 Laos Fr. Protectorate
1932 Absolute monarchy ends in Thailand
1937 Admin. of Burma separated from India
1941 Japanese overrun Indo-China, Burma and Thailand
1946 French Indo-China partially independent
1948 Burma regains independence
1949 Laos, Vietnam and Cambodia independent within French union
1950–4 French and Communists at war in Indo-China
1954 Cambodia fully independent
1955 South and North Vietnam fully independent
1959 New constitution in Thailand
1964–73 Vietnam War: Vietnam unified under rule of Communist N
1971 Communists from South invade Laos
1975 Communists take control in Laos

Era bands:
BC | AD | 1000 1100 1200 1300 1400 1500 1600 1700 1800 1900

300 BC–AD c.850 CHINESE DOMINATION OF VIETNAM
c.850–1200 RISE OF BURMA
1300–1600 THAI DOMINATION
1600–1800 OPENING UP OF EUROPEAN TRADE
1852–1941 EUROPEAN COLONIAL RULE
1948– INDEPENDENCE

Population by Country
Total: 141 million

Thailand 33%
Laos 2.5%
Burma 24%
Kampuchea 3.5%
Vietnam 37%

Population by Religion

Buddhism 56%
Conf./Dao./Budd. 34%
Communist Party 1%
Min. rel. 9%

Rice—food for millions
In central Thailand rice plants are cultivated in nursery beds, and then transplanted to the paddies at the beginning of the monsoon season in May.

The monsoon winds, sweeping across the Indian Ocean, bring to mainland Southeast Asia long rainy seasons that are ideal for rice production, and this region has become known as "the rice basket of the world." The heavy rainfall also causes extensive soil erosion, so that the rivers have a high silt content and build up deltas of fertile alluvium at their mouths. It is here, on the coasts and in the agriculturally rich valleys, that the major civilizations of the past were formed. Permanent-field, irrigated-rice cultivation was practiced, and large kingdoms with complex social organizations were established. In the highlands, however, where wet-rice cultivation was impracticable, dry rice was grown by small groups of shifting cultivators.

China, as well as India, has had considerable cultural influence in this area. Easy sea accessibility brought trade with China and cultural influences from Sri Lanka to the Malayo-Polynesian people of the area, and Indianized states emerged in the Mekong delta (Funan) and the Annam coast (Champa) before the second century AD. Funan's Sanskrit traditions were inherited by the Mon-Khmer, who founded the mighty Khmer Empire during the ninth century in Angkor. At the height of its power in the twelfth century the Khmer Empire controlled the entire Mekong valley up into central Laos, and most of present-day Thailand. Materially dependent on the large-scale cultivation of rice, its remarkably complex irrigation system necessitated a high degree of social organization. The king was looked upon as a *Chakravartin* (Universal Monarch) and his palace conceived as the center of the earth. The snake god of an earlier fertility cult survived in the form of the Indian *Naga*, and became a central motif in the Hindu-Buddhist art and architecture of the area. Another great state that flourished during this period was Pagan, founded on the Irrawaddy by the Burmans in the ninth century; it became a famous center of Buddhist learning and architecture.

In 1253 Kublai Khan's conquest of Yunnan hastened a final wave of Tai speakers into Burma and northern Indo-China. A series of Tai principalities grew up along the Chao Phraya and Upper Mekong valleys, during the thirteenth and fourteenth centuries, out of which the states of Thailand and Laos were later formed. The Tai conquerors, like the Burmans, adopted Theravada Buddhism from their Mon subjects, and this became the dominant faith of the region.

During the British colonization of Burma and the French colonization of Indo-China in the nineteenth century, Chinese immigrants came into Southeast Asia as indentured laborers, small farmers and traders, and they remain the largest single minority in the area today, acting as middlemen between rice producers and centralized authority. In the past century they have come to control much wholesale and retail trade and some industry and banking. Japanese occupation during World War II weakened colonial power, and the Union of Burma was formed after independence in 1948, as a federation of ethnically diverse states. The partial granting of independence to French Indo-China in 1946 resulted in the outbreak of the long, and economically crippling, Indo-China Wars, from which Vietnam, Laos and Kampuchea have emerged with Communist governments.

Southeast Asia remains predominantly rural, with rice the main crop in the fertile lowlands, where people such as the Central Thai continue their long tradition of irrigated agriculture. Some of the more marginal highland regions are still inhabited by shifting cultivators, such as the Hmong, but their way of life is threatened by modern developments.

The Central Thai

The Central Thai, originally of the Chao Phraya river-basin area, now number over twelve million. They have expanded southward into the Malay peninsula, while intermarriage has occurred with Chinese immigrants and Malays. During Thailand's period of absolute monarchy, which lasted until a peaceful military coup in 1932, social ranks were differentiated by entitlement to labor, under a centralized feudal-bureaucratic system known as the *sakdina*. The labor of the peasants was compulsorily mobilized by the king's officials for irrigation projects or warfare, and there also existed two distinct categories of slave— hereditary bondsmen and debt-clients. Although slavery was abolished in 1905, traces of the sakdina system persist, in the vertical patron-client relationships that characterize Thai society.

A typical Thai village is either a "ribbon" settlement alongside a road or canal, or a cluster of houses surrounded by paddies. The Thai house is usually built of teak or bamboo and is raised from the ground by wooden stilts to avoid snakes and flooding. The predominant economic activity is wet-rice cultivation. Transplanting the rice, and harvesting it at the end of

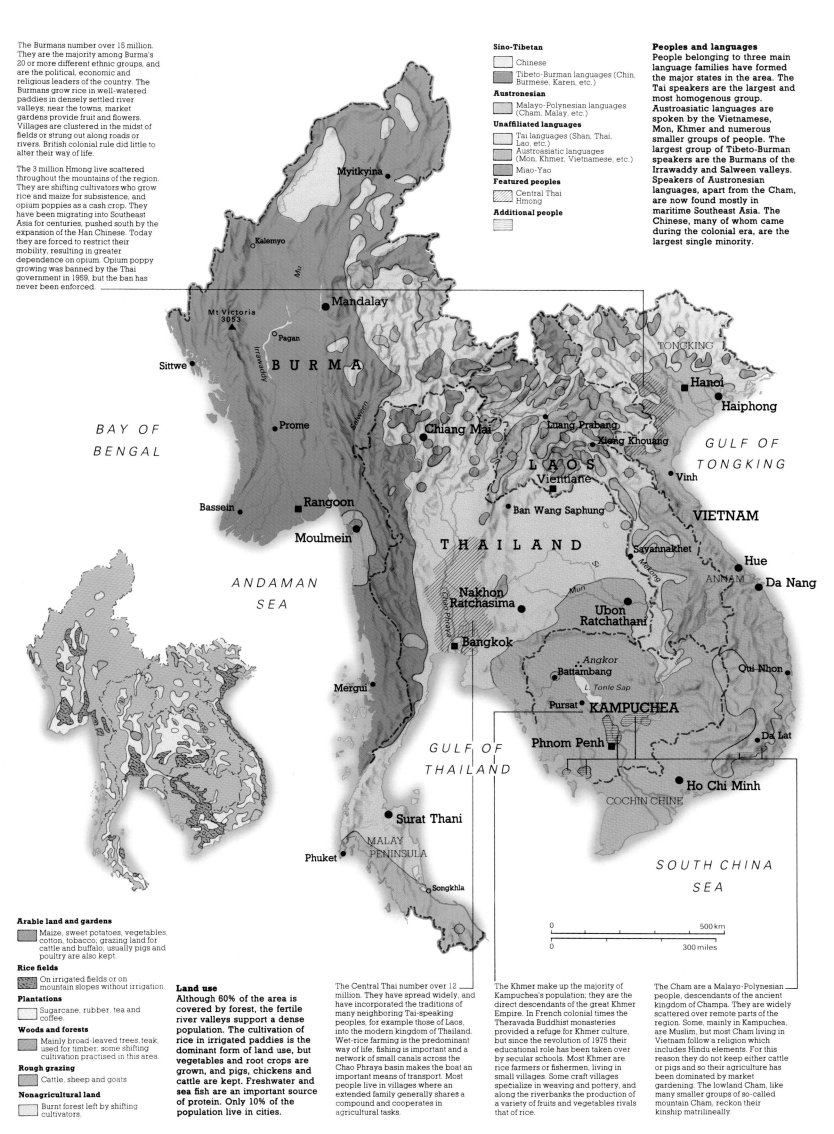

The Burmans number over 15 million. They are the majority among Burma's 20 or more different ethnic groups, and are the political, economic and religious leaders of the country. The Burmans grow rice in well-watered paddies in densely settled river valleys; near the towns, market gardens provide fruit and flowers. Villages are clustered in the midst of fields or strung out along roads or rivers. British colonial rule did little to alter their way of life.

The 3 million Hmong live scattered throughout the mountains of the region. They are shifting cultivators who grow rice and maize for subsistence, and opium poppies as a cash crop. They have been migrating into Southeast Asia for centuries, pushed south by the expansion of the Han Chinese. Today they are forced to restrict their mobility, resulting in greater dependence on opium. Opium poppy growing was banned by the Thai government in 1959, but the ban has never been enforced.

Sino-Tibetan
☐ Chinese
☐ Tibeto-Burman languages (Chin, Burmese, Karen, etc.)
Austronesian
☐ Malayo-Polynesian languages (Cham, Malay, etc.)
Unaffiliated languages
☐ Tai languages (Shan, Thai, Lao, etc.)
☐ Austroasiatic languages (Mon, Khmer, Vietnamese, etc.)
☐ Miao-Yao
Featured peoples
☐ Central Thai
☐ Hmong
Additional people
☐

Peoples and languages
People belonging to three main language families have formed the major states in the area. The Tai speakers are the largest and most homogenous group. Austroasiatic languages are spoken by the Vietnamese, Mon, Khmer and numerous smaller groups of people. The largest group of Tibeto-Burman speakers are the Burmans of the Irrawaddy and Salween valleys. Speakers of Austronesian languages, apart from the Cham, are now found mostly in maritime Southeast Asia. The Chinese, many of whom came during the colonial era, are the largest single minority.

BAY OF BENGAL

ANDAMAN SEA

GULF OF TONGKING

GULF OF THAILAND

SOUTH CHINA SEA

Myitkyina

Kalemyo

Mt Victoria 3053

Pagan

Sittwe

BURMA

Mandalay

Prome

Chiang Mai

Luang Prabang

Xieng Khouang

TONGKING

Hanoi

Haiphong

LAOS

Vientiane

Vinh

VIETNAM

Bassein

Rangoon

Moulmein

Ban Wang Saphung

THAILAND

Savannakhet

Hue

ANNAM

Da Nang

Nakhon Ratchasima

Ubon Ratchathani

Mun

Bangkok

Angkor

Battambang

L. Tonle Sap

Qui Nhon

Mergui

Pursat

KAMPUCHEA

Da Lat

Phnom Penh

COCHIN CHINE

Ho Chi Minh

Surat Thani

MALAY PENINSULA

Phuket

Songkhla

0   500 km
0   300 miles

Arable land and gardens
☐ Maize, sweet potatoes, vegetables, cotton, tobacco; grazing land for cattle and buffalo; usually pigs and poultry are also kept.

Rice fields
☐ On irrigated fields or on mountain slopes without irrigation.

Plantations
☐ Sugarcane, rubber, tea and coffee.

Woods and forests
☐ Mainly broad-leaved trees, teak, used for timber; some shifting cultivation practised in this area.

Rough grazing
☐ Cattle, sheep and goats

Nonagricultural land
☐ Burnt forest left by shifting cultivators.

Land use
Although 60% of the area is covered by forest, the fertile river valleys support a dense population. The cultivation of rice in irrigated paddies is the dominant form of land use, but vegetables and root crops are grown, and pigs, chickens and cattle are kept. Freshwater and sea fish are an important source of protein. Only 10% of the population live in cities.

The Central Thai number over 12 million. They have spread widely, and have incorporated the traditions of many neighboring Tai-speaking peoples, for example those of Laos, into the modern kingdom of Thailand. Wet-rice farming is the predominant way of life, fishing is important and a network of small canals across the Chao Phraya basin makes the boat an important means of transport. Most people live in villages where an extended family generally shares a compound and cooperates in agricultural tasks.

The Khmer make up the majority of Kampuchea's population; they are the direct descendants of the great Khmer Empire. In French colonial times the Theravada Buddhist monasteries provided a refuge for Khmer culture, but since the revolution of 1975 their educational role has been taken over by secular schools. Most Khmer are rice farmers or fishermen, living in small villages. Some craft villages specialize in weaving and pottery, and along the riverbanks the production of a variety of fruits and vegetables rivals that of rice.

The Cham are a Malayo-Polynesian people, descendants of the ancient kingdom of Champa. They are widely scattered over remote parts of the region. Some, mainly in Kampuchea, are Muslim, but most Cham living in Vietnam follow a religion which includes Hindu elements. For this reason they do not keep either cattle or pigs and so their agriculture has been dominated by market gardening. The lowland Cham, like many smaller groups of so-called mountain Cham, reckon their kinship matrilineally.

Mainland Southeast Asia 2

the rains, were traditionally occasions when *awraeng*, a form of reciprocal labor exchange, would take place within the village. Although this still occurs, land-owners now often hire laborers instead.

Fishing is the next most important household economic activity, especially along the coastline and in the inland canals and streams of central Thailand. Many Thai farmers also keep pigs or poultry near the home, and increasingly maize, garlic, peanuts and soybeans are being planted. Some investment in insecticides and fertilizers has occurred, and in certain areas large-scale irrigation and hydroelectric schemes have transformed traditional agriculture.

The shift away from subsistence farming toward cash crops has led to the proliferation of market centers in provincial capitals and rural areas. Women play a conspicuous role in these new markets, since traditionally they have been concerned with business and trading activities. The impact of capital investment, however, has forced many peasants into debt, into tenancy, and finally into complete landlessness.

Theravada Buddhism remains an essential feature of Thai life, and at most major undertakings or life crises, such as marriages, housebuilding or funerals, monks are invited to officiate. Every Thai male is expected to spend at least a brief period as a monk before marriage. The local *wat* (Buddhist monastery) can become a storehouse of presents given by the villagers, and act as a communication center, guiding and structuring Thai social life. Many days are set aside for special visits to the *wat*, and on some the *wat* organizes temple fairs, providing a variety of entertainments for fund-raising purposes. The *wat* also provides a social insurance against old age and poverty, since men may become monks at any time of life.

Older beliefs in spirits have been incorporated into the Buddhist ethos. Thus, during housebuilding, ceremonies are held to appease the subterranean serpents, Nagas, and at sickness, departure on a long journey and other important turning points in an individual's life cycle, a *sukhwan* (soul-calling rite) is held, when threads are attached to the person's wrists to bind his wandering *khwan* (vital essence).

The Hmong

The Hmong (Miao or Meo) of whom there are over three million, are located in the mountainous uplands of northern Thailand, Laos, Vietnam, and southern

A Hmong childhood
On the outskirts of their village in northern Thailand a group of Hmong children play with a wooden cart. Bringing up children is the responsibility of both parents, and the father plays a special role when a new baby is born, looking after the next eldest child and taking it everywhere with him.

Inland fishing
Most fishing takes place in inland waters, fish being caught with dip or scoop nets as well as in traps and baskets as demonstrated by these Malay peasants. Sometimes poles and spears are used, or a particular kind of tree bark is beaten into the water, producing a poison that stuns the fish.

The world in a temple
Buddhist buildings are laid out on the Indian principle—with each section representing an aspect of the material or spiritual world: the base represents Mount Meru, the mythical world mountain, the plinth and the central sections represent body and spirit, or the earth and heavens, and the spire represents the Buddha or Nirvana. Giving gifts of food, money or goods to the temple is important for a Buddhist—in this way he is believed to obtain great merit. Visitors may also bring small pieces of gold leaf, which they apply to the *wat*, thus constantly renewing its gold surface. As gold is the color of immortality, such an offering is considered to aid the renunciation of wordly wealth and the attainment of other-wordly peace.

China. Their preference for high altitudes of 900–1,500 meters (3,000–5,000 feet) is the outcome of a lengthy process of southerly expansion by the Han Chinese, which has forced many marginal communities into inaccessible regions. For several centuries the Hmong have migrated into Indo-China, and, since the late nineteenth century, into Thailand. Hmong history has been characterized by frequent rebellions against centralized authority, often linked with Messianic Christian beliefs.

The Hmong, who are shifting cultivators of dry rice and corn, also cultivate opium poppies as a cash crop. After two to three years cultivation, dry-rice fields should ideally be left fallow for twelve to fifteen years. Opium poppies, on the other hand, may be grown successfully on the same land for ten years or longer, as they will tolerate relatively infertile soil. As fertility is reduced, individual households or whole villages move to new locations, sometimes over two hundred miles away. However, the migration of impoverished lowland farmers into the hills, combined with government restrictions on shifting cultivation, has reduced this mobility. The Hmong are increasingly forced to cultivate secondary forest areas for longer periods, and this does not allow the soil sufficient time to regenerate. As yields drop drastically, rice must be purchased from the lowlands and dependence on opium as a cash crop is therefore increased.

The Hmong are divided into clans modeled on the Chinese surname groups, and are subdivided into lineages based on the household. A household may consist of several families, by the time sons of the householder have acquired wives and children of their own, and it forms the primary unit of production. Ideally each village is inhabited by members of a single clan, but often representatives of two or more clans may live in the same village. Wide-reaching cultural divisions, such as "blue" or "white" Hmong cross-cut the kinship boundaries, and are marked by strong distinctions of language, custom and costume.

Hmong must marry outside their clan. Marriages, including child betrothals, are negotiated between the families of prospective parents, except in rare cases of elopement or marriage by capture. Marriages are celebrated with great pomp and expense, and divorce is rare, since it involves the girl's family returning the brideprice. Child labor is an important feature of Hmong economic organization, and the adoption of children is quite common.

In their social organization and belief system, the Hmong show traces of Chinese influence, but other beliefs, such as those in the spirits of ancestors, remain uniquely Hmong. Elaborate rituals conduct the souls of the dead to their resting places, and shamans are called in to exorcise evil spirits during sickness, a ceremony that often involves animal sacrifice.

A major festival takes place around the new year, once the rice harvest is in. It is celebrated at staggered intervals between December and February, allowing villagers to attend the ceremonies of other villages. Local spirits are invited, large quantities of food and liquor are consumed, sword dances may be performed, buffalo fights staged, and rows of courting couples play catch with colored cloth balls. Items of clothing, forfeited as penalties for dropping the ball, may provide an excuse for further meetings and eventual love matches. Considerable sexual freedom is permitted at this time of year.

During the Indo-China Wars of the mid-twentieth century, many Hmong communities were utterly destroyed by indiscriminate bombing in the "free-fire" zones. Thousands of destitute and homeless Hmong refugees have now been resettled in France, Australia, Canada, French Guiana and the United States, and more in "evacuation camps" in Thailand await transportation. The dispersion of the Hmong poses new problems of cultural adaptation for a people noted for their strong sense of ethnic unity, and it remains to be seen whether their traditional resilience will prove equal to the exigencies of life in exile.

Exotic headdress of the Akha
The Akha are a hill people practicing shifting cultivation. Most of them are found in northern Thailand inhabiting roughly the same region as the Hmong, but small groups also live in the hills of Burma, Laos and southwest China. The women's elaborate headdresses, decorated with silver, are part of their everyday costume. The Akha still practice their traditional spirit worship.

Meaning through movement
Classical Thai dance-drama blends epic and theater with dance and music. Episodes from the great Hindu epic the Ramayana or from traditional Thai and Hindu folk stories are performed. Actors usually remain mute while the dialogue is sung by members of a chorus seated with the orchestra.

Khon, the older, more austere form of masked pantomime, are traditionally performed mainly by men, while in *Lakhon* women also take part. High, pointed headdresses modeled on court costume are worn, and meaning is expressed through the use of *mudras*, or particular positions of the hands and fingers, in relation to bodily postures.

"The embroidery people"
The Hmong sometimes refer to themselves as the "embroidery people," and tribal subdivisions of the "blue," "white" and "flowery" Hmong were traditionally marked by the women's clothing. Appliqué may be combined with embroidery for sashes, turbans or the skullcaps worn by the men. Much of an unmarried girl's time is spent weaving costumes from hemp on a loom worked by a foot pedal; in Thailand some craft work is sold to tourists.

Indonesian Archipelago 1

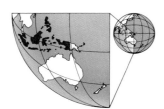

Sailing as far as Africa and India with their cargoes of spices, the early Indonesians brought back the religions of foreign lands. From these alien traditions grew a culture of baffling complexity where violence and beauty go hand in hand, where the eternal oppositions—of good and evil, male and female— rule everyday life, and where simple peasants live by aristocratic ideals.

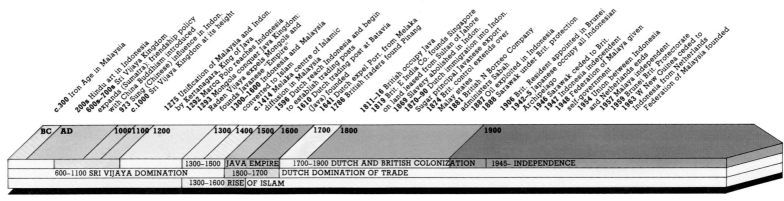

BC / AD	1000 1100 1200	1300 1400 1500 1600	1700 1800	1900			

1300–1500 JAVA EMPIRE   1700–1900 DUTCH AND BRITISH COLONIZATION   1945– INDEPENDENCE

600–1100 SRI VIJAYA DOMINATION   1500–1700 DUTCH DOMINATION OF TRADE

1300–1600 RISE OF ISLAM

Population by Country
Total: 204 million

Indonesia 69%

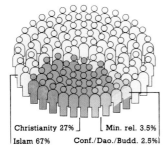

The Philippines 23%   Malaysia 7%
Sing./Bru. 1%

Population by Religion

Christianity 27%   Min. rel. 3.5%
Islam 67%   Conf./Dao./Budd. 2.5%

Land use
In the east, and upland areas of the west, shifting cultivation is the main land use. The lowlands and valleys, particularly on Java, Bali and Sumatra are used for irrigated rice cultivation by peasant farmers who also keep animals and grow vegetables. Plantations of export crops on Kalimantan, Sulawesi and Sumatra date from colonial times.

Arable land

Maize and cassava, potatoes, other vegetables, groundnuts, soya beans and tobacco.

Rice fields

Irrigated and dry rice are both grown.

Plantations

Rubber, coconuts, oil palms, sugarcane, tea, coffee and a variety of spices.

Woods and forests

Coniferous and broad-leaved trees, especially teak and mahogany, used for timber, firewood, charcoal, resins, gums, oils, fibres and medicines; some shifting cultivation practised in this area.

Rough grazing land

Cattle and goats in Indonesia; buffalo elsewhere; pigs and poultry also important.

Nonagricultural land

Industrial and urban areas.

The Indonesian people call their country *tanah air*, meaning literally "land and water." This archipelago, with its bewildering variety of peoples, comprises over 13,500 islands and spans more than 4,800 kilometers (3,000 miles). For over 2,000 years the role of the Indonesians in overseas trade has opened the islands to foreign cultural influences, and powerful Hindu, Buddhist and Islamic empires have left their mark upon Indonesian society.

The whole region is inhabited by Austronesian-speaking peoples, known popularly from their geographical spread as Malayo-Polynesians. They were once thought to have been pushed out of southern China by a population explosion, but it is doubtful if any land-based people could so easily have become expert sailors and navigators. Whatever their origin, they colonized a broad belt of tropical islands where they live by fishing and agriculture. Throughout the region the rich volcanic soils and favorable climate allowed the accumulation of substantial surplus resources, which permitted the development of a stratified society and the emergence of a social elite.

Recent archaeological discoveries have challenged the orthodox view that agriculture and civilization were imported into Southeast Asia from India and China, as the names Indo-China and Indonesia suggest. It is probably more accurate to think of indigenous technology and cultural institutions being added to and exchanged by Indonesian traders who ventured as far as India and Africa at least 2,000 years ago. By the seventh century AD Hindu-Buddhist empires flourished and laid claim to large parts of the archipelago. Successive civilizations, boasting immense monasteries and universities, rose and fell and with the decline of the trade-based empire of Srivijaya came the emergence of a different kind of state, depending on rice cultivation. This required the centralized organization of irrigation, and the stress was consequently on cohesion—the king was seen as the center of the kingdom, and ultimately the pivot of the universe.

From the thirteenth century onward, Islam spread from the Middle East along the trade routes, and by the end of the sixteenth century the Hindu courts had fled to Bali in the face of militant Muslim encroachment. At the same time, the Dutch began fighting for control of the Moluccan spice islands and trade routes. The base for Dutch colonization of the archipelago was Java and as internal peace was established, the island's population grew dramatically.

Indonesian societies are very varied but three principal types can be recognized—Hinduized societies based on rice cultivation, mercantile Islamic coastal peoples, and tribal groups on the remoter mountains and islands. Apart from these three groups, there are also the Chinese who were encouraged by the Dutch to settle in Java as their agents and middlemen.

Hindu influence survives principally in Bali and in the center of Java. The dominant people of Java are the Javanese and the centers of their culture are the aristocratic courts, which nestle among the volcanoes forming the island's backbone. The millions of peasant farmers who eke out a living from overcrowded rice terraces define themselves and their culture in terms of aristocratic ideals of behavior and language.

Islam is dominant among the coastal and mercantile societies, which are found mostly on the shores of Sulawesi, Kalimantan and across much of Sumatra.

The Minangkabau are Muslim traders and farmers who have migrated widely in the archipelago. In contrast to the peasants of Bali and Java, they have been pioneer farmers of commercial cash crops since the early days of Dutch plantation development. Their complex system of land rights is traced through women.

The Javanese inhabit what is politically and economically the most important island in the archipelago, and although they are predominantly Muslim, there is a group in the interior who follow a mixed Buddhist/Hindu religion. Peasants, led by the village headman, work on the agricultural estates of noble landholders.

They vary from the Bugis of southern Sulawesi, who are the great sailors of the archipelago, to the Malays, who are both sailors and agriculturists, to the more settled Sumatran peoples like the Minangkabau, who have been brought extensively into the wider market system by the Dutch development of plantations.

In contrast to the overpopulation of Java and Bali, the vast expanse of Kalimantan is sparsely settled by small groups of Dayak, except around the coastal areas. Dayak peoples are generally egalitarian, and the largest social unit is usually the longhouse, essentially a village built on stilts as a defense against enemies and floods. The staple crop is hill rice, grown in forest clearings prepared by slashing and burning the trees.

Among the Dayak and many other tribal peoples in central and eastern Indonesia, as well as in the Philippines, head hunting was widespread and warfare endemic, although sporadic. Many reasons have been offered for head hunting but none is really adequate, and it is probably wrong to look for a single explanation. Although booty was taken, this was secondary to the value placed on heads.

The smaller islands of eastern Indonesia present curious contrasts, since the inhabitants practice simple settled or shifting agriculture, but possess richly complex cosmologies. Not just nature, but everything, from the house and village to society as a whole, is organized by rigorous principles of symbolic opposition into complementary categories such as good:bad; male:female; superior:inferior and so on.

The major cultural division in Indonesia is that between Hindu and Muslim, but there is a very rich indigenous tradition and culture which cuts across many of the ostensible divisions, so that in its diversity the Indonesian archipelago achieves a curious unity. The many contrasts as well as the common themes are illustrated by the Hindu peasants of Bali and the Muslim Minangkabau of Sumatra.

The Balinese
Bali, together with Java, dominates the rest of Indonesia politically, although the two islands make up only 5 percent of the land area. Bali was among the last islands to be subjugated by the Dutch, for it has no natural resources and is protected by the dangerous

The Kalinga's ability to preserve their traditional life style is partly due to their character as fierce and dangerous warriors. Numbering 40,000, their ideas about justice—meaning the right of each village to assert its interests by the use of force—remain unchanged, despite economic advances.

Kalinga recovery from illness
Kinsmen and friends celebrate the recovery of one of their number with a feast supplied by all those present; if they are rich it may include meat.

The vast expanse of central Kalimantan is sparsely settled by groups of Dayak, egalitarian people with little organized leadership. Like the mountain people of Sulawesi and the Philippines, the Dayak are traditionally head-hunters. Many now grow cash crops or work on plantations or for logging companies.

Peoples and languages
Most languages belong to the Austronesian family, Bhasa Indonesian and Malay being the most widely used, with 80 million speakers. The former is the *lingua franca* of the region. The 2 languages differ from each other only in the spelling systems imposed: by the Dutch in Indonesia and the British in Malaysia. Continued reforms and technical vocabularies are encouraging a divergence into separate languages.

Austronesian
- West Indonesian languages (Malay and Bahasa Indonesian, Javanese, Dayak, Balinese), Tagalog, Iloko, Buginese, etc

Sino-Tibetan
- Chinese

Unaffiliated languages
- Austroasiatic languages (Jakun, Semang, Senoi)

Featured people
- Balinese
- Minangkabau

Additional people

The Balinese are an ancient, literate, Hindu people, whose aristocracy and peasantry are closely linked. Their economy is based on the intensive cultivation of rice on terraces cut into the volcanic rock of mountain slopes.

The Bugis are the most mobile of the Muslim seafaring peoples. They became notorious as pirates after Europeans disrupted their traditional trading system in the colonial period. Today they are interisland traders and rice farmers. Many women are skilled silk weavers, often earning most of the family's cash income.

Mt Pulog 2929

LUZON

Manila

PHILLIPINES

SOUTH CHINA SEA

SULU SEA

MINDANÃO
Davao

SIA
BRUNEI

Gunung Kinabalu 4101

SABAH

CELEBES SEA

Manado

SARAWAK

BORNEO

KALIMANTAN

MOLUCCAS ISLANDS

SULAWESI (CELEBES)

IRIAN JAYA
Djaja Peak 5030
NEW GUINEA

Banjarmasin

NESIA

BANDA SEA

JAVA SEA

Ujung Pandang (Makasa)

ARAFURA SEA

MATRA Surabaja

FLORES SEA

BALI

TIMOR

Kupang

TIMOR SEA

0   600 km
0   400 miles

Indonesian Archipelago 2

seas that surround it and the equally violent people who inhabit it. This has often puzzled Europeans who have confused the Balinese concern for aesthetics and religion with their own utopian ideals. Toward the north of Bali lies a chain of volcanoes and crater lakes, from which radiate rivers that have cut deep gorges into the soft volcanic rock. The kingdoms on the long alluvial plain to the south therefore have unusual shapes, like strips stretching from the coast far into the mountains. This laid the pattern for interminable local wars since rival aristocratic families would send out junior branches to try to control outlying regions of the kingdoms, especially in the interior where water supplies were vulnerable. As a result, minor princes are to be found in many villages, so that court and peasant culture are closely linked, giving Balinese culture a peculiar vitality.

Bali is heavily overpopulated and the economy is based upon the peasant cultivation of irrigated rice on terraces. Although most families also keep cattle, pigs or chickens, and cultivate some vegetables, it is in intensive farming of rice that the Balinese excel, whether in ingenuity in building aqueducts and tunnels for water or in methods of transplanting and tillering to increase yield. Before colonization, the power of the princes to command the labor of the peasantry permitted them to build large estates. With political changes, however, such sources of income have been cut off, while the princes' heavy ritual obligations to the peasantry remain. Thus differences in wealth are declining sharply. Being Hindu, the Balinese divide the population into castes, and the higher the caste, the more scrupulous the observation of moral and religious rules. The basis of caste membership is birth within a ranked kin group. While the principle of hierarchy is agreed, exact placing of any group may be disputed. The main criteria are myths of origin, traditional status privileges (especially the number of tiers allowed on one's funeral bier), and ritual purity. The latter is expressed in terms of accepting cooked food and, most critically, of sexual relations and marriage with others. A Balinese never takes certain types of food from those who are lower, and men may not take women who are higher, traditionally on pain of death. It is what is taken into the body—food or semen—which is polluting, and women are therefore allowed to rise through the system.

Politics, to the Balinese, is one of life's main entertainments. While wars were bitter and bloody, the dramatic presentation of each side played a major part in public evaluation of the outcome. Similarly, the great royal rituals of marriage and cremation were central to the maintenance of authority over the peasantry. In stark contrast to ideals of caste hierarchy, villages are

Peoples of the sea
The homeland of the Bugis is in the southern part of Sulawesi but they travel throughout Indonesia and Malaysia in their large ocean-going sailing vessels. Here they often form new settlements and an extended family may well have its members thousands of miles apart. Once pirates, who were often hired by the Balinese for slave raids, they now carry cargoes of local produce or imported goods. There are few sights as magnificent as thousands of Buginese ships tacking between large modern vessels as they make their way into Singapore.

Cremation of a Brahman
The Balinese celebrate 4 great cycles of Hindu rites: the first ensures safe birth, the second placates evil spirits, the third worships the gods and the fourth purifies the dead. Death creates the problem of separating the soul from the corpse; this is achieved by washing the body in holy water followed by cremation and disposal of the ashes in a river or the sea. Princes and priests are carried on magnificent biers pulled by animals that reflect the hierarchy—white bulls are used for priests and the unmarried, black bulls for the less pure.

Houses of the Minangkabau
Elaborately carved houses such as these are widely found among the Minangkabau of Sumatra. Much prestige hinges on the size of the building and on the magnificence of the carving and roofs. The adaptation of corrugated iron sheeting to traditional roof design reflects the ingenuity of the Minangkabau.

run by councils of notional equals, each family having equal representation regardless of wealth.

A central theme of Balinese society, as in other Indonesian cultures, is the ambiguity and negotiability of most legal and cultural rules. The key lies in the general Indonesian concept of *adat*, a term that means "order" or "the way of the world." Each group, human, animal and divine, has its place in this order—it is the *adat* of pigs to be eaten by men and the *adat* of demons to injure men. *Adat* is not fixed but changes according to circumstance, and much thought is given to deciding what is fitting at any moment.

Adat is important in understanding religion in Bali, which is famous for its elaborateness and intensity. In theory the Balinese are Hindu and deities with Indian names are worshiped in innumerable of temples throughout the island, but each social group also has its own temple and god. The link between local temple gods and their Hindu counterparts is often unclear, as are the reasons for invoking them, and the Balinese expend substantial time and effort on temple ceremonies the ends of which are largely obscure. The key is the notion of *adat*, for temple ceremonies are meeting points between gods and men where changes in the rules governing their lives can be negotiated through the process of spirit possession. As the Balinese see it, the duty of the gods is to uphold ideals, but also to make these intelligible and appropriate to the changing circumstances of the world.

The Minangkabau of western and central Sumatra

The Minangkabau are a Muslim people whose homeland lies in the mountain areas of Sumatra. They are farmers of cash crops but have also been extensively

Heads for status
The tattoos on this Kalinga's chest and shoulders indicate his status as a successful head-hunter. For the Kalinga and many other peoples in this region, the taking of heads was once a necessary qualification for any serious political position within the community.

Height and purity
Priests sit facing Gunung Agung, Bali's highest peak and identified by the Balinese as the sacred mountain Meru. Height is an important index of purity. Shrines for the gods tower above the priests, who themselves sit on pedestals far above the congregation.

engaged in trade, and have migrated widely throughout the archipelago and into Malaysia. One reason for this wanderlust may be found in local economic and social conditions. Much of the Dutch plantation development was based in Sumatra, and from the nineteenth century onward the Minangkabau were forced into a wider economy. The Minangkabau are notable because clan membership and rights in land are traced through women, while men marry out into alien families, where they have no authority beyond their own household. Formally, women are under the authority of their brothers, but as these may well be far away, women tend to have wide influence and power. In such a system the pressures on men to escape and seek their fortunes elsewhere are great.

Traditionally, the villages of the Minangkabau were largely autonomous, each with its own *adat*—here understood as the system of laws and customs on which order at any moment was based. Each village was composed of intermarrying groups based on notional kin ties, and the *adat* was that of whichever group first settled there and cleared the forest. Two intermarrying groups are represented in each village, known as the Koto-Piliang and the Bodi-Caniago. The former is associated with hierarchical rules of status and punitive law, and the latter with a more egalitarian and restitutive form of justice. Local political issues are decided by a council of clan representatives drawn from each group, and their decisions are directed by whichever style of law and custom holds in the village. Nowadays the formal administration consists of a headman, who is responsible to his superiors in the government bureaucracy, but despite this politics still tend to follow traditional lines.

Although the two out-marrying kin groups are bound together by their mutual need for marriage partners, there is an intense rivalry between them. The two halves are further identified with all the major conceptual divisions of the Minangkabau world: land versus sea, hierarchy versus equality and so on. In the past, members of the two sides annually fought symbolic battles in the bush. The system of conceptual oppositions remains important and is very typical of Indonesian societies.

The conversion of the Minangkabau to Islam has raised various difficulties both in law and ritual. Islam is biased toward the transmission of property rights through males, whereas *adat* demands that it be through females. Similarly the symbolic system through which the Minangkabau order their lives is entirely alien to Islam. In general the Minangkabau resolve the potential conflict by stressing *adat*, but strict Muslims among them feel that the religious rules should have primacy.

Animals, gods and men
In Bali's Hindu tradition the terrifying Indian goddess Kali is unknown, but Durga, who in India is benevolent, has acquired her dreaded characteristics. The witchlike figure of Rangda, portrayed here by a giant puppet, is seen as a manifestation of Durga. The puppet's mask is carved by a master craftsman, who must imbue it with mystical power by sitting up throughout the night in a cemetery. The monkeys are figures of fun in the dance, which is being performed here for tourists. Monkeys are of great importance on Bali for they represent a borderline between animals and humans; the Balinese emphasize the differences that separate men from animals, and have a horror of appearing animallike— babies are prevented from crawling on all fours, and in later life the teeth are filed down so that they do not resemble animal fangs. Demons and gods, however, are depicted as hairy, long-fanged beasts. In the case of the gods this does not imply animallike qualities, but is simply a way of representing their nature.

Oceania

The Pacific is the world's greatest ocean—some 100 million square kilometers (63 million square miles) of open water, with most of its innumerable volcanic and coral islands lying in a vast equatorial belt. The name "Oceania" is a reminder that these islands were populated by sailors and navigators, and the remotest—Easter Island—was peopled over 1,000 years before Magellan sailed across the Pacific in 1519–21.

Australia and New Guinea were the first to be settled, with human populations established 30,000 to 40,000 years ago. Although these countries were linked at various times by a land bridge, there was always a sea gulf separating them from the Asian mainland which the first people must somehow have crossed. New Guinea and Australia were thus an entry point into the Pacific, but beyond exploration of the islands that now make up Melanesia, the early population remained confined to this region. Indeed, there were vast areas of land for these

hunter-gatherers to exploit, and for those who moved into the interior of Australia, or the highlands of New Guinea, the sea which had brought them to their new lands eventually become remote and unknown.

The Australian Aborigines remained as hunter-gatherers until recent times, but the peoples of New Guinea were probably among the first in the world to adopt agriculture, for there is archaeological evidence strongly suggesting crop cultivation as long as 9,000 years ago. The major food crops were tubers—taro and yam—along with coconut, banana and sugarcane. All these plants were domesticated in southeast Asia or in New Guinea itself. Thus, the indigenous peoples of Australia and Melanesia made use of their natural resources in very different ways, but in both cases people lived in small-scale communities in which political power was achieved through personal skill in production, organization or warfare.

Polynesia and Micronesia
On 4 June 1976, a small canoe sailed into Papeete harbor, Tahiti. It was a double canoe, built in traditional Polynesian style, carrying a crew of seventeen. Tahitians were crowding the waterfront and standing in the surf—it was the largest crowd in the island's history, some 15,000 people. The canoe they were welcoming had sailed from Hawaii, over 4,000 kilometers (2,500 miles) away, navigated only by star positions and wave patterns. What the Tahitian crowd were welcoming was an achievement which spoke of an essential shared identity between Pacific islanders. For the people of Polynesia and Micronesia the sea has always been a link as much as a barrier, and it is as "islanders" that many of them think of themselves.

The original expansion of Asian peoples into the Pacific was a huge enterprise in terms of the distances traveled and the risks taken. It began about 5,000 years ago—much later than the settlement of New Guinea and Australia—and was carried out in canoes, some large enough to carry a hundred passengers. The movement eastward was gradual and the Marquesas Islands were not settled until about 2,000 years ago or less, while New Zealand remained uninhabited until 1,000 years ago. Its settlers, the ancestors of the Maori, came from eastern Polynesia and quickly expanded into its huge, empty, fertile lands. Initially the Maoris lived mainly by gathering, and by hunting New Zealand's curious flightless birds, but they later became fulltime agriculturists.

Agriculture was practiced throughout the islands of the Pacific, and the crops grown were essentially the same as those of New Guinea. The soils of the volcanic islands are extremely fertile, producing good harvests, while the sea provided fish to supplement the diet. In this bountiful natural environment, the Polynesians and Micronesians developed elaborate stratified societies, where high birth and rank were important political factors.

Paradise lost
For many of the people of Oceania, the European colonial era resulted in the destruction of their world. The great sailing ships of the eighteenth and nineteenth centuries brought settlers who seized their lands, disrupted their economies, and spread diseases to which the indigenous people had no resistance. The Australian Aborigines suffered the greatest losses both in numbers and territory. They were rapidly dispossessed of the fertile coastal areas of Australia, and became associated in the popular mind with the desert existence in the interior, where some groups managed to survive. Welfare policies have since drawn many to the poverty-stricken fringes of urban life, while mineral discoveries have given new value to their home territories and made the question of Aboriginal land rights a crucial issue.

European settlement in Australia and New Zealand has produced a dominant white population which greatly outnumbers the indigenous people, but the same is not true of Polynesia and Micronesia. Here every ethnic group is, in a sense, a minority—Indians are found in Fiji, Vietnamese and Indonesians in New Caledonia, Americans in Hawaii, Japanese throughout Micronesia and Chinese on most islands of the Pacific. However, the economic exploitation of Polynesia that characterized the colonial era has continued, and the twentieth century has seen new dislocations. In Micronesia, for example, whole populations have had to move, because large phosphate deposits have been discovered and their islands literally dug away. Certain islands in French Polynesia have been used for testing nuclear weapons, resulting in the disruption of the inhabitants' way of life, and pollution of their environment with radioactive wastes. Of all the indigenous people of the area, those who have suffered least outside interference are the half-million highlanders of Papua New Guinea, who were only "discovered" in the 1930s. Much of their traditional way of life has survived up to now, but contact with the modern world is resulting in rapid change.

The traditional canoes of Polynesia

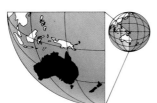

For the Aborigines, sacred features of the landscape, and belief in the Eternal Dreaming – a parallel, mystical life – were the focus of society. For the Maori it was the tribal house, *symbolizing the body of a revered ancestor. But the European settlers swept aside these ancient ways of life, as they exploited the fertile soil, the gold and other riches of their new lands.*

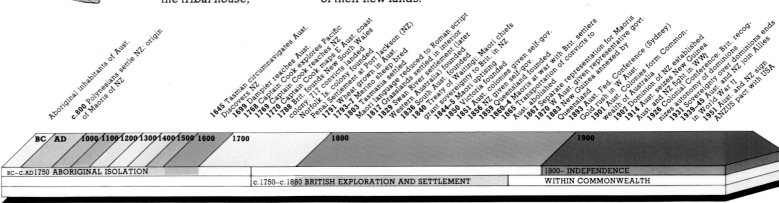

Timeline labels:
Aboriginal inhabitants of Aust. origin
c.800 Polynesians settle NZ; origin of Maoris of NZ
1645 Tasman circumnavigates Aust.
Discovers NZ
1699 Dampier reaches Aust.
1768 Captain Cook explores Pacific
1769 Captain Cook reaches NZ
1770 Captain Cook maps E. Aust. coast
1788 Brit. founds New South Wales colony; 717 convicts landed
Penal Settlement at Port Jackson (NZ)
Norfolk Is. colony founded
1791 Wheat grown in Aust.
1793-7 Merino sheep bred
1803 Tasmania settled
Maori language reduced to Roman script
1817 Grasslands settled in interior
1829 Swan River settlement (later Western Australia) founded
1836 South Aust. founded
1840 Treaty of Waitangi: Maori chiefs grant sovereignty to Brit. in NZ
1844-5 Maori uprising
1850 Victoria founded
1851 Aust. colonies given self-gov.
1856 NZ given self-gov.
1859 Queensland founded
1860-4 Maoris at war with Brit. settlers
1865 Transportation of convicts to Aust. abolished
1867 Separate representation for Maoris
1870 W. Aust. given representative govt.
1883 New Guinea annexed by Queensland
Gold rush in W. Aust.
1901 Aust. colonies form Commonwealth of Australia (Sydney)
1907 Dominion of NZ established
1914 Aust. seizes New Guinea
Aust. and NZ fight in WWI
1926 Colonial Conference: Brit. recognizes autonomy of dominions
1931 Sovereignty over dominions ends
1939-45 Aust. and NZ fight in World War II
1951 Aust. and NZ sign ANZUS pact with USA

BC AD 1000 1100 1200 1300 1400 1500 1600 1700 1800 1900

BC–c.AD 1750 ABORIGINAL ISOLATION
c.1750–c.1880 BRITISH EXPLORATION AND SETTLEMENT
1900– INDEPENDENCE WITHIN COMMONWEALTH

Population by Country
Total: 18 million

Australia 82% — New Zealand 18%

Population by Religion

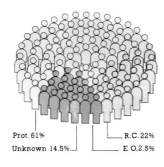

Prot. 61% — R.C. 22%
Unknown 14.5% — E.O. 2.5%

Indo-European
☐ Germanic language (English)

Austronesian
☐ Polynesian language (Maori)

Unaffiliated languages
☐ Australian languages (Aranda, Murngin, etc.)

Featured peoples
Maori
Australian Aborigines

Peoples and languages
Traditionally oriented Australian Aborigines are today found mostly in the Arnhem Land area of the Northern Territory, in the Kimberleys, and in the central regions. In the last, dialects of the Western Desert language are spoken. In Arnhem Land the dominant languages are, in the western sector, Gunwinggu and in the northeastern sector, dialects of Malag or Yolngu. In the Kimberleys, Walmadjeri is fast becoming a main *lingua franca*. All are distinctive languages, and it is uncertain that they belong to a single group. Most of the Maoris, about half of whom still speak their own language as well as English, live on North Island. They are a largely urbanized population.

Australia is a land of vast open spaces, with only 6 percent of its territory above 600 meters (2,000 feet). One third of the country is extremely arid with an average rainfall of less than 25 centimeters (10 inches), and another third is semidesert, with about twice this amount of rain. The sparse rainfall is also irregular and some areas may go for years without rain. New Zealand presents a striking contrast, with its relatively well-watered, mountainous islands and its temperate climate. These marked differences in climate affected the indigenous people of the region and are still influential today, so that Australia and New Zealand are, in many respects, different countries.

Australia was discovered and settled by man at a much earlier date than New Zealand and by people of a different racial stock. The first Australians came from the northwest about 40,000 years ago, when the sea level was much lower than it is today, and the sea journey, probably made on rafts, much shorter. New Zealand, on the other hand, was settled by Polynesians who came from islands in the Pacific Ocean over 1,000 years ago. The Maoris are generally more heavily built than the Aborigines, with lighter skin and straighter hair. Although their arrival in New Zealand was relatively recent, by the time European colonists reached the country they had settled throughout both islands, except

Arnhem Land, an area of bush, woodland, jungle and swamps, is inhabited by Aborigines who have preserved much of their traditional way of life. Boys are circumcised in a semi-public ceremony at about 7 years of age, after which they share a common camping place.

ARAFURA SEA
Torres Strait
TIMOR SEA
Darwin
ARNHEM LAND
CORAL SEA
Gulf of Carpentaria
INDIAN OCEAN
Mornington Island
Great Barrier Reef
NORTHERN TERRITORY
QUEENSLAND
GREAT SANDY DESERT
MACDONNELL RANGE
Fortescue
Alice Springs
SIMPSON DESERT
GREAT DIVIDING RANGE
Ashburton
GIBSON DESERT
AUSTRALIA
L. Eyre
WESTERN AUSTRALIA
Brisbane
GREAT VICTORIAN DESERT
SOUTH AUSTRALIA
L. Torrens
Darling
Kalgoorlie
L. Gairdner
Newcastle
NULLARBOR PLAIN
NEW SOUTH WALES
Murrumbidgee
Sydney
Perth
Swan
Great Australian Bight
Adelaide
Canberra
VICTORIA
Melbourne
TASMAN SEA
TASMANIA
Hobart

Aborigines who previously lived in the Gibson Desert belonged to the Western Desert culture. They were semi-nomadic, and life was relatively harsh, but some food was almost always available even during bad periods. Stone tools were still used by these Aborigines until recently.

Some Aranda of central Australia are still employed on pastoral stations, as were Aborigines in other Northern Territory and Kimberley areas. Much of their old way of life and traditional culture has changed radically, and most have been converted to Christianity.

The Lardil Aborigines live on Mornington Island which is rich in food resources, and they still rely largely on traditional methods of hunting and gathering. They gather turtles' eggs, roots, yams and berries, and hunt wallabies, turtles, geese, lizards and dugongs (aquatic mammals).

0 600 km
0 400 miles

Sale of Merino sheep
Australia is the world's most important producer of wool, exporting 95% of the wool she produces. Most sheep are Merinos, bred from a Spanish flock imported in the 19th century. These sheep are tolerant of very dry conditions, and can even survive in regions with only 38 cm (15 in) of rain a year. Small farms in these areas can be ruined by a flood or bush-fire, and most farms cover very large areas to minimize the effect of local disasters.

in the least accessible uplands of North Island. The Maoris initially lived by hunting and gathering, but later adopted agriculture, growing taro and sweet potato as staples. The Aborigines, however, were seminomadic hunter-gatherers; in the arid regions this was the only viable economy, but even in the more favorable parts of Australia they did not practice any form of agriculture, and the dog, which they brought with them from their Asian homeland, was their only domesticated animal.

The earliest European contact with this region was made by Portuguese ships in the fifteenth century. Cook extensively charted the coastlines in 1769, and settlement by Europeans began in the late eighteenth

century, when the British Empire underwent a rapid expansion. The use of Australia as a penal colony from 1788 until the midnineteenth century added thousands of convicts to those who voluntarily came to settle.

In New Zealand, settlement by Europeans, mainly traders supplying timber, flax and foodstuffs to Australia and servicing the whaling ships of the southern fisheries, took place from about 1800 onward. Protestant missionaries of the Church Missionary Society were well established by 1815, and the Maori language was rendered into Roman script by British scholars as early as 1820. By 1840, many Maoris were familiar with Maori translations of the Bible and were literate in their own language. British rule was formalized by the Treaty of Waitangi (1840), which recognized the status of Maori chiefs in exchange for cession to Britain. After 1840 a period of sporadic warfare between the Maori and the settlers, mainly over land, but also over sovereignty, occurred. By its conclusion virtually no part of Maori life was untouched by European culture. Many Maoris were bilingual, most chiefs were literate (they had corresponded extensively with the colonial government) and Christianization was widespread. Traditional Maori social organization was profoundly affected by the end of intertribal warfare, the defeats in the land wars with the settler governments, and by the economic and cultural changes that had occurred.

Settlers in both countries introduced livestock, mainly sheep and cattle. Intensive sheep farming became the predominant activity throughout New Zealand, and remains a major part of the economy. In Australia, cattle and sheep are raised on huge farms or "stations" of 40,000 hectares (100,000 acres) or more, the only successful method in such arid conditions. Because so much of New Zealand is suitable for agriculture, the traditional Maori way of life disappeared very rapidly, but the harshness of much of Australia kept the European settlers out and left some Aboriginal groups to pursue their hunter-gatherer economy well into the twentieth century. It was the Aborigines of the southern regions who fared the worst, as they were excluded from their own fertile lands and obliged to live on the outskirts of European settlements. Many died as a result of maltreatment, shooting or introduced diseases. Their traditional culture was rapidly altered, but many retained their Aboriginal identity.

Wool was a vital part of Australia's initial prosperity, but it was the discovery of gold that helped to establish Australia's reputation as a land of opportunity, drawing waves of immigrants from Britain and other parts of Europe. The gold boom lasted from 1851 until about 1910, and in addition to Europeans, thousands of Chinese came into Australia in search of gold. The mining of gold has now declined, but since the end of the nineteenth century Australian wealth has been derived mainly from its extensive resources of other minerals. Uranium, bauxite, nickel and tungsten are among the most important elements mined today.

Since 1945, a new pattern of life has emerged in both countries. Although fundamentally agrarian in economy, both Australia and New Zealand have become intensively urbanized societies and each has, or is developing, an industrial base. As a result of this, Maoris in New Zealand have moved rapidly into urban areas, particularly Auckland, while the search for mineral wealth has disrupted Aboriginal life on those lands which had previously been free from the encroachment of large numbers of Europeans.

Australian Aborigines
Excluding the Torres Strait Islanders, the Australian Aborigines number about 125,000, although only about 46,000 of these are of full Aboriginal descent. Aborigines once occupied the entire continent, including Tasmania; at that time they numbered at least 300,000 and were mostly concentrated around the coasts and permanent waters. They could be divided into 500 or so "tribes" according to differences of language, territory and shared social identity. Members of neighboring groups interacted in trade, exchange and religious affairs, but there was no direct communication across the continent and no overall name existed which covered them all.

Along the northern coasts Aborigines became used to Indonesian visitors long before the first European settlers arrived in 1788, but the European invasion was

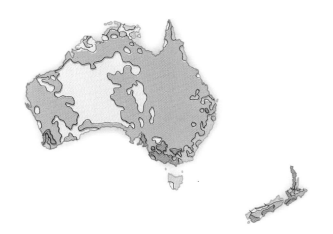

Arable land, gardens and permanent grassland
Mainly wheat; also oats, barley, fodder crops, potatoes, other vegetables; grazing for sheep, dairy and beef cattle.

Orchards and plantations
Sugar cane, oranges, grapes, apples, pears, apricots, peaches, plums, bananas and pineapples.

Woods and forests
Coniferous and broadleaved trees, especially eucalyptus, used for timber and paper; includes some rough grazing land.

Rough grazing land
Limited grazing, mainly for sheep and beef cattle in Australia, better grazing in New Zealand; includes some arable land.

Non-agricultural land
Desert, salt lakes, Aboriginal reserves, mountain peaks, industrial and urban areas.

Land use
Pastoralism is the dominant land use. In most of New Zealand sheep and cattle are farmed intensively, and the export of agricultural products forms the basis of New Zealand's economy. In Australia there is extensive grazing for sheep in the temperate south and for cattle in the subtropical north. In the more productive areas, pastures may be broken up every few years and fodder or cash crops grown before regrassing. Only in the south of New Zealand and in the eastern, southern and southwestern coasts of Australia do arable farming and fruit growing predominate.

NORTH ISLAND

Auckland

Waikato

NEW ZEALAND

Wellington

Christchurch

SOUTH ISLAND

PACIFIC OCEAN

The early Maoris hunted giant birds, known as moas, which stood 350 cm (12 ft) high. These birds became extinct, probably through over-hunting, about 1,000 years ago. Agriculture was adopted at about the same time, warfare became far more common, and the Maoris' culture underwent a change. Maori culture today is a blend of Maori and European elements. Tribal identity, the Maori language, and a measure of local self-government have remained, as have aspects of Maori customs, although syncretized with Christian beliefs and practices.

Australia and New Zealand 2

drastically different, for the new settlements expanded into Aboriginal territories and interfered with natural resources. Clashes followed, but the Aborigines soon learned that their only course was to adapt and submit. European diseases caused many to die, and in zones of intensive European settlement, a part-Aboriginal population came to replace the original people. Traditional life disappeared from most of the southwest and southeast, but Europeans did not overrun the whole country at once. Some Aboriginal groups, mainly in the center and the north, had a breathing space and they were able to keep much of their own culture and way of life.

All Aborigines were once seminomadic, hunting and gathering over a recognized territorial range in fairly small groups. Within this range, specific sites were owned by members of local descent groups, who were responsible for their ritual upkeep. Such descent groups were exogamous and their members had special bonds with shape-changing mythic beings, sometimes in human, sometimes in animal or other form. Religion was the main source of authority, and of rules for everyday as well as sacred affairs. It provided inspiration for music, song-poetry, myths, dancing, painting and sculpture. Two basic features of Aboriginal culture were a close emotional relationship to the land and the view that the same life essence was shared by all living things. The major mythic beings had shaped the landscape and created people, and they remained eternally present at their named sites.

The mythic beings were a buffer between Aborigines and the unpredictability of the land and climate in which they lived. Many religious rituals focused on renewal and seasonal fertility, representing change as a pattern within a framework of continuity. In the same way human birth and death were seen against a background of eternal spiritual existence, a concept often translated as the "Eternal Dreaming." Children born into this setting were certain of their social, personal and "eternal" identity. The Aborigines' division of labor between young and old, between men and women, was based on interdependence. Women contributed most consistently to the family diet and they had an important role in religion and in everyday life. However, men's roles in public and religious affairs were more conspicuous and on a more corporate basis. Polygyny was permitted almost everywhere, but in most areas monogamy was more common. Marriage was a normal expectation for everyone and early betrothal, especially for girls, was customary in some

Celebrating sun and surf
Surf carnivals are unique to Australia and are likely to take place at any of the more popular beaches during the summer months. These lifesavers (lifeguards) are taking part in a march on one of Sydney's beaches. The lifeguards put on spectacular and competitive displays of the essential skills of their profession—swimming races, lifesaving of dummies and dramatic surf-boat races in which crews of 5 men row longboats out against the breaking surf. They are frequently up-ended by massive rollers which jettison the crew into the sea amid a welter of oars. Those crews skillful enough to get out beyond the surf then have to maneuver their boat to catch an incoming wave in order to get back. Sydney has 56 km (35 miles) of surfing beaches, of which Bondi Beach is the most famous. The bronzed surfing fraternity epitomize Australia's sporting, outdoor image.

areas. Marriages were often arranged, but this did not necessarily mean lack of affection.

Aborigines had a flair for organizing their small social groups, and for ensuring cooperation in everyday affairs, but they were vulnerable when faced with external pressures. They relied on lessons learned in the past, and these became less relevant and useful under changing circumstances with increasing European intrusion and interference.

By 1936–40 the Australian government's "protection" and segregated-control policies toward the Aborigines were giving way to what was called assimilation. In the aftermath of World War II, many Aborigines were sceptical and disillusioned, and the aim of assimilation was interpreted as the final destruction of their traditions and identity. The policy was officially modified in 1965 to counteract this impression, but social protest was becoming more widespread and at the same time the Aboriginal population was steadily increasing in size.

Following the Gove Peninsula Land Rights dispute (1968–71), the Woodward Aboriginal Land Rights Commission has paved the way for granting land rights to Aborigines in the Northern Territory. The gradual liberalization of official policies, and some financial

Aboriginal life
Polygyny was permitted by all Aboriginal groups but monogamy was the most common form of marriage. The taking of several wives depended on the inclination of the man concerned, and was primarily for economic reasons and to sustain and develop a wider network of relationships, which could be a responsibility but also an advantage. This Aborigine of Arnhem Land has 10 wives, 7 of whom are pictured here. Returning from a successful hunting trip with a pelican to help feed his sizeable family, he proudly displays his rifle, a weapon which has now largely replaced traditional implements. These included spears, clubs and boomerangs, although the boomerang was not found everywhere in Australia. The spear was used in combination with a *woomera* (spear thrower), which enabled the hunter to propel the spear accurately over distances of 55 m (180 ft). During the dry season, from April to September, the Aborigines of Arnhem Land scattered in small groups, relying mainly on hunting. In the wet season they remained in semipermanent camps, eating berries, meat, vegetables and fish. As in many hunter-gatherer societies, women supplied much of the food.

Land of the Porou
From Hikurangi Mountain the Ngati Porou, a powerful Maori group, are able to see all their tribal land. By siding with the British during the land wars, the Ngati Porou were able to keep their lands, while 1¼ million hectares (3 million acres) were confiscated from other Maoris. Good grazing land such as this covers most of New Zealand, and pastoralism has replaced the traditional Maori economy of subsistence cultivation.

Dance for a Queen
The *haka* (dance) involves exaggerated facial expressions which can express either welcome or aggression. Here it is being performed to celebrate the coronation of Queen Te Ata, monarch of the Maori tribes of the Waikato valley. These tribes appointed a sovereign during the 19th-century land wars; although not accepted as monarch by other tribes the "Maori Queen" has symbolic significance for all Maoris.

which has given us the word "taboo") are seen as violations of the social order, and of the relationship of people to their past.

Maori political organization in the past focused on aristocratic descent, which conferred *mana* (prestige) on individuals but gave them no automatic right to rule. Inherited *mana* had to be validated through distinction in a number of fields—economic pursuits, art, leadership in war, oratory, knowledge and wisdom. Although women had different roles, women of distinction, equal or superior to that of men, abound in traditional history.

The center of Maori life is the *marae*, a courtyard and complex of buildings of which the *whare hui* (communal house) is the center. The *marae* (strictly the courtyard but also including the house) is bound by *kawa* (strict rules of custom) and by *tapu*, which vary according to tribal custom. In the north all ritual is conducted within the *whare hui*, where the dead lie in state, people sleep, and speeches and discussions are carried on; in other areas greater use is made of the courtyard. Because of its *tapu* no food can be taken into the *whare hui*, and formal arrangements discriminating between *manuhiri* (visitors) and *tangata whenua* (the people of the land) are made in the precedence of rituals, and in sleeping places. Within the *whare hui*, which is usually named after an ancestor, the people are held to be within the body of the ancestor, and this symbolism is expressed in the carvings and other decorations, and in the formal arrangement of objects within the communal house.

Social and cultural life for Maoris moves between two poles, as *taha Pakeha* (part of the wider, white-dominated society) and *taha Maori* (part of Maori life). *Taha Maori* means the acceptance of communal interest, knowledge of Maori language and customs, and obligations outside those of kinship (but expressed in kinship terms) to other Maori people. Even for the most acculturated Maoris, *taha Maori* can be reasserted with intense and devastating results. The death of a relative, for example, brings a powerful communal response in which the apparently isolated individual will find himself or herself caught up, obligations of mourning completely overriding the demands of everyday urban life.

Contemporary Maori life thus consists of a series of compromises at every level between the wider New Zealand society and Maori society. In this some Maoris succeed and find fulfillment, but others, especially as they grow older, submerge themselves deeply in *taha Maori*. Others again become hopeless and alienated misfits, homeless minds in their own culture and deviants outside it. In the 140 years since the Treaty of Waitangi, the problems of conserving Maori culture and identity have brought forth varied responses—war, passive resistance, religious syncretism and innovation, and political activity. Since the late 1970s, however, self-conscious cultural and political movements such as Mana Motuhake and the Waitangi Action Committee have arisen, and these movements point to a more militant assertion of Maori identity.

backing from State and Federal governments, have provided opportunities for the growth of self-determining, decentralized communities in the center and north. On the basis of traditional Aboriginal culture, or symbols of that culture, a new Aboriginal heritage is being shaped. Inevitably it includes Australian-European elements, but it is a significant development, emphasizing roots in a past that can never be recovered by most people of Aboriginal descent.

The Maoris of New Zealand

The Maoris, who number about a quarter of a million, are now a largely urbanized population, but many still have ancestral interests in land and tribal links which bind them to rural communities.

The Maori people are divided into tribes which are identified with particular regions. Such tribes had no corporate identity in the past but acknowledged common ancestry from canoe migrants, who first settled *Aotearoa* (New Zealand). Members of these tribes can recite the names of ancestors who traveled in the canoes, and trace detailed genealogies from them. The corporate groups of Maori society are the *hapuu*, a named group tracing descent from a fairly recent ancestor, and the *whaanau*, an extended family group of some five generations in depth. Since descent may be traced through either parent, and beyond first cousins, kinship networks ramify widely and there are no formal marriage prohibitions. The central metaphor of Maori culture is kinship, not only in terms of human relations but also in terms of a metaphysical relationship of the human being with the natural and supernatural worlds. For example, violations of *tapu* (the Maori word is derived from the same Polynesian term

Preserving Maori traditions
A Maori woman prepares the leaves of a flaxlike plant for the traditional *piupiu* dancing skirt. The leaves are boiled in a hot spring to soften them, and then dyed. Those that have been boiled and dyed can be seen drying in the background. These skirts are a reminder of the Maoris' Polynesian ancestry.

Polynesia, Micronesia and Melanesia 1

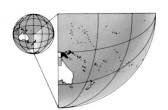

Sunshine and dancing, sexual freedom and feasting—this was the myth that European explorers wove around the volcanic islands of Polynesia. But these same Europeans brought with them destruction for the indigenous people, through disease and forced labor. The Pacific Islands are still idyllic, but traditional life styles survive in only a few of the islands.

Population by Region
Total: 6 million
Melanesia 61%

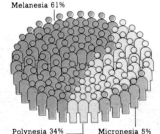

Polynesia 34% Micronesia 5%

Population by Religion

Non-script. 39% R. Catholicism 26%
Min. rel. 15% Protestantism 20%

Navigators of the South Seas Polynesians make their canoes from single logs. Much larger versions of such canoes were used by their ancestors to colonize the Pacific Islands.

Stretching southeast from the Asian mainland is a volcanically active zone, part of the destructive "ring of fire" that encircles the Pacific Ocean. The tips of the innumerable volcanic cones pepper this vast tract of the Pacific, forming the islands of Polynesia and Micronesia. Traveling in large canoes, Mongoloid groups, possibly from China or Formosa, began to reach these islands 5,000 years ago. They moved from island to island as one people, and thus preserved their common language and culture. Fiji, Samoa and Tonga were settled between 3,000 and 2,000 years ago and from there the Polynesians pushed eastward, colonizing Easter Island 1,600 years ago and Hawaii 1,300 years ago. Reaching the larger land masses of Melanesia to the southwest, they encountered Australoid people who had been there for as long as 35,000 years before them. The linguistic diversity of present-day Melanesia (especially New Guinea where more than 1,000 different languages are spoken) is in sharp contrast to the linguistic homogeneity of Polynesia and Micronesia, and reflects its far longer history of settlement and the extensive barriers to communication caused by the rugged terrain.

The cultural themes of Polynesia and Micronesia also present a contrast with those of Melanesia. Polynesian and Micronesian societies show a remarkable uniformity and are deeply marked by principles of rank and chiefship. Rank is hereditary and on the larger islands it has led to highly stratified societies with royal lineages. An impressive feature of these Polynesian societies was their capacity to erect massive stoneworks, such as the famous *ahu* statues of Easter Island.

Melanesian societies were generally smaller in scale and far more egalitarian, with the cultural emphasis on the ceremonial exchange of goods. Their leaders, or "big-men," achieved status through their own efforts in warfare and in amassing and exchanging material goods. These differing emphases—on rank and on exchange—have survived to the present day, despite the effects of colonization. However, they are not exclusive, for there is some hereditary ranking in Melanesian societies and the exchange of valuables is of importance in Polynesia.

The earliest home of agriculture in the Pacific region was the remote central highlands of New Guinea, where archeologists have found evidence of irrigation channels 9,000 years old. This makes New Guinea one of the most ancient agricultural sites in the world, ranking with the Fertile Crescent of the Middle East. The first crops were probably taro, bananas and sugarcane. The domesticated pig was introduced about 9,000 years ago and the sweet potato was brought from America, perhaps by Spanish ships, about 300 or 400 years ago. These are the main foods, together with fish, coconuts and yams.

Western mythology builds a picture of the Pacific Islands as lands of plenty—of sunshine, beauty, dancing, feasting and ceremonies—but the image obscures the terrible depredations that accompanied European incursions from the sixteenth century onward. The earliest ravages were by disease. Tubai and Raivavae, islands which lie to the south of Tahiti, lost two thirds of their populations in an epidemic introduced by a visiting ship. The Pacific Islanders had no resistance against diseases such as influenza, tuberculosis, dysentery, smallpox and measles, nor against venereal diseases, whose spread was accelerated by the sexual freedom of Polynesian society.

The activities of missionaries in undermining traditional values and the introduction of guns, liquor and opium, wreaked further havoc. Slave trading in the mid-nineteenth century was followed by "blackbirding," a legalized form of labor recruitment, in which islanders were transported to Australia or to Fiji, to work on cotton plantations for pitifully low wages. At the same time, 60,000 Indians were brought into Fiji by the British to work the sugar plantations, and Indians today outnumber the indigenous Fijians.

The initial phase of discovery, pacification and mission influence, was followed by intensive commercial exploitation, with one particular resource or crop becoming important on each major island. Politically, the area was divided up between the British, French, Dutch and German governments, and in World War II it served as a battleground for the world powers.

The effect of colonization was to destroy many societies in the Pacific islands and, associated with the adoption of Christianity, many local cults sprang up, often called "cargo cults." These cults are usually headed by a leader or leaders with charismatic influence, often appearing as a prophet. At one extreme the cults have as their objective securing large amounts of European wealth and power by magicoreligious means; at the other extreme, the cults

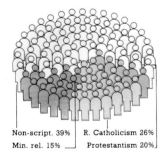

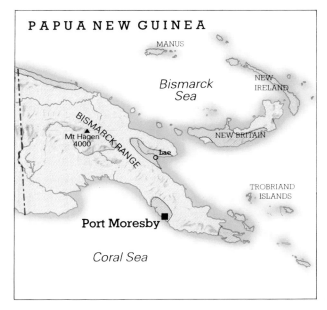

PAPUA NEW GUINEA

MANUS

Bismarck
Sea

NEW
IRELAND

BISMARCK RANGE

Mt Hagen
4000

NEW BRITAIN

Lae

TROBRIAND
ISLANDS

Port Moresby

Coral Sea

The 60,000 Melpa were virtually isolated in the central highlands until the arrival of Europeans in the 1930s, but since their traditions have affinities with the capitalist system they have adapted well to modern life. Today almost all the Melpa are cash croppers of coffee and vegetables, and some have become rich businessmen and politicians. Although interclan warfare is banned by the government, it still threatens to erupt periodically between the competitive and now land-hungry clans.

Just over 9,000 people live on the dozen or so islands that are surrounded by the single coral reef of Truk. The staple food is breadfruit, which is stored in pits. Fish are caught within the reef by the women, and in the open sea by the men. Matrilineal clans are divided into lineages which own land and property, and on marriage most men go to live with the families of their wives. Several generations of kin live close together and eat food cooked in a common hearth. Age and sex are the basic sources of authority.

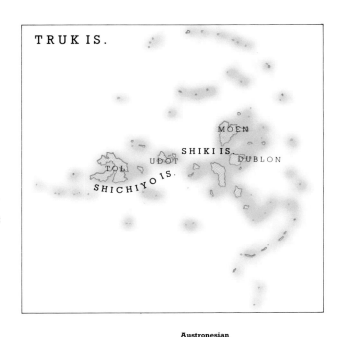

TRUK IS.

MOEN

SHIKI IS.

UDOT   DUBLON

TOL

SHICHIYO IS.

Austronesian

Polynesian languages (Samoan,
Tahitian, Tongan, etc.);
Micronesian languages (Trukese,
etc.); "Melanesian" languages
(Fijian, Kiriwina, Motu, etc.)

Indo-European

Germanic language (English)

Unaffiliated languages

Other languages (Melpa, etc.)

Featured people

Samoans of Western Samoa
Melpa of Mount Hagen

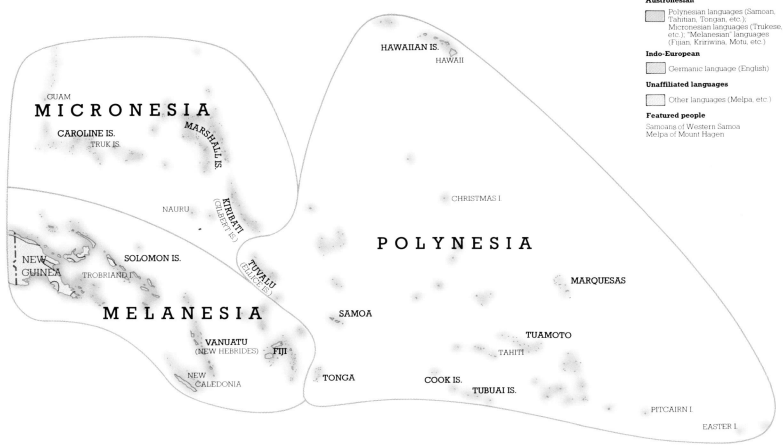

HAWAIIAN IS.

HAWAII

GUAM

MICRONESIA

CAROLINE IS.

MARSHALL IS.

TRUK IS.

CHRISTMAS I.

NAURU

KIRIBATI
(GILBERT IS.)

POLYNESIA

NEW
GUINEA

SOLOMON IS.

TUVALU
(ELLICE IS.)

MARQUESAS

TROBRIAND I.

SAMOA

MELANESIA

TUAMOTO

VANUATU
(NEW HEBRIDES)   FIJI

TAHITI

NEW
CALEDONIA

TONGA   COOK IS.

TUBUAI IS.

PITCAIRN I.

EASTER I.

TROBRIAND
OR
KIRIWINA IS.

KAILEUNA I.

Losuia

KITAVA I.

MUWO I.

The four main coral islands of the Trobriands support rich yam gardens, industriously cultivated by the population of 14,000. Men take part in a complex system of ceremonial exchange, known as *kula*, which necessitates long canoe voyages. Many ritual objects, such as carved and painted canoe prows, are of great beauty and are now produced for tourists. Descent is matrilineal; each man receives a harvest gift of yams from his wife's brother, and boys return to their maternal uncle's territory at maturity.

The 150,000 Samoans of Western Samoa have retained much of their traditional way of life, unlike the islanders of American Samoa, who receive massive economic assistance from the United States. The Western Samoans live in villages of between 100 and 1,000 people. Many grow bananas, coconuts or cocoa for cash. Breadfruit, bananas, taro, yams and sweet potatoes form the bulk of the diet, sometimes supplemented by fish, shellfish, crabs, pigs or chickens. The Samoans have blended Christianity with their traditional values.

WESTERN SAMOA

SAVAII

Apia

UPOLU

Peoples and languages
Fijian is politically the most important Austronesian language in Melanesia, while Samoan, Tongan and Tahitian are important in Polynesia. In Micronesia, Chamorro (spoken on Guam), Gilbertese, Trukese and Marshallese are the major languages. They are spoken by between 20,000 and 150,000 people, and all have a rich oral tradition, although until missionaries introduced the Roman alphabet, Easter Island was the only community to have a script. The linguistic homogeneity of Polynesia contrasts with the diversity of New Guinea, where there are over 1,000 distinct languages. The coastal people of New Guinea speak Melanesian languages which are Austronesian in structure, while the inland regions are occupied by people of different origin (thought to be distantly related to the Australian Aborigines) who speak Papuan languages.

Polynesia, Micronesia and Melanesia 2

develop into political movements uniting people in a program for social and economic advancement.

Today the great majority of the islands and archipelagos are politically independent, albeit with economic aid from their previous colonial masters. America still controls Hawaii, American Samoa and most of Micronesia, however, and Britain, France and New Zealand retain small territories. The western part of New Guinea, Irian Jaya, is now incorporated into the Indonesian Republic. Despite the disruptive effects of colonization, some of the societies of this region have survived. The Samoans of Western Samoa and the Melpa of New Guinea are two such societies, and they illustrate clearly the difference in cultural emphasis between Polynesia and Melanesia.

Samoans of Western Samoa

Despite centuries of contact with the western world, the Samoans are one of the few Polynesian peoples who have succeeded in retaining much of their traditional way of life, which they call *fa'a Samoa*. About 150,000 people live on the two main islands of Western Samoa with its generally fertile soil, on which coconuts, cocoa and bananas are grown for cash. Bananas are sold only to New Zealand, which maintains close economic ties with Samoa and also provides wage employment for Samoan migrants. These migrants send money home, since in the modern economic system money earned by young men in wage labor is subject to the demands of their kin. There have been attempts to improve cattle, fish and timber production, and tourism has been encouraged, but not at the expense of stifling Samoan tradition.

For day-to-day subsistence, the men make canoes and fish in the open sea, while the women do the heavy agricultural work, make *tapa* barkcloth, weave pandanus leaves into mats and do some reef fishing. The staple root crops are taro, yams and sweet potatoes,

which are cooked with coconut for flavoring. Pigs and poultry are killed for ceremonial occasions.

A Samoan normally belongs to his father's *'āiga* (descent group), and each *'āiga* has certain *matai* names (titles of rank) to bestow on its most promising men. The relative rank of the *matai* names is fixed, and determines where each *matai* sits in the *fono* (village council). All this is in keeping with the general Polynesian principle of inherited titles, but the Samoans depart from this general rule in so far as there is election to some titles.

Each household (households vary in size from three or four people to as many as twenty) has a *matai* at its head, and he is in charge of land claims, the organization of labor and the settling of disputes among them. The most important *matai* from each village traditionally requires a girl, related to him by female ties, to be his *taupo* (princess). She should be beautiful and skilled at dancing, so that she can act as village hostess to visitors. The *taupo* is expected to be a virgin and is eventually married to an important *matai* from a neigh-

Mekeo warrior
The Mekeo live in a fertile area of Papua New Guinea. Contact with the modern world is eroding traditional patterns of social behavior.

Moka—aggressive gift giving
Moka originated from the system of compensation which took place after wars. With the abolition of warfare, *moka* has assumed distinctly aggressive overtones, the larger the gift, the greater the status of the giver and the greater the obligation of the recipient to repay the giver.

Imposing beauty of the Melpa
At *moka* dances both sexes wear flamboyant headdresses. When standing still they look like statues on display: when they move, it is with stately grandeur. The care which they lavish on personal appearance is also expended on their gardens and important ceremonial grounds.

boring village with whom *tonga* (fine mats) are exchanged, *tonga* being traditional property that is always exchanged through women. Male personal property is known as *oloa*, as is wealth or goods, such as radios, obtained from Europeans.

Meetings of the village *fono* are conducted in a highly ceremonious way, and *tulafale* (orators) make the speeches for the *matai*. Before a meeting can start, the traditional ritual of kava drinking must take place and it is the special task of the *taupo* to prepare and serve the kava. A libation is also offered to the deities and spirits. Over the years the *matai* system has been well integrated into the modern system of government at national level. Samoans have long been influenced by missionaries, and most are Christian.

Melpa of Papua New Guinea

The Melpa, of whom there are now roughly 60,000, belong to a branch of peoples who first entered Melanesia some 40,000 years ago. They live in the central highlands of Papua New Guinea, near Mount Hagen. Although linked to the coasts by a network of trade ties, they were effectively cut off from the rest of the world until European explorers entered their region in the early 1930s. The Melpa welcomed the Europeans when they found that they brought highly valued marine shells, especially pearly shell, that had previously trickled only slowly into their area via trade routes. To the Melpa, these had a special importance, as they were required for *moka*, that is, ceremonial exchanges of pigs and valuable shells.

The Melpa do not live in villages but have small scattered settlements that usually comprise the homestead of a man and his family. The men sleep separately from the women, children and pigs, and there are small huts in each settlement where the women are secluded during menstruation.

At marriage, the bridegroom's subclansmen and maternal kin pay high bridewealth for a wife, who will work for him and help him to accumulate wealth for *moka* exchanges. After marriage, close ties are maintained with the wife's family, using *moka* exchanges.

In the large settlements, there is a clan ceremonial ground, outside the communal men's house, which the ancestors' spirits are said to inhabit. The area is surrounded by a high fence, and only those men initiated in the cult can enter. The ghosts of dead kin guard morality and strike wrongdoers with sickness; their sins can be expiated only by confession and sacrifice. Theft is common, and is dealt with by counter-theft, compensation payments and sometimes physical violence. Within each clan, big-men have informal powers of arbitration.

The big-men run large settlements, have other men working for them, have several wives, and give credit—mainly in the form of pigs and cash—to anyone requiring it. The more they lend out the greater their prestige, and therefore power. Each big-man wears a set of *omak* (bamboo tally sticks) around his neck, and these show how much credit he has provided. Big-men have adapted very easily to the capitalist system as its basic method of working is so similar to their traditional one. Although Melpa society

Open house in Samoa
Samoan houses have no walls. Blinds made from palm leaves provide a degree of privacy when they are lowered in the evening. There are usually 30 to 40 households in a Samoan village, each one presided over by a *matai*. Households tend to be fluid: children frequently shift from one house to another taking advantage of the hospitality of one of their relatives. This has a moderating effect on overly strict parents, for children are always able to find protection outside the home. The *fono*, attended by all the *matai*, takes place in the ceremonial house—a much larger version of the dwelling houses. Junior *matai* do not have the right to sit with a post at their backs and they are therefore said to be of "between the posts" ranks.

Suffering for status
At one time all young Samoan boys were required to endure the painful tattooing ceremony. Polynesians who, along with the Japanese, were the greatest exponents of this art, believed that extensive tattooing reflected high social status. In some cases the whole body was tattooed, even the tongue.

is basically egalitarian, there is still a hierarchy of social classes: major big-men, minor big-men, ordinary citizens, and men too poor to marry.

Traditionally there is a clear division of labor between the sexes. Men clear gardens and plant sugarcane and bananas; women till and weed them, and plant brassicas, taro and sweet potatoes. Some crops, such as yams, are planted by either sex, as are introduced crops such as coffee, maize and manioc. Gardens are well protected against pigs, which are let out to forage in the nearby forests by day. At night the women lure them back to the settlement by hand-feeding them sweet potatoes.

Nowadays, all Melpa are cash croppers, and some have emerged as rich businessmen and politicians. Melpa traditions continue alongside modern elections, sales of coffee, vegetable marketing, visits to town by motor vehicle and membership of either the Lutheran or the Catholic church. Differences of wealth are apparent, and young men who resent their neighbor's riches involve themselves in violent bouts of drinking, partly as a means of protest. In the precolonial past, they would have been warriors, and values associated with bravado and physical prowess are still maintained by men, who contrast themselves strongly with women. Cash wealth and differences in education are gradually introducing social patterns based on economic class, and money has entered Melpa ceremonial *moka* exchanges.

Warfare used to be very prevalent among the Melpa and their neighbors, and a complex system of allies and enemies, based on clan traditions, gradually built up. After a dispute with a minor enemy, the Melpa preferred to do a *moka* exchange, as the women from these clans were potential wives. However, major enemies never intermarried, and so physical violence was the normal way of settling these disputes.

Male dominance was reinforced by this warfare; but today it is bolstered by fertility cults directed to a female goddess, women being excluded from these rites. Meanwhile the traditional position of men is being challenged by women's possession of money, through vegetable sales and shares in coffee money.

Generally the Melpa have not been adversely affected by recent social change, but their lives are now altering rapidly. If the *moka* is abandoned, the chief framework of Melpa society will have collapsed.

Trobriand yam house
High-ranking men may head a polygynous household. They may also have a yam house built for them by junior members of the family and by political supporters as a mark of respect. The owner of the yam house benefits considerably from this system as the builders are required to fill the house with yams after every harvest. Trobriand islanders are primarily an agricultural people and fishing is of secondary importance. Harvest produce is divided according to a household's needs and its gift and prestige requirements. Being a matrilineal society, the gifts are made by the man to his maternal kin. All Trobriand villages follow the same pattern of two concentric rings of houses: the inner ring are store houses, the outer ring are dwelling huts. The space in the center of the inner circle is used for dances, feasts and is also the village burial ground.

North America

North America is a continent with two histories—an early history of colonization and settlement by Mongoloid hunter-gatherers who crossed from Siberia during the Ice Age, and a second history of conquest and development by Europeans, beginning in the sixteenth century. To both waves of settlers it has proved a land of plenty, rich in natural resources, but their attitudes to the use of those resources could not have been more different. For most Indians, a profound respect for the earth demanded that each tree cut down, each animal killed was carefully used to the full. To the Europeans, however, the land and its products were raw material to be manipulated and exploited as they pleased. The great gulf between the two is reflected in the lament of a Wintu Indian holy woman: "How can the spirit of the earth like the White man ... Everywhere the White man has touched it, it is sore." It is reflected, too, in the dramatic difference in population

figures, for the Indians of North America numbered only a million or so when the European colonists first arrived, while the same land area now supports over 250 million people.

The first Americans

It is still not certain when the first groups of people crossed from Asia into America, although they are known to have traveled on dry land, for the lowering of the sea level during the Ice Age drained the Bering Strait, creating a corridor of land between the two continents. Their migration was probably not a deliberate one, and they may well have wandered into this vast, uninhabited continent as a result of following the herds of animals which they hunted. Slowly these early hunters moved southward, perhaps along an ice-free corridor in the eastern foothills of the Rocky Mountains. They spread through the vast, empty lands, hunting mammoths and other large mammals. But with the receding of the ice sheets,

the climate changed and their descendants were forced to adopt a new way of life. Most remained as hunters or hunter-gatherers, pursuing smaller animals and exploiting plant foods, but some later learned the skills of agriculture from those tribes which had settled in the valleys of Central America. As the population expanded, distinct cultures emerged in different areas although common themes still linked the widely scattered groups. A feeling of reverence for nature was strong among all Amerindian tribes, and agriculture was abhorred by some because it involved scarring the face of "mother earth." Social systems were, on the whole, simple, and the complex hierarchical civilizations of South and Central America had no parallel in the north.

The European influx

Although others may have reached America earlier (and the Vikings had temporarily colonized Greenland in about AD 1000), it is Columbus who is usually credited with its discovery, and he who misnamed its inhabitants "Indians." Reaching the Caribbean islands in 1492, he believed that he had circumnavigated the world and was standing on the shores of "Farther India" – islands in the Indian Ocean. The Spanish conquistadors who followed him were largely interested in South America and the fabled golden treasures of Eldorado, and they made only limited headway in the north. Although Dutch traders and French fur-trappers penetrated the northeast during the sixteenth century, large-scale colonization of North America only really began with the British settlers of the seventeenth century.

The early English colonists, aided by the labor of African slaves, built up the economy of their new lands so rapidly that by 1775 they were strong enough to fight for independence from Britain. The newly independent nation, full of optimism for the future and requiring workers for its growing industry, opened its gates to the poor and oppressed of Europe. The nineteenth century saw a great influx of immigrants—first from northern Europe, but later from southern Europe—who were rapidly absorbed into the American "melting pot." What they sought was freedom from prejudice and injustice, and the opportunity to build a life of prosperity by their own efforts. This ethos remains strong in American society, and the man who has "pulled himself up by his bootstraps" is still the hero of the American Dream.

Relations between north and south—the former with its history of Puritan ideals, the latter a glittering aristocratic society whose wealth was based on slave labor—grew ever more tense as the Union expanded and in 1861 civil war broke out. With their victory, the northerners brought an end to slavery and the blacks embarked on the long process of integration into free society, a process which, though still not complete, has rapidly advanced in the past twenty-five years. Meanwhile, the expansion westward continued and the Indians lost yet more of their lands. At the turn of the century, their population was at an all-time low, and disease was rife among the demoralized survivors.

The twentieth century has seen the wealth and influence of North America expand enormously, as modern technology has been applied to exploiting its vast resources. The United States has developed at an unparalleled rate, despite the setbacks of the 1930s depression, while Canada, still governed directly by Britain until 1931, has grown less rapidly. With its growing affluence, the United States has been drawn back into the political affairs of its old homelands in Europe, and thence into the politics of the rest of the world. From a position of detachment in the first half of the century, the United States has moved to one of close involvement in the affairs of other nations, and has fought a succession of foreign wars. Since World War II, rivalry with the USSR has been the focus of foreign policy and the spur, not only for a massive buildup in arms, but also for tremendous advances in space exploration, sending an American to the moon in 1969, and unmanned craft to Jupiter, Saturn and Uranus in the 1980s.

Monument Valley in southwest America, a Navajo reservation

Amerindian North America 1

"We did not think of the great open plains, the beautiful rolling hills, and winding streams with tangled growth, as 'wild.' Only to the white man was nature a 'wilderness' and only to him was the land 'infested' with 'wild' animals and 'savage' people. To us it was tame. Earth was bountiful and we were surrounded with the blessings of the Great Mystery."
A Sioux Chief.

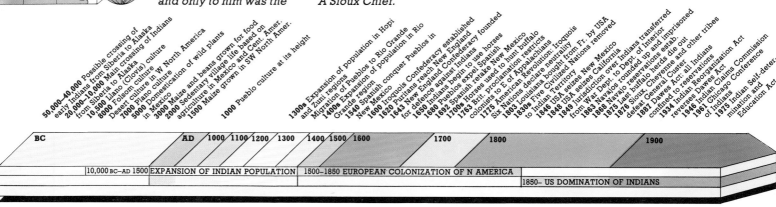

Timeline labels:
50,000–40,000 Possible crossing of early Indians from Siberia to Alaska
20,000–10,000 Main crossing of Indians from Siberia to Alaska
10,500 Llano (Clovis) culture
8000 Folsom culture in W North America
7000 Plano culture
5000 Domestication of wild plants in Mexico
3000 Maize and beans grown for food in Cent. Amer.
2000 Sedentary village life based on agriculture in Mexico and Cent. Amer.
1500 Maize grown in SW North Amer.
1000 Pueblo culture at its height
1300s Expansion of population in Hopi and Zuni regions
Migration of Pueblos to Rio Grande region
1400s Expansion of population in Rio Grande region
1540 Spanish conquer Pueblos in New Mexico
1600 Iroquois Confederacy established
1620 Puritans reach New England
1643 New England Confederacy founded for defence against Indians
1650 Indians begin to use horses
1680 Pueblos expel Spanish
1692 Spanish retake New Mexico
1700s Horses used to hunt buffalo
1763 Brit. proclamation restricts colonists to E. of Appalachians
1775 American Revolution: Iroquois Six Nations declare neutrality
1803 Louisiana bought from Fr. by USA
1830s Five Civilized Nations removed to Indian Territory
1846 USA seizes New Mexico
1848 USA seizes California
1849 Jurisdiction over Indians transferred from War Dept. to Dept. of Interior
1863 Navajos rounded up and imprisoned
1868 Navajo reservations estab.
1875 Last buffalo herds die out
1876 Sioux defeat General Custer
1887 Dawes Act: all Indians confined to reservations
1934 Indian Reorganization Act reverses Dawes Act
1946 Indian Claims Commission estab.
1961 Chicago Conference of Indians
1975 Indian Self-determination and Education Act

| BC | AD | 1000 | 1100 | 1200 | 1300 | 1400 | 1500 | 1600 | 1700 | 1800 | 1900 |

10,000 BC–AD 1500 EXPANSION OF INDIAN POPULATION
1500–1850 EUROPEAN COLONIZATION OF N AMERICA
1850– US DOMINATION OF INDIANS

Population by Residence
Total: 1½ million

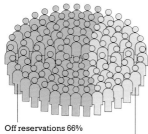

Off reservations 66%
On reservations 34%

Round house
The hogan is the traditional Navajo dwelling. Made of logs and earth, hogans are either hexagonal or octagonal in shape, with a dome-shaped roof. In the center of the roof is a hole through which smoke from the domestic fire can escape. This shape was ideally suited to accommodate the religious ceremonies of the Navajos, as well as providing a weatherproof shelter. With the availability of man-made materials, however, the original hogan design has been modified, and cement is often used instead of earth. Many Navajos have now abandoned hogans altogether.

The earliest archaeological finds in North America which can be securely dated are 11,500 years old, although the ancestors of the Amerindians may in fact have migrated from Siberia at a much earlier date. These first immigrants hunted mammoths and other now-extinct animals on the high plains of North America as the glaciers were retreating at the close of the Ice Age. Later they turned their attentions to the bison and camels which ranged the plains region. As the larger animals died out, these people were replaced by other groups who gathered wild plants and hunted smaller game, as well as exploiting the rich marine resources of the coastal regions.

In western North America the surviving populations turned to plant seeds and roots for the bulk of their subsistence and developed the Desert Culture, which later formed the basis for the agricultural societies of the Pueblo Indians. In the eastern forest regions the early hunters turned to the exploitation of forest products and the utilization of mussels and fish, and developed a variety of cultures which continued into the sixteenth and seventeenth centuries. The hunting of buffalo intensified in the Plains area and the hunting of caribou and other migratory animals continued in the northern interior forests of what is now Canada.

The domestication of plants in Central America and the gradual spread of agriculture northward into portions of what is now the United States had a profound effect on many Indian groups. Present evidence indicates that the domestication of maize, beans and squash took place in the central Mexican plateau before 5000 BC, and reached the southwestern regions of North America around 1500 BC. Here there was also a long developmental period, and agriculture was not firmly established until some 2,000 years ago.

North America is usually divided into some ten to twelve culture areas—geographical regions occupied by tribes with generally similar culture patterns. The divisions between groups are not clear cut since in most areas there is no close relationship between the distribution of languages, physical types and culture patterns. Some culture areas, such as the Great Basin in western North America, show considerable time depth, with little major change from 8000 BC to the present, whereas the Plains culture, with its utilization of the horse, introduced by Spanish explorers in the sixteenth century, flourished for only a short time.

The social and political organizations of the Indians showed a surprising variety of forms but did not attain the high level of development reached in Central and South America, despite the diffusion of agriculture and other practices from Mexico. Everywhere in North America the local group or band was important. In a few regions, such as the Great Basin, the bands were small and made up mainly of related families, but in more favorable areas, such as California and on the Plains, the local groups might have a lineage or clan organization, or develop into larger composite bands with a central political structure and a feeling of tribal unity. Where agriculture made permanent settlements possible, the village or town organization was usually composed of clan or moiety groups and had a centralized religious and political structure. Warfare was endemic in some regions, such as the Great Plains, but much of North America was generally peaceful.

In almost all areas of North America there were seasonal movements in connection with the food quest. Frequently the local group inhabited a winter village and broke up into smaller family groups during the summer. But in some regions the patterns were reversed, as among the Plains tribes, where the bands wintered separately and came together in the tribal camp circle during the summer for buffalo hunting, ceremonies and warfare. Only among the Pueblo Indians, and to a lesser extent the southeastern tribes and the Iroquois, were there sedentary dwellings occupied throughout the year.

The early English and French settlers were dependent on the Indians for food and initially treated them as sovereign nations with whom treaties were made. At first, colonial frontiers expanded rather slowly and pressures on the Indians to move further west were not too great. During the wars for control of North America, both the French and British recruited Indian allies, and the Iroquois confederacy played an important role in the defeat of the French. In the "Proclamation of 1763" the British Crown established the Appalachians as the western boundary for colonial settlement, and attempted to keep control of trade. If this boundary could have been maintained for a period, American Indian history might have been different, but the Crown was unable to enforce its decision and the line was soon breached by the colonists.

The American Revolution, which began in 1775, was one of the turning points in American Indian history.

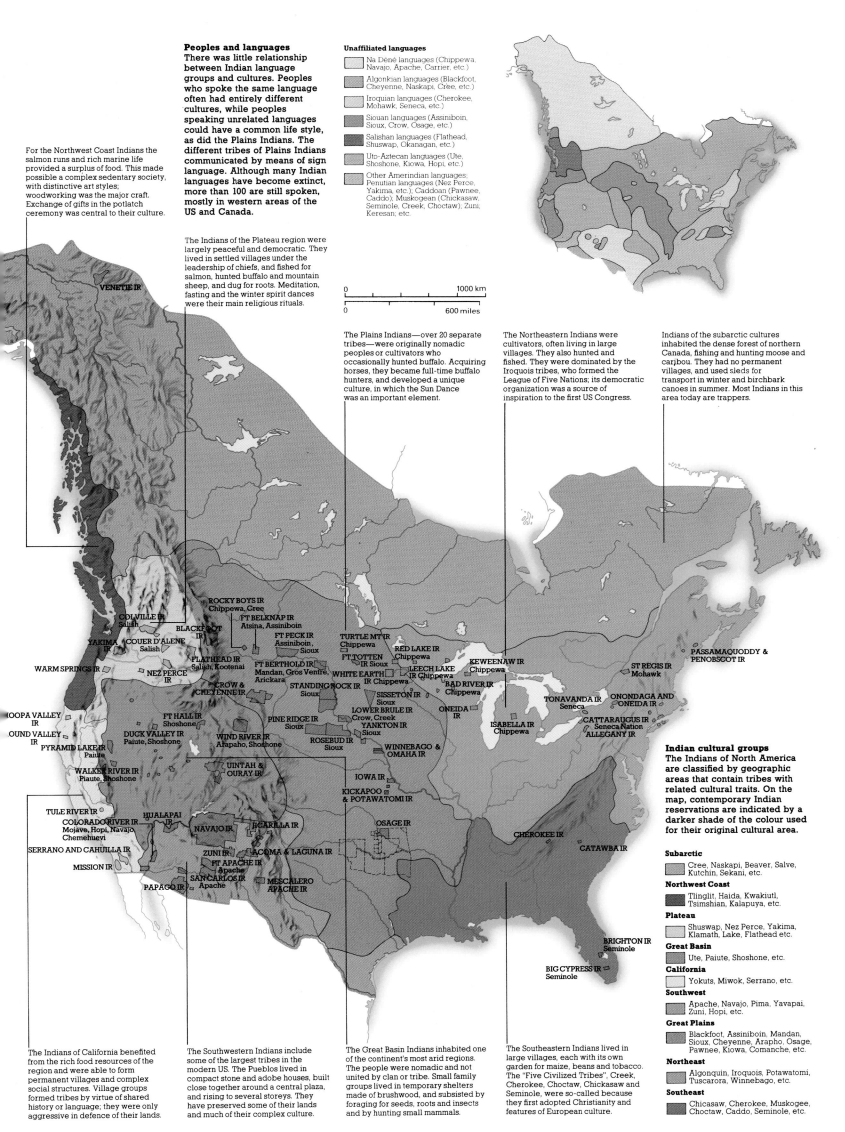

Peoples and languages
There was little relationship between Indian language groups and cultures. Peoples who spoke the same language often had entirely different cultures, while peoples speaking unrelated languages could have a common life style, as did the Plains Indians. The different tribes of Plains Indians communicated by means of sign language. Although many Indian languages have become extinct, more than 100 are still spoken, mostly in western areas of the US and Canada.

Unaffiliated languages

- Na Déné languages (Chippewa, Navajo, Apache, Carrier, etc.)
- Algonkian languages (Blackfoot, Cheyenne, Naskapi, Cree, etc.)
- Iroquian languages (Cherokee, Mohawk, Seneca, etc.)
- Siouan languages (Assiniboin, Sioux, Crow, Osage, etc.)
- Salishan languages (Flathead, Shuswap, Okanagan, etc.)
- Uto-Aztecan languages (Ute, Shoshone, Kiowa, Hopi, etc.)
- Other Amerindian languages; Penutian languages (Nez Perce, Yakima, etc.); Caddoan (Pawnee, Caddo); Muskogean (Chickasaw, Seminole, Creek, Choctaw); Zuni; Keresan; etc.

For the Northwest Coast Indians the salmon runs and rich marine life provided a surplus of food. This made possible a complex sedentary society, with distinctive art styles; woodworking was the major craft. Exchange of gifts in the potlatch ceremony was central to their culture.

The Indians of the Plateau region were largely peaceful and democratic. They lived in settled villages under the leadership of chiefs, and fished for salmon, hunted buffalo and mountain sheep, and dug for roots. Meditation, fasting and the winter spirit dances were their main religious rituals.

The Plains Indians—over 20 separate tribes—were originally nomadic peoples or cultivators who occasionally hunted buffalo. Acquiring horses, they became full-time buffalo hunters, and developed a unique culture, in which the Sun Dance was an important element.

The Northeastern Indians were cultivators, often living in large villages. They also hunted and fished. They were dominated by the Iroquois tribes, who formed the League of Five Nations; its democratic organization was a source of inspiration to the first US Congress.

Indians of the subarctic cultures inhabited the dense forest of northern Canada, fishing and hunting moose and caribou. They had no permanent villages, and used sleds for transport in winter and birchbark canoes in summer. Most Indians in this area today are trappers.

Indian cultural groups
The Indians of North America are classified by geographic areas that contain tribes with related cultural traits. On the map, contemporary Indian reservations are indicated by a darker shade of the colour used for their original cultural area.

Subarctic
Cree, Naskapi, Beaver, Salve, Kutchin, Sekani, etc.

Northwest Coast
Tlinglit, Haida, Kwakiutl, Tsimshian, Kalapuya, etc.

Plateau
Shuswap, Nez Perce, Yakima, Klamath, Lake, Flathead etc.

Great Basin
Ute, Paiute, Shoshone, etc.

California
Yokuts, Miwok, Serrano, etc.

Southwest
Apache, Navajo, Pima, Yavapai, Zuni, Hopi, etc.

Great Plains
Blackfoot, Assiniboin, Mandan, Sioux, Cheyenne, Arapho, Osage, Pawnee, Kiowa, Comanche, etc.

Northeast
Algonquin, Iroquois, Potawatomi, Tuscarora, Winnebago, etc.

Southeast
Chicasaw, Cherokee, Muskogee, Choctaw, Caddo, Seminole, etc.

The Indians of California benefited from the rich food resources of the region and were able to form permanent villages and complex social structures. Village groups formed tribes by virtue of shared history or language; they were only aggressive in defence of their lands.

The Southwestern Indians include some of the largest tribes in the modern US. The Pueblos lived in compact stone and adobe houses, built close together around a central plaza, and rising to several storeys. They have preserved some of their lands and much of their complex culture.

The Great Basin Indians inhabited one of the continent's most arid regions. The people were nomadic and not united by clan or tribe. Small family groups lived in temporary shelters made of brushwood, and subsisted by foraging for seeds, roots and insects and by hunting small mammals.

The Southeastern Indians lived in large villages, each with its own garden for maize, beans and tobacco. The "Five Civilized Tribes", Creek, Cherokee, Choctaw, Chickasaw and Seminole, were so-called because they first adopted Christianity and features of European culture.

Amerindian North America 2

The forces unleashed by the revolution undermined the power and independence of the surviving Indian nations to such an extent that they could no longer bargain from a position of equality, but were relegated to the status of "dependent nations," whose lands were subject to confiscation or forced sale. Following the war, pressures for the removal of all Indians to lands west of the Mississippi became more intense, and when Andrew Jackson was elected President the removal policy was put into effect. In the 1830s the Five Civilized Nations were removed to Indian Territory (now the state of Oklahoma), along with most of the remaining groups of eastern Indians. The Civil War (1861–1865) dealt a further blow to Indian independence as they were caught between the contestants and lost much of their remaining land and possessions.

From the 1860s to the 1880s the Sioux and the Apache tribes were defeated by government forces, and at the same time, the pressure from white settlers increased. This led to the Dawes Act of 1887, which allotted reservation lands to heads of families, the surplus being thrown open to white settlement. The objective was to hasten assimilation of Indian populations, but the main result was to reduce Indian lands from 57 million hectares (140 million acres) to less than 20 million hectares (50 million acres) between 1887 and 1933. Indian society became demoralized and there was a loss of population through epidemics.

In the 1930s President Roosevelt radically changed the directions of Indian policy and supported the Indian Reorganization Act, which reversed the provisions of the Dawes Act by stopping further allocation of Indian lands to settlers and allowing Indian peoples to have a greater role in deciding their future. The Indian population reached its lowest level around the turn of the present century, but in recent years there has been a dramatic reversal, with Indian populations often increasing at a faster rate than the white majority. There is also a new pride in being Indian and many Indian ceremonies have been revived.

The Iroquois Indians

The five tribes which made up the original Iroquois confederacy—the Mohawk, Oneida, Onondaga,

Cayuga and Seneca—were well established in the Finger Lakes region (now part of upper New York State) when European traders first penetrated the area in the sixteenth century. The Iroquois numbered only a few thousand but their skill and courage as warriors and their talent for political organization allowed them eventually to control the entire region between the Ohio river and the Great Lakes, as far west as the Mississippi river.

The Iroquois kinship system was based on matrilineal clans known as *owachira*, and these were grouped into two divisions which were of political and ceremonial significance. In the early seventeenth century each clan segment or lineage lived in a longhouse, within which there were several nuclear families or "firesides." The husbands joined their wives' longhouse after marriage. Women did most of the agricultural work, leaving the men free to hunt or go on war expeditions. The villages, made up of several longhouses, were fairly small and they moved on every few years when the soil became exhausted.

Stitch in time
Many traditions of Navajo life survive on the reservations today but adaptations have been made to the life style of 20th-century America. Daily household chores are done by the women, who also spin and dye wool for weaving. Now, however, the rugs and blankets that are woven are often sold to tourists visiting the reservation. Here a woman spins wool outside the traditional hogan. Children and men herd sheep and goats amid the spectacular scenery of the southwest United States, but the living to be made by most reservation Indians, from either pastoralism or craftwork, is meager. Intensive land use has led to soil erosion on many reservations. In modern American terms, most Navajos live below the poverty line.

Images in sand
Navajo sand paintings express the fundamental religious beliefs of the tribe. Navajo philosophy sees the world made up of Earth Surface People and Holy People. The well-being of Earth Surface People is dependent upon care in thought and deed, and in order to preserve harmony with the universe, Navajos live according to a set of religious rules. The sand paintings depict myths and legends that tell how the world was formed, explain characteristics of the animal world, and describe the deeds of Holy People. One such Holy Person is Changing Woman, the only all-benevolent Navajo god, who created humans and gave them maize. Other gods include the Wind and Thunder People, who possess both negative and positive qualities.

Around AD 1600, or possibly even earlier, the Iroquois tribes established a confederation on the model of their tribal council, probably as a result of pressures from neighboring Algonkian-speaking tribes together with their new French allies. The confederacy, or League of the Iroquois, operated through a council composed of fifty *sachems* (chiefs) drawn from the five tribes. Each position was hereditary in a particular lineage, with the women nominating the holder of the chieftainship (always a man) who was then installed by the council. Each tribe voted as a unit, and the League could only act when the members were unanimous. Highly successful at first, the confederation broke up when the tribes could not agree on whom to support in the Revolutionary War.

The Iroquois had a number of major religious ceremonies centered on sacred masks, carved from wood, which were kept in the longhouse. The ceremonies were concerned with the agricultural cycle or with the curing of illness, and a major festival took place at midwinter to celebrate the arrival of the new year. At the death of a *sachem* the League conducted a condolence ceremony and ritually installed his successor.

The Iroquois were initially successful in controlling the fur trade, and aided the British against the French. But with the defeat of the British forces by the Americans in the Revolutionary War, those who had sided with the British fled to Canada and in 1780 they were given lands on the Grand river, where they still reside. Those who remained in the United States were granted small reservations in the 1890s. In the period of disorganization following the destruction of their communities in New York State, the Iroquois became very demoralized and abuse of alcohol was a serious problem. But in about 1800, a new religious movement arose, called the Handsome Lake religion, after its founder, who claimed to have received a revelation from the Great Spirit. Handsome Lake preached a return to Iroquois values and a modification of agriculture and social life, with the men taking a more responsible role than they had done traditionally. This had the beneficial effect of satisfying the missionaries and officials who were now in charge. Today the Handsome Lake teachings form the basis for the longhouse religion of the non-Christian Iroquois, both in Canada and on their small reservations in New York State. In recent years the Iroquois have been in the forefront of the Indian cultural renaissance, struggling to maintain their lands in the face of development projects and to revitalize the longhouse as a symbol of their governing council.

The Navajo Tribe

The Navajo Indians, who now reside on a reservation of almost 6.5 million hectares (16 million acres) in northern Arizona and New Mexico, are currently the largest American Indian tribe, numbering 130,000 or more. Their ancestors, like those of the Apaches, were Athapaskan-speaking hunters in what today is southern Canada, who migrated to the southern plains and adjacent mountain regions of the southwest, arriving in about AD 1500. Once there, they gradually differentiated into separate tribes, some remaining in the plains as typical buffalo hunters and others, like the Chiricahua and Mescalero Apache, adapting to the resources of the various southwestern environments. The Navajo rapidly learned agricultural skills from their Pueblo neighbors, and the *Apaches de Navaju*

Amerindian rights
Walter Echo Hawke is a Pawnee and a qualified attorney. He works for the Native American Rights Fund, in Boulder, Colorado, and is seen here studying a child custody dispute involving an American Indian woman. The progress of American Indians toward determining their own way of life in modern America has been somewhat erratic. The attempts of the US government to cater for Indian culture within the wider society culminated in 1970 in the granting to reservation Indians the right to choose and administer their own system of government and implement their own education, health and antipoverty programs. This has had some success, but the dissemination of information about rights in a broader sense is often difficult.

New homes from old
In the Hollywood image of the American West all Indians live in teepees, but this type of tent—a conical framework of poles covered with about 20 buffalo hides—was, in fact, only used by the Plains Indians. A great variety of house designs were seen among other North American Indians. Homes were built from wood, earth or mud. Adobe—mud mixed with straw, molded into bricks and dried in the sun—was used by the Pueblo Indians to construct their impressive villages. Traditional houses still predominate on many reservations and here a Seminole woman, living in Ochopee in the Florida Everglades, strips bark from logs to construct a tent. Bark covered the tents of many tribes, while the Iroquois used bark to build their longhouses.

Fire brigade
The Allegany Indian Reservation Fire Department is a volunteer fire-fighting service run by Seneca Indians. Although based on the reservation, the service is extended to the nearby city of Salamanca, New York State. The Department also runs an ambulance to ferry Seneca Indians to the hospital in Salamanca. This service, established about 6 years ago, has contributed to the process of assimilating the Seneca into American society. Too often, however, the Indians feel bitter and alienated, particularly because their employment prospects are limited.

are first described in 1626 as living in the Chama valley of northern New Mexico and cultivating "broad fields" in the Pueblo manner. Archaeologists have now confirmed this seventeenth-century Navajo settlement.

During the seventeenth and eighteenth centuries the Navajos raided both Pueblo and Spanish settlements, obtaining horses and sheep, and traded with the Eastern Pueblo Indians for pottery and woven cloth. When the Pueblo Revolt of 1680–92 temporarily drove the Spaniards out of New Mexico, Pueblo refugees from Spanish reprisals fled to the mountains and joined the Navajo communities. During this period there was considerable intermarriage and the Navajos adopted weaving and pottery making and added Pueblo elements to their matrilineal clan system. They also borrowed Pueblo ceremonies and myths, adapting them to their own purposes.

During the eighteenth and nineteenth centuries the Navajo were gradually forced westward by Spanish attacks, but the Spaniards finally withdrew as a result of the Mexican Revolution of 1821. The United States took over New Mexico and the government set about pacifying the Navajo and Apache raiders. This was finally accomplished by Colonel "Kit" Carson in 1864, when some 8,000 Navajos were rounded up and incarcerated for four years at Bosque Redondo. In 1868 a treaty was signed with the Navajo allowing them to return to a portion of their old reservation and to continue their pastoral and agricultural activities.

In the century since their return, the Navajo have grown tenfold in population and have developed new occupations, such as weaving fine blankets and rugs, and working in silver. Today their large reservation can only support about half of their total population and many Navajos live and work in neighboring cities. On the reservation areas, which have been added to periodically, Navajo life has retained much of its native character. They hold on to their language tenaciously and live in native-style housing in extended family groups, centered on a head woman and her daughters. Sheep herding and subsistence agriculture are important and the traditional crops—maize, beans and squash (marrowlike vegetables)—are still the main ones grown, although fodder crops are now produced to be sold for cash.

The sixty or more matrilineal clans provide a means of organizing the larger population, and their ceremonial system centers on rituals for the restoration of harmony between man and nature. The Navajo have some fifty ceremonial chants for curing illness. These may last as long as nine days and are carried out by singers, who learn them by a long apprenticeship.

In the 1920s the Navajo were encouraged to develop a Tribal Council and were aided in exploiting the mineral resources, including oil, coal and uranium, which have been found on their reservation. The Navajo were active in World War II and after the war became more interested in education for their children. Today, with excellent leadership, they are making progress in solving their own problems with the aid of the government, while maintaining their language and their essential values.

Canada and the United States 1

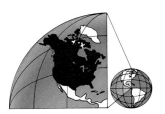

"Give me your tired, your poor, your huddled masses yearning to breathe free ..." Escaping the confines of tradition, class privilege and bigotry, European settlers came to America in untold millions to build society anew. With abundant resources and economic liberty they created a nation whose wealth, technology and power are unrivalled in the modern world.

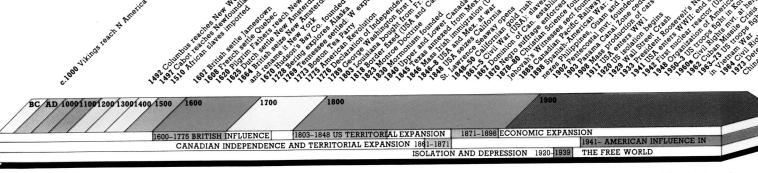

c.1000 Vikings reach N America
1492 Columbus reaches New World
1497 Cabot reaches Newfoundland
1510 African slaves imported
1607 British settle Jamestown
1608 French settle Quebec
1620 Pilgrim Fathers reach New England
1625 Dutch settle New Amsterdam
1664 British seize New Amsterdam and rename it New York
1670 Hudson's Bay Co. founded
1728 Bering explores Alaska
1769 Tennessee settled; W expansion
1773 Boston Tea Party
1775 American Revolution
1776 Declaration of Independence
1789 George Washington first Pres.
1803 Louisiana bought from Fr. by USA
1818 Border fixed (USA and Can.)
1823 Monroe Doctrine
1830 Mormonism founded
1840 Upper and Lower Canada united
1845 Texas annexed from Mex. by USA
1846-8 USA and Mex. at war
1848 USA seizes California
1848-50 Californian gold rush
1861-5 Civil War (USA); slavery abol.
1867 Dominion of Can. established
1870 Negro suffrage enforced
1878-80 Christian Science founded
1885 Canadian Pacific Railway runs
1895 Jehovah's Witnesses sect founded
1898 Spanish-American War; USA an-nexes Philippines, Guam and Puerto Rico
1902 Pentecostal mvt. founded (USA)
1903 Panama Canal Zone ceded to USA
1908 Mass production of cars (USA)
1917 USA enters WWI
1920 US isolation begins
1929 Wall Street Crash
1933 President Roosevelt's New Deal
1941 USA enters WWII; end of isolation
1942 First nuclear reactor (USA)
1948 Organization of American States
1950-3 US troops fight in Korean War
1960s Civil Rights mvt. at height
1962 Cuban Missile Crisis
1963-73 US troops fight in Vietnam War
1964 Civil Rights Bill
1973 Detente with China

BC AD 100 1000 1100 1200 1300 1400 1500 1600 1700 1800 1900

1600–1775 BRITISH INFLUENCE
1803–1848 US TERRITORIAL EXPANSION
1871–1898 ECONOMIC EXPANSION
CANADIAN INDEPENDENCE AND TERRITORIAL EXPANSION 1861–1871
1941– AMERICAN INFLUENCE IN
ISOLATION AND DEPRESSION 1920–1939 THE FREE WORLD

Population by Region
Total: 218 million

W USA 15%
S USA 28%
NE USA 21%
E CANADA 7%
W CANADA 2%
N Central USA 25%
Atlantic (Can.) 1%
Prairies (Can.) 1%

Population by Religion
Minority religions 47%

R. Catholicism 25%
Protestantism 26%
E.O. 2%

The vast fertile lands of North America presented themselves to the early colonists as a virtually empty country, where society could be built anew, free from the shackles of privilege, prejudice and tradition they had left behind in Europe. Such freedom nurtured the development of a capitalist economy and this, combined with the natural riches of the continent, have made the United States and Canada two of the wealthiest nations on earth. With wealth has come power, and the United States, a newly emerged nation of small farmers only 300 years ago, now exerts influence over millions of people far beyond its national boundaries.

The area of the United States is 9,500,280 square kilometers (3,678,896 square miles) including Alaska and Hawaii. In this expansive geographic area there is tremendous variation in the climate, from the bitter cold of the central plains, where the temperature often falls to between $-30°$ and $-45°C$ ($-25°$ to $-50°F$) in January, to the deserts of the southwest, where the midday temperature in July may be $40°C$ ($105°F$) or higher. Tornadoes, hurricanes, blizzards, floods and droughts are all experienced, but despite these hazards the land is amazingly productive and the United States and Canada are suppliers of grain to the world. Canada's geographic area is even greater than that of the United States, with an area of 10 million square kilometers (3,830,000 square miles), although much of this is barren arctic waste—or so it was regarded before its vast mineral wealth was discovered.

The first Europeans to settle in North America were Spaniards pushing north and west from what is now Mexico, and Frenchmen who moved southwest from Nova Scotia to establish trading posts, such as Quebec in 1608. By 1663 the French territories were made into a royal colony and named New France. The first effective English settlement was at Jamestown, Virginia, in 1607, and English colonists drove a wedge into the continent from the Middle Atlantic states, eventually confining the French to Quebec and Montreal. They surrendered in 1759 and all Canada passed into British hands. Colonial America was overwhelmingly English despite the presence of other Europeans and a large population of African slaves.

English colonization was firmly based in the production of crops for the European market—tobacco, indigo, cotton, rice and sugar—or in the production of goods and services to support the slave plantations of the Caribbean—codfish, lumber and ships. By the late eighteenth century, however, they had developed enough local craft production and nascent industry to be on the way to economic self-sufficiency. The thirteen colonies were able to join together against Britain, and fight a successful revolutionary war, because they already had a sound economy.

The United States, formally created by the Constitutional Convention of 1787, was not a homogenous nation, economically or socially. There were considerable differences between the Puritan settlements of the north (which had started with the landing of the *Mayflower* in Massachusetts in 1620) and the plantation colonies of the south, with their aristocratic life style and their slave-based economy. Conflict between the north and the south was nothing new, but by the 1850s it began to move inexorably toward a confrontation on the question of whether slavery could be introduced into new states as they were added to the Union.

Civil war broke out in April 1861 and at the end of the war, in 1865, slavery was abolished, sending the south into a long period of economic decline from which it has only recently begun to recover. Meanwhile, the northern industrial economy, fueled by the westward expansion of the rail network and the remarkable burst of technological innovation in the late nineteenth century, was not halted until the great depression of the 1930s. This halt proved to be only temporary, but it led to the massive growth of government regulation and social legislation which is being questioned as contrary to the spirit of free enterprise.

Originally the United States was largely a farming nation, but agriculture has become steadily more efficient until it employs a very small proportion of the population. Farm workers today form a mere 2.8 percent of the total population compared with 25 percent in 1930 and almost 90 percent in 1770. Similarly the proportion of workers engaged in the "blue collar" categories (craft and factory workers, and nonfarm laborers) has fallen steadily until now they comprise only one third of the work force. The United States is a wealthy country with a per capita gross national

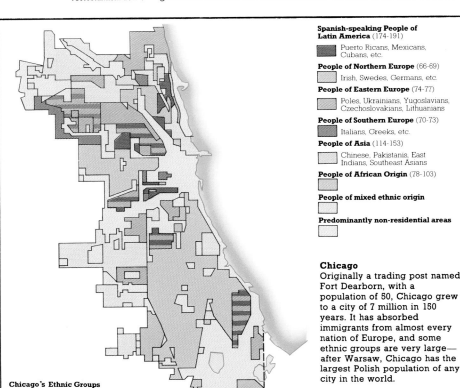

Spanish-speaking People of Latin America (174-191)
- Puerto Ricans, Mexicans, Cubans, etc.

People of Northern Europe (66-69)
- Irish, Swedes, Germans, etc.

People of Eastern Europe (74-77)
- Poles, Ukrainians, Yugoslavians, Czechoslovakians, Lithuanians

People of Southern Europe (70-73)
- Italians, Greeks, etc.

People of Asia (114-153)
- Chinese, Pakistanis, East Indians, Southeast Asians

People of African Origin (78-103)

People of mixed ethnic origin

Predominantly non-residential areas

Chicago
Originally a trading post named Fort Dearborn, with a population of 50, Chicago grew to a city of 7 million in 150 years. It has absorbed immigrants from almost every nation of Europe, and some ethnic groups are very large—after Warsaw, Chicago has the largest Polish population of any city in the world.

Chicago's Ethnic Groups

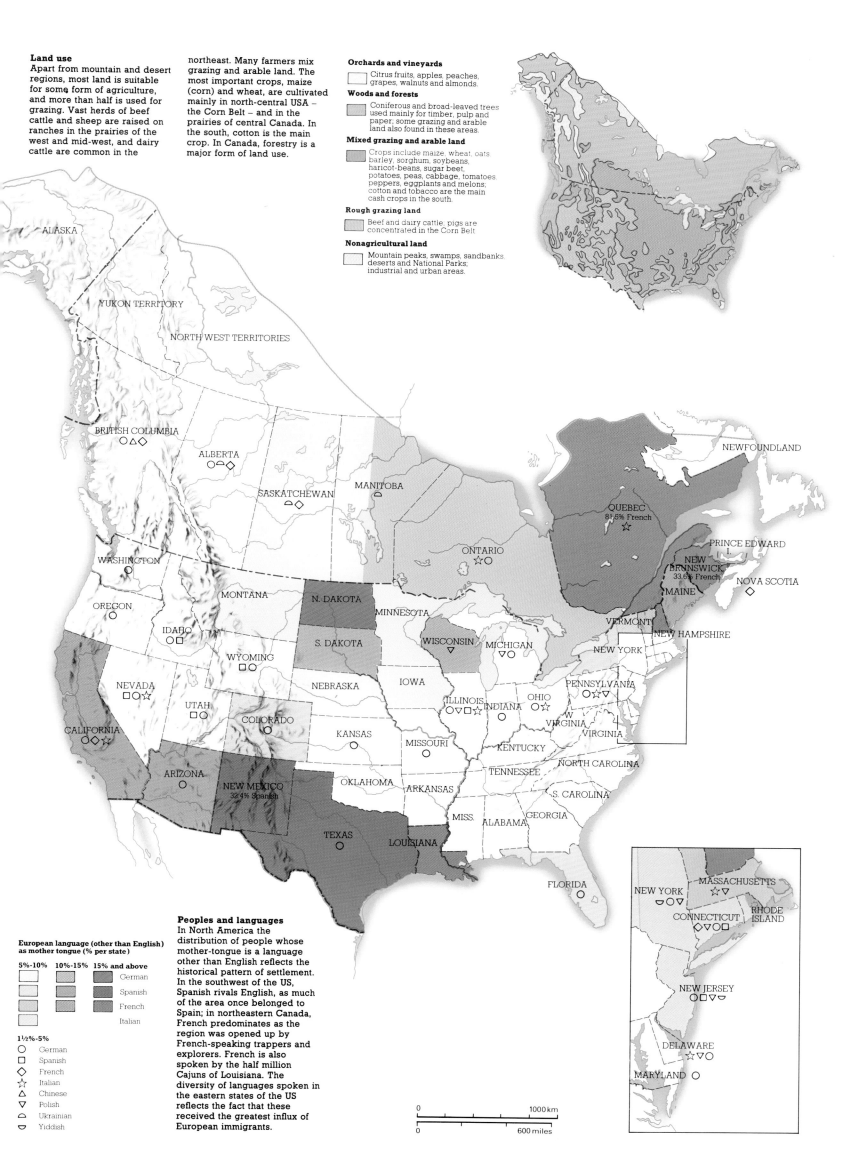

Land use
Apart from mountain and desert regions, most land is suitable for some form of agriculture, and more than half is used for grazing. Vast herds of beef cattle and sheep are raised on ranches in the prairies of the west and mid-west, and dairy cattle are common in the northeast. Many farmers mix grazing and arable land. The most important crops, maize (corn) and wheat, are cultivated mainly in north-central USA – the Corn Belt – and in the prairies of central Canada. In the south, cotton is the main crop. In Canada, forestry is a major form of land use.

Orchards and vineyards
Citrus fruits, apples, peaches, grapes, walnuts and almonds.

Woods and forests
Coniferous and broad-leaved trees used mainly for timber, pulp and paper; some grazing and arable land also found in these areas.

Mixed grazing and arable land
Crops include maize, wheat, oats, barley, sorghum, soybeans, haricot-beans, sugar beet, potatoes, peas, cabbage, tomatoes, peppers, eggplants and melons; cotton and tobacco are the main cash crops in the south.

Rough grazing land
Beef and dairy cattle; pigs are concentrated in the Corn Belt

Nonagricultural land
Mountain peaks, swamps, sandbanks, deserts and National Parks; industrial and urban areas.

European language (other than English) as mother tongue (% per state)

5%-10%   10%-15%   15% and above
German
Spanish
French
Italian

1½%-5%
○ German
□ Spanish
◇ French
☆ Italian
△ Chinese
▽ Polish
⌒ Ukrainian
▽ Yiddish

Peoples and languages
In North America the distribution of people whose mother-tongue is a language other than English reflects the historical pattern of settlement. In the southwest of the US, Spanish rivals English, as much of the area once belonged to Spain; in northeastern Canada, French predominates as the region was opened up by French-speaking trappers and explorers. French is also spoken by the half million Cajuns of Louisiana. The diversity of languages spoken in the eastern states of the US reflects the fact that these received the greatest influx of European immigrants.

QUEBEC
81.5% French

NEW BRUNSWICK
33.6% French

NEW MEXICO
32.4% Spanish

0   1000 km
0   600 miles

Canada and the United States 2

product in 1979 of $10,630—higher than any country except West Germany, Sweden and Switzerland, and fifty-five times that of India. However, income is unevenly distributed so that about 12 percent of individuals were living below the poverty level in 1979.

Both Canada and the United States, but particularly the latter, have been sustained from the first by the idea of a new beginning, and by an optimism which assumes that all problems are capable of rational solution in a world which can be made ever more perfect. This utopianism has survived to the present, although it has been hard pressed to contain the trauma of industrial development and the diversity created by the immigration of millions of people.

The nineteenth century saw a fresh wave of immigration to the United States which brought some nine million people from the British Isles and northern Europe between 1820 and 1880; a great many of these were Irish peasants fleeing from the horrors of famine in their homeland. Another twenty-three million came between 1880 and 1930, but northern Europeans were now outnumbered by east Europeans, Italians, Greeks, Spaniards and Portuguese. Since 1924, immigration has been at much lower levels, but it has further diversified the population, bringing in Cubans, Puerto Ricans, Mexicans, Chinese, Japanese and Vietnamese.

Language use is a sensitive index of assimilation and in the United States non-English-speaking immigrants quickly adopted English, and the use of their original languages, even in the home, fell off sharply in the generation born in the United States. The same has been true in Canada, but here the original French population have retained their own language. Because of the stagnation of the Canadian economy and the absence of significant industrialization, the French population has largely remained in conservative rural Catholic communities. An upsurge of French nationalist sentiment after World War II threatened to take Quebec out of the confederation, and an uneasy compromise which recognizes Canada to be a bilingual state has not altered the fact that only 13.4 percent of the population is bilingual, most of them French Canadians who also speak English.

The normal American family is on the whole independent of wider kinship units, both residentially and economically, and thus well suited to life in a society where mobility is necessary. At the same time the family is emotionally supportive, providing a "haven in a heartless world." The mother plays an important role as the focus of emotional ties, in contrast to the competitive, male-dominated working world.

Almost every immigrant group went through a phase when its family life was considered to be disorganized, and it is currently the blacks who are going through this phase. A higher proportion of blacks than whites live in poverty, with high unemployment, substandard housing and poor education—conditions which foster teenage pregnancy and marital separation, creating large numbers of female-headed households. At the same time there is an increasing proportion of black families following middle-class norms and even moving out of the cities into the suburbs.

Some aspects of contemporary middle-class family life, however, are coming to look more like the supposedly disorganized patterns of the lower class. There are significant increases in the divorce rate, in the number of children born out of wedlock and in the number of couples living together without being married. But rising divorce rates do not signal a lessening of Americans' belief in family life, and the rates of family formation and remarriage remain high. It is the belief that the family should be based upon the personal love relationship of husband and wife that induces people to abandon the marriage when they are no longer "in love."

If patterns of family life converge upon an American type the same is true of religion. Widespread participation in religious organizations (many of which are ethnically differentiated) is being accompanied, paradoxically, by a progressive secularization of belief and even ignorance of religious content. The Bible is ubiquitous. Jews maintain active synagogues and many have increased their commitment to religious doctrine. Many Roman Catholics increasingly question the infal-

libility of the Pope and approve of birth control, but these opinions do not keep them from church.

In spite of widespread church membership and repeated outbreaks of enthusiasm and new sect formation, some writers argue that religiosity in America converges upon a broad national "civil" religion. Expressed through churches and recognizing a transcendent God, it nevertheless draws upon American history for its revered events and personages—the Declaration of Independence, the Constitution, the Gettysburg Address, Memorial Day, George Washington, Abraham Lincoln, John Kennedy and even the Moon Landing.

The people of Chicago

The city of Chicago displays the peculiar quality of American life to advantage. It sprang up almost overnight. In 1830 only fifty people lived in a fort and trading post at the silted up mouth of the Chicago River on the shores of Lake Michigan. By 1937 the river had been opened up and Chicago was becoming the main center for the collection and shipping of the products of midwestern agriculture. All the main transcontinental rail routes which developed in the 1870s ran through Chicago, encouraging it to become a major industrial as well as trading area, and it received its

Spaghetti junction
Interconnecting flyovers, like this one in San Francisco, are the hallmark of most North American cities. American society places a huge emphasis on mobility and is first among world car manufacturers; 83% of all families own a car and 28% own two or more cars. The number of motor vehicles registered between 1940 and 1970 has more than tripled from 32 million to 108 million. In metropolitan areas 7 out of 10 trips are made in private cars, which are used for even the shortest trips. Such mobility has stimulated the growth of sprawling suburbs, dispersing the community and creating cities with no real center.

Sweet choice
A small child presented with a multiple choice of sweet-vending machines, unerringly homes in on the "right" brand. In common with children in other wealthy, industrialized nations, American children are a prime target of the television advertisers, and at an early age they are familiar with a range of products such as electronic toys, food and clothes. Presented with a panoramic range of glossy artifacts, and imbued with the belief that what is new, clean and shiny is better than what is old, they expect a constant supply of new things, irrespective of whether their parents can afford them.

The floating forest
This logging camp on the Campbell River in British Columbia uses the river to float the cut timber downstream to the saw mills or pulp mills. Without the rivers Canada's logging industry would not be economically viable. Processing the timber actually in the forests would not be feasible, since the harsh weather would prevent work in winter and there would be the problem of transporting the finished products to the cities. Canada's coniferous forest covers 4.4 million square km (1.7 million square miles) or nearly one half of the total land area. Canadian timber production is amongst the highest in the world and Canadian pulp is estimated to supply half the newspapers in Europe and North America. Douglas fir, the major economic species in British Columbia, has been overexploited in the past, but better forest management techniques have now been introduced in most regions.

Green parade
March 17th—St Patrick's Day—is widely celebrated in the USA. Like other ethnic groups, the Irish have become part of the American "melting pot," and real cultural differences, separating them from other groups, have long since disappeared. Nevertheless, the idea of ethnicity and separate identity is cherished because of the political power wielded by ethnic minorities. Originally formed by immigrants for mutual support, the ethnic communities became pools of votes to be mobilized by politicians in exchange for practical help, thus creating the city political machines.

share of immigrant labor from Europe. When foreign immigration diminished after 1915, Chicago became a major destination for blacks moving from the south, a trend not reversed until the 1970s. By 1980 the population of the greater metropolitan area was 7,058,000, and of the three million people living in the city itself about 40 percent were black.

Chicago's leading citizens are justifiably proud of the city's progress over the past 150 years. Its museums, architecture, symphony orchestra, opera companies, hospitals, universities and scientific research centers are among the best in the world and they have been financed by the proceeds of industry and trade. The business elite has always been largely White Anglo-Saxon Protestant (WASP) and they resided originally in luxurious houses built in the city after the great fire of 1871. Some remain in the "Gold Coast," a

sector of high-income housing along the lakefront, but most have moved out to create exclusive suburbs to the north of the city.

At the lower end of the status scale, ethnic clustering of immigrants was typical in the nineteenth century, as can be seen in maps drawn up in 1895. These show that within a typical low-income section there were representatives of fourteen different ethnic groups, all living in close proximity. Today ethnic neighborhoods are more segregated as a result of secondary movement, which took place once people became more prosperous. Different groups were established around churches or synagogues, supposedly to preserve national culture and community life. But it was precisely within these communities that language loss occurred, religion became more secular and family life was Americanized, for people did not live in isolation. They were drawn into the discipline of industrial labor and the cultural influence of state schools.

Black migrants have had a very different experience since racial discrimination has, until very recently, kept them confined within the area of their original settlement. Beginning from a small area just south of the vice district, the city-within-a-city occupied by blacks grew as the pressure of population made it desirable for whites to sell property in neighboring areas. However, the large expansion in the period during and after World War I was not accomplished without race riots, bombings and signs of racial hostility. Black reaction to discrimination produced extreme forms of separatist sentiment, embodied in such movements as Garvey's Back to Africa movement in the 1920s and Elijah Muhammad's Black Muslim movement in the 1950s and 1960s. But this has not represented the aspirations of many blacks, and indeed these movements have generally reversed their aims over time. Since blacks were some of the earliest immigrants to America they were among the first to become assimilated into the developing national culture. At the same time, a black subculture was created out of the experience of segregation. Its basis was the folk culture of black slaves, sharecroppers and industrial workers—their speech, music, religion, art and cuisine—and the literature of the black intelligentsia.

In spite of all their difficulties, many blacks have prospered and provided community leadership, which shows clearly that their aims and values are in the mainstream of the nation. The late Martin Luther King Jr has joined the pantheon of national heroes. In Chicago the annual Bud Billiken's Day parade, originally devised to honor black newspaper delivery boys, is now comparable to St Patrick's Day parade and not even an Irish mayor would miss it.

The big dipper
Since 1830, when the Mormon Church was founded, the USA has witnessed the birth of a great number of minority faiths. The Calvary Church is one of the more recent Christian offshoots. Founded in 1970, it shares certain characteristics with the Fundamentalist and Evangelical Churches. The Calvary Church is situated on the Costa Mesa on the Pacific Ocean and to become a member of this Church, initiates have to be baptized. This is not the usual sprinkling with water but requires complete immersion—fully clothed—in the sea. These group baptisms take place 4 or 5 times a year—during the fine weather.

South and Central America

The great land mass that stretches from the banks of the Rio Grande in the north to the rugged cliffs of Tierra del Fuego in the south possesses, despite its geographical and ethnic diversity, a unity that is represented by its name—Latin America. Throughout this vast area (except for those places where the French, Dutch and British gained small footholds, in the Caribbean and the Guianas), Spanish and Portuguese influence has been supreme, and their languages remain an important unifying factor.

The Spaniards, from their first settlements in the Antilles at the end of the fifteenth century, conquered and colonized Mexico, Central America and the Andean countries, spreading southward until checked in Chile by the Araucanian Indians, a people who had also set the limit to Inca expansion in that direction. A second Spanish movement, starting from the east coast, embraced the lowland region which is divided

today between Argentina, Uruguay and Paraguay. Meanwhile, the Portuguese (whose right to settle in South America arose from a mistake in the 1494 Treaty of Tordesillas, which was designed to partition the world between the two Iberian powers) colonized the coast of Brazil.

The Spanish and Portuguese were faced with very different types of society and terrain. The highlands of Mexico, Central America and the Andes were the homes of civilizations—Aztec, Maya and Inca—which in many respects were as advanced as those of the Old World. The conquests of these states, although extraordinary feats of arms, proved relatively easy once control was gained over the central authority, since the administration of the whole state then fell into the conquistadors' hands. Although rebellions by native peoples were not uncommon, Spanish control was never seriously threatened until the early nineteenth century wars of independence, which were instigated by those of Spanish descent. In lowland South America, and to a lesser extent in the Caribbean, the problems facing colonialists were very different. In this area, not simply each tribe, but often each settlement, was an autonomous unit and had to be dealt with individually so that control over the lowlands was only achieved in a piecemeal fashion.

The size of the Indian population when Columbus arrived in 1492 is unknown, and estimates vary widely, so that it is impossible to give an accurate figure for the reduction in numbers which occurred following the European conquest. However, the loss of life was very great, and some authorities estimate that 95 percent of the indigenous population died. The reasons for this disastrous decline include warfare and slavery, but above all it resulted from diseases, such as smallpox, measles and influenza, which the Europeans brought with them and to which the Amerindians had no resistance. The present-day distribution of Amerindians in the Caribbean and Latin America is very uneven. In the regions most densely populated in preconquest times—Mexico, Central America and the Andes—there remains a large, and in places growing, Amerindian component in the population. Thus the living descendants of the Maya still inhabit their traditional homelands, and in the central Andes the language of the Incas is kept alive by Quechua peasants. But in the Caribbean, the first area to suffer the brunt of European intrusion, no pure-blooded Indians survive, and this is equally true of the coastlands of Brazil and the grasslands of Argentina and Uruguay. In the more infertile and inhospitable regions, such as the Gran Chaco, a greater number of Indians is found, and in the remoter parts of the Amazonian forest there are still a few Indians carrying on a traditional way of life. However, in most places where the Indians have survived physically they have at the same time suffered cultural loss, and today are barely distinguishable from the mestizo peasants. Their way of life is now a blend of traditional customs and those learned from four centuries of Spanish contact.

The ethnic mosaic

The ethnic and racial composition of Latin America has become yet more complex as immigrants from all over the world have poured into the area. Some were brought forcibly, such as the African slaves, shipped across the Atlantic in their hundreds of thousands, to work in sugar plantations in the West Indies and Brazil. Today, the descendants of these slaves form an important component of the population in many areas, and a few, such as the Maroons or Bush Negroes of Surinam, who are descended from escaped slaves, have retained much of their original African culture. Others came willingly but did not necessarily plan to stay. These included the Asian indentured laborers who were brought in following the abolition of slavery; their descendants make up over half the population of the Republic of Guyana, a former British colony. Of their own freewill, and keen to make a fresh start in this new world, came Germans, Italians, Scandinavians and migrants from most parts of Europe. In the last few decades many immigrants have come from the Far East, particularly from Japan, and these people have prospered in both rural and urban areas. It has not been unusual for those of the same nationality to form colonies where much of their traditional language and culture has survived—the Welsh-speaking community of Patagonia is a striking example of this.

The peoples of Latin America and the Caribbean thus form a mosaic of many different ethnic and racial elements. The contrasts in ways of life, too, are striking. In the cities, modern office blocks, factories and villas are flanked by ornate seventeenth-century Spanish houses and surrounded by the makeshift dwellings of the urban poor. In the forest, the Amerindian in his village clearing may look up to see a jet airliner bound for another continent, carrying passengers who are his compatriots, yet who inhabit an entirely different world and have no understanding of his culture.

Pilgrims at the shrine of Christ of the Snow Star in the Andes

Mexico and Guatemala

In this region were born the most impressive civilizations of ancient America. On the central Mexican plateau, the bloodthirsty but splendid empire of the Aztecs flourished, while to the east the Mayan Empire fostered the study of astronomy and complex mathematics. Today a vigorous mestizo culture combines ancient and modern elements in a uniquely colorful society.

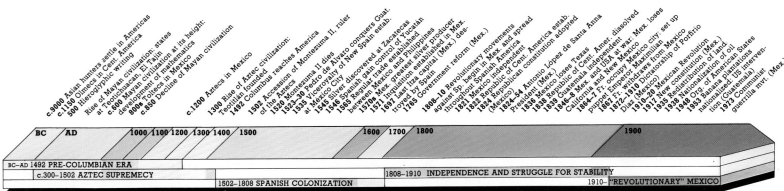

Timeline events:
c.9000 Asian hunters settle in Americas
c.1150 Olmecs in Cent. America
500 Hieroglyphic writing
Rise of Mayan civilization: states at Teotihuacan, El Tajin
c.600 Mayan civilization at its height: development of mathematics
800s Toltecs in Mexico
c.850 Decline of Mayan civilization
c.1200 Aztecs in Mexico
1300 Rise of Aztec civilization: Teotitlán founded
1492 Columbus reaches America
1502 Accession of Montezuma II, ruler of the Aztecs
1520 Montezuma II dies
1523–30 Pedro de Alvaro conquers Guat.
1535 Mexico City: Viceroyalty of New Spain estab.
1545 Silver discovered at Zacatecas
1546 Spanish gain control of Yucatán
1565 Regular trade established between Mex. and Philippines
1570s Mex. greatest silver producer
1571 Inquisition established in Mex.
1697 Last Itza capital (Mex.) destroyed by Spain
1765 Government reform (Mex.)
1808–10 Revolutionary movements against Sp. begin in Mex. and spread throughout Spanish America
1821 Mexico independent
1822 Republic of Cent. America estab. (Mexico)
1824 Republican constitution adopted
1824–54 Antonio López de Santa Anna President (Mex.)
1836 Mexico loses Texas
1838 Republic of Cent. Amer. dissolved
1839 Guatemala independent
1846–8 Mex. and USA at war: Mex. loses California and New Mexico
1864–7 Ft. occupy Mexico city: set up puppet Emperor Maximilian (Mex.)
1867 Ft. withdraws from Mexico
1872–1910 Dictatorship of Porfirio Diaz (Mexico)
1910–20 Mexican Revolution
1917 New constitution (Mex.)
1935 Redistribution of land
1938 Nationalization of oil
1948 Org. of American States
1953 Banana plantations nationalized: US intervention in Guatemala
1973 Communist guerrilla mvt. (Mex.)

Timeline periods:
BC–AD 1492 PRE-COLUMBIAN ERA
c.300–1502 AZTEC SUPREMECY
1502–1808 SPANISH COLONIZATION
1808–1910 INDEPENDENCE AND STRUGGLE FOR STABILITY
1910– "REVOLUTIONARY" MEXICO

Population by Country
Total: 75 million

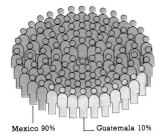

Mexico 90%   Guatemala 10%

Population by Religion

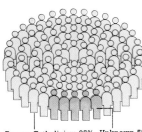

Roman Catholicism 95%   Unknown 5%

Rituals of the past
Many Mexican villages celebrate fiestas which involve colorful processions. These Totonac Indians are taking part in the fiesta of Corpus Christi at Popantla. In a later stage of the ceremony, 5 participants will climb to the top of a 30m (100 ft) pole. One plays a drum on a tiny platform while the 4 others leap head first toward the earth, having first secured themselves to the pole by means of a rope around the waist. The ropes are coiled around the top of the pole, and as they slowly unwind the dancers describe graceful circles around the pole, their arms outstretched like birds' wings. This strange ritual predates the arrival of the Spanish conquistadors but has been syncretized with Roman Catholic practice.

In central Mexico, the great chain of mountain ranges that extends from Alaska to Tierra del Fuego fans out to enclose a high plateau which has a pleasant, temperate climate. It was here that some of the most elaborate and hierarchical of ancient Amerindian civilizations arose, and here too that the Spanish invaders of the sixteenth century established the first strongholds of colonial rule. Today, Mexico, and its immediate neighbor Guatemala, lie midway between North and South America. Although themselves Spanish speaking, they have cultural links with both halves of the continent, and the technological development they have experienced in recent years is largely due to the economic influence of the United States.

This region is characterized by a great variety of climates, ranging from the aridity of the northern deserts to the high temperatures and humidity of the southern central zones. The best area for agriculture is the central Mexican plateau, and it is here that the greatest densities of population are found. The mountainous terrain limits agricultural production in southern Mexico and Guatemala and turns most rivers into unnavigable torrents, rushing through deep canyons.

While the first Amerindian settlers of this region were undoubtedly hunter-gatherers, the cultivation of maize seems to have begun some seven or eight thousand years ago. With the adoption of agriculture, permanent villages were established, the houses being built of sun-dried *adobe* bricks, similar to those still used by some Indians today. The people of these earliest settlements had a simple culture, but about 3,000 years ago they were succeeded by far more complex civilizations, such as that of the Olmecs, whose stone sculptures—gigantic heads weighing several tons—are found on the Gulf coast, particularly at Veracruz.

The Olmecs were followed by a string of other civilizations, notably the Zapotec, Mixtec, Toltec and Tarascan, which left behind them the ruins of gigantic ritual centers. In the last two centuries before the Spanish conquest, the Aztecs, descendants of a warlike northern people, overthrew surrounding tribes to create a vast empire covering much of the region.

The other great civilization of Mexico was that of the Maya, who dominated the Yucatán peninsula, southern Mexico, Guatemala and part of Honduras from about 2,500 years ago until the time of the Spanish conquest in the sixteenth century. The Maya were not only great builders but also highly skilled astronomers and mathematicians, and their achievements are all the more impressive for being based on a relatively simple economy. The Maya peasants practiced shifting cultivation of maize and vegetables, and after the decline of the splendid temple-cities (which began for unknown reasons before the arrival of the Spanish conquistadors) they continued this way of life.

The Spanish conquest of Mexico began in 1519 and in a surprisingly short space of time the vast Aztec Empire had been subdued. The country was given the name of New Spain and remained under the Spanish crown for three centuries, during which time many of the institutions and customs of modern Mexico were developed. The Spanish king also sent out groups of friars and through their efforts the majority of Indians were converted to Christianity.

In 1821 Mexican nationalists declared independence from Spain for both Mexico and Guatemala, but as there was no tradition of democracy, both countries were plagued by revolts and civil wars. Aggression from outside added to the problems—in 1846 the United States provoked a war which ended with the loss of almost half Mexico's territory. Even today, political upheaval continues to plague Guatemala, but since 1920 Mexico has been relatively peaceful, and has made great progress economically. It is now a modern country with an extensive network of roads and railroads, efficient airlines, ambitious projects of electrification and irrigation, and a booming oil industry. At the same time, there are still Indians living in much the same way as their ancestors did in the days of the Aztec and Maya Empires. Four-and-a-half centuries after the Spanish conquest there remain substantial populations who are Indian in race, culture and language, while *mestizos* (those of mixed ancestry) account for 70 to 75 percent of the total population.

Guatemalan market
The colorful clothes of these Guatemalan Indians combine traditional Indian styles with those of 17th-century Europe, acquired from the Spanish conquistadors. Every village has its own fashions and color combinations. Living in the central highlands, these descendants of the Maya scratch a meager living from tiny plots of land. Their crops include beans, squash, potatoes and maize, and their equipment is limited to hoes, machetes and digging sticks. Surplus crops are exchanged at the weekly village markets, where the products of local potters and weavers are also on sale. In spite of attempts at land reform, most peasants remain very poor. A mere 2% of landowners—Europeans and *mestizos*—own over 70% of the land, and commercial plantations account for much of the best farmland, producing coffee, bananas, sugar and cotton for export to North America.

Indians and mestizos of Mexico

The Indian groups of Mexico differ greatly in language, dress and customs, and in the extent to which they adhere to their traditions. There are still some groups of Mixtecs whose appearance and way of life have changed little since before the Spanish conquest. They live in simple *adobe* huts, work their fields with digging sticks, spin and weave their own cotton cloth, and have no domestic animals either for traction or the transport of goods. Normally the women go naked above the waist, and shoes are never worn. Maize is the staple food and is eaten mainly in the form of *tortillas*—unleavened bread.

In villages that are more closely linked to the market economy, however, the traditional Indian dress is often replaced by clothes approximating to the European fashions worn by *mestizos*—this change blurs outward distinctions and facilitates the Indians' integration with the *mestizo* population. Economic interaction with *mestizos*, and the influence of schools and non-Indian teachers, make some Indians wish to become part of the *mestizo* culture. The first steps in this direction, after the abandonment of the traditional dress, are the adoption of a different style of housing and the use of Spanish as the domestic language.

Indians and *mestizos* are not separated by rigid barriers and may be on friendly terms, but such relations are never those between equals, and this is reflected in attitudes to marriage. *Mestizos* tolerate the marriage of a *mestizo* with an Indian woman, since he can raise her to his own status, but disapprove of a *mestizo* girl marrying an Indian man.

The *mestizos* themselves, although conscious of their partly Indian ancestry, identify culturally with the European pattern of life. However, they have an ambivalent attitude to both their Indian and their Spanish heritage—three hundred years of colonial rule, during which numerous laws and royal decrees discriminated against *mestizos*, set up considerable antipathy to European domination. The leaders of the Revolution of 1911 did away with all such legal discrimination and even made some efforts to reverse the process of hispanicization by salvaging something of the indigenous civilization. Large funds are now devoted to the excavation and restoration of prehispanic monuments, and the modern Mexican is perhaps prouder of the architectural achievements of the Maya and the Zapotecs than of the Baroque churches gracing all major towns.

The great mass of the urban population in Mexico is of *mestizo* stock, and even the *mestizos* of rural areas have developed some urban traits. While the Indians, with their various distinct languages, stand for cultural regionalism, the *mestizos* represent an all-Mexican culture which is based on Spanish tradition and Catholicism, but prides itself nevertheless on a distinctly Mexican identity.

The racial mixture in Mexico is paralleled by a syncretism of ancient and new elements in the realm of belief, with pagan ideas adapted to Christian practices. While statues of Christ and the Virgin Mary are carried through Mixtec villages at Easter, the men put on fantastic masks and paint their bare bodies with ancient symbols and figures of animals. Ostensibly they represent Jews clamoring for the crucifixion of Christ, but they also symbolize the spirits and demons of the pagan past. Similarly the Aztec fascination with death survives in many present-day customs. In the days preceding the feasts of All Saints and All Souls skulls made from sugar and decorated with silver and gold leaf are sold in all the markets of Mexico. Sumptuous meals for the dead are prepared in many homes and placed on special altars, for on All Souls day the dead are believed to visit their old homes.

The Tarahumara are noted for their strenuous relay races, which may cover 300 km (200 miles). A rugged and taciturn people, they have preserved their ancient way of life by retreating into the most inhospitable mountain areas.

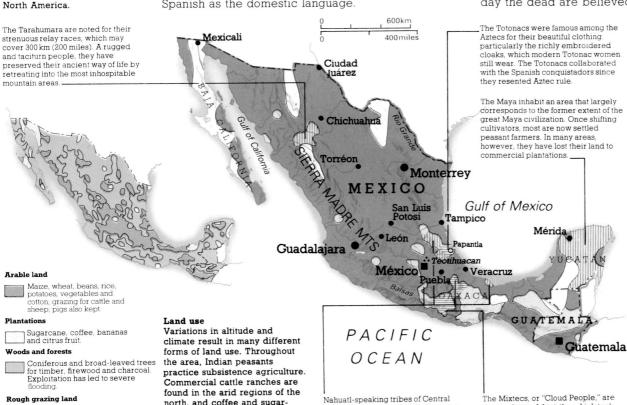

The Totonacs were famous among the Aztecs for their beautiful clothing, particularly the richly embroidered cloaks, which modern Totonac women still wear. The Totonacs collaborated with the Spanish conquistadors since they resented Aztec rule.

The Maya inhabit an area that largely corresponds to the former extent of the great Maya civilization. Once shifting cultivators, most are now settled peasant farmers. In many areas, however, they have lost their land to commercial plantations.

Peoples and languages
In Guatemala, 45% of the 6,800,000 population are of Indian descent and speak an Amerindian language, while the rest speak Spanish. In Mexico, however, Spanish is the main language and of a population of 67 million, only about 2¼ million people speak an Amerindian language; of these, about 1¼ million also speak Spanish. Many of those in the bilingual group are of solely Indian descent, although most mestizos living in Indian areas are familiar with the local Indian language. There are about 50 different Amerindian languages in this region. The largest Indian group is that of the Nahuatl-speaking tribes of the Mexican central plateau, whose language was once spoken by the Aztecs. The Zapotec and Mixtec languages survive in the region of Oaxaca.

Arable land

Maize, wheat, beans, rice, potatoes, vegetables and cotton; grazing for cattle and sheep; pigs also kept.

Plantations

Sugarcane, coffee, bananas and citrus fruit.

Woods and forests

Coniferous and broad-leaved trees for timber, firewood and charcoal. Exploitation has led to severe flooding.

Rough grazing land

Cattle in arid and semiarid areas.

Nonagricultural land

Mainly desert, swamps, mountain peaks, saltflats and lime-rich hardpans.

Land use
Variations in altitude and climate result in many different forms of land use. Throughout the area, Indian peasants practice subsistence agriculture. Commercial cattle ranches are found in the arid regions of the north, and coffee and sugarcane plantations in the south coastal zones. In the temperate climate of the central Mexican plateau many different grain and fruit crops flourish.

Nahuatl-speaking tribes of Central Mexico have preserved the language of the Aztec Empire. Another relic of their past is a belief in homeopathy, which features herbal steam baths, taken either individually or ceremonially in family groups.

The Mixtecs, or "Cloud People," are descendants of the tribe which took over the Oaxaca region after the decline of the Zapotecs in AD 1000. Their culture was noted for its superb craftsmanship in gold, silver and precious stones.

Indo–European

Romance language (Spanish)

Unaffiliated languages

"Amerindian" languages (Maya, Quiche, Mixtec, Zapotec, Otomi, Tarahumara, Nahuatl, Totonaco, etc.)

Featured people

Mestizos

Additional peoples

Central America and the Caribbean 1

On the Caribbean islands and the Central American isthmus, the peoples of the Americas, Europe and Africa have mingled to produced a vibrant, colorful Creole culture, whose vitality springs in part from their resistance to slavery and suffering. The legacy of those times remains in the crippling poverty that stems from economic dependence on cash crops such as sugarcane and bananas.

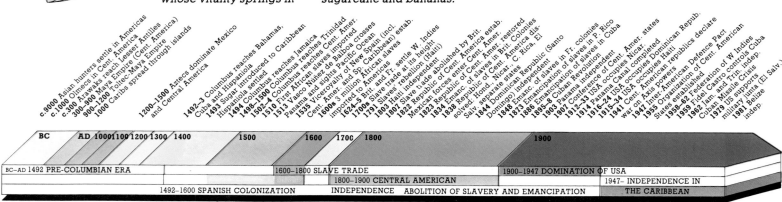

BC	AD 1000 1100 1200 1300 1400	1500	1600 170C 1800	1900

BC–AD 1492 PRE-COLUMBIAN ERA — 1600–1800 SLAVE TRADE — 1900–1947 DOMINATION OF USA
1800–1900 CENTRAL AMERICAN — 1947– INDEPENDENCE IN
1492–1600 SPANISH COLONIZATION — INDEPENDENCE — ABOLITION OF SLAVERY AND EMANCIPATION — THE CARIBBEAN

Population by Country
Total: 43 million

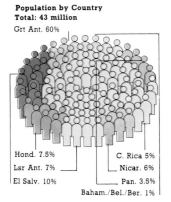

Grt Ant. 60%

Hond. 7.5% — C. Rica 5%
Lsr Ant. 7% — Nicar. 6%
El Salv. 10% — Pan. 3.5%
Baham./Bel./Ber. 1%

Population by Religion

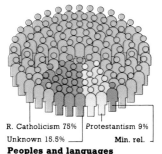

R. Catholicism 75% — Protestantism 9%
Unknown 15.5% — Min. rel.

Peoples and languages

People of African origin are numerically dominant; their languages are Afro-European creoles and they share a distinctive Caribbean culture. Not all creole languages are mutually intelligible, but most creole speakers are also fluent in the dominant European language. The descendants of Europeans form a separate group, as do the Asians, particularly Hindi and Tamil speakers. These Asians have resisted creole culture by retaining their languages and their Hindu or Islamic religion. Small groups of Amerindians survive, mainly in Central America.

Indo–European

Romance languages (Spanish, Papiamento, French, French Creole)

Germanic languages (English, English Creole)

Indo–Aryan language (Hindi)

Unaffiliated languages

"Amerindian" languages (Guaymi Miskito, Cuna, etc.)

Featured peoples

Garifuna
Mopan Maya

Additional peoples

The 2,000 Mopan Maya are the descendants of a sophisticated and learned civilization which, unlike other major civilizations, was based on shifting cultivation, without the use of the wheel, the plow or even beasts of burden. The Mopan Maya are still shifting cultivators but they have lost the best land to plantations, and are restricted to reservations in the less productive areas.

The 80,000 Garifuna, or "Black Carib," are the descendants of Carib Indians and escaped African slaves who inhabited Dominica and St Vincent but were transported to the Bay Islands off Honduras by the British in 1797 and from there spread to Central America. They now occupy coastlands stretching through three countries, but still speak the same language, Carib, and share a distinctive culture which combines African and indigenous elements. A few Black Caribs remained on St Vincent and their descendants are found there today, alongside Yellow Caribs, who are mainly of Indian descent. A small Black Carib population is also found on Trinidad where some fled after a volcano erupted on St Vincent in 1812.

GRAND BAHAMA IS
GREAT ABACO IS
ELEUTHERA IS
ANDROS
CAT IS
SAN SALVADOR
EXUMA
LONG ISLAND
ACKLINS ISLAND
THE BAHAMAS
CAICOS ISLAN

Havana   Matanzas   Santa Clara
Pinar del Río   CUBA
Yucatan Channel
Camagüey   Holguín
Baracoa
Santiago de Cuba   Cap-Haïtien
Gonaïves   HISPAN
Pue
Pla
DOMI
REP
San
Domingo
HAITI
Port-au-Prince

GREATER
CAYMAN IS
Montego Bay
JAMAICA   May Pen
Kingston
ANTIL
L

YUCATÁN PENINSULA

MEXICO

BELIZE   Belize

ISLAS DE LA BAHIA

CARIBBEAN

La Ceiba
San Pedro Sula
HONDURAS
San Salvador   Tegucigalpa
EL SALVADOR   San Miguel   Puerto Cabezas
León   NICARAGUA
Managua   L. de Managua
L. de Nicaragua
AR

PACIFIC

COSTA
Volcano de Chiriqui 3477
San Jose   RICA   Limón   Colón   CANAL ZONE
Volcano Irazu 3432   PA   Panama
David   NA   MA
Santiago   Gulf of Panama

0		600 km
0		400 miles

The contemporary peoples of the Caribbean and Lower Central America are the products of nearly five centuries of colonial domination. Although this vast tropical region is characterized by immense cultural, historical and environmental diversity, the countries within it all have the heritage of European colonialism in common. Some preconquest peoples survive today, but most of the population are of mixed ancestry, descended from Europeans, Africans and Asians.

The Caribbean islands, or West Indies, extend in a 3,000-kilometer (2,000-mile) arc from Venezuela to Cuba. They include the Greater Antilles (Cuba, Hispaniola, Jamaica and Puerto Rico), the Bahamas and the Lesser Antilles. Except for the Greater Antilles and Trinidad, all the islands are under 1,700 square kilometers (650 square miles) and most are much smaller than this. With a subtropical climate, the region boasts extensive fertile land suitable for agriculture.

The Caribbean coastal lowlands of Central America extend from Belize to Panama. This region receives high rainfall and is covered with heavy tropical vegetation. The cooler interior region of Lower Central America is mountainous, with interspersed plateaus and valleys, while the narrow Pacific coastal plain is relatively dry.

Despite the fertile land, widespread poverty is characteristic of the whole area. Today most rural people are poor peasant farmers or plantation laborers. Many areas are heavily overworked; and economic hardship, both in the towns and the countryside, is further exaggerated by extreme population density—as high as 600 per square kilometer (1,550 per square mile) on Barbados.

When Columbus and the Spanish conquerors arrived in 1492, they treated the indigenous people harshly. On Hispaniola it is estimated that, by 1540, the population had declined to less than 500 as a result of European diseases and slave labor. The Bahamas were raided for slaves and were severely depopulated by 1542, as were many other islands. Only a few isolated pockets of indigenous people survived in the Caribbean after the

The mixed blessing of tourism
Perfect beaches are one of the features that attract tourists to the Caribbean islands. Tourism in Jamaica provides seasonal employment, but much of the financial benefit is lost since most of the hotels are foreign owned. This is a common problem in the Caribbean, and one not confined to tourism. The colonial period created economies based on exporting a few agricultural commodities (notably sugar) which can fluctuate greatly in price. The islands produce few of their own basic requirements and none are self-sufficient in food, as a result they are crippled by massive import bills.

Indentured laborers from China, Java and India as well as Europe were brought to work on the plantations after slavery was outlawed, and their descendants add to the complex cultural pattern of the islands. Hindi speakers make up half the population of Trinidad, Tamil is spoken on Martinique, while Chinese and Javanese speakers are settled on Trinidad, Jamaica and Cuba.

sixteenth century, and today the only prominent "indigenous" groups are the Caribs of Dominica and St Vincent. Who in fact are of mixed ancestry.

The Spanish introduced African slaves to Hispaniola in the sixteenth century, and in the early seventeenth century British and French settlers brought European indentured laborers to work on tobacco plantations. The rapid growth of plantation sugar production after 1636 encouraged the importation of millions of West African slaves by British, French, Spanish and Dutch planters over the next two centuries. This produced a distinctive and complex hierarchical society, a continuing feature of which is the class system and an emphasis on skin color in defining social status. Following the British emancipation of slaves in 1834, the immigration of East Indian and other Asian laborers added to this complexity, particularly in Trinidad.

As a result, while a common Amerindian heritage has to some extent influenced Caribbean culture, the major influences have been European and African; today the Creole cultures, which are a combination of these two influences, are numerically dominant in the Lesser Antilles, Haiti, Jamaica and the Bahamas. Except for Haiti, which seized its independence from France in 1803, all the Caribbean islands remained at least nominal colonies until the twentieth century, some changing hands frequently; the British colony of Antigua only gained its independence in 1981. There are still five British dependencies, two French *départements* and one self-governing Dutch possession.

As in the Caribbean, the arrival of Europeans at the beginning of the sixteenth century devastated the population of Lower Central America through disease. The Spanish settlements were poor and provincial, limited primarily to the Pacific plain and the upland western regions. As many native groups died out, the dominant rural population became *mestizo* (of mixed ancestry) overseen by the urban elites of Spanish descent. In the British-influenced areas along the entire eastern coast, the settlers intermarried with both the indigenous people and West African slaves. In Belize, the Creole population, like the Creole population of the Caribbean, is of mixed African-British descent.

Of the many small groups of indigenous peoples in Lower Central America, the Garifuna, occupying the entire Caribbean coast from eastern Honduras to central Belize, and the Mopan Maya in southern Belize together illustrate both the cultural diversity of the region and the effects of European colonization.

The Garifuna of Central America

The Central American Garifuna are descendants of Carib Indians and escaped Negro slaves who inhabited Dominica and St Vincent during the seventeenth and eighteenth centuries. An aggressive people, their ancestors resisted British and French control and in 1797 were forcibly removed to the Islas de la Bahía, off Honduras. They gradually spread along the coast, reaching Belize by 1802 and intermarrying with local people of African descent. Nearly 80,000 Garifuna

Land use
Maize, root crops and beans are the main subsistence crops. Large plantations and ranches are found in lowland areas, with smaller farms in the uplands. Many areas in the Caribbean are heavily overworked.

Arable land

Maize, rice; root crops such as manioc, beans and plantains are the staple crops; tobacco and cotton grown for cash.

Plantations

Sugarcane, coffee, bananas, cocoa, spices and coconuts.

Permanent grassland

Primarily beef and dairy cattle; pigs are also kept.

Woods and forests

Coniferous and broad-leaved trees provide timber, paper and pulp; some shifting cultivation is still practised in this area.

Rough grazing land

Beef cattle, often on extensive ranches in central America; pigs are also kept in the Caribbean.

Non-agricultural land

Badly drained coastal areas, mountain peaks.

Central America and the Caribbean 2

occupy fifty-one towns and villages along a 650-kilometer (400-mile) stretch of the Caribbean coast from Dangriga in Belize to Plaplaya in Honduras. The Garifuna are the largest constituent of these communities, although other ethnic groups live in them as well. The population today is predominantly African in origin, but the Garifuna speak an Amerindian language and have retained some of the Carib cultural traditions. They are gifted linguists and speak other languages, the most common ones being English and Spanish.

Nearly all Garifuna settlements are located by the sea, and traditional villagers depend heavily on the products of fishing. In addition to fishing, the men's tasks include hunting, particularly for deer and wild birds, cooperative house building, growing cash crops, and craft activities, although craft production has declined in the face of economic modernization. Manioc, from which cassava bread is made, is the chief crop, grown in small scattered plots by means of shifting cultivation. Today many Garifuna men migrate to the major towns and ports of the Caribbean coast in search of wage labor and some have emigrated to other countries, in particular to the urban centers of the United States and Canada.

Owing to the long absences of adult men from their home villages, Garifuna women must often cope with domestic tasks without the help of their husbands. The women are the principal subsistence horticulturists, food preparers and domestic workers. Older women live with their daughters and are primarily responsible for rearing their young grandchildren. Mothers "loan" their small children to other unrelated households, where the children help with household tasks. Sometimes children are even loaned to white middle- or upper-class families.

Young men and women continue to live in their natal households throughout their twenties, even though

Community labor
Men of the village of Soufriére on the island of Dominica work to repair a road damaged by heavy rain. Sometimes community labor is voluntary; more often it is paid for on a daily basis.

Learning in the sun
Children on the island of Nevis enjoy an open-air lesson. The islands are now trying to combat a high rate of illiteracy—a legacy of poor education in the past.

they may have children as a result of informal marriages. The husband contributes to the support of his children, who remain in the mother's household, until he has set up a separate house for the family; he will usually do this by the time he is thirty. If a marriage does not survive, both the man and the woman will restore their ties with their own natal households, the children remaining with the mother.

Childbirth among the Garifuna includes the custom of *couvade*, whereby men are expected to remain relatively idle for a month or more after the child is born and to abstain from all sexual intercourse for forty-days. Infants are baptized—ordinarily as Roman Catholics—following a cleansing ritual performed nine days after the birth. The death of a Garifuna is marked by a nine-night wake of Catholic prayers, the last of which involves the recounting of folk tales, drumming and dancing. The wake is regarded as the farewell to the lingering and potentially hostile *afurugu*, the spirit-double of the *iuani* (heart-soul), which leaves human company immediately following death.

While all Garifuna are nominal Christians, mainly Roman Catholics, many have kept to their traditional beliefs and rituals. They believe in numerous spiritual forces that interact with humans—most feared is a group that includes the malevolent *ufie* (ghosts), *mafia* (forest demons) and *agaiuma* (river-dwelling spirits). The *agaiuma* are particularly dangerous and are believed to appear to men as seductive women. With the aid of his spirit helpers the *búiai* (shaman) is responsible for protecting humans from these dark powers. The *gubida* (ancestor spirits) may either reward or punish an individual, depending upon the ceremonial attention paid to them. The *búiai* may diagnose an illness as due to neglect of the ancestor spirits, prescribing an offering ritual to appease them. The most elaborate of these is the *dogó* rite, which is held by the *búiai* in a special ancestor house (*gaiunare*) and involves group singing and dancing, drumming, sacrificial offerings of seafood and fowl to family ancestors, and possession by the ancestral spirits.

While retaining their traditional beliefs within the local practice of Christianity, the Garifuna participate fully in the modern political and economic systems of their respective countries. Belizean Garifuna, for example, are a highly literate population, and many hold responsible positions throughout the country, in business, government, education and the Church.

The Mopan Maya of southern Belize

The Mopan Maya are among the descendants of the great lowland Maya civilization whose Classic Period (AD 300–900) was characterized by sophisticated ceremonial and civic architecture, hieroglyphic writing, mathematics and astronomy. At the time of the Spanish conquest the temple cities had begun to decline, but the Mopan Maya still had a flourishing culture with many of the characteristics of the classic civilization. Disease and forced migrations under Spanish rule resulted in the diminution of their numbers. Spanish missionary activity brought about many changes in

their culture, but they have remained an ethnically and linguistically distinct group and have retained many Maya cultural traditions.

Approximately 2,000 Mopan Maya inhabit four principal communities in the inland Toledo district of southern Belize. The Belize Mopan are mainly descendants of migrants who left San Luís in neighboring Guatemala in 1883, bringing the traditions of their patron, San Luis, with them.

The Mopan are traditionally shifting cultivators, planting on land within reservations set aside for community use by the Belize government. Their principal crops are maize, beans, root vegetables and rice.

A Caribbean hazard
The climate in this region is usually balmy, but storms originating in the Atlantic increase in strength as they move westward and highly destructive hurricanes occur frequently in the Caribbean, except in the very south. The hurricane season lasts from June to November. In 1979 Hurricane David ravaged Dominica. The government has now begun to build concrete-block houses that are able to withstand such onslaughts.

They also maintain orchards, some of which are now privately owned. Agriculture is primarily a male pursuit, as is hunting, gathering and freshwater fishing. In the past, related men cooperated voluntarily in agricultural work groups, but much agricultural work is now done by mutual hiring. Many younger men find temporary wage labor in agriculture elsewhere.

In contrast to the Garifuna, where male absence often leads to the dominance of females in the household, the Mopan household is firmly controlled by the husband-father. The family, generally consisting of a couple and their children, is the basic economic unit. Women's work is primarily domestic, and children are expected to help the parent of the same sex. Traditional marriage ceremonies precede fulltime cohabitation, and many couples are also married in Catholic ceremonies by the resident priest in San Antonio. As elsewhere in South America, *compadrazgo* (co-godparenthood) is an important means of integrating households in a wider sphere of mutual obligations.

Village government is dual in character. On the one hand it still incorporates the nineteenth-century *alcalde* (mayor) system—the *alcalde* is an experienced older man, elected to serve as the moral focus of the community, hear village court cases, organize *fagina* (cooperative community labor and sponsor an annual thanksgiving ceremony. On the other hand, there is a village council of seven elected members which deals with government agencies.

Life is changing rapidly among the Mopan as educational and economic opportunities outside the village increase. However, few families leave their home village permanently, and Mopan cultural identity remains strong. Although Mopan cosmology, involving a complex hierarchy of traditional Maya deities, has declined in recent years, native medicine and sorcery remain important.

Echoes of the Maya past
While some fiestas of the Mopan Maya are primarily of Catholic and Spanish folk origin, the fiesta of San Luis Rey shows strong Mayan influence. This festival features a masked deer dance, the ritual feeding of the masks and the consumption of much alcohol. A large greased pole is erected which the male participants attempt to climb. This pole is said to represent the sacred and universal "tree of life."

Bananas for export
Bananas, sugar, coffee and coconuts are the major cash crops of the Caribbean. US companies introduced banana plantations to this region in the late 19th century and ownership remains largely in foreign hands; mass export of bananas did not begin until the 20th century. Most Garifuna men used to work in the banana industry, but after the economic depression of the 1930s such opportunities grew scarce.

Andes and the Western Seaboard 1

Among bleak, windswept peaks of the Andes, Indian peasants, with a timeless acceptance of hardship, continue a way of life that predates the magnificent Inca Empire. Far below them, in the arid coastlands, modern cities mushroom around the old Spanish colonial centers, offering a new and affluent life style for some, but attracting many others to a life of hopeless poverty.

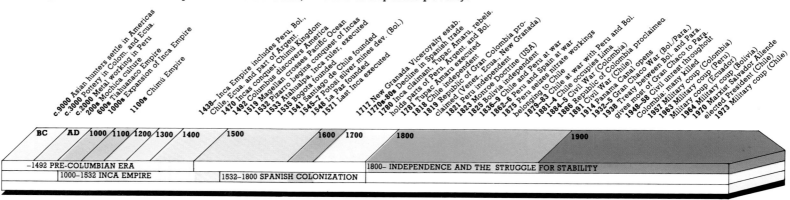

c.9000 Asian hunters settle in Americas
c.3000 Pottery in Colom. and Ecua.
c.2000 Metal working in Peru
200s Mochica culture
600s Tiahuanaco Empire
1000s Expansion of Inca Empire
1100s Chimú Empire
1438- Inca Empire includes Peru, Bol., Chile, Ecua. and part of Argent.
1470 Incas conquer Chimú Kingdom
1492 Columbus discovers America
1519 Magellan crosses Pacific Ocean
1532 Pizarro begins conquest of Incas
1533 Bogotá founded; Inca ruler executed
1535 Atahualpa, Inca ruler, executed
1541 Santiago de Chile founded
1545-7 Potosí silver mines dev.
1548 La Paz founded
1571 Last Inca executed
1717 New Granada Viceroyalty estab. (Bol.)
1770s-80s Decline in Spanish trade
1780 Inca claimant, Tupac Amaru, rebels, holds parts of Peru, Argent. and Bol.
1781 Tupac Amaru executed
1818 Chile independent
1819 Republic of Gran Colombia pro-claimed (Venez., Ecua., New Granada)
1821 Peru independent
1823 Monroe Doctrine (USA)
1823 Bolivia independent
1836-9 Chile at war with Peru and Bol.
1862-6 Peru and Spain at war
1875 Peru seizes nitrate workings belonging to Chile
1879-83 Chile occupies Lima
1881-4 Civil War (Colombia)
1884-5 Republic of Colombia proclaimed
1891 Civil War (Chile)
1914 Panama Canal opens
1932-5 Gran Chaco War (Bol./Para.)
1938 Treaty between Bol. and Para. gives most of Gran Chaco to Para.
1948-58 Civil unrest throughout Colombia; many killed
1957 Military coup (Colombia)
1963 Military coup (Ecuador)
1964 Military coup (Bolivia)
1970 Marxist Salvador Allende elected President (Chile)
1973 Military coup (Chile)

| BC | AD | 1000 | 1100 | 1200 | 1300 | 1400 | 1500 | 1600 | 1700 | 1800 | 1900 |

-1492 PRE-COLUMBIAN ERA
1000-1532 INCA EMPIRE
1532-1800 SPANISH COLONIZATION
1800- INDEPENDENCE AND THE STRUGGLE FOR STABILITY

Population by Country
Total: 69 million

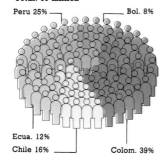

Peru 25% — Bol. 8%
Ecua. 12%
Chile 16% — Colom. 39%

Population by Religion

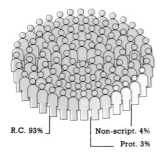

R.C. 93% — Non-script. 4%
Prot. 3%

Potato harvesting in the Andes
Quechua workers on a highland hacienda bring in the potato harvest. The potato was first domesticated on the *puna*, where little else will grow.

The west coast of South America is a land of astonishing contrasts, dominated by the massive Andean chain. Through a combination of tropical latitudes and high mountains, the Andes are a mosaic of ecological zones. In Colombia, Ecuador and northern Peru the chain is relatively narrow, with tropical jungle along the Pacific coast; in southern Peru and Bolivia it broadens out to the high *puna*—a bleak, windswept tableland, 4,000 meters (13,000 feet) above sea level, with the vast waters of Lake Titicaca at its center. At these latitudes the coastal strip is a desert broken by patches of riverside irrigation. In northern Chile the broad belt of the Atacama desert cuts across the Andes, and south of the desert the country consists mainly of highland heath and scrub steppe, becoming harsher farther south. Over the whole region this tremendous diversity is reflected in the wide variety of products—from potatoes and pasturage for llamas and alpacas in the *puna*, to crops such as maize, beans and squash in the irrigated temperate valleys and cotton and sugar along the coast.

Such ecological diversity has had a strong and persistent influence on the social and political life of the whole region. Before the arrival of the Spanish conquerors in the sixteenth century the area was the cradle for some of the most sophisticated civilizations of the New World, such as the coastal Chimú (four-teenth century) and the highland Inca (fifteenth century). To the north of the *puna*, where the Andean chain narrows, small chiefdoms, such as the powerful Chibcha, abounded; to the south the area was inha-bited by politically uncentralized farmers and herders, the most numerous, linguistically, being the Arauca-nians. Farther south still, the inhospitable environment supported groups of hunter-gatherers.

With the introduction, by the Spanish, of European diseases and the brutal imposition of forced labor in the gold and silver mines, many native cultures were destroyed. Others, however, survived hispanicization and some were actually reinforced. Today the term "Indian" refers to people displaying traditional cultural traits such as an indigenous mother tongue, while *mestizo*, although in theory meaning someone of mixed ancestry, in fact denotes fluency in Spanish and a "western" cultural orientation. The *mestizos* have become the skilled workforce of the towns.

As in other culture areas in South America, since World War II there has been a dramatic increase in migration from the countryside to the urban coastal areas, due partly to the pressure on the land of an expanding rural population and partly to wartime industrial expansion. Every major city is now ringed by a belt of shanty towns, and the Indian migrants are being assimilated into the urban working class.

The Indian peasant masses have on the whole had little influence over the successive civilian and military governments of the Andean countries. However, since World War II Bolivia, Peru and Chile have all intro-duced agrarian reform measures designed to benefit estate tenants and plot holders. Some haciendas in Peru have been expropriated and turned into co-operatives, worked by the former labor-tenants under state management. Of the surviving Indian peoples, the contrasts of environment and culture are best seen in the Quechua of the Cuzco region of southern Peru and the Mapuche of central Chile.

Quechua of the Cuzco region

Cuzco, the capital of the Inca Empire, was captured by the Spanish in 1533 and two years later they estab-lished their own capital on the coast which was to become the prosperous industrial city of Lima. Under the Spanish those highland Indians removed to the coast as a workforce rapidly lost their language and native identity; in the high Andes, however, the In-dians generally retained both. Quechua was the un-written language of the Incas and it has given its name to the descendants of those Indians once ruled by the Inca Empire, now numbering some three million.

The Quechua of southern Peru live in closely knit communities that derive from the ancient *ayllus*, kin-based local groups that predated the Incas and on which the fundamental organization of their empire was based. The Spanish introduced administrative arrangements that recognized the custom of corporate land tenure and protected the territories of the *ayllus* from encroachment. The first republican government of Peru withdrew this protection by breaking up Indian communal lands into private plots, and many com-munities subsequently disappeared. Others, however, survived into the twentieth century, and the constitu-tion of 1920 restored the protection by recognizing the Indian community as a legal entity.

Quechua communities are now based on territory rather than on kinship, though they often display a high degree of endogamy. The community owns all the

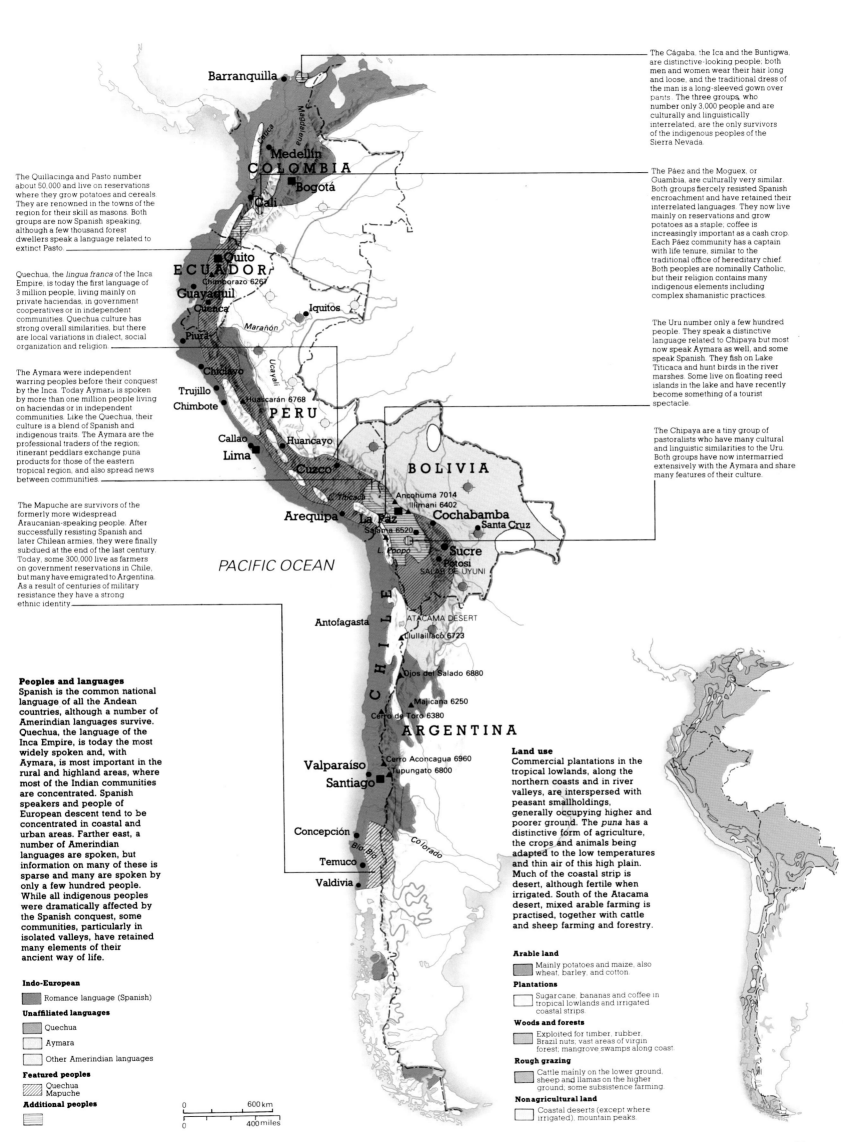

The Cágaba, the Ica and the Buntigwa, are distinctive-looking people; both men and women wear their hair long and loose, and the traditional dress of the man is a long-sleeved gown over pants. The three groups, who number only 3,000 people and are culturally and linguistically interrelated, are the only survivors of the indigenous peoples of the Sierra Nevada.

The Páez and the Moguex, or Guambia, are culturally very similar. Both groups fiercely resisted Spanish encroachment and have retained their interrelated languages. They now live mainly on reservations and grow potatoes as a staple; coffee is increasingly important as a cash crop. Each Páez community has a captain with life tenure, similar to the traditional office of hereditary chief. Both peoples are nominally Catholic, but their religion contains many indigenous elements including complex shamanistic practices.

The Quillacinga and Pasto number about 50,000 and live on reservations where they grow potatoes and cereals. They are renowned in the towns of the region for their skill as masons. Both groups are now Spanish speaking, although a few thousand forest dwellers speak a language related to extinct Pasto.

The Uru number only a few hundred people. They speak a distinctive language related to Chipaya but most now speak Aymara as well, and some speak Spanish. They fish on Lake Titicaca and hunt birds in the river marshes. Some live on floating reed islands in the lake and have recently become something of a tourist spectacle.

Quechua, the *lingua franca* of the Inca Empire, is today the first language of 3 million people, living mainly on private haciendas, in government cooperatives or in independent communities. Quechua culture has strong overall similarities, but there are local variations in dialect, social organization and religion.

The Aymara were independent warring peoples before their conquest by the Inca. Today Aymara is spoken by more than one million people living on haciendas or in independent communities. Like the Quechua, their culture is a blend of Spanish and indigenous traits. The Aymara are the professional traders of the region; itinerant peddlars exchange puna products for those of the eastern tropical region, and also spread news between communities.

The Chipaya are a tiny group of pastoralists who have many cultural and linguistic similarities to the Uru. Both groups have now intermarried extensively with the Aymara and share many features of their culture.

The Mapuche are survivors of the formerly more widespread Araucanian-speaking people. After successfully resisting Spanish and later Chilean armies, they were finally subdued at the end of the last century. Today, some 300,000 live as farmers on government reservations in Chile, but many have emigrated to Argentina. As a result of centuries of military resistance they have a strong ethnic identity.

PACIFIC OCEAN

Peoples and languages
Spanish is the common national language of all the Andean countries, although a number of Amerindian languages survive. Quechua, the language of the Inca Empire, is today the most widely spoken and, with Aymara, is most important in the rural and highland areas, where most of the Indian communities are concentrated. Spanish speakers and people of European descent tend to be concentrated in coastal and urban areas. Farther east, a number of Amerindian languages are spoken, but information on many of these is sparse and many are spoken by only a few hundred people. While all indigenous peoples were dramatically affected by the Spanish conquest, some communities, particularly in isolated valleys, have retained many elements of their ancient way of life.

Indo-European
▨ Romance language (Spanish)

Unaffiliated languages
▨ Quechua
□ Aymara
□ Other Amerindian languages

Featured peoples
▨ Quechua
▨ Mapuche

Additional peoples
▨

Land use
Commercial plantations in the tropical lowlands, along the northern coasts and in river valleys, are interspersed with peasant smallholdings, generally occupying higher and poorer ground. The *puna* has a distinctive form of agriculture, the crops and animals being adapted to the low temperatures and thin air of this high plain. Much of the coastal strip is desert, although fertile when irrigated. South of the Atacama desert, mixed arable farming is practised, together with cattle and sheep farming and forestry.

Arable land
▨ Mainly potatoes and maize, also wheat, barley, and cotton.

Plantations
□ Sugar cane, bananas and coffee in tropical lowlands and irrigated coastal strips.

Woods and forests
▨ Exploited for timber, rubber, Brazil nuts; vast areas of virgin forest; mangrove swamps along coast.

Rough grazing
▨ Cattle mainly on the lower ground, sheep and llamas on the higher ground; some subsistence farming.

Nonagricultural land
□ Coastal deserts (except where irrigated), mountain peaks.

0 — 600 km
0 — 400 miles

Barranquilla
Medellín
COLOMBIA
Bogotá
Cali
Quito
ECUADOR
Chimborazo 6267
Guayaquil
Cuenca
Iquitos
Marañón
Piura
Chiclayo
Ucayali
Trujillo
Huascarán 6768
Chimbote
PERU
Callao
Huancayo
Lima
Cuzco
BOLIVIA
L. Titicaca
Ancohuma 7014
Illimani 6402
Arequipa
La Paz
Cochabamba
Sajama 6520
Santa Cruz
L. Poopó
Sucre
Potosí
SALAR DE UYUNI
Antofagasta
ATACAMA DESERT
Llullaillaco 6723
Ojos del Salado 6880
Majicana 6250
Cerro de Toro 6380
CHILE
ARGENTINA
Cerro Aconcagua 6960
Valparaíso
Tupungato 6800
Santiago
Concepción
Colorado
Bío Bío
Temuco
Valdivia

183

Andes and the Western Seaboard 2

land, and each member has a right to plots for pasture and cultivation. Once the plots were reallocated every year, according to family needs, but now the rights are inherited. The community organizes the annual cleaning of the main irrigation channels. This task may be accompanied by a religious festival that typifies the beliefs of the Indians, incorporating both pre-Inca and Catholic elements. The festival is a ritual dramatization of the fertilization of the Earth Mother, known as *Pachamama*, by the spirits of the lakes and marshes; however, to the modern Quechua, *Pachamama*, the life-giving spirit that makes the grass and crops grow, is identified with the Virgin Mary.

With such beliefs in the spirits of natural phenomena, such as mountains, lakes and rivers, the Quechua are only nominally Catholic. Each community has its cycle of religious fiestas dedicated to local patron saints and to the universal feasts of the Church. Some fiestas attract tens of thousands of devotees from the surrounding regions because particular shrines are said to possess miraculous powers. Although the cost of a local fiesta is substantial it is not shared by the community. Instead, one man is elected—or more often forced—to become the fiesta's *mayordomo*, and he must then meet all the expenses for that year. These include the hire of musicians, decoration of the church altar and the saint's image, and the provision of food and drink for the revellers. The *mayordomo* gains considerable prestige, which may enable him later to make a bid for political power in the community's ruling body, the *varayoq*, but the fiesta itself may ruin him financially. Some men spend the rest of their lives paying back the debts incurred.

The community's cohesiveness is expressed not only through the fiesta but also through the system of co-operative labor, whereby kin, neighbors and friends help each other with their work. For everyday tasks, this takes the form of *ayni* (exchange labor), according to which a day's labor is repaid with a day's labor on the same or a similar task. For jobs such as housebuilding *mink'a* (festive labor) is used, the sponsor providing food, drink and musical entertainment for his worker guests. Increasingly, however, wealthier community members tend to rely on wage labor rather than on the traditional collaboration.

The Quechua grow a variety of crops, including maize, barley, quinoa and potatoes. Llamas, alpacas and sheep are kept for their wool, which is woven into the brightly colored shawls and ponchos still worn by the peasants. Pigs and cattle are kept for meat, and

Traditional division of labor
Men weave *bayeta*, a coarse cloth for sacking, trousers and skirts, on Spanish upright looms. Women tend to weave traditional decorative designs for shawls, ponchos and belts. The chemical dyes, now replacing natural dyes, give the yarn a brighter color.

The Corpus Christi fiesta
Spanish colonial rule produced a number of common cultural features throughout the Andean area. The most distinctive is the complex of Catholic fiestas. There is considerable regional variation, however, since local religions have become syncretized with Catholicism.

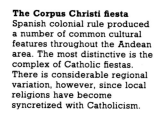

mules for transport along the precarious mountain pathways. Most households also keep cavies, a kind of guinea pig, whose meat is considered a delicacy and is served at community festivals. Some communities today still retain control over widely separated lands at different altitudes. Q'ero, for example, 88 kilometers (55 miles) east of Cuzco, has lands ranging in altitude from 2,000 meters (6,500 feet) to over 3,900 meters (12,800 feet), the highest and lowest zones separated by a distance of only 40 kilometers (25 miles).

For the most part agricultural and pastoral production is geared to subsistence, but a limited volume of produce is exchanged or sold outside the community. In some areas there are special exchange partnerships between individuals in different ecological zones. Not all produce is disposed of in this way, however, and markets also play a role. Highland peasants buy and sell at the local weekly village markets, where they can obtain fruit and coca leaves from the *montaña* zone in the eastern foothills, as well as industrial manufactures from the coastal region, such as plastic bowls, knitting needles, cutlery and radio batteries. Quechua communities in the Cuzco region are also visited by itinerant Aymara traders.

Present-day Mapuche engage primarily in farming, cultivating a variety of crops including corn, potatoes, beans, chili peppers and quinoa. Formerly it was the women who did most of the agricultural work while the men engaged in interlineage warfare and in fighting the Spanish. Cash-crop cultivation is now carried out by the men, the women tending the household vegetable gardens. Another change has been the replacement of the once numerous llama herds by horses, sheep, cattle and pigs. Those Mapuche who served in the Spanish colonial army became excellent cavalrymen and thereafter the horse was adopted as a means of transport. Today, as a result of population pressure and declining land productivity, many of the Mapuche living on reservations are very poor.

Ever since the sixteenth century there have been large-scale migrations of Araucanians into Argentina, many of them seeking asylum from the reprisals that followed their periodic uprisings against the Spanish authorities. For the last century the Mapuche have fought a losing battle through the courts. The Allende government (1970–73) did give them some security, but recent legislation allows reservation land to be split up and sold. The Mapuche suffered persecution for their support of Allende and many have migrated east across the Andes in search of better economic opportunities.

For those Mapuche remaining on the reservations, if a man is to marry he must choose a woman from another patrilineage—that is, from another reservation. Bridewealth formerly consisted of llamas but is now a token payment in cattle and craft goods such as ponchos, blankets and silver jewelry. In addition the groom is allocated a plot of land by his father. Occasionally dramatized bride-capture is practiced. When a groom cannot accumulate sufficient bridewealth, the couple elope, and a traditional ceremony takes place later when the bridewealth is paid.

The Mapuche are nominally Catholic but are particularly noted for their shamanistic practices. A reservation without a shaman is regarded as especially liable to spiritual attack, causing illness or death among its members. Shamans contact their spirit-helpers in order to combat these evil spirits and to diagnose the cause of death. The role of shaman was formerly passed from father to son, but shamans are now usually women, the role passing to a daughter or close kinswoman. Special shamanistic ceremonies known as *machitun* are held, when the neophyte demonstrates her newly acquired skills before the more experienced shamans. In the curing rite itself, the shaman passes into a trance, massages or manipulates the affected parts of the patient and blows smoke and water in four directions over the patient's body. The rite is accompanied by drumming on a tambourine and may include ventriloquism and sleight of hand. A successful shaman can amass considerable wealth by Mapuche standards. This shamanistic complex is similar among Siberian and other Arctic peoples.

The Uru of Lake Titicaca
These Indians fish and hunt birds in the marshes. A few live on floating reed islands. Their boats are made from totora reed and ichu grass and have a trapezoidal rigged sail. The craft is highly maneuverable even in narrow riverways, and can withstand violent storms.

Mapuche shamanism
The sacred *rewe* tree to the right of this *machi* (female shaman) has both religious and shamanistic significance. Her drum and rattle, both made from gourds, are part of her essential ritual equipment. All illnesses and even accidents are attributed to evil spirits, and the shaman struggles to exorcize these during seances, helped by her familiar spirit.

Quechua exchange labour
The Quechua organize their work by means of *ayni*, or exchange labor. In this plowing team one man operates the wooden foot-plow (whose design dates back to Inca times), a second adds fertilizer, and a third puts in seed potatoes. The team works on the fields of each team member in turn, the sponsor for the day providing food and the narcotic coca leaves that Andean peasants habitually chew.

The complex network of associations within the community is the essential fabric of a Quechua peasant's life, but relationships with outsiders may also be important. The strongest of these is the *compadrazgo* bond, formed when a couple, chosen as godparents for a new baby, are bound for life to the baby's parents in ritual kinship. The *compadrazgo* bond is Christian in origin, but it need not be initiated at baptism: a second opportunity arises at the child's first hair cutting, an occasion of traditional significance. When a *compadrazgo* relationship is set up with a couple in a separate community, it often develops into a partnership for the exchange of produce, which benefits both sides, especially if they inhabit different ecological zones.

Mapuche of central Chile

The Mapuche are the survivors of the once vast population of Araucanian farmers and herders, whose territory in aboriginal times covered much of central Chile. Today the number living on government reservations is estimated at 300,000 and they occupy the area between the Bio-Bio river and the town of Valdivia. Although they all refer to themselves as Mapuche (people of the land), the Andean Mapuche refer to those on the coast as Lafquenche and to the sub-Andean Mapuche as Puelche.

The Mapuche successfully resisted Spanish and later Chilean hegemony until the end of the nineteenth century, when they were finally subdued and placed on small reservations. Until then they had traditionally lived in localized patrilineages, each headed by a man known as the *lonko*. Title to reservation lands was vested in the *lonko*, and though this title was not heritable the *lonko* is still regarded as the *de facto* owner of the land of his patrilineage. The *lonko's* position was further strengthened by the fact that patrilineages grew larger and stronger as the pressure on reservation land limited the opportunities for new lineages to hive off.

Amazonia and the Eastern Seaboard 1

To the thousands of Indian tribes who once roamed the Amazon basin, the jungle was a provider of food and shelter, but to the gold-hungry Europeans it was a deadly trap of venomous insects and piranha-infested rivers. Now the sharp edge of modern technology is finally making inroads on the once impregnable forest, destroying both its people and its wildlife.

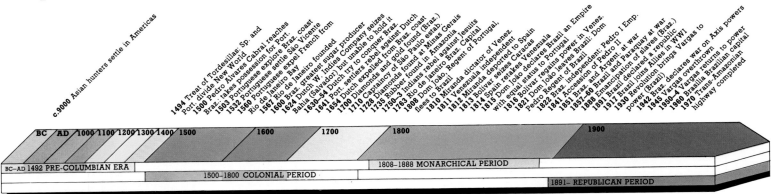

c.9000 Asian hunters settle in Americas
1494 Treat of Tordesillas: Sp. and Port. divide New World
1500 Pedro Alvares Cabral reaches Braz.: takes possession for Port.
1503 Portuguese explore Braz. coast
1532 Portuguese settle São Vicente
1560 Portuguese expel French from Rio de Janeiro Bay
1567 Rio de Janeiro founded
1600 Braz. greatest sugar producer
1624 Dutch W. Indies Company seizes Bahia (Salvador) but unable to hold it
1630–54 Dutch try to conquer Braz.
1641 Port. settlers rebel against Dutch
1654 Dutch expelled from Braz. coast
1700 Diamonds and gold found (Braz.)
1710 Captaincy of São Paulo estab.
1728 Diamonds found in Minas Gerais
1735 Rubber found in Amazonia
1750–3 Indians rebel against Jesuits
1763 Rio de Janeiro Braz. Capital
1808 Dom João, Regent of Portugal, flees to Brazil
1810 Miranda dictator of Venez.
1811 Venezuela independent
1812 Miranda deported to Spain
1813 Bolivar seizes Caracas
1814 Spain retakes Venezuela
1815 Dom João declares Venezuela with equal status to Portugal an Empire
1816 Bolivar regains power in Venez.
1821 Dom João leaves Brazil: Dom Pedro Regent of Brazil
1822 Braz. independent: Pedro I Emp.
1831 Accession of Pedro II
1851 Braz. and Argent. at war
1852–60 Brazil and Paraguay at war
1888 Emancipation of slaves (Braz.)
1891 Brazil declared a republic
1917 Brazil joins Allies in WWI
1930 Revolution brings Vargas to power (Brazil)
1942 Braz. declares war on Axis powers
1945 Vargas overthrown
1950–4 Vargas returns to power
1960 Brasilia Brazilian capital
1970 Trans-Amazonian highway completed

BC	AD	1000	1100	1200	1300	1400	1500	1600	1700	1800	1900

BC–AD 1492 PRE-COLUMBIAN ERA
1500–1800 COLONIAL PERIOD
1808–1888 MONARCHICAL PERIOD
1891– REPUBLICAN PERIOD

Population by Country
Total: 138 million

Brazil 89%

Venezuela 10%
Guyana 0.5%
Suri./Fr. Gui. 0.5%

Population by Religion

RC 88.5%
Unknown 10%
Min. rel. 1.0%

Highway through the forest
The Trans-Amazon highway—for much of its length a dirt track—is accelerating the destruction of the few remaining Amazonian Indians.

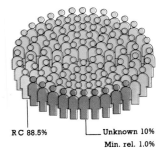

Dense tropical rain forest covers some 6,000,000 square kilometers (2,300,000 square miles) of lowland South America, and is the home of hundreds of Amerindian groups, a few of which have remained isolated in the jungle until the present day. The vast forest and its labyrinth of waterways have remained largely unexploited by non-Indians until recently. Apart from the brief nineteenth-century rubber boom, it is only within the last couple of decades that the region has been opened up to major development projects—roads, cattle ranches, timber and mineral extraction. Development entails ever increasing deforestation which, as well as destroying wildlife and often initiating an irreversible process of soil erosion, threatens the way of life of the remaining indigenous people in the region.

South America has been inhabited by Amerindians for at least 10,000 years, but it is difficult to say how long the Amazon basin itself has been inhabited, since archaeological dating here is inconclusive. There is a great deal of variety between the indigenous societies in this area, but they have in common a life style based on small communities, which is largely in keeping with the ecological balance of the tropical forest. Most engage in seasonal hunting, fishing and gathering, combined with shifting cultivation; until the arrival of the Europeans there was sufficient land for each tribe to move its village site every few years. Some tribes developed trade partnerships prior to European contact, but many were self-sufficient, although intra- and inter-tribal warfare was common.

At the time of the arrival of Europeans, the more culturally advanced Indian tribes were situated in the floodplains of the Amazon (the *várzea*), and along the Caribbean and Atlantic coasts. Given the accessibility of this area to white colonization, the introduction of slavery and the Indians' lack of immunity to European diseases, the *várzea* and coastal tribes soon became virtually extinct. The lowland Indian population is estimated to have numbered several million before the arrival of Europeans, although such figures are controversial and unreliable. Today, there are about 120 tribes left, and the Indian population of the Brazilian Amazon amounts to no more than 150,000.

Portuguese domination of the Amazonian area was the result of a treaty agreed with Spain in 1494, before European exploration of South America had even begun. The first permanent Portuguese settlement was established near São Paulo in 1532, but the Portuguese did not develop much of the hinterland and never set up the strong central government characteristic of the Spanish colonies. However, the northern coastland of the region—the fabled Pearl Coast—was controlled by Spain and here there was more exploration. The decimation of the indigenous peoples resulted in a severe shortage of labor and Negro slaves were imported in such great numbers that by the eighteenth century they formed the bulk of the population in Colombia and Venezuela.

Gold—the prime motivation of many early colonists—was found in the Mato Grosso and Goiás regions in the early seventeenth century, along with many different kinds of precious stones. Prospectors quickly opened up the area, and further incursions were made by groups of roving bandits, often numbering several thousand in size, whose treatment of the Indians was despicable even by the standard of the time. These bandits often became involved in armed clashes with Jesuit missionaries, who had first entered the region in the sixteenth century and who had converted a great many Indians to Christianity.

It was not gold but rubber that was instrumental in opening up the most densely forested parts of Amazonia. This curious material had been discovered very early on, but it only became useful when Charles Goodyear devised the vulcanization process in 1840. The rubber boom was spectacular, opening the Amazon to international shipping and fostering the growth of a magnificent city, Manaus, but it did not bring prosperity to the Indians. Many were exterminated in the search for rubber trees and those hired as tappers by the concession owners found themselves inextricably trapped in debt bondage—they were given manufactured goods on credit to be paid for in rubber, but the prices were adjusted by the owners so that the debt could never be repaid. The rubber boom ended in 1912, when Malayan plantations, using Brazilian rubber-tree seed, proved far more lucrative, but rubber is still tapped on a small scale.

Between 1810 and 1825 independence was gained by almost all the countries of South America. Only the Guianas—small footholds gained by Britain, France and Holland—remained colonies, and of these French Guiana is still a *département* of France. Following independence, Brazil's prosperity slowly increased,

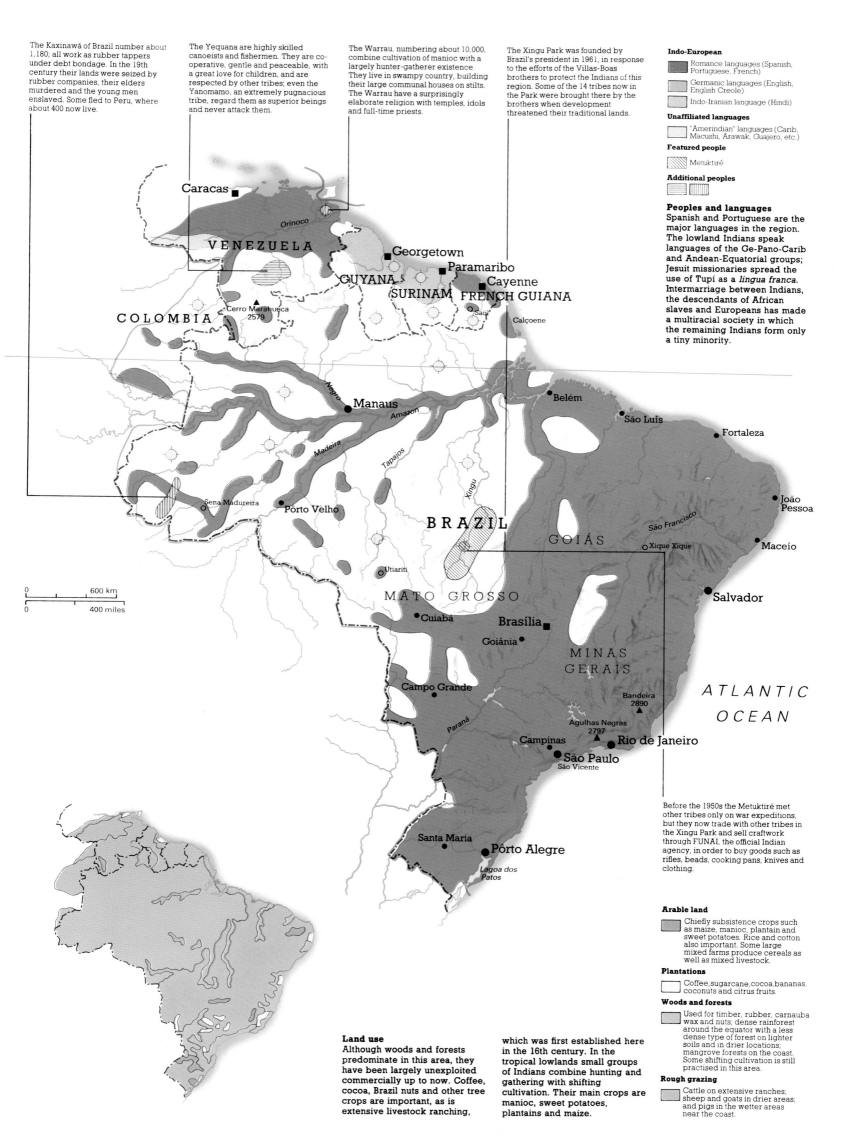

The Kaxinawá of Brazil number about 1,180; all work as rubber tappers under debt bondage. In the 19th century their lands were seized by rubber companies, their elders murdered and the young men enslaved. Some fled to Peru, where about 400 now live.

The Yequana are highly skilled canoeists and fishermen. They are co-operative, gentle and peaceable, with a great love for children, and are respected by other tribes; even the Yanomamo, an extremely pugnacious tribe, regard them as superior beings and never attack them.

The Warrau, numbering about 10,000, combine cultivation of manioc with a largely hunter-gatherer existence. They live in swampy country, building their large communal houses on stilts. The Warrau have a surprisingly elaborate religion with temples, idols and full-time priests.

The Xingu Park was founded by Brazil's president in 1961, in response to the efforts of the Villas-Boas brothers to protect the Indians of this region. Some of the 14 tribes now in the Park were brought there by the brothers when development threatened their traditional lands.

Indo-European

Romance languages (Spanish, Portuguese, French)

Germanic languages (English, English Creole)

Indo-Iranian language (Hindi)

Unaffiliated languages

"Amerindian" languages (Carib, Macushi, Arawak, Guajero, etc.)

Featured people

Metuktiré

Additional peoples

Peoples and languages
Spanish and Portuguese are the major languages in the region. The lowland Indians speak languages of the Ge-Pano-Carib and Andean-Equatorial groups; Jesuit missionaries spread the use of Tupí as a *lingua franca*. Intermarriage between Indians, the descendants of African slaves and Europeans has made a multiracial society in which the remaining Indians form only a tiny minority.

Before the 1950s the Metuktiré met other tribes only on war expeditions, but they now trade with other tribes in the Xingu Park and sell craftwork through FUNAI, the official Indian agency, in order to buy goods such as rifles, beads, cooking pans, knives and clothing.

Arable land

Chiefly subsistence crops such as maize, manioc, plantain and sweet potatoes. Rice and cotton also important. Some large mixed farms produce cereals as well as mixed livestock.

Plantations

Coffee, sugarcane, cocoa, bananas. coconuts and citrus fruits.

Woods and forests

Used for timber, rubber, carnauba wax and nuts; dense rainforest around the equator with a less dense type of forest on lighter soils and in drier locations; mangrove forests on the coast. Some shifting cultivation is still practised in this area.

Rough grazing

Cattle on extensive ranches; sheep and goats in drier areas; and pigs in the wetter areas near the coast.

Land use
Although woods and forests predominate in this area, they have been largely unexploited commercially up to now. Coffee, cocoa, Brazil nuts and other tree crops are important, as is extensive livestock ranching, which was first established here in the 16th century. In the tropical lowlands small groups of Indians combine hunting and gathering with shifting cultivation. Their main crops are manioc, sweet potatoes, plantains and maize.

187

Amazonía and the Eastern Seaboard 2

but poor coffee harvests and rising oil prices have undermined the economy, while the building of the new capital, Brasília, involved the country in massive debts and generated a spiral of inflation. As in other South American countries, the population is increasing at such an alarming rate that educational and welfare facilities are unable to keep pace. Venezuela is more fortunate in having oil reserves that have made it one of the wealthiest countries in South America.

With massive developments in the Amazon basin since World War II, the decline of the indigenous people has continued and even accelerated. The main instrument of development is a vast road system, the Trans-Amazon highway, inaugurated in 1970. The highway has dislodged many previously uncontacted Indian groups and these, together with previously contacted tribes, are now struggling to preserve a land base. The Metuktiré are an example of a tribe that are now, for the first time, experiencing the impact of the modern world. Many of the traits they have developed for survival in the rain forest—flexibility, resourcefulness, cooperation and mutual assistance—are seen also in the *favelados*, who eke out a living in a very different sort of environment, the urban centers of modern Brazil.

The Metuktiré of the Xingu Park, central Brazil

Peaceful contact was first established with the Metuktiré in 1953, although they were well known before then for their attacks on white settlers. In 1971 a highway cut off the northern area of the Xingu Park and the Metuktiré were requested to move south of this road, abandoning their traditional land. Half refused to move, but the rest now live in the village of Kretire, some 20 kilometers (12 miles) south of the highway. The population of Kretire is around 160, while the number of Metuktiré north of the highway is about 130; like all recently contacted groups their numbers have been severely reduced by European diseases.

The Metuktiré have so far maintained a largely traditional life style, based on shifting cultivation. A forest site is felled for all village food plots to be planted side by side, and plots are cultivated for about three years. Traditional crops include manioc, sweet potatoes, maize, tobacco and cotton, but other crops, such as bananas, rice, pineapples, sugarcane and pumpkins have been introduced more recently.

In the rainy season, the Metuktiré reside in spacious circular villages, but during the dry season the village splits up and the people travel in small bands on long hunting and gathering trips. Hunting remains an important male task, although fishing is now the main source of protein. With the aid of a rifle, rather than the traditional bow and arrow, the men hunt wild pigs, tapirs, armadillos, deer, jaguars, monkeys and turtles. Fish are caught by hook and line, bow and arrow, or by poisoning. Wild honey is collected by men, and both men and women gather wild fruits and berries.

The Metuktiré are endogamous, each village forming an autonomous unit. Each household normally shelters an extended family, and on marriage—signalled by the birth of a child—a man moves to the house of his parents-in-law, remaining there for the

Lip plug: symbol of manhood
Piercing and ornamentation of the lower lip is a widespread tradition among Amazonian tribes. It is done only to men, and the lip ornament symbolizes male attributes—prowess in war and oratory. This Metuktiré wears the traditional wooden lip disc, but the use of this is now dying out among the Metuktiré, to be replaced by a short string of beads threaded through the lower lip, a style of ornament favored by other tribes in the region. The future of the Metuktiré is far from certain. The Xingu Park, where they live, has already been whittled down in size, and a law passed in 1972 gives the government the right to remove Indians from their territory if this is seen to be in the best interests of economic development or national security.

Houses over the Amazon
Along the banks of the Amazon a special form of agriculture has developed. During the season when the river is in flood *terra firme* (cleared forest soil) is cultivated; when the waters recede the farmers turn their attention to the *várzea* (fertile river margins). The same subsistence crops—rice, manioc, beans and maize—are grown on both, but on the *várzea* jute is also grown and cattle grazed. The cattle are kept in floating corrals.

Sugar power
In a Brazilian factory, sugar is transformed into alcohol for motor fuel—part of Brazil's drive to reduce oil imports and bring down its massive national debt. To produce the raw material, sugar, many peasants practicing subsistence agriculture have been forcibly removed from their land so that sugarcane plantations can be established. The same peasants are then reemployed as plantation workers at low wages and on an irregular seasonal basis. Attempts are now being made to develop a process that uses manioc as the raw material in this process, rather than cane sugar. Credit facilities have been manipulated to encourage the purchase of alcohol-fueled cars—3 years' credit is available for these, but only 1 year for gasoline-driven cars.

rest of his life. Sexual differentiation of roles begins at an early age. Girls care for their younger siblings, accompany their mothers to the food plots and learn the art of body painting. Young boys learn to use the bow and arrow and listen to the recitation of myths in the men's assembly house in the center of the village.

At night, after assembly in the men's house, each man retires to his wife's household, where every nuclear family has a separate sleeping place and hearth. The men within a household take turns in fishing and hunting, and a man normally delivers his catch to his wife, who gives one portion to her parents and another to her husband's mother and sisters. Men are obliged to assist their fathers-in-law in house building and food-plot clearance.

The Metuktiré are noted for the richness of their ceremonies, which take place on numerous occasions, notably the maize harvest, the initiation of boys at puberty, and the death of an adult. The dancing and singing is performed mainly by the men. The Metuktiré have a great many myths, which explain such things as the acquisition of fire from the jaguar, and the gift of certain crops from a "star woman." They use herbal remedies to counteract evil spirits and have a *shaman* who communicates with the dead. Much attention centers on the socialization of the individual—the ears of both sexes are pierced at birth so that they may "hear" well, that is, obey social etiquette.

The name is the most important item of Metuktiré inheritance—it is passed to a newborn child from a relative other than the parents, along with a specific ceremonial role and the use of certain items of ceremonial dress. Since each personal name is chosen from a finite set and ascribes a social role, an individual is perpetuated by passing on his name to a child. In this way Metuktiré society reproduces, role by role, its stock of specialized ceremonial knowledge.

Traditionally there were two or more chiefs within a village, plus a number of *shamans*, but a new type of chief has arisen—the *capitão*, who is bilingual and deals with outsiders. The two types of chief coexist, but the *capitão* now overshadows the traditional chief.

Favelados of Brazil

Almost every city in Brazil, regardless of its size, has a *favela*—a shanty town of makeshift shelters constructed on land which is illegally occupied. In the last forty years the size of the *favelas* has steadily increased, and this is a pattern that can be seen in cities throughout South America. The underlying causes of the expansion of *favelas* are related not only to migration from rural areas, but also to natural growth, for their birth rates exceed those in the metropolitan areas as a whole. In Brazil, another factor contributing to the growth of *favelas* is the way in which industrialization has occurred, since industry is in general highly capitalized and thus absorbs little labor.

Despite variations among *favelas* in terms of their history and the proportion of urban area they occupy, there are aspects of social organization which are found generally. Regular employment is exceptional among the inhabitants of the *favela*, commonly known as *favelados*. Most depend on a combination of casual labor, domestic service, small-scale production, trading and various other activities. In a small town on the Amazon for example, a *favela* household might include several generations of kin as well as *sócios* (fictive kin) who all contribute by raising ducks, fishing, sewing, washing automobiles, trading, and collecting and selling fruit. Each individual might be thought to be "self-employed," but the actual economic unit is the rather loosely defined household. Far from being a marginal form of existence, such an organization is highly flexible and responsive to changing circumstances.

Worshiping the sea goddess
Cults of spirit possession are widespread in Brazil, where they give the poor a sense of identity and a release from the squalor and misery of *favela* life. The cults are syncretic, drawing their inspiration from Catholicism, Amerindian and West African religions. In the cult of Iemanja, the Goddess of the Sea, gifts of combs, mirrors, ribbons and perfumes are offered in recognition of her vanity. Frenzied dancing takes place on the beach before the participants rush headlong into the sea—each year a few are drowned. In southern Brazil one of the more unusual possession cults has the Volkswagen car as its object of veneration.

The materials used to construct the *favela* buildings vary from cardboard and plastic sheeting to cinder blocks and wattle. Public utilities are limited, with many houses drawing electricity from a single meter. Water not infrequently has to be fetched from distant public taps, and sewage facilities are makeshift. But despite their appearance, *favelas* are not disorganized in a social sense, and close cooperative relationships exist between households. Assistance in establishing newcomers and the exchange of information about jobs, building materials and other resources are an important part of *favela* life.

The contradictory status of *favelas* as "unofficial" cities which may nonetheless account for 30 percent of the population (as in Rio de Janeiro), is reflected in many ways. While *favelas* are generally looked down on, they are also the context in which the most potent syncretic (Afro-Brazilian) cultural practices operate. For example samba schools—organizations which prepare costumes, floats, and dance routines for use during carnival—are a product of the *favelas*.

Two faces of a city
The contrasts between Brazil's 35 million living below the poverty line and the 5% who earn 39% of the national income, is starkly illustrated by Rio de Janeiro's sprawling *favelas*, seen against a backdrop of modern skyscrapers. Although no longer Brazil's capital, Rio remains the cultural center of the country and a major tourist resort. The luxury suburb of Copacabana, which has mushroomed around the beach of the same name, exemplifies the stark contrasts within Brazil's city life: by day the beach is packed with wealthy tourists, to whom vendors from the *favelas* sell food, drinks and cigarettes; by night the streets are the haunt of prostitutes, while the beach is a resting place for destitutes without even a shanty house to go to.

Argentina, Paraguay and Uruguay

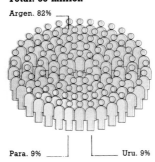

Across the Pampas of America's southernmost lands vast fields of wheat and corn undulate in the wind. Thousand-strong herds of cattle graze, tended by gauchos, who spend most of their lives on horseback. Of the many tribes of Indians who once roamed these open plains or stalked jaguars in the dense forest, only a tiny handful have survived to the present day.

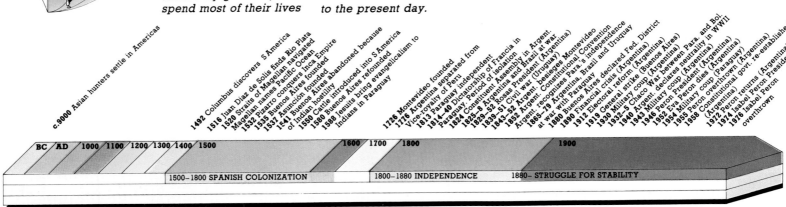

c.9000 Asian hunters settle in Americas
1492 Columbus discovers S America
1516 Juan Diaz de Solis finds Rio Plata
1520 Straits of Magellan navigated
Magellan names Pacific Ocean
1532 Pizarro conquers Inca Empire
1535 Buenos Aires founded
1537 Asunción founded
1541 Buenos Aires abandoned because of Indian hostility
1550 Cattle introduced into S America
1580 Buenos Aires refounded
1588 Jesuits bring evangelicalism to Indians in Paraguay
1726 Montevideo founded
1776 Argentina separated from Vice-royalty of Peru
1813 Paraguay independent
1814–40 Dictatorship of Francia in Paraguay. Period of isolation
1824 Constituent Assembly in Argent.
1825–8 Argentina and Brazil at war
1829–52 Rosas President (Argentina)
1839–51 Civil war (Uruguay)
1843–52 Argent. besieges Montevideo
1852 Argent. Constitutional Convention
1865–70 Argentina, Brazil and Uruguay at war with Paraguay
1880 Argent. recognizes Para.'s independence
1890 Financial crisis (Argentina)
1912 Electoral reform (Buenos Aires)
1919 General strike (Buenos Aires)
1930 Military coup (Argentina)
1932–5 Chaco War between Para. and Bol.
1940 Argent. declares neutrality in WWII
1946 Peron President (Argentina)
1952 Eva Peron dies (Argentina)
1954 Military coup (Paraguay)
1955 Peron overthrown (Argentina)
1958 Constitutional govt. re-established (Argentina)
1972 Peron returns (Argentina)
1974 Isabel Peron President (Argentina)
1976 Isabel Peron overthrown

| BC / AD | 1000 | 1100 | 1200 | 1300 | 1400 | 1500 | | 1600 | 1700 | 1800 | | 1900 |

1500–1800 SPANISH COLONIZATION   1800–1880 INDEPENDENCE   1880– STRUGGLE FOR STABILITY

Population by Country
Total: 33 million

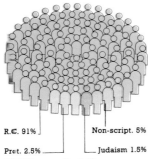

Argen. 82%

Para. 9%   Uru. 9%

Population by Religion

R.C. 91%   Non-script. 5%

Pret. 2.5%   Judaism 1.5%

Dividing up the kill
The Chamococo still go hunting when they cannot find paid work. They hunt with dogs and rifles instead of the old bow-and-arrow or lance.

The countries of the southeastern cone of South America have populations of predominantly European ancestry and since the beginning of the twentieth century they have been more directly linked with the world economy than any other region of Latin America, being major exporters of cereals and meat. Wheat and maize are grown, and great herds of cattle and sheep raised on the vast plains of the region, particularly on the fertile Pampas grasslands.

The entire region was once inhabited by small groups of nomadic hunter-gatherers, but most of these people were displaced or annihilated by nineteenth-century European settlers. The indigenous people have now very largely disappeared, except in the less accessible forest regions and on the Chaco, an inhospitable area characterized by extremes of temperature and alternating periods of drought and flooding. Only in Paraguay has the Indian culture had any impact on the majority of the population, which both culturally and physically is *mestizo* (of mixed ancestry).

The dependence of the three countries' economies on ranching and mechanized agriculture has concentrated the wealth and most of the political power in the hands of the large landowners. In Uruguay reforms were carried out at the beginning of the twentieth century, when the only welfare state in Latin America was created, and in Argentina President Peron did much to improve the situation of the workers. In the late 1960s, however, both countries suffered economic crises and social unrest, which resulted in the military taking control of their governments. Since the mid-1970s small-scale farming and home industries have become increasingly uneconomic in the face of competition from the modern agroindustries and large numbers of people are moving to the cities in search of

work, or becoming wage laborers on the mechanized farms. At the same time, areas that had previously been thought unfit for agriculture have been brought into production and great tracts of forest felled for timber and to create pasture. Thus the habitat of the few Indian peoples who have survived in the remoter regions of Paraguay and northern Argentina is being steadily destroyed and their future gravely threatened. For some, such as the Chamococo, the impact of the modern world has, in any case, already undermined their culture, but others, such as the Mbya, continue to cling to their traditions and resist integration.

Chamococo of the Paraguay river
The Chamococo number at most only about 1,500 people and are divided into two groups: the Ebidoso (or Chamococo Manso) and the Tomaraha (or Chamococo Bravo). They inhabit the upper reaches of the Paraguay river, living in settlements on the outskirts of small towns.

Traditionally the Chamococo were nomadic hunter-gatherers inhabiting the arid scrub forests of the central Chaco. According to their own legends they left the forest, probably in the eighteenth century, under the leadership of the warrior chief Basebuk, and began to settle along the banks of the Paraguay river. Once there, they continued to hunt, trading their animal skins with the occupants of the garrison towns of Fuerte Olimpo and Forte Coimbra. At this time the eastern bank of the river was occupied by the Mbayá-Guaykuru, who continually raided the Chamococo for slaves, and under these conditions the garrison towns offered the Chamococo a degree of security.

In the late nineteenth century, as the upper Paraguay river began to be occupied by European ranchers and logging companies, the Chamococo soon found themselves becoming more dependent on wage labor. Their lands were fenced off and given over to grazing cattle; they found that even to enter the property they needed the permission of the new landowner. Today they work as ranch hands or as peons in the lumber camps, usually taking on *changas* (poorly paid short-term employment). Some work in the illegal but more lucrative business of hunting cayman or trapping jaguar for their skins. Products of the forest are now of little importance in the Chamococo's diet, and although hunting and fishing remain as activities to occupy the periods without work, most items have to be bought from the store.

Some of the women take on poorly paid work, such as washing clothes, carrying water and cutting firewood, for European or *mestizo* patrons. This is particularly true of older women who do not have small children to care for, and those whose husbands have to work away from the village. In some cases the woman's work represents virtually the only income for the family since the men are often without work.

In the Chamococo's traditional clan system membership was inherited in the male line, both sons and daughters belonging to the clan of their father. Nowadays this clan system has almost completely disappeared as a large number of Chamococo are *mestizos*. Unless they have a Chamococo father, they have found themselves excluded from the system, which they therefore tend to deride. The young no longer take the advice of their elders, or share their ideals—many simply want to be "like Paraguayans." The Chamococo now practice a type of fundamentalist Christianity, originally brought to them by North American missionaries, which to some extent has assimilated elements of their traditional mythology.

Mbya of the Paraguayan forest

In contrast to the Chamococo the Mbya, who probably number about 15,000, show little sign of being assimilated into the peasant culture of rural Paraguay. They are the descendants of those Guarani who remained outside the Jesuit *reductions*—large townships run along paternal socialist lines. As in the era of the reductions (1607–1767), the Mbya of today are still unwilling to compromise their strongly held religious beliefs, which are extremely complex and extend into all aspects of their lives. They will therefore abandon their homes rather than submit to external authority.

The Mbya are basically horticulturists, although they depend to some extent on hunting small animals and on collecting forest products: honey, fruits and the leaves of a shrub from which *yerba maté* (a beverage rather like tea but drunk from a gourd or cow horn through a metal straw) is made. Their gardens are fairly small, usually covering 1–1.5 hectares (2½–4 acres) and the main crops include yucca, maize, squash and beans, as well as a number of medicinal herbs. The men carry out the heavier agricultural tasks, such as clearing the forest, and the women help in weeding and harvesting.

Their villages are usually located in the more remote parts of the forest and the most isolated groups are subsistence farmers. Some Mbya grow very small quantities of cash crops, such as maize, which are sold by the men to the *acopiador*, a wholesaler who is also a storekeeper and who provides goods on credit for the promise of cash crops. The usual means of transport is on foot, very few Indians having horses or ox-carts.

Those Mbya living in areas of "private property" are usually unable to utilize more than about two acres of land without risking the anger of the landowner. As this is insufficient for subsistence needs, many Mbya, especially the younger men, now go off for long periods to seek wage labor, although sooner or later they return to the main village. Another reason frequently given for these temporary migrations is a man's desire to escape from the excessive demands of his in-laws. During the first few years of marriage a man is expected to live with his wife's family and to perform bride service for them; this may include work in their gardens, hunting, collecting forest products, and even payments in cash. Apart from this there are no formal rites of marriage, and there is no inheritance as an individual's belongings are destroyed at death.

Leadership amongst the Mbya is unusually pronounced for an Amerindian people, some Mbya headmen acting in a very authoritarian manner. In many communities the leaders have adopted the hierarchy of the Paraguayan military, the headmen of larger villages calling themselves "generals," and the lower ranking leaders—usually heads of extended families or small groups working for patrons—calling themselves "captains" or "lieutenants." Even the boys of ten to twelve years old are not exempt from this system, being the conscripts who carry out menial tasks such as clearing the village paths and working in the general's gardens.

It is uncertain how much this system owes to Paraguayan culture, and it seems possible that the military titles have simply been grafted onto a preexisting hierarchy based more on mystical knowledge and understanding than on straightforward political power. The village headmen are invariably the masters of ceremony in the prayers and dances that mark the important stages of the agricultural cycle, such as planting. The generals are the only people empowered to carry out the initiation ceremonies in which the young men have their lips pierced, thus allowing them to wear the *tembeta* (lip plugs), which are considered the traditional mark of Mbya manhood.

Many groups of indigenous peoples, speaking a variety of Amerindian languages, still inhabit the Chaco. Originally they lived by fishing, hunting, gathering and simple horticulture. Today, like the Chamococo, they eke out a living as ranch hands, or work on sugarcane plantations or in factories. Many live near the mission stations.

Only in Paraguay are the people predominantly mestizo. Spanish is the official language, but Guarani is the language of the home and most people are bilingual. Their Guarani heritage is strongly fictionalized and serves as a focus for nationalist sentiment. In recent years many Japanese and Koreans have settled in towns within Paraguay.

Although the Mbya still inhabit the remoter areas of tropical forest, many other groups of Guarani-speakers are now being pushed out of their forest regions by settlers and logging companies. These include the Guayaki, a nomadic people who are some of the last true hunter-gatherers still following their old way of life in South America.

Inhabitants of the bleak Patagonian plateau include the descendants of hardy 19th-century Welsh settlers who landed at Puerto Madryn and colonized the Chubut valley, where they devised a system of irrigation that allowed the land to be cultivated. Most still speak Welsh as well as Spanish, and their traditional culture has largely survived.

Peoples and languages

The original Amerindian inhabitants of this region spoke a large number of very diverse languages, the majority of which are now extinct. These indigenous people make up only 1% of the region's present population; they live in Paraguay and northern Argentina. Only in Paraguay is an indigenous language, Guarani, still widely used. The dominant languages are those of the European settlers, notably Spanish speaking.

Indo-European

- Romance language (Spanish)
- Celtic language (Welsh)

Unaffiliated languages

- Amerindian languages

Featured peoples

- Chamococo
  Mbya

Additional peoples

The mainstay of the economy
On the Pampas and the Chaco there are huge cattle ranches where the cattle often run semi-wild. The gauchos brand and vaccinate the cattle, check and repair the boundary fences and organize the occasional *rodeo* (head count). For low wages and basic food rations they work long hours on horseback, often sleeping outside.

Land use

On the immense grasslands of the region cattle and cereals are produced, but the arid Patagonian plateau is devoted to sheep-farming. The forest regions have the oldest European settlements; here smallholdings and huge agro-industries coexist, producing cash crops. Extensive forest clearance in eastern Paraguay is causing soil erosion.

Arable land and plantations

- Mainly wheat and maize; some cotton, soybeans, rice, tea, sugarcane and fruit, particularly grapes.

Permanent grassland

- Grazing for cattle.

Woods and forests

- Coniferous and broadleaved trees, used mainly for firewood and building timber.

Rough grazing

- Vast areas supporting cattle and sheep at very low density.

Nonagricultural land

- Mountain peaks, salt flats and urban areas.

Glossary

A

aboriginal
Pertaining to the original inhabitants of a region, generally those in occupation prior to European contact.

affinity
A relationship established by marriage. A person's parents-in-law, sister-in-law, etc, are his affines.

age grade
A stage, or role, in a formalized system based on AGE SETS. The age grades of a given society are ranked hierarchically on the basis of age; the members of the age set occupy one of the senior grades exercising political control.

age set
A group of individuals, usually males, whose ages fall within a particular interval (say, five years) and who progress together in the course of their lives through the age-linked roles of their society. These roles may be formalized into AGE GRADES.

agnate
A male kinsman on the father's side, for example grandfather, father's brother, father's brother's son, etc. *See also* PATRILINY.

ancestor cult
A religious cult in which the ancestors are believed to influence the affairs of their living descendants. The ancestor spirits may be propitiated through prayer or sacrifice, supplicated to withdraw their malign influence or bestow their blessings, or invoked to punish wrong-doers.

animism
The attribution of spiritual power to natural phenomena.

anthropology
See CULTURAL ANTHROPOLOGY, ETHNOLOGY, PHYSICAL ANTHROPOLOGY, and SOCIAL ANTHROPOLOGY.

avunculocality
A pattern of residence, found mainly in societies with MATRILINEAL DESCENT, in which a man lives in the home or village of his mother's brother.

B

bilateral descent
The tracing of DESCENT equally through both males and females at every generation. Bilateral descent gives rise to widely ramifying KINSHIP links.

bilateral descent group
A DESCENT GROUP based on the principles of BILATERAL DESCENT; an ancestor-focused KINDRED. Unlike UNILINEAL DESCENT GROUPS, bilateral descent groups are not mutually exclusive but overlap with one another, so that a person belongs to several.

bilineality *See* DUAL DESCENT

bilocality
A pattern of residence, found mainly in societies with MATRILINEAL DESCENT, in which a married couple lives alternately with the husband's kin and the wife's kin.

brideprice *See* BRIDEWEALTH

bride service
The custom whereby a man works for his father-in-law for a period in the early years of marriage, to "earn" his bride.

bridewealth
The transfer of material goods on marriage from the groom and/or his kin to those of the bride, in return for rights which may include the bride's sexual, domestic and reproductive services. The transfer commonly creates an alliance between the two families.

C

Capitalism
Economic system in which property and the means of production are privately owned. Capitalism embraces the notions of freedom of choice, the profit motive, individual enterprise and efficiency through competition. In practice, however, under a capitalist system governments actively participate in economic regulation, although to a much lesser extent than that found under COMMUNISM or SOCIALISM.

cargo cult
A millenarian cult of the type common in colonial and postcolonial Papua New Guinea, characterized by a belief in the imminent delivery—usually by the ancestors—of quantities of manufactured goods, the "cargo." Cargo cults demand varying degrees of discipline from their adherents to hasten the arrival of the cargo. A cargo cult may at first require a return to earlier INDIGENOUS religious practices, but may later display SYNCRETISM between indigenous religion and Christianity.

cargo system
A system of ranked religious or politico-religious offices found in many Latin American communities. The offices typically entail the financing of fiestas. A person occupies a number of different offices successively in the course of his life, beginning with the junior posts and progressing to the more senior, with intervals of a few years between each office. Those who have occupied the senior offices enjoy great prestige, and the community leaders are drawn from amongst them. (From the Spanish *cargo*, office.)

cash crop
A crop grown for sale, as distinct from a SUBSISTENCE CROP.

caste
One of the hereditary groups into which Hindu society is divided. At the most general level there are four ranked castes—Brahmans (priests), Kshatriyas (rulers and soldiers), Vaishyas (farmers and merchants), and Shudras (craftsmen, servants and laborers)—to which must be added the outcastes—the Untouchables or Harijans (butchers, tanners, cobblers, sweepers, night-soil removers, etc). At the regional and local levels, these categories are further divided into numerous subcastes (*jatis*), each with its own occupation. Castes and subcastes are characteristically ENDOGAMOUS. (From the Portuguese *casta*, race or lineage.)

clan
A group of people who recognize DESCENT from a common ancestor, the founder of the clan. This founder may be a mythical personage. A clan may comprise a number of LINEAGES.

class
A group of people who define themselves, or who are defined by others, according to their role in the economic or political system of their society.

cognatic descent *See* BILATERAL DESCENT

collateral kin
Relatives belonging to a person's own generation, such as siblings, first cousins and second cousins. *See also* LINEAL KIN.

colonialism
The formation, by a people or country, of settler communities involving political and/or economic control of foreign territories. The phrase "internal colonialism" is sometimes used to refer to domination within a STATE by one exclusive power group. *See also* NEOCOLONIALISM.

common market
A form of economic integration in which there is free internal trade, a common external TARIFF, and the free movement of labor and capital among partner states. The European Economic Community (EEC) is an example.

Communism
A theory of society based on the ideas of Karl Marx and Friedrich Engels, according to which CAPITALISM gives way to the complete public control of the means of production, distribution and exchange. The term commonly refers to the beliefs and institutions of people claiming allegiance to the theory.

compadrazgo
A bond of ritual kinship between the parents and GODPARENTS of a child, found in certain Christian CULTURES. The bond usually entails the exchange of goods and services between the *compadres* (coparents), either on the basis of reciprocity or of PATRON-CLIENT-AGE between the godparents, who are the patrons, and the parents, who are the clients. (From the Spanish *compadrazgo*, coparent-hood.)

conjugal family *See* FAMILY, CONJUGAL

consanguinity
Relationship between kin defined in terms of blood ties, as opposed to one of AFFINITY.

consensual union
A sexual relationship established through the mutual consent of both partners.

corporate group
A group treated for political or legal purposes as if it were a single person. Members of the group may have certain rights vested in it. UNILINEAL DESCENT GROUPS frequently act as corporate groups.

couvade
The custom whereby a man takes to his bed when his wife gives birth to a child. (From the French *couver*, to hatch.)

cross-cousin
A first cousin traced through an opposite-sex SIBLING of a person's parent, that is the father's sister's child (PATRILATERAL cross-cousin) or the mother's brother's child (MATRILATERAL cross-cousin).

cultural anthropology
The study of cultural and social diversity based upon an investigation of CULTURE and material artifacts. Social relations are here seen as part of culturally patterned behavior. *See also* SOCIAL ANTHROPOLOGY.

culture
All knowledge that is aquired by man by virtue of his membership of a society. A culture incorporates all the shared knowledge, expectations and beliefs of a group.

D

democracy
Political system in which citizens are involved in some way in the ruling of society. In parliamentary democracy the will of the people is expressed indirectly, through elected representation in more than one party. Democratic centralism depends on a one-party system.

dependency
A partially self-governing territory attached to a colonial power.

dependency theory
A theory which analyzes UNDERDEVELOPMENT as the consequence, at least in part, of foreign exploitation.

descent
The relationships between the living and their ancestors. Descent may be traced through males, females or both.

descent group
A group of people who trace DESCENT from a common ancestor. Descent groups may be PATRILINEAGES, MATRILINEAGES or BILATERAL DESCENT GROUPS.

double descent *See* DUAL DESCENT

double unilineal descent *See* DUAL DESCENT

dowry
Wealth endowed upon a woman as a marriage settlement. In some cases where HYPERGAMY is practiced, the dowry has the effect of enhancing a lower-status woman's eligibility for marriage. In others it represents a PREMORTEM INHERITANCE.

dual descent
The tracing of DESCENT according to both PATRILINEAL and MATRILINEAL principles in the same society. A person thus belongs to two DESCENT GROUPS. Certain rights and duties are inherited patrilineally, while certain others are passed on matrilineally.

E

endogamy
The practice of marrying exclusively within one's own group, for example one's CASTE, CLASS or village. *See also* EXOGAMY.

ethnic group
A group having a sense of identity founded upon perceived cultural and/or physical criteria.

ethnocentrism
The tendency to view and evaluate other CULTURES from the standpoint of one's own, often disparagingly.

ethnography
A detailed description of the CULTURE and social organization of a particular people or group.

ethnology
The study of the histories and interrelations of different CULTURES. The term is still used on the Continent, and to a lesser extent in North America, where the meaning is CULTURAL ANTHROPOLOGY with a greater historical emphasis.

exogamy
Marriage to a person outside one's own group, for example to a member of another LINEAGE or CLAN. *See also* ENDOGAMY.

extended family *See* FAMILY, EXTENDED

F

family, conjugal
The family in which a person is a spouse/parent; a person's "family of procreation."

family, extended
A family spanning three generations and comprising a set of SIBLINGS with their parents, spouses and children.

family, joint
A set of SIBLINGS who hold property jointly, and share earnings and consumption equally.

family, matrifocal
A family focused on a woman or women, frequently a set of sisters, to which husbands have only loose attachments. The matrifocal family is a marked feature of many Caribbean societies.

family, natal
The family into which a person was born; a person's "family of orientation."

family, nuclear
A family comprising a husband, wife and their children.

family, stem
A family spanning three generations and comprising a husband, wife, their children, and the parents of either spouse.

feudalism
A politico-economic system in which land is held by subjects (VASSALS) on condition of loyalty or service to a superior.

G

GATT: General Agreement on Tariffs and Trade
An international body set up in 1947 to investigate ways and means of reducing the TARIFFS levied on internationally traded goods and services.

genealogy
A record of the DESCENT of a person or group through named ancestors.

godparent
A person who sponsors another at a RITE OF PASSAGE, typically baptism in Christian cultures.

Green Revolution
The increase in grain production associated with the scientific development of new dwarf hybrid varieties of wheat and rice. This has resulted in higher grain yields for some farmers in developing countries but has not brought about the massive general increase in food production originally expected.

gross domestic product (GDP)
The total monetary value calculated at market prices of all final goods and services produced in an economy over a given period of time, usually one year.

gross national product (GNP)
The sum total of all incomes that accrue in a particular geographical region over a given period of time, usually a year, ie GDP, plus all incomes that accrue to residents of that region from their investments in foreign countries, less incomes that accrue to foreigners as a result of their investments in that region.

H

hacienda
An agricultural estate or ranch in Latin America. (From the Spanish *hacienda*, farm.)

hunting and gathering
A way of making a living by gathering wild fruits, nuts, leaves, roots, honey, grubs or birds' eggs, and hunting wild animals.

hypergamy
A form of marriage in which women marry men of superior rank.

hypogamy
A form of marriage in which women marry men of inferior rank.

I

IBRD: International Bank for Reconstruction and Development (World Bank)
An international financial institution forming part of the United Nations. One of its main objectives is to provide development funds to Third World nations in the form of interest-bearing loans and technical assistance.

ideology
Literally, the science of ideas. In social science it commonly refers to the way of thinking characteristic of a particular class or group. More generally, it is used to describe theories, such as Fascism and Marxism, which prescribe political action to change and reorganize society.

IMF: International Monetary Fund
An autonomous international financial institution set up in 1944. Its main purpose is to regulate the international monetary exchange system, in particular to control fluctuations in exchange rates of world currencies in order to alleviate severe balance-of-payments problems.

imperialism
Domination of one people or country by another. The domination can be economic, cultural, political or religious.

incest prohibition/taboo
The prohibition of sexual relations between close kin. Although incest prohibitions are found in all societies, the degrees of KINSHIP which they specify vary widely.

income per capita
The total GNP of a country divided by the total population. Income per capita is often used as an economic indicator of the levels of living and development. However, it takes no account of the often dramatic differences in income distribution.

indentured labor
A form of employment in which the laborer is bound to his employer for a specified period.

indigenous
Pertaining to the native people or CULTURE of a region.

infant mortality
The deaths among children between birth and one year of age. Infant mortality rates give the number of deaths per 1,000 live births.

inflation
A period of general price increases as reflected, for example, in the consumer and wholesale price indices. More generally, the phenomenon of rising prices.

initiation
A RITE OF PASSAGE in which a person is invested with a special role. The term commonly refers to the promotion of young people to adulthood, but may also be applied to the admission of individuals to a religious cult.

J

joint family *See* FAMILY, JOINT

K

kindred
A group of people related to one another through BILATERAL DESCENT. Kindreds may be ancestor focused (ie include all the descendants of a given ancestor) or ego focused (ie defined by the relationships of each individual; thus each person's kindred group includes a different set of individuals, except in the case of full SIBLINGS, who share the same kindred); the latter may be of first-cousin range, second-cousin range, etc. Kindreds are not mutually exclusive but overlap with one another. *See also* COLLATERAL KIN, LINEAL KIN.

kinship
A blood relationship or a relationship viewed as such, for example the relationship between a couple and their adopted child. Kinship is sometimes opposed to AFFINITY. *See also* COLLATERAL KIN, LINEAL KIN.

kula
The system of ceremonial exchange among peoples of the eastern archipelago of Papua New Guinea. The system entails the circulation and exchange of two kinds of valuables between men on different islands, shell necklaces moving clockwise around the islands and shell bracelets moving counterclockwise. A person takes part in the kula to enhance his prestige and political influence. (From the Melanesian *kula*, to exchange ceremonial gifts.)

Glossary

L

ladino *See* MESTIZO

laissez faire
Literally "allow to do," an expression often used to represent the notion of free enterprise. (From the French.)

latifundia
Extensive agricultural estates or ranches, characteristic of certain social systems. (From the Latin *latus*, broad; *fundus*, farm.)

levirate
The inheritance of a widow by her husband's kinsman, usually a brother, who then fathers children in the name of the dead man.

life crisis
A stage in the physical, social and emotional maturation of a person, for example birth, puberty, marriage and death.

life expectancy (at birth)
Period of time, normally in years, that a baby is expected to live after it has been born alive.

lineage
The direct descendants in line from a common ancestor or ancestress; frequently used to refer to a UNILINEAL DESCENT GROUP.

lineal kin
A person's relatives in the ascending and descending generations, such as grandparents, parents, children and grandchildren. *See also* COLLATERAL KIN.

M

magic
The art of influencing the course of events by occult means, often with the help of spells and the presumed control of supernatural forces; may be used for positive, socially approved purposes or for negative, anti-social purposes. The conventional distinction between magic and religion is difficult to draw in many cultures.

matriarchy
The exercise of political and/or domestic control by women. In practice this is an extremely rare practice. *See also* MATRILINEAL DESCENT.

matriclan
A CLAN based on the principle of MATRILINEAL DESCENT.

matrifocal family *See* FAMILY, MATRIFOCAL

matrilateral
Pertaining to the mother's side. A person's matrilateral kin are those to whom he is related through his mother.

matrilineage
A LINEAGE based on the principle of MATRILINEAL DESCENT: a UNILINEAL DESCENT GROUP so formed.

matrilineal descent
The tracing of DESCENT through females. According to this system, social identity, status, political office, material goods, etc, pass down the generations from a man to his sister's son.

matriliny *See* MATRILINEAL DESCENT

matrilocality *See* UXORILOCALITY

mestizo
A person with mixed Spanish and Amerindian ancestry and a Hispanic cultural orientation; pertaining to this cultural orientation, as distinct from Amerindian cultures. (From the Spanish *mestizo*, mixed breed.)

millennarianism
The belief in the imminence of a new epoch of happiness and well-being.

miscegenation
The blending of RACES.

moiety
One of two balanced halves into which a social group is divided, commonly on the basis of KINSHIP.

monogamy
The rule or practice of having only one spouse at a time.

monogenism
The theory of the DESCENT of all human beings from an original single pair.

monopoly
A market situation in which a product that does not have close substitutes is being produced and sold by a single seller.

monotheism
Religious beliefs based on the recognition of a single, unique deity.

N

natal family *See* FAMILY, NATAL

nation
People sharing the same language and CULTURE and a sense of identity associated with presumed common origins. Nations do not necessarily coincide with STATES. (From the Latin *natalis*, birth.)

nationalism
IDEOLOGY according to which all people owe a supreme loyalty to their NATION. Nationalist sentiment, drawing upon and extolling a common CULTURE, language and history, can be a powerful unifying force. Particularly strongly developed in 18th- and 19th-century political theory.

neocolonialism
The maintenance of economic and/or political dominance in former colonies which are officially self-governing. *See also* COLONIALISM.

neolocality
A pattern of residence in which a married couple establishes a new home, away from the homes or villages of both their parents.

neophyte
A novice; a person newly admitted to a social role, political office, or religious cult.

nomadism
A life style involving frequent shifts of residence which is associated with certain modes of SUBSISTENCE, for example PASTORALISM and HUNTING AND GATHERING.

nuclear family *See* FAMILY, NUCLEAR

O

obsequies
Funeral rites and solemnities.

OECD: Organization for Economic Co-operation and Development
An organization of 20 countries from the western world. Its major objective is to assist the economic growth of its member STATES by promoting cooperation and to undertake technical analysis of national and international economic trends.

OPEC: Organization of Petroleum Exporting Countries
An organization consisting of the 13 major oil-exporting countries of the Third World which acts as a "cartel" to promote their joint national interests.

Oxfam
Formerly the Oxford Committee for Famine Relief, an international charity, formed in World War II and registered as a charity in 1948. It attempts to alleviate suffering due to poverty or natural misfortune in all parts of the world. As a result of its policy to educate people so that they can solve their own problems, nearly three-quarters of Oxfam's budget is devoted to long-term projects in the areas of agriculture, nutrition, family planning and medicine.

P

parallel cousin
A first cousin traced through a same-sex SIBLING of a person's parent, that is the father's brother's child (PATRILATERAL parallel cousin) or the mother's sister's child (MATRILATERAL parallel cousin).

pastoralism
A way of making a living by keeping herds of domesticated animals.

patriarchy
The exercise of political and/or domestic control by men. This may be found even in societies with MATRILINEAL DESCENT.

patriclan
A CLAN based on the principle of PATRILINEAL DESCENT.

patrilateral
Pertaining to the father's side. A person's patrilateral kin are those to whom he is related through his father.

patrilineage
A LINEAGE based on the principle of PATRILINEAL DESCENT; a UNILINEAL DESCENT GROUP so formed.

patrilineal descent
The tracing of DESCENT through males. According to this system, social identity, status, political office, material goods, etc, pass down the generations from father to son.

patriliny *See* PATRILINEAL DESCENT

patrilocal *See* VIRILOCAL

patrimony
A right, office or estate inherited from a person's father.

patron-clientage
An arrangement found in some stratified societies whereby a client seeks the permanent favor or protection of another of higher status (patron), in return for support, loyalty, goods and services.

peasant
A country dweller, usually engaged in small-scale subsistence cultivation, who pays rent or taxes in cash, labor or kind to a political superior or to the STATE. (From the Old French *paisant*, from *pais*, country).

peon
In Latin America, a day-laborer. A debt-peon is a laborer trapped in employment through debts owed to his employer. In India, an office messenger. (From the Spanish *peon*, day-laborer.)

per capita income *See* INCOME PER CAPITA

physical anthropology
The study of man's biological diversity.

polyandry
The practice of one woman having two or more husbands at the same time.

polygamy
The practice of having more than one spouse at a time.

polygyny
The practice of one man having two or more wives at the same time.

polytheism
The recognition of more than one deity.

potlatch
A ceremony common among Amerindian groups of the northwest coast of North America in which large quantities of material goods were given away by the sponsor to his guests, or even destroyed. Potlatches were manifestations of power. They were held in order to make legitimate the changes of status in RITES OF PASSAGE, and to assert claims to political superiority. (From the Kwakiutl *potlatch*, giving.)

powwow
A feast, dance or conference among Amerindians of North America. (From the Algonkin *powah*, ceremony.)

premortem inheritance
The passing of wealth to an heir before the death of the holder.

purdah
The seclusion of women from men or strangers. (From the Urdu and Persian *pardah*, veil or curtain.)

R

race
A breeding population differing from other populations of the same species in the frequency of one or more genes. External characteristics such as skin color and hair type are now regarded as biologically dubious criteria for distinguishing human races, and have been replaced by more clear-cut characteristics such as bloodgroups. Whatever the criteria selected, there are no sharp breaks between racial categories. Racial categories must be distinguished absolutely from groups based upon shared language or cultural traits, since cultural features are not linked with genetic characteristics.

rites of passage
A rite marking or effecting a person's change of status, especially a change associated with a LIFE CRISIS.

S

sedentarization
The transition from SHIFTING CULTIVATION to SEDENTARY CULTIVATION, or from NOMADISM to settled residence, especially as part of government policy towards PASTORALISTS and HUNTER-GATHERERS.

sedentary cultivation
Cultivation of a fixed territory, permitting settled residence.

segmentary lineage system
A KINSHIP system in which there is complementary opposition between LINEAGES of equivalent size. In such a system, two lineages opposed to each other at one level of GENEOLOGICAL segmentation are united at a higher level. Thus in one context group X may stand in opposition to group Y; but in another context groups X and Y will unite as group W in opposition to group Z.

shamanism
A religious practice in which a specialist priest (*shaman*) makes contact with spirits or supernatural agencies for the purposes of worship, healing, or the warding off of misfortune. Shamanism commonly involves SPIRIT POSSESSION. (From the Tungus *shaman*, a priest.)

shifting cultivation
A pattern of cultivation in which land is cropped for a few years until it loses its fertility, then abandoned and allowed to regenerate. Shifting cultivation is practiced in areas of low population density, and may be associated with pastoral NOMADISM. *See also* SLASH-AND-BURN CULTIVATION, SWIDDEN AGRICULTURE, PASTORALISM.

sib
A set of SIBLINGS; a grouping based on this set.

sibling
One of two or more children having one or both parents in common.

Sinicization
The tendency of minority ethnic groups to adopt elements of the dominant Han Chinese culture.

slash-and-burn cultivation
A form of SHIFTING CULTIVATION in which a plot is cleared, in forest or scrub, by cutting down and then burning the natural veg-

etation. The plot is cultivated for a few years and then abandoned for an extended period. After regeneration it may again be cleared and cultivated.

social anthropology
The study of social and cultural characteristics of diverse ethnic groups based upon investigations into different forms of social organization. CULTURE is here treated as a vehicle for social relations. *See also* CULTURAL ANTHROPOLOGY.

Socialism
A system of social and economic organization in which property is owned not by private individuals but by the community, in order that all may share fairly in the wealth produced. Many different forms of socialism exist in both theory and practice, differing mainly in their interpretation of how much property the individual should be allowed, what definition of "the community" is used—whether it be the factory, the town or the state—and to what degree individual liberty is subordinated to the requirements of the society as a whole.

sororate
The custom by which a man's dead wife is replaced by her sister, who then becomes wife to the same man.

spirit possession
The temporary occupation by a spirit or supernatural agency of a person's body. Spirit possession may involve trance states, and is a feature of some forms of SHAMANISM.

state
An autonomous self-governing political unit, usually with a centralized hierarchical power structure which may or may not be democratically elected. It may sometimes, but does not necessarily, coincide with a NATION. *See also* DEMOCRACY.

stem family *See* FAMILY, STEM

subsistence
Basic means of making a living. The principal non-industrial modes of subsistence are HUNTING AND GATHERING, PASTORALISM, SHIFTING CULTIVATION and SEDENTARY CULTIVATION. Many societies practise combinations of these forms of subsistence.

subsistence crop
A staple crop grown for consumption, as distinct from a CASH CROP.

subsistence economy
An economy in which production is geared to consumption rather than sale.

swidden agriculture
(From Old Norse *svithningr*, clearing land by burning) *See* SLASH-AND-BURN CULTIVATION

syncretism
The fusion of elements of two or more religious systems into a single cult. The term typically refers to the process whereby features of a world religion are blended with local patterns of ritual and belief.

T

taboo
The setting apart of an object, act or person by means of prohibitions or supernatural sanctions; something so set apart. (From the Tongan *tabu*, holy and unclean.)

tariff
A fixed percentage tax on the value of an imported commodity levied at the point of entry into the importing country.

transhumance
A form of NOMADISM found among certain pastoralists, involving the regular seasonal movement of livestock between summer and winter pastures, the former usually being at high altitudes and the latter in lowland valleys. *See also* PASTORALISM.

tribe
An ETHNIC GROUP in preindustrial, traditional societies. A tribe is usually associated with a territory and is ideally an autonomous political unit. (From the Latin *tribus*, a division of the Roman city state.)

"trickle down" theory of development
The prevalent view of the 1950s and 1960s, in which development was seen as a purely economic phenomenon in which rapid gains in the overall growth of GROSS NATIONAL PRODUCT and PER CAPITA INCOME of the developing countries would automatically bring benefits (ie "trickle down") to the poorest people in the form of jobs and other economic opportunities.

U

UNCTAD: United Nations' Conference on Trade and Development
A body of the United Nations whose primary objective is to promote international trade and commerce with special emphasis on the trade and balance-of-payments problems of developing nations.

underdevelopment
Economic situation in which there are persistent low standards of living with the following characteristics: absolute poverty, low INCOME PER CAPITA, low rates of economic growth, low consumption levels, poor health services, high death rates, high birth rates, vulnerability to and dependence on foreign economies, and limited freedom of choice. *See also* DEPENDENCY THEORY.

unilineal descent group
A descent group based on the tracing of DESCENT through one line only. Such a group may be a PATRILINEAGE or a MATRILINEAGE.

use rights *See* USUFRUCT

usufruct
The right of using and enjoying the produce, benefits or profits of another's property, provided that the property remains undamaged. The term is commonly employed in relation to land. (From the Latin *usus*, use; *fructus*, fruit.)

uterine
Born of the same mother.

uxorilocality
A pattern of residence in which a married couple lives in the natal home of the wife.

V

vassal
One who holds land or privileges from a superior, and owes loyalty and homage to him. *See also* FEUDALISM.

virilocality
A pattern of residence in which a married couple lives in the natal home or village of the husband.

voodoo
The SYNCRETIC religious system of Haiti, combining elements of Christian liturgy with African SPIRIT POSSESSION and seen by its adherents as a form of Christianity.

W

wage labor
Labor rendered to another for cash.

witchcraft
Belief in the power of certain persons to harm others by mystical means. The conventional distinction between witchcraft, the innate or psychic power to harm, and sorcery, the use of MAGIC for the same end, is difficult to draw in many cultures.

General Index

General Index

General Index

Index of Place Names

Page numbers in *italic* refer to
   diagrams or to photographs and
   their captions.
Page numbers in **bold** refer to maps.

Index of Place Names

Index of Place Names